Britain and Italy in the Era of the Great War

This is an important reassessment of British and Italian grand strategies during World War I. Stefano Marcuzzi sheds new light on a hitherto overlooked but central aspect of the war experiences of Britain and Italy: the uneasy and only partial overlap between Britain's strategy for imperial defence and Italy's ambition for imperial expansion. Taking Anglo-Italian bilateral relations as a special lens through which to understand the workings of the Entente Cordiale in World War I, he reveals how the ups and downs of that relationship influenced and shaped Allied grand strategy. Marcuzzi considers three main issues – war aims, war strategy and peace-making – and examines how, under the pressure of divergent interests and wartime events, the Anglo-Italian 'traditional friendship' turned increasingly into competition by the end of the war, casting a shadow on Anglo-Italian relations both at the Peace Conference and in the interwar period.

Stefano Marcuzzi is a Marie Curie fellow at the University College Dublin, an analyst in emerging challenges at the NATO Defense College Foundation and an external fellow at Boston University.

T0364225

Cambridge Military Histories

Edited by

JENNIFER D. KEENE, Chapman University

HEW STRACHAN, Professor of International Relations, University of St Andrews, and Emeritus Fellow of All Souls College, Oxford

GEOFFREY WAWRO, Professor of Military History and Director of the Military History Center, University of North Texas

The aim of this series is to publish outstanding works of research on warfare throughout the ages and throughout the world. Books in the series take a broad approach to military history, examining war in all its military, strategic, political and economic aspects. The series complements Studies in the Social and Cultural History of Modern Warfare by focusing on the 'hard' military history of armies, tactics, strategy and warfare. Books in the series consist mainly of single-author works – academically rigorous and groundbreaking – which are accessible to both academics and the interested general reader.

A full list of titles in the series can be found at:
www.cambridge.org/militaryhistories

Britain and Italy in the Era of the Great War

Defending and Forging Empires

Stefano Marcuzzi

University College Dublin

CAMBRIDGE
UNIVERSITY PRESS

Shaftesbury Road, Cambridge CB2 8EA, United Kingdom

One Liberty Plaza, 20th Floor, New York, NY 10006, USA

477 Williamstown Road, Port Melbourne, VIC 3207, Australia

314–321, 3rd Floor, Plot 3, Splendor Forum, Jasola District Centre, New Delhi – 110025, India

103 Penang Road, #05–06/07, Visioncrest Commercial, Singapore 238467

Cambridge University Press is part of Cambridge University Press & Assessment, a department of the University of Cambridge.

We share the University's mission to contribute to society through the pursuit of education, learning and research at the highest international levels of excellence.

www.cambridge.org
Information on this title: www.cambridge.org/9781108932684

DOI: 10.1017/9781108924009

First published 2020
First paperback edition 2022

A catalogue record for this publication is available from the British Library

ISBN   978-1-108–83129-1   Hardback
ISBN   978-1-108-93268-4   Paperback

To the memory of my great grandfather,
Corporal Vincenzo Nicolini, awarded
the Silver Medal of Military Valour
during the retreat from Caporetto,
and of his son, Faustino

Contents

Figures

Maps

Acknowledgement

This volume, has been a novel and tough experience, in especial need of the synergies and collaborations that go into making a book. At the academic level, I wish to thank above all my mentor at Oxford, Professor Sir Hew Strachan. I marvel at how fortunate I was, and what an encouragement he was to a young man who was not quite sure what he wanted to do. Rob Johnson was another key figure in my Oxonian training, widening my research horizons into strategic studies and geo-politics. My DPhil research, from which the present volume flows, also benefitted from the sharp eyes of Adrian Gregory, who evaluated it *in itinere*, and of Richard Bosworth and John Gooch who examined it at the viva voce. It was a rare privilege for me to enjoy the comments of the two leading Italianists in the UK. By challenging some of my conclusions, they stimulated further thinking on how, under the pressure of divergent interests and wartime events, the Anglo-Italian traditional friendship turned increasingly into competition by the end of the war. Beyond my Oxonian network, Nicola Labanca's generosity has been a great support.

For their truly outstanding advice, I must thank a vast number of scholars who animated my research at various stages. Some have been supportive for longer periods, such as Cathal Nolan, William Philpott, Andrea Ungari, Richard Hammond, Jonathan Krause, John Horne and Vanda Wilcox. Others I have met at international conferences or via Skype, inspired my work; among them, John Peaty, Daniela Luigia Caglioti and Stéphane Audoin-Rouzeau. Carlo Fumian, Piero Del Negro, Marco Mondini, Carlotta Sorba, Giovanni Focardi and Giulia Albanese taught me the job at Padua University and have been an inexhaustible source of stimulation and collaboration ever since. An important mention goes to my first teachers, and true examples to follow, Susanna Fincato, Rossella Verbani and Mario Simonato. A sad but fond thought goes to the memory of Silvio Lanaro, my supervisor in Padua, who took special care of me both at the university and at the Scuola Galileiana di Studi Superiori.

I owe a huge debt to the staff of both Italian and British archives, especially the Archivio di Stato, the Archivio Storico del Senato, the Archivio della Farnesina, the Archivio Storico dello Stato Maggiore dell'Esercito and the Archivio dell'Ufficio Storico della Marina (Rome); the National and Maritime Archives (London) and the Bodleian Special Collections (Oxford). I thank the archivists for their professionalism and passion. Alyson Price and Michael Barbour, whom I met during my stay at the EUI Florence, were of great help as well. I also wish to thank some high-rank officers from the UK, Italy and NATO for helping me reconsider the significance of World War I in the current shaping and implementation of coalition strategies. Among them are General Sir Michael Rose, Admiral Cristiano Bettini, General Giorgio Battisti, General Giuseppe Morabito and Colonel Ian Hope.

Writing a book in a language different to my own, whilst looking for a job and performing multifarious duties in various collaborative projects, could not have been accomplished without the moral support of a handful of irreplaceable people. I wish to express special thanks to my old friends, Alessio Terzi and Alexandros Giannakoulas. The former has shared my passion for history and battles since we were teenagers, and later was among the first to read my early works. The latter, a brilliant DPhil fellow at Oxford and a close friend ever since, has been relentless in his encouragement. Our discussions on military affairs, from Thutmose III to von Manstein – and our recurrent *excursus* on James Bond – might have had some elements of the nerdish, but they were important to me more than Alexandros can know. Finally, to my wonderful family, Franco, Maria and Mara, and to Giorgia, for the cheer and understanding through the three years that this project dominated my life and, more often than not, absorbed my limited spare time. They were the Old Guard protecting my castle and spurring me on.

Introduction

Literature on alliance and coalition warfare has generated a tendency to consider alliances in an aggregate manner, blurring the distinction between multilateral and bilateral partnerships, and especially overlooking the impact of the latter within the context of the former.[1] However, alliances are rarely symmetric and coherent wholes. This calls into question the capacity of traditional approaches to coalition warfare to understand the root dynamics of intra-alliance management in conflict.

World War I offers a patent example. The conflict, which began on 28 July 1914, initially saw the Triple Entente of Great Britain, France and Russia – aligned with Serbia – facing the Central Powers of Germany and Austria-Hungary. Almost immediately, Belgium was forced into the western Allied block by a German invasion. In time, about twenty countries joined one side or the other – though many sustained little or no fighting, whilst some belligerents such as Russia dropped out before the war ended on 11 November 1918. Among those who joined the heaviest fighting were the Ottoman Empire and Bulgaria (on Germany's side), and Italy, Romania and the United States (on the Allies' side). Some, like Italy and Romania, did so by shifting their pre-war alliances. Each country entering the conflict brought with it its own expectations, prejudices, preferences and reservations, especially regarding allies with whom they had never previously cooperated. Inevitably this led the belligerent countries to form special bilateral or multilateral partnerships within their alliances which were particularly important for those countries, which sustained heavier fighting. War in 1914–1918 became so complex and so multifaceted that strategy had to balance the demands of competing theatres of war, to coordinate the frequently divergent aims of allies and to stir each country's social and economic resources. Finally, the belligerents had to consider how to address these issues not only at war but also in

---

[1] H-Y. Yang, 'A study on role-based approach to bilateral alliances in Northeast Asia', *Journal of International and Area Studies*, XXIII, 1, June 2016, pp. 33–57.

the peace that would follow. A British maritime strategist, Julian Corbett, in 1911 called this 'major strategy' in order to distinguish it from 'minor strategy', which was the art of campaigning. He also occasionally used the descriptor 'grand strategy', and the latter term gained currency.[2]

In this context, the study of bilateral relations as a special lens through which to understand the workings of alliances at war provides a focus on the balance of power within allied blocks and illuminates how preferential partnerships affect allied grand strategies. Keith Neilson, Kathleen Burk, Elizabeth Greenhalgh, Gary Shanafelt, Holger Herwig, Alexander Watson, Ulrich Trumpener and Jehuda Wallach took this approach to World War I studying Anglo-Russian, Anglo-American, Anglo-French,Austro-German and German-Turkish relations, respectively.[3] The present volume fills a gap in this field, by providing a study of Anglo-Italian relations during the Great War and the Paris Peace Conference. It argues that Britain was Italy's main partner within the Entente, and that Rome sought to make London the guarantor of the promises upon which Italy joined the Allies. This expectation assumed that Britain and Italy enjoyed special geopolitical, economic, cultural and historical ties. A widespread idea in the Italian governing class, this was a minority feeling in Britain, which expected Italy to be an important contributor to the Allied victory and a stabilising force in the post-war settlement, but which continued to see France – and later the United States – as its main partner. The expectations that each country had of their alliance were largely unfulfilled, casting a shadow on their relations in the post-war period. I argue that this happened because of Anglo-Italian incompatibility in three key areas: war aims, war strategy and peace-making. These areas, which together constituted the grand strategy of both countries, have been studied in the past but never fully assessed as a whole.

The first issue, which is also the main focus of this book, is the uneasy and ultimately insufficient overlap of Britain's strategy for imperial defence

---

[2] H. Strachan, 'The Strategic Consequences of the World War', *The American Interest*, IX, 6 June 2014.

[3] K. Neilson *Strategy and Supply: the Anglo-Russian Alliance 1914–17* (Boston: Allen & Unwin, 1984); K. Burk, *Britain, America and the Sinews of War, 1914–1918* (London: Routledge, 1985); E. Greenhalgh, *Victory through Coalition: Britain and France during the First World War* (Cambridge: Cambridge University Press, 2005); G. W. Shanafelt, *The Secret Enemy: Austria-Hungary and the German Alliance 1914-1918* (New York: Columbia University Press, 1985); H. H. Herwig, *The First World War: Germany and Austria-Hungary 1914–1918* (London: Arnold, 1997); A. Watson, *Ring of Steel: Germany and Austria-Hungary at War, 1914–1918* (London & New York: Allen & Basic, 2014); U. Trumpener, *Germany and the Ottoman Empire 1914–1918* (Princeton: Princeton University Press, 1968); J. L. Wallach, *Anatomie einer Militärhilfe: die preussisch-deutschen Militärmissionen in der Türkei 1835–1919* (Düsseldorf: Droste, 1976). Luca Micheletta studied Anglo-Italian relations in the post-war years: *Italia e Gran Bretagna nel primo dopoguerra. Le relazioni diplomatiche tra Roma e Londra dal 1919 al 1922*, 2 vols. (Rome: Jouvence, 1999).

and Italy's ambition for imperial expansion. Hew Strachan, David Stevenson, John Gooch and David French, among others, have studied British strategy in World War I at length and, though with different hues, they share a conclusion that Britain's main reason for fighting in the war was to defend its Empire and its supremacy among the great powers from the threat posed by German military ambitions.[4] French added that such supremacy was to be defended against Britain's allies too.[5] Analysis of Anglo-Italian relations during the war and its immediate aftermath proves him right, but the real problem is to put this British strategic principle into perspective. Britain was not initially fighting for conquest, but the developments of the war convinced its policymakers that the Empire's security and supremacy would be better achieved by gaining control of vast territories belonging to their enemies. The fact that the British possessed many of these by the end of the war – having conquered them first-hand with only limited support from their allies – was a not insignificant stimulus to that conclusion. Britain was still thinking defensively, but what changed were the means to achieve its security, as defeating German militarism was now deemed insufficient. So British war aims were not fixed at the opening of the conflict, rather they developed progressively in a flexible approach to war and peace diplomacy.

For Italy, the 'least of the great powers',[6] World War I was, from the beginning the opportunity for which many Italian statesmen had been waiting, to complete national unification through the annexation of the 'unredeemed lands' – Italian territories under Habsburg rule – and to gain a place among the major powers through imperialist expansion in the Balkans, Asia Minor and Africa. For many years, this was not fully recognised by Italian historians. Afflicted by an intellectual narrow-mindedness, and possibly by an inferiority complex, Italian scholarship has rarely looked at other schools, limiting itself to enlightening Italy's actions only to Italians. In the years following the war many authors, including Gaetano Salvemini, Francesco Tommasini and Luigi Salvatorelli[7] set to track a reasonable, progressive and honourable shift

---

[4] Strachan, 'The Battle of the Somme and British Strategy', *The Journal of Strategic Studies*, XXI, 1, 1998, pp. 79–95; D. Stevenson, *1917. War, Peace, and Revolution* (Oxford: Oxford University Press, 2017); J. Gooch, *The Plans of War: The General Staff and British Military Strategy c.1900–1916* (New York: Wiley & Sons, 1974); D. French, *British Strategy and War Aims, 1914–1916* (London & Boston: Allen & Unwin, 1986).

[5] French, *The Strategy of the Lloyd George Coalition, 1916–1918* (Oxford: Clarendon, 1995).

[6] R. Bosworth, *Italy, the Least of the Great Powers: Italian Foreign Policy before the First World War* (London & New York: Cambridge University Press, 2005).

[7] G. Salvemini, *La politica estera italiana dal 1871 al 1915* (Milan: Barbera, 1944), p. 20; F. Tommasini, *L'Italia alla vigilia della guerra: la politica estera di Tommaso Tittoni*

in alliances from Vienna and Berlin to London, Paris and Petrograd, justified by the hostile attitude of the old allies and legitimate Italian national claims. Some, like Mario Caracciolo, argued explicitly that Italy's war had not been imperialistic.[8] Later Mario Toscano and Brunello Vigezzi stressed the need for a broader analysis of Italy's geopolitical competition with its former allies, but even these scholars did not manage to get to the heart of the imperialist urges of a part of the Italian political elite.[9] They were indirectly supported by Arno Mayer when he argued that Italy's choice between war and peace was one of domestic rather than foreign policy.[10] The present volume, on the other hand, argues that Italy's imperial ambitions played a crucial role in the Italian intervention and in the shaping of its war aims.

Such ambitions did not escape Anglo-Saxon historians. Richard Bosworth linked Liberal and Fascist Italy's foreign policies,[11] arguing that the break between the two periods emphasised by Italian historians[12] is in fact less clear-cut than Italians like to think; Gooch stressed the impact of Italian Balkan appetites in Italy's choice to enter the fray in 1915.[13] Once again, the problem is to put the Italian imperialist thrust into perspective. In fact, it did not reflect a coherent plan for expansion: it was a somewhat schizophrenic impulse of conservatives and nationalists, which produced a dramatic confrontation with Italian democrats and neutralists. The lack of a coherent design, as well as a significant gap between imperialist ambitions and the real potential of the country, would impact negatively on Italy's efforts to become a genuine great power. Furthermore, this increased Italy's claims throughout the war and the Peace Conference. By taking a wider and comparative perspective, this book aims to show how the geopolitical goals of Britain and Italy, which in 1914–1915 seemed compatible and

(Bologna: Zanichelli, 1934), pp. 35 ff.; I. Bonomi, *La politica italiana da Porta Pia a Vittorio Veneto (1870–1918)* (Turin: Einaudi, 1944), p. 206; L. Salvatorelli, *La Triplice Alleanza. Storia diplomatica 1877–1912* (Milan: Istituto per gli Studi di Politica Internazionale, 1940), p. 17; E. Decleva, *L'Italia e la politica internazionale dal 1870 al 1914. L'ultima fra le grandi potenze* (Milan: Mursia, 1974), p. 167.

[8] M. Caracciolo, *L'Italia e i suoi Alleati nella Grande Guerra* (Milan: Mondadori, 1932).
[9] M. Toscano, *Il Patto di Londra* (Pavia: Pubblicazioni della Facoltà di Scienze Politiche, 1931); B. Vigezzi, *L'Italia di fronte alla Prima guerra mondiale (1914–1915)*, vol. I, *L'Italia neutrale* (Milan & Naples: Ricciardi, 1966).
[10] A. Mayer, *Politics and Diplomacy of Peacemaking. Containment and Counterrevolution at Versailles, 1918–1919* (London: Weidenfeld & Nicolson, 1967), p. 675.
[11] Bosworth, *Italy, the Least*, pp. 18–19.
[12] B. Croce in *Il Giornale d'Italia*, 9 July 1924; Bosworth, *Italy and the Approach of the First World War* (London & Basingstoke: Macmillan, 1983), pp. 28–50.
[13] Gooch, *The Italian Army and the First World War* (Cambridge: Cambridge University Press, 2014).

even mutually supportive, grew increasingly irreconcilable by the end of the war. This discrepancy hinted at possible future conflict.

Connected to the problem of war aims is the debate on how the Italian intervention was brought about. As mentioned, the issue of involving neutral countries in the fighting was recurrent in World War I, yet negotiations over Italy's entry were arguably the most complex of all. Italian and non-Italian historians have interpreted them oppositely. Whilst the former have either justified Italy's shift in alliance with the need to complete national unification,[14] or welcomed it as a model-pragmatism,[15] the latter described Italy as a bargainer which, in true Machiavellian fashion, offered its services 'for sale to the highest bidder'.[16] This left a historiographical gap which the present volume aims to fill, taking into account the feelings and complex dynamics running through the Italian ruling class and public opinion, which motivated Italy's ambiguous attitude, as well as the often-forgotten yet crucial part played by Britain in forcing Italy out of its neutrality – not least by what some have termed 'coercive diplomacy'.[17] The way in which such negotiations were conducted indicated a trend in inter-Allied relations in the years that followed. Of the Entente nations, Britain was the most determined to have Italy in the Alliance and encouraged Italian imperialist ambitions with the Treaty of London, which promised Rome substantial territorial gains in exchange for Italy's support. Rome thus saw Britain as the guarantor of the London Treaty.

Other problems in Anglo-Italian relations emerged during the war as a result of conflicting evaluations of Italy's contribution to the final victory. Those writers on British strategy devoted little attention to the importance of Italy in Britain's strategic thinking, while Italian scholars such as Mario Isnenghi and Giorgio Rochat, authors of the best volume on Italy's war, did not grasp the degree to which Italy's experience was shaped by its 'special partnership' with Britain, especially in the maritime and financial spheres. Yet Italy proved recalcitrant to abide when Britain, which remained the leading power in the Entente until America

---

[14] See above-mentioned authors, and especially Caracciolo.

[15] M. Isnenghi, G. Rochat, *La Grande Guerra, 1914–1918* (Florence: La Nuova Italia, 2000).

[16] Strachan, *The First World War: A New Illustrated History* (London: Simon & Schuster, 2003), p. 120; C. J. Lowe, F. Marzari, *Italian Foreign Policy, 1870–1945* (London & Boston: Routledge & Keegan Paul, 1975), pp. 133–150; Stevenson, *1914–1918: The History of the First World War* (London: Penguin, 2012), pp. 110–112; W. Gottlieb, *Studies in Secret Diplomacy during the First World War* (London: Allen & Unwin, 1957), pp. 146–149, 198; M. Thompson, *The White War. Life and Death on the Italian Front (1915–1919)* (London: Faber, 2008), p. 25.

[17] B. A. Ellman, S. C. M. Paine eds., *Naval Coalition Warfare. From Napoleonic Wars to Operation Iraqi Freedom* (London & New York: Routledge, 2008), p. 154.

overshadowed it, tried to coordinate the Allied war effort: Rome saw in British attempts to dictate Allied strategy, an intention to preserve British resources at the expense of Italy. Such strategic contrasts spurred James Burgwyn to conclude that Italy's alignment with the Allies 'was always a *mésalliance*'.[18] Some Italian historians share that view. Luca Riccardi, author of the main work on Italian war diplomacy, holds that Italy found in its new Entente partners 'allies' but not 'friends';[19] Salvemini called Italy a 'provisionary ally',[20] a term re-evoked by Maria Grazia Malchionni as 'occasional travel companion'.[21] This reading needs integrating with an account of the efforts made – largely by Britain – to bridge differences and an evaluation of the ambiguous results. Furthermore, historians have so far been oblivious to the fact that Italy's entry did not present only an obvious coordination problem, but it also provided the original allies with an opportunity to manipulate the newcomer in their own disputes. A deeper analysis of Anglo-Italian relations during the war, then, can shed light on how the Entente functioned, and how the ups and downs in this bilateral relation shaped Allied global strategy.

A corollary to British complaints that Italy was little cooperative was the criticism about the efficacy of Italy's war. It is all too familiar, thanks to the remarkable number of works that downplay Italy's contribution. These reflect Allied frustration at realising that Italy's entry did not deliver the final blow to the Central Powers as initially hoped. Italy was accused of fighting only where it served its empire project, and Allied criticisms encroached upon the operational and tactical levels. More recently, scholars such as Gooch, Stevenson and Vanda Wilcox have challenged the traditional view of the Italian front as a marginal and almost peaceful war theatre, by revealing to non-Italians how destructive that front really was and how cardinal was Italy's support for the Entente. Not only did Italian intervention prove to be the major diplomatic success for the Allies, but it also changed the geopolitical chessboard of the conflict, depriving the Central Powers of just the support they would have needed to win the war before the United States joined. Indeed, any military expert asked to consider a hypothetical what-if Italy had

---

[18] H. J. Burgwyn, *The Legend of the Mutilated Victory: Italy, the Great War, and the Paris Peace Conference, 1915–1919* (Westport, CT & London: Greenwood, 1993), p. 2.

[19] L. Riccardi, *Alleati non amici. Le relazioni politiche fra l'Italia e l'Intesa durante la prima guerra mondiale* (Brescia: Morcelliana, 1992).

[20] Salvemini, 'La diplomazia italiana nella grande guerra', in *Dal Patto di Londra alla Pace di Roma. Documenti della politica che non fu fatta* (Turin: Gobetti, 1925), pp. 750–752.

[21] M. G. Melchionni, *La vittoria mutilata. Problemi ed incertezze della politica estera italiana sul finire della Grande Guerra (ottobre 1918–gennatio 1919)* (Rome: Ed. Storia e Letteratura, 1981), p. 147.

remained neutral or had joined Germany's allies, would perhaps conclude total or partial victory for the Central Powers. Without the Italo-
Austrian front, Vienna could probably have crushed Serbia earlier than
1916 and could have contributed significantly to an earlier downfall of
Russia. These consequences of prolonged Italian neutrality would have
been aggravated by an Italian attack on France in the south, by a joint
Italo-Austrian naval effort hampering Allied operations and trade routes
in the Mediterranean, and by a potential Italo-Turkish offensive in Egypt
from Italian Libya and Ottoman Palestine, had Italy joined the Central
Powers. Finally, the performance of the Italian army (*Regio Esercito*) and
navy (*Regia Marina*) was worthier than usually appreciated, given the
means at their disposal and the geographic features of their operational
theatres.[22] To understand why this was never grasped by Italy's allies, one
needs to look at the persistent stereotypes by which any country tended to
look at its partners, and to analyse the different propaganda techniques
each Ally used to promote its cause. Alliances, of course, consist of
individuals from different cultures, including military subcultures.
Thus, a war of coalition 'demands compromise, the sacrifice of cherished
assumptions, and a deep understanding of Allied concerns, aims, and
fears'.[23] Britain and Italy had different understandings of this problem, as
we shall see. Inefficient inter-Allied communication was indeed one of the
main faults in the Entente's war. It hampered Allied solidarity and mutual
understanding, no less than military coordination. Italy's failure in this
respect had a notable impact on its relations with its allies – especially
Britain.

The Peace Conference at Versailles (Paris) provided the stage where
differences mounted throughout the war converged and collided.
Traditionally, there has been a tendency to analyse the war and the
making of the peace as two separate things. Studies of the Paris Peace
Conference, including works of excellence by Margaret MacMillan and
Leonard Smith[24] follow this approach. Mayer did consider how domestic
politics from 1917 onwards influenced the peace talks,[25] but the process
of peace-making began earlier than 1917, at least in Britain. It was in the
summer of 1916 that a reflection on the British scheme for peace-making

---

[22] Stevenson, *1917*, p. 213; V. Wilcox, *Morale and the Italian Army during the First World War* (Cambridge: Cambridge University Press, 2016); Gooch, *Italian Army, cit.*

[23] W. Murray, R. Hart Sinnreich, J. Lacey eds., *The Shaping of Grand Strategy. Policy, Diplomacy, and War* (Cambridge: Cambridge University Press, 2011), p. 28.

[24] M. MacMillan, *Peacemakers. The Paris Peace Conference of 1919 and Its Attempt to End War* (London: Murray, 2001); L. Smith, *Sovereignty at the Paris Peace Conference of 1919* (Oxford: Oxford University Press, 2018).

[25] Mayer, *Political Origins of the New Diplomacy, 1917–1918* (New Haven: Yale University Press, 1959).

began to develop as part of a broader debate on British war aims. The scope of Britain's war, the military strategy necessary to achieve it, and the diplomatic tactics needed to capitalise on victory, were a continuum, rather than three successive steps, in the minds of British policy- and strategy-makers. Each of the three elements influenced the others. This does not mean that the process of preparing for peace while waging war was coherent. But it does mean that, in the case of Britain, peace-planning was approached in an increasingly systematic way and Versailles was just the implementation phase – not even the culmination of the process, for the peace settlement continued to be adjusted in the years that followed. In other words, when approaching the issue of warfare and peace-making, we ought to bear in mind that history is a living process. The present book thus follows the approach of Burgwyn and Erik Goldstein. The former was the first to examine Italy's grand strategy from the intervention to the Peace Conference, seeing the result of the latter as a direct outgrowth of Italy's wartime disputes with its allies. The latter author studied British peace-making from 1916 to 1920.[26] This book complements those works, expanding the analysis into new aspects such as naval developments, financial negotiations and propaganda, and at times proposing a different reading of events. My aim is to show how the diverging approaches to peace-making in Britain and Italy shaped their war strategies as well as their diplomacy at Versailles – and, more specifically, how the absence of an early peace-planning phase in Italy weakened Rome's position. In turn, this wrenched Italy's liberal institutions. The domestic policy–foreign policy interplay highlighted by Mayer, when it works in one direction because of the repercussions of the former on the latter, also works in the opposite direction because international success or failure, can consolidate or crumble a country's political and institutional system.[27]

Finally, a longer perspective on peace-making leads to a partial revision of the literature on the Italian failure at Versailles. Traditionally, the claim of the British, American and French statesmen that the unsatisfactory – to Italy – result was caused by Italy's wild demands and stubborn refusal to come to a 'just' compromise at the peace talks have been accepted by historians. It seemed coherent with the widespread and solid prejudice that saw Italian foreign policy, from the unification onwards, as unreliable by nature – made of repeated 'diplomatic conjuring'.[28] So, little credence

---

[26] E. Goldstein, *Winning the Peace. British Diplomatic Strategy, Peace Planning, and the Paris Peace Conference, 1916–1920* (Oxford: Clarendon, 1991).

[27] Decleva, *L'incerto alleato. Ricerche sugli orientamenti internazionali dell'Italia unita* (Milan: Angeli, 1987), p. 8.

[28] Bosworth, *Italy, the Least*, p. 297.

has ever been given to the assertion of Italian statesmen that they had good reasons to believe Italy had been deceived.[29] While critics of the Italian position argue that the Italian 'mutilated victory' was pure myth invented by frustrated nationalists deprived of imperialist booty, Burgwyn holds that 'the notion of the mutilated victory was at least a half-truth that grew out of the stresses and strains of Italy's wartime diplomacy'.[30] Now, however, discovery of the private papers of the Italian and British ambassadors, Guglielmo Imperiali and Sir Rennell Rodd provides new insights into this question, which had tremendous consequences for Europe in the years to come.

The structure of the book is meant to find a balance between a purely chronological order and a thematic order. In the case of Anglo-Italian relations in World War I, this is facilitated by the fact that various diplomatic issues became urgent in sequence. That is where the chapter division originates, though there is a limited movement back and forth in time in some chapters, which bows to topic consistency – this, I hope, need not be confusing for the reader. The first part of the volume details how Britain and Italy turned their traditional friendship into an alliance, bringing Italy into the Entente. It highlights how contested this process was, both domestically and internationally, and on what premises it was accomplished. The second part studies how such differences influenced the Entente's war. The third part of the volume is dedicated to the decline in Anglo-Italian relations in the final act of the war and the Peace Conference, the battle of Caporetto in October 1917 being taken as the turning point, which marked a significant shift in Italy's position within the Entente.

The end of the story presented difficulties in its own right. There was no official end to the Peace Conference; the signature of the German Treaty on 28 June 1919 is taken as a symbolic conclusion of the conference, but work continued on the Austrian and Turkish Treaties, and a final Near East settlement was achieved only at Lausanne in 1923. Then the Versailles Treaty was revised at Locarno in 1925. Italy and Britain had interests in all these treaties – in fact, Italy was more involved in the Austrian and Turkish treaties than in the German. Thus, ending the story with the grand ceremony of 28 June 1919 seemed unsatisfactory. On the other hand, stretching the narrative to the Lausanne and Locarno Conferences would have risked losing sight of the connection between war and peace-making strategies, which the volume aims to emphasise:

---

[29] S. Sonnino, *Diario (1916–1922)*, 3 vols. (Bari: Laterza, 1972); V. E. Orlando, *Memorie (1915–1919)* (Milan: Rizzoli, 1960).
[30] Burgwyn, *The Legend*, p. 1.

later treaties, though assessing problems that originated in the war were motivated by post-war politics, and they were dealt with by an altogether different group of European political leaders. This is particularly true in the case of Italy, where the rise of Benito Mussolini in 1922 is generally taken as a turning point between World War I and post-war periods. The latter argument is debatable, a point made by Bosworth and others.[31] Indeed, the fascist overthrow of Liberal Italy had little impact on the protracted negotiations for a final European and Mediterranean settlement, as it largely failed to reverse Italy's downgrade. The book ends when Italy's imperial ambitions were shattered with the official rejection of the London Pact, made by Italy's Entente allies in June 1919. Coupled with the earlier rejection of the 1917 colonial treaty, this 'mutilated' Italy's victory. It also coincided with the downfall of Italy's last War Cabinet, and the eclipsing of the last statesmen who had led Italy into the war and the Peace Conference. The Epilogue links this showdown with a less crucial yet not insignificant event, which had continuity with the peace talks that cannot be ignored – the apparent end of the Fiume crisis with the expulsion of the legion of Italian nationalist occupants of the city under Gabriele D'Annunzio. It was a symbolic close of Italy's wartime aspirations.

By looking at the Anglo-Italian 'special partnership', I seek to offer an original account of how bilateral relations modelled coalition warfare in World War I. The book aspires to go beyond classic diplomatic history by giving greater attention to the implementation – not just the shaping – of war strategies. The volume contextualises these strategies within the social and political backdrop of the period, including its cultural aspects – though this is not a work of cultural history; this book is primarily about the grand strategy of war and peace – with some intrusions into operational and tactical details – where the three main issues of war aims, war strategy and peace-making are put into perspective and analysed in their evolution. For each of the three areas, the book highlights how the different approaches of Britain and Italy generated expectations that conflicted with reality, creating disappointment and mutual recrimination and ultimately corroding Anglo-Italian relations. It is also pregnant with considerations on the making of strategy today.

Because of the centrifugal forces that were at play, the Entente-Italy 1914–1915 talks have still much to say about the relations between belligerent and neutral countries, as well as about the turning of longer-lasting alliances into heterogeneous ad hoc fighting groups. That of Britain and Italy is also an emblematic case study of how first-class powers

---

[31] Bosworth, *Italy, the Least*, pp. 18–19; Burgwyn, *The Legend*, p. 319.

and emerging powers can conduct coalition warfare – and of what problems they usually face in the process. It also shows how crucial aspects in the shaping of national grand strategies were influenced by internal dynamics. The applicability of grand strategy makes particular sense today, especially to the world superpowers such as the United States, China and Russia, all of which have to unite maritime capabilities to those of land power, to project power at a distance and to acquire and lead lesser allies. Moreover, the damage to Allied solidarity, mutual understanding and military coordination made by mistrust and poor communication within the Entente reveals that the communication of strategic intentions, war experiences and national views on matters of allied interest are far from merely a question of diplomacy. In such context, maintaining any strategic continuity at all required supplementary efforts on the part of statesmen, diplomats and generals – which, even in a war of *matériel*, highlights the importance of individuals.

Another aspect of the functioning of alliances is the issue of how to attack hostile alliances and how to respond to an attack at the core of your alliance. The Entente, for example, made extensive strategic use of propaganda against the enemy. By contrast, it had to respond to the use by the Central Powers of revolution as a strategic weapon. This raises the problem of adaptability and flexibility of a fighting coalition. It has both a strategic and an operational significance, and they remain with us today. The impact of interoperability, for example, was made vividly clear in a speech by the US Chief of Naval Operations, Michael Mullen, at the seventeenth International Seapower Symposium in September 2005: 'Perhaps the most profound effect of today's challenges', Mullen claimed, 'is the increased value of cooperation between friends, allies, coalition partners, and like-minded nations'.[32] The Entente response to such issues, yet again, cannot be neglected by those interested in the changing character of war. Last but not least, the case of Italy in 1918–1919 demonstrates that, although indispensable to waging a successful war, operational success is not sufficient for strategic or geopolitical success. Perhaps obvious to military history aficionados, that was a lesson that many others, including the Germans in World War II, and the Americans in Vietnam, Iraq, and elsewhere would come to learn first-hand.

---

[32] M. Mullen, 'Keynote Address', in J. B. Hattendorf ed., *Seventeenth International Seapower Symposium: Report of the Proceedings, 19–23 September 2005* (Newport: Naval War College Press, 2006), pp. 4–5.

Part I

Making the Anglo-Italian Entente
(1911–1915)

1   Context

Turning a friend into an ally might appear to be an easy job. The case of Britain and Italy at the outbreak of World War I shows how uneven and contested such a process really is. Anglo-Italian friendship was an obvious element of European international relations in the *Belle Époque*. Britain had sponsored Italian unification in 1861, which was subsequently consolidated mainly thanks to the *Pax Britannica*; furthermore, the two countries had strong commercial ties; they shared the same liberal values and seemed to have close colonial and Mediterranean interests.

When World War I broke out, it appeared that Anglo-Italian ties would play a crucial part in determining Italian choices in foreign policy. The conflict was ignited on 28 June 1914 by the assassination of Archduke Ferdinand, heir to the Austro-Hungarian throne, in Sarajevo. Austria-Hungary accused its neighbour, Serbia – a rival in Balkan affairs – of having aided the assassins, and sent an ultimatum demanding humiliating concessions. When Serbia rejected it, Austro-Hungary declared war. The domino-effect was quick. Russia, feeling obliged to protect a fellow Slav nation, begun mobilisation, spurring a declaration of war by Germany, Austria-Hungary's main ally, on 1 August. This implied war with France, which Germany declared on 3 August. Italy refused to follow suit, proclaiming its neutrality. The war involved Britain on 4 August, when Germany's famous Schliffen plan, designed to knock France out of the conflict in a few weeks before concentrating on Russia, led German forces to violate neutral Belgium. A British Expeditionary Force (BEF) landed in France on 12 August, whilst the French launched their own offensive in Alsace-Lorraine. This was driven back with enormous losses on both sides. The main German thrust towards Paris was halted on the Marne River between 6 and 12 September, after which a series of clashes northward led to the First Battle of Ypres in October, and the stabilisation of the western front from the English Channel to the Swiss border. Both parties dug in, seeking shelter from devastating machine gun and artillery fire: trench warfare had begun.

Britain applied its usual maritime strategy – one that had been successful against Napoleon a hundred years earlier: a blockade of the Central Powers to strangle their economies. The Germans responded with a counter-blockade thanks to the new submarine weapon, challenging British supply routes. In the meantime, Austria-Hungary failed to defeat Serbia, whilst Russia's invasion of East Prussia blundered into disaster at the battles of Tannenberg (26–30 August) and the Masurian Lakes (7–14 September). Austro-Hungarian offensives in the east against Russia nonetheless failed to capitalise on German victories. Russian weakness encouraged an Ottoman intervention on the side of the Central Powers, opening a new front in the Middle East and North Africa. The war raged in the oceans and European colonies as well, with French and British forces kept in check by inferior German troops in Africa for a couple of years – in East Africa, for the duration of the conflict – whilst German possessions in the Pacific were soon occupied by troops of British dominions Australia and New Zealand. As winter closed in, a new Austro-Hungarian offensive in Serbia was shattered, together with the widespread expectation that the conflict would last a few months.

In this context, secret talks on possible Italian intervention took place. In the summer of 1914, such talks were dominated by Anglo-Italian conversations that seemed to lead to a quick shift on the part of Italy from its allies of the Triple Alliance to the Triple Entente. But soon less obvious factors burst onto the scene causing the negotiations to drag on for nine months. Arguably, the talks succeeded only when Britain took the lead in the Entente diplomatic action. From an analysis of Anglo-Italian relations during Italy's neutrality, therefore, we can draw some general conclusions about the problems facing alliances at war when dealing with neutrals and attempting to involve them in the conflict. First, deep-rooted stereotypes can have a greater impact on diplomatic action than is generally appreciated, and the role of individuals can be crucial in bridging differences and influencing national policies. Second, there is a fundamental difference between the war aims of belligerent countries – focussed on the immediate need to end the war successfully and as quickly as possible – and those of neutrals willing to enter the fray – focussed on the terms of their participation and the fulfilment of those terms. Third, the impacts of economic warfare and of political espionage in influencing neutrals are often overlooked aspects that can ultimately prove more effective than traditional diplomatic instruments. Finally, alliances are rarely born overnight and, however good the relations between two countries, they are not generally based on ideals and shared values, but on convergence of interests and on the art of compromise.

2   Traditional Friendship

The student of European international relations in 1914 could argue that relations between Great Britain and Italy had always been friendly *despite* the British and the Italians. The two peoples were not without some common traits and a certain mutual respect, but what prevailed were the deeper-rooted stereotypes by which they knew each other. For the British, the Italians were a rough, immature, disorganised and essentially faint-hearted people. The Italians, for their part, reacted with a mixture of admiration, envy and resentment.

True, the British ruling class admired the history and values bequeathed by ancient Rome, when London was only an outpost of its empire, and the artistic conquests of the Renaissance. And also true, they supported the Italian Risorgimento.[1] More tellingly, the wider British public, in Queen Victoria's words, 'went mad' for some of its protagonists, Giuseppe Garibaldi above all. This was evident in the triumphant welcome Garibaldi received on his visit to Britain in 1864.[2] Other protagonists of the Risorgimento enjoyed less success. In 1856 Victor Emmanuel II, then still king of Sardinia-Piedmont, had made a marriage proposal to Princess Mary of Cambridge, cousin to Queen Victoria and sister of Lord Cambridge, Chief of the British General Staff. In the view of Camillo Cavour, Sardinia's Prime Minister, such an alliance would have proved extremely valuable to the prospect of unifying Italy under the Savoy. The princess had politely declined the proposal, declaring quite frankly to Queen Victoria that she found the prospect of spending her lifetime with such a 'rough man' unattractive.[3] More generally, one can argue that neither the enthusiasm for the Risorgimento and the living legend of Garibaldi nor that for

---

[1] S. Patriarca, *Italianità. La costruzione del carattere nazionale* (Bari: Laterza, 2010), p. 12.
[2] See: P. Milza, *Garibaldi* (Milan: Longanesi, 2013).
[3] BOD, Clarendon papers, box C.136, Clarendon to Marochetti, 20 September 1856; E. Di Nolfo, 'Il mancato matrimonio di Vittorio Emanuele II con la Principessa Mary di Cambridge', *Il Risorgimento*, XIX, 1967, pp. 93–111.

ancient Rome, however powerful, ever led to a real British interest in Italy as a new European power. For the British, once the adventure of the Risorgimento was over, Italy was largely unknown and the Italians were an essentially indecipherable people.

The attention of the British public was revived in 1911 with the publication of George M. Trevelyan's *Garibaldi and the Making of Italy*. Trevelyan, a well-known British historian, wrote a trilogy covering the Risorgimento. *Garibaldi and the Making of Italy* was the final volume, published to coincide with the fiftieth anniversary of Italy's unification. The Risorgimento, in Trevelyan's view, was a step forward in 'man's long march to civilisation'. Garibaldi was the hero, 'the rover of great spaces of land and sea, the fighter against desperate odds, the champion of the oppressed, the patriot, the humane and generous man all in one'. Italy was described as a nation reborn, rising up from its ruins, no longer 'the home of ghosts, but the land which the living share with their immortal ancestors'.[4] However, Trevelyan believed that 'the comic element is never long absent in Italy'[5] and investigated the reason for this discrepancy:

Some people regard the Italians as sentimental idealists. ... Others condemn them as materialists. Materialism and idealism are found side-by-side in much sharper contrast than in England. ... Foggy like his climate, the Englishman ... makes an indistinguishable blur of ideal and material motives for action. ... The Italian, on the other hand ... thinks that he is guided in an action either by grovelling self-interest or by lofty ideals, and he makes no ploy about saying the one or the other. ... But most Italians are materialists one day and idealists the next. Hence their mercurial character.[6]

In the same year another book on Italy portrayed a different picture. Published in Germany and translated across Europe, Thomas Mann's *Death in Venice* described the *Bel Paese* with heavy and grotesque traits: the Italians were a nation of greedy liars and Italy the country of decadence, corruption, poverty, and both physical and moral illnesses. Mann evoked Italian stereotypes that had been circulating in Northern Europe since the late Middle Ages: the Italian character was corrupted by Catholic superstition, indolence, the typical 'Mediterranean effeminacy' and the immorality of Niccolò Machiavelli.[7]

---

[4] G. M. Trevelyan, *Garibaldi's Defence of the Roman Republic* (London: Longmans Green, 1907), pp. 11–16.

[5] Trevelyan, *Garibaldi and the Thousand* (London: Longmans Green, 1909), p. 41.

[6] Trevelyan, *Scenes from Italy's War* (London: T.C. & E.C. Jack, 1919), pp. 11–12.

[7] H. Heller, *Anti-Italianism in Sixteenth-Century France* (Toronto, Buffalo, London: University of Toronto Press, 2003).

Trevelyan and Mann described the two viewpoints from which the British public knew Italy – and the latter quickly became more widespread. Trevelyan believed that the decline of British sympathies towards Italians began after the unification of Italy, when Italian elites were 'no longer constrained to live in exile in England'. At the same time, there was 'a diminution of mutual business connections relatively to those formed with the other countries'.[8] Since then, the *Bel Paese* was, for the British, primarily a holiday destination. It did not do much good to Italy's reputation as a new European power. British visitors were enthusiastic about the artistic and naturalistic beauties of the Peninsula but had a much lower impression of its inhabitants, who 'wasted their time in promenades' or 'tender, if not licentious gallantries', and lived in a 'state of satisfied subjection'.[9] A British guidebook in 1905 warned that it was only the sun which helped redeem Italy 'from a sort of vulgarity or the suspicion of a kind of hideous squalor'.[10] Some found this predilection for the morbid, this kaleidoscope of beauty and poverty, singularly odd, even exciting. As Bosworth noted, a British noblewoman travelling around Italy wrote: 'Civilisation, cleanliness and comfort are excellent things, but they are sworn enemies to the picturesque'.[11]

This view of Italy as a young country taking its first step towards civilisation – with rather poor results – was confirmed by Italian politics.[12] *The Times* correspondent Henry Wickham Steed described Rome as a place of 'bedraggled untidiness' where 'the game of politics [seemed] to be played according to other rules than those to which I had been accustomed'.[13] Sir Francis Bertie, the British ambassador to Rome from 1903 to 1905, declared: 'Italy was like a woman with two lovers whose jealousy of each other she utilised for her own profit'.[14] One British journalist wrote: 'To find an English resident in Italy who is not perpetually in a state of only semi-suppressed irritation with the Italians is a thing so rare as to be remarkable. "They are like children", is the stock criticism'.[15] Bosworth

---

[8] Trevelyan, *Scenes*, pp. 35–36.

[9] M. O'Connor, *The Romance of Italy and the English Political Imagination* (New York: St Martin's Press, 1998), p. 47.

[10] N. Douglas, *Old Calabria* (London: Secker & Warburg, 1915).

[11] Bosworth, *Italy and the Approach*, p. 3.

[12] J. Tilley, *London to Tokyo* (London: Hutchinson, 1942), p. 32.

[13] H. W. Steed, *Through Thirty Years, 1892–1922. A Personal Narrative*, 2 vols. (London: Heinemann, 1924), I, pp. 103–104.

[14] British Documents on the Origins of the War 1898–1914 (BD), vols. I–IX (London: G. P. Gooch, H. Temperley eds., 1926–1935), FO800/173, Bertie to Mallet, 15 April 1905.

[15] R. Bagot, *My Italian Year* (London, 1911), p. 2.

underlined that such impressions were to prove long-lasting – the British continued to say much the same things about Fascist Italy.[16]

Of course, the Italians were not the only people the British stereotyped – the Irish provided another obvious case.[17] It is also important to stress that such stereotyping was to a degree self-inflicted. Italian intellectuals and patriots tended to see the degenerated Italian character as the main reason for the decline of the *Bel Paese* in world politics.[18] The very word 'Risorgimento', taken to indicate the process of reunification of the country, implied, as a necessary first step, a moral regeneration of the Italian people.[19] Many Italian intellectuals condemned Italian idleness (*beatissimo far niente*, 'happy sitting around'), indolence and individualism as the main national vices,[20] whilst Pasquale Villari, the most popular historian of Liberal Italy, attributed Italy's weakness to its 'illiterate people, ignorant professors, impossible diplomats, and incapable generals'.[21] As Silvana Patriarca highlighted, this reveals that Italian stereotypes were deeply internalised by the Italian elites, but the latter hoped that Italy could redeem itself from its hundred-year-long thraldom.[22] Needless to say, they judged the Risorgimento incomplete when the Italian Kingdom was proclaimed in 1861, partly because Rome, Venice, Trento and Trieste were not included, but also because the hoped-for moral regeneration of Italians had not yet occurred – in fact, Italy had needed foreign aid to be unified.[23]

To fully redeem Italy, the majority of Italian intellectuals suggested taking Britain as a model.[24] They admired the British and saw their empire as the modern version of the Roman Empire. This feeling was nonetheless accompanied by a sense of frustration which turned into an inferiority complex. Many Italian elites knew their people were considered inferior

---

[16] Bosworth, *Italy and the Approach*, p. 5.
[17] T. Eagleton, F. Jameson, E. W. Said, *Nationalism, Colonialism, and Literature* (Minneapolis & London: University of Minnesota Press, 1990).
[18] M. Pickering, *Stereotyping. The Politics of Representation* (Basingstoke & New York: Palgrave, 2001); F. Venturi, 'Il movimento riformatore degli illuministi meridionali', *Rivista Storica Italiana*, 74, 1962.
[19] Patriarca, *Italianità*, pp. 6, 13.
[20] C. Balbo, *Le speranze d'Italia* (Naples: Gemelli, 1848); G. Leopardi, 'All'Italia', in *Canti* (Naples: Starita, 1835); G. Mazzini, 'Interessi e principii', *La Giovine Italia*, 1832); C. Lozzi, *Dell'ozio in Italia*, 2 vols. (Turin: Unione Tipografico-Editrice, 1870–1871); D. Carina, *Dell'ozio in Italia. Osservazioni* (Forlì: Gherardi, 1871); F. De Sanctis, *Saggi critici* (Naples: Morano, 1890).
[21] P. Villari, 'Di chi è la colpa? O sia la pace e la guerra', *Il Politecnico*, IV, 2, 1866.
[22] Patriarca, *Italianità*, p. 15.
[23] M. D'Azeglio, *I miei ricordi* (Florence: Barbera, 1867); De Sanctis, *Storia della letteratura italiana*, 2 vols. (Naples: Morano, 1870–1871).
[24] G. Ferrero, *L'Europa giovane. Studi e viaggi nei paesi del nord* (Milan: Treves, 1897), pp. 420–421; Balbo, *Pensieri sulla storia d'Italia. Studi* (Florence: Le Monnier, 1858), p. 513.

and at times reacted angrily. Vincenzo Cuoco, Vincenzo Gioberti and Pasquale Turiello responded to anti-Italian generalisations by proclaiming the superiority of Italian civilisation,[25] whilst Paolo Mantegazza and Napoleone Colajanni rejected the idea of an 'Anglo-Saxon superiority' point-blank.[26] They particularly disliked the British stance as 'masters' of Europe, adopted with an arrogance that was often unbearable, particularly when British success rested not on battles fought in pursuit of ideals, as in France, 'the country of the "rights of man"',[27] but on commercial and financial wealth. Some in Italy commented sarcastically that both sectors, banking and finance, had an Italian origin, as had jurisprudence, the art of western war and political science. Hence the Anglo-Saxon swagger was even less tolerable when it did not admit 'the ancient debts of England to Italy'[28] – an increasingly spiteful discourse, no less fed on stereotypes than that of the British.

The British view of Italy was overall based on the reports of diplomats and journalists, or the impressions of travellers and visitors. The impression of Britain held by Italians, however, was founded also on the experience of Italian immigrants living in Britain – some 20,000 in 1914.[29] Rome tried to keep in touch with emigrants, so that they would feel they were 'Italian citizens'. In the Ten Commandments for the Italian Abroad, the strongest advice was, along with obedience to the laws of the host country, the need to remember that one was always Italian, to speak Italian, to introduce oneself as Italian and as far as possible to marry within the Italian community so that the children would be educated as Italians. This policy discouraged complete integration and aggravated the usual problems of stereotyping and racism Italians experienced in Britain. Although Bosworth is quite right in noting that culture shocks of this kind were likely to be experienced by those southern Italians who moved to Northern Italy, rather than abroad,[30] the frustration that Italian immigrants felt in Britain at an only partial integration certainly did little to encourage mutual sympathy between the Italians and the British.

This is not a place to discuss the limits and artificiality of the mutual stereotypes, but it is important to bear them in mind because they had

---

[25] V. Cuoco, *Platone in Italia*, F. Nicolini ed. (Bari: Laterza, 1928), p. 259; V. Gioberti, *Del primato morale e civile degli italiani*, G. Balsamo-Crivelli ed., 2 vols. (Turin: Unione Tipografico-Editrice, 1920), II, p. 147; P. Turiello, *Governo e governati in Italia. Saggio*, 2 vols. (Bologna: Zanichelli, 1882), p. 108.

[26] Patriarca, *Italianità*, pp. 98 ff.; N. Colajanni, *Italiani del Nord e italiani del Sud (con 133 tavole numeriche e 31 tavole geografiche)* (Turin: Bocca, 1901), p. 53.

[27] Burgwyn, *The Legend*, p. 11.   [28] Trevelyan, *Scenes*, pp. 35–36.

[29] F. Coletti, 'Dell'emigrazione italiana', in P. Blaserna, *Cinquanta anni di storia italiana*, 3 vols. (Milan: Hoepli, 1911), III, p. 81.

[30] Bosworth, *Italy and the Approach*, p. 5.

a huge impact on Anglo-Italian political relations. It should come as no surprise to the reader to know that, throughout the second half of the nineteenth century, British policymakers never considered Italy as a potential ally. British views on Italian foreign policy were epitomised by a famous remark by A. J. P. Taylor: 'There were few real secrets in the diplomatic world [before 1914], and all diplomats were honest, according to their moral code'. This was accompanied by a footnote: 'It becomes wearisome to add "except the Italians" to every generalisation. Henceforth it may be assumed'. The 'childish', 'grotesque' and 'rascally' Italian people, governed by 'corrupt, Masonic politicians',[31] seemed to have very little to offer as an ally – and its reliability was almost non-existent.

Italy's interests in a British alliance were stronger. The years after unification were characterised in Italy by consolidation policies. Benedetto Croce metaphorically called that period the 'prose' of the administrative settling-in following the 'epic' feats of the Risorgimento.[32] In foreign policy, this included the rather spasmodic search for allies. Because of its recent origins, Liberal Italy could not call on a tradition of foreign policy to guide it. Italy was too weak to dictate the rules of the European concert but not so submissive that it would passively accept those of others. The nation struggled between two opposing lines of conduct: resign itself to being a second-class power, focussing on internal consolidation, or behave like a great power. Whichever of the two paths was followed, it would be necessary to garner support from a nation more concerned with urgent social and economic needs.[33]

On one principle Italian policymakers agreed: Italy could not stand alone in the European concert. Doubts, reservations, uncertainties and opposing views were, however, frequent regarding the road to take and the travelling companions to choose. Naturally, this was not a purely Italian situation. For any country, the choice to stand with one side or another implies responding to both internal and international rationales, to fears and hopes; no decision of this kind has ever been taken evenly. Yet it seems that foreign policy in Liberal Italy took on more dramatic hues because of the fundamental fragilities that unification had not overcome.[34] The political elite of Liberal Italy was generally aware of the structural limits of the country and lived in fear of losing what they had gained with such difficulty – Italy. This collective phobia that a major failure in foreign policy might lead to a collapse of the country can be found in the memoirs of Italian statesmen, in the works of poets and writers,[35] and in

---

[31] Ibid., p. 97.   [32] Croce, *Storia d'Italia dal 1871 al 1915* (Bari: Laterza, 1927), p. 399.
[33] Decleva, *L'incerto alleato*, p. 13.   [34] Burgwyn, *The Legend*, p. 7.
[35] Croce, *L'Italia dal 1914 al 1918: pagine sulla guerra* (Naples: Ricciardi, 1919); E. Corradini, *La patria lontana* (Milan: Treves, 1910) and *La guerra lontana* (Milan:

military provisions drawn up immediately after the 'liberation' of Rome in 1870. Italy had recently clashed with France, its ally in the 1859 Second War of Independence against Austria, over the dispute between Italy and the papacy on papal sovereignty over Rome. So the main Italian fear, which would remain alive for many years, was of a French attack undertaken with Vatican complicity. Visual evidence of this are the ruins of the so-called *Campo Trincerato Romano*, a line of fortifications erected to defend the strip of territory surrounding the capital. Work continued until 1891, an indelible symbol of a permanent state of fear.[36] On the opposite side of Italy's northern frontier with France was Austria, Italy's traditional enemy, still in possession of the Italian provinces of Venice, Trento and Trieste when the Italian Kingdom was proclaimed and awaiting its opportunity to retake Milan. Liberal Italy needed an ally that could neutralise Austria and deter France, and most Italian politicians favoured Britain. The long and low Italian coastline made friendship with the main maritime power imperative; Italy depended on British imports; the two countries had similar liberal institutions; and Italian statesmen were convinced that only British support would prevent their infant state from being strangled in its cradle by its neighbours. Their hopes were to be frustrated. London was interested in keeping strong commercial ties and good political relations with Rome since Italian friendship prevented any direct threat to British Mediterranean routes from the ports of La Spezia and Taranto, and British exports benefitted from the Italian market. But that was about it – a point made clear by William E. Gladstone, Prime Minister between 1868 and 1894.[37]

In 1866 Italy signed an alliance with Prussia, a continental power looking for expansion and unification of the fragmented German states. As the unification of Italy and Germany was proceeding in parallel, it seemed an obvious alliance. Indeed, it proved fruitful, as the two partners managed to defeat Austria, bringing about the Italian annexation of Veneto. However, the military developments of the 1866 campaign – which saw Italian reverses on land and at sea compensated by Prussia's decisive victory at Sadowa – made it an unbalanced alliance. It was not renewed on the eve of the Franco-Prussian War, and a rather isolated Italy could only look incredulously at the rapid Prussian triumph over the French Empire in 1870–1871. Furthermore, in 1879 Germany and Austria-Hungary signed a treaty of mutual defence, the Dual Alliance – also known as the Central

---

Treves, 1911); A. Oriani, *Fino a Dogali* (Milan: Galli, 1889), *La disfatta* (Milan: Treves, 1896) and *La rivolta ideale* (Naples: Ricciardi, 1908).

[36] S. Ferretti, P. Guarini, A. Giovannelli, A. Grimaldi, L. Tamborrino eds., *Operare i forti. Per un progetto di riconversione dei forti militari di Roma* (Rome: Gangemi, 2009), p. 11.

[37] C. Seton-Watson, *Storia d'Italia dal 1870 al 1925* (Bari: Laterza 1967), pp. 38 ff.

Powers alliance. Now Italy's former German ally and Italy's deadliest enemy were in an unprecedented *combinazione*, and Italian security seemed more precarious than ever. The previous year, the first Italian colonial ambitions had been frustrated at the Congress of Berlin – a significant setback for Italian diplomacy, which had for some years tried to gain French and British consent to an Italian expansion into Tunis. In 1881 France occupied Tunisia – a further humiliation for Italy, which shattered any possibility of a rapprochement with France in the short run. The following year, exploiting Italian dread of a potential encirclement by France in the west, Germany in the north and Austria-Hungary in the east, Berlin proposed to Rome an alliance with the Central Powers. Otto von Bismarck, the demiurge of the Second Reich, sought a Mediterranean ally in case another Franco-German conflict erupted over the question of the German occupation of Alsace-Lorraine (1871). The proposal caused intense debate in Italy, and it was a turning point in the fundamental question of Italy's status among the European powers: entering the alliance would have officially brought Italy into the club of the great powers; rejecting it would have left Italy isolated. A formal alliance also meant clear obligations: Italy would have to support its new allies militarily in the case of aggression by other powers; it would have to give up its claims for the Italian territories under Habsburg rule – the *terre irredente*, 'unredeemed lands'; and it would have to agree to a complex system of mutual compensation with Austria-Hungary in the case of unilateral expansion of either of the two former enemies in the Balkans. There were further implications. The alliance was clearly anti-Russian and anti-French, and despite the recent dispute with Paris, large sectors of the Italian ruling class and public opinion – including Prime Minister Agostino Depretis – still looked more favourably towards the 'Latin sister' than to Austria-Hungary. On the other hand, Depretis' Foreign Minister, Pasquale Stanislao Mancini, favoured the alliance. The decisive push was given by King Umberto I, a conservative monarch who openly sponsored the 'block of order', Germany and Austria-Hungary. On one thing they all agreed: no alliance must jeopardise Italy's good relations with Britain.[38] So Mancini posed one condition to Berlin and Vienna for the successful conclusion of the alliance: a declaration annexed to the treaty should be signed by the three powers stating explicitly that the alliance 'shall not in any case be directed against Britain'. Berlin and Vienna agreed. On 20 May 1882 the Triple Alliance was born.[39]

---

[38] G. Giordano, *Cilindri e feluche. La politica estera dell'Italia dopo l'Unità* (Rome: Aracne, 2008), pp. 219–225.

[39] J. Grenville, B. Wasserstein eds., *The Major International Treaties of the Twentieth Century. A History Guide with Texts* (London & New York: Routledge, 2013), p. 38.

The Mancini declaration shows that, although Italy had found the continental alliance it had been looking for since its unification, the fear among its policymakers that Italian security was threatened by neighbouring powers had not vanished. Rather, it had evolved into a permanent mistrust of everyone, be they allied or hostile countries – after all, one of the newly acquired allies was none other than the most recent and deadliest enemy. As paradoxical as it might sound, Italy – a country that very few seemed to trust because of its repeated shifts in alliances in the search for a real ally – mistrusted the other powers even more. In such a context, Italy desperately wanted to maintain its good relations with the strongest world power. In fact, Rome kept trying to extract a British commitment towards Italy even after the signature of the Triple Alliance Treaty, especially as it was not initially incompatible with the latter. That same year, Italy had some success: Britain indulged the first wave of Italian colonialism, as the Italians took possession of Assab (Eritrea). British generosity was a political calculation. The outbreak of the Mahdist revolt in Sudan threatened British interests in Eastern Africa, and London would rather see the Red Sea coast in the hands of a traditional friend than in those of Islamist fanatics or, even worse, a stronger power – France. In 1884, as the Egyptian garrisons retreated from the coast and the Mahdist revolt gained ground, Gladstone encouraged the Italians to occupy Massaua and, possibly, launch a military expedition to help relieve the siege of Khartoum.[40] The city, however, fell on 25 January 1885, and London informed Rome that it intended to leave Sudan for the time being and that consequently it would not support any further Italian advance in the region.[41] Some Italian statesmen reprimanded British egoism, reviving the stereotypical image of England as a nation of bankers and shopkeepers, only interested in Italy where the 'sacred British interests'[42] were at stake. Alberto Blanc, Foreign Minister, considered British foreign policy 'short-sighted, petty, and full of contradictions', disrespectful of the 'true friends of England'.[43]

Many Italian politicians nonetheless continued to emphasise Anglo-Italian special friendship and tried to capitalise on it. In 1887, Italian Foreign Minister Carlo Felice Di Robilant proposed to Lord Salisbury, who was several times the Secretary of State for Foreign Affairs between 1878 and 1900, an Anglo-Italian agreement to preserve the Mediterranean status quo. He promised to support Britain in Egypt, in exchange for

---

[40] C. Seton-Watson, *Storia d'Italia*, p. 140; Sonnino, *Diario*, I, p. 125.
[41] Gooch, *Italian Army*, pp. 17–18.
[42] G. Imperiali di Francavilla, *Diario 1915–1919* (Soveria Mannelli: Rubbettino, 2006), p. 132.
[43] Quoted in C. Seton-Watson, *Storia d'Italia*, p. 206.

British support 'of Italy's actions in any part of the Northern Africa littoral, and particularly in Tripolitania and Cyrenaica'. Salisbury conceded warily that any 'collaboration' between the two Governments should be decided 'according to circumstances'.[44] Further attempts by Robilant to get a formal British obligation failed; yet in the summer of 1890 the Italian minister extolled Salisbury's declaration that, should the Mediterranean status quo be altered, Italy could occupy Ottoman Tripoli.[45] This spurred Italian conviction that Italy was 'the *protégée* of Great Britain'.[46] Prime Minister Antonio Di Rudinì, a determined supporter of an Anglo-Italian special partnership, declared to the Italian Senate on 29 June 1891 that he could imagine 'no issue' in which Italy's position 'was not identical to that of England'. Quite tellingly, this declaration was made as a corollary to Rudinì's announcement of Italy's renewal of the Triple Alliance; it almost suggested that the renewal was subordinate to Anglo-Italian understanding. But it also exaggerated Britain's commitment towards Italy.[47] Salisbury was resolutely against any alliance limiting Britain's freedom of action.[48] Despite his reputation as a friend of Italy among Italian diplomats,[49] he privately called the Italians 'sturdy beggars'[50] that could be kept 'in England's camp' with a few 'small sugar plums'.[51] He also disliked the increased Italian African ambitions. So, he mellifluously suggested that Rome act in the colonies 'with the greatest caution and patience' – de facto putting on ice any Italian aspirations in North Africa.[52] Salisbury's successor, Lord Lansdowne, was equally determined to avoid any formal alliance with Italy. His main preoccupation was to preserve British detachment from European affairs: an Anglo-Italian alliance might cause Britain some trouble with other continental powers, such as France.[53] Lansdowne's view was in line with a new principle that dominated British foreign policy. It became known as 'splendid isolation', and however artificial this definition might be it certainly reflected the widespread idea in the British governing class that Britain, being geographically isolated and unchallenged at sea, should concentrate on its global

---

[44] Ibid., p. 146.   [45] Sonnino, *Diario*, I, pp. 220, 389.

[46] S. Quartararo, *Roma fra Londra e Berlino* (Rome: Bonacci, 1980), p. 35.

[47] W. Walters, 'Lord Salisbury's Refusal to Revise and Renew the Mediterranean Agreements', *The Slavonic Review*, 29, 1950, p. 283.

[48] A. J. P. Taylor, 'British Policy in Morocco, 1886–1902', *The English Historical Review*, LXVI, 260, 1951, pp. 350–353; Lowe, *Salisbury in the Mediterranean* (London: Routledge & Keegan Paul, 1965), p. 85.

[49] C. Seton-Watson, *Storia d'Italia*, p. 206.

[50] J. L., Glanville, *Italy's Relations with England 1896–1905* (Baltimore: Furst, 1934), p. 31.

[51] BOD, Rodd private papers [uncat.], Rodd to Cromer, 8 September 1902.

[52] C. Seton-Watson, *Storia d'Italia*, p. 159.

[53] TNA, FO800/132/28, Lansdowne to Currie, 12 December 1900.

interests, its industrial growth and its domestic political reforms, instead of European politics.[54]

Anglo-Italian relations in the second half of the nineteenth century, therefore, were characterised by some apparently contradictory principles. The two peoples clearly did not love each other, despite some strong values they held in common – which were more emphasised in Italy than in Britain. Geopolitically, Britain was a country that did not need – nor did it wish to have – allies; Italy was a country that looked for allies and found them elsewhere. Both Britain and Italy were willing to keep mutually friendly relations, but despite repeated Italian invitations for a stronger collaboration, Britain was not happy to concede. The changing geopolitical context at the turn of the century would significantly challenge some of those principles.

---

[54] Hart Sinnreich, 'About turn: British strategic transformation from Salisbury to Grey', in Murray, Sinnreich, Lacey eds., *Shaping of Grand Strategy*, p. 114.

3   Crumbling Principles

3.1   Descended from Olympus

In the last decade of the nineteenth century the principle of 'splendid isolation' in British foreign policy wavered, and by the turn of the century it had virtually come to an end. The Empire faced a progressive redistribution of global economic and military power. Britain lost its agricultural self-sufficiency becoming, for the first time in its history, an importer of food; it suffered an alarming decline in its industrial and technological advantage, particularly with respect to Germany and the United States; it struck growing protectionism on its global trade balance; it also witnessed the modernisation and enlargement of continental armies, accompanied by the rapid development of railroads, which affected Britain's main strategic advantage – the ability to transport its armed forces farther and faster than any of its potential adversaries. The Boer Wars (1880–1881 and 1899–1902) shattered Britain's confidence in the capacity of its army to face a first-class opponent.[1] Last, but perhaps most disturbing, Britain was confronted with increased threats to its worldwide maritime supremacy.[2]

Altogether, these factors produced concern about the British Empire's security and prosperity. As John Charmely wrote, 'for [Britons] ... it seemed as though everywhere they looked Britain's position was crumbling, in Africa, in the Near East, in the Far East, the challenges were mounting, and an isolated Britain ... appeared to have no strategy for dealing with it'.[3] Speculation about the likely causes and the course of a future war became a well-established and highly popular literary genre

---

[1] J. Darwin, *The Empire Project. The Rise and Fall of the British World-System 1830–1970* (Cambridge: Cambridge University Press, 2009), p. 258.
[2] Hart Sinnreich, 'About turn', p. 116.
[3] J. Charmley, *Splendid Isolation? Britain, the Balance of Power, and the Origins of the First World War* (London: Hodder & Stoughton, 1999), p. 232.

in Britain, with a steady rise in the output of semi-fictional accounts of conflicts between London and one or more of the other great powers.[4] The perception of the geopolitical and operational environment by British policymakers changed profoundly, and with it the strategic arrangements needed to maintain Britain's world supremacy.[5] Consequently, Britain's relationship with the other major powers also changed. Britain was the natural defender of the status quo, for it had more to fear than to gain from any readjustment in world power. Hence it renewed investment in military and naval programmes – such as the Naval Defence Act of 1889 and the Esher reforms (1906–1909) – and it pursued more active and flexible diplomacy in Europe.[6]

Italy was part of the new equation. In the late 1880s, traditional Anglo-French colonial competition and the expansion of Russia into Persia, Central Asia, the Far East and the Eastern Mediterranean made France and Russia obvious opponents of Britain. In 1887, Britain signed a naval agreement with Italy and Austria-Hungary aimed at preserving the Mediterranean status quo. In the following years, Rome tried again to promote 'a British alliance',[7] encouraging Vienna to welcome London into the Triple Alliance. This proposal was based on the assumption that 'England would much more easily be inspired by solidarity towards the Austro-German block' if Italy was part of the *combinazione*.[8] A veto, however, came from Berlin, owing to the tension that had begun gradually and fatally to ruin Anglo-German relations. In 1896, Germany rejected the Italian request to renew the Mancini declaration in attachment to the third renewal of the Triple Alliance. More and more it seemed that the German Reich would challenge the British world system. The threat of a Franco-Russian attack on Britain indeed faded in the early twentieth century, even though the 1894 Franco-Russian alliance had made any deterrence on them in the Mediterranean harder. After securing the British position at the periphery of the Empire through the Treaty of Hay-Pauncefote (1901) with the United States and the Anglo-Japanese alliance of 1902, London made tenacious efforts to reconcile with France and Russia.[9] Lord Lansdowne managed to agree with Paris to a comprehensive settlement of outstanding disputes in the imperial sphere, which cleared the way for the Anglo-French Entente Cordiale of

---

[4] J. Lawrence, *The Rise and Fall of the British Empire* (London: Abacus, 1995), p. 334.
[5] Gooch, 'The Weary Titan: Strategy and Policy in Great Britain, 1980–1918', in W. Murray, M. Knox, A. Bernstein eds., *The Making of Strategy: Rulers, States, and War* (Cambridge: Cambridge University Press, 1997), p. 305.
[6] Darwin, *The Empire Project*, p. 269.
[7] TNA, FO45/716, memoranda from Rome ns. 26–33, 31 January 1894.
[8] Sonnino, *Diario*, I, pp. 513–518.   [9] Hart Sinnreich, 'About turn', p. 134.

1904. This was followed by the Anglo-Russian convention of August 1907, which terminated an eighty-year cold war in the Middle East and Asia.[10] The Anglo-Russian agreement was largely the personal achievement of the new Secretary for Foreign Affairs, Sir Edward Grey, who succeeded Lansdowne on the Liberal Party's return to power in 1905.[11]

Born in 1862 and first elected to parliament at the age of twenty-three, Grey belonged to a generation for which the expansion of the British Empire must have had a certain sense of inevitability. He was famous for his love of nature and his horror of war, and some, including David Lloyd George – president of the Board of Trade at the time – had doubts about his commitment to relaunch Britain's role as the world's superpower. Prime Minister Henry Campbell-Bannerman, on the other hand, appreciated Grey's diplomatic skills and was convinced that he was the right man to preserve British interests, with the smallest risk of resorting to war to do it. In a sense, Lloyd George was right: Grey was uninterested in expanding the Empire further. He believed that Britain should now concentrate on developing and protecting what territory it possessed, and he saw alliances with European partners as key.[12] His diplomatic approach proved successful regarding France and Russia, but Germany posed a rather different challenge. The shift between Bismarkism and the *Weltpolitik* favoured by the young and energetic Kaiser Wilhelm II was epitomised by an ambitious programme of ship construction which would provide Germany with a fleet of forty-five battleships and thirty-two cruisers by 1920.[13] In addition, the schedule for dreadnought construction by Germany's Mediterranean allies, Italy and Austria-Hungary, from 1908 onwards caused further concern in Britain.[14] These were responses to the Anglo-French and Anglo-Russian ententes which had caused the Anglo-Italo-Austrian Mediterranean agreement to lapse. Together, the armed races in the North Sea and the Mediterranean posed an unprecedented threat to British command of the waves.[15] Britain's response was twofold. On the one hand, it scheduled a substantial modernisation and redistribution of British naval forces in order to secure the North Sea, and on the other, it resorted to diplomacy to defuse the Mediterranean threat.

[10] Lawrence, *The Rise and Fall*, p. 338.
[11] K. Robbins, *Sir Edward Grey. A Biography of Lord Grey of Fallodoon* (London: Cassell, 1971), p. 159.
[12] Robbins, *Politicians, Diplomacy and War in Modern British History* (London & Rio Grande: Hambledon, 1994), pp. 165, 173.
[13] This project was revised by 1914 to give a total of sixty-one battleships by 1928: Lawrence, *The Rise and Fall*, p. 335.
[14] Darwin, *The Empire Project*, p. 261.   [15] Hart Sinnreich, 'About turn', p. 140.

The radical reconstruction and redeployment of the navy began in 1904 under the direction of the First Sea Lord Admiral John Fisher. British squadrons in the Pacific, South Atlantic and western hemisphere were withdrawn, and those in the Far East reduced in number. Most of the navy's capital ships were reorganised into three battle fleets: a Mediterranean Fleet based at Malta, an Atlantic Fleet based at Gibraltar and a Channel Fleet operating from home ports. Inevitably, this strengthened the British position in the North Sea at the expense of the Mediterranean.[16] Nonetheless, one British diplomat believed that Britain had an additional card to play in the region, which had been too often undervalued: Anglo-Italian traditional friendship.

A rare figure in the Foreign Office in his openly pro-Italian attitude, Sir James Rennell Rodd became British ambassador to Italy in 1908. Born in 1858, he was a descendant of the then famous geographer James Rennell. A graduate of Balliol College, Oxford, he had a lively interest in literature and had published a book of poetry, *Rose Leaf and Apple Leaf*, with an introduction by Oscar Wilde. Rodd had begun his diplomatic career in 1883, earning his first major posting in Egypt in 1894.[17] In 1901, he was promoted to first secretary at the British embassy in Rome, where he worked for two years under the ambassador Lord Currie, 'an old friend'.[18] Later Rodd was posted to Sweden before returning to Rome as ambassador. Unanimously recognised as a cultured classicist, Rodd was a reserved and gentle man. He had a true love of Italian history, art and culture, and – possibly the only person in the entire British hierarchy – he admired the Italian people. He appreciated in particular the generosity, the 'love for justice' and the tenacity of the ordinary Italian people, who had often to rely solely on their own energy and resources, on the so very Italian 'art of getting by', to make up for the failings of a disorganised state perceived as removed from them.[19] From his arrival in Rome, he began to encourage Grey to look beyond preconceived notions about Italy.

Diplomatically, Rodd agreed with Grey that the days of Olympian detachment were over. However, he was concerned that London's new links with France and Russia could bring Britain more firmly into the anti-German camp, decreasing its freedom of action significantly. So Rodd tactfully suggested that Grey should exploit the notoriously see-sawing relations Italy had with its Austro-Hungarian and German partners, to turn Rome into a British ally in the Mediterranean. This would secure the Mediterranean once and for all, and the precarious position the Central

---

[16] Lawrence, *The Rise and Fall*, pp. 336–345.   [17] *The London Gazette*, 22 October 1901.
[18] Sir J. Rennell Rodd, *Social and Diplomatic Memories 1902–1919*, 3 vols. (London: Arnold & Co., 1925), III, p. 2.
[19] F. Martini, *Diario 1914–1918*, G. De Rosa ed. (Verona: Mondadori, 1966), p. 34.

Powers would consequently face in southern Europe would make it impossible for Germany even to think that it could wage a successful war against the Allies. On 6 May 1909, Rodd stressed that it was only the fear of 'its weakness vis à vis Germany that keeps Italy in the Triple Alliance'. But once this was removed by assuring Italy the support of another strong ally, Rome 'would have no reason to stay in the Triple Alliance'.[20] Rodd tended to undervalue how such a massive diplomatic interference of Britain in that alliance might provoke a German reaction, instead of deterring it. In other words, he might have precipitated war when he tried to prevent it.

Grey was cautious about Rodd's suggestions, and whilst confirming his intention to strengthen Anglo-Italian ties, he did not push his policy to the point of upsetting the Triple Alliance.[21] But Rodd remained convinced that the descendants of the Romans and the 'new Romans' of Britain were natural allies, and should become so formally, sooner or later. A major crisis in Italy's relations with its allies might remove the impediments that had so far prevented a shift in alliances. The Italo-Turkish War of 1911–1912 gave Rodd the chance to bring home his case.

3.2   'The Great Proletarian, She Has Risen!'

Italy's foreign policy up to the end of the nineteenth century followed three main principles. The first was to find allies. The second was to preserve peace and the status quo, avoiding any war with a major power that might result in national collapse if Italy were defeated. The third was to keep good relations with Britain. The first dogma was repeatedly questioned as Italy wavered from one ally to another in search of a trustworthy partner; the second collapsed in 1911.

The Triple Alliance did not end Italian uncertainties in foreign policy: where the Italo-Prussian alliance of 1866 had proved unbalanced, the Triple Alliance soon proved even more frustrating for Italy. True, it brought Italy concrete advantages in allowing Rome to fight its cold war with France in the Mediterranean and to start Italy's colonial adventure with its back covered by powerful allies. But the latter never really treated Italy as an equal, and in time this exacerbated Italy's relations with its allies – especially Austria-Hungary. Furthermore, Vienna and Berlin made a strong case against any further Italian expansion when, in the first decade of the twentieth century, Italian colonial appetites shifted

[20] TNA, FO800/64, Rodd to Grey, 6 May 1909.
[21] C. J. Lowe, M. L. Dockrill, *The Mirage of Power*, 3 vols. (London & Boston: Routledge & Kegan Paul, 1972), I, pp. 92 ff.

from the Horn of Africa to Libya and Asia Minor. This new wave of Italian colonialism coincided with the country's industrial development, particularly in the northern regions. A greater self-confidence spurred Rome to relaunch its imperial project which had been suspended after the 1896 defeat at Adowa in Ethiopia. Italy slowly became the country more interested in altering the status quo, at least in the Mediterranean.[22] The imperialist thrust was arguably a legacy of the Risorgimento. On the one hand, the Risorgimento glorified the liberal principles of freedom, self-determination of the peoples and democratic government. On the other, however, it called for a rebirth of the military virtues of the Italians, and a return to the feats of ancient Rome. Some, like Garibaldi, saw a contradiction between the two, and opposed any war of conquest. Many others did not see any inconsistency between national rebirth and national expansion. Rather, they saw inevitability in the process. A wave of nationalism that swept Italy at the turn of the century led to the founding of the Italian Nationalist Association (*Associazione Nazionalista Italiana*, ANI) in 1910, under the influence of Enrico Corradini and Giovanni Papini. Although divided between supporters of different kinds of nationalism – authoritarian, democratic, moderate and revolutionary – the ANI was unanimous in pressing for the creation of an Italian empire. Corradini linked leftism with nationalism by claiming that Italy was a 'proletarian nation' that was being exploited by international capitalism, which penalised it economically and kept its people divided on class lines.[23]

The Italian press echoed nationalist slogans calling for revenge for the humiliation suffered in Ethiopia. Italy's first imperialist journal, *Il Regno*, founded by Corradini in Florence in 1903, exalted 'a proud spirit of conquest',[24] recalling Turiello's claim, made after an earlier Italian colonial setback at Dogali in 1887, that if Italy did not succeed in the colonial race, it would never be a first-class power.[25] Italian ambitions progressively expanded into Europe as well, reviving irredentist claims on Italian territories held by Vienna (Trento and Trieste), France (Nice and Savoy) and, to a minor degree, Britain (Malta).[26] The nationalist journalist Virginio Gayda, the Trieste-born irredentist Alessandro Dudan and the Trieste-born writer Scipio Spalater also viewed Austro-Hungarian ambitions in the Balkans, as well as expansionist aspirations by the Balkan

[22] Burgwyn, *The Legend*, p. 8.
[23] 'Manifesto of the Italian Nationalist Association', in J. Leib Talmon, *The Myth of the Nation and the Vision of Revolution: The Origins of Ideological Polarization* (Berkeley & Los Angeles: University of California Press, 1982), p. 484.
[24] P. L. Occhini, 'Né fanciulli né semidei', *Il Regno*, 29 November 1903.
[25] Turiello, *Governo e governati*, I, pp. 7–8.   [26] Quartararo, *Roma*, pp. 33, 59.

states themselves – Serbia above all – with equal mistrust.[27] Italian eyes focussed on Albania, which was 'for Italy what the Low Countries were for Great Britain': a buffer state that should be safeguarded and, if necessary, occupied to prevent any other power from setting up home seventy miles from the Italian Adriatic coast.[28] Italian nationalists, who found their charter in Filippo Tommaso Marinetti's 1909 *Manifesto of Futurism*, glorified courage, discipline, duty, self-sacrifice, honour and war to rectify once and for all, the bad qualities of the Italian people.[29] Of course, the cult of the nation, of militarism and of war (which brought from Darwinism the theory of natural selection and applied it to the human species) was a common cultural feature in all of Europe at the time – the success of futurism outside Italy is illustrative.[30] Yet in Italy, partly because of the unsatisfactory results of the Risorgimento and partly because of the legacy of ancient Rome, these ideas took on a distinctively expansionist form. None of the ambitious and vocal Italian nationalists, however, seemed to have a coherent imperial design. Moreover, they tended to ignore the gap between ambitions and the real potential of the country. Truth was that Italy had arrived late to the colonial race, and its relative weakness in international affairs meant that it was dependent on the acquiescence of the other great powers towards its empire-building. Furthermore, Italy's geographic location doomed it to sharp conflicts of interest with both European alliances.[31] As a consequence, Italian policy-makers were reactive to events and approached opportunities for expansion with sharp pragmatism.

First, Italy secured its position in the south, signing two treaties with Britain in 1894 and 1902 on the mutual spheres of influence in East Africa and the Mediterranean;[32] then it made a rapprochement towards France in 1900 through a secret agreement recognising French interests in Morocco in exchange for French recognition of Italian interests in Tripoli. In 1902 – given the defensive nature of the Triple Alliance Treaty – Italy signed a non-aggression pact with France.[33] In line with these agreements, Rome supported Paris at the Algeciras Conference of

---

[27] F. Caccamo, 'Italy, the Adriatic and the Balkans: From the Great War to the Eve of the Peace Conference', in V. Wilcox ed., *Italy in the Era of the Great War* (Leiden & Boston: Brill, 2018), pp. 122–125; V. Gayda, *La crisi di un impero. Pagine sull'Austria contemporanea* (Turin, 1913); A. Dudan, *La monarchia degli Asburgo. Origini, grandezza e decadenza: con documenti inediti*, 2 vols. (Rome, 1915); G. Amendola, *Carteggio*, E. D'Auria ed., 5 vols. (Rome & Bari, then Manduria, 1986–2006), III, docs. 49, 90.
[28] C. Seton-Watson, *Storia d'Italia*, p. 37.   [29] Quoted in Patriarca, *Italianità*, p. 137.
[30] See D. Ottinger ed., *Futurism* (Paris & Milan: Five Continents, 2009).
[31] Burgwyn, *The Legend*, p. 37.   [32] Bonomi, *Politica italiana*, p. 206.
[33] S. R. Williamson, *The Politics of Grand Strategy: Britain and France Prepare for War, 1904–1914* (London: Ashfield, 1990), p. 6.

1906, which established a French protectorate over Morocco. Prince Bernhard von Bülow, the German chancellor, called it the *Giro di Valzer* policy: like a young woman at a ball, Italy could dance with more than one gentleman as long as she came back to her husband at the end of the dance.[34] And Rome's partner, Berlin, was not happy with the prospect of Italy taking Tripoli. In 1891 article 9 was integrated into the Triple Alliance Treaty, providing German support to Italian expansion in North Africa, but made it conditional to the overall geopolitical situation. Throughout the first decade of the twentieth century, Berlin was worried that an attack on the Ottoman Empire, the 'sick man of Europe', might bring about the collapse of the European concert.[35] Vienna was less tolerant.[36] In 1908, while a large part of the Italian army was deployed in Southern Italy to assist the local population hit by the Messina earthquake, Franz Conrad von Hötzendorf, Chief of Staff of the Austro-Hungarian army, proposed a pre-emptive attack on Italy to shatter once and for all its ambitions to become a genuine great power. Emperor Franz Joseph opposed the plan, but when it became known in Italy, mistrust towards the Austrians inevitably grew stronger. As usual, tension within the Triple Alliance brought Italy closer to the Entente. In 1909, in response to Austria-Hungary's unilateral occupation of Bosnia and to Vienna's refusal to give any compensation to Italy – as provided for by article 7 of the Triple Alliance Treaty – Rome signed a secret Italo-Russian convention at Racconigi aiming to prevent any further Austro-Hungarian expansion in the Balkans.[37] At the same time, Rome intensified its diplomatic action in London to gain British consent for the Libyan operation. Italian Prime Minister Giovanni Giolitti, a left-wing liberal, master in the political art of *trasformismo* – the method of making a flexible, centrist coalition government which isolated the extremes of the Left and the Right – believed that the conquest of Libya would satisfy the nationalists, strengthen Italy's prestige and provide a solution to the problems of Southern Italy's population growth. Libya was to become a promised land for Italian proletariats.[38]

The man charged with selling this plan to London was Guglielmo Imperiali di Francavilla, the new Italian ambassador to Britain. Son of the Campanian Marquis Francesco Imperiali and of the noblewoman

---

[34] G. Giolitti, *Memorie della mia vita*, 2 vols. (Milan: Garzanti, 1945 [1922]), II, p. 329.

[35] B. Vandervort, *Verso la quarta sponda, la guerra italiana per la Libia (1911–1912)* (Rome: Ufficio Storico dello Stato Maggiore dell'Esercito [USSME], 2012), p. 226.

[36] Documenti Diplomatici Italiani (DDI), 4th series, vols. VII–VIII, doc. 24, Avarna to San Giuliano, 30 April 1911.

[37] Decleva, *L'Italia e la politica*, p. 167.

[38] C. L. Killinger, *The History of Italy* (Westport: Greenwood, 2002), pp. 127–128.

Clementina Volpicelli, he was of the same age as Rodd, born in August 1858. A graduate at the University of Naples, Imperiali entered the political division of the Italian foreign ministry, nicknamed the Consulta, in 1882. He made his reputation in Washington in 1891, during the so-called New Orleans lynching crisis, which sparked off the most serious diplomatic incident between Italy and the United States until World War II. Following the massacre of Italian emigrants, the young diplomat managed to obtain from the US Government reparations for the families of the victims, restoring relations with Washington to their 'close' and 'cordial' status.[39] After postings in Brussels, Berlin, Sofia and Belgrade, Imperiali arrived in Constantinople in 1904, with the mission of preserving the balance of power in the Balkans and the Mediterranean. When he was posted to London in 1910, his task was essentially reversed.

Imperiali replaced Antonino di San Giuliano, who was to become Italian Foreign Minister. San Giuliano's most important achievement in London had been the Anglo-Italian agreement on the spheres of influence in Ethiopia of 13 December 1906, which had left him with an impression that London had no intention of seeing the status quo in the Mediterranean upset. When he met with Imperiali in May 1910, before returning to Italy, San Giuliano informed his successor that Grey viewed the potential disintegration of the Ottoman Empire with apprehension. Furthermore, he confided to Imperiali that Italy's reputation as a trustworthy partner was not very high. In order to have London make an exception in Italy's favour, to its principle of defending the status quo, Rome needed to give Britain clear guarantees. Though suffering from frequent neuralgias, which made it difficult for him to work non-stop for hours, Imperiali established close relations with Grey and won the sympathy of Foreign Office officials, thanks to his loquacity and frankness.[40] The Italian ambassador shared with Rodd the desire to turn the traditionally good Anglo-Italian relations into a special partnership, and possibly an alliance, although, unlike his British colleague, he would not take personal initiatives to this end. To gain British support for further Italian expansion, Imperiali gave Grey two guarantees: first, Italy would not cause the disintegration of the Ottoman Empire; second, Italy could be relied upon as a stabilising force in the Mediterranean. In other words, Italy was not just a German outpost in the Mediterranean, and its

---

[39] F. G. Orsini, 'Vita diplomatica di Guglielmo Imperiali', Preface to Imperiali, *Diario*, pp. 24, 45–48.
[40] Rodd, *Memories*, III, p. 178.

expansion in Libya would not become a trampoline for German penetration into North Africa.[41]

The international context favoured Imperiali's mission. France had already agreed to Italy taking Libya, and Grey wished to ensure against any Italo-French entente potentially inimical to London. Furthermore, Germany, in order to avoid upsetting the Triple Alliance, eventually pressed Constantinople to give Italy special concessions in Tripoli, and it was imperative that Britain would not remain the only power to oppose Italian interests.[42] Finally, the Admiralty saw in an Italian expansion into Libya 'nothing detrimental to British interests in the Mediterranean'.[43] On 26 July 1911, Imperiali could inform Rome that Britain would not intervene in support of Turkey on Libya.[44] Later, some commented that Grey was no Salisbury and lacked the nerve to tell the 'sturdy beggars' bluntly where they stood in the European hierarchy; but Grey had a more delicate situation to cope with than his predecessors.[45] Nevertheless, when he gave his green-light to Imperiali he was thinking in terms of backing up Italy diplomatically at Constantinople – as Germany was doing[46] – to help Rome gain substantial economic concessions in Libya. He never meant to encourage Rome to embark on an attack.[47] So when Italy issued its ultimatum to Constantinople on 27 September, and then declared war on 29 September, Grey made a strong protest to Imperiali against Italy's aggression as 'very embarrassing to the [Entente] Powers'.[48] To Rodd he wrote in irritation: 'Italians have been very foolish in putting out their foot so far in this Tripoli business'.[49] The British press was uniform in denouncing the 'immoral' Italian action.[50] The Italian press and intellectuals, on the other hand, cheered at Giolitti's bold move. Scipio Sighele, a nationalist, declared upon Tripoli's fall: 'The foreigners did not believe that we could do what we did; maybe we, incorrigible self-critics and self-denigrators, didn't either'.[51] Giuseppe Prezzolini, a future

---

[41] Imperiali was favoured by an apparent Anglo-German rapprochement in the spring of 1911: DDI, 4, VII–VIII, Imperiali to Di San Guliano, docs. 25, 53, 57: 3 May, 11 and 19 June 1911.

[42] BD, IX, n. 231, Grey to Nicolson, 19 September 1911.

[43] E. Serra, *L'intesa mediterranea del 1902* (Milan: Giuffré, 1957), pp. 180–181.

[44] DDI, 4, VII-VIII, doc. 104, Imperiali to San Giuliano, 26 July 1911.

[45] Lowe, 'Grey and the Tripoli War, 1911–1912', in F. H. Hinsley ed., *British Foreign Policy Under Sir Edward Grey* (Cambridge: Cambridge University Press, 1997), p. 322.

[46] DDI, 4, VII–VIII, doc. 223, Pansa to San Giuliano, 26 September 1911.

[47] Lowe, 'Grey and the Tripoli War', p. 316.

[48] DDI, 4, VII–VIII, doc. 254, Imperiali to San Giuliano, 29 September 1911.

[49] TNA, FO800/64 Grey to Rodd, 14 November 1911.

[50] W. C. Askew, *Europe and Italy's Acquisition of Libya* (Durham, NC, 1939), pp. 67–69.

[51] S. Sighele, 'Quello che abbiamo compiuto', in E. Scaglione ed., *Primavera italica. Antologia delle più belle pagine sulla guerra italo-turca* (Naples: Bideri, 1913), pp. 572–573.

anti-fascist, saluted war as proof of the birth of the 'new Italy'.[52] Even the socialist poet Giovanni Pascoli was jubilant: 'The great proletarian, she has risen!' he declared.[53]

Rodd was rather excited. He believed that Italy would soon become 'a more important factor in the Mediterranean', and, because the Triple Alliance was to expire at the end of the year, now was the moment to attract Rome more firmly into the British orbit. To begin with, he urged Grey to do everything he could to halt anti-Italian comments in the British press. In Italy, he reported, 'they were intensely sensitive about public opinion in England'.[54] Grey had an awkward matter in his hands. So far, the British geopolitical principles of defending the status quo and keeping good relations with Italy had overlapped. Now they seemed incompatible. He consulted with his officials at the Foreign Office and was probably surprised to find that an increasing number began to favour a pro-Italian orientation in British policy, and some openly bought Rodd's point. Gerald Fitzmaurice, an expert in Turkish affairs, deprecated the traditional policy 'that Italy should remain in the enemy's camp' and commented that 'one can't help wonder whether it would not be safer to have her in the Anglo-French camp'; and Louis Mallet, a special *progeté* of Grey, minuted: 'Italy is doing us a service in her attack on the Turkish Empire'.[55]

On 16 October, Rodd informed Grey of the content of the Mancini declaration, which Italy had repeatedly tried to have reinserted in the Triple Alliance Treaty. Rodd had only now managed to get, 'in a very confidential manner', details of the Mancini clause and how it had been rejected by Germany. And he suggested Grey that Britain should look for just that kind of understanding with Italy. There was 'no doubt' that Italy and Austria-Hungary were in competition in the Balkans – with the exception of their common anti-Serbian stance – and it was 'quite conceivable that [their] alliance may not stand the strain of the next "opportunity" on the eastern side of the Adriatic'. As things now stood, 'an overt proposal of Italy to her allies to allow her to contract out in our favour' seemed unrealistic; so, Rodd proposed a secret Anglo-Italian pact that would dispel any possibility of an Anglo-Italian confrontation, particularly as Italy's new Libyan colony would border on Egypt.[56] A few days

---

[52] G. Prezzolini, *Italia 1912. Dieci anni di vita intellettuale (1903–1912)*, G. M. Simonetti ed. (Florence: Vallecchi, 1984), p. 51.

[53] G. Pascoli, 'La Grande Proletaria si è mossa', in Rochat, *Il colonialismo italiano* (Turin: Loescher, 1973), pp. 87 ff.

[54] TNA, FO800/64, Rodd to Grey, 10 October 1911; Rodd to Grey, 3 October 1911.

[55] Ibid., 371/1252, Minute by Mallet to Grey, 2 October 1911.

[56] Ibid., 800/64, Rodd to Grey, 16 October 1911.

later, Rodd came up with a more detailed and audacious proposal. In a conversation with Camille Barrère, French ambassador to Rome, the latter had proposed a tripartite agreement 'between England, France and Italy for reciprocally guaranteeing their position in the Mediterranean'. Such an agreement 'between the three Powers most interested in the Mediterranean and North Africa', would have deprived the Triple Alliance of any *raison d'être*, 'as far as Italy is concerned', and would have 'put an end to all the talk about Malta as an object of irredentism'.[57] Throughout November, December and January, Rodd kept suggesting that London make Italy a fourth partner in the Triple Entente whilst Barrère did the same to Paris. Rodd emphasised the doubts that Giolitti had confessed to him about renewing the Triple Alliance.[58] It does not seem that Rodd would insist in his efforts out of personal ambition: he saw his post in Italy as the peak of his diplomatic career. He simply had a sincere mania for everything Italian. He wished to see Italy victorious and satisfied, and he believed that could happen only if Italy ultimately joined Britain.[59] Seeing the two countries he loved the most, united in an alliance was arguably his deepest challenge and a very personal mission.

Although he agreed that the Moroccan, Bosnian and Libyan crises had widened the gap between Italy and its allies, 'so that her foreign policy has tended to become more and more associated with that of England, France and Russia',[60] Grey was not enthusiastic about drawing Italy out of the Triple Alliance in 1912. He was irritated with the Italians for having resorted to war, and he also knew that British public opinion was utterly hostile to Italy, especially when news came of the atrocities of Italian soldiers in Tripoli. The situation worsened when Italy extended the war by attacking the Dardanelles and occupying the Dodecanese islands in the spring of 1912. Rome did so in order to force Constantinople to sue for peace – and it worked; but this move sparked greater anti-Italian reaction in Britain.[61] This time, strategic objections came from the Admiralty: 'Possession by Italy of naval bases in the Aegean Sea would imperil our position in Egypt, would cause us to lose our control over our Black Sea and Levant trade ... and would expose in war our route to the East via the Suez Canal'.[62] Any alignment with Italy as a prelude to

---

[57] Ibid., Rodd to Grey, 25 October 1911.
[58] Ibid., Rodd to Grey, 6 November 1911; Rodd to Grey, 25 January 1912.
[59] C. Seton-Watson, 'Britain and Italy 1914–1915: the role of Sir Rennell Rodd', in A. Migliazza, E. Decleva ed., *Diplomazia e Storia delle relazioni internazionali. Studi in onore di Enrico Serra* (Milan: Giuffré, 1991).
[60] TNA, FO800/64, Rodd to Grey, 23 August 1909.
[61] Lowe, 'Grey and the Tripoli War ', p. 320.
[62] TNA, FO800/356, Nicolson to Bertie, 23 May 1912.

enticing it from the Triple Alliance was now increasingly remote: Grey resolved to remain neutral in the ongoing conflict.[63]

As Rodd feared, this paved the way for the seventh renewal of the Triple Alliance on 5 December 1912. When he realised the Anglo-Italian alliance he had pushed for would not materialise, Rodd wrote Grey regretting the missed opportunity. His telegram is one of the sourest he ever wrote, and one of the very few in which he dared to get close to

Map 3.1 The British and Italian empires at the outbreak of World War I, 1914

---

[63] Robbins, *Politicians, Diplomacy and War*, p. 149.

questioning his superior's policy: 'There is of course one line of argument which might have been used with some effect to the Italians' to bring about a different outcome. 'They might have been told that Aehrenthal's[64] days are numbered, that he and the old emperor are their only friends in Austria, and that if they wished to safeguard their future, they had best do so before it became . . . too late'. Rodd concluded:

Recent events . . . and the position Italy will eventually hold in the Mediterranean . . . do seem very considerably to change the conditions under which her association in the Triple Alliance might be regarded by us. . . . And it seems not inconceivable that some opportunity might then present itself, for which it would be well not to be unprepared.[65]

Britain and Italy had never been closer to an alliance than in 1911–1912. Although Grey's desire to reduce any alteration to the European status quo had ultimately favoured Italy's re-alignment to the Triple Alliance, the domino-effect sparked by Italy's attack on the Ottoman Empire would bring about a deadly escalation of violence in the Balkans, which would lead to the major crisis of 1914.

[64] Alois Lexa von Aehrenthal, Austro-Hungarian Foreign Minister.
[65] TNA, FO800/64, Rodd to Grey, 5 December 1912.

4   Pushing Friendship into Alliance

4.1   Becoming Allies: The Impact of 'Common Values'

The war, although war had been in the air for so long, came quite unexpectedly in the summer of 1914, above all in Britain and Italy.[1] The former had arguably underestimated the July crisis, being more focussed on the internal dispute over suffrage and the crisis in Ireland.[2] Italy, on the other hand, had been much more wary, since the Serbian affair involved one of its allies and one of its neighbouring countries; yet Vienna, being content with Berlin's 'blank cheque', had not taken the trouble of consulting Rome before issuing its ultimatum to Belgrade on 23 July. So, it shocked both Britain and Italy. From an analysis of their attitudes at the peak of the crisis, we may also conclude that both countries tried hard to prevent war. Their joint effort brought London and Rome once again closer to one another and seemed to confirm that Italy really belonged to the block of the western liberal powers rather than the Central Powers. This cooperation to save peace became the basis for the subsequent negotiations to wage war together.

In London the Liberal Government led by Herbert H. Asquith initially hoped that, in the event of war, Britain could remain a 'spectator'.[3] Four senior members of the Cabinet, including Lloyd George, Chancellor of the Exchequer, were ready to resign if the country became involved in a European war. Grey seemed determined to stay out of it, despite the possibility that the Austro-Serbian affair would escalate into a greater war between Austria-Hungary (and possibly Germany) and Russia, Serbia's ally.[4] However, some in Whitehall, like Eyre Crowe, William Tyrrell, and

[1] C. E. Playne : *The Pre-War Mind in Britain* (London: Allen & Unwin, 1928), p. 391.
[2] Robbins, *Edward Grey*, p. 278.
[3] Strachan, *The First World War*, 3 vols. (Oxford: Oxford University Press, 2001), I, p. 94.
[4] Robbins, *Edward Grey*, p. 293.

the new permanent Under-Secretary, Arthur Nicolson, warned him that if war broke out, British interests would require London to intervene to avoid German rule over the continent.[5] For the moment, both Asquith and Grey stood on the fence.

In Rome the new Prime Minister, Antonio Salandra, had been in power for just three months when the crisis arose. Rodd called him 'a man of the highest principle and integrity', though many considered him as merely a stop-gap premier.[6] Instead, Salandra proved to be a skilled and ambitious politician: in an attempt to create a new balance within the liberals, which Giolitti had tended to move to the Left, he progressively shifted power back to the Right. He played on slippery ground, as Giolitti still controlled a large sector of parliament, which mirrored the anti-war feelings of most Italians. Salandra was furious with Vienna and Berlin for having adopted a hard line with Serbia without consulting Rome – as provided for by the Triple Alliance Treaty. To him it was an open violation of the alliance, and further proof that Italy was treated more like a client than an ally. Furthermore, he would not forget that Italy and Austria-Hungary had recently had a diplomatic clash over their spheres of influence in Asia Minor, so he was not ready to go to war to defend purely Austro-Hungarian interests in the Balkans – Italy would be reduced to a satellite of the Habsburgs if Vienna took Serbia.[7] San Giuliano shared his opinion, but feared that an escalation of the conflict might force Italy to choose between Germany and Britain.[8]

So, when Vienna issued the Serbian ultimatum, the anxious eyes of Italian statesmen looked first to London rather than to Vienna. On 25 July, San Giuliano instructed Imperiali to inform Grey that Italy looked favourably on joint peace initiatives even though its position towards Germany was rather delicate.[9] In Rome, Rodd, shocked by the crisis and caught up with other preoccupations – his family was in Hamburg and was desperately trying to get back home – shared San Giuliano's opinion that Britain and Italy, because of their common liberal values and their long tradition of commitment to international law, should act in concert to preserve peace. The following day, after Austria-Hungary had broken off relations with Serbia, Grey proposed to all the powers involved in the crisis, a conference of ambassadors to be held in London to address the Serbian question. Late that night, Rodd telegraphed San Giuliano's reply that Italy favoured the conference but

---

[5] Hinsley, *British Foreign Policy*, pp. 36–43. [6] Rodd, *Memories*, III, p. 221.
[7] Burgwyn, *The Legend*, p. 18.
[8] G. Ferraioli, *Politica e diplomazia in Italia tra XIX e XX secolo. Vita di Antonino di San Giuliano (1852–1914)* (Soveria Mannelli: Rubbettino, 2007), p. 814.
[9] DDI, 4, XII, doc. 502, San Giuliano to De Martino, 25 July 1914.

could not unilaterally support the British appeal for a suspension of military preparations during the talks before consulting Berlin and Vienna. This reservation defused Grey's initiative, but Salandra had no choice, if he was not to irritate his partners, who had already complained about the lack of Italian support. San Giuliano confessed to Rodd that he feared Vienna would retaliate for it, one day. This was not an encouraging starting-point. 'So began the hectic week of desperate effort to close the flood-gates against the tide', noted Rodd in his diary.[10] Nevertheless, San Giuliano became convinced that only the British threat, backed by Italian mediation, could make Germany pause on the edge of the precipice. So he tried again on the 28th, publicly re-stating Italy's support for the ambassadors' conference in London, this time informing Grey that he would fully support any British peace initiative. It was too late. In British eyes, Italy wanted 'to square the circle'. Without 'exposing herself to a change of faith she wants to remain in the Triple Alliance and yet not go to war with France. ... No Anglo-Italian "formula" can solve this ethical problem'.[11] The same day, Austria-Hungary declared war on Serbia; the following day Russia began general mobilisation. On 2 August, the day following Germany's declaration of war on Russia, Salandra called an emergency council of ministers. Giulio Rubini, Minister of Finance, and Domenico Grandi, Minister of War, declared that the country was not ready to enter another war, particularly as the army was still heavily committed in Libya. Grandi informed his colleagues that the new Chief of Staff, Luigi Cadorna, who had assumed command little more than a week before, had issued a confidential memorandum on the state of the army:[12] less than half of it was equipped with uniforms, munitions reserves amounted to only 700 rounds per rifle, heavy artillery, grenades, and transportation vehicles were insufficient; given the casualties suffered in Libya, only 26,000 officers were available, but the general staff thought 90,000 were needed to manage mobilisation for a European war. Furthermore, the only strategic options for the moment were an offensive deployment against France, which included the despatch of five Italian corps to the Rhine, or a defensive one in the

---

[10] Rodd, *Memories*, III, pp. 183, 196–201, 213.

[11] BD, X, n. 2, doc. 449, Crowe memorandum, 29 July 1914.

[12] Cadorna, *La guerra alla fronte italiana. Fino all'arresto sulla linea del Piave e del Grappa (24 maggio 1915–9 novembre 1917)* (Milan: Treves, 1923), pp. 2–20; 'Condizioni dell'Esercito alla data dell'assunzione in carica del nuovo Capo di Stato Maggiore dell'Esercito, S.E. il Tenente Generale conte Cadorna', Italian General Staff memorandum in D. Cellamare, 'La preparazione e la mobilitazione generale dell'esercito italiano all'inizio della Prima Guerra Mondiale', Ministero della Difesa: www.carabinieri.it/editoria/rassegna-dell-arma/la-rassegna/anno-2006/n-2-aprile-giugno/studi/la-preparazione-e-la-mobilitazione-generale-dell'esercito-italiano-all'inizio-della-prima-guerra-mondiale

east: no plans existed for an offensive against Austria-Hungary. Unfortunately, only two out of seventeen corps in the army were in full efficiency.[13] In apparent contradiction with his report, Cadorna suggested an immediate mobilisation to expand his military apparatus with new recruits. Some Italian statesmen were astonished that 'in two years of full powers and unlimited means at their disposal, spending one billion and a half lire, our military administration has not been able to provide the army with the needs for an offensive war of any kind'.[14] Since all the ministers agreed that the Austro-Hungarian aggression towards Serbia did not give rise to a *casus foederis*, Salandra concluded that neutrality was fully justified, and declared it that night. Rodd did not conceal his relief: '*J'en suis heureux parce que ça nous rapproche*', he said to Ferdinando Martini, the Colonial Minister.[15]

Indeed, Italian neutrality was cheered in the Entente capitals. On 2 August Germany had issued its ultimatum to Belgium, demanding passage through Belgian territory, and on 3 August Berlin declared war on Paris. Italy's neutrality allowed the French to transfer 350,000 men from the Italian frontier to the north – in Barrère's opinion, it saved France when the German invasion came a few days later[16] – and encouraged London to issue its own ultimatum to Berlin demanding the respect for Belgian neutrality. Petrograd went one step further, proposing to draw Italy 'to our side, promising Valona and freedom of action in Albania'.[17] French President Raymond Poincaré was ready to do so. The Franco-Russian offer was promptly made to the Italian ambassador in Petrograd, Andrea Carlotti, by the Russian Foreign Minister, Sergei Sazonov.[18] These early diplomatic exchanges over the question of Italian shift in alliance have often been overlooked. Anglo-Saxon scholarship, in particular, has tended to describe negotiations as a result of Italy's initiative:

---

[13] M. Mondini, *Il Capo. La Grande Guerra del generale Luigi Cadorna* (Bologna: Il Mulino, 2017), p. 143.

[14] Sonnino, *Diario*, II, p. 15. The military staff, on the other hand, had been complaining for some time that it had insufficient financial means. See: 'Cenni su provvedimenti indispensabili per migliorare le condizioni dell'esercito', Italian General Staff memoradum quoted in full in A. Salandra *La neutralità italiana 1914–1915. Ricordi e pensieri* (Milan: Mondadori, 1928). Such complaints were in fact typical of all European armed forces at the time: R. Bencivenga, *Saggio critico sulla nostra guerra* (Rome: Tipografia Agostiniana, 1930).

[15] Martini, *Diario*, pp. 9–12, 26.

[16] G. Fasanella, A. Grippo, *1915. Il fronte segreto dell'intelligence. La storia della Grande guerra che non c'è sui libri di storia* (Milan: Sterling & Kupfer, 2014), p. 72. Trevelyan and C. Seton-Watson shared this view: Trevelyan, *Scenes*, p. 5; C. Seton-Watson, *Storia d'Italia*, p. 486.

[17] F. Payot ed., *Documents diplomatiques secrets russes* (Paris: Payot, 1928), p. 215; C. Sabini, *Le fond d'une querelle. Documents inedits sur les relations franco-italiennes 1914–1915*, 2 vols. (Paris: Grasset, 1921), II, pp. 299–230.

[18] Salandra, *L'intervento, 1915: ricordi e pensieri* (Milan: Mondadori, 1930), pp. 5–6, 23–24.

Rome offered its services to both the Entente and the Central Powers, and then stood 'for sale to the highest bidder'.[19] In reality, the initiative came from the Entente, and both Salandra and San Giuliano were very cautious towards it. They kept Sazonov's offer secret and replied in kind but vague terms only on 14 August. First, they needed to be sure about London's position regarding the war. San Giuliano said to Olindo Malagodi, editor of *La Tribuna*, a popular Giolittian newspaper, that Italy's policy now 'depended necessarily on Britain's'.[20] Personally, he would rather want London stayed out of the expanding conflict: in such a case, Italy and Britain could act as a neutralist pressure group. On the other hand, if London were to enter the battle, the room for manoeuvre for Italian diplomacy would be drastically reduced – and as a 'great power', Italy would start feeling the need to enter the conflict.[21] Senator Luigi Albertini wrote as much to his wife: 'Heaven help us if we stay out of this conflict, unless Britain also stays out. In other words, if England enters, we shall have to march, either with Austria or against her'.[22] A breach had begun to appear in the apparently resolute Italian neutralism.

News of the British intervention on the evening of 4 August made Italian neutralists waver even more. The official argument in favour of Britain's declaration of war on Germany was the Belgian issue. Grey had preached intervention as a matter of principle, although with little enthusiasm. Asquith too had become convinced that, after making 'every effort any government could possibly make for peace', Britain must honour its obligations with Belgium and France. In his memoirs, Grey admitted that he was more concerned with the defence of the British world-system,[23] whilst David French emphasised that the ultimate goal of Asquith was that Britain should emerge from the conflict as the dominant power over both its enemies and its allies.[24] As other European statesmen did, both Grey and Asquith gave their intervention an idealist *façade*:[25] Britain would go to war to stand for the liberal values of freedom, justice, and the rule of law, and to eradicate Prussian militarism.[26] All those British

---

[19] Strachan, *New Illustrated History*, p. 120; Bosworth, *Italy, the Least*, p. 401, *Italy and the Approach*, p. 132. Italian historians argued the opposite: Albertini, *Le origini*, p. 356; Toscano, *Patto di Londra*, p. 28. Mario Caracciolo went so far as to talk of the 'wranglings of governments, later Allied, to get us to intervene': Caracciolo, *L'Italia e i suoi Alleati*, p. 21.

[20] O. Malagodi, *Conversazioni della guerra 1914–1919*, 2 vols., B. Bigezzi ed. (Milan & Naples: Ricciardi, 1960), I, p. 17.

[21] Bosworth, *Italy, the Least*, p. 377.

[22] L. Albertini, *Epistolario: 1911–1926*, 4 vols., O. Barie ed. (Milan: Mondadori, 1968), I, *Dalla guerra di Libia alla Grande Guerra*, p. 392.

[23] E. Grey, *Twenty-Five Years 1892–1916*, 2 vols. (London: Hodder & Stoughton, 1925), II (here and henceforth), pp. 15, 157–158.

[24] French, *British Strategy*, pp. XI–XIII.   [25] Robbins, *Edward Grey*, p. 295.

[26] *The Manchester Guardian*, 7 August 1914.

Cabinet members who had promised to resign in the event of war did so, except Lloyd George whom the Prime Minister convinced to stay.[27] British public opinion, after some major anti-war demonstrations in the previous days, reacted rapidly to the Government action. Some cheered the opportunity of becoming the major power in Europe after the war; others greeted the coming conflict with a mixture of determination and apprehension, rather than with any great enthusiasm.[28] In general, the British public swung quite solidly behind intervention.[29] As John Keiger has noted, a country extremely divided a few days earlier, was suddenly united by the war.[30]

In Italy, the opposite occurred. A disorganised minority of interventionists began to press the Government to enter the war with the argument that neutrality would ultimately alienate both the Central Powers and the Entente. Irredentists of the Risorgimento tradition advocated war on Vienna to take back Italy's 'unredeemed lands'; others, from the colonial circles, strove to take Tunisia from France; yet others did not care much about which side Italy should support. The case of Alfredo Rocco, a popular nationalist spokesman, was emblematic: he first wanted Italy to side with the Central Powers and then with the Entente, as long as it entered the war and stirred the energy of the nation. These interventionists were confronted by an equally disorganised, though larger group of Italian socialists and catholics – usually rivals – preaching neutrality alongside Giolittian liberals. None of these groups had a coherent policy and they badly lacked coordination.[31] The only statesman who seemed to have a clear view on the matter at this stage, was the Colonial Minister, Martini.

One of the most cultured of Salandra's ministers, a former professor of history and literature at the University of Pisa and a prolific writer, Martini had been a brilliant governor of Eritrea from 1897 to 1907. He loved French *civilisation*, was fluent in French and had a great admiration for Britain. He called the British 'the modern Romans', and looked to their liberal institutions as a model. Not surprisingly, Martini was a determined anti-Austrian, and took upon himself the task of rallying those who favoured the 'liberal sisters' of the west against the German 'block of order', to re-launch the feats of the Risorgimento. Martini was

[27] Strachan, *The First World War*, I, pp. 94–97.
[28] S. Audoin-Rouzeau, A. Becker, *La violenza, la crociata, il lutto: La Grande Guerra e la storia del Novecento* (Turin: Einaudi, 2000), p. 62.
[29] *The Daily News*, 4 August 1914.
[30] J. F. V. Keiger, 'Britain's "union sacrée" in 1914', in J-J. Becker, S. Audoin-Rouzeau eds.: *Les sociétés européennes et la guerre de 1914–1918* (Nanterre: Université Paris X, 1990).
[31] Isnenghi, Rochat, *Grande Guerra*, pp. 84, 121.

a skilled orator, and in a series of feverish meetings in Rome in early August, he pressed his colleagues to join the Entente. Britain's intervention proved a very strong argument. The Italians were confident that they could defend the Alps successfully against an Austro-Hungarian invasion, but their coasts were exposed to Royal Navy attacks: 'Half our coastal cities would be destroyed the first day', Martini repeated. Furthermore, the Italian colonies would be cut off from the motherland in the event of war with Britain, not to mention Italy's dependence on British raw materials.[32] It was not difficult for Martini to bring his colleagues in the Government onto his side regarding the need to avoid war with Britain, particularly as the naval Chief of Staff, Paolo Thaon di Revel, confirmed that the *Regia Marina* could not take on the Royal Navy. Convincing them that Italy should fight in the Entente was a rather different thing. But, as an idealist, Martini believed that Anglo-Franco-Italian liberal values, and the prospect of completing the Risorgimento, could lead to a shift in alliances rather evenly. Rodd of course shared his view. The two were good friends and their desire to see Italy siding with the Allies led them occasionally to bypass their respective Governments, making promises they had no authority to make. Already on 2 August had Martini guaranteed to both Barrère and Rodd that Italy would never support the Central Powers. In so doing, he was overstepping Salandra, but Martini believed that he was acting in 'the real national interest'. For his part, Rodd agreed with Winston Churchill, First Sea Lord, that war between Italy and Britain would have been 'a crime against history and against nature' and he went on to propose a special Anglo-Italian partnership within the Entente, promising that 'England will always be happy to give Italy everything she desires' to fulfil the Risorgimento.[33]

On 9 August, Imperiali joined the Martini-Rodd duo. He reported to San Giuliano on two confidential meetings he had had on 6 and on 9 August with Alfred Rothschild, a former director of the Bank of England. Rothschild had told Imperiali 'in top secrecy' that the British 'political, financial and military circles' were happy to offer Italy territorial gains if it were to contribute to the triumph of 'the cause of peace' over German militarism – for it was 'certain that Austria and Germany could not hold out at length against all the great powers'. As a personal comment, Imperiali added that an alliance based on the liberal values of the Risorgimento tradition should be taken seriously, and that a special

[32] Martini, *Diario*, pp. 11–17.
[33] Rodd, *Memories*, III, p. 226; Martini, *Diario*, pp. 11–17, 87; TNA, ADM1/8365/1, Italy and the War. Notes and Comments on Italy's position and prospects. Position of British and German Fleets. Miscellaneous notes and Correspondence from the First Lord's Office relating the earlier subjects, 1914.

Anglo-Italian partnership within it would guarantee a durable post-war equilibrium: 'The friendship between Italy and Britain ... considering the common interests of the two Governments ... will enable us to count always on British aid, should such a balance be threatened by a victorious and strengthened France'.[34] To Martini, he wrote that the war should be promoted as the Fourth War of Independence, and 'it would be a pity to miss an opportunity that may not come again'.[35]

Grey finally made an offer on 11 August: Britain would support Italy's claims for the 'unredeemed lands' in Trentino, Trieste and Northern Dalmatia (Istria), in exchange for an immediate commitment to the Entente. Rodd discussed the proposal privately with Martini before delivering it to Salandra. Rodd, who confessed that he considered Italy his 'second motherland', and who wished to spend his 'lifetime in Italy', expressed his personal wish to see Italy's desires come true with such a passion that Martini would 'never forget the hours spent with him tonight'.[36] Where Sazonov's early offer was based on the promise of limited Italian expansion in the Balkans, Martini, Rodd, Imperiali and Grey sponsored an Anglo-Italian alliance based mainly on ideals, 'nature' and 'history', with the prospect of fulfilling Italy's national unification by acquiring the 'unredeemed lands'. This was consistent with the democratic principles that officially motivated Britain's war.

Unfortunately, the club of idealist promoters of the Anglo-Italian entente underestimated the realities of politics. Whereas Italian interests did not clash with those of Britain, they did with France and Russia. The French were not happy to discuss Italian irredentist ambitions for fear that some French territories like Nice and Savoy would eventually be included in the list, and Dalmatia was an issue for Russia. The only justification for Italian Dalmatian claims would be that the Venetian Republic had dominated large parts of the region until 1797, but Sazonov considered that a feeble argument. Possibly offended by the tepid Italian reaction to his own proposal, he made it clear to Grey that he would not support Italian expansion in what was now Slav territory.[37] Grey was also disappointed by the lack of a firm Italian commitment. This was caused by a series of circumstances. First, early French reverses had encouraged San Giuliano to play dilatory tactics to avoid rushing the country into war on the losing side. This seemed to confirm the less benevolent stereotypes about Italy's Machiavellian policy, but in the context of the traditional Italian phobia of a fatal failure in foreign policy,

---

[34] DDI, 5, I, docs. 85, 155 and 242, Imperiali to San Giuliano, 6, 9 and 14 August 1914.
[35] Martini, *Diario*, p. 46.   [36] Ibid., pp. 33–34.
[37] Lowe, Dockrill, *Mirage of Power*, II, pp. 171 ff.

it is understandable. San Giuliano believed that what was ultimately at stake was not this or that colony, nor national prestige or honour, but the very survival of Italy.[38] He was encouraged in his caution by reports from the Italian military attachés in Allied countries. Major Enrico Greppi emphasised from London that an increasing number of officials both in the War Office and in the Admiralty suspected the war would be longer than initially envisaged, and that early misunderstandings between the French and the British commands favoured the Germans. On 20 September, he reported that any offensive seemed to produce 'only partial results' with 'very slow progresses' leaning towards a form of attrition.[39] Lieutenant-Colonel Giovanni Breganze, military attaché in Paris, the very same day came to a similar conclusion: 'Perhaps the war of movement has ended and the war of position begins'.[40] So, San Giuliano preferred to wait in the hope that the conflict would produce mutual exhaustion of France and Austria-Hungary.[41] After all, Italy was still far from ready for war; Salandra needed time to change the diplomatic, political and psychological attitudes of the political elite, and to gather public support.[42] Rome's ambiguous attitude revived British prejudices about Italy not being a worthwhile partner,[43] with the effect that when Imperiali produced an extensive list of Italy's conditions to Grey, largely inspired by the principle of nationality, the latter treated these as little more than an academic exercise. Though confirming his support in principle, Grey added, 'we could not pledge ourselves to any of these things till Italy stated definitely that she was prepared to join us'.[44] Although negotiations were kept alive, mainly by Rodd, Salandra and San Giuliano throughout September, the possibility of a rapid and positive outcome had vanished. The sudden death of San Giuliano on 16 October marked the end of the first round of the talks.

Common values and traditional friendship had proven insufficient to bring about an Anglo-Italian entente and Italy's intervention on the Allies' side. Both Italian and Allied statesmen knew that negotiations might revive, but they would be characterised by a more pragmatic and less enthusiastic tone and would be based on geopolitical interests rather than ideals.

---

[38] DDI, 5, I, doc. 281, San Giuliano to Salandra, 16 August 1914.

[39] L. Scoppola Iacopini, 'Le relazioni dell'addetto militare italiano a Londra', in F. Anghelone, A. Ungari eds., Gli addetti militari italiani alla vigilia della Grande Guerra 1914–1915 (Rome: Rodorigo, 2015), pp. 57–59, 68.

[40] G. Pardini, 'Sul campo di battaglia: le relazioni dell'addetto militare italiano a Parigi, 1914–1915', in Ibid., pp. 105–107.

[41] DDI, 5, I, doc. 55, San Giuliano to Salandra, 4 August 1914.

[42] TNA, FO371/2008/39916–7, Rodd to Grey, 13 August 1914.

[43] Robbins, Edward Grey, p. 307.

[44] DDI, 5, I, doc. 223, Imperiali to San Giuliano, 12 August 1914.

4.2   Becoming Allies: The 'Carrot and the Stick' Policy

Two days after San Giuliano's death, Salandra addressed the Italian parliament and proclaimed a new principle in Italian foreign policy: *sacro egoismo* (sacred egoism). He would from now on lead the nation with 'the firmest strength of spirit, [and a] serene vision of the real interests of the country ... which should not exclude, where necessary, prompt action. ... A spirit [is needed], free from every preconception, every prejudice, every feeling other than boundless and exclusive devotion to our homeland – sacred egoism for Italy'.[45] Although it was little more than a declaration of patriotism, without any specific implication other than the intent to keep Salandra's hands free, it had huge consequences both in the domestic and international arenas. Domestically, it gave further impetus to the interventionist campaign. Internationally, it delivered the impression that Italy was raising the price of its intervention but was also getting ready to enter the war; so both the Central Powers and the Entente discussed the opportunity to accept Italy's terms, and eventually raced for Rome's support.[46]

The shift in Italian desiderata was personified by the new Foreign Minister, who took office on 31 October. Sidney Sonnino was a peculiar figure in the Italian establishment. Son of an Italian Jew and a Welsh mother, he grew up an Anglican; as such, he was fluent in English and had a special admiration for Britain.[47] This was not acritical but was shaped around Sonnino's biases. He had always been a loner – he escaped his graduation party and photograph[48] – and was known to be pragmatic rather than an idealist like Martini. His unrequited love for Marchioness Bianca Capranica del Grillo[49] had arguably aggravated his introversion, and possibly stimulated a cynicism. He had little faith in British or Italian parliamentarianism – his early work *On the Representative Government in Italy*, published in 1872, cast a negative evaluation of the 'excessive compromises' that were needed to keep power in liberal institutions.[50] Of Britain, he admired not the institutional system, but the Empire's strength. In time, Sonnino became 'a traditional, conservative, leading figure in the old party of the Italian bourgeoisie',[51] serving as Finance Minister in 1893–1896 and as Prime Minister in 1906 and 1909–1910. Less experienced in diplomacy than San Giuliano, he was nonetheless more ambitious, and dreamt of making Italy a genuine great power

---

[45] Salandra, *L'intervento*, p. 150.   [46] Bosworth, *Italy, the Least*, p. 19.

[47] C. Seton-Watson, 'Britain and Italy', p. 217.

[48] C. Montalcini, *Sidney Sonnino* (Rome: Tipografia della Camera dei Deputati, 1926), p. 14.

[49] Sonnino, *Diario*, I, p. 111.   [50] Montalcini, *Sonnino*, pp. 14, 27.

[51] Isnenghi, Rochat, *Grande Guerra*, p. 312.

through expansion in the Adriatic and the Eastern Mediterranean.[52] This ambition, coupled with his rough, stubborn character,[53] earned Sonnino the accusation of being the demiurge of a selfish war and the 'archvillain of the peace ... oblivious to the democratic spirit'. Burgwyn considered him 'out of touch with the modern era',[54] and Bosworth called Sonnino 'Italy's worst-ever Foreign Minister'.[55] Yet Sonnino also had intelligence and perseverance that made him, in Salandra's eyes, the right man for a policy of 'sacred egoism', and that enabled Sonninio to stay in office for the duration of the war, unlike any of his European counterparts.

Sonnino followed the old Italian policy that Italy could not afford a major defeat, or it might 'disintegrate'. A second principle that guided him was a marked mistrust of all European powers, particularly France, Austria-Hungary and the Slav countries – including Russia. On 2 August, he was even ready to support Germany, but the British intervention changed everything. Not that he trusted Britain more than others; but he was better disposed towards it, especially as he was convinced that the Empire's resources would ultimately triumph. On 7 November, he made his first visit as Foreign Minister to Rodd. The latter told Sonnino what he most wanted to hear – that Britain could discuss offers to Italy 'without consult-ing her allies'.[56] Sonnino reciprocated by saying that he was determined to strengthen Anglo-Italian special ties, a point he repeated on 27 November and 19 December.[57] Sonnino's customary suspiciousness, however, inspired his third and more important foreign policy principle: good accounts make for good friends. He acknowledged that, should Italy join the Entente, it would find brothers-in-arms 'very much estimable, no doubt', but whose interests partially diverged from Italy's; so he wanted a detailed pact that would become a binding document at the peace table.[58] In this aspect, he had the support of the armed forces. General Giovanni Ameglio pushed him to get *patti chiari* (clear pacts) from the British in exchange for Italian support. Ameglio, a veteran of the Libyan war who would become governor of the colony in 1915, thought mainly in colonial terms, so he listed the ports of Zeila and Djibouti, including their British and French hinterlands, and the chain of Ethiopian mountains along the Nile, as Italian desiderata.[59] The *Regia Marina*, by contrast, was more interested in gaining 'Adriatic supremacy' – a phrase coined at the time by the Secretary-General to the Consulta, Giacomo De Martino, and

---

[52] Mondini, *Il Capo*, p. 267.   [53] Imperiali, *Diario*, p. 140.
[54] Burgwyn, *The Legend*, pp. 2, 17.   [55] Bosworth, *Italy and the Approach*, p. 134.
[56] Sonnino, *Diario*, I, pp. 9, 72; II, pp. 10–12, 22–23, 43, 50.
[57] TNA, FO800/65, doc. 80, Rodd to Grey, 7 November 1914.
[58] DDI, 5, III, doc. 816, Sonnino to Imperiali, 16 February 1915.
[59] Sonnino, *Diario*, I, pp. 32–33.

adopted by Sonnino himself.[60] The Entente's early offer had unleashed the starving dogs of Italian imperialism: their ambitions were nothing new, but for the first time they assumed a clearer and more determined shape. Sonnino's plan developed over several months. A first draft of Italian demands was sent to Imperiali on 8 November and included: Trentino, Trieste, Istria up to the Quarnaro and Valona; the Dalmatian islands were to be neutralised, and Italy's interests in the Eastern Mediterranean recognised by the Entente powers; in particular, Italy would replace German and Austro-Hungarian spheres of influence in Asia Minor.[61] It was not a real imperial project yet, but it departed from the irredentist aspirations of the Risorgimento tradition – and from Grey's original offer.

Martini privately protested this unexpected development. He sponsored a *piccola guerra* (small war) against Austria-Hungary for the liberation of the 'unredeemed lands'; he never wanted to invade non-Italian territories. Sonnino replied that 'unredeemed brothers' lived equally in Trieste and in Istria. Martini rebuffed him: 'Unifying all the territories where Italians live would mean conquering almost the whole world'. On one point, however, the two agreed: Italy should seek a special partnership with Britain. This convergence prevented a split in the interventionist wing of Salandra's Government. It was, however, based on two very different assumptions. Martini believed that London could be trusted as a guarantor of Entente promises to Italy because of the impact of public opinion on British liberal institutions, which made any British Government commitment a truly national decision. Sonnino had very little regard for the public – 'Who cares about public opinion', he used to say. 'Once a monarch orders, the people must obey'.[62] Nor was he much impressed by Asquith's claim that Britain was fighting for 'freedom', 'justice' and the extirpation of militarism; rather, he believed Britain's real motives were geopolitical. Sonnino needed a special partnership with London only because it was the leading power in the Entente and could push the others to accept Italy's terms. He would not commit himself before Grey made an official – though secret – declaration in favour of the Italian claims. This should be done, he stressed once more, through bilateral negotiations as 'it would be better not to deal with France and Russia directly at present'.[63]

Unfortunately, Salandra's *sacro egoismo* speech had produced a revival of anti-Italian sentiment in London.[64] Influential members of both the

---

[60] DDI, 5, II, doc. 164, annex 4, De Martino to Salandra, 31 October 1914, and annex 5, Sonnino to Salandra [...] November 1914.

[61] Sonnino, *Carteggio 1914–1922*, P. Pastorelli ed. (Bari: Laterza, 1974), pp. 51–63.

[62] Martini, *Diario*, pp. 15, 103.   [63] Lowe, Dockrill, *Mirage of Power*, II, p. 175.

[64] Burgwyn, *The Legend*, p. 16.

Cabinet and the Foreign Office including Churchill and Nicolson – usually pro-Italian – had been disgusted by it. Rodd was the only one left to justify the Italian Prime Minister's seemingly 'selfish national motives' claiming that 'taken in their context, there is nothing ungracious in their point. The speaker was indicating the qualities indispensable to a statesman who, in so grave a moment, had to maintain the continuity of policy'.[65] Despite Rodd's pleas, Grey found himself in a rather unpleasant position. On the one hand, he had to overcome internal opposition to the prospect of bowing to Italian appetites; on the other, he now saw Italy's intervention as a factor of the greatest importance for several reasons. The first was, quite simply, that numbers count, especially in a war of attrition. Italy could mobilise two million men; the prospect of a longer war than anticipated, combined with the increasing munition shortage, made Italy's support very important. Smashing the Triple Alliance by attracting one of its members onto the Entente side would also be a diplomatic score, which could produce a domino-effect, encouraging other neutrals to join the Allies. All members of the Entente agreed on these points, though with different hues. Yet Grey was especially interested in getting Italy on-board for two additional reasons: he saw no fundamental conflict between Italy's and Britain's war aims (contrary to his allies); and Italy's intervention would serve particularly British strategy.[66]

In the opening phases of the war, British strategy followed its traditional lines: 'Naval and economic pressures, supplemented by limited liability on land'. The despatch of the BEF – a small army, based on volunteering – was in line with the assumption that the main burden of the fight on land was to be shouldered by Britain's continental allies.[67] Such allies, however, were failing expectations. As Britain moved towards a more manpower-oriented strategy, it would have benefitted more than others from the addition of a new continental ally. At sea, Britain aimed to blockade the Central Powers, and this required securing the Mediterranean – for which the addition of Italy could be crucial.[68] This explains the unprecedented sympathy by the wider British public towards Italy as the war drifted towards its first winter. Despite some bitter comments about Italian 'tenacious bargaining' by British statesmen,[69] Major Greppi noted an increasing confidence that Italy's entry would be 'decisive'. Austria-Hungary 'would have never borne a third front after

[65] Rodd, *Memories*, III, p. 224.   [66] Lowe, Dockrill, *Mirage of Power*, II, pp. 180–181.
[67] Strachan, 'Battle of the Somme', pp. 79, 81–83.
[68] French, *British Strategy*, pp. 82–88; *Strategy of Lloyd George*, p. 40.
[69] D. Lloyd George, *The Truth about the Peace Treaties*, 2 vols. (London: Gollancz, 1938), II, p. 27.

Russia and the Balkans'. Repeated rallies before the Italian embassy by Italian sympathisers were accompanied by articles in *The Times*, *The Observer*, and *The Spectator*, which praised the Italian Government for having remained neutral in the summer and predicted an inevitable rupture between Rome and Vienna. Greppi was a meticulous observer of the British public, not just of its armed forces: he also recorded comments on British society, economy and politics. A convinced anglophile, in good relations with Asquith and King George V, Greppi was so gratified by British flattering in the autumn of 1914 that he concluded Britain would make 'any concession' to get Italy in. British enthusiasm about a possible Italian entry was apparently so contagious that Greppi, despite his own reports on the lengthening of the war, became convinced that an offensive of the Italian army, 'well organised, confident in its own strength and its commanders, not worn out' by the fighting, could be the turning point in the conflict.[70]

As British public opinion cheered at Italy, a parallel development that pushed Grey to precipitate Italy's intervention was the arrival of the former German chancellor, von Bülow, in Rome in December.[71] The Kaiser had charged him with gaining Rome's support by promoting an Italo-Austrian reconciliation. Bülow soon realised that Italy's intervention on the side of the Central Powers was impossible;[72] so he concentrated on preventing Italy's shift in alliances. He exploited his contacts in the Italian ruling class and business sector, as well as the Vatican, to promote a neutralist campaign. He bought or financed several newspapers, including *La Stampa* (Turin), *Il Secolo* (Milan), *Il Mattino* (Naples), *Il Popolo Romano*, *La Vittoria*, *La Concordia* and *La Vita* (Rome), all of which echoed Bülow's promise that Vienna would compensate Italy's neutrality with some territories in the 'unredeemed lands'. He also went as far as trying to corrupt Italian members of parliament (MPs) to expand further the anti-war majority in the Chamber.[73] Bülow found in Giolitti a strong ally. The latter mocked those who thought that a 'small war' was possible:[74] if Italy entered the conflict, it would have to fight a world war. Giolitti was convinced that the country was not ready to do this and he feared social unrest. He wrote in *La Tribuna*: 'I strongly believe, considering the present situation of Europe, that very much

---

[70] Scoppola Iacopini, 'Le relazioni', pp. 65–72. See also: M. Brignoli, 'Edoardo Greppi. Londra 1914–1915', *Studi Storico-Militari*, 1999 (Rome: USSME, 2000), pp. 573–672.
[71] Salandra, *L'Intervento*, pp. 19–20.   [72] Burgwyn, *The Legend*, p. 15.
[73] Fasanella, Grippo, *1915*, pp. 56–85; C. Augias, *Giornali e spie. Faccendieri internazionali, giornalisti corrotti e società segrete nell'Italia della Grande Guerra* (Milan: Bur, 1994).
[74] Salandra, *L'intervento*, pp. 248 ff.; G. De Rosa, Preface to Martini, *Diario*, p. XXXII.

[*parecchio*] can be obtained without war'.[75] These initiatives caused the interventionist front, which had seemed to gain some ground in the previous weeks, to retreat significantly. Public opinion might have been of little importance to Sonnino, but both Salandra and the King would not reject it completely.[76]

At the same time, Martini, 'Rodd's informant in the Italian Cabinet',[77] told the British ambassador that Sonnino had made an overture to Vienna. Appealing to article 7 of the Triple Alliance Treaty, Sonnino had asked for Trento and Trieste as compensations for Austro-Hungarian occupation of Belgrade.[78] Historians have debated Sonnino's move at length. Some saw a sincere desire in his initiative to reconcile with Vienna;[79] others interpreted it as an attempt 'to keep the Central Powers quiet until he was ready to join the Entente'.[80] We will probably never know Sonnino's real thoughts, as he did not confess them in his diary. Salandra, on the other hand, claimed that, at that point, he had already chosen the Entente.[81] As a matter of fact, Italo-Austrian negotiations produced very little, as Vienna was adamant about keeping Trieste, its main Adriatic port, off the table. Nonetheless, Salandra urged Sonnino not to break negotiations, for 'breaking with the Central Powers would leave us at the Entente's discretion, with no possibility to insist on those preliminary guarantees that we asked for'.[82] The Italian move was not just an attempt to buy time, it was also a diplomatic weapon to put pressure on the Allies – Grey above all – to accept Italy's terms. In the meantime, Italian marines landed in Valona on 25 December and made it an Italian outpost in Albania. The operation was organised against Cadorna's advice, who believed that no less than one army corps was needed to maintain control of Albania.[83] Sonnino overruled the Chief of Staff in the first of many civil-military clashes in the Italian war. When Rodd protested Sonnino's first Balkan adventure, the latter claimed that it was not an imperialistic, but a defensive, move against well-known Serbian aspirations. Italy simply wanted to prevent 'any other power from going there'.[84]

The combination of Bülow's mission and Sonnino's talks with Vienna and unilateral Balkan move, produced a schizophrenic debate within the Foreign Office. Was Italy about to swing once more towards its traditional

---

[75] Giolitti, *Memorie*, II, pp. 529–530.   [76] Sonnino, *Diario*, II, p. 10.

[77] Lowe, Dockrill, *Mirage of Power*, II, p. 175.   [78] Martini, *Diario*, p. 272.

[79] Isnenghi, Rochat, *Grande Guerra*, pp. 140 ff.

[80] Lowe, Dockrill, *Mirage of Power*, II, p. 176. In Martini's words: 'Simulate negotiations with the Central Powers, and in the meantime arm, prepare mobilisation, and be ready for any circumstance': Martini, *Diario*, p. 22.

[81] Salandra, *L'Intervento*, p. 193.

[82] DDI, 5, I, doc. 420, Salandra to Sonnino, 18 December 1914.

[83] Mondini, *Il Capo*, p. 267.   [84] Sonnino, *Diario*, II, p. 63.

allies? Throughout December and January, Asquith, Grey and Nicolson repeatedly asked Imperiali about the effects of Bülow's propaganda on Italian public opinion, and Grey promised that he would do all he could to counter anti-Italian feelings in his Cabinet. Although he did not expect an Italian intervention in the winter, it was clear that he waited anxiously for some assurances.[85] He would not wait passively, however. Grey's response to the unexpected Italian developments was twofold. On the one hand, he charged Rodd with promoting pro-Entente propaganda in Italy to counter Bülow's efforts; on the other, Grey resorted to economic warfare to put pressure on Salandra and the Italian business sector. The first part of the plan aimed at Italian public opinion; the second, at both public opinion and the Government.

Rodd coordinated his campaign with Barrère. They financed interventionist newspapers such as *Il Corriere della Sera*, *Il Giornale d'Italia*, *Il Resto del Carlino* and *Il Secolo XIX*, and enlisted militant intellectuals like D'Annunzio, Marinetti and Corradini to strengthen the interventionist cause. Rodd and Barrère also encouraged some Italian socialists, such as Benito Mussolini and Leonida Bissolati, to embrace it. Mussolini was a young journalist and anti-war activist with political ambitions. French and British money helped turn him into a fervent interventionist in the autumn of 1914, when he resigned as director of the socialist newspaper *Avanti!*, and founded *Il Popolo d'Italia*, an interventionist paper largely financed by Rodd and Barrère. Mussolini was expelled from the Socialist Party and began a head-on confrontation with his former colleagues Filippo Turati, Camillo Prampolini and Armando Borghi, who preached neutrality following the socialist 'solidarity amongst the peoples'. Socialist divisions weakened the neutralist camp.[86] Trevelyan, who was in Rome at the time, noticed a great increase in historical appeals to the Risorgimento in Italian literature. He described the Italian interventionist campaign as the peaceful 'masterpiece of a people whose oldest political tradition, dating from before Ciceruacchio, Rienzi and Appius Claudius, is the 'politics of the *piazza*', and considered 'the touchstone of enthusiasm for the war' to be 'friendliness to England'.[87] It was an utterly biased view of Trevelyan's Italophilia. In reality, the Italian debate on intervention soon became heated and increasingly out of control. Whereas the early Italian interventionists and irredentists had had the tacit support of the King, Mussolini's agitators were mad dogs. Their propaganda became increasingly violent and anti-institutional, promoting slogans against parliament – perceived as weak and anti-patriotic – and against the monarchy itself.

---

[85] DDI, 5, I, docs. 373, 406, 473 and 476, Imperiali to Sonnino, 12, 15 and 24 December 1914.
[86] Augias, *Giornali e spie*, pp. 167–168.   [87] Trevelyan, *Scenes*, pp. 19, 28, 30.

'We want war', Mussolini repeated in the *piazze*. 'And if you, Majesty, who has, under article 5 of the Statute [constitution] the right to call up our men ... refuse to do so, you will lose your crown'.[88] Costanzo Premuti, an active interventionist, summarised the motto of Mussolini's men: 'We shall not have war until we break neutralism with our daggers, terrifying all the enemies of intervention'.[89] On 13 January 1915, Martini wrote in his diary in astonishment that he feared that protracted neutrality would lead to a collapse of the monarchy and Sonnino agreed with him. Although the interventionists remained a noisy minority, they seemed ready to unleash a civil war.[90] So the British policy to exacerbate deliberately Italian domestic divisions in order to counter German propaganda and strengthen the interventionist cause, originally aimed at the Italian people, proved an effective stimulus for the Government too.

Economic pressure proved even more effective. In August 1914, the British had established a blockade of the Central Powers. In the Mediterranean, all types of cargo coming from the Atlantic, including those heading to neutral countries, were intercepted and often confiscated.[91] These measures were not originally designed to influence the behaviour of the neutral countries, but they soon proved a key instrument in doing so, particularly in Italy. Throughout the autumn, the British progressively removed the distinction between different types of war contraband, absolute or conditional, and they began to detain all cargo whose details on import and destination were not specified. These included goods such as oil, vegetable seeds, fish, textiles, cotton, minerals and metals, sanitary materials and raw materials, which Italy badly needed.[92] Salandra found himself in an uncomfortable position: on the one hand, he did not want to jeopardise his understanding with London, but he needed to protect Italian economic interests and to defend Italy's trade with its neighbouring countries, including its allies of the Central Powers. Martini himself had an unprecedented argument with his friend Rodd, when the former noted that the British policy towards Italy had very little to do with 'traditional friendship'.[93] The British consular service expressed criticism

---

[88] De Rosa, Preface to Martini, *Diario*, p. XLII.
[89] C. Premuti, *Come Roma preparò la guerra* (Rome: Società Tipografica Italiana, 1923), p. 230.
[90] Martini, *Diario*, p. 302.
[91] K. Neilson, 'Reinforcements and Supplies from Overseas: British Strategic Sealifts in the First World War', in G. Kennedy ed., *The Merchant Marine in International Affairs 1850–1950* (London & Portland: Routledge, 2000).
[92] C. Garzía Sanz, 'El poder de John Bull en la Gran Guerra. Visiones de la diplomacia italiana sobre la neutralidad', *Historia y Política*, 33, 2015.
[93] Martini, *Diario*, p. 183.

of London's severe initiatives: Montgomery Carmichael, the British consul in Livorno, appealed to the British Government to alleviate their measures, which went 'against the Entente's interests'. British naval interference in Italian trade risked diminishing British prestige: 'I am distressed at not being able to defend my country's action as well as her policy'.[94] Indeed 'British egoism' became one of the main arguments behind German propaganda in Italy.[95] But Grey was unmoved. British commercial policy endured, and became stricter.[96] It was no doubt successful in raising with the Italian Government, the question of whether prolonged neutrality was worth the price of a potentially serious economic crisis. British trade restrictions were superimposed on an economy suffering from the closure of the Dardanelles by the Ottomans, which cut Russian grain supplies to Italy. By February 1915, the price of grain imports in Italy had increased by 20 to 25 shilling per ton,[97] and the Italian press began to blame the Government for driving the country into economic recession. All major newspapers expressed similar fears, and even the neutralist *Italia Nostra* acknowledged that war might be necessary for 'economic and commercial' reasons.[98] Imperiali, for his part, believed that the only way to make the British relax their blockade was for Italy to join them in the war.[99]

In the last months of Italy's neutrality, British economic policy towards Italy became more elaborate. Andrew Percy Bennett, the commercial attaché in Rome, and Gerald Campbell, British consul in Venice, launched a commercial campaign through the British chambers of commerce in Italy.[100] It was meant to 'counter German influence in principal [Italian] ports and business hubs' by establishing a system for the supervision of contraband; to promote the Entente cause amongst Italian commercial communities by influencing 'the Italian merchant mind' through British commercial partners and local newspapers; and to strengthen Italian economic dependence on Britain. British consuls

---

[94] TNA, FO170/817, Charmichael to Rodd, December 1914.
[95] M. Borsa, *Italia e Inghilterra* (Milan: Società Editoriale Italiana, 1916), p. 5.
[96] García-Sanz, 'The end of neutrality? Italy and Spain in the Mediterranean theatre on the Great War', in J-L. Ruiz Sánchez, I. Cordero-Olivero, C. García-Sanz eds., *Shaping Neutrality throughout the First World War* (Saville: Editorial Universidad de Sevilla, 2015), p. 234.
[97] 'L'Italia di fronte alla questione del grano', *Corriere delle Puglie*, 2 February 1915.
[98] G. Battagliai, 'Imitiamo la Bulgaria!', *Italia Nostra*, 17 January 1915; 'Il problema granaio. Polemiche e constatazioni', *La Stampa*, 2 February 1915; 'Dimostrazione per il grano ad Andria', *Il Popolo d'Italia*, 2 February 1915; 'Un forno assalito a Sassari', *Il Giornale d'Italia*, 3 February 1915; 'Così parlò il Finanziere Bonomi', *Avanti!*, 2 February 1915; E. Pantaleoni, 'San Gennaro o Salandra?', *Il Giornale d'Italia*, 3 February 1915.
[99] TNA, FO170/825 Grey to Rodd, 12 August 1914; Rodd, *Memories*, III, p. 229.
[100] García-Sanz, 'End of neutrality?', p. 236.

were charged with the task of introducing commercial vetoes or blacklists in their districts. Percy Bennet appointed special agents to the major Italian ports to gather commercial intelligence on Italian firms trading with 'the enemy'.[101] The British consular service also issued strong appeals to their fellow nationals living in Italy to do everything in their power to discover any attempt to get contraband across Italian frontiers: 'All patriots became spies for the British sake'.[102] Once again, this interference in Italian domestic affairs was met with some criticism, particularly from the Committee on Restriction of Enemy Supplies in London.[103] But it also proved successful in mobilising Italian merchant communities against the Central Powers. Italian patriots and interventionists saw it as an opportunity to fight long-established German influence over Italy's economy, and to 'Italianise' the country's industry and the national financial network.[104] This put further pressure on Salandra, for it proved that large branches of the Italian business sector, as well as 'local workers and lower classes', when faced with the choice of supporting either the British or the Germans, would rather back the former.[105] Moreover, rumours came from London that a part of the British establishment wished to further 'blackmail Italy by closing the Gibraltar strait to its commerce'.[106]

Anglo-Italian exchanges, far from leading to an Anglo-Italian entente, had, in the autumn and winter of 1914–1915, produced Anglo-Italian arm-wrestling. Both countries used the 'carrot and the stick' tactic to influence each other. Italy was ready, if invited, to offer its services to the Entente, and form a special alliance with Britain; on the other hand, it threatened to remain neutral in exchange for minor concessions from the Central Powers, if Britain failed to accept Italian terms and to have them accepted by the other Entente powers. Britain was ready to do so, had Italy made a firm commitment first. To encourage it, London exploited its maritime and economic power, and used its financial wealth to influence Italian press and political elites – and thus public opinion – by all legal and illegal means. Italy was turned into a battlefield of espionage, propaganda and commercial war, and its sovereignty was repeatedly

---

[101] TNA, FO382/192, Rodd to Grey, 17 February 1915.

[102] García-Sanz, 'British Patriots and Spies in Italy (1914–1915): Fighting the Enemy of the Neutral Front Line', in A. Biagini, G. Motta eds., *The First World War: Analysis and Interpretation*, 2 vols. (Newcastle: Cambridge Scholars Publishing, 2015), I, pp. 192–196.

[103] TNA, FO382/193, Bennet to Rodd, 25 February 1915.

[104] L. D. Caglioti, 'Why and how Italy invented an enemy aliens problem in the First World War', *War in History*, XXI, 2, 2014, pp. 142–169.

[105] García-Sanz, 'British Patriots and Spies', p. 196; Trevelyan, *Scenes*, pp. 16–12.

[106] Sonnino, *Diario*, II, p. 32.

violated to drag it into the war. The rather simplistic version of the 'Machiavellian Italian' being 'for sale to the highest bidder', should take account of the active role played by the British authorities to force Italy's decision.

Salandra yielded at last. In mid-February, he concluded that diplomatic games were no longer possible; on the 16th, he instructed Sonnino to send Imperiali a revised draft of Italian conditions for the Entente and on 4 March Imperiali delivered it to Grey with the commitment that the latter had so long awaited: Rome was willing to enter the war. If they had to fight, however, both Salandra and Sonnino agreed that they must fight for the greatest possible advantage. Sonnino's final conditions reflected this conclusion. His earlier proposal had set the Italian frontier at Quarnaro, so as to include Trieste and Istria. The new memorandum,[107] instead, included Southern Dalmatia and its Adriatic islands, as well as colonial gains in Africa and Asia Minor – territories that were much harder to justify in liberal and democratic values.[108] In his diary, the Italian ambassador noted in dismay: 'If this request should be met, it will give rise to a wealth of problems from the promoters of the principle of nationality!'[109] Sonnino justified his extended claims under the principle of 'strategic security'. Naturally, such a concept is relative and can be extended indiscriminately. So, whereas South Tyrol was vital to the protection of Trentino, Dalmatia was touted as indispensable to secure Italian dominance over the Adriatic, whilst portions of Asia Minor and Africa were crucial to guarantee a long-term balance of power. Inspired by the principle of *sacro egoismo*, Sonnino had integrated and overlapped the liberal-democrats' aspirations to national unification with the imperialist ambitions of Italian nationalists and conservatives.

Imperiali and even Martini ended up in concert with him. 'After all', noted Imperiali, 'if we risk so much we are quite right to ensure the absolute supremacy in the Adriatic!'[110] Beyond this self-persuasion, however, as a well-seasoned diplomat, Imperiali had grasped the dangerous path that Italy was about to tread, presenting territorial claims grounded on two very different principles: one of unification of the 'unredeemed lands' according to the principle of nationality; the other of pure imperialist expansion, albeit masked by the fancy words of 'strategic security'. Moreover, Italy's imperialist thrust was far from welcome

---

[107] ASSR, Fondo Imperiali, b. 2, f. 10, Patto di Londra, Telegrammi, sf. Memorandum delle condizioni e dichiarazioni di non concludere pace separata, 16 February 1915.

[108] Around 230,000 German-speaking Tyrolese, 700,000 Slavs and 650,000 Italians lived in the territories claimed by Italy: Thompson, *White War*, p. 31.

[109] Imperiali, *Diario*, p. 132.   [110] Ibid., pp. 132–136.

in the Entente capitals: it needed to be either accepted or dissolved by the Entente for the alliance to be concluded.

4.3   Becoming Allies: The Art of Mediation

After Rome's commitment to the Entente, the intricate and tiring negotiations on Italy's intervention entered a new phase. The talks moved to London on Italy's request: partly to ensure secrecy – the Foreign Office did not release communiqués to the press – and partly to deliver a clear political message that Italy wished to make Britain – the only Entente power towards which Italian sympathies were 'unanimous and universal' – its main partner in the Alliance, and the guarantor of anything that would be agreed upon. Imperiali emphasised to Grey that Italy counted on Britain to bridge past Italo-Russian, and especially Italo-French differences. Giving 'full satisfaction' to Italy, he maintained, would benefit Britain: 'Harmony of views' and 'lack of substantially divergent interests', made it convenient to London 'to strengthen and expand the position of Italy, [Britain's] true friend in the Adriatic and the Mediterranean'. In the latter region, Imperiali continued, London's past and, even more so, future relations with its original Entente partners might not be as 'perpetually clear and easy as those with Italy'.[111] Grey skirted any pledge to give 'full satisfaction' to Italy; he was 'very irritated' by Sonnino's final claims, especially in the colonies.[112] But he did take it upon himself to reconcile Italian interests with those of the other Entente powers. This provided a classic illustration of Grey's complaints of the difficulties in tripartite diplomacy – 'It was no uncommon situation for three different suggestions to be made'.[113]

The main opposition to the alliance was Russia. The original promoter of Italy's entry into the Entente now strongly disapproved of Italian war aims, particularly Rome's demand for the whole of Dalmatia down to the Narenta, together with the offshore islands and the Sabbioncello peninsula – which affected Serbian interests and included territories largely inhabited by Slavs. Sazonov also feared that 'any fresh collaboration would complicate peace negotiations'. A fourth power might try to disunite the original Entente members 'for its own personal profit'.[114] Sazonov's position was initially met with sympathy in the Foreign Office and in the British Cabinet, which agreed 'that these [Italian claims] were very sweeping claims'.[115] Nicolson declared: 'Sazonov is quite right:

---

[111] DDI, 5, III, doc. 67, Imperiali to Sonnino, 9 March 1915.
[112] Imperiali, *Diario*, p. 39.   [113] Lowe, Dockrill, *Mirage of Power*, II, p. 169.
[114] Grey, *Twenty-Five Years*, p. 206.   [115] Hinsley, *British Foreign Policy*, p. 417.

Dalmatia is Slav and anxious to unite with Croatia. ... We will have a Southern Slav question with Italy in place of Austria'.[116] A corollary to these objections was Britain's anxiety to prevent a disintegration of the Habsburg Empire – a preoccupation shared in Paris.[117] Grey, however, pointed out that the common object of France, Britain and Russia was 'to finish this war as quickly as possible on satisfactory terms'. Again, he stressed that Italy's participation alongside the Entente would be 'the turning point in the war'.[118] To repel the Italian overture, after all Britain had done to bring it about, seemed 'the height of folly' – and the power refused 'may go to Germany, who will readily offer attractive conditions'.[119]

Beneath Grey's common sense lay other considerations, which he discussed with his British colleagues. He had initially reasoned that Italy's war aims would not affect British interests. Now, however, it seemed obvious that Italy's *sacro egoismo*, if vetoed in the Balkans, would be directed elsewhere. When discussing potential revisions of Sonnino's terms, Imperiali had mentioned to Grey, both Smyrna and Alexandretta, as well as territories in British Somaliland and the Egypt-Libya border.[120] It was therefore crucial for Britain to limit, as much as possible, Italian colonial claims, favouring Italian imperialism in the Balkans instead. This also served to counter-weigh Britain's original allies. It proved a strong point. Though accepting the overriding necessity of the immediate cession of Constantinople to Petrograd, no one in the British Cabinet was reconciled to 'the emergence of Russia as a strong Mediterranean naval power'.[121] Many were suspicious about Petrograd's aspirations in the Balkans and Persia.[122] Asquith was explicit that he would rather see Dalmatia in Italy's hands than in Russia's.[123] Both Horatio Kitchener, Secretary of State for War, and Churchill agreed. They were adamant that Britain should take Alexandretta under its control to keep 'command of the sea in the Mediterranean', and saw the defeat of Germany as a prelude to re-launching British domination in the south 'against France and Russia'.[124]

Sonnino then was rather convincing when he pointed out that 'the Dardanelles opened', Russia would have become 'a first-class maritime

---

[116] TNA, FO371/2008/57905, Nicolson minute on Buchanan, 7 October 1914.
[117] Robbins, *Edward Grey*, p. 309.
[118] TNA, CAB37/127 Grey to Bertie and Buchanan, 22 March 1915.
[119] Grey, *Twenty-Five Years*, p. 207.   [120] Ibid., p. 188.
[121] Lowe, Dockrill, *Mirage of Power*, II, pp. 177–181.
[122] BOD, Asquith papers, vol. 25, Memorandum by Winston Churchill, Naval Estimates, 1914–1915, 10 January 1914; TNA, FO800/374, Nicolson to Hardinge, 11 June 1914.
[123] Ibid., CAB37/126/21, Asquith to the King, 24 March 1915.
[124] Hinsley, *British Foreign Policy*, p. 418.

power in the Mediterranean and we [Italians and British] could not work to create an additional base for her in the Adriatic'.[125] He also maintained that the Sabbioncello peninsula and the Dalmatian islands were indispensable for the strategic security of Italy: 'It would not be worth going to war to liberate ourselves from the overbearing Austrian domination in the Adriatic if we then found ourselves in the same conditions of weakness [towards] a league of ambitious young South Slavic states'.[126] Asquith admitted that Sonnino's strategic case was 'very strong', as 'under the conditions of modern maritime warfare their coast will never be safe if the Dalmatian islands can be used by a rival power as a shelter and basis for submarines and destroyers'. He concluded: 'The importance of bringing in Italy without delay appears to be so great that it was agreed to give a general consent to what she asks and to press on Russia to do the same'.[127] He saw the Italian intervention as part of a strategic triptych that included a lightning Anglo-French amphibious offensive on Constantinople through the Dardanelles and a push to Balkan neutrals to join the Allies. If successful, these three Entente enterprises would have brought the war to an end by June.[128]

Once the decision in favour of Italy was taken, Grey encouraged Théophile Delcassé, French Foreign Minister, to accept the bulk of Italian claims in the Adriatic, and to press Russia to remove its veto. At the same time, he pressed Italy to compromise at least on the Cursola islands with the argument that Sonnino's 'excessive claims' would 'not only involve a sacrifice of the principle of nationality … but would permanently disturb relations between Italy and her new neighbours'.[129] Rodd advised him quite frankly: 'Price of Italian cooperation involves sacrifice of Dalmatia. … Can we afford to renounce their cooperation on account of Cursola islands?'[130] Grey then proposed to Imperiali a different scheme: Italian strategic interests could be covered by taking the offshore Dalmatian islands and imposing the neutralisation of the Slav coastline: 'That would be a solution that I could really press against Russian objections'.[131] Imperiali and Rodd had a hard time to soften Sonnino. By 6 April, they seemed doomed to failure.[132] Top-secret despatches and telegrams ran back and forth to prevent a dead end. Grey

---

[125] Sonnino, *Diario*, II, pp. 121–123.
[126] DDI, 5, III, doc. 104, Sonnino to Imperiali, 14 March 1915; doc. 164, Sonnino to Imperiali, Tittoni and Carlotti, 21 March 1915.
[127] TNA, CAB37/126/21, Asquith to the King, *cit.*   [128] French, *British Strategy*, p. 87.
[129] Quoted in Lowe, 'Britain and Italian Intervention, 1914–1915', *The Historical Journal*, XII, 3, 1969.
[130] TNA, CAB37/127/11, n. 181, Rodd to Grey, 2 April 1915.
[131] Ibid., 126/21, Grey to Rodd, 25 March 1915.
[132] DDI, 5, III, doc. 260, Sonnino to Imperiali, 3 April 1915.

was on the brink of physical collapse. He was suffering from the strain brought on by overwork and bad eyesight. Eventually, Sonnino conceded that Italy would leave to Serbia the coast from Cape Planka to the Voyusa, including Spalato and the five neighbouring islands, provided that all these were neutralised and that Italy obtained all the other islands and the peninsula of Sabbioncello. But only when Delcassé gave his support to the British was it possible to get around the difficulties of quadrangular interests and overcome what Asquith called 'Sazonov's piddling little points'.[133] Left alone, Sazonov began to come round. He added one final condition – that Italy should not take part in any operations in the Dardanelles Straits – and consented to the remaining Italian claims 'as long as nothing was said publicly about this'.[134] The ban on Italian action in the Straits presented no problem as this had never been envisaged in Rome. Instead, Italy asked for direct British support to its war effort in

Figure 4.1 Marquis Guglielmo Imperiali, Italian ambassador to Britain, with General Luigi Cadorna, Italian Chief of Staff, and Lord Kitchener, British Chief of Staff in London

[133] Lowe, Dockrill, *Mirage of Power*, II, p. 169.
[134] Hinsley, *British Foreign Policy*, p. 420. Though signing it, Sazonov continued to consider the Treaty of London 'a setback in Russian diplomacy': Burgwyn, *The Legend*, p. 35.

financial and material aid. London agreed on a loan of £50 million and allowed Italy to purchase 230 Maxim machine guns.[135]

The Treaty of London was signed in secrecy on 26 April 1915. Imperiali confessed that he was deeply moved that day.[136] Rodd was jubilant. He finally saw the objective of his efforts come to fruition and wrote a long praise of the Italian people in his memoirs.[137] It was, in many ways, a triumph of Grey's tenacious diplomacy, of Sonnino's pragmatism, and of the conciliatory skills of Rodd and Imperiali.

---

[135] Cellamare, 'La preparazione', *cit.*   [136] Imperiali, *Diario*, p. 151.
[137] Rodd, *Memories*, III, p. 257.

5   The Contested Treaty

Although the Treaty of London was a great achievement – it proved the only major diplomatic victory of the Entente until 1917 – it was also a *chiaroscuro*. It defined in detail the post-war Italian gains in Europe (Trentino and South Tyrol, up to the Brenner; Trieste and Istria as far as Quarnaro, but without the Italian city of Fiume in Croatia; Dalmatia down to Sabbioncello; and a protectorate over the largest part of Albania).[1] The treaty however failed to define in equally clear terms Italy's colonial gains. Articles 9 and 13 stated that, in the event of an Anglo-French partition of the Ottoman Empire and the German colonies, Italy would 'obtain a just share of the Mediterranean region adjacent to the province of Adalia', and 'some equitable compensation' in Africa.

Imperiali had pressed Sonnino to demand detailed colonial compensations, but Grey had opposed it, and the Italian Foreign Minister had given in, content with an assurance that the matter would be discussed in the future.[2] The treaty also called for close Allied cooperation: military, naval and financial conventions were to be drawn up setting the conditions for Italy's coordination with Britain, France and Russia in the fight 'against all their enemies' – thus denying the possibility of Italy waging a 'small war' against Austria-Hungary alone. The latter point was particularly critical in the light of Italy's insufficient military preparation. Moreover, by the time Italy declared war on 23 May, the Allies had lost the initiative in their respective spring offensives: the Russians had lost Lemberg (Lvov), and were in full retreat eastwards, whilst the Anglo-French landing at Gallipoli had been bloodily stemmed.[3] It was difficult in these circumstances to persuade the Balkan states that the addition of Italy would bring about a swift defeat of the Central Powers. Thus, the expected domino-effect in favour of the Entente never materialised.

---

[1] ASSR, Fondo Imperiali, b. 2, f. 10, Patto di Londra, Telegrammi, Testo del Patto di Londra, art. 16.
[2] Imperiali, *Diario*, p. 177.   [3] Hinsley, *British Foreign Policy*, p. 422.

The London Treaty also caused some resentment in both Britain and Italy. Rumours about its contents elicited severe protests from Serbo-Croat communities in the Entente capitals, especially London, where Slav committees were stronger.[4] Here they were supported by British intellectuals such as Steed, Arthur Evans and Robert Seton-Watson. Steed had a particular enthusiasm for the Slav cause, according to Rodd because he had lived for years, 'filially I believe rather than maritally', with a South Slav woman,[5] and regarded the treaty as a betrayal of the basic principles for which the Allies were fighting.[6] Evans, correspondent of *The Times* from Paris, agreed, and correctly predicted that the population in Austria-Hungary would resist the Italian invader fiercely.[7] Seton-Watson saw Grey at the beginning of May to protest against the treaty. By awarding Dalmatia to Italy, he claimed, the Foreign Minister had robbed Britain of the moral right to denounce the German conquest of Belgium: 'This treaty was the work of a small group of diplomatists following thoroughly Metternichian principles'. He also insisted that the content of the treaty be made public. Grey kindly replied: 'You are quite right: in time of peace all secret treaties are wrong and detestable; so is the use of poison gas; but in a great war, you will be driven, in self-defence, to the use of both'.[8] Regarding Seton-Watson's ethnical objections, Grey confessed: 'We cannot stretch the principle of nationality to the point of risking success in war'. Far from satisfied by Grey's reply, Seton-Watson kept promoting the Slav cause throughout the war with several bitter pamphlets directed as much against Italian appetites as against Grey's pusillanimity.[9]

Salandra too had to battle to have the London Pact approved. He presented parliament with the *fait accompli* on 4 May, after Italy had been, for eight days, allied with both the Entente and the Central Powers – a unique case in history.[10] Salandra's *escamotage* was meant to overcome the neutralist majority in the Chamber, but it failed, and the Prime Minister had to resign. King Victor Emmanuel III rejected his resignation and invited him to reshuffle his Cabinet. Giulio Rubini

---

[4] DDI, 5, I, doc. 688, Imperiali to Sonnino, 23 January 1915; Grey, *Twenty-Five Years*, pp. 206–208.

[5] Quoted in MacMillan, *Peacemakers*, p. 124.

[6] A. J. May, 'Seton-Watson and the Treaty of London', *The Journal of Modern History*, XXIX, 1, March 1957, pp. 42–47.

[7] R. W. Seton-Watson, *R. W. Seton-Watson and the Yugoslavs. Correspondence 1906–1941*, British Academy & UOZ eds., 2 vols. (London & Zagreb: Institute of Croatian History, 1976), I, p. 182, Seton-Watson to Herbert Fisher, 9 October 1916.

[8] Grey, *Twenty-Five Years*, p. 161.

[9] R. W. Seton-Watson, *The Balkans, Italy, and the Adriatic* (London: Nisbet & Co., 1915); 'The Failure of Sir Edward Grey', *English Review*, XXII, 1916, pp. 135–161.

[10] Martini, *Diario*, pp. 389 ff.

(Minister of Finance) and Domenico Grandi (Minister of War), who had opposed an Italian rearmament for financial reasons, were replaced with Paolo Carcano and Vittorio Zupelli, both pro-Entente: by supporting this move, the King played a decisive part in pushing parliament to approve the new alliance.[11] Eventually, in the so-called radiant days of May 1915, when Italy marched against Austria-Hungary, the war seemed to reunite the political and economic forces of the nation. Beneath the surface, however, there remained the difference between those who wanted war and those who had adapted to it. In time, the friction between the two groups would increase dramatically.[12]

The way the Treaty of London was created, as well as its content and domestic reactions to it in both Britain and Italy, illustrates the main patterns of the Entente's war diplomacy in the years to come. 'Business is business, above all for the British', was Imperiali's comment, and it summarised quite effectively the nature of the new alliance.[13] This was largely brought about by Anglo-Italian discussions and was based on a special Anglo-Italian entente, but by the time it was concluded mutual sympathy motivated by shared values and traditional friendship had melted away, and had been replaced by a convergence of interests which, however, were threatened by inter-Allied competition. In this context, Britain acted as a mediator in the Entente, with the twofold goal of strengthening the Alliance and of defending British interests by diverting the war aims of the other Entente members away from its own. It was a contradictory policy, for it encouraged mutual competition amongst the other Allies, thus damaging Allied solidarity. Italy was equally ambiguous in presenting territorial claims based on two conflicting principles. Furthermore, the essence of the Anglo-Italian special partnership was never formally addressed.

Italian policymakers had always considered Anglo-Italian ties to be somehow exceptional – but they had tended, more often than not, to overemphasise them. Consequently, Italian statesmen held Britain a special interlocutor throughout the months of neutrality – at times the only interlocutor. Now they considered it a special ally, and it seems clear that they looked to London as the guarantor of the London Pact. But Britain never made an equally clear promise on the latter point. Key British figures such as Grey and Asquith looked favourably on Italy, mirroring the expectation of the wider British public that Rome could deliver the decisive blow to the Central Powers and serve British war aims;

[11] A. Ungari, 'La scelta di un Re', in G. Orsina, A. Ungari eds., *L'Italia neutrale 1914–1915* (Rome: Rodorigo, 2016), p. 92.
[12] Isnenghi, Rochat, *Grande Guerra*, p. 314.   [13] Imperiali, *Diario*, p. 150.

but Greenhalgh made a good point that France, because of its military weight and the tight Anglo-French collaboration on the western front, remained prominent in British eyes.[14] One might therefore wonder whether the Anglo-Italian partnership was really 'special'. For the Italians it was such; for the majority of the British establishment, the specialness of the bilateral relation was relative, although they would at

Map 5.1 The Treaty of London of 1915

[14] See: Greenhalgh, *Victory through Coalition*, cit.

times encourage Italian assumptions throughout the war, to keep the Italians quiet. Anglo-Italian relations in the conflict were therefore based on, and responded to, rather different expectations. Moreover, British and Italian war aims were less compatible than it seemed, for London fought to defend its world supremacy against both enemies and allies whereas Italy fought for expansion. Waging a successful war of coalition in this context was far from easy.

A handful of British and Italian diplomats and statesmen had turned traditional Anglo-Italian friendship into an alliance, bringing about Italy's intervention in World War I on the side of the Entente. How they would play out the complex nature of this alliance and its contradictions, under the pressure of unpredictable military developments, remained to be seen.

Part II

Integrating Italy into the Triple Entente (Spring 1915–Summer 1917)

6   Context

Implementing treaties and policy papers, particularly when they are the result of a precarious compromise between multiple international players, is notoriously troublesome in the functioning of coalitions. A coalition grand strategy is shaped by usually conflicting national war aims, which are the products of distinct domestic considerations and strategic views. That is why general agreements are often followed by implementation documents providing an operational framework. These, however, are rarely flexible enough to survive contact with the enemy, as well as unpredictable situational changes. The implementation of the London Treaty is a clear example. Shortly after signing the pact, the Allies drew up military, naval and economic conventions providing the operational framework for its implementation; instead of simplifying Allied relations, they provided a diplomatic and political battleground. Three major issues followed, corresponding approximately to three distinct phases in Allied relations up to summer 1917. The first issue was the nature of Italy's war. The content of the London Treaty was kept secret; the Italian Government presented the war to the Italian public as the Fourth War of Independence against Austria-Hungary, following the suggestion of the liberal-democrat promoters of the intervention. In Salandra's words, it would be *la nostra guerra*, 'our war', a 'holy war' for national unification.[1] The immediate consequence of this was Italy's failure to declare war on Germany and Turkey. This obviously conflicted with the reality of a coalition war; it hampered Allied coordination and revived anti-Italian sentiment in the Entente countries. Such sentiment was exacerbated by Italy's failure to promote effectively the Italian cause and the real reasons behind its ambiguous position, which is revealing of the crucial role of propaganda in allied countries.

---

[1] 'Our war is a holy war' said Salandra in a speech at the Campidoglio, on 2 June 1915: *La nostra guerra è santa* (Rome: Tipografia del Senato, 1915).

These Italian failings were particularly relevant in view of the global developments of the war. The second half of 1915 saw severe Entente setbacks in Poland in August; in the Balkans where Allied forces failed to breakthrough at Gallipoli and Salonika; in the Middle East where the British were beaten at Ctesiphon in November; and on the western front where Anglo-French autumn offensives in Artois, Champagne and at Loos were bogged down with enormous losses. The need for better Allied coordination became increasingly clear – but Italy seemed to fight its own war. Britain played a key role in progressively involving Rome in the wider war of the Entente, as in Italy's declaration of war on Turkey in August 1915 and on Germany one year later. Yet Allied war diplomacy proved slow and inefficient, leading to diplomatic fiascos in the Balkans. This raises the question of whether diplomacy retains a role in wartime or whether it is eclipsed by the power of arms.

A second phase in the confrontation between Italy and its allies opened when attention shifted to the colonial question, leading to further contrasts dictated by the unexpected alteration in Allied war aims. Here Britain, which now devoted greater attention to the Middle East and supported an anti-Ottoman Arab revolt – proved a crucial mediator and probably prevented a fatal split in the Entente. This phase coincided with the disappointing results of Allied coordination in early 1916. The Allies scored a few notable successes, including Russia's Erzurum offensive on the Caucasus front in January 1916, the Brusilov offensive in Galicia on 4 June and the battle of Jutland on 31 May – the only major naval battle of the war, where the British suffered heavier losses but nonetheless claimed victory as the German ships withdrew and did not to re-emerge from their ports for the remainder of the war. But the Allies were battered into exhaustion at Verdun (21 February–18 December) and the Somme (1 July–18 November). The Central Powers were favoured by their central position, which allowed them to shift troops from one front to another faster and to support each other better. Yet they too were bleeding. This was the moment when early reflections on peace-making began in Britain, significantly shaping Britain's war strategy in the following months.

In view of a lengthening of the war, the isolation suffered by Italy was detrimental to the Allied cause. A third phase in Allied relations began in early 1917, when Britain made overtures to Italy, directed by the new Prime Minister Lloyd George, as part of the first serious attempt to shape an Allied grand strategy. This phase coincided with dramatic changes in war scenario: Germany's submarine campaign, the Russian Revolution and the American intervention. It shows the deep interplay of domestic and international politics, but it also reveals the difficulty of changing the nature of a strategy originally made of rather distinct national wars into a coherent grand strategy. As early peace talks failed and Italy reconciled with its Entente allies at St Jean de Maurienne (19 April), the great Allied offensives of mid-1917 – the Nivelle offensive, the Kerensky offensive, Third Ypres and the Tenth and Eleventh Isonzo offensives – remained largely in line with previous independent strategic approaches.

7   Turning Papers into Policies
The Implementation of the London Treaty

7.1   The Military Convention

Close Allied cooperation provided for by the London Pact was based on the conventions signed by the Allies during May 1915, when Italy enjoyed a one-month extra-time to speed up its military preparations. Britain had a particularly important role for two reasons: it was Italy's partner in the most important of the three conventions, the financial one, and it was the country that committed itself to mediate between Italy and France over the naval convention.

Allied land cooperation was regulated by the military convention signed on 21 May 1915.[1] Article 4 provided for Italy and Russia to concentrate their main efforts against Austria-Hungary in coordination with Serbia, so as to crush the Habsburg Empire on three sides.[2] On paper, it was a brilliant plan. However, on 2 May a joint Austro-German offensive routed the Tsarist forces in Galicia and drove them back more than 130 kilometres, taking some 400,000 prisoners.[3] This impeded any Russian assistance to Italy when it declared war. The Serbian attitude also proved disappointing: the Serbs had been fighting their own war of survival, and by the summer of 1915, their losses had cut Serb manpower in half.[4] Furthermore, the Serbs harboured strong suspicions towards Italy. The Serb delegation in Petrograd was convinced that 'the worst enemy is not Austria-Hungary, but Italy'.[5] The Serb hereditary prince, Alexander Karađorđević, confided to a Russian diplomat that he found the idea of collaborating with the Italians 'revolting'.[6] Supporting the

---

[1] Rochat, 'La Convenzione militare di Parigi (2 maggio 1915)', *Il Risorgimento*, VIII, 3, 1961, p. 155.
[2] DDI, 5, III, doc. 687, Carlotti to Sonnino, 14 May 1915.   [3] Riccardi, *Alleati*, p. 23.
[4] C. Seton-Watson, *Storia d'Italia*, p. 523.
[5] P. H. Michel ed., *La question de l'Adriatique, 1914–1918: Recueil de documents* (Paris: Costes, 1938), p. XLIV; L. Valiani, *La dissoluzione dell'Austria-Ungheria* (Milan: Il Saggiatore, 1966), pp. 113–114.
[6] F. Caccamo, 'Italy, the Adriatic', p. 134.

Italian advance on Trieste was the least of Serbian worries, especially since Belgrade was not a signatory to the London Treaty: it did not feel obliged to follow its dictates.[7] Italo-Russo-Serbian coordination proved impossible from day one.

To make matters worse, the Italian Government had ordered mobilisation only on 22 May, so Cadorna could not launch his major offensive earlier than 23 June, by which time the Austro-Hungarians had managed to raise the number of their divisions in Italy from 15 to 22.[8] Cadorna was still superior 2:1, but on the Italian front numbers were counter-balanced by other factors. The frontline was 650 kilometres from the Italo-Swiss border to the Adriatic Sea. It ran through snow-covered peaks as high as 3,000 metres in the north; in the east, it followed the Isonzo River snaking from the Julian Alps down to the sea with plateaus (the main of which was the Carso) some 800 metres high. Slopes, heights and crests between 100 and 2,000 metres high crowned these plateaus in what was a perfect defensive position. Battle-hardened Austro-Hungarian veterans commanded by General Svetozar Boroëvić defended the high ground, which they had fortified in advance. They enjoyed a clear view of the enemy and its movements, whereas the Italians could barely see them.[9] Cadorna had other disadvantages too. His forces lacked hand-grenades, machine guns and munitions. Cadorna had no more than 71 aircraft (largely Blériot-Gnome monoplanes) for reconnaissance and could deploy only 28 heavy siege batteries (mostly 140A howitzers and 149G mortars) and 96 field batteries. Few 280 mm and 305 mm howitzers were available, designed for coastal defence and almost impossible to move on land.[10] Scarce in numbers and weak in calibres, the Italian artillery was also poor in quality – within the year 139 guns exploded out of malfunction.[11] Such limitations did not discourage Cadorna's ambition. He planned to take up a defensive stance in the Trentino (1st Army), launching his offensive in the Carnia (4th Army) and across the Isonzo on two directions: the main attack fell to the left wing (2nd Army), its goals being Ljubljana and later Vienna, with Trieste as a secondary objective to be reached by the right wing (3rd Army). His grand strategic design was to be fed by 'energetic' and 'improvised' assaults on the part of his subordinate commanders.[12] At the tactical level, his instructions were outlined in his circular *Attacco frontale e ammaestramento tattico*, published in February,

---

[7] Salandra, *La neutralità italiana*, p. 324.
[8] P. Pieri, *L'Italia nella Prima Guerra Mondiale (1915–1916)* (Turin: Einaudi, 1965), p. 78.
[9] DDI, 5, IV, doc. 137, Cadorna to Salandra, 9 June 1915.
[10] Cellamare, 'La preparazione', *cit.*   [11] Gooch, *Italian Army*, pp. 107.
[12] AUSSME, H5, b. 17, f. 1, n. 203, Cadorna ai Comandanti della 2ª & 3ª Armata, 16 May 1915.

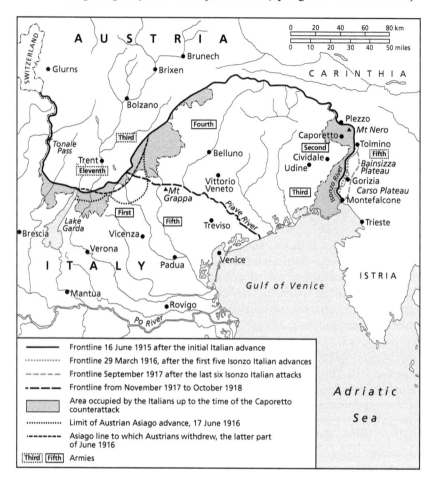

Map 7.1 The Italian Front, 1915–1918

which preached frontal assaults as the doctrinal dogma for infantry units.[13]

It is striking how little Cadorna's plans had benefitted from what had so far happened on other fronts. Italian historians have emphasised that the reports from Greppi and Breganze lacked a coherent analysis of operations on the western front in 1914–1915, and in fact confirmed the bias of the more traditionalist Italian commanders (Cadorna among them) by

[13] Ibid., Comando del Corpo di Stato Maggiore, Attacco frontale e ammaestramento tattico, Circolare 191 del 25 febbraio 1915, Rome 1915.

stressing the relevance of manoeuvring in the opening phases of the war and encouraging expectations about a cathartic Italian intervention.[14] But they also stressed the unprecedented impact of new technologies – including machine guns, heavy guns, aircraft and gas projectiles – on the battlefield, and how they impeded decisive results.[15] Offensives, Breganze wrote, turned into 'true hecatombs', and to be successful they would have required 'an overwhelming superiority, which no one seems to have'.[16] Greppi sent Cadorna detailed tactical suggestions: 1) Any attack must be preceded by the 'complete destruction of barbed wire by the artillery', which would need an 'almost endless' amount of ammunition and 2) 'When infantry attacks, artillery must target uninterruptedly the terrain behind the enemy first line to inhibit the arrival of reinforcements'.[17] Despite their contradictions, such reports were clear enough to make a commander pause and wonder whether waves of frontal infantry assaults with little artillery support available could really lead to decisive breakthroughs – especially on the adverse terrain the Italians found ahead.

Unfortunately for the Italians, Cadorna grasped the need for greater industrial mobilisation and the importance of manpower, both of which led him to ask repeatedly for larger resources to expand the army during the neutrality period; but he would not renounce his Napoleonic dreams.[18] As highlighted by Marco Mondini in his thorough biography of Cadorna, offensive biases were a common trait in western military culture at the time. Cadorna was no exception.[19] His stubbornness however goaded his preconceptions. Nor would he listen to those who called the latter into question – rather he would sack them, as he did with the commander of the 3rd Army, General Luigi Zuccari, two days before the war began.[20] Like Sonnino, Cadorna was a centraliser. Until August 1917, he preferred not to create a 'modern headquarters'[21] with a large operations bureau that would analyse operations in detail, learn

[14] Rochat, 'La preparazione dell'esercito italiano nell'inverno 1914–1915 in relazione alle informazioni disponibili sulla guerra di posizione', *Il Risorgimento*, XIII, 1, 1961; Mondini, *Il Capo*, p. 127.

[15] Scoppola Iacopini, 'Le relazioni', pp. 70–71.

[16] Pardini, 'Sul campo di battaglia', p. 109.

[17] AUSSME, G29, b. 68, f. 1, R. trasmessi nel 1915, rapporto 18 aprile 1915.

[18] Ibid., H5, b. 17, f. 3, Provvedimenti pel caso di una lunga campagna di guerra. Organizzazione di nuove unità, Cadorna to Salandra, 21 May 1915; A. Gatti, *Un Italiano a Versailles, dicembre 1917-febbraio 1918* (Milan: Ceschina, 1958), pp. 425–426; *Caporetto. Diario di guerra* (Bologna: Il Mulino, 1997), pp. 77, 141.

[19] Mondini, *Il Capo*, pp. 175–177.

[20] See G. L. Baio, *Il milite noto. Il generale Luigi Zuccari 'primo morto' della Grande Guerra* (Bergamo: Papini, 2015).

[21] A. Barbero, *Caporetto* (Bari: Laterza, 2017), p. 56.

lessons and make grounded plans. Despite its name of *Comando Supremo* and its size,[22] Cadorna's headquarters in Udine, some 45 kilometres behind the frontline, was run by a handful of loyal friends and followers. Many began to call it 'the Udine Ministry', where 'adulators had unfortunately ended up prevailing'.[23] Cadorna's subordinates had mixed opinions of him; some, like Colonel Angelo Gatti, admired him almost acritically;[24] others, like General Luigi Capello, disliked him and competed with him – which encouraged Cadorna's paranoid centralism.[25] General Enrico Caviglia, more balanced, described Cadorna as an 'incomplete' commander: 'He saw clearly the grand strategic problems, but lacked touch on the immediate situation'.[26] Quite interestingly, Martini, influenced by Cadorna's obstinacy in his Isonzo offensives, thought the opposite: 'He is a tactician ... not a strategist'.[27] Not surprisingly, Cadorna held a uniformly low opinion of politicians and tried to extract the greatest possible autonomy from the Government[28] – which did not help to establish a coherent war policy. Yet, again like Sonnino, Cadorna was more multifaceted than has been traditionally portrayed. He compensated for his monopolism with an *élan*, a determination and an energy that had few equals at the time, and that are all the more impressive in a man his age (he was 65 years old in 1915). The Italian army would benefit much from his organisational talent. Rodd regarded him 'as one of the great soldiers in the war',[29] and the Austro-Hungarian general Alfred Krauß, called Cadorna 'the greatest of the Italians'.[30]

Three days into the war, Cadorna ordered all his subordinates in the frontline, except those in the 1st Army to act 'offensively with daring' to gain 'as much territory as possible' in preparation for the decisive assault when he had assembled enough men. He was disappointed. Preoccupied with sabotages to their communication lines once they entered enemy territory, Italian generals were overly cautious in their opening moves.[31]

---

[22] In 1915, the *Comando Supremo* included more than a thousand officials: Mondini, *Il Capo*, p. 247.

[23] Quote by Don Minozzi, a clergyman very influential in the Italian Command: Barbero, *Caporetto*, p. 55.

[24] Gatti, *Caporetto*, p. 22.

[25] G. Minozzi, *Ricordi di guerra* (Amatrice: Tipografia Orfanotrofio maschile, 1956), pp. 29–30.

[26] E. Caviglia, *La dodicesima battaglia (Caporetto)* (Milan: Mondadori, 1933), pp. 254–258.

[27] Martini, *Diario*, p. 579.   [28] Mondini, *Il Capo*, pp. 105, 263.

[29] Rodd, *Memories*, III, p. 256.

[30] Barbero, *Caporetto*, p. 53; A. Krauß, *Il miracolo di Caporetto. In particolare lo sfondamento di Plezzo*, E. Cernigoi, P. Pozzato eds. (Valdagno: Rossato, 2002), p. 22. In a letter to his wife, Conrad termed Cadorna's dismissal the main Austro-Hungarian achievement at Caporetto: L. Brignoli, *Il generale Luigi Cadorna, Capo di Stato Maggiore dell'esercito (1914–1917)* (Udine: Gaspari, 2012), p. 78.

[31] Isenghi-Rochat, *Grande Guerra*, pp. 165–167.

In irritation, Cadorna sacked the commander of the 1st Cavalry Division, Nicola Pirozzi, and later Luigi Nava, commander of the 4th Army, the first of 217 generals, 255 colonels and 337 lieutenant-colonels he would fire throughout the war.[32] Convinced, as were many of his colleagues throughout Europe, that discipline and will were what mattered most in war, Cadorna aimed to 'remove all hesitation and give everyone the necessary offensive spirit'.[33] But Italian preparatory assaults across the Isonzo found strong defences protected by barbed wire that made lightening manoeuvres chimerical. Frustrated, Cadorna began to suspect that it was in fact necessary to proceed 'methodically and with patience, in the hope that the latter will not shrink in our impatient people'.[34] Yet the Italian soldiers proved their worth when they were well led. In the night between 15 and 16 June, two *Alpini* battalions (mountain troops), under General Donato Etna, assaulted Mount Nero, the highest peak (2,245 metres) dominating the eastern bank of the Isonzo, which the Austro-Hungarians considered impregnable thanks to its precipitous cliffs. The *Alpini* climbed the cliffs at night and took the summit by sunrise in hand-to-hand combat. George Trevelyan, who was on the Italian front commanding a unit of the British Red Cross, called it 'as fine a feat of arms and mountaineering combined as stands on record in history'.[35]

The next week Cadorna launched his first major offensive. It offered the inaugural evidence of endemic odds. The first was the terrain. The rocky ground made digging and re-supplying extremely difficult and exposed the soldiers to an additional shower of rock fragments as sharp as knifes at every shell explosion. It also produced 'unforeseen and crippling tactical consequences'.[36] Divisions found it impossible to keep their cohesion during the attacks because slopes, bluffs, ravines and rocks split their linear formation into fractions, with the result that they were beaten back fraction by fraction upon reaching the enemy position. And when they broke through, the Italians were exposed to counter-attacks for much longer than their allies on the western front, because the rough terrain and the lack of good roads slowed down the movement of their reserves. Another nasty surprise was the quality of Austro-Hungarian defences. Trevelyan witnessed the attack on Mount Sabotino, in the Gorizia sector:

Sabotino was a stronghold of nature and of art. ... Athwart this immense natural glacis the Austrians had ... blasted out in the limestone surface a deep trench, which the Italians called ... the *trincerone*. They had also hollowed out for

---

[32] Gooch, *Italian Army*, p. 105.
[33] L. Cadorna, *Lettere famigliari*, R. Cadorna ed. (Milan: Mondadori, 1967), Cadorna to his wife, 30 May 1915, p. 105.
[34] DDI, 5, IV, doc. 137, *cit.*   [35] Trevelyan, *Scenes*, p. 88.
[36] Gooch, *Italian Army*, p. 101.

themselves great chambers in the rocks, where thousands of men could shelter during the preliminary bombardments. ... Against these previously prepared defences the Italians on the open glacis of the mountain had to push forward such trenches as they could improvise, scraping them out in the interstices of the rocks. ... It was a contest of unequal terms.[37]

The battle ended on 7 July with a few Italian bridgeheads established on the eastern bank of the Isonzo.[38] In London, news of the offensive came in dribs and drabs. Kitchener and Robert Crewe – Lord President of the Council – visited Imperiali anxiously asking for news. 'We advance slowly but, it seems, confidently', the ambassador replied, though he admitted that the enemy 'called victory all along the line'. At the end of June, Kitchener was already sending Cadorna tactful suggestions to spur the Italian advance. Enemy lines, he revealed, could be bent with great effort, but they were 'extremely difficult to break'. He stressed that modern warfare favoured the defender, and recommended surprise attacks. He also concluded that greater Allied collaboration was needed.[39] In the

Figure 7.1 A trench at 150 metres from the enemy, with Palenik mountain held by the Austro-Hungarians

---

[37] Trevelyan, *Scenes*, pp. 47–49.   [38] C. Seton-Watson, *Storia d'Italia*, p. 521.
[39] Imperiali, *Diario*, pp. 173–181; DDI, 5, IV, docs. 246 and 317, Imperiali to Sonnino, 23 and 30 June 1915.

Figure 7.2 Italian *Alpini* climbing a steep slope in the opening phases of the war

following days, Allied representatives met at the French headquarters in Chantilly for the first time to discuss better coordination, and agreed upon concerted actions.[40] Cadorna urged Serbia in particular to take the offensive 'in accordance with the Italo-Russian Pact' and emphasised this in his reply to Kitchener.[41] Crowe, however, reminded the Italians that it was inconvenient to push Serbia to attack: it would have further damaged their battered army – the sole force that impeded 'the Germans to put pressure directly onto Bulgaria and to link up with

---

[40] R. A. Doughty, *Pyrrhic victory: French Strategy and Operations in the Great War* (Cambridge, MA: Belkna, 2005), pp. 176–180.
[41] DDI, 5, IV, doc. 343, Cadorna to Sonnino, 5 July 1915.

Turkey'.[42] It was a matter 'of degree', intervened Sonnino: Serbia did not need to use all of its army, but it needed to follow the Allied military convention.[43]

No assistance came from Belgrade, but this did not dissuade Cadorna that with better preparations a general breakthrough was in sight. On 18 July, he launched his Second Isonzo offensive. He attacked on a wide front to keep the enemy unsure of his real objectives, but in doing so, he nullified his numerical superiority. The artillery fire, far from being focussed on key sectors, was dispersed along the front.[44] Early Italian successes encouraged optimism in London. Imperiali expected the fall of Gorizia and cheered at the 17,000 Austro-Hungarians who marched into captivity. But the Italian attack faded and, in the end, produced only local advances. In two weeks, 'nothing new, nor positive' came from the front. Disillusion was high in London. Publicly British statesmen praised Italian operations, but privately they were disheartened. Imperiali found Nicolson 'very depressed', and the latter called the present phase of the war 'the most critical for the Allies'. Warsaw had fallen, and the Italian operations proceeded 'ways too slowly', admitted Imperiali.[45] The Italians chiefly blamed the Serbs for their failures. 'On the lower Isonzo, the arrival of fresh enemy forces from the Serbian frontier continues', lamented Cadorna,[46] who came to suspect a secret Austro-Serbian agreement preparatory to a ceasefire between Vienna and Belgrade. He concluded in a rage: 'Had Serbia been Allied with Austria she would not have acted differently from what she has'.[47] The British were next on Italy's complaint list, because they had not yet delivered the machine guns purchased in May. Initially, Kitchener had delayed their despatch on the grounds that 'before giving our machine guns to Italy we need to ensure in what direction they will fire', yet he remained unmoved even after Italy had declared war.[48] Imperiali's repeated pleas were in vain,[49] as were Rodd's, who insisted that 'a greater impulse to Italy's war' might accelerate 'the war's end'.[50] Even Trevelyan, who recurrently noted the cordial comradeship between his men and the Italian soldiers, acknowledged that 'in those early days a special difficulty existed. I became aware ... that Italy did not believe that England was pulling her full weight'.[51]

What was lacking from Italy was a clear explanation of the unexpected and bitter realities of its theatre of war. This reflected another early fault in

---

[42] Sonnino, *Diario*, II, p. 171.

[43] DDI, 5, IV, doc. 358, Sonnino to Imperiali, 6 July 1915.

[44] Mondini, *Il Capo*, p. 149.

[45] Imperiali, *Diario*, pp. 186–202; DDI, 5, IV, doc. 333, Imperiali to Sonnino, 3 July 1915.

[46] Ibid., doc. 499, Cadorna to Sonnino, 30 July 1915.   [47] Salandra, *L'intervento*, p. 325.

[48] DDI, 5, IV, doc. 364, Imperiali to Salandra, 7 July 1915.

[49] Ibid., doc. 371, Imperiali to Sonnino, 8 July 1915.   [50] Sonnino, *Diario*, II, p. 221.

[51] Trevelyan, *Scenes*, pp. 30–33.

the Italian war, which was to become endemic: miscommunication. Cadorna conveyed little information to either the press or the policymakers. He had severely reduced the communication and press corps of the *Comando Supremo* – contrary to what happened in the other European armies.[52] Cadorna's bulletins were meagre, nebulous and sometimes rather mendacious. He did little to share with his allies, the particulars of Italy's war, its material difficulties, and the mammoth efforts made to overcome them. Foreign visitors were not welcome at the frontline, something Trevelyan regretted very much: having witnessed the realities of the Italian war, and the valour of the Italian troops, he was convinced that notwithstanding their failures, their performance would have earned respect, had a British representative seen the battlefield.[53] Since May, Italian casualties had been some 60,000, slightly more than Austria-Hungary's 58,000.[54] Given the advantage of defence over offence, and of the Austro-Hungarian position over the Italian, it is remarkable that the *Regio Esercito* had inflicted almost equal losses upon its enemy. Likewise remarkable is the morale of the defenders, many of whom were Slavs fighting viciously to repulse the Italian invasion.[55] They had suffered a casualty rate of one in three without breaking. This was neither appreciated abroad, nor did Italian representatives give special relevance to the Italian victory at Mount Nero – apparently the news never came to Imperiali who never mentioned that significant success in his detailed diary. Instead, vague news came about 'the valour of our troops' and their 'slow but constant progresses'. Imperiali was forced to confess: 'I don't see things clearly' – which was embarrassing when he had to confront British generals or statesmen.[56] This was true also for Italian diplomats elsewhere, as we shall see.

The Italians had envisaged a promenade to Vienna.[57] Their allies expected just as much. Now those hopes were dispelled, and Italy's contribution to land operations proved far less pivotal than expected.

7.2   The Naval Convention

The war at sea increased inter-Allied frustration. In the summer of 1914, an Anglo-French naval convention established a division of labour between the Royal Navy and the French *Marine Nationale*. The former would concentrate in the North Sea facing the bulk of the

---

[52] Mondini, *Il Capo*, p. 106.
[53] Trevelyan, *Scenes*, p. 199. No more welcome were Italian journalists and politicians: Mondini, *Il Capo*, pp. 118, 270–275.
[54] Gooch, *Italian Army*, pp. 108–113.   [55] Mondini, *Il Capo*, p. 165.
[56] Imperiali, *Diario*, pp. 182, 186, 193, 205.   [57] Mondini, *Il Capo*, p. 159.

German navy; the latter would take on the Austro-Hungarian *k.u.k. Kriegsmarine* plus the German *Mittelmeerdivision*, consisting of the battle cruiser *Goeben* and the light cruiser *Breslau*, in the Mediterranean. French Admiral Augustin de Lapeyrère was made Allied Commander-in-Chief in the Mediterranean. His strategy reflected the Mahanian principle of securing command of the sea by engaging and defeating the enemy fleet.[58]

The war however began on a sour note when the *Mittelmeerdivision* managed to escape to the Dardanelles and was subsequently included in the Turkish fleet. Lapeyrère was disappointed by the cautious attitude of the Austro-Hungarian Chief of Staff, Anton Haus, who wisely refused to engage the superior French fleet in open waters. Rather, he concentrated his three dreadnoughts and nine pre-dreadnoughts in the Northern Adriatic, and sent his cruiser flotilla – three armoured cruisers and three light cruisers – to Cattaro at the southern tip of Dalmatia, without leaving the Adriatic. On 16 August 1914, Lapeyrère tried unsuccessfully to provoke him into battle by passing through the Straits of Otranto at the mouth of the Adriatic. Lapeyrère realised that geography compensated the Austro-Hungarians for their numerical inferiority since the Eastern Adriatic coast is mostly rough, protected by a chain of islands with internal passages that the Austro-Hungarians could easily defend and navigate sheltered from outside attack. Moreover, the new submarine weapon was a constant threat to his battleships, so Lapeyrère opted for a 'distant blockade' of Austria-Hungary, analogous to the British blockade of Germany in the North Sea, transferring the bulk of the French navy to Corfu to guard the mouth of the Adriatic.[59]

Early French failures played a crucial part in shaping Allied naval strategy when, in early May 1915, Allied delegates met in Paris to draw up a new naval convention which included Italy. The Italian delegate, Mario Grassi, presented a bold proposal from Revel following the same offensive principle that had inspired Lapeyrère: a joint Allied force was to neutralise the Austro-Hungarian fleet with a single blow, clearing the Adriatic in the first hour of Italy's war. Because the favourable geography of the Austro-Hungarian shore required a significant preponderance of forces – especially light craft, which the Italians lacked – Revel asked for Anglo-French support in the shape of 6 battleships, 24 destroyers and as many minesweepers and torpedo craft for anti-submarine

[58] A. T. Mahan, *Sea Power in its relations to the War of 1812*, 2 vols. (New York, 1903), II, pp. 51–52; Mahan, *The Influence of Sea Power upon History 1660–1783* (Boston, 1890), pp. 287–288.

[59] L. Sondhaus, *The Great War at Sea. A Naval History of the First World War* (Cambridge: Cambridge University Press, 2014), pp. 97, 111, 128.

duties as possible.[60] The French, however, rejected the proposal on the grounds that a massive naval operation in the relatively narrow Adriatic basin without proper intelligence on the enemy was too risky, and they were also adamant that no French capital ships should be re-deployed north of Otranto.[61] The British were also unhappy with the prospect of providing the Italians with naval reinforcements. They had already despatched men and ships for the Dardanelles operation, which was promoted by Churchill and launched on 25 April.[62] So, the British believed that the *Regia Marina* should deal with the *k.u.k. Kriegsmarine* without further aid – an idea reflecting the generally low opinion they had of the Austro-Hungarian navy. The Italians, on the other hand, having a higher opinion of the *k.u.k Kriegsmarine,* which they had confronted unsuccessfully in 1866, insisted that the slight superiority they enjoyed over it called for a joint operation.[63]

Revel was so dissatisfied with his new naval allies that he issued a memorandum to Sonnino on 5 May, stressing his apprehension about Italy being left to take the full burden of the fight at sea. If sufficient Allied forces were not made available for the Adriatic operation, he would rather refuse concluding the naval convention and rely on the Italian force for a strictly defensive war. Sonnino, for his part, called Tommaso Tittoni, the Italian ambassador in Paris, urging him to inform the French Government that unless a real cooperation was agreed upon, it would not be possible to conclude the naval convention, and this would invalidate the entire Treaty of London. Sonnino even suspected that the inadequate support offered by the Entente allies showed a secret intention to avoid the annihilation of the Austro-Hungarian fleet, mirroring Anglo-French preoccupation that the Habsburg Empire should not emerge from the war badly weakened.[64] The British tried to mediate. Both Rodd and Capitan William Boyle, British naval attaché to Rome, stressed to London that the Italian fear of France becoming an 'overwhelming' maritime power in the Mediterranean was far from absurd if the *Regia Marina* was severely weakened by its lone fight against the *k.u.k. Kriegsmarine.*[65] Churchill went to Paris to press for a compromise, promising to support Italy 'as far as possible' despite the

---

[60] DDI, 5, III, doc. 637, Sonnino to Tittoni, 9 May 1915; Sonnino, *Diario*, II, p. 16; M. Gabriele, 'La Convenzione navale italo-franco-britannica del 10 maggio 1915', *Nuova Antologia*, 1972–1973, April-May 1965.

[61] C. Seton-Watson, *Storia d'Italia*, p. 522.

[62] Sondhaus, *Great War*, pp. 131; 172–173.

[63] Italy's fleet included three dreadnoughts, nine pre-dreadnoughts, ten armoured cruisers: Ibid., p. 59.

[64] DDI, 5, III, doc. 637, *cit.*

[65] P. G. Halpern, 'The Anglo-French-Italian naval convention of 1915', *Historical Journal*, XIII, 1, March 1970, pp. 106–129.

Admiralty's little confidence in the efficiency of the Italians. To support Churchill, Tittoni pressed Grassi very hard to sign the convention on 10 May, before Revel could raise further objections.[66]

The convention created the First Allied Fleet in the Adriatic under Revel. It consisted of the bulk of the Italian fleet, twelve French destroyers, four British light cruisers, four British pre-dreadnoughts and as many submarines and minesweepers as possible. If the First Allied Fleet was to move to the Northern Adriatic, a Second Allied Fleet would be assembled in the south under Lapeyrère, consisting of Allied ships not already allotted to the First Fleet. Lapeyrère remained the overall Allied Mediterranean commander with Revel as his subordinate, but the Italians insisted that any Allied force operating in 'the Italian sea' be put under Italian command; so in the event that the Second Allied Fleet entered the Adriatic, Lapeyrère would be subordinated to Revel.[67] This tortuous command chain was – to at least one commentator – a classic expression of the 'parochial mind' symptomatic of 'the disease called national prestige', and proved a serious impediment to any Allied coordination.[68] This was particularly deleterious given the nature of the Adriatic operations.

The main strategic problem for the Allies in the Adriatic was how to induce the Austro-Hungarians to sortie for a naval battle under conditions favourable to the Allies. Unfortunately, the limited capacity of the Italian ports, combined with the need to guard Austro-Hungarian naval bases both in the upper and lower Adriatic, forced the Allies to split their forces between Venice, Taranto and Brindisi; this apart from the French reserve at Corfu – a substantial waste of resources.[69] Furthermore, none of the four parts of the Allied armada was strong enough to anticipate a success, if it met the whole Austro-Hungarian fleet.[70] The Allies would have to converge on the enemy from different directions before engaging in full-scale combat. As the Austro-Hungarians were not passive – they frequently raided the Italian coast, which, unlike the Eastern Adriatic littoral, is open and much easier to attack[71] – the plan sounded reasonable. But the complexity of this manoeuvre posed unprecedented

---

[66] DDI, 5, III, doc. 606, Imperiali to Sonnino, 7 May 15; L. Aldrovandi Marescotti, *Nuovi ricordi e frammenti di diario*, (Milan, 1938), Revel to Aldrovandi Marescotti, 8 May 1915, p. 222.

[67] Sondhaus, *Great War*, p. 131.

[68] Halpern, 'Anglo-French-Italian naval convention', p. 128.

[69] Halpern, *A Naval History of World War I* (London: University College London, 1994), p. 159.

[70] A. Thomazi, *Guerre navale dans l'Adriatique. La marine française dans la grande guerre 1914–1918* (Paris: Payot, 1925); Ufficio Storico della Marina (USM), *La Marina Italiana nella Grande Guerra*, 8 vols. (Florence: Vallecchi, 1935–1942), I, pp. 435–439.

[71] Halpern, *The Battle of the Otranto Straits. Controlling the Gateway to the Adriatic in WWI* (Bloomington: Indiana University Press, 2004), p. 1.

challenges to the Allied navies. It required prompt reactions and rapid decision-making. Instead, the ambiguous Allied hierarchy, exacerbated by bad signal communications, allowed the Austro-Hungarians repeatedly to slip through Allied fingers.[72] The situation deteriorated when, in mid-summer 1915, the Germans sent their own submarines to the Adriatic in support of the Austro-Hungarians. This was an undesired consequence of the Dardanelles campaign, and unleashed the first experiment in unrestricted submarine warfare in the Mediterranean. Moreover, the fact that Italy was not at war with Germany created an intricate situation because the Italians could not attack German U-boats in Austro-Hungarian bases. In contrast, U-boats masquerading as Austro-Hungarian submarines, attacked all enemy and neutral vessels – including Italian – in the Adriatic and Mediterranean. To face the new threat, the British proposed the creation of a drifter barrage across the Straits of Otranto aimed at trapping enemy submarines in the Adriatic. Revel initially rejected the plan, for it would have left Italy alone to face the U-boats with its inadequate light craft. He was forced to accept it at the end of the summer after the British made any Allied naval support conditional upon Italian participation in the Otranto barrage.[73] The barrage essentially turned Allied strategy from an offensive-based approach into a strategy of containment. The rationale behind it was that submarines could be blocked from passing through relatively narrow straits – a tactic already implemented, with mixed results, in the English Channel. Physical issues, however, made its replication at the mouth of the Adriatic far more ambitious – and far less realistic. The English Channel is 33.1 kilometres wide at the Strait of Dover; by comparison, the Otranto Channel is 72 kilometres wide, and the currents are stronger. Furthermore, it was misleading to talk of a barrage, or even of a 'line' of drifters, which suggested a continuous line of small ships with nets. Only a portion of the over 60 drifters involved was in service at the same time on the line, as many of them needed repairs or lacked personnel.[74] The barrage also caused further conflicts over the prickly question of command: because neither the Italians nor the French were inclined to put their units at the mouth of the Adriatic under the command of the other, the barrage was assigned to Rear Admiral Cecil Thursby, commander of the British Adriatic Squadron, who, however, remained nominally subordinate to Revel.[75] The Otranto experiment proved largely ineffective.

---

[72] Halpern ed., *The Royal Navy in the Mediterranean* (Aldershot: Gower, 1987), p. 2.
[73] Sondhaus, *Great War*, p. 165.
[74] NMRN, Limpus MSS, Thursby to Limpus, 28 September 1915.
[75] AUSM, b. 498, f. 3, Contributo dalla Marina inglese all'Italia durante la guerra 1915–1918.

Disillusion about a quick naval victory, mutual recrimination about the Otranto flop, and the prospect of a permanent Austro-Hungarian naval thorn in their flesh strained Allied relations.[76] Revel blamed his allies for the failure to knock out the *k.u.k. Kriegsmarine* in the opening phases of Italy's war and for the ineffective Otranto strategy.[77] Their limited collaboration strengthened Revel's conclusion that Italy, being the only Entente power to be in close contact with a modern enemy fleet in the Mediterranean, must prevent debilitating losses in its confrontation with Austria-Hungary, in order to defend Italy's military and diplomatic place in the post-war settlement. So, he would not launch any major Adriatic operation until adequately supported by his allies with the light craft he badly lacked.[78] The British and French began to think that Italy's entry into the war 'instead of relieving our burden in the Mediterranean, as might have been expected', had the effect of 'increas[ing] it materially'.[79] This was hard for them to accept, particularly because reports from British and French naval attachés repeatedly stressed that the Italian attitude had become increasingly cautious, and that the Italian battleships were largely unused;[80] the Italian 'lack of offensive spirit' became a mantra.[81] Admiral Louis Dartige du Fournet, who replaced Lapeyrère as Allied Mediterranean Commander in October 1915, repeatedly expressed his disappointment in the 'defensive' nature of Italian plans.[82] Wilfred Tomkinson, who commanded British submarines in the Adriatic, claimed that the Italian crews 'seemed to seek any excuse for not going out',[83] whilst Thursby, stated bluntly: 'The Italians lack initiative, avoid responsibility, and are not accustomed to Fleet work'.[84]

Italy's allies suggested to Revel that, if he was not going to launch any major Adriatic operation, he could at least provide assistance to Allied transportation operations in the Mediterranean. He replied that the short distance between Dalmatia and Italy forced him to scatter his limited light

[76] Sondhaus, *Great War*, pp. 8–9, 168.
[77] AUSM, b. 497, f. 2, Cooperazione interalleata durante la guerra marittima mondiale in Mediterraneo, Memorandum di Revel, 8 August 1917.
[78] E. Cernuschi, *Battaglie sconosciute. Storia riveduta e corretta della Regia Marina durante la Grande Guerra* (Vicenza: Edibus, 2014), pp. 25 ff.
[79] J. S. Corbett, *History of the Great War Naval Operations. Based on Official Documents*, 3 vols. (London & New York: Longmans & Green, 1920–1923), II, p. 395.
[80] Lieutenant W. E. Parry, *Diary*, Parry MSS 71/19/1, 14 November 1916. Quoted in Halpern ed., *The Royal Navy*, p. 186.
[81] TNA, FO371/2685/65037, Nicolson to Rodd, 21 January 1916; Rodd papers, Hardinge to Rodd, 28 June and 23 August 1916.
[82] Halpern, *Naval War*, p. 270.
[83] CCC, Tomkinson MSS, 170/2, Tomkinson Diary, 18, 22 and 25 October; 2 and 4 November 1915; 31 January; 13 March 1916.
[84] BL, Jackson MSS, Thursby to Jackson, 12 May 1916.

craft along the Adriatic coast to 'battle and repulse' potential enemy raids that might materialise quickly and unexpectedly. The British protested that he should not be preoccupied with keeping a significant part of his forces in the Adriatic for that purpose, because Austro-Hungarian raids could do little damage.[85] Revel remained adamant that 'There are domestic political necessities ... which in Italy cannot be ignored', hinting at the need to keep the consensus over the war and avoid a social revolution.[86] Revel's allies were not impressed by his explanation. Captain Herbert W. Richmond, British liaison officer with the Italian fleet, grumbled that the Italians had surrendered their sea to the Austro-Hungarians 'in spite of [Austro-Hungarian] inferior naval force & without fighting an action!' He concluded bluntly: 'They [Italians] had better sell their Fleet & take up their organs & monkeys again, for, by Heaven, that seems more their profession than sea-fighting'.[87]

The volley of Allied criticism of the *Regia Marina* not only reinforced anti-Italian stereotypes that were widely shared in the Royal Navy; it also influenced post-war literature. Naval experts of the war like Paul Halpern and Lawrence Sondhaus have described Revel as a 'defensive-minded' strategist, who imposed an 'essentially defensive character' on Italian operations;[88] this hampered the overall Allied Mediterranean strategy, because 'from the start the Italians ... seemed willing to concede the Adriatic to the enemy'.[89] Hence, Austro-Hungarian control of the waves, which was to last to the end of the war.[90] Such vulgate is a myth. Revel's principle was that 'at sea defence is ensured only by offence'.[91] During the Libyan war, Revel had conducted some of the boldest actions of the *Regia Marina* in the Dodecanese,[92] and his proposal for a joint Allied Adriatic operation was distinctively offensive. This is confirmed by his general plan for operations issued to all Italian admirals at the beginning of hostilities:

Our primary objective must be the destruction of enemy naval forces. In consequence, any unit of the fleet, when finding itself in conditions of at least tactical parity, must engage in full, with little concern for the inevitable losses, in order to destroy the enemy, or at least put it out of action.[93]

---

[85] AUSM, b. 498, f. 18, Definition and allocation of the Japanese and United States Reserves and their maximum contribution in the Mediterranean.
[86] USM, *Marina italiana*, VI, p. 387.
[87] Quoted in Halpern, *Naval History*, pp. 150, 153.
[88] Halpern, *Naval War*, pp. 99, 272.   [89] Sondhaus, *Great War*, pp. 132–138.
[90] Ibid., p. 316; Halpern, *Naval War*, p. 439. See also Burgwyn, *The Legend*, p. 177.
[91] V. Grienti, L. Merlini: *Navi al fronte. La Marina Militare italiana e la Grande Guerra* (Parma: Mattioli, 2015), p. 59.
[92] E. Ferrante, *Il grande ammiraglio Paolo Thaon di Revel* (Rome: USM, 2018).
[93] AUSM, b. 354/4, Viale, 'Piano generale delle operazioni in Adriatico', 18 April 1915.

Like Cadorna, however, Revel was shocked by the realities of the war. His allies' lack of collaboration and submarine warfare hindered his schemes. When the Italians lost the armed cruiser *Garibaldi* and the large cruiser *Amalfi* in the early stages of the war to enemy torpedoes, Revel realised that he needed to fight a very different kind of war. Not surprisingly, he came to the same conclusion as the French in 1914: capital ships were of little value in the Adriatic, and they must be preserved until a major naval engagement against enemy capital ships could be fought.[94] This, however, does not mean that he intended to remain passive in the meantime. He encouraged his subordinates to attract the enemy into battle with provocatory sorties by Italian and, when available, Anglo-French light craft, bombarding the enemy bases despite all geographical odds, and chasing the Austro-Hungarians any time they emerged.[95] By the end of the war, Italian actions numbered ninety-six dwarfing the *k.u.k. Kriegsmarine*'s fifty-one sorties.[96]

Italy's allies never appreciated this. One possible reason was that the *Regia Marina* operated largely alone, the other Allies contributing to just nineteen actions throughout the war.[97] In part, inter-Allied misinterpretation was exacerbated by Revel's cold and stormy character, which did not help to establish mutual empathy. Many senior Allied naval officers mentioned his inflexible attitude as an impediment to Allied collaboration. Admiral Howard Kelly, commander of the British cruisers at Brindisi, found Revel 'a real tough nut' and for Admiral William Sims, commander of US forces in European waters from mid-1917 '[Revel] delivered his opinions with an insistence which indicated that he entertained little doubt about their soundness [and] was not particularly patient if they were called into question'.[98] Once more, these criticisms must be qualified. Quite possibly, as an experienced admiral with 38 years of service, Revel disliked being taught the job by uneasy allies. Yet the early developments of the war suggest that Revel's character was not the main problem. As the summer faded, and the war at sea, like that on land, shrank into a stalemate, it was more inter-Allied prejudices, mutual competition, differing strategic views, together with antithetical evaluations of the strength of the *k.u.k. Kriegsmarine* and its potential, that made a coherent maritime strategy impossible for the Allies. But Italy was already being held mainly responsible.

---

[94] USM, *Marina Italiana*, III, pp. 215–220.
[95] N. Morabito, *La Marina italiana in guerra 1915–1918* (Milan: Marangoni, 1933), pp. 26–27.
[96] Marcuzzi, 'From the Adriatic to the Mediterranean. Italy in the Allied Naval Strategy (1915–1918)', *War in History*, XXVII, 3, 2018, p. 465.
[97] Ibid.   [98] Halpern, *Naval War*, pp. 84–85.

Figure 7.3 Portrait of Paolo Thaon di Revel, Italian Chief of Naval Staff for most of the war

7.3 The Financial Convention

The financial convention was a bilateral agreement between London and Rome, which tied Italy's war to Britain more than to the other countries of the Entente. To appreciate its importance, one needs to understand Italy's distinctive approach to war economy.

In 1914, Italy's annual national income was 20 billion lire. The cost of the war quickly rose to about one billion lire per month. Unlike many of the other belligerents, Italian politicians did not delude themselves that they could pass the cost of the war on to the defeated. The dominant idea was that 'the longer the war, the less easy it would be to make the defeated pay [an] indemnity'.[99] Instead, Italian politicians hoped that the war would be financed by their allies. The use of external finance reflected a political awareness that standards of living could not be strained without breaking the fragile political and social support for the war.[100] The

[99] L. Einaudi, *La condotta economica e gli effetti sociali della guerra italiana* (Bari: Laterza, 1933), p. 30.
[100] B. Stringher, *Su le condizioni della circolazione e del mercato monetario durante e dopo la guerra* (Rome: Toniolo, 1920), p. 92.

conflict was thus financed in small measure (16 per cent) by increased taxation, a proportion comparable to France's 14 per cent and Germany's 13 per cent, though far below Britain's 30 per cent.[101] Not surprisingly, the lira weakened steadily throughout the war: by early 1918, it had lost over 40 per cent of its value relative to the pound. External weakness and political constraints on taxation meant that monetary expansion financed the war by another 16 per cent and took place in two stages: in the early months of the conflict, when opposition to the war had not yet been silenced by censorship, and after the Caporetto defeat in October 1917. Together with 'strained distribution channels and spreading shortages of labour and goods', this contributed 'to sharp bouts of inflation at politically delicate moments'.[102]

Francesco Galassi and Mark Harrison highlighted three main aspects of the Italian war economy: first, the management of domestic supply, and the creation of industrial giants such as FIAT, ILVA, Ansaldo and Breda; second, the issue of war finance, both public and private, the choice between monetisation, taxation and debt and the role of the Bank of Italy in directing public policy; third, the external balance, exchange, debt and imports. The challenge of Italy's external balance during the conflict was to put an economy lacking raw materials, and especially fossil fuels, in a condition to fight an extended industrial war. Furthermore, 25 per cent of all Italian imports until 1915 came from the Central Powers. Now Italy must multiply its imports from the western powers while simultaneously adapting to a war economy. This dual and brisk change extenuated Italy's difficulties: its domestic resources were being reallocated away from exports to military goods, the substantial emigrants' remittances and tourist revenues were shrinking, and the foreign private capital market was largely gone. Since depreciation failed to free significant resources for the war, Italy had to borrow from its allies, not knowing whether its post-war export prospects would earn the foreign exchange necessary to repay the debts.[103]

Financial matters were not dealt with in detail in the London Treaty. Article 14 stated rather vaguely that Britain would 'assist' Italy in raising a loan of 'no less than £50 million' on the London market 'at equitable terms'. Turning these fine words into reality proved difficult. Allied

---

[101] C. P. Kindleberger, *A Financial History of Western Europe* (London: Allen & Unwin, 1984), p. 292; Strachan, *First World War*, I, pp. 864–873.

[102] F. L. Galassi, M. Harrison, 'Italy at war, 1915–1918', in S. Broadberry, M. Harrison eds., *The Economics of World War I* (Cambridge: Cambridge University Press, 2005), p. 5.

[103] Ibid.; During the war Great Britain, India and Egypt provided from 25.9 to 28.3 per cent (the United States from 40.7 to 42.7 per cent): Einaudi, *Condotta economica*, pp. 64, 90.

finance ministers first met in February 1915, establishing a close liaison between their central banks and agreeing on a policy for joint foreign loans and credit for lesser allies.[104] The Anglo-Italian financial convention, signed in Nice on 5 June, followed this principle, but proved a double-edged sword, especially for Italy. The withdrawal of the £50 million British credit was to be made in instalments that could not exceed £2 million per week. The rest of the loan was secured by Italian annual treasury bonds.[105] The British however were worried by the weakness of the pound relative to the dollar, and refused to grant a real loan, conceding only an opening of credit. This restricted the possibility that Italy could independently resort to the British financial market. Sonnino, who was also reluctant to export much gold at the beginning of Italy's war, defined the British stance as 'mean'.[106] In the end, Italy agreed to deposit one sixth of the sum in gold with the Bank of England and secure the rest with a bond swap, pegging the lira at 28 to the pound (up 2.20 lire from the pre-war rate, but down 3 lire from the average 1915 exchange rate of 31.00 lire) and agreeing to do 'everything possible' to avoid encouraging gold flows from Britain.[107]

These early Anglo-Italian disagreements were made grimmer by the fact that the British loan soon proved insufficient to match Italian war needs. The Italian Treasury Minister, Carcano, was the object of strong criticism in the Italian parliament throughout the summer, for not asking the British for a bigger loan. Carcano, however, thought it shameful that the last of Italy's wars of independence was heavily financed by others.[108] The financial convention, therefore, proved as inadequate as the other two in establishing the successful Allied cooperation envisaged by the London Treaty. It was just three months into Italy's war, and the conditions of its participation needed to be significantly revised.

---

[104] W. Philpott, *Attrition. Fighting the First World War* (London: Little Brown, 2014), p. 189.
[105] DDI, 5, III, doc. 609, Sonnino to Imperiali, 8 May 1915.
[106] Sonnino, *Diario*, II, p. 172.   [107] Galassi and Harrison, 'Italy at war', pp. 17–21.
[108] Einaudi, *Condotta economica*, p. 33.

8 Dealing with Recalcitrant Allies
Shaping Italy's War

8.1 'La nostra guerra'

Disenchantment about Italy's intervention came at a time when London was facing grave problems. The first was the shortage of munitions, which had begun in the winter of 1914–1915 and lasted for much of 1915. It spurred the British Government to create a separate ministry entrusted to Lloyd George, charged with the task of industrial mobilisation. A second problem was the manpower shortage. Voluntary recruiting declined in the second half of 1915: 135,263 men enlisted in May, but only 95,413 in July, and by early January 1916, the army was 250,000 men below establishment.[1] In mid-summer 1915, the British Government confronted the possibility of introducing conscription for the first time. The debate became heated among three camps: those who preached conscription, such as George Curzon, Churchill and Lloyd George; those who were opposed in principle, but tended to see it as inevitable – among them Grey, Arthur Balfour, First Lord of the Admiralty, and Henry Lansdowne, Minister without portfolio; and those, like Reginald McKenna, Chancellor of the Exchequer, and Asquith, who opposed conscription for economic and ethical reasons.[2] The debate was put on ice when Minister of Education Arthur Henderson expressed his concern that British workers, many of whom were denied the right to vote, would strongly resist fighting for a government they had no part in electing. For the moment, the British had little choice but to ask for greater Allied efforts.[3]

Italy, in particular, was falling below expectations. Its failure to join the other Allies in the war on Turkey and Germany created a common opinion in Britain, France and Russia that Italy wanted its own empire but was not ready to fight for it, in violation of the London

[1] Strachan, 'Battle of the Somme', p. 86.
[2] DDI, 5, IV, doc. 776, Imperiali to Sonnino, 21 September 1915; Imperiali, *Diario*, p.189.
[3] French, *British Strategy*, p. 131.

Treaty.[4] Historians too have considered Salandra's delaying tactics as 'flimsy excuses ... not to declare war'.[5] In reality, Salandra was ready to honour his undertakings – though with little enthusiasm. His problem was that most of his ministers disapproved of declaring war on Constantinople and Berlin. Already on 12 June, Salandra had brought the question of an Italian declaration of war on the Ottoman Empire to the Cabinet as a preliminary step on expanding Italy's war.[6] Sonnino had supported him, and so had Carcano and Martini. The main promoter of a 'small war' aligned himself with the standard-bearer of Italian imperialism in part to honour his promise to Rodd that he would sponsor the Entente's war *tout court*; in part because he understood that Italy could hardly benefit from a potential partition of Anatolia under article 9 of the London Treaty, if Rome did not fight Constantinople. But five ministers were either opposed or 'not entirely favourable'.[7] They feared the financial burden of a wider war, and considered it premature to escalate a conflict for which Italy was ill prepared:[8] the Italian people, they said, could tolerate a defensive campaign, in which Italians may even perform 'miracles', but they would not support a war of aggression.[9] Of course, a purely defensive war was not possible, but the Government must keep promoting the conflict as a war of liberation, not of conquest.[10] This was the closest it could get to the ideal of 'defensive war', which was promoted by the other belligerents in order to cement their public opinions. Moreover, scepticism about the Dardanelles expedition was high at the Italian court. The King's military adjutant, Colonel Francesco Avogadro, believed that 'the Dardanelles campaign is doomed to failure, because it has been poorly prepared'.[11] British 'obsession' with 'the ever more apparent difficulties in the Dardanelles' did not help to involve the Italians.[12] Throughout July, Sonnino played dilatory tactics, much to Grey's frustration.[13] Sonnino passed the buck onto the *Comando Supremo* who 'excludes absolutely the possibility of extracting men, weapons and resources' from the main front 'for any operation in the Dardanelles' – from

---

[4] R. Poincaré, *Au Service de la France. Neuf années de souvenirs*, 10 vols. (Paris: Plon, 1926–1933), VI, p. 224.

[5] Burgwyn, *The Legend*, p. 38; F. Ponteil, *La Méditerranée et les Puissances* (Paris: Payot, 1964), pp. 118–125.

[6] TNA, FO371/2376/72729, Rodd to Grey, 14 June 1915.   [7] Martini, *Diario*, p. 445.

[8] Riccardi, *Alleati*, p. 56.   [9] Martini, *Diario*, p. 328.   [10] Riccardi, *Alleati*, p. 35.

[11] F. degli Azzoni Avogadro, *L'amico del Re. Il diario di guerra inedito dell'aiutante di campo di Vittorio Emanuele III* (Udine: Gaspari, 2009), p. 103.

[12] DDI, 5, IV, doc. 86, Imperiali to Sonnino, 3 June 1915.

[13] TNA, FO371/2376/74983, Rodd to Grey, 9 June 1915.

which Italy had been barred by Russia during the Treaty of London negotiations, after all.[14] Privately, however, he confessed that his main concerns were domestic: 'Any talk ... of such an operation ... would rightly alarm our public opinion',[15] which was already preoccupied with 'the dangers mounting around us due to the Russian retreat, to Serb hesitation, and to the overall situation which has badly worsened since we signed the London Treaty'.[16]

The question of Rome's declaration of war on Berlin was even more complicated. It provides a further example of the huge impact of domestic problems on military strategy. The Italo-German partnership had been much stronger than the Italo-Austrian. Germany maintained an influence over the Italian business sector, the press and intellectuals.[17] Moreover, Salandra's ministers believed that Russian failure to honour the Allied military convention relieved Italy of the duty to commit itself to further military endeavours. Finally, Cadorna, who had a reverential fear of the German army, warned the Government that the Italo-Swiss frontier was 'totally undefended' and that a potential German invasion through Switzerland would be fatal.[18] In conclusion, Italy was not ready to fight a total war. Confronted with strong opposition from his ministers, Salandra feared a split in the Government and resolved that 'at least until the general conditions of the war changed' he would go no further than to break diplomatic relations with Berlin and Constantinople unless, of course, either of them attacked first. This never happened, and Italy found itself in an uncomfortable political and diplomatic limbo. To aggravate matters, Salandra did not explain the real reasons behind his policy to either his diplomats or his allies. He wished to avoid being perceived as a weak Prime Minister, so he limited himself to instructing Imperiali to reassure the British that the obligations of the London Pact would be honoured as soon as possible.[19] Rodd instead, grasped from Martini, the political fragmentation within the Cabinet, but he was not informed of the crucial problem of Italy's poor military preparedness.[20] Imperiali and Rodd, who had spared no effort to promote Italy's intervention on the side of the Entente, now felt rather embarrassed by the disappointing attitude of the Italian Government. With scarce information about Salandra's intents, they could do little to avoid a bitter inter-Allied confrontation. As

---

[14] DDI, 5, IV, doc. 342, Salandra to Imperiali, 5 July 1915.   [15] Imperiali, *Diario*, p. 199.
[16] DDI, 5, IV, doc. 358, *cit.*; Sonnino said quite the same to Barrère: Sonnino, *Diario*, II, pp. 172–173.
[17] Isnenghi, Rochat, *Grande Guerra*, pp. 82–83.
[18] Cadorna, *Altre pagine sulla Grande Guerra* (Milan: Mondadori, 1925), p. 44.
[19] DDI, 5, IV, doc. 342, Salandra to Imperiali, 5 July 1915.
[20] Rodd papers, Rodd to Grey, 2 September 1915.

a result, Britain, France and Russia began to bring greater pressure on Italy to embrace the Entente's war.[21]

France and Russia wanted to adopt a hard line. They believed that Rome's ambiguous stance denoted a secret Italo-German agreement of non-belligerency,[22] and threatened to make the London Treaty public so as to hold the Italian Government to its word.[23] London believed that revealing the treaty would badly affect the Allies' relations with Belgrade, so it opted for a softer approach. Grey took upon himself the task of pushing Italy with patience and determination, to commit itself beyond its immediate military horizon.[24]

8.2   Exploiting British Financial Supremacy

The diplomatic deadlock was broken at the end of July, thanks to a Russian request made to Italy one month earlier: Petrograd needed a quick despatch of 300,000 Italian Wetterli rifles to speed up its military reorganisation after the defeats suffered in the spring.[25] Sonnino had replied that Italy could not despatch weapons overseas, but the Foreign Office realised that the Russian appeal gave Britain the opportunity to propose an exchange to Sonnino: if Italy agreed to hand over the rifles to Russia and follow the Entente's line regarding Turkey and Germany, it could contract a new loan with the British Treasury on advantageous terms. Sonnino could not guarantee the Russians would get the arms – first he had to overcome the opposition of the War Minister – but he welcomed the opportunity of a financial arrangement additional to that of Nice to cope with the steady increase in spending; Sonnino thought it was necessary to raise $200 million as soon as possible.[26] Rodd was happy to relay the request to Grey, but on a condition that Italy reciprocated with a greater military effort. This forced Sonnino and Salandra to press hard their colleagues in the Cabinet to declare war at least on Turkey.[27] As the balance in the Government swung progressively in his favour, Salandra gave the green-light for a massive press campaign to prepare Italian public opinion for the break with the Ottomans.[28] Finally, on 21 August, Rome declared war on Constantinople.

Now that the first of the British requests had been fulfilled, Sonnino telegraphed Imperiali the text of Italy's loan request.[29] The first half of the

[21] Riccardi, *Alleati*, pp. 83 ff.
[22] ADMAEF, Guerre 1914–1918, Italie, vol. 563/2, Paléologue to Delcassé, 11 July 1915.
[23] Ibid., vol. 563/61 Cambon to Delcassé, 25 May 1915.   [24] Riccardi, *Alleati*, pp. 84 ff.
[25] Sonnino, *Diario*, II, pp. 168–169.
[26] DDI, 5, IV, doc. 781, Sonnino to Imperiali, 22 September 1915.
[27] Martini, *Diario*, pp. 490–491.
[28] DDI, 5, IV, doc. 577, Imperiali to Sonnino, 12 August 1915.
[29] Ibid., doc. 788, Sonnino to Imperiali, 23 September 1915.

loan was to be quickly negotiated in the United States as part of the credit that the other Allies were also contracting. The rest was to be obtained by the opening of a credit with the Bank of England. The latter operation was to be secured by the transfer of Italian Treasury bonds maturing after one year but renewable. Sonnino also requested the elimination of the clause in the Nice agreement concerning the need to back the loan with gold, or at least its reduction to the equivalent of one-tenth of the value of the loan.[30] Imperiali presented the proposal to Grey at the end of September. Grey forwarded it to McKenna,[31] but informed Imperiali that the supply of rifles to the Russians was a precondition for any negotiation on financial issues.[32] If Italy refused, Britain would reduce its naval units in Taranto.[33]

British blackmail proved successful.[34] However, when all seemed settled, a problem arose regarding the timing of the money transfer – McKenna proposed the end of 1916 while Imperiali requested that it be completed in no more than nine months.[35] Twice in October McKenna stalled and laid down new terms or one more condition: the Italian Government had to inform Britain what it wanted to purchase from each country and then Britain would supply the product where it could. This would have badly limited Italy's purchases from markets other than the British; in particular, France was to be excluded – an example of Britain's policy to use its financial relations with a minor partner to strengthen its economy at the expense of its strongest ally, who was a potential future competitor.[36] Imperiali held this clause an unacceptable restriction of his Government's freedom of action.[37] McKenna replied that he was trying to do everything possible to satisfy Italy but that he could not harm British interests.[38]

On 3 November, the British Treasury proposed a new arrangement: Britain would provide £125 million, of which £52 million would be available for purchases on markets outside Britain, provided that London could raise the US funds adequate to meet its promises to all Allied Governments.[39] The director of the Bank of Italy, Bonaldo Stringher, was increasingly disillusioned. He proposed to raise the figure

---

[30] TNA, FO371/2374/135852, Rodd to Grey, 1 October 1915.
[31] DDI, 5, IV, doc. 781, Imperiali to Sonnino, 28 September 1915.
[32] Ibid., doc. 890, Imperiali to Salandra, 10 October 1915.
[33] Ibid., doc. 894, Imperiali to Sonnino, 11 October 1915.
[34] Imperiali, *Diario*, p. 208; DDI, 5, IV, doc. 925, Sonnino to Imperiali, 18 October 1915.
[35] Ibid., docs. 937 and 942, Imperiali to Sonnino, 19 and 20 October 1915.
[36] ASMAE, t.gab. 2188/519 and 2259/531, Imperiali to Sonnino, 25 and 30 October 1915.
[37] DDI, 5, V, doc. 40, Imperiali to Sonnino, 1 November 1915.
[38] Riccardi, *Alleati*, p. 88.
[39] DDI, 5, V, doc. 55, Imperiali to Sonnino, 3 November 1915.

for Italian purchases on foreign markets to £74 million, while Sonnino specified that the exclusion of the French market was 'completely inappropriate'.[40] Sensing an imminent Anglo-Italian clash, Imperiali tried to bridge the differences emphasising the increasing financial glitches Britain was facing and reassuring Sonnino that 'here the intention to support us is really genuine'.[41] In Rome, Rodd echoed Imperiali stating that Britain's control on Italian purchases 'has no object except to ensure that we shall not compete against each other as buyers in the same market'.[42] On 5 November, Italy agreed to 'expand as much as possible' its purchases in Britain.[43] However, on 6 November, McKenna raised the stakes once again with one more clause for Stringher: the right for Britain to suspend the transfer of funds in case of a financial crisis.[44] Moreover, he rejected the Italian request to raise to £80 million the credits to be spent outside the British market, granting no more than £60 million (later increased to £65 million). When Imperiali protested, Grey 'pointed to our [Italian] situation vis à vis Germany with a tactful, delicate allusion to the financial operation'.[45] Britain was raising its requests yet further, demanding an Italian declaration of war on Germany. The Italian Government refused to link the financial operation to its attitude towards Germany, but it did accept all other British terms. The agreement was signed on 19 November. Imperiali and Stringher did not conceal their discontent.[46] Another reason for Italian complaints – made repeatedly by Carcano – was that London had not signed any agreements with Rome like those made with Paris to assist bilateral exchanges. London replied that 'similar arrangements' had 'only been possible because France was able to send a substantial amount of gold in proportion to the credits set up'. To ease the situation, the monthly sum that Britain made available to the Italian Government for exchange purposes was trebled from £1 million to £3 million per month.[47] The new funding would be granted according to 'Italian requirements', based on the programmes of the Commissariat of Supplies and the Ministry of Weapons and Ammunition, whose representatives in Rome formed the General Committee of Procurement chaired by Vincenzo Giuffrida.[48]

[40] ASMAE, t.gab. 1396, Sonnino to Imperiali, 3 November 1915.
[41] Ibid., t.gab. 2370/550, Imperiali to Sonnino, 5 November 1915.
[42] Rodd papers, McKenna to Rodd, 4 May 1916.
[43] ASMAE, t.gab. 2359/547, Imperiali to Sonnino, 5 November 1915.
[44] DDI, 5, V, doc. 64, Imperiali to Sonnino, 6 November 1915.
[45] Imperiali, *Diario*, p. 217.
[46] DDI, 5, V, doc. 100, Imperiali to Sonnino, 14 November 1915.
[47] Rodd papers, Bonar Law to Rodd, 23 March 1917.
[48] S. Crespi, *Alla difesa d'Italia in guerra e a Versailles* (Milan: Mondadori, 1937), p. 127.

The British were satisfied with the result.[49] They had persuaded the Italians to accept almost all of their clauses. In addition, the financial issue had proved decisive in getting Italy to declare war on Turkey and to increase Rome's commitment within the Entente's supply chain. For its part, Italy had succeeded in getting a larger loan than originally planned, but on conditions that were already limiting its financial autonomy. Delays, and less than full cooperation on the part of Britain's hard-pressed war industries in delivering the Italian contracts, caused further grumbling in Rome throughout the early months of 1916. Equally resented was the condition imposed by Britain that Italian purchases abroad be handled exclusively through Allied supply organisations. London would not yield because it wished to avoid further pressures on the pound. As the war went on these concerns only grew, so that London increasingly insisted that Italian purchases involving US raw materials or component parts had to be paid for in dollars. In 1915, however, Italy still retained some room for manoeuvre because the extent of its external weakness had not yet become fully apparent.[50]

8.3   The Balkan Swamp

Italy's declaration of war on Constantinople catapulted Rome onto the stage of the Balkan theatre. In theory, it was an Entente success, for it marked an Italian involvement beyond the Italian front. As it turned out, however, it proved yet another disappointing affair, at least initially, for it did not produce an immediate military commitment, and it muddled further the complex diplomatic confrontation in the region. Confident of its capacity to reconcile the distinct interests of its turbulent allies, London once more acted as the mediating power in the Alliance, with the aim of producing a common Entente policy to acquire as many Balkan states as possible as allies. This time, however, London's task was exacerbated by the need to reconcile not just the interests of the Entente powers but also those of the regional powers.

Grey's approach to war diplomacy did not make his job any easier. His assumption was that war diplomacy was completely dependent on military factors, and thus the diplomats were in no position to question the judgements and priorities of the generals.[51] This idea was shared by Asquith and Nicolson, with the result that both the Prime Minister and the Foreign Office deferred to Kitchener and to the Chiefs of Staff even on

---

[49] TNA, FO371/2371/175822, Note of the Foreign Office on Anglo-Italian Financial Agreement, 22 November 1915.
[50] Galassi, Harrison, 'Italy at War', p. 20.
[51] TNA, CAB37/160/20, Memo by Grey, 27 November 1916.

those occasions when other politicians had put forward wiser proposals. Asquith and Grey failed to appreciate the integral connection between strategy and diplomacy and how one can assist the other, if properly coordinated. Grey, in fact, seemed to welcome the gap between diplomatic and strategic planning, for it gave him an illusion of freedom.[52]

This was epitomised by the British approach to the Balkan question. Grey's policy in the region at the outbreak of the war was 'to promote a confederation of the Balkan States', resurrecting the Balkan League that had defeated Turkey in 1913, and which this time could form a neutral bloc. Balkan traditional rivalries, however, made a confederation chimerical. Serb-Bulgarian enmity over Macedonia was endemic, going back to the late nineteenth century, and had been made worse by the Serb annexation of Bulgarian Macedonia at the end of the Second Balkan War (1913). That conflict had also added Greece and Romania to the list of Bulgaria's inveterate enemies. Turkey's entry into the war prompted Grey to renounce the idea of Balkan neutrality and press the Balkan states to join the Entente. Lloyd George and Churchill advocated an expedition to Salonika as an Allied base to attack Constantinople to give effective support to Grey's design, but Kitchener opposed the proposal arguing that the Entente's priority was the western front. Grey hesitated, in the end aligning himself with the War Secretary. The Salonika project was replaced with the Dardanelles operation, more complex and riskier, which resulted in a deadly boomerang for the Allies. The Gallipoli stalemate increased Allied need for help to unlock the situation, but it also made it more difficult for the Entente to get that help. Not until the Dardanelles proved an ultimate disaster in autumn 1915, did the British reconsider the Salonika operation, but by then Germany had the upper hand in the diplomatic battle in the region. Determined that he should prevent the Balkan states joining the Allies, Eric von Falkenhayn, German Chief of Staff, unleashed an offensive in the east, first breaking the Russians at Gorlice in May, and then turning on Serbia in October: a concentration of power that effectively supported German diplomacy in the Balkans.[53] Berlin enjoyed a major advantage over its enemies in leading relatively smoothly the overall strategy of the Central Powers, whereas the Allies were usually divided.[54]

In May 1915, Allied efforts focussed on Bulgaria, arguably the strongest of the Balkan powers. The result of strenuous negotiations between Britain, France and Russia produced an extensive list of territorial gains

[52] Lowe, 'Italy and the Balkans, 1914–1915' in Hinsley ed., *British Foreign Policy*, pp. 517–519.

[53] Lowe, Dockrill, *Mirage of Power*, II, pp. 184 ff.

[54] Rodd, *Memories*, III, pp. 262–264.

for Sofia if it joined the Allies, including the return of Serbia's Macedonian acquisitions in exchange for compensations in Bosnia-Herzegovina and on the Adriatic coast. The Entente would put pressure on Athens to cede Kavala to Bulgaria in exchange for gains in Asia Minor and promised to endorse talks between Bulgaria and Romania on Dobruja, which had passed from Bulgaria to Romania at the end of the Second Balkan War. Finally, the Allies pledged financial aid to Bulgaria.[55] The main issue with this package was that the Entente offered territory, which was only partly within its power to dispose of. Only such territory as the four powers might win from Turkey could actually be offered in any exchange; the rest depended on the *placet* of neighbouring countries. The inclusion of Italy in the talks in the summer of 1915 added a fresh problem, since Rome, albeit in principle happy to welcome new allies, was the only Entente power that opposed the prospect of a stronger Serbia on the Adriatic coast.[56] With Italy objecting to Serbian compensations, all that the Allies were now free to offer to Bulgaria was the territory that had been left to Turkey in 1913. Unfortunately, this was not 'what Bulgaria most wanted' which was 'a port on the Aegean and the fulfilment of its "national aspirations" in Macedonia; and these concerned Greece and Serbia'. Vasil Rodoslavov, the Bulgarian Prime Minister, insisted that the Allies pressed those countries to make territorial sacrifices in his favour, and he refused to make a clear commitment to the Allied cause until he was satisfied.[57]

The issue of Serbian concessions to Bulgaria and Serbian Adriatic compensations evolved into a dispute between Rome and Belgrade, with the former blaming Serbia's 'unspeakable' refusal to coordinate military operations with Italy, whilst Serbia complained that it had been kept in the dark about Italy's claims in Dalmatia.[58] The other Allies inclined towards Belgrade, feeling that they had a special obligation towards the first victim of Austro-Hungarian attack. To ease the negotiations, London suggested disclosing the Italian Adriatic gains provided for under the London Treaty to Serbia, thereby setting up open and fair talks with Belgrade;[59] Sonnino opposed it. He held that such an initiative would not soften Serbia, rather it would encourage it to demand a round of negotiations regarding the Treaty itself. He also feared that 'revealing details of the London Agreements would only serve to create agitation in Italy, where tempers would flare against all the supporters of Italian Dalmatia'. In other words, he wanted to preserve Italian imperialist

[55] DDI, 5, IV, doc. 54, Cucchi Boasso to Sonnino, 30 May 1915.
[56] Riccardi, *Alleati*, p. 111.   [57] Grey, *Twenty-Five Years*, pp. 195–196.
[58] Imperiali, *Diario*, p. 171; DDI, 5, IV, doc. 155, Imperiali to Sonnino, 11 June 1915.
[59] Ibid., doc. 189, Sonnino to Imperiali, Tittoni, Carlotti and Squitti, 15 June 1915.

claims from potential objections of both Serbia and the Italian liberal-democrats.[60] Serbia reacted to Sonnino's veto by occupying Northern Albania, an area of primary Italian interest. This brought Italo-Serbian relations close to a breakdown. Sonnino was also disappointed by the timid complaints of the other Allies about the Serbian action.[61] Grey's indulgence was particularly irritating and encouraged a wider Anglo-Italian rift. On 1 August, Grey proposed to offer Serbia, in exchange for its Macedonian concessions to Bulgaria, 'the entire territory west and south of the Drava and Danube, stretching west as far as and including Agram, and south to the frontier with Dalmatia, with part of the Adriatic coast including Fiume, Spalato, Ragusa, Cattaro, S. Giovanni di Medua and the relative hinterland'.[62]

Sonnino was astonished. Martini was shocked. Not only did the British not condemn Belgrade's decision to detach troops from the Austro-Serbian front to conduct what the Italians termed 'a useless operation' in Albania, but the British now made offers to the Serbs that openly violated the Treaty of London. Grey justified his proposal as a necessary sacrifice for the common cause, but Sonnino protested that Serbian actions were illegitimate – unlike Italy's move into Albania, which he insisted on portraying as not imperialistic but defensive.[63] Of course, he failed to mention that the same might well hold true for Serbia – and Serb desire to seize part of the Albanian coast could also be rationalised on military grounds as an attempt to open a retreat route in the case of enemy encirclement. Sonnino's counter-proposal to Grey was as follows: instead of giving satisfaction to Bulgaria at the expense of Serbia, and to Serbia at the expense of Italy, it would be better to concede Russian territory in Bessarabia to the Balkan powers. If Russia wished to be the 'protector' of the Balkan states, it should demonstrate benevolence, granting what for Russia, given its size, would be 'minimal' concessions to its precious client-states.[64] Not surprisingly, this produced Russian complaints that its 'Western allies were saving themselves at her expense'.[65] Serbia too found Grey's proposal unsatisfactory: Belgrade was ready to bow to Bulgarian exigencies only if it was granted Croatia, the strategic district of Skopje in Macedonia and substantial financial aid, and it also required to be welcomed as a fifth partner of the Entente.[66] Grey's scheme

---

[60] Imperiali, *Diario*, p. 178.
[61] DDI, 5, IV, doc. 105, Sonnino to Imperiali, Tittoni and Carlotti, 6 June 1915, on Italian reaction; doc. 115, Imperiali to Sonnino, 7 June 1915, on British reaction.
[62] Ibid., doc. 510, Sonnino to Imperiali, Tittoni and Carlotti, 1 August 1915.
[63] C. Seton-Watson, *Storia d'Italia*, p. 524.
[64] Sonnino, *Carteggio*, p. 515, Salandra to Sonnino, 26 June 1915.
[65] Grey, *Twenty-Five Years*, p. 209.
[66] DDI, 5, IV, doc. 695, Squitti to Sonnino, 1 September 1915.

collapsed. He was frustrated with Italy and badly disappointed by Serbia, which, despite the massive support it had received from the Allies, including Grey's diplomatic openings at the expense of Rome, proved 'quite intractable'.[67]

Meanwhile, equally teasing negotiations were taking place regarding Greek concessions to Bulgaria in Thrace, which Athens stubbornly opposed. Sonnino's solution to this impasse was that the Entente should act with greater firmness and choose one partner who would guarantee the greatest support without attaching conditions to already signed agreements. Obviously, his preference was for Bulgaria rather than Serbia or Greece.[68] He insisted that chasing all the Balkan states would foster the idea that they were all indispensable, which, in turn, would only increase their claims. Salandra too thought that it was high time the Allies did as the Germans did, which was, not to 'negotiate' but to 'impose'.[69] Such ideas were shared by Rodd, who thought it logical that 'we could not satisfy everyone'. Sonnino, Rodd believed, 'adopted a practical and unsentimental line. ... He held that a huckstering policy of offering a little here and a little there was a mistake. You will never get to the end of certain appetites'.[70] France joined Sonnino's position: Delcassé suggested giving Macedonia and Thrace to Bulgaria and risk the consequences – what Crewe called 'Delcassé's manner of telling Greece and Serbia that they may go to the devil'.[71] This course gained the support of Lloyd George, Churchill and Lord Robert Cecil in London; Grey, Crewe and Asquith were opposed. Although their position seemed hopeless, they insisted that it was 'just conceivable that for once honesty may be the best policy'.[72] Apart from the moral aspect, there was a practical consideration – the danger of fatally irritating Serbia and Greece without being sure of getting Bulgaria. Imperiali, for his part, agreed with the latter group.[73] It may be imagined how busy the telegraph was throughout September as Grey kept trying to bring in Bulgaria without offending Serbia, Greece and Romania.[74]

The mammoth difficulty of coming to a common line domestically, having it approved by the Allied Governments, and then sticking to it vis à vis neutral powers – the inescapable dilemma of fighting a coalition war – proved insuperable for the Entente in the 1915 Balkan negotiations. In

---

[67] Grey, *Twenty-Five Years*, p. 196.
[68] See: P. Pastorelli, 'Le relazioni fra l'Italia e la Serbia dal luglio 1914 all'ottobre 1915', in Pastorelli ed., *Dalla prima alla seconda Guerra mondiale. Momenti e problemi della politica estera italiana (1914–1943)* (Milan: LED, 1996).
[69] DDI, 5, IV, doc. 525, Salandra to Imperiali, Tittoni and Carlotti, 5 August 1915.
[70] Rodd, *Memories*, III, p. 263.   [71] Lowe, Dockrill, *Mirage of Power*, II, p. 194.
[72] TNA, CAB37/130/29 Asquith to the King, 30 June 1915.
[73] DDI, V, IV, doc. 92, Imperiali to Sonnino, 4 June 1915; Imperiali, *Diario*, p. 167.
[74] Lowe, Dockrill, *Mirage of Power*, II, p. 205.

a desperate effort to preserve Bulgarian neutrality at least, the Allies and their Bulgarian sympathisers attempted to buy the country's grain harvest and create a food crisis. This affair was revealed to the Bulgarian Government, and the perpetrators were arrested. On 6 September, Sofia signed a secret convention pledging its services to the Central Powers.[75] In exchange, it was granted the whole of Macedonia, an ample range of other territories and a war loan of 200 million francs with an additional supplementary loan if the war lasted longer than four months.[76] As Grey put it, 'the bird offered by Germany was not only a bigger and brighter bird, but seemed to be coming nearer to the hand'. Although the final outcome seemed to Grey in retrospect almost inevitable,[77] the Entente's diplomatic setback had the effect of an earthquake in the Alliance. In France, it contributed to the collapse of the Viviani Cabinet and the *Union Sacrée*.[78] Victor Emmanuel III was disheartened.[79] Imperiali confessed: 'I have never in all these years seen such a massacre as that of the negotiations between Bulgaria and the Entente powers'.[80] Rodd, too, brooded that Grey had not adopted Sonnino's firmer line: 'Looking back on the discussions ... I cannot but think that had the Allies rejected all sentimental considerations the chance was at one time open to them of securing the cooperation of Bulgaria'.[81]

The scale of the *débâcle* became fully clear in October, when Austria-Hungary, Germany and Bulgaria invaded Serbia from three sides. In a race against time, the British and the French despatched two incomplete divisions to Salonika, establishing a beachhead of what would become the Macedonian front, aimed at preventing the collapse of Serbia. It proved insufficient, partly because the Italians refused to join in, partly because Greece put forward a fierce diplomatic opposition to the expedition. Italian refusal was, once again, largely justified by Sonnino on military grounds. In reality, Cadorna was not deaf to Serb appeals. Though rejecting the impossible Allied request for 150,000 Italian men, he was ready to divert 'a strong division, made of three infantry brigades, a couple of *Bersaglieri* battalions, and adequate artillery and logistic support', some 30,000 men in all. But Zupelli was concerned that, 'once involved in the gears of a Balkan war, we would get sucked in with no limits in time or commitment'.[82] Salandra, for his part, suspected that 'we will be forced

[75] Bulgaria's talks with the Entente however continued until 14 September.
[76] M. A. Yokell, *Sold to the highest bidder? An investigation of the diplomacy regarding Bulgaria's entry into World War I*, M.A. thesis (Richmond: University Press, 2010), pp. 102–103.
[77] Grey, *Twenty-Five Years*, pp. 198, 225.   [78] Poincaré, *Au Service*, VII, p. 197.
[79] Avogadro, *L'amico del Re*, p. 97.   [80] Imperiali, *Diario*, p. 183.
[81] Rodd, *Memories*, III, p. 268.
[82] DDI, 5, IV, doc. 966, Zupelli to Cadorna, 25 September 1915; doc. 967, Cadorna to Zupelli, 26 September 1915.

to do something in Albania, in which case there can be no Salonika'.[83] Sonnino concluded that it was through 'its maximum effort' on 'the Austrian front' that the Italian army would 'cooperate to alleviate pressure ... on Serbia'.[84] Cadorna's Third Isonzo offensive (18 October–4 November), however, failed to divert significant Austro-Hungarian forces.[85]

The final impediment to the Salonika operation came from Athens, which, impressed by the Entente's Bulgarian and Dardanelles blunders, refused to support what seemed to be an Allied lost cause.[86] The forth-coming elections in Greece played a crucial role in this new Entente misfortune. Greece was torn by the conflict between King Constantine I and his former Prime Minister, Eleftheros Venizelos of the Liberal Party. The former was affiliated with the German royal family and favoured the Central Powers, whereas the latter considered Greece as a close ally of Britain and was determinedly anti-Turkish. Although the electoral body supported Venizelos, Constantine forced Venizelos to resign on 21 February 1915 and replaced him with the conservative leader Dimitrios Gounaris. In a few months, the crisis reached its peak (the 'National Schism') between the supporters of Venizelos, who created their own Government in Salonika, and the official Government of Athens. To prevent a civil war, the King called for general elections in December, which, however, Venizelos boycotted. The Allies monitored the Greek situation in apprehension, and were, as usual, divided over the affair: London and Paris favoured Venizelos' return to power, harbouring the hope that he would intervene in the war on their side. Rome feared Venizelos' ambitions in Epirus and Asia Minor, which conflicted with Italian interests, and hoped that Constantine would get rid of him once and for all.[87] In such a context, Grey concluded: 'We cannot send more troops to Salonika ... without being assured of the cooperation of Greece'.[88]

This gloomy scenario also jeopardised the third Balkan negotiation of the Entente, that with Romania. Bucharest was bound to the Central Powers by a secret treaty of 1883, but when war broke out Romanian Prime Minister Ion Brătianu proclaimed his neutrality, claiming, like Italy, that Austria-Hungary was the attacker and not the attacked.

---

[83] Ibid., V, doc. 48, Salandra to Sonnino, 2 November 1915.
[84] Ibid., doc. 52, Sonnino to Imperiali, Tittoni and Carlotti, 3 November 1915.
[85] Gooch, *Italian Army*, pp. 115–118.
[86] DDI, 5, IV, doc. 718, Sonnino to Imperiali, Tittoni, Carlotti and Cucchi Boasso, 7 September 1915.
[87] Ibid., doc. 131, Imperiali to Sonnino, 9 June 1915.
[88] Grey, *Twenty-Five Years*, p. 220, Grey to Bertie, 6 October 1915.

Throughout 1915, Romania was courted by the Allies, but talks were hampered by the same territorial issues that had led to the Bulgarian fiasco – Romania asking for compensations in Serbian territory and Serbia rejecting the request. Now with Russia in retreat, Serbia almost prostrate, Greece deeply divided, and the Allies paralysed by their chronic divergences, it had become dangerous for Romania to depart from neutrality.[89] Consequently, Serbia did not receive substantial support from either the Allies or Balkan countries. Between 10 November and 4 December, the Serbs made a last and desperate attempt to join the two Allied divisions that had made a limited advance from the south, but were unable to gather enough forces due to the pressure from the north and east. They failed to break through Bulgarian lines and turned south and west in full retreat through Montenegro and Albania. The Allies organised an emergency naval evacuation to save what remained of the Serbian army. Ironically, the evacuation was largely carried out by the Italian navy, although Italo-Serb rivalries had contributed significantly to the crisis. It was a notable success for the *Regia Marina*, now commanded by Luigi di Savoia, Duke of the Abruzzi – Revel had resigned in October because of chronic differences with the Navy ministers over the power and functions of the chief of the naval staff.[90] A glamorous cousin of the King, Abruzzi was younger and more aggressive than Revel; he managed to plan a logistically impeccable rescue operation with very short notice, concentrating the bulk of the Italian fleet in enemy waters and coordinating successfully with his allies despite intense aerial attack from the enemy pursuing the fugitives.[91] In four months, the *Regia Marina* made 584 journeys back and forth, the *Marine Nationale* made 168, and the Royal Navy 77.[92] In all, some 200,000 Serbs, mostly soldiers and some refugees embarked on Allied transport ships that carried them to various Greek islands; later, they joined the Salonika front for the remainder of the war. The Serb authorities did not reciprocate Italian efforts, excluding Rome from the formal thanks they offered to the other Allies for their rescue.[93] The Italian contribution has remained badly underestimated to this day, and at least two experts of World War I neglected it altogether.[94] By

---

[89] Ibid., p. 208.

[90] Grienti, Merlini, *Navi al Fronte*, p. 33. Italian Ministers of Marine were as follows: Leone Vitale from the outbreak of war until 24 September 1915; Camillo Corsi from 30 September 1915 to 16 June 1917; Arturo Triangi from 16 June to 16 July 1917; and Alberto De Bono from 16 July 1917 to 23 June 1919.

[91] NMRN, Limpus MSS, Thursby to Limpus, 2 December 1915; Thursby to Limpus, 13 December 1915; Thursby to Limpus, 22 December 1915.

[92] Morabito, *Marina italiana*, pp. 108–110.   [93] F. Caccamo, 'Italy, the Adriatic', p. 136.

[94] Sondhaus, *Great War*, p. 167; Burgwyn, *The Legend*, p. 46.

10 February 1916, the Serbian campaign was over in bitterness and recrimination.

From May 1915 to the end of the year, the Entente had suffered one setback after another in the Balkans. The Dardanelles campaign had resulted in a disaster and led to Churchill's resignation; Greece and Romania remained anchored to their neutrality; Bulgaria had joined the Central Powers; Serbia was now occupied and, as a consequence, Germany opened the railway line from Berlin to Constantinople, managing to prop up its weaker partner, the Ottoman Empire.[95] British efforts to involve Italy in the global war of the alliance had so far cast a partial success. They had increased the Allied supply chain and had brought about Italy's declaration of war on the Ottoman Empire, but they had failed to produce a common Entente policy on the Balkan question.

8.4   Yearning for Land Coordination

Entente failures to attract new allies revived the inter-Allied dispute over Italo-German neutrality. Now more than ever Britain, France and Russia needed direct support in their struggle against the Teutonic colossus. Italian lack of commitment against Germany had not been compensated for by successes on the Isonzo, where Cadorna's Third and Fourth offensives (the latter ended on 5 December) made little progress. Trevelyan recorded that the fighting had been carried out 'under the most discouraging conditions of cholera and winter weather', and was 'a story of which any race could well be proud'.[96] Put into perspective, such efforts were arguably more important than they seemed in late 1915. Since the beginning of the war, Italian casualties had been 232,000, as opposed to 135,000 Austro-Hungarian. Though numerically fewer, Austro-Hungarian losses were higher proportionally: Italian casualties were 23 per cent of the forces engaged, compared with 40 per cent of the Austro-Hungarian forces.[97] Attrition was made grimmer for the Austro-Hungarians by a progressive Italian build-up. Throughout the winter, Italian infantry divisions grew from 35 to 42, artillery was doubled and the Italians learned to fight on mountainous terrain, building new roads, excavating underground caverns and shelters to reduce losses and installing cable cars (*teleferiche*) to bring in supplies and ammunition.[98]

But taking stock of the first semester of Italy's war, the other Allies saw little reason for enthusiasm. Rodd reported that the evaporation of Italian hopes for a quick victory had strengthened the already strong Giolittian

[95] Imperiali, *Diario*, pp. 235–236.   [96] Trevelyan, *Scenes*, p. 55.
[97] Gooch, *Italian Army*, p. 118.   [98] Trevelyan, *Scenes*, p. 63.

party and that many Italians were convinced that Germany would win the war.[99] British agents in Italy began to doubt that Rome would be loyal to the Alliance: 'As long as the Government can control the popular sentiment, Italy will stand by us, but if it gets out of control – for example, after a defeat – or if people get tired of the war, ... then the same thing will happen as after the battle of Adua in Abyssinia',[100] when Francesco Crispi's Government had collapsed and Italy had sued for peace. In Britain, disenchantment with the impact of Italy's intervention was coupled to increasing disappointment about the Italian role in Allied strategy. Italy was described as a 'recalcitrant ally'[101] focussed on its 'private war' with Austria-Hungary.[102] Such claims were reinforced by Sonnino's refusal to join the Salonika operation. Rodd entreated an Italian participation informing Sonnino that Britain would send 'substantial forces and artillery to Salonika as well as some heavy guns'. Russia and France 'will also reinforce Salonika and His Majesty's Government earnestly hope[s] Italy will similarly give the utmost assistance sending, if possible, two divisions'. Sonnino politely declined the request, claiming that Cadorna 'did not think it possible to detract forces from our front'.[103] In fact, Cadorna oscillated between scepticism and support for an Italian participation at Salonika (he calculated that it could divert Austro-Hungarian forces from the Isonzo),[104] and the General Staff was largely in favour of it.[105] Once again, it was the politicians, including Salandra, who opposed an expansion of Italy's war for domestic reasons.

In November and December the British press unleashed one of its periodic anti-Italian campaigns. Italy's *sacro egoismo* was presented as one of the main causes for the Balkan failures, and Italy was described as a half-ally. Italy's failure to participate in joint operations was emphasised, whereas the role of the Italian navy in the Serbian rescue was practically ignored.[106] The Italian press responded with a volley of 'endless recriminations against selfish Britain'. British and Italian mutual stereotypes dramatically resurfaced leading to a significant cooling in relations. More importantly, Imperiali began to harbour suspicions that

---

[99] J. Whittam, *The Politics of the Italian Army* (London: Croom Helm, 1977), pp. 195–196.

[100] TNA, CAB37/142/7, MacDonogh, Note respecting the attitude of Italy, 3 February 1916.

[101] Halpern, *The Naval War in the Mediterranean 1914–1918* (Annapolis: Naval Institute Press, 1987), p. 374.

[102] C. Seton-Watson, *Storia d'Italia*, p. 525.

[103] Sonnino, *Diario*, II, pp. 55–61, 253–254.

[104] DDI, 5, VI, docs. 73, 138 and 177, Cadorna to Sonnino, 5, 19 and 24 July 1915.

[105] Ibid., V, doc. 493, Salandra to Sonnino, 22 February 1916.

[106] L. Tosi, *La propaganda italiana all'estero nella Prima Guerra Mondiale* (Udine: Del Bianco, 1977), pp. 38–47.

something big was taking shape behind the scenes of Allied relations, on which he had no clear intelligence. Repeated 'mysterious' visits of Grey to Paris, as well as equally furtive meetings between Nicolson, Cambon and Alexander Benckendorff, Russian ambassador to Britain, in London seemed to suggest that Britain, France and Russia were discussing matters that they were not inclined to share with Italy. On 15 November, exploiting Rodd's presence in London on home leave, Imperiali met him for lunch and tested him. Rodd did not open up; he praised Sonnino, stating that Britain had 'all faith in him', but stressed once more that Asquith urged an Italian involvement in the war on Germany. Beneath the cordial tone of the meeting, lay an inexplicable silence over Anglo-Franco-Russian intentions. The two ambassadors nonetheless promised each other to press their respective Governments to placate the press and restore traditional Anglo-Italian understanding.[107] They enjoyed little success. Only in February 1916 did Imperiali notice some benevolence towards Italy in *The Times* (an article titled 'What Italy has achieved' gave a surprisingly positive account of Italian military operations) and the *Westminster Gazette* – '*Pour une fois*' exclaimed the ambassador.[108] These were likely the result of Rodd's warning to Grey that 'the more frequent anti-Italian complaints in the British press, the more difficult it was for Salandra to bring his ministers onto his side on the German matter',[109] but British openings were not reciprocated. When Imperiali pressed Rome to moderate the Italian press, he received a cold reply from Salandra. The British – 'insular merchants', in the Prime Minister's words – were postponing negotiations regarding the supply of vital goods to Italy as retaliation for the Italian failure to declare war on Germany, pursuing a 'mean mercantilism and [an] economic exploitation even of Allied nations'.[110] Predictably, it would not take long before the British press resumed its bombardment on the young ally.[111]

The French were blunter. The new Prime Minister, Aristide Briand, was determined to push Italy to 'engage fully in the war'.[112] Discussions on Italy's involvement were part of a broader debate on improving Allied coordination. Briand sought greater Allied integration in both the strategic and operational spheres. He proposed a permanent Allied body meeting periodically in Paris. This plan updated the Chantilly one. That conference had simply called for synchronised offensives, which had proved ineffective – the French had failed in Artois and the British at Loos; furthermore, Briand wished to include the diplomats in future

---

[107] Imperiali, *Diario*, pp. 144, 216–217; 218–219; 258.
[108] *The Westminster Gazette*, 'Italy and the Adriatic'; Imperiali, *Diario*, pp. 244–249.
[109] TNA, FO371/2685/45813, Rodd to Grey, 4 March 1916.
[110] DDI, 5, V, doc. 236, Salandra to Imperiali, 26 December 1915.
[111] Imperiali, *Diario*, pp. 256–264.   [112] Quoted in Riccardi, *Alleati*, p. 233.

meetings for a better coordination of war diplomacy and strategy.[113] At the end of November 1915 Briand tested the British and the Russians. Whilst the former accepted with apparent enthusiasm, the latter urged that whoever was not engaged against all the enemies of the Entente should be excluded from the talks[114] – an obvious reference to Italy. Briand replied that the best way to bring about an Italian declaration of war on Germany was to extend Rome's involvement in the Allied strategy.[115] On

Map 8.1 The Western Front 1914–1918

[113] French, *British Strategy*, p. 111.

[114] ADMAEF, Guerre 1914–1918, Dossier Général, vol. 988/117, note by Quai d'Orsay, 21 November 1915.

[115] Riccardi, *Alleati*, p. 234.

7 December, Sazonov gave his consent, at which point Briand shared his proposal with the Italian ambassador to Paris, Tittoni.[116] Sonnino's reply on 15 December was not encouraging. The Foreign Minister expressed 'the greatest reservation' on Briand's proposed body, which he saw as a 'useless stage setting'.[117] After all, Allied military representatives had just met again at Chantilly to plan for their offensives in the new year.[118] They had agreed on 'a concerted sequence of summer offences on all the European fronts' to deny the Central Powers the possibility of moving troops from one front to another. The French and British would attack together on the River Somme.[119] The main effort would fall on the French army, but the British would significantly expand their contribution thanks to the introduction of conscription from January 1916.[120] The British also expected to expand their artillery by 1,090 heavy guns so that the army could have a total of 9,881 guns of all calibres, of which 7,240 should be in the field by March 1916.[121]

In these circumstances, it was not clear how Briand's project overlapped with the Chantilly Conferences. Throughout January and February, Briand reiterated his suggestions for a novel Allied body, without however moving Sonnino. The latter was preoccupied that adhering to a French project might shift the balance of power in the Alliance away from London and towards Paris. Traditional Italo-French competition in the Mediterranean suggested against any initiative that might strengthen the position of Paris in the Entente. Furthermore, Sonnino disliked the idea of an Allied body charged with 'the unification of Allied diplomacy'. He had been disturbed by recent attempts on the part of his allies to revise the London Pact in order to meet shorter-term objectives in the war; he would not provide any roundtable where immediate wartime needs might compromise Italy's war aims.[122] Finally, he assumed that Briand's body would renew requests for Italian participation on the Macedonian front.[123] None of this was known abroad. Briand suspected that Sonnino mistrusted Tittoni, who, being based in Paris, would likely represent Italy in the meetings.[124] Sazonov would happily cut negotiations.[125] In theory, Grey's approach

[116] ASMAE, t.gab. 2808/500, Tittoni to Sonnino, 7 December 1915.
[117] Ibid., t. 1808, Sonnino to Tittoni, 15 December 1915.
[118] DDI, 5, IV, doc. 911, Sonnino to Salandra, 14 October 1915.
[119] Stevenson, *1917*, p. 5.
[120] D. R. Woodward, *Lloyd George and the Generals* (Newark: University of Delaware Press, 1983), pp. 76–77.
[121] Strachan, 'Battle of the Somme', p. 84.   [122] Riccardi, *Alleati*, pp. 238–241.
[123] DDI, 5, V, doc. 369, Sonnino to Tittoni, 25 January 1916.
[124] ADMAEF, Guerre 1914–1918, Dossier Général, vol. 988/136, Briand to Barrère, 14 January 1916.
[125] Ibid., vol. 988/134, Paléologue to Briand, 6 January 1916.

was precisely to subordinate Allied post-war ambitions to the needs 'of the common cause', as he had told Sonnino during the Bulgarian negotiations; in this sense, Sonnino was right to be suspicious. Yet the initial British eagerness for Briand's scheme proved less than expected when it came to give London's final approval. Grey confessed to Imperiali that he had given his assent 'in principle', but he saw no urgency to unify Allied diplomacy:[126] it threatened his freedom of manoeuvre, and Grey too was preoccupied that the Briand project would result in a de facto shift in the leadership of the Alliance to France.[127]

When Briand visited Asquith on 21 January, he elicited from the latter the consent to 'multiply exchanges of views' between Allied heads of state, 'coordinating diplomatic and military action'.[128] But shortly afterwards London presented its own project for coordination, which envisaged no novel body but a greater role for military attachés. Tellingly, the reference to Paris as the basis for future Allied meetings was omitted.[129] Further contrasts erupted with the French over the planning of the Anglo-French summer offensive. According to the Chantilly agreement the main thrust was to be preceded by preliminary attacks to wear down the enemy forces. But the French Chief of Staff, Joseph Joffre, and the Commander of the BEF, Sir Douglas Haig, could not agree on just where such operations should be launched – each part suspicious that the other was anxious to avoid the strain of the opening phase of the operation.[130] So, the Allies were not united, and the discrepancy between Italy's position and that of the other Entente members was less clear-cut than traditionally described. On one thing – Rome's failed declaration of war on Berlin – London, Paris and Petrograd were aligned (with London as a mediator); on how to improve cooperation the Allies tended to oscillate according to circumstances and to their own national interests.

With full Russian support and ambiguous British backing, Briand travelled to Rome to settle the matter with Sonnino and Salandra. He visited Rodd, who suggested to him that 'the right policy to adopt [with the Italians] was never forcing the note but at the same time using all our opportunities to keep our Italian Allies in line, while treating them with even exceptional consideration'.[131] On 10 February the Salandra-Briand

---

[126] DDI, 5, V, doc. 271, Imperiali to Sonnino, 4 January 1916.
[127] Riccardi, *Alleati*, p. 237.
[128] DDI, 5, V, doc. 352, Tittoni to Sonnino, 22 January 1916; TNA, FO971/2685/15037, FO to Rodd, 22 January 1916.
[129] ASMAE, t.gab.segr. 184/29, Imperiali to Sonnino, 22 January 1916. The Italians were equally unenthusiastic about the British proposal: t.gab. 211/92, Imperiali to Sonnino, 24 January 1916.
[130] French, *British Strategy*, pp. 181–182.
[131] TNA, FO371/2685/30699, Rodd to Grey, 12 February 1916.

meeting was interlocutory.[132] Sonnino was tougher. He did not object to more frequent Allied meetings, but restated his doubts about an additional 'useless apparatus'.[133] Briand obtained a plenary conference in Paris in March, preceded by a summit of Allied military leaders.[134] To him, it was a start.[135]

The Germans, however, frustrated Allied plans. On 21 February they unleashed a major offensive on the French town of Verdun, which lay in a salient formed during the German invasion of 1914. It resulted in one of the most horrific battles of the war, where infantry divisions were destroyed almost as fast as they could be fed into the line. By December, when the offensive was called off, the French had lost some 377,000 men, and the German 337,000.[136] Such a desperate struggle had immediate consequences: first, the French had to divert more and more divisions from the planned Somme offensive to the Verdun meat-grinder, eventually reducing the French contribution on the Somme to 13 divisions against 20 British divisions; thus, the supporting role of Kitchener's New Armies became the principal effort. The Somme, furthermore, was de facto reduced from an ambitious 'decisive battle' to a relief offensive aimed at attracting German reserves away from Verdun.[137] The French expected such an attack to begin as soon as possible, but the British were not ready.[138] A second consequence of Verdun was renewed French pressure on their allies for better coordination. Briand awaited the forthcoming conference in Paris anxiously, and raised his expectations of the meeting.[139] He was frustrated by repeated Italian delays.[140] Salandra gave instructions to General Carlo Porro, Italian representative to the preliminary military conference of 12 March, to avoid any undertaking that bound Italy to increase its military commitment.[141] Sonnino, for his part, was only anxious for the imminent meetings to avoid 'any discussion on the future peace and its terms',[142] so he opposed the participation of lesser allies, including Serbia, to prevent any talk on the Adriatic settlement. By the end of the month allied meetings had achieved

[132] DDI, 5, V, doc. 433, Salandra to Sonnino, 11 February 1916.
[133] Ibid., doc. 436, Sonnino to Tittoni, 11 February 1916.
[134] Ibid., doc. 448, Sonnino to Tittoni, 13 February 1916.
[135] ADMAEF, Guerre 1914–1918, Dossier Général, vol. 858/160, Confidential memorandum by Quai d'Orsay, 18 February 1916.
[136] Philpott, *Attrition*, p. 226.
[137] Philpott, *Bloody Victory: The Sacrifice on the Somme and the Making of the Twentieth Century* (London: Little Brown, 2009), pp. 81, 86.
[138] Strachan, 'Battle of the Somme', p. 85.
[139] DDI, 5, V, doc. 874, Tittoni to Sonnino, 24 May 1916.
[140] Ibid., doc. 565, Sonnino to Salandra, 8 March 1916.
[141] Ibid., doc. 493, Salandra to Sonnino, 22 February 1916.
[142] Ibid., doc. 585, Sonnino to Imperiali, Tittoni, Carlotti, Koch, Carignani and Galanti, 12 March 1916.

only 'minimal results'.[143] Of the four final resolutions of the plenary confer-ence, the first made an abstract appeal to greater Allied 'diplomatic and military' coordination; no plans were included in the records to implement those words. The second and third resolutions called for greater mutual support in the economic sphere, endorsing an Allied economic conference in Paris to be held '*prochainement*'. The last resolution recommended an enlargement of the Allied bureau for naval freights management based in London.[144]

The Briand experiment had resulted in much ado about nothing and was never repeated. Italy was somewhat responsible for this outcome, but the British had also been far from consistent in their policy. In the end, the Allies resorted to doing what they did best – namely mounting parallel offensives on their respective fronts as a form of indirect support to the French. Synchronisation was poor, however, and results disastrous. Cadorna's Fifth offensive on the Isonzo (6–15 March) made minimal progress and was cancelled after two weeks. The surprisingly low losses of some 2,000 men on each side[145] aroused Allied suspicions that the Italians had not fought seriously. Robertson was so irritated by Porro's delaying tactics that he would have happily 'kicked him in the stomach'.[146] Lloyd George deduced that the Italians were not of 'any great assistance' in the war, their only service being to hold down 'a large force of Austrians'.[147] Kitchener began to think that Italy could be more useful to the Allied cause if – given its 'overabundance of men' – it consented to send to France and Britain some thousand workers that could replace 'French and British factory labourers, thus reinforcing their respective armies'.[148] As for the Russian relief offensive, it was launched on 18 March at Naroch and led to 100,000 losses without diverting one single German division from France.[149]

Renewed Allied criticism put Imperiali in a crossfire, as Salandra blamed him for not being able to calm British nerves. Imperiali began to suspect that the Prime Minister was planning to replace him. The arrival in London of Edmondo Mayor, a new Italian delegate charged with the supplies negotiation, seemed to overshadow the ambassador. Imperiali's suspicion seemed to be confirmed when he was given an unexpected leave in Italy on 26 March. Back in Rome, he found 'indifference, dumb hostility against the war, unfair criticism and unfounded complaints'. In a series of tough

---

[143] Riccardi, *Alleati*, pp. 247–248.
[144] DDI, 5, V, doc. 650, Conclusions of the Paris inter-Allied Conference, 28 March 1916.
[145] Gooch, *Italian Army*, p. 148. [146] Quoted in French, *British Strategy*, p. 184.
[147] TNA, CAB42/14/12, War Committee minutes, 30 May 1916.
[148] DDI, 5, V, doc. 828, Imperiali to Sonnino, 17 May 1916.
[149] Riccardi, *Alleati*, pp. 215–218.

but frank meetings with Salandra and Sonnino, he was confirmed at his post. Salandra, Imperiali noted, looked 'depressed and tired', like 'a person frightened by the burden of the responsibility he has shouldered, almost regretting it'. The Prime Minister lamented that Britain 'does not sufficiently appreciate our military action'. Imperiali once more urged him to consider a declaration of war on Germany. 'Slowly, slowly, we'll get there', Salandra replied. 'We have given our word', insisted Imperiali. 'Yes, yes, you are right. Try to persuade them to show patience'. The ambassador shook his head: 'Fine, but it won't be easy'. Salandra's conclusion was that something had to be done quickly to improve Italy's reputation abroad, or Rome would be completely isolated within the Entente.[150]

8.5   The Limitations of Italian Overseas Propaganda

Salandra's apprehension about the feeble empathy between Italy and its allies reflected a long debate within the Italian Government about the best policy to promote the Italian cause in Allied countries. The Italian failure in this context was the result of two distinct issues which overlapped: the first was inefficient communication and the second was the lack of a strategic vision of overseas propaganda.

In the diplomatic field, as in the military, the former problem originated with an obsession among the leading Italian figures with secrecy and centralisation of power. Sonnino limited as much as possible information regarding Italy's war aims so as to avoid any spread of the content of the London Treaty, which he believed would hinder his diplomatic designs; he was equally unhappy with the idea of sharing with his allies the development of Italy's war, above all its military difficulties; finally, Sonnino insisted upon supervising every Italian communication to Allied and neutral countries, discouraging any personal initiative on the part of Italian diplomats. This obviously tended to paralyse Italian diplomacy. When Italian representatives abroad were asked about Italy's position on matters of Allied interest, it was not unusual that they simply would not know what to say. For example, no clear justification was given for Rome delaying its declarations of war on Turkey and Germany. Italian representatives made veiled complaints about their 'absolute ignorance on the whole matter',[151] coupled with frequent appeals to Sonnino for information, which were largely ignored.[152]

[150] Imperiali, *Diario*, pp. 228, 240, 256–258.
[151] DDI, 5, V, doc. 785, De Bosdari to Sonnino, 8 May 1916.
[152] Justus, alias Giulio Casalini, *V. Macchi di Cellere all'ambasciata di Washington. Memorie e testimonianze* (Florence: Bempoard, 1920), p. 42; DDI, 5, IV, docs. 157, 226, 315, and 432, Bonin Longare to Sonnino, 10, 11, 30 June, and 15 July 1915; docs. 17, 413, 617,

This problem was aggravated in dealing with foreign public opinions. In order to improve its reputation abroad, Italy needed to create a narrative of its war including its sacrifices and its achievements, for the wider public. Only through a coherent propaganda strategy carried out through a variety of channels, could Italy generate a closer empathy with its allies and dispel long-lasting anti-Italian stereotypes. Unfortunately, many Italian states-men and diplomats failed to appreciate how important propaganda was in a modern conflict.[153] Italian politicians were convinced that politics should be carried out only in the offices of power by a handful of able persons and tended, rather naïvely, to dismiss propaganda as a 'useless' and 'unfair' tool. Italian representatives abroad were not in the habit of shifting from the traditional patterns of diplomatic behaviour: they dealt with sovereigns, prime ministers, foreign ministers, their peers, but rarely with the wider political, journalistic or intellectual world of the countries where they were posted. This idea was generally shared by the entire European political elite in 1914, but by the time Italy entered the war, the other belligerents had realised how important propaganda was, both at home and abroad. Propaganda offices had been created to boost the morale of the nation, to weaken the enemy's will to fight and to promote each country's war aims to international public opinion.[154]

In Britain, for example, Grey regarded public opinion as a factor that, although unfit to exercise democratic control over a country's foreign policy, could vitally influence its formulation. In his speeches and despatches, the use of 'public opinion' was often a convenient device, put forward in support of a certain course of action, but this was not inconsistent with the recogni-tion that at some point British foreign policy had to meet with popular approval.[155] The attention devoted to domestic public opinion spurred the British Government to cultivate international public opinion too, so as to strengthen the British image and cause. Asquith set up several propaganda agencies coordinated by Charles Masterman, ex-president of the National Insurance Commission, with offices at Wellington House, London. Masterman surrounded himself with experts, including academics like James Headlam-Morley, and the novelist Anthony Hope. The team focussed on both domestic and overseas propaganda:

A pattern of work was laid down for each of the 'national' sections. First, each had to study the foreign press and keep in touch with the trend of public opinion in the country with which it was dealing. Secondly, each section was to translate and

and 689, Squitti to Sonnino, 26 May, 12 July, 18, 26, and 31 August 1915; and anonymous note with no specified date, but probably from De Martino to Sonnino, in ASMAE, b. 54.

[153] Mondini, *Il Capo*, p. 105.   [154] Tosi, *Propaganda*, pp. 13, 37–45.
[155] Robbins, *Politicians*, pp. 126–127.

publish any matter likely to have a favourable effect on that opinion. . . . Thirdly, each was to deal directly with individuals . . . encouraging press correspondents in England and any distinguished visitors to the country 'to take a right view of the actions of the British Government since the commencement of the war'. . . . Special representatives were sent . . . abroad to report on the condition of public opinion and to recommend methods of allaying dissatisfaction with or opposition to British policy.[156]

Although coordinating the efforts of the various bodies under Masterman's control was a problem,[157] which led the British Government to reorganise the bureau periodically, Wellington House succeeded in building a 'literature' of the British contribution to the war that was also, in the wider sense, a literature of peace, for it emphasised that the British aimed at defeating German militarism and guaranteeing a 'just peace'. This narrative took the form of books, pamphlets, posters, various publications and official speeches by statesmen and sovereigns. These documents were distributed abroad and by June 1915, two and a half million copies were already circulating; eight months later this figure was seven million. Illustrated papers were published in several languages, and telegraph agencies opened branches in several European cities to disseminate pro-Britain accounts of the war. In January 1916, control of propaganda was placed in the hands of the Foreign Office, thus improving coordination of propaganda initiatives for the purposes of diplomacy.[158]

Italy was ages behind in this process. The creation of a body for propaganda overseas, with clear and coherent guidelines to promote the Italian cause, was both slow and contradictory for two main reasons. First, Sonnino strongly opposed any propaganda abroad. Second, Italy lacked the financial resources to carry out a massive propaganda campaign. Sonnino's opposition was a consequence of his elitist dismissal of public opinion as a political agent. He ardently opposed any 'leak', as he called it, to the Italian press and public, let alone foreign press and public.[159] Not only were Italian representatives abroad typically little informed of Sonnino's designs, but they were not urged by the Italian Government to share what they knew or to explain Italy's point of view to a wider public. Instead, they were encouraged to endure their natural tendency to elude any unofficial diplomatic network. Sonnino's instructions were to deny or rectify

---

[156] M. L. Sanders, 'Wellington House and British Propaganda during the First World War', *The Historical Journal*, XVIII, 1, March 1975, pp. 119–146.

[157] TNA, INF4/4b, Report on propaganda arrangements by Robert Donald, 9 January 1917, pp. 3–19.

[158] Sanders, 'Wellington House', p. 122.   [159] Sonnino, *Diario*, I, pp. 321–322.

unfair accounts about Italy in the international press, but he never provided detailed counter-arguments. Not surprisingly, the ideal motivating Italy's war – the desire for unification – had little hold on international public opinion, whilst expressions such as 'our war' and 'sacred egoism' had a notable – and negative – impact.[160]

The first Italians to realise these limits were newspaper correspondents abroad. On 7 February 1916, Antonio Albertini wrote from Petrograd to his brother Luigi, the editor of the *Corriere*, that Russian public opinion considered Italy a second-rate ally. Russians wondered why Italy did not send troops to the Balkans, did not declare war on Germany and did not advance 'ten kilometres a day on the Carso'. The Russian press could offer no explanation on this because they had no information from Italian diplomats.[161] Renzo Larco made similar observations in the *Corriere* at the beginning of April, stressing the difference between the Italian approach and that of France and Britain in Russia. An unsigned comment, which Luciano Tosi attributed to editor Albertini,[162] followed the article reprimanding the Italian Government: 'Where is our propaganda action? ... In this war, nations need to be "cultivated" for them to keep producing trust, and trust between nation and nation is no less necessary to the fortunes of war than trust of each in his own Government'.[163] The following month, Mario Borsa, London correspondent of the *Secolo*, submitted a memorandum through journalist Ugo Ojetti to the Information Office of the Italian *Comando Supremo*,[164] describing British propaganda in detail and suggesting it be taken as an example. Borsa echoed Guglielmo Emanuel's editorial of 8 March describing the Wellington House Bureau for the *Corriere* readers: the attitude of British diplomats had moved from a sort of 'splendid isolation' at the outbreak of the war to a more open attitude:

Not only has [Britain] sent groups of Italian, French, Russian, American, Dutch and Swedish reporters to visit both the front and the fleet, but it has also invited a group of Russian writers ... to visit Britain, its arms factories, military camps, yards and fleet.[165]

Emanuel concluded: 'The British example needs to be copied more than anywhere else in Italy, where ... Government contact with foreign public opinion does not seem to exist at all'. This torrent of criticism spurred

---

[160] Tosi, *Propaganda*, pp. 38–40.   [161] Albertini, *Epistolario*, pp. 552–555.
[162] Tosi, *Propaganda*, p. 39.
[163] 'Il pubblico, la stampa e l'Italia', *Il Corriere della Sera*, 12 April 1916.
[164] U. Ojetti, 'L'Italia e l'Inghilterra e la guerra di domani', *Il Secolo*, 31 May 1916.
[165] G. Emanuel, 'Quel che fa l'Inghilterra per mettere in rilievo il suo sforzo', *Il Corriere della Sera*, 8 March 1916.

those Italian politicians with more modern ideas, such as Martini and De Martino, to suggest a coherent propaganda strategy to Sonnino and Salandra.[166] Martini urged Sonnino to invite Allied politicians and journalists to visit the Italian front, so that they could realise *de visu* 'the obstacles we have to overcome'.[167] De Martino went one step further and submitted, on 14 February 1916, a report to Salandra analysing anti-Italian feelings in the Allied countries. His conclusion was that such sentiment risked leading to Italy's isolation at the end of hostilities, so he proposed a vast 'defensive' and 'counter-offensive' propaganda operation to be coordinated by the Consulta. He also insisted that it was crucial to send trusted employees of the Consulta overseas to explain to Italian diplomats the importance of a systematic propaganda campaign.[168] Imperiali was one of the very few Italian diplomats who agreed with De Martino. Although initially opposed to any propaganda in Britain,[169] Imperiali scanned the British press and in the spring of 1916 was so disturbed by anti-Italian feelings in London, and by Grey's repeated 'outbursts', that he urged the Government 'to provide rapidly a thorough explanation to clarify this unpleasant situation and make things right'.[170] So, when he met Salandra in Rome, on 29 April, he was happy to find that the latter had begun to come round. Sonnino, however, proved immovable. His fundamental objection was financial: any propaganda campaign would fail unless Italy acquired many newspaper publishers, as Germany and Austria-Hungary had done – something Italy could not afford to do.[171] Salandra – who considered himself a disciple of Sonnino in the art of politics – tended to bow to his judgement.[172] So, he resorted to implementing only two minor initiatives in the summer of 1916, neither of which needed the consent of the Consulta. The first was to allocate 45,000 lire to produce publications on the Italian contribution to the war.[173] The second initiative was the establishment of the Central Committee of Propaganda for the Italian Adriatic, with Giovanni di Cesarò, Sonnino's nephew, as the Chairman. Its main task was to separate the Czechs from the Yugoslavs and to induce the former to support Italian ambitions in the Adriatic.[174]

---

[166] DDI, 5, IV, docs. 571 and 619, Imperiali to Sonnino, 11 and 18 August 1915.
[167] Martini, *Diario*, p. 580.
[168] ACS, Carte Presidenza del Consiglio, b. 19–29-7, De Martino to Sonnino, Relazione, 14 February 1916.
[169] DDI, 5, IV, doc. 927, Imperiali to San Giuliano, 10 October 1915.
[170] Ibid., V, doc. 823, Imperiali to Sonnino, 16 May 1916.
[171] Sonnino, *Carteggio*, pp. 499–500; 690.   [172] Tosi, *Propaganda*, p. 22.
[173] ACS, Carte Presidenza, b. 19–11-10, f. 4.
[174] G. Pitacco, *La passione adriatica* (Bologna: Cappelli, 1928), p. 56.

These insufficient government initiatives were partly compensated for by the action of pro-Italian committees and organisations abroad. In the summer of 1914, the private associations of interventionists had sprung up all over Italy: the most active were *Trento e Trieste*, *Dante Alighieri* and *Pro Patria*. When war broke out, these committees opened branches abroad and were joined by emigrants' associations. However, these were essentially nationalist and irredentist groups; their political initiatives reflected their own hopes for annexations. Since these groups ignored the contents of the London Pact, their claims often went beyond the terms of the Treaty itself. They failed to appreciate that, at least at the propaganda level, the war needed an idealist veneer. Promoting nationalist and annexationist slogans served only to exacerbate Italy's growing isolation, for it gave the impression that Rome was not fighting for the ideals of justice and freedom, as the other powers claimed to be doing, but for personal gain – thus strengthening, not dissipating, the 'greedy and Machiavellian Italian' stereotype.[175] Thus, despite Allied mistakes and divisions, the legend grew that Italy was the chief cause of Allied blunders.[176] Salandra's failure to stem the steady deterioration of Italy's reputation amongst its allies had profound consequences on Allied relations in 1916.

8.6   Italy's War Relaunched

The price of Italy's isolation became evident to Imperiali when comments in the British press in mid-May made reference to the 'full agreement' between Britain, France and Russia on Turkey. Imperiali's suspicions in February were justified. There had, indeed, been discussions between Italy's allies regarding the fate of the Turkish Empire, and a general understanding was reached in the spring of 1916 without Italy having been consulted. Imperiali was, of course, unaware of the content of such talks. Back in London, he saw Grey on 15 May, seeking clarification, but was left with an unpleasant impression: coldness and irritation, both unusual in the minister. At the end of the month, the Foreign Minister confirmed that talks had occurred between the three original Entente members on the post-war colonial settlement. Imperiali's requests for further details were met with annoyance: 'Why should it always be me to act as inter-Allied herald'. Imperiali listed for Grey what he considered the 'natural reasons' for that: Italian 'extreme trust' in Grey; Britain's role

---

[175] Tosi, *Propaganda*, p. 86.
[176] TNA, FO371/2263/100758 Grey to Rodd, 31 July 1915; Burgwyn, *The Legend*, pp. 41 ff.

in the Treaty of London negotiations; and the 'traditional friendship that ties us to England'. It was a proclamation of Italy's understanding of the Anglo-Italian partnership, but Grey remained adamant that the results of the talks would not be shared until the half-way nature of Italy's war had been resolved.[177] Offended, the Italians replied that 'England contributes to the lengthening of the war by keeping one million men immobile in Flanders, and everything seems to suggest they will remain there until the end of the war'. Compared with such a passive attitude, the question of Italian declaration of war on Berlin was one of a 'Byzantine' nature.[178]

This was the climate of Anglo-Italian relations when the Austro-Hungarian offensive in Trentino struck. Later called *Strafexpedition*, a 'punitive expedition' against the treacherous ally, it was launched on 15 May with the ambitious aim of breaking through the Italian lines south of Trentino into the Venetian plain, cutting off the main body of the Italian army engaged on the Isonzo. The initial success of the offensive was spectacular, and reached Asiago on 28 May. The Italians were outgunned 10:1, but they followed Cadorna's orders to defend every inch of terrain, mounting desperate counter-attacks to regain lost ground. Their losses amounted to 76,000 men, as opposed to 30,000 Austro-Hungarians, but they eventually managed to halt the enemy.[179] Italian appeals for help accelerated Russian preparations for an offensive in Galicia.[180] General Aleksei Brusilov had scheduled his attack for July to coincide with the Somme offensive, but launched it on 4 June, taking the Austro-Hungarians off-guard. By forcing the Austro-Hungarians to divert forces eastwards, Brusilov's offensive gained credit for relieving the Italians in 1916, although, on 2 June, Cadorna had already issued a bulletin announcing the failure of the enemy offensive in Trentino.[181] Austro-Hungarian attacks nonetheless continued in the following days. Cadorna's optimistic bulletin might have been aimed at pre-empting arguments that Italy had been saved by Brusilov. If that was his intention, Cadorna failed. Imperiali noted bitterly that British authorities held little doubt that Italy owed its survival to its allies more than to its own soldiers.[182] He was partially relieved when Cadorna formed a new reserve army gathering troops from the Isonzo, ten divisions in total, and counter-attacked *en masse* on 16 June – another 70,000 Italians and 53,000 Austro-Hungarians were lost, and the latter were now in

---

[177] Imperiali, *Diario*, pp. 183, 264, 288; DDI, 5, V, doc. 820, Imperiali to Sonnino, 16 May 1916.
[178] Ibid., doc. 874, Tittoni to Sonnino, 28 May 1916.
[179] Isnenghi, Rochat, *Grande Guerra*, pp. 188 ff.
[180] DDI, 5, V, doc. 840, Sonnino to Cadorna, Imperiali, Tittoni and Carlotti, 20 May 1916.
[181] Pieri, *L'Italia*, pp. 103 ff.   [182] Imperiali, *Diario*, p. 272.

Figure 8.1 Italian infantry patrol at a mountain station

Figure 8.2 Italian *Alpini* on the march on the Adamello (Trentino), 1916

retreat.[183] After months of strained inter-Allied relations, Imperiali commented, 'it was a pleasure to walk through the streets of London today and read posters which read *Italian Victory*'.[184]

The army's resistance, however, could not prevent the collapse of the Salandra Government on 10 June. The British did not sympathise with the political instability of their young ally. Rodd was particularly upset by the replacement of his friend Martini with Gaspare Colosimo, a Giolittian.[185] Despite Rodd's praise of Martini, their personal relations had significantly cooled in recent months, due, as we shall see, to repeated Anglo-Italian disagreements in North Africa. Martini left the Government disillusioned with the outcome of his longed-for Anglo-Italian 'special partnership'.[186] Victor Emmanuel III called Paolo Boselli to set up a 'national Government' along the lines of the French *Union Sacrée*; its key figures were Vittorio Emanuele Orlando, Minister of Justice and the Interior, Ivanoe Bonomi and Leonida Bissolati – both transformist socialists, appointed as Public Works Minister and Minister of Government Assistance, respectively. The latter proved particularly important in keeping Cadorna in check.[187] Boselli's most difficult choice was of the Foreign Minister. He liked Tittoni, but the British grimaced over his past neutralist sympathies.[188] Grey preferred Sonnino by all means. Despite his stormy character, Sonnino was a guarantee of continuity in Rome's foreign policy alongside the Entente. Boselli was not deaf to Grey's opinion, and confirmed Sonnino at his post.[189] The swift resolution of the government crisis was a relief for Britain.[190] Italian public opinion, on the other hand, viewed the new Government with some scepticism. Boselli, aged 72, was considered too old, and curiously enough he was leading a national coalition, which he had initially thought would be 'foolishness'.[191] Despite his ultimate failure, Boselli's job has recently been reassessed by Italian historians. The establishment of a wider political coalition made it easier to mobilise the nation for war. A Ministry of Arms and Munitions was created to coordinate political and technical mobilisations and was entrusted to the energetic General Alfredo Dallolio.[192] Italy now faced World War I with a fresh commitment.

---

[183] Isnenghi-Rochat, *Grande Guerra*, p. 194.   [184] Imperiali, *Diario*, p. 281.
[185] Rodd, *Memories*, III, pp. 294–296.
[186] Martini was 'mortified and irritated:' DDI, 5, IV, doc. 483, Imperiali to Sonnino, 27 July 1915.
[187] Isnenghi, Rochat, *Grande Guerra*, pp. 312–317.   [188] Imperiali, *Diario*, p. 275.
[189] Riccardi, *Alleati*, p. 284.
[190] TNA, FO371/2685/126986, Rodd to Grey, 26 June 1916.
[191] P. Melograni, *Storia politica della Grande Guerra (1915–1918)* (Rome & Bari: Laterza, 1969), p. 193.
[192] Isnenghi, Rochat, *Grande Guerra*, p. 318.

Boselli's first priority was to reaffirm Allied solidarity.[193] He was encouraged to expand Italy's venture by two main factors. The first was the extraordinary effort made by the British and French on the Somme on 1 July. The attack dispelled Italian reservations on British 'limited' commitment on land.[194] Initially, it seemed that developments on the Russian and Italian fronts favoured the offensive. Falkenhayn had to raise the number of German divisions in Russia from fifty-two to seventy-six throughout the summer to prevent a collapse of the Austro-Hungarian army. This did not, however, coincide with a reduction in German forces in the west – where German divisions in fact grew from 112 to 121 by November, when the Allied offensive ended.[195] Falkenhayn's defences on the Somme, furthermore, proved impregnable. Famously, the massive Allied bombardment caused limited damage to German bunkers, and the supposedly swift Allied advance bogged down almost immediately in a grid of gun and machine gun fire. In part, this was a consequence of British preparations: on paper, Britain deployed an unprecedented one and a half million men supported by 1,538 guns – but of these, only 468 were heavy and 1,070 were field guns. To speed up production, the British had curtailed quality.[196] The first day on the Somme was the worst day in the history of the British army in terms of casualties: 57,470 of whom 19,240 were killed.[197] The Allies had badly underestimated the enemy's defences, and the scale of its reserves. At the end of the battle, British and French forces had penetrated 10 kilometres into German-occupied territory, at the cost of 419,000 British and 204,000 French casualties.[198] The German army also suffered about half a million losses,[199] but it survived the battle, and successfully assisted its Austro-Hungarian partner against Brusilov. The Chantilly scheme appeared in tatters.

Pressure grew once again on Italy to complement Allied efforts. The French urged the Italians to take part in a new offensive on Bulgaria, which now seemed the last theatre where the Allies might gain 'decisive results' by the end of the year.[200] Together with the

---

[193] Albertini, *Venti anni di vita politica*, part 2 (here and henceforth), *L'Italia nella Guerra Mondiale*, 2 vols. (Bologna, 1951), I, p. 305.

[194] Trevelyan, *Scenes*, p. 33.

[195] W. Miles, *Military Operations, France and Belgium, 1916: 2nd July 1916 to the End of the Battles of the Somme*, in *History of the Great War Based on Official Documents by Direction of the Historical Section of the Committee of Imperial Defence*, 36 vols. (London: Imperial War Museum & Battery Press, 1992 [1938]), II, p. 555.

[196] Strachan, 'Battle of the Somme', p. 85.

[197] R. Prior, T. Wilson, *The Somme* (Boston: Yale University Press, 2005), p. 119.

[198] G. Sheffield, *The Chief: Douglas Haig and the British Army* (London: Aurum, 2011), pp. 194–197.

[199] Philpott, *Bloody Victory*, pp. 602–603.

[200] DDI, 5, V, doc. 537, Carlotti to Sonnino, 3 March 1916.

Russians, the French asked Italy to send one division to Salonika.[201] Cadorna conceded one brigade.[202] Paradoxically enough, now it was the British who hesitated, as Sir William Robertson, Chief of the Imperial General Staff, expressed no enthusiasm for an offensive until Romania had joined the war.[203] The French and Russians, however, considered an Allied show of force as the final push to Brătianu.[204] After a conversation with Allied military attachés on 24 July, Cadorna approved the Franco-Russo plan and promised one division. Boselli endorsed Cadorna's conclusion that the defeat of Bulgaria would result in 'a most compromising situation for the Central Powers'.[205] In Boselli's mind, military considerations were intertwined with diplomatic ones. A second factor spurring his decision – which was arguably more important than the first – was preoccupation about the secret Allied colonial talks from which Italy was excluded. Imperiali had repeatedly advised that 'we should fear more serious consequences' should the other Allies take Italy's limited observance of the London Treaty 'as a pretext to justify their lack of support to the integral realisation of our agreed claims' at the end of the war.[206] Both Sonnino and Salandra had not been deaf to such arguments – that Britain was not ready to intercede for Italy on the colonial question was particularly off-putting[207] – but in the final months of his Government, Salandra's position was so precarious that he felt he lacked 'the moral strength' necessary to push the King to sign another war declaration.[208] This was not the case for Boselli: he understood that a satisfactory solution to the colonial question was 'closely linked to the military sacrifices Italy was prepared to make'.[209] So, he gave the green-light for the Salonika offensive, breaching for the first time the principle of 'our war'. This was complemented by a renewed Allied offer to Romania, which included Austro-Hungarian Transylvania and strong military support. As a further concession to his allies, Boselli signed the agreement undertaken by Britain, France and Russia at the economic conference in Paris in June, which bound Italy to cease trade relations with the

[201] Ibid., doc. 136, Sonnino to Imperiali, Tittoni, Carlotti and Cadorna, 17 July 1916.
[202] Ibid., doc. 138, Cadorna to Sonnino, 19 July 1916.
[203] AUSSME, E2, b. 14, Delmé-Radcliffe to Cadorna, 10 June 1916.
[204] DDI, 5, VI, doc. 82, Tittoni to Sonnino, 7 July 1916.
[205] Ibid., doc. 177, Cadorna to Sonnino, 24 July 1916.
[206] Ibid., V, doc. 882, Imperiali to Sonnino, 30 May 1916; VI, docs. 105 and 211, Imperiali to Sonnino, 11 July and 1 August 1916.
[207] G.D. Gifuni ed., *Il diario di Salandra* (Milan: Pan, 1969), pp. 44–50.
[208] DDI, 5, V, doc. 896, Salandra to Sonnino, 27 May 1916.
[209] Gooch, *Italian Army*, p. 178.

neutral countries, companies and private persons whose business was in whole or in part under enemy control.[210] Thus, the British objective to complete the blockade of the Central Powers was achieved. Only one issue remained to fill the gap between Italy and its allies: Germany. The final turn in the diplomatic dance was determined by events on the battlefield.

Having repulsed the Austro-Hungarian offensive in Trentino, Cadorna planned a new attack in the east. He made full use of his solitary geographical advantage over the enemy – the inner line of communications – by transferring thirteen divisions from Trentino back to the Isonzo undetected and launched the Sixth Isonzo battle on 6 August. Cadorna's objective was the strategic city of Gorizia, which formed a salient in the front.[211] For the first time, the Italians had concentrated a mass of artillery in a small area: 1,200 guns – 400 of them large-calibre – and 800 new heavy trench mortars or *bombarde*. Hard fieldwork supervised by an emerging officer, Colonel Pietro Badoglio, had excavated an intricate grid of trenches, tunnels and caverns in the limestone, often by night, until the front lines were as close as 30 metres to enemy trenches. Cadorna called it 'a classic example of field fortification and of the offensive preparation of terrain'.[212] Thus, the attackers were at the enemy's front lines before its forces had recovered from the bombardment – an unexpected feat for the Italians. The Sabotino – insuperable for so long – fell in 38 minutes.[213] The Austro-Hungarians had arguably underestimated the capacity of the Italians to mount another offensive after two months of continuous bitter fighting. The 3rd Italian Army took Gorizia on 9 August.[214] The 'liberation of Gorizia' did not cause a crisis in the Austro-Hungarian defence system, which reformed on the second line of mountains above Trieste, but it did have a resounding effect in Italy and abroad. It was the first great Italian victory of the war. 'British press enthusiastic', wrote Imperiali.[215] Cadorna reassured Boselli that the Swiss-Italian frontier was now fortified, and he felt confident that he could repulse even a German attack. The Italian Government at this point felt strong enough to declare war on Germany, which Boselli did on 28 August together with Brătianu.[216] This produced 'new heights of optimism' in British circles.[217] Allied expectations for a quick victory at

---

[210] J. Brown Scott, 'Economic Conference of the Allied Powers', *The American Journal of International Law*, X, 4, October 1916, pp. 845–852.

[211] Marcuzzi, 'The Battle of Gorizia (6–17 August 1916): A Turning Point in Italy's War', MWP Working Papers, 14, *Cadmus*, 2017, p. 2.

[212] See: F. Zingales, *La conquista di Gorizia* (Rome: USSME, 1925).

[213] Isnenghi, Rochat, *Grande Guerra*, p. 197.   [214] Thompson, *White War*, p. 175.

[215] Imperiali, *Diario*, pp. 297–301.   [216] Sonnino, *Diario*, II, p. 201.

[217] French, *British Strategy*, p. 205.

least over Bulgaria would once again prove over-optimistic, but Rome was now fully committed to the world war.

Britain had played a crucial part in altering Italy's political stance of May 1915, based on the principle of *la nostra guerra*. Italy's decision to join the Allies in the war on Turkey and Germany – which Burgwyn attributed to Sonnino's pressure on Italian prime ministers[218] – was in fact largely the result of a staunch British diplomatic effort. Though Britain was as resolute as France and Russia not to consider Italy a trustworthy partner until the latter fully embraced the Entente's war,[219] London enjoyed more success than its partners in bringing that about, because it could exploit its financial power and because it enjoyed more consideration from Italy. This does not mean that the Anglo-Italian alignment was absolute. Contrasts remained acute, and at times different alignments were formed within the Entente – such as between Italy and France – impeding a common strategy. But overall, partly through mediation, partly through blackmail, and partly thanks to Italian victories, the main inter-Allied political differences of 1915 had been bridged, at least on paper. Unfortunately for the Entente, the colonial question, where the diplomatic game now moved, would turn out to be another minefield.

---

[218] Burgwyn, *The Legend*, p. 39.   [219] Riccardi, *Alleati*, pp. 266 ff.

9   Peripheral Competition

9.1   African Distractions

The first year of Italy's war had shaken some assumptions upon which the Anglo-Italian entente had been based. The effectiveness of their shared values as a bonding agent, the impact of Italy's intervention and strategic collaboration had proved disappointing. One principle remained, however, which seemed to be a solid foundation of Anglo-Italian relations: the convergence of geopolitical interests, or at least the absence of geopolitical competition. This held on both sides. Rome and London had never clashed geopolitically: Grey, Sonnino, Rodd and Imperiali agreed that Anglo-Italian interests were 'absolutely identical', and that 'Italy must work hand in hand with England not only during the war but after the war'.[1] The colonial question that erupted over the Allied partition of the Ottoman Empire challenged this last assumption and brought to the fore a fundamental conflict between Britain's war aims and those of Italy.

To appreciate this fully, we need to take a step back to 1915 in North Africa, where Anglo-Italian interests diverged over the Senussi problem and the management of the Libyan-Egyptian border. The Senussi (or Sanusi) were a Muslim political-religious Sufi order which spread along the caravan routes of North Africa setting up hostels and religious schools for the itinerant Bedouin tribesmen of the region. Its influence grew especially in Egypt and Cyrenaica, and in the twentieth century turned military. Although originally opposed to the Turks, the Senussi joined them in the war against the Italian invaders in Libya in 1911–1912. After the withdrawal of the Ottomans, the Senussi took the lead in the resistance in most of the country, holding out in the deep desert regions while the Italians held most of the towns and coast and the Cyrenaica plateau.

---

[1] TNA, FO371/2685/126986, Rodd to Grey, 26 June 1916.

In contrast, the Senussi had positive relations with the Anglo-Egyptian authorities, who tolerated their proselytising and commercial activities.[2] The outbreak of World War I led to a convoluted situation. The Ottoman Sultan proclaimed *jihad* against the Entente powers in autumn 1914, but, upon German request, he excluded Italy from its targets, to avoid rushing Rome into the Entente. This distinction was purely academic, especially when the Turks were heavily involved in financing and supplying Libyan rebels with the aim of destabilising – and maybe one day recapturing – the Italian colony. Italy was de facto affected by the *jihad*, led in Libya by Sayyid Ahmed al-Sharif, the new Grand Senussi. On the other hand, he was not willing to fight the British, despite their being legitimate targets of the *jihad*.[3] The British, for their part, were preoccupied with the defence of the Suez Canal. In the first two years of the war, the Turks had the upper hand in the Middle Eastern theatre. They forced the British into retreat in Mesopotamia and, between January and February 1915 advanced from Southern Palestine across the Canal into Egypt. Such expedition, led by German General Kress von Kressenstein, was repulsed by British defenders. During the next few months, von Kressenstein launched a series of raids and attacks in an attempt to disrupt traffic on the Canal.[4] In this context, the British chose to appease the Senussi, indulging their arms smuggling across the Egyptian-Libyan border, which fed anti-Italian guerrillas, and even promising the Senussi an autonomous emirate in Cyrenaica if they undertook to keep the *jihad* away from Egypt.[5]

Italy's entry into the conflict exacerbated this prickly scenario. Italy was now a proper target for the *jihad*, and that obviously strengthened anti-Italian resistance in Libya. Cadorna's desperate need for soldiers to be sent into the European cauldron led to a reduction of the Italian garrison in Libya, coupled with a gradual Italian withdrawal from the inner regions and the plateau to the coast. The rebels seemed to have a tangible opportunity to force the Italians into the sea, and they maintained the momentum, tormenting the Italian posts and their retreating columns with ambushes, hit-and-run attacks and occasionally large-scale assaults. By the end of July 1915, Italian dominion was reduced to a few coastal cities, such as Tripoli, Homs, Benghazi and Tobruk. Yet Cadorna was eager to concentrate on the European theatre. Salandra and Sonnino maintained

---

[2] S. Hadaway, *Pyramids and Fleshpots. The Egyptian, Senussi and Eastern Mediterranean Campaigns, 1914–1916* (Straud: Spellmout, 2014), p. 98.

[3] A. Del Boca, *Gli italiani in Libia*, 2 vols. (Milan: Mondadori, 1993), I, p. 261.

[4] A. Bruce, *The Last Crusade: The Palestine Campaign in the First World War* (London: Murray, 2002), pp. 26–27.

[5] Del Boca, *Italiani in Libia*, I, pp. 262 ff.

that the Libyan theatre was a sideshow in Italy's war, but nonetheless one that could not be ignored or abandoned – Italy must defend at least its last beachheads, or it might not be able to claim back the colony. Italy's fight in Libya evolved into a parallel war, which would end only in 1931 with the fascist reconquest of rebel territory.[6] It was typically dirty colonial warfare, with barely any prisoners taken on either side, deadly rebel raids, unsuccessful Italian chases – which usually led to rebel ambushes of the pursuers – and frequent Italian reprisals on civilians. In the fortifications along the coast, 35,000 men were crammed, largely infantry, faced by some 20,000 *mujahidin*, highly mobile and armed with modern rifles smuggled by German and Turkish agents. To contain the rebel thrust in the summer of 1915, Italy urged Britain to stop Senussi trafficking of weapons and munition across the Egyptian border and to put pressure on the order to come to an agreement with Rome.[7] London, however, adopted dilatory tactics, admitting that Italian and British interests on the Senussi matter did not coincide.[8]

Salandra was much annoyed with the British for their inaction. On 5 July 1915, he wrote to Imperiali that the Italian setbacks in Libya were a direct consequence of 'the behaviour of England' which 'let the Senussi rebellion against us be fed in every way, even after we formally became allies'.[9] Imperiali agreed that such an attitude was 'incompatible' with the Anglo-Italian alliance,[10] but Grey limited himself to dismissing Italian complaints as 'exaggerated'. As long as he served as Colonial Minister, Martini was in the frontline of the Italian diplomatic efforts to agree upon a common Anglo-Italian policy in North Africa. He presented Rodd with detailed reports about British acquaintance and even complicity with the Senussi smuggling, favoured by the activity 'of a British officer whom they pronounce Ruel [Leopold Royle]'. Rodd, rather surprised by the precision of Italian intelligence, promised to persuade Grey to press General John Maxwell, British commander in Egypt, to 'make it understood among the Senussi that they cannot be friends to Britain and enemies to Italy at a time'.[11] Maxwell kept regular mail communication with al-Sharif, suggesting to him 'from friend to friend' to give up any potential anti-British design, but his correspondence makes no reference to Italy.[12] The situation did not improve during the summer, so that a disheartened Martini concluded that

[6] N. Labanca, *La guerra italiana per la Libia, 1911–1931* (Bologna: il Mulino, 2012), p. 11; Del Boca, *Italiani in Libia*, I, pp. 293 ff..

[7] Sonnino, *Diario*, II, pp. 29–30.

[8] R. Astuto, 'Ferdinando Martini e l'Inghilterra', *Rivista delle Colonie*, IV, 287, April 1943, p. 287; DDI, 5, IV, doc. 435, Sonnino to Imperiali, 16 July 1915.

[9] Ibid., doc. 342, Salandra to Imperiali, 5 July 1915.

[10] Ibid., doc. 371, Imperiali to Sonnino, 8 July 1915.   [11] Martini, *Diario*, pp. 271, 518.

[12] R. McGuirk, *The Sanusi's Little War. The Amazing Story of a Forgotten Conflict in the Western Desert, 1915–1917* (London: Arabian Publishing), pp. 298–310.

Rodd must have little influence on his Government. The Italian minister also began to suspect that the British were not unhappy to see Italy expelled from Libya. Martini enjoyed more 'examples of the brotherhood of dear England'. The British unilaterally occupied Karaman on the Sudanese-Eritrean border, and the Hanish-Zucur archipelagos off the Eritrean shore. It was difficult to present this as a pre-emptive action against the Turks; rather, it seemed to mark the limits of Italian colonial ambitions in the region. The occupied territories were so close to the Italian Eritrean colony 'that their seizure is something more than *sans façons*, it is pure contempt of our rights'. Martini was exasperated: 'A more unfaithful attitude than that of England towards us in Africa is impossible to imagine'. He shared his disappointment with Rodd and few others though, for he believed that the day Britain's attitude were to be known in Italy 'Italian sympathies [for the British] would severely decline'.[13]

Italian protests pushed the British to explicate their territorial projects better. At the end of July, Rodd came up with a proposal that would manage both the Senussi problem and the standing issue of the Libyan-Egyptian border, which had never been precisely delineated. It reflected al-Sharif's desire, repeatedly expressed to Maxwell, to avoid the Italian annexation of Jaghbub and Cufra, 'holy places and religious centres for us'.[14] The former was an Italian claim in British territory, the latter formally belonged to the Libyan colony, but the Italians had never succeeded in occupying it. Rodd suggested: 'There are territories belonging to England (Siwa, Jaghbub), and others belonging to Italy (Cufra). We could unite them and create a sultanate for the Senussi'. Martini replied he would 'never accept' such a proposal. Personal relations between Rodd and Martini cooled. The former insisted that a compromise was needed, which included some Senussi claims; the latter repeated that the Senussi must be considered an enemy of the Entente, and could not, in any ways, be trusted. British confidence in their capacity to keep the Arabs under control, and even to lead them into an anti-Turk revolt, seemed to Martini proof that 'Rodd and his superiors live in a world of sweet fallacies'. He would rather believe the opposite, that it was the Turks who could march to Suez, repeating their failed Canal expedition of February 1915, this time fomenting Senussi raids into the region to distract British forces. No one seemed to take this possibility seriously, however.[15] The turning point came in September, when Senussi forces

[13] Martini, *Diario*, pp. 480, 506, 541, 608–609.
[14] Sayyis Ahmad al-Sharif al-Sanusi to Maxwell, 26 July 1915, in McGuirk, *Little War*, p. 300.
[15] Martini, *Diario*, pp. 499, 556; DDI, 5, IV, doc. 100, *cit.*, annex: Crewe to Imperiali n. 65995/15, 2 June 1915.

invaded Egypt. After months of bargaining, they embraced the project sponsored by Enver Bey, Pasha and Ottoman Minister of War, aimed at breaking British power in Egypt. Al-Sharif and Nuri Bey, half-brother of Enver, marched from Cyrenaica, whilst Ali Dinar, the Sultan of Darfur, marched from the south. Their surprise attack caught the British off-guard and led the *mujahidin* to occupy Siwa, El Bahariya, Farafra and Mogara before being re-supplied by German submarines at Sollum on 12 November and heading towards Mersa Matruh. In the meantime, another revolt led by Ulad Ali broke out in Egypt.[16] Martini could not help thinking that the British deserved it: 'The English have acted towards us not even as good neighbours – let alone allies. Now they reap the rewards of their Senussi appeasement – those rewards which we predicted they would reap'.[17]

These developments coincided with the Allied debate on coordination initiated by Briand in the autumn of 1915. As mentioned, Italy was not at all enthusiastic about it as far as the European theatre was concerned, but Martini sponsored a similar solution in the colonies. He held that 'if the front of our war has to be a common one, it must include our colonies too'.[18] Instead, the British kept acting independently, as Maxwell intercepted and beat Nuri Bey and al-Sharif at the battle of El-Hzalin in December.[19] At the beginning of 1916, the British launched a larger operation led by General William Peyton to clear the Egyptian Mediterranean coast. It continued throughout February despite huge logistical problems, but though leading to British reoccupation of Sidi Barrani and Sollum, it failed to break the *mujahidin*, who retreated towards the Libyan border and the inner oases. The lengthening of the fight spurred Anglo-Italian cooperation, at last. Grey and Kitchener agreed that Peyton should coordinate with the Italian garrison in Libya. An agreement officially endorsed this on 13 March,[20] and Briand also accepted to interdict any trafficking with the Senussi from French Tunisia.[21] The campaign was fought using traditional and new methods of warfare, a strategy begun by the Italians who had pioneered the military use of aeroplanes in the Italo-Turkish war. The British exploited the internal combustion engine to drive on the desert and fly over it, adding a new dimension of speed and mobility to their operations, which was beyond the capacity of the Senussi to challenge. The British and the

---

[16] Ibid., doc. 515, Imperiali to Sonnino, 2 August 1915.   [17] Martini, *Diario*, p. 597.
[18] DDI, 5, V, doc. 458, Martini to Sonnino, 14 February 1916.
[19] Del Boca, *Italiani in Libia*, I, p. 317.
[20] ASMAE, Libia, b. 122/9, f. 76, n. 2286; DDI, 5, V, doc. 441, Sonnino to Serra, 12 February 1916.
[21] Ibid., doc. 460, Tittoni to Sonnino, 15 February 1916.

Italians also conducted espionage and sowed dissent among Senussi leaders. On 25–26 July 1916, a British raiding force from Sollum and Italian cars from Bardia converged on a *mujahidin* party at Wadi Sanal in Libya, scattering the Senussi and giving a clear message that there would be no sanctuary on either side of the border.[22] More combined Anglo-Italian actions led, in November, to the defeat of Ali Dinar, who fell in battle. Nuri Bey and al-Sharif fled to inland Marmarica and to the oasis of Jaghbub, respectively.[23] With the defeat of the Senussi, the second Turkish-German attempt to undermine British interests in Egypt collapsed. The war against the rebels continued, however, until a precarious armistice with the Senussi was signed in April 1917.[24]

Despite the Anglo-Italian rapprochement – which originated from military difficulties and not from a convergence of geopolitical interests or the desire for Entente integration in the colonial theatre – British policy in Africa shook Italian trust in the 'preferred ally'. This stimulated a more autonomous and ambitious thinking in Italian colonial policy, although ambitions were rarely matched by Italian means. Martini, for example, began to think that 'because we cannot count on the loyalty and not even on common interests of our allies and their agents, we will have to count on their errors'. British management of the Egyptian crisis, in his eyes, demonstrated that British 'contempt for the natives' and the consequent overconfidence in British capacity to keep them under control, had undermined London's ability to deal with 'the forces of Islam'. Martini began to dream of a greater role for Italy in North Africa and the Middle East as the protector of the Arabs, exploiting the historic Arab hatred for Britain and France. Through an Italian agent, Guelfo Civinini, he made overtures to Bey el-Masri, an ambitious leader of anti-Italian resistance in Cyrenaica, who led an Arab society aiming to create an independent Arab state in Arabia, and was looking for a European protector. Civinini offered him Italy's support, in exchange for Arab surrender of any claims in Libya. The project, wrote Martini, was to be implemented as much as possible behind Britain's back.[25]

Although nothing came out of this plan, it is indicative of the state of Anglo-Italian relations in the summer of 1916. Martini summarised it: 'When they find it advantageous, the British act independently; when it is convenient to them to act differently, they do as if we had common interests'.[26] Given Italy's partial commitment to the Entente's war at

---

[22] G. MacMunn, C. Falls, *Military Operations: Egypt and Palestine, From the Outbreak of War with Germany to June 1917*, in *History of the Great War*, I, pp. 134–140.

[23] Hadaway, *Pyramids and Fleshpots*, pp. 98–106.

[24] Labanca, *Guerra italiana*, pp. 130–136.   [25] Martini, *Diario*, pp. 376, 522.

[26] Ibid., pp. 608.

the time, this could be easily reversed. When Boselli came to power, he was determined to improve this state of affairs, but the colonial talks of 1916–1917 would widen the gap.

9.2   The Dispute on Asia Minor

The issue of Allied partition of the Ottoman Empire was even more problematic than the Anglo-Italian dispute in Africa. Initially, the Allies tended to look unfavourably upon the prospect of a disintegration of the Empire, which they considered an important element of Mediterranean stability. Grey, in particular, was willing to adhere to his principle of avoiding fresh conquests even after Turkey had entered the war and, in any case, he found the whole question premature. 'If we won the war, spheres of interest would have to be defined', he held, but 'what we needed first was to concentrate on winning the war'. In November 1914, however, the Russians advanced into the Caucasus and announced that they 'must not be expected at the end of the war to withdraw from what they had conquered in Asia Minor'.[27] The French put forward claims for the whole of Cilicia as well as Syria. Asquith's War Committee found them 'excessive', but the demands of the other Allies convinced the British that, should they 'leave the other nations to scramble for Turkey without taking anything ourselves, we should not be doing our duty'.[28] Some members of the Cabinet, such as Herbert Samuel, the President of the local Government board, advocated the annexation of Palestine as a 'buffer between French territory to the north and British-dominated Egypt to the south'.[29]

Negotiations took place in spring 1915 and again between February and May 1916. Under the Sykes–Picot Agreement signed on 16 May 1916, Russia was to push its frontier south-westwards into Asia Minor, taking Armenia, Erzerum, Trabzon and Northern Kurdistan, plus Constantinople as agreed in 1915. France was to annex a strip of Asia Minor west of the new Russian frontier, running down to Adana and the gulf of Alexandretta, and continuing along the Syrian coast to Northern Palestine. Britain was granted Mesopotamia from Baghdad to the Persian Gulf and the larger part of Palestine. Remaining territories in Anatolia would form a new Turkish state.[30] It is important to stress that the British Government was still following a defensive principle, but this now included expansion of the Empire as a necessity to guarantee its

[27] Grey, *Twenty-Five Years*, pp. 230–231.
[28] TNA, CAB42/2/14, War Committee, 19 March 1915.
[29] French, *British Strategy*, p. 82.
[30] Lloyd George, *War Memoirs*, 2 vols. (London: Odhams, 1938), II, p. 1084.

protection. David French has suggested that the reason for this controversial British policy lay in the contradiction between Britain's *façade* of 'war for justice and liberty', and its real objective, which was to defend British supremacy.[31] This is confirmed by the development of the colonial talks throughout the war. Asquith and Grey had initially assumed that their goal of ensuring British prominence in order to avert any future threat to the Empire could be attained simply by strengthening British naval power and maintaining British military and financial superiority vis à vis opponents as well as allies.[32] Now, however, the prospect of an expansion of Allied powers required London to follow a similar path. Of course, the line between this concept of imperial defence and direct imperialism was thin; in time, it would blur further and then evaporate. On the other hand, British surrender of Alexandretta to the French, against which both Kitchener and Churchill had made a very strong case,[33] was part of a series of colonial concessions by Grey to Paris – including Mosul and the provisional occupation of the greater part of Cameroons[34] – intended to gain French support for a new Arab kingdom in Syria.[35] The prospect of an Arab homeland served to ignite a British-led anti-Turk revolt in the Middle East. Despite Martini's scepticism, London did manage to mobilise at least some of 'the forces of Islam', and the Arab anti-Turk revolt was officially initiated in early June 1916.[36] The Sykes–Picot Agreement, far from being solely a post-war settlement provider, had therefore important and immediate repercussions in the conflict. The adhesion of Italy to the Entente risked nullifying this compromise.

During the first phase of the colonial talks, Italy was excluded because it was still neutral. During the second round, however, Italy was a member of the Entente, yet it was kept in the dark. When the Treaty of London was agreed, Britain, France and Russia signed a secret memorandum stating that Italy's entry into the alliance could not modify the colonial conditions that were being discussed.[37] The London Pact granted Italy Adalia in the case of an Allied partition of Turkey, plus undefined compensation aimed at creating an 'equitable' Mediterranean equilibrium; in

---

[31] French, *Strategy of Lloyd George*, pp. XII-XII.   [32] French, *British Strategy*, pp. 220 ff.

[33] TNA, CAB24/2/5, War Council, 10 March 1915.

[34] FO officials lamented: 'If Grey is allowed a free hand – like in this instance – he will fritter away all our bargaining powers before the conclusion of the war': W. R. Louis, *Great Britain and Germany's Lost Colonies 1914–1919* (Oxford: Oxford University Press, 1969), pp. 61–62.

[35] Grey promised the Arab leader Sherif Hussein bin Ali 'the districts of Damascus, Homs, Hama and Aleppo': Robbins, *Sir Edward Grey*, pp. 309–310.

[36] Hinsley, *British Foreign Policy*, p. 448.

[37] Toscano, *Gli accordi di San Giovanni di Moriana* (Milan: Giuffré, 1936), pp. 64–65.

fact, only Adalia was allotted to Italy in the Sykes–Picot Agreement – no additional gains counterbalanced the extensive acquisitions of the other Allies. On 28 August 1916, Imperiali met Grey with confidence: Italy had just declared war on Berlin; so now, at last, the colonial question could be discussed. Grey welcomed the ambassador and did not even wait for Imperiali to mention the colonial agreement, but introduced it himself: 'I am going to stir up the question of Asia Minor', he said, and promised to keep the Italian ambassador updated.[38] Whilst Imperiali waited for news, Sonnino quivered with impatience. As days and then weeks, passed without news, he began to think that his allies might not have been sincere in their promises. Rodd repeatedly reminded Grey that sharing the content of the colonial agreement with Italy was both fair and wise, as 'the conditions contemplated were bound to become known sooner or later'.[39] The Foreign Minister however played for time.[40]

The apparent indifference towards Rome led to the Italian myth of the anti-Italian colonial plot. Sonnino, Imperiali and even Cadorna denounced a 'deliberately malevolent attitude towards Italy' and became convinced that the original Entente members were conniving behind Italy's back to prevent their minor ally from becoming a genuine imperial power.[41] This interpretation was reflected in Italian post-war literature.[42] It is misleading. The idea of a prolonged and coordinated plot gives too much credit to the capacity of the original Entente members to be consistent in their policies. True, they agreed that Italian imperialism should be confined to the Adriatic region; they had given vague assurances of colonial concessions to Italy purely to speed up the conclusion of the London Pact, yet none of them was happy to have Italy joining in on the colonial question. That being said, however, when the event materialised Anglo-Russo-French unity typically broke down. The only power in direct competition with Italy in Asia Minor was France, whose area of influence extended to Mersin and now included Alexandretta. It seemed obvious that if the Italians were assigned territory beyond Adalia, the first zone of influence to be weakened would be the French, as it bordered on the Italian. So, Paris was the most stubborn opponent to any Italian involvement in Asia Minor negotiations. Russia was more preoccupied that including Italy in the talks would lead to a revision of the Anglo-Russo-French agreement of 1915, which had granted Petrograd the possession of Constantinople. Re-opening the talks might have enabled the western powers to withdraw from this obligation, which they had

---

[38] Imperiali, *Diario*, p. 303.   [39] Rodd, *Memories*, III, pp. 266–267.
[40] DDI, 5, VI, doc. 417, Imperiali to Sonnino, 12 September 1916.
[41] Ibid., doc. 865, Imperiali to Sonnino, 18 December 1916; Imperiali, *Diario*, p. 273.
[42] See M. Caracciolo, *L'Italia e i suoi Alleati, cit.*

entered reluctantly. Thus, Petrograd opposed an Italian involvement, but more for its mistrust of the West than for a specific anti-Italian colonial competition at this stage.[43]

Grey had his own problems with Italy's request. The latter had materialised at a time when the first round of post-war planning had begun in Asquith's Cabinet. This was prompted partly by the Sykes–Picot talks (which stimulated greater reflection on British desiderata), and partly by the inconclusive Somme offensive. Based on the latter, Lord Lansdowne argued the possibility of a peace not originating from a decisive Allied victory. In August, the British Government was the first among the belligerents to authorise reports by ad hoc committees on the prospects for peace-making. The initial phase of the debate was essentially academic, but it must not be overlooked, for it stretched to the Imperial War Cabinet session of 1917. Among those who submitted memoranda on the matter were Robertson, Balfour and the Minister of Munitions, Edwin Montagu. Asquith also requested a memorandum from the Foreign Office, entrusted to Tyrrell and Sir Ralph Paget.[44] The first report to be submitted, on 29 August, was Montagu's. He was indifferent to the claims of Britain's allies and focussed on a 'Carthaginian peace' with Germany.[45] Two days later, Robertson circulated his memorandum. It suggested peace negotiations based upon three principles: the balance of power in Europe; the maintenance of British maritime superiority; and the preservation of a weak power in the Low Countries. It also recommended leaving Germany 'reasonably strong on land, but to weaken her at sea'. Austria-Hungary should be reduced but not dismantled, so as to counter-balance 'the power of Russia' on land, and to prevent the Mediterranean from becoming 'a French and Italian lake'. To that end, Vienna should be guaranteed possession of the Adriatic port of Fiume.[46] Balfour's report came in next, on 4 October. In order to achieve 'a durable peace', it sponsored 'the double method of diminishing the area from which the Central Powers control the men and money required for a policy of aggression, while at the same time rendering a policy of aggression less attractive by rearranging the map of Europe in close agreement with what we rather vaguely call the principle of nationality'.[47]

---

[43] Riccardi, *Alleati*, pp. 314–315, 332–333, 342–349, 404.

[44] Goldstein, *Winning the Peace*, p. 10.

[45] TNA, CAB29/1/P-3, The Problems of Peace, 29 August 1916.

[46] Ibid., CAB41/18/10, Robertson, General Staff Memorandum submitted in accordance with the Prime Minister's Instructions, 31 August 1916; CAB29/1/P-4, General Staff Memorandum Submitted in Accordance with the Prime Minister's Instructions, 31 August 1916.

[47] Ibid., CAB37/157/7, Memo by Balfour, 4 October 1916.

Although they did not make any specific reference to Asia Minor, these reports advocated a *divide et impera* (divide and rule) diplomatic strategy and discouraged any significant enlargement of Britain's allies. Neither did they mention any role for Italy beyond the Treaty of London. If anything, Balfour's insistence on the principle of nationality, if accepted as one of Britain's cardinal principles of peace-making, might even call that treaty into question. Neither Asquith nor Grey found any stimulus to involve Italy in the colonial question in such reports. In fact, the Foreign Minister was still waiting for the Foreign Office memorandum to be completed when Sonnino's requests for details multiplied. Although Grey denied it,[48] this might have further slowed Allied notification to Italy. Exasperated, Sonnino made a scene to Rodd on 9 September reminding him that it was Grey who had opposed a detailed wording on Italian colonial claims in the Treaty of London; and now he dropped all responsibilities. 'I did not expect all this, least of all from Grey, whom I had always tried to make the epicentre of all our most important negotiations with the Allies'. He concluded bluntly: 'I cannot accept on behalf of my country the part ... of inferiority and pupillage. Rather I shall leave my post telling my fellow countrymen that they can condemn me because I was lacking in prudence and in awareness, trusting in the loyalty and good faith ... of [the] Allied Governments'.[49] To placate Sonnino, Grey pushed France and Russia to share the colonial agreement with Rome on the grounds that '*la continuation de la ligne de conduite maintenant l'Italie dans l'oscurité, tend à créer une atmosphère malhereuse de froideur et de suspicion vis à vis des Alliés*'.[50] This caused him some criticism from his subordinates. George Grahame, a British official in Rome, found that the Foreign Minister was too sensitive to Italian theatrical displays.[51] Grey went one step further, promising to Imperiali: 'Either the agreements reached with France and Russia are consistent with what was agreed with Italy [in the London Treaty], which must be fully honoured, or they are not. If they are, there is nothing to discuss; if they are not, we shall discuss making them consistent'. Imperiali called it a 'clear and honest reply'.[52] This opening meant not only that the colonial agreement would soon be notified, but also that it was open to discussion. By making this overture to Italy, however, Grey unilaterally broke the Allied tripartite

---

[48] Rodd papers, Hardinge to Rodd, 5 September 1916.
[49] Ibid., Rodd to Hardinge, 9 September 1916; TNA, FO371/2780/179796, Hardinge to Crewe, 11 September 1916; Sonnino, *Diario*, II, pp. 37–40.
[50] ADMAEF, Guerre 1914–1918, Italie, vol. 571/109, British note to the French Government, 31 July 1916.
[51] BL, Bertie papers, ADD, MSS63043, f. 220, Grahame to Bertie, 29 September 1916.
[52] Imperiali, *Diario*, p. 311.

memorandum of April 1915, which denied any modification of Allied colonial arrangements. That of course led to renewed Franco-Russian opposition.[53] The inter-Allied clash continued throughout September, with Britain, France and Russia blaming each other before Italy for the ill-justified delay in the communication,[54] until Grey forced the Franco-Russian hand and delivered the articles of the Sykes–Picot Agreement to Imperiali in October.

Their contents infuriated Sonnino. By denying Italy any compensation additional to the province of Adalia, the other Allies had left a huge disproportion between their future possessions and Italy's. The principle of an 'equitable' Mediterranean equilibrium had remained words on a page.[55] Sonnino presented his own claims to the British Government, privately, on 18 October. They now included the Vilayets of Aidin and Konya, and since 'without Adana and the port of Mersin, the territory of Konya would have no value',[56] the latter provinces were also included. By 4 November, when the Italian terms were presented to France and Russia, Sonnino added Smyrna to the list because of its strategic location and the commercial ties it had with Italy.[57] If accepted, these claims would turn Italy from an Adriatic power with some Mediterranean bases into a fully-fledged Mediterranean power with its own colonial empire.[58] The Italian imperial project was now complete. Predictably, it produced strong recriminations in the Allied capitals. The French saw their suspicions come true, for the greater part of Sonnino's claims belonged to French-allotted territory. Russia had fresh objections: Sonnino's claim of Smyrna, which dominated the Dardanelles, now led to open Italo-Russian competition in the Eastern Mediterranean. Grey's reaction to the expanded Italian imperial project is one of the trickiest issues of the war. Officially, he protested the size of Sonnino's claims, but did not dismiss them.[59] In reality, he was very preoccupied for at least three reasons. First, the potential collapse of the Sykes–Picot Agreement would put its military implications, including Anglo-French coordination in support of the Arab revolt, back into question, with unpredictable consequences in the war. Second, Sonnino's claim of Smyrna conflicted with British designs in the Aegean, where Grey had begun to imagine a post-war regional settlement that could favour British war strategy.

---

[53] Riccardi, *Alleati*, pp. 314–315.   [54] Sonnino, *Diario*, II, p. 44.
[55] Riccardi, *Alleati*, pp. 344–345.
[56] DDI, 5, VI, doc. 572, Sonnino to Imperiali, Carlotti and Ruspoli, 16 October 1916.
[57] Ibid., doc. 400, Tittoni to Sonnino, 12 September 1916.
[58] Riccardi, *Alleati*, pp. 355–358.
[59] DDI, 5, VI, doc. 587, Imperiali to Sonnino, 19 October 1916; TNA, FO371/2780/ 190952 and 2780/229908, Grey to Rodd, 18 October and 14 November 1916.

Expecting the return to power of Venizelos in Greece – which would materialise in June 1917 – Grey planned to use Smyrna as 'exchange goods' to obtain Greek intervention on the side of the Entente; alternatively, Smyrna was to become the main port for the new Turkish state after the war. Finally, Italy's vast colonial claims would significantly alter the post-war settlement in the Mediterranean.[60] This led to unprecedented Anglo-Italian geopolitical competition. The last pillar of the Anglo-Italian alliance that had not yet been challenged by war events began to crumble.

This clash was exacerbated by Grey's lack of understanding for the unexpected Italian ambitions, as emerges from many confidential documents addressed to Rodd.[61] In particular, the Foreign Office insisted that Italy had no interest in either Mersin or Smyrna, so it could not understand their claim. A commercial tradition linking Smyrna to Italy did exist, but the fundamental problem here was that the Italians claimed Smyrna and Mersin *precisely* because their interests were not yet well established and Sonnino wished to widen them. Italy was fighting in World War I to become a genuine great power, and its ambitions turned towards those places, which offered the greatest commercial opportunities. From the Italian point of view, Mersin and Smyrna were of crucial economic interest for they were the opposite ends of the only trans-Anatolian railway: without them – or at least one of the two – any Italian ambitions in Asia Minor were devoid of meaning. For the British, and even more so for the French, such demands were both absurd and dangerous. Throughout October, Grey groped like a blind referee of a football match degenerated into a brawl. Truth was, Grey simply did not have a plan to respond to a steady increase in Italian colonial demands. His only option was an Allied colonial conference to be held by the end of the year. Both Paris and Petrograd, however, rejected the proposal. They blasted London for its decision to share the Sykes–Picot Agreement with Rome and to concede that it was open to revision, and held Grey responsible for the chaotic situation thus produced. They held that if Britain wished to satisfy Italy it would have to agree to compensations in the British Empire, as neither Paris nor Petrograd was ready to reduce its own claims in Asia Minor.[62]

In light of this reply, the new Italian Colonial Minister, Colosimo, elaborated an alternative proposal. Italy would surrender the largest part of its demands in Asia Minor except for Adalia; in turn, Rome

---

[60] Rodd papers, Hardinge to Rodd, 29 November 1916.
[61] Ibid., Hardinge to Rodd, 13 September 1916; 14 February, 17 April, 18 and 22 May 1917.
[62] Riccardi, *Alleati*, pp. 346–351.

would be granted compensations on the Tunisian-Libyan and Libyan-Egyptian borders, and in the Red Sea.[63] This shouldered the largest burden of Italian compensations onto the British Empire and was, of course, an indirect response to British policy of Italian containment in Africa. The proposal shocked the Foreign Office. The new permanent Under-Secretary, Charles Hardinge, former Viceroy and Governor-General of India, who had recently replaced Nicolson, wrote to Rodd that those Italians who believed Britain would repay Italy's services in the war with its own territories were misled:

We always regard with suspicion Italian contentions in the Red Sea … and we have no intention of allowing them [Italians] under any pretext to get over on to the Eastern coast. It was on account of the danger from Italian aspirations that we hoisted our flag … on some of the islands in the Red Sea off the coast of the Hedjaz. … Why should we be prevented from doing so by any agreement with Italy, who should be content with the considerable coast line now under her occupation on the western shore of the Red Sea. … It is clear that the Italians intend to open their mouths very wide.[64]

Upon British refusal, Sonnino returned to his Asia Minor scheme, and he instructed Imperiali to prepare the ground for the conference that Grey had proposed. The ambassador, however, came up against evasive or dilatory British responses throughout that autumn.[65] Grey was still trying to figure out what minor British concessions to make to Italy or, alternatively, what British concessions to make to France to have it indulge some Italian claims. To calm Italian nerves, Grey re-stated to Lord Cromer, in a letter copied to Rodd, his intention to cooperate with Rome: 'If Italy continues to fulfil her part in the war, she must have whatever has been promised to her when she entered the war'.[66]

The problem, however, was to define exactly the colonial promises to Italy, for the nebulous wording of articles 9 and 13 of the London Pact encouraged conflicting interpretations according to the distinct national interests of each Allied power. In autumn 1916, therefore, inter-Allied tensions, which until then had largely focussed on the issues of improving coordination and widening the Italian participation in the war, were developing into a more specific geopolitical competition. Unfortunately, just at the time when this new diplomatic confrontation was becoming

---

[63] CUL, Hardinge papers, 25, fs. 65 and 230, Rodd to Hardinge, 9 and 23 September 1916, quoted in J. Fisher, *Curzon and British Imperialism in the Middle East, 1916–1919* (London & Portland: Cass, 2005), pp. 66–67.

[64] Rodd papers, Hardinge to Rodd, 13 September 1916.

[65] Imperiali, *Diario*, pp. 298, 305, 309, 324.

[66] Rodd papers, Grey to Cromer, 5 October 1916.

tense, the cards of British domestic politics were shuffled in a new political storm: the crisis in Asquith's Government.

9.3   Change of the Guard and Diplomatic Stalemate

The collapse of Asquith was not unexpected. His Cabinet had sailed through troubled waters since the outbreak of the war with two reshuffles in summer 1914 and in autumn 1915, largely due to the ineffectual handling of the war – limited coordination of military operations on the most distant fronts, the shell crisis and the acquiescence of Asquith and Grey to Kitchener being obvious examples. Lloyd George had become the main critic of Asquith, and by early December 1916 openly threatened to overthrow him.[67] Asquith's attempts to keep the situation under control or to mediate with Lloyd George failed. On 5 December, he crossed to the opposition and remained leader of the Liberal Party, while the conservatives formed a Government under the leadership of Lloyd George – a liberal but backed by a minority of his liberal colleagues.[68] 'Lloyd George was thus a Prime Minister without a Party, while the Unionists were a party without their own Prime Minister' is David French's sardonic comment.[69]

Asquith's failure was one of strategy as well as war policy. His Cabinet had calculated that the war would reach its zenith in 1917. Britain should save its strength for that moment to win not only the war but also the peace:[70] 'The Asquith Coalition wagered that the Central Powers ... would sue for peace before Britain had gone bankrupt'. But the calculations were wrong. Military pressure on Germany had not been decisive, and Britain was bleeding financially as well as physically. By the time Lloyd George came to power, Britain's dependence on American funds and supplies was already evident. A memorandum by John Maynard Keynes, a key figure at the Treasury, which was circulated by Cecil (Under-Secretary for Foreign Affairs and Minister of Blockade) in the Cabinet on 6 November 1916 highlighted that 'of the £5,000,000 which the Treasury had to find daily for the prosecution of the war about 2 million had to be found in North America'.[71] Lansdowne on 13 November, defined as 'incalculable' the financial burden accumulated by Britain.[72] Keynes' conclusion was that 'if things go on as at present,

---

[67] Imperiali, *Diario*, p. 342.   [68] Stevenson, *1914–1918*, pp. 148–149; 269–271.
[69] French, *Strategy of Lloyd George*, p. 13.
[70] French, 'The Meaning of Attrition, 1914–1916', *English Historical Review*, CIII, 407, 1988, pp. 385–405.
[71] TNA, CAB42/23/7, Memorandum by R. Cecil, 6 November 1916.
[72] Ibid., 37/159/32, Memorandum by Lansdowne, 13 November 1916.

I venture to say with certainty that by next June or earlier the President of the American Republic will be in a position, if he wishes to dictate his own terms to us'.[73]

The fundamental aim of the new Government remained the same as its predecessor – to have Britain triumph as the dominant power in Europe. But, to do so, it would be necessary to change step.[74] Greater industrial, material and moral mobilisation, as well as government efficiency, was necessary. Lloyd George and Robertson, who detested each other,[75] agreed that the war would not be over in 1917, but in 1918 or later. If Britain did not rationalise resources, it would not survive. Lloyd George was critical not only of Asquith's war management; he was equally dissatisfied by the lack of coordination among the Allies, who were still pursuing 'a policy of drift'.[76] It was imperative to change that too. Focussing on theatres considered peripheral, Lloyd George thought, would favour Allied cooperation and could lead to victories that would soothe public opinion.[77] He later summarised the qualities he thought necessary of a 'Chief Minister of the Crown in a great war': courage, composure, judgement, vision, imagination and initiative, strengthened by 'continuous consultation with experts'.[78] There is little doubt that Lloyd George possessed many of such qualities. Born in 1863 to Welsh parents, he had nearly twenty-five years of political experience. He had served as President of the Board of Trade (1905–1908) and Chancellor of the Exchequer (1908–1915). Asquith had appointed him to the Munitions Ministry in May 1915, and to the War Office in the summer of 1916 when Kitchener died in a U-boat attack. His long experience had taught Lloyd George how to seize the day, how to extricate himself from troubled waters, when to accommodate associates and when to stand firm. At the Munitions Ministry, he revealed his energetic skills as an organiser, as well as his strong personality in confronting the military.[79] Lloyd George's activity at the War Office aggravated his arm-wrestling with the generals as well as with those politicians and journalists who supported direction of the war by the General Staff. In October 1916, Asquith asked Lloyd George to give his 'word of honour' that he had

[73] J. M. Keynes, The financial Dependence of the United Kingdom on the United States of America, 10 October 1916, in MLC, Keynes papers, JMK/T/14, Treasure official 1915–19: war finance. Papers concerning the state of Anglo-American relations, September 1916.
[74] French, Strategy of Lloyd George, pp. 5–6.
[75] C. Cross ed., Life with Lloyd George: The Diary of A. J. Sylvester, 1931–1945 (London: Macmillan, 1975), p. 80.
[76] Quoted in French, British Strategy, p. 91.
[77] French, Strategy of Lloyd George, pp. 7, 16.   [78] Lloyd George, Memoirs, I, p. 602.
[79] Grey, Twenty-Five Years, pp. 242–244.

'complete confidence' in Haig and Robertson and held them irreplace-able. It was untrue, but Lloyd George complied, revealing another quality that would serve him well in the future – namely the ability to tell people what they wanted to hear when he wished to avoid a head-on confrontation.[80] He would not give up completely, however. In November, Lloyd George reasserted his right to express his opinion on strategy,[81] and that became one of his main characteristics when he came to power.

To improve efficiency, Lloyd George chose only four other ministers to work alongside him in his new War Cabinet: three conservatives – Lord President of the Council and Leader of the House of Lords, Curzon; Chancellor of the Exchequer and Leader of the House of Commons, Andrew Bonar Law; and Minister without portfolio, Lord Milner – plus Arthur Henderson, the sole Labour representative.[82] The new Foreign Secretary, Balfour; the Foreign Under-Secretary, Hardinge; the Secretary of State for War, Edward Stanley (Lord Derby); and Sir Edward Carson, who replaced Balfour as First Lord of the Admiralty, would also often take part in Cabinet meetings in an advisory capacity. A secretariat was appointed under Maurice Hankey, to streamline Cabinet work.[83] Lloyd George hoped that this simplified structure would eliminate the delays and inefficiencies of Asquith's large Government. But it was impossible to remove differences of opinion, just as it was to curb internal rivalries, which would shake the War Cabinet. During 1917, several sub-committees were created to cope with the amount of work. In December 1916, however, Lloyd George was highly satisfied with the War Cabinet he had set up. Of course, Robertson did not agree. He considered Lloyd George an opportunist and the new members of the Cabinet 'quite as bad as the last lot'.[84]

The outcome of the government crisis had two major consequences in the Asia Minor question. First, it paralysed British diplomacy for nearly two months, leading to a stalemate in negotiations. Second, and more important as far as Italy was concerned, it led to the replacement of a group of statesmen and diplomats with whom the Italians had estab-lished strong political and personal ties. This process had begun with the replacement of Nicolson, usually pro-Italian, with Hardinge. With the

---

[80] American President Wilson later remembered: 'He [Lloyd George] is slippery as an eel, and I never know when to count on him': Burgwyn, *The Legend*, p. 230.
[81] Woodward, *Field-Marshal Sir William Robertson: Chief of the Imperial General Staff in the Great War* (Westport: Praeger, 1998), pp. 64–65, 71–72.
[82] French, *Strategy of Lloyd George*, p. 17.
[83] M. Hankey, *Government Control in War* (Cambridge: Cambridge University Press, 1945), pp. 41–42.
[84] French, *Strategy of Lloyd George*, p. 30; Stevenson, *1917*, p. 123.

departure of both Asquith and Grey in December, the British makers of the Anglo-Italian entente had gone. Not by chance, Imperiali predicted that Italy would find itself 'in a mess' when the British Cabinet changed. He mistrusted Lloyd George, and feared serious repercussions on foreign policy in the case of Grey's departure. In his diary, the Italian ambassador praised the honesty of the British minister, and described him as a friend of Italy.[85] One might conclude from the analysis of Anglo-Italian relations under Grey that the vision of Grey as pro-Italian is exaggerated. On one thing, however, Imperiali was right: despite inevitable and even significant differences, Italy could count on Grey as a man willing to listen and talk. The fact that Imperiali and Grey had worked together for so long was also important: they knew each other well and undoubtedly respected each other, which certainly helped their management of Anglo-Italian relations. So, despite the stormy moments they got through, Imperiali was moved when he visited Grey to say goodbye, and told him 'how difficult it is for me to separate myself from him'. The same applied to Asquith.[86]

Imperiali's preoccupation deepened when he heard that Balfour was to become Foreign Minister. The ambassador dismissed the news laconically: 'Can't understand it'.[87] Balfour was known to have a little-concealed contempt for Italians – although he was diffident and scornful of many British colleagues too, a *façon d'être* known as the 'Balfourian manner'. Harold Begbie, a journalist, described it as follows: 'This Balfourian manner ... has its roots in ... an attitude of convinced superiority which insists in the first place on complete detachment from the enthusiasms of the human race, and in the second place on keeping the vulgar world at arm's length'.[88] Curzon, who knew Balfour well, formed a bad opinion of him: 'His seeming indifference to petty matters, his power of dialectic, his long and honourable career of public service, blinded all but those who knew him from the inside to the lamentable ignorance, indifference and levity of his regime'.[89] But Lloyd George recognised Balfour's political value as a former premier, and his intellect and pliability.[90] Equally ill-disposed towards the Italians, whom he considered 'a most grasping and unreasonable people',[91] was Hardinge. Thanks to his energetic character, he soon became the most important personage at the Foreign Office after

[85] Imperiali, *Diario*, pp. 84, 342–343, 348.
[86] DDI, 5, VI, docs. 806 and 854, Imperiali to Sonnino, 7 and 16 December 1916.
[87] Imperiali, *Diario*, p. 345.
[88] H. Begbie (as A Gentleman with a Duster), *Mirrors of Downing Street: Some Political Reflections* (New York & London: Knicherboker, 1921), pp. 76–79.
[89] Quoted in MacMillan, *Peacemakers*, p. 425.
[90] French, *Strategy of Lloyd George*, p. 19.
[91] BL, British Embassy, Rome, Add. Ms. 63045, f. 37, Grahame to Bertie, 6 January 1917.

Balfour.[92] Unsurprisingly, Imperiali had never got on with him – he found Hardinge 'rigid and cold'.[93] The new Foreign Under-Secretary had been shaken by the attempt on his life in India in 1912 and by the sudden loss of his wife in 1914, followed by the death of his eldest son from war wounds. He had always tended to be imperious, and these experiences exaggerated this tendency. Furthermore, he was openly pro-Austrian: 'We have no desire to dismantle Austria-Hungary', he repeated, and he would be satisfied to see 'the Austrian Empire composed of autonomous states in personal union with the Emperor'.[94]

Another distinctive trait of the new British Cabinet was the increase in imperialists. The most ardent among them were Curzon and Milner. They believed that Britain's key objective should be to deprive Germany 'of those parts of the globe – France, Belgium, Syria, Palestine, Mesopotamia, South and East Africa, and the Pacific – where it could menace Britain's imperial communications'. These were the 'irreducible minima' required to safeguard 'Britain's own security'. On the other hand, the objectives of their allies – such as 'the national aspirations of the subject nationalities of the Austro-Hungarian Empire', including Italians, and the achievement 'of French aims in Alsace-Lorraine' – were secondary. Also Balfour, Cecil – who deputised for him – and Hardinge, though with different hues, put more emphasis on British desiderata in the Middle East.[95] They rejected Grey's tendency of giving his allies British concessions to bring them into line with British designs and reconcile their claims. Grey's colonial concessions to France, though they had paid off in the Sykes–Picot talks, marked a dangerous precedent for they encouraged the other allies to put forward claims in the British Empire itself. Instead, Britain should adopt a tough line and 'speak very strongly' on 'the final settlement of the Turkish question'[96] – which meant preventing both the French and the Italians from making any major gains in the region.

Altogether, such ideas marked a shift towards a more aggressive version of British security and defence policy. This tendency was already evident in the final months of Asquith's rule, but now it became predominant in the Cabinet – and found an eager ear in Lloyd George. Opposition by Lloyd George to the Second Boer War in 1900 has stimulated an assumption that he was not an imperialist. In reality, though usually critical of British imperial management, he was nonetheless a proud guardian of the

---

[92] Hinsley, *British Foreign Policy*, p. 525.   [93] Imperiali, *Diario*, p. 278.
[94] Hardinge MSS, vol. 25, Hardinge to Bertie, 15 September 1916.
[95] French, *Strategy of Lloyd George*, pp. 18–19, 64.
[96] TNA, CAB37/162/12, Memo by Cecil, 22 December 1916; Hardinge MSS, vol. 26, Hardinge to Rodd, 25 October 1916.

Empire.[97] His early thoughts on how to secure British priorities were widely influenced by Paget and Tyrrell's memorandum. This was the most important report thus far produced on the British approach to the setting of the post-war order. It had been circulated in Asquith's Cabinet shortly before its downfall, but had not been discussed.[98] Lloyd George found it 'an impressive document, well informed, bold and far-seeing'.[99] The memorandum's premise was that no peace settlement would be satisfactory to Britain unless 'it promises to be durable'. To that end, Paget and Tyrrell advocated 'the principle of nationality' as 'one of the governing factors in the consideration of territorial arrangements after the war' – provided that it was not pushed so far as 'unduly to strengthen any state, which is likely to be a cause of danger to European peace in the future'.[100] In view of the increased claims by Britain's allies – the reference to Asia Minor was patent – Paget and Tyrrell recommended that the British attitude 'should be guided by circumstances generally and British interests in particular'.[101] Tellingly, they made no reference to an Italian role in the colonies, and noted with concern Britain's commitment under the Treaty of London. The latter 'unfortunately constitutes a very distinct violation of the principle of nationality and there is consequentially no doubt that it involves the risk of producing the usual results, namely irredentism, and lack of stability and peace'.[102] Lloyd George agreed completely on this point. Paget and Tyrrell were confident that 'there is every prospect of the parties [Italy and the Austrian and Balkan minorities] reaching a satisfactory settlement by direct friendly negotiation', which was utterly untrue. As mentioned, Sonnino had no intention to re-discuss the London Treaty with either allies or enemy minorities. By unilaterally putting forward an option of voluntary revision of the Treaty, Paget and Tyrrell instilled in the British Cabinet a false expectation. Finally, Paget and Tyrrell were the first to preach a flexible diplomatic strategy that could be modified according to geopolitical and military developments.[103] The Foreign Office memorandum contained the embryo of principles that were to become key in the final British peace-making strategy. It reinforced the view that Britain should pursue a *divide et impera* policy; it also introduced the idea that the British diplomatic approach from now on should be ever more pragmatic, attentive of the realities of the war more than the agreements already made. Though not advocating a revision of either the London or the Sykes–Picot

---

[97] MacMillan, *Peacemakers*, p. 51.   [98] Goldstein, *Winning the Peace*, p. 10.
[99] Lloyd George, *The Truth*, I, p. 32.
[100] TNA, CAB29/1/P-5, quoted in Goldstein, *Winning the Peace*, pp. 11–12.
[101] Lloyd George, *The Truth*, I, pp. 37–41.   [102] Goldstein, *Winning the Peace*, p. 12.
[103] Lloyd George, *The Truth*, I, pp. 27–28, 37, 45.

pacts, Paget and Tyrrell's memorandum insinuated for the first time that Allied treaties were not unalterable – a voluntary amendment was possible and desirable.

Although unaware of all this, Imperiali foresaw increasing difficulties for Italy in the Asia Minor dossier, when negotiations resumed. He telegraphed Sonnino that, with Lloyd George, Balfour and Hardinge now in power, he feared finding himself 'one against three'.[104] Imperiali formed a slightly different opinion of Lloyd George when they met for the first time on 23 December. Imperiali was positively impressed by Lloyd George's interest in fronts beyond Flanders. In particular, the British premier wished to strengthen cooperation with Italy: he proposed an Anglo-French-Italian naval conference to better coordinate action in the Mediterranean, a meeting with Sonnino, and a common solution for the still unresolved Greek question. He did not talk of Asia Minor though, which made Imperiali suspicious.[105] A few days later, on 2 January, Imperiali tested him: 'What matters to me above all ... is to see a close and constant contact established between Rome and London on the basis of common interests – to my mind the best, and perhaps the only, remedy to halt the intrusiveness of the French'. The reference to Asia Minor was clear, but Lloyd George let it drop diplomatically with a smile. Imperiali's conclusion was that Lloyd George did intend to strengthen Anglo-Italian collaboration, but that he would leave management of the Asia Minor negotiation to the anti-Italian Balfour-Hardinge duo. Lloyd George had other priorities: turning the strategies of the individual Entente powers into a more coherent Allied grand strategy. It was only as part of this renewed Allied cooperation, not as an independent diplomatic question as Imperiali and Sonnino wanted, that Asia Minor would be discussed.[106]

---

[104] Imperiali, *Diario*, p. 348.
[105] DDI, 5, VI, docs. 892, 893 and 894, Imperiali to Sonnino, 23 December 1916.
[106] Imperiali, *Diario*, pp. 343–349, 355.

10 Shaping Allied Grand Strategy

10.1 New Strategic Options for 1917

In January 1917 Lloyd George's intuition to shift the focus of the Allies from the western front to minor theatres in order to circumvent the seemingly insuperable German defences in the west, took a more concrete form by defining three new priorities: winning the war in the Middle East, breaking Austria-Hungary in Italy and restoring Russian morale and material strength so that it could regain the initiative in the east and distract German reserves from the other theatres. If successful, this plan would eliminate Germany's main allies, Constantinople and Vienna, and force Berlin to sue for peace.[1] To Lloyd George, it seemed more promising than the usual plan to launch synchronised offensives on the individual Allied fronts, which had been confirmed at a further Chantilly Conference in November 1916.[2] However, involving Italy and Russia in Lloyd George's grand strategy was far from straightforward. The British premier tried to do this by organising two Allied conferences in Rome and Petrograd.

Lloyd George's attention was drawn to the Italian front by Charles Delmé-Radcliffe, the British military attaché in Rome, who suggested that the Italians would welcome direct Allied support in their advance towards Trieste.[3] Furthermore, a visit to Rome would enable new members of the British Cabinet to meet with their Italian counterparts, especially Sonnino, who was generally hostile to meetings abroad because the Italian political situation impeded long stays away from the capital. The Rome Conference (5–7 January), was presided over by Boselli, but Lloyd George took the lead in the talks. He proposed an Allied offensive on the

---

[1] TNA, CAB28/2/IC15a, Lloyd George, memorandum circulated by the Prime Minister to the delegates, 5 January 1917.
[2] Stevenson, *1917*, p. 6.
[3] TNA, CAB42/19/2, Hankey to Lloyd George, 8 December 1916.

Isonzo to be launched by the bulk of the Italian army supported by Anglo-French troops transferred from the west. Not surprisingly, the French mounted a fierce opposition. Robertson and Haigh also opposed the plan from the onset, both unwilling to divert their forces towards peripheral fronts.[4] In contrast, Cadorna welcomed the proposal.[5] Yet Sonnino feared that the Anglo-French allies would take all the credit for a victory in Italy, so he instructed the Italian delegates to take a 'passive' line.[6] Without Sonnino's support, Cadorna too pulled back. Lloyd George's proposal gradually lost ground until it fizzled out.[7] Lloyd George's setback was partly compensated for by an unprecedented Allied convergence on the Greek question although it was a secondary object of the conference. Throughout the autumn of 1916 Anglo-French pressure on Athens to enter the war in exchange for territorial gains in Asia Minor had increased,[8] leading to the landing of a small Allied contingent at Piraeus on 1 December. The attempt to force Constantine's hand had failed when the Allied troops had faced the Greek regular army, and had been compelled to evacuate.[9] The Italians had protested against Anglo-French intrusions in Greek affairs, and remained resolutely in support of the King against Venizelos, an 'astute and turbulent character', in Imperiali's words.[10] The other Allies however, considered Venizelos 'a staunch friend' of the Allied cause.[11] Lloyd George later called him 'the greatest Greek statesman since Pericles'.[12] By contrast, Hardinge described Constantine in venomous terms:

Those dirty Greeks appear to be playing their usual dirty game, and ... Elliot [British ambassador to Greece] is sending me correspondence that has been intercepted between Tino [Constantine] and the German Military Attaché, which ... proves conclusively that the King is involved in the plot against the Allies by which the Bulgarians and the Turks take over the whole of Greece.[13]

In Rome the French demanded stronger action against Constantine, giving a free hand to the French (and Allied) commander at Salonika, Maurice Serrail. This proposal raised British suspicions that the French

[4] Riccardi, *Alleati*, pp. 382–386.
[5] DDI, 5, VII, doc. 113, Cadorna to Sonnino, 17 January 1917.
[6] Orlando, *Memorie*, pp. 97–103.
[7] Sonnino, *Diario*, III, pp. 98 ff; C. Seton-Watson called it 'the greatest Italian mistake in the whole war': *Storia d'Italia*, p. 533.
[8] See an anonymous note in: ADMAEF, Guerre 1914–1918, Dossier Général, vol. 991/ 31–34.
[9] G. B. Leon, *Greece and the Great Powers, 1914–1917* (Thessaloniki: Institute for Balkan Studies, 1974), pp. 400–411, 434.
[10] DDI, 5, VI, doc. 364, Imperiali to Sonnino, 1 September 1916.
[11] Grey, *Twenty-Five Years*, p. 173.   [12] Quoted in MacMillan, *Peacemakers*, p. 364.
[13] Rodd papers, Hardinge to Rodd, 23 August 1916.

Figure 10.1 The British ambassador to Italy, Rennell Rodd, with David Lloyd George in Rome during the inter-Allied Conference of 5–7 January 1917

planned to establish their own influence in the region and turn Greece into their preferential ally in the Eastern Mediterranean. So, although they disagreed on the Venizelos issue, Lloyd George and Sonnino joined forces and managed to push the French to agree on a common Entente note for the Greek Government. It stated that the Allies were determined to protect their armies at Salonika, which now numbered 150,000 men and included the Italian 35th division, against the menace posed by Greek forces in their rear.[14] This could be done only if such forces were transported to the Peloponnese as soon as possible. If the

---

[14] G. Menoni, 'La Campagna di Macedonia 1916–1918', *Storia Militare*, 33, June 1996, p. 22; G. B. Leontaritis, *Greece and the First World War* (Boulder: East European Monographs, 1990), pp. 332–334.

Greek Government had not responded to the Allied note within 48 hours of its receipt, the Allies would assume full liberty to safeguard their armies by other means.[15] This ultimatum managed to put pressure on Constantine without reaching a breaking point and without bowing to Venizelos. To Imperiali it seemed to be 'a triumph of our own thesis'.[16] It did not bring about a solution of the Greek question – Greece remained firmly neutral – but it did bring Italy and its allies back together on the matter and offered proof of the Allied potential for properly coordinated war diplomacy.[17] The British premier was satisfied with the result.[18] On 10 January, back in London, Lloyd George informed Imperiali of the excellent impression Sonnino had made on him: 'Tenacious, pertinacious, but you know at once where you are with him'. Lloyd George's praises were echoed in the British press, especially the *Observer*, which defined Sonnino as 'the most cool and most firm of the European statesmen', in whom British public opinion placed complete trust. Imperiali commented: 'Fine, but [Lloyd George] seemed to me somewhat disappointed by the difficulties set up by our "Mars" [Cadorna] to the implementation of Lloyd George's preferred plan that is the offensive on our front!'[19] The aversion to Cadorna would remain strong in the British Prime Minister: 'Cadorna's lukewarmness was fatal', he repeated.[20] In reality, the figure mainly responsible for the failure of his plan was Sonnino, precisely the person who had made the best impression on him.

Lloyd George's satisfaction with the outcome of the Rome Conference cannot hide his failure to change the traditional lines of Entente strategy. This was confirmed by the subsequent conference in Petrograd at the end of January. Called, once again, on Britain's initiative, its aim was to deal with the growing crisis in Tsarist Russia. The country was on the brink of revolution and the Allies' priority here was to prevent it. Milner, Gastone Doumergue, the French Colonial Minister, and Vittorio Scialoja, Minister without portfolio in the Italian Cabinet, led the respective delegations. They arrived in Petrograd on 29 January, where they formed committees to address each specific problem – political, economic and military.[21] Formal meetings started on 1 February and continued until the 20th. Between meetings, the delegates travelled around trying to gain a first-hand impression of Russia's conditions. They found the country in a

[15] Lloyd George, *Memoirs*, I, p. 857.   [16] Imperiali, *Diario*, p. 359.
[17] ADMAEF, Guerre 1914–1918, Italie, vol. 574/123–125, Barrère to Briand, 29 January 1917.
[18] Lloyd George, *Memoirs*, I, p. 858.   [19] Imperiali, *Diario*, p. 358.
[20] Lloyd George, *Memoirs*, I, p. 858.
[21] G. Petracchi, *Diplomazia di guerra e rivoluzione. Italia e Russia dall'ottobre 1916 al maggio 1917* (Bologna: Il Mulino, 1974), pp. 57–88, 393.

deplorable state of disorganisation, muddle and disorder, 'rent with faction, permeated with German propaganda and espionage, eaten up with corruption'.[22] Russia was suffering from what Stevenson termed a 'double blockade' as Germany barred the Baltic Sea and Turkey the Dardanelles, and from an unprecedented crisis in grain production.[23] Its army was not broken yet, but the defeats suffered by Romania in November and December 1916 added a burden to the Russian army, which it simply could not manage.[24] Russian commanders were already delaying their participation in the new Chantilly offensives, claiming that any expectation of a Russian contribution earlier than May was unrealistic.[25]

The Petrograd Conference proved a race against the odds. The British decided to establish a mission in Russia to accelerate the weapons' supply;[26] but they refused to assume onerous financial burdens – which was what the Russians most wanted. London was suspicious of how the Russians would use Allied resources.[27] To avoid a dead end, the Russians suggested that the conference delegates at Petrograd should form a permanent Allied commission to deal with Allied cooperation.[28] This would give them more time to press their case for aid; it would also create an unprecedented political integration. Doumergue found the Russian suggestion very interesting and proposed a wider commission of delegates from each Allied Government, a sort of Allied coordinating body.[29] The Italians objected that a rigid structure for political and diplomatic direction would complicate matters, rather than simplify them. Though privately they agreed that greater integration within the Entente was necessary, they had no instructions from Sonnino regarding Allied coordinating bodies and suspected that the Foreign Minister would disapprove of any initiatives on the matter. Once again, the Allies agreed that their collaboration was inadequate, but they diverged over a possible solution.[30] As on previous occasions, London tried to reconcile the French and Italian positions. The British delegates, at Italy's request, approved a watered-down version of the French proposal, according to which meetings 'would be held at any time and period which appear convenient', but without making them 'too numerous to be effective'.[31]

---

[22] Lloyd George, *Memoirs*, I, p. 932.   [23] Stevenson, *1917*, pp. 92–93.

[24] TNA, WO106/1088, Knox despatch, 31 March 1917.

[25] Ibid., CAB28/2, War Cabinet session of 7–20 February 1917.

[26] Ibid., CAB23/1 War Cabinet 57, War Cabinet minutes, 6 February 1917.

[27] DDI, 5, VII, doc. 198, Carlotti to Sonnino, 1 February 1917.

[28] Ibid., doc. 237, Carlotti and Scialoja to Sonnino, 6 February 1917.

[29] Aldrovandi Marescotti, *Guerra diplomatica: ricordi e frammenti di diario* (Milan: Mondadori, 1938), pp. 91–100.

[30] Riccardi, *Alleati*, p. 396.

[31] DDI, 5, VII, doc. 300, Carlotti and Scialoja to Sonnino, 15 February 1917.

It proved little more than a rhetorical solution.[32] Thus the conference – the last one in which the Tsar's Government participated – produced little practical effect.

The consequence of this became clear in early March (late February according to the Russian calendar) when food riots, demonstrations and a mutiny at the Petrograd garrison forced Nicholas II to abdicate on the 15th. A Provisional Government was formed, supported by liberals and moderate socialists. It pledged to continue to fight alongside the Allies but renewed its request for greater Allied support. The other Allies agreed in principle. Real power in Russia after the February Revolution, however, lay with the socialist leaders of the Petrograd Soviet of Workers' and Soldiers' Deputies, who were elected by popular mandate – unlike the ministers of the Provisional Government. They openly supported a separate peace and promoted a strong anti-war propaganda 'both in the Duma and in the army'.[33] Following the situation with apprehension, Luigi Aldrovandi Marescotti, an aide to Sonnino concluded that, unless some unforeseeable development intervened, Russia would no longer play an active role in the war.[34]

10.2   Peak of Imperialist Clash

The embarrassing stalemate over Allied grand strategy spurred Lloyd George to look for a solution to the colonial question, hoping that this would ease Allied collaboration, and especially soften Italy, which had proved unreceptive to his proposals. Negotiations to address Italian colonial claims began on 29 January in London and lasted through mid-March, presided over by Balfour.

Balfour adopted a more ambitious scheme aimed at guarding against potential alteration of the Sykes–Picot Agreement by strengthening British influence in the Eastern Mediterranean. The progressive weakness of the Russian diplomatic stance was accompanied by a growing influence of the French in the Middle East, as a consequence of their decision to join the Palestinian campaign. This had been discussed during the Sykes–Picot talks, but now that it was about to become a reality it spurred British anxieties that the French may want to 'put a finger in any Palestinian pie that might be baking'.[35] They must be kept at bay. As for the Italians, Grahame advised London not to be 'bluffed' into making exaggerated concessions in Asia Minor by the devious bargaining tactics of 'Southern

---

[32] ADMAEF, Guerre 1914–1918, Dossier Général, vol. 992/105, Paléologue to Briand, n.d.
[33] DDI, 5, VII, doc. 504, Porro (Romei) to Sonnino, 18 March 1917.
[34] Riccardi, *Alleati*, p. 437.   [35] Lloyd George, *Memoirs*, II, p. 1084.

peoples'.[36] Balfour needed no encouragement, and was determined that any Italian gains in the region should be satisfied at the expense of the French – so as to counter-balance potential increase of French influence elsewhere. The cherry on top of Balfour's colonial cake was his secret design to take Smyrna under British influence. Thus, London would be able to control the Russians at Constantinople, the Italians in Southern Anatolia and the French in Eastern Anatolia, reaffirming British predominance in the Near East. Balfour's justification for this open violation of the Sykes–Picot Agreement was the solid economic interests the British already had in the Smyrna region, above all the Smyrna–Aidin railway that had been constructed by a British company and whose stocks the Italians had tried unsuccessfully to buy.[37] For Balfour's plan to become a reality, Italian ambitions on Smyrna had to be removed, as Hardinge explained to Rodd:

> My own feeling is very strong on the subject of Smyrna, which, in my opinion, we ought under no circumstance whatsoever to cede to Italian exigencies. They have no interests at all there, while ours are of the greatest importance, and in the zone that has now been delimited for them all important foreign interests are purely British.[38]

This shift in British ambitions in Asia Minor[39] has usually been unheeded but is important because it re-shaped Allied colonial talks and contributed significantly to drag on the imbroglio. It also epitomises the British tendency to pit London's allies-rivals against one another in order to preserve its own supremacy. Rome too changed its diplomatic approach at the London Colonial Conference. Whereas Sonnino's earlier policy had been to seek a general agreement that integrated Italy's claims with the colonial pacts of the other allies, this time he aimed at winning over British support as a preliminary step to a new arrangement that could subsequently be imposed on the Russians and the French. He instructed Imperiali, representing Italy at the conference, to manoeuvre so as to break the Anglo-French axis and make the Anglo-Italian entente the catalyst of Allied colonial agreements. However, Balfour's scheme made Britain as tough as France towards Italian imperial designs, so Imperiali looked for decisive support where he was going to find firm opposition. Given his orders to take an 'inflexible' line regarding Italy's ambitions,[40] negotiations looked set for a head-on collision.

---

[36] BL, ADD, MSS 63045, f. 37, Grahame to Bertie, *cit.*
[37] Petricioli, *L'Italia*, pp. 361 ff.   [38] Rodd papers, Hardinge to Rodd, 7 March 1917.
[39] Despite the opposition of Drummond, the British line on Smyrna was reinforced by Lord Drogheda: TNA, FO371/3043/12848, Memorandum by Lord Drogheda, 'Italy and the partition of the Turkish empire', 17 January 1917.
[40] DDI, 5, VII, doc. 118, Imperiali to Sonnino, 18 January 1917.

In the first session of the conference, on 29 January, Cambon, the French delegate, presented a Franco-Russian scheme, which slightly extended Italian gains from Adalia towards Konya, without however including Konya itself, Mersin, Adana or Smyrna.[41] Imperiali undertook to demolish the arguments put forward by the Russians and French and 'with some energy' opposed their objections on Smyrna.[42] Balfour remained *super partes*. He did not deny Italy's rights to 'equitable compensations', but he did not wish to 'breach understandings already in place with France'.[43] Balfour proposed a report be prepared by Mallet – former British ambassador to Constantinople – on the 'real' value of the areas offered to Italy and France so as to determine the size of each power's gains. Thus, he tried to turn an Allied negotiation into a bilateral Italo-French confrontation, with Britain acting as arbitrator. He also astutely evaded any reference to Smyrna. Imperiali received Balfour's proposal coldly and, though not rejecting it, declared that he would not feel bound by any result that came out of Mallet's report.[44] In the following days, Imperiali tried to knit together some personal contacts to prepare the ground for the next conference session. To establish an Anglo-Italian deal, he visited Lloyd George on 9 February, in an attempt to by-pass Balfour. He was disappointed. The British premier considered that prolonged discussions on Asia Minor could, in the end, 'be academic if, at a certain point, the Allies should not become masters of the territories to be taken from Turkish domination'.[45] Lloyd George encouraged Imperiali to accept whatever came out of Mallet's report, so as to restore Allied solidarity and concentrate on Lloyd George's priority: Allied cooperation to win the war. There would be time, when victory was gained, to discuss the post-war order in more detail, maybe re-adjusting the colonial arrangements. Sonnino thought the opposite: his priority remained to have Italian claims solemnly recognised, so as to avoid nasty surprises at the Peace Conference, and urged Britain to 'remove … the French and Russian objections to our requests'.[46]

Behind what seemed a personality clash lay a profound methodological difference. Lloyd George adopted as flexible a diplomatic approach as possible, prioritising what he considered Allied strategic necessities. He was inspired by the reports of the committees established to formulate an

[41] Riccardi, *Alleati*, pp. 403–406.
[42] DDI, 5, VII, doc. 179, Imperiali to Sonnino, 30 January 1917.
[43] N. M. Toraldo-Serra, *Diplomazia dell'imperialismo e questione orientale: la spartizione dell'impero ottomano e la nascita del problema palestinese, 1914–1922* (Rome: Bulzoni, 1988), pp. 67–72.
[44] Riccardi, *Alleati*, p. 404.
[45] DDI, 5, VII, doc. 263, Imperiali to Sonnino, 9 February 1917.
[46] Ibid., doc. 273, Sonnino to Imperiali, 11 February 1917.

early peace-making strategy, which stressed the need to look beyond paper agreements and to define the guiding principles to be followed in order to secure British interests – leaving it to the Prime Minister to reconcile these proposals when they were incoherent and to harmonise them with war strategy. No such committees were established in Italy to aid Sonnino develop a more flexible diplomatic line and to consider new options in negotiations. Sonnino remained convinced that Italy's interests would be secured by establishing detailed pacts in wartime that made peace negotiations at the end of the war as smooth and straight as possible – almost irrelevant, in fact, as far as Italy was concerned; military considerations and strategic planning fell beyond his preoccupations. On the contrary, Lloyd George understood that any treaty would count little if it became incompatible with the overall military and geopolitical situation. For him, the colonial agreement was not an end, but a means to reconcile Allied strategy and achieve victory. To Sonnino's credit, it must be remembered that he was not the Italian premier. It was Boselli who should harmonise Italian strategy and diplomacy and coordinate with the other allies. But like Salandra, he tended to avoid head-on confrontations with Sonnino – and with Cadorna, who was equally opposed to any commingling of military and political issues.[47]

Military-civilian arm-wrestling over the war's direction was frequent in all belligerent countries. The Italian anomaly was the exceptional influence of Sonnino, a Foreign Minister who enjoyed more authority than the premier, and who was extremely jealous of his responsibilities. Throughout the winter, Sonnino opposed any attempt by Boselli to pursue a broader diplomatic strategy through a new Ministry of Propaganda, entrusted to Scialoja. Boselli's move originated from reiterated pressure by De Martino and Ojetti, who revealed that French and British propaganda had contributed 'almost as much as that of the Central Powers' to eclipsing Italy's role in the war. The persistent lack of a 'narrative' of the Italian war, which presented Italian claims as legitimate compensations for Italy's sacrifices, exacerbated Rome's isolation on the colonial question.[48] Sonnino's hostility was a 'formidable hurdle', though the inadequate funds made available to the new ministry – less than two million lire in the whole of 1917 – proved just as detrimental.[49] Whilst Italian propaganda remained insufficient, Italian

---

[47] Mondini, *Il Capo*, pp. 260–268.
[48] ASSR, Senato del Regno, Legislatura XXIV, Discussioni, Tornata del 4 luglio 1916, pp. 2590–2591; ASMAE, Carte Italia, 1916–1918, b. 111, f. 1152.
[49] ASCD, Relazione della Commissione d'Inchiesta sulle spese di Guerra, doc. XXI della Camera dei Deputati, XXVI Legislatura, vol. I, 52, pp. 85–87; Tosi, *Propaganda*, pp. 57, 69, 84.

nationalists accused Britain and France of being 'indifferent' to the needs of Italy, 'the Mediterranean convict'. Senator Leopoldo Franchetti, with the tacit support of the Colonial Minister, Colosimo, began a noisy campaign calling Asia Minor the 'natural outlet' of Italian colonialism. He provided Boselli and Sonnino with a memorandum signed by 3,000 Italian politicians and intellectuals, which nailed down what the Italian war aims should be according to the signatories: Trento, Trieste, Istria, Dalmatia, the 'exclusive domination of the Adriatic', Djibouti, an Ethiopian protectorate, an extension of the Libyan borders, and Southern Anatolia from Smyrna to Alexandretta. The Italian nationalist Luigi Federzoni called it 'the fundamental chart of our rights in the Adriatic and Mediterranean'.[50] Whereas in Britain an inclination had emerged in favour of reducing Italian gains, in Italy the Government was pressed to widen them.

On 12 February, the Entente delegates met again. Balfour presented Mallet's report: the main Italian claims, Smyrna and Mersin, were 'not even mentioned'. Instead, Italy would get the whole Konya district, and minor portions of the Adana region removed from the French zone.[51] Imperiali refused even 'to enter the discussion' on such a basis. Balfour asked: 'If you do not want to discuss the matter, why the meeting?' Imperiali replied politely, but firmly, that he would not accept such an unfair treatment of Italy. Balfour appeared irritated. 'I shall telegraph Rodd', he said. 'Telegraph by all means', replied Imperiali. In his diary, the ambassador regretted the 'bad mood' at the end of the session.[52] An equally bitter note ran through Hardinge's letter informing Rodd:

The Conference of Ambassadors on the Asia Minor question is making no progress whatever. ... Imperiali has only one argument, and that is that the Italian Government were so badly treated in the agreement having been made behind their backs in 1915, that it is necessary for the Powers to give Italy material compensation for this apparent slight. On the other hand, the demands of Italy are perfectly fantastic. Italy has not fired a single shot against the Turks anywhere. ... Why Italy should claim more than others is beyond my comprehension.[53]

Together with Hardinge's criticism of Italy came Balfour's blame of Imperiali, who was considered less and less cooperative. In reality, the ambassador was not assuming a personal position but was simply following Sonnino's strict instructions – without any great enthusiasm.[54] At the same time, though, Imperiali was offended by the aloofness of Balfour

---

[50] C. Seton-Watson, *Storia d'Italia*, p. 181.
[51] DDI, 5, VII, doc. 325, Drummond to Imperiali, 17 February 1917.
[52] Imperiali, *Diario*, pp. 360–370.
[53] Rodd papers, Hardinge to Rodd, 14 February 1917.
[54] Toscano, *Gli Accordi*, p. 218.

and Hardinge whose barely concealed contempt for Italians emerged quite clearly in such situations and whose 'indecisive and snooty attitude tries my patience dearly'. On the 19th, the atmosphere was almost unbearable. Imperiali commented: 'Balfour ... avoids me. ... In this way we are reaching breaking-point'. Imperiali felt badly upset, as he could not understand why London was so stubborn in resisting Italian 'legitimate' aspirations: 'Here they are incomprehensibly blind. They had such a wonderful chance to consolidate Italy's friendship and they stupidly let it go. I regret Grey's departure'.[55]

The next day, Imperiali received Sonnino's comments on Mallet's report. The Italian minister re-stated his claims to Adana, Smyrna and Mersin, stressing that 'before parliament and the country my position has become extremely distressful and difficult due to the behaviour of the Allied Governments'.[56] The ambassador replied proposing a new scheme maintaining uncompromising attitude on Smyrna and accepting greater flexibility on other claims.[57] In turn, Sonnino urged the ambassador to make an attempt to talk privately with the British. He suggested trying Lloyd George as a possible ally,[58] but Sonnino ignored that Imperiali had already played that card on his own initiative. The ambassador felt powerless and was rather irritated also with Sonnino, who 'first gives me that hateful part to play and now wants me to make this up and in all this does not let me understand fully what his real thoughts are'. It took 'the patience of a saint to understand the blessed man'.[59] Eventually, Sonnino accepted Imperiali's suggestion, making Smyrna Italy's priority.[60] Imperiali submitted a memorandum on the revised Italian claims to Balfour on 1 March.[61] Unfortunately, Smyrna was the very claim Balfour was not ready to give up. So, where Imperiali was confident that he had by-passed French opposition by accepting a compromise on Adana and Mersin he now ran into a firmer – and unexpected – British veto. Balfour's reply came on 14 March and was essentially a replica of Mallet's proposal, which Balfour claimed was 'fair'. Imperiali snubbed him: 'You are completely wrong'. 'But you are asking too much claiming Smyrna and Mersin', retorted Balfour. 'And you', insisted Imperiali, 'have excluded both. How can we talk on this basis? Without Smyrna there is no point'. Shortly after this meeting, Imperiali warned Lloyd George: 'If Asia Minor is not settled, Sonnino will go'. The Prime

---

[55] Imperiali, *Diario*, pp. 370–373.
[56] DDI, 5, VII, doc. 337, Sonnino to Imperiali, 20 February 1917.
[57] Ibid., doc. 337, Imperiali to Sonnino, 20 February 1917.
[58] Ibid., doc. 355, Sonnino to Imperiali, 23 February 1917.
[59] Imperiali, *Diario*, p. 375.   [60] Riccardi, *Alleati*, p. 410.
[61] DDI, 5, VII, doc. 395, Sonnino to Imperiali, 1 March 1917.

Minister replied: 'That would be fatal!' Imperiali rebutted: 'It depends on you'.[62]

In the days that followed, talks increased mutual recriminations. In the end both Balfour and Sonnino concluded, in agreement with the French and Russian delegates, that no significant changes were in sight[63] – better to take a break than risk breaking up. The curtain was brought down on the London Colonial Conference, which marked the peak of inter-Allied diplomatic clashes in 1917. Imperiali did not hide his concern that the awful outcome of the discussion would 'leave behind it bitterness and resentment'.[64]

10.3   Ships, Torpedoes and Blockades

Although Lloyd George's attempt to cement political and land coordination in the Entente fell far behind his expectations at the beginning of 1917, the British premier was confident that he could achieve better results in the maritime and economic spheres. He sponsored an Allied naval conference in London in January, which he again left to specialists. The meeting was much needed in view of the inefficient Allied coordination against enemy submarines, especially in the Mediterranean. Thanks to the faults of the Otranto barrage, by the end of 1916, submarine warfare had extended throughout the Mediterranean.[65] It became critical in January 1917 when Germany revived its unrestricted U-boat campaign, which had been interrupted in May 1915 to appease Washington after 123 Americans had died in the sinking of the RMS *Lusitania*.[66]

By resuming unrestricted submarine warfare, the Germans deliberately risked involving the United States in the conflict – American intervention would indeed follow on 6 April – but they had calculated that the economies of the Allied nations would collapse before the Americans could play any significant part in the war. German and Austro-Hungarian U-boat flotillas were now stronger in numbers and quality and tended to use the deadly torpedo weapon – where previously they had often used submarine guns to attack enemy vessels. The U-boats became the main threat to the vital Allied trade routes, and to the lines of communication with Allied expeditionary forces abroad. They were expected to raise the average monthly sinkings from 400,000 to 600,000 tonnes and to frighten off at least half the neutral vessels. It was a defensive and counter-offensive strategy at once, which applied a counter-blockade to the Allies. Admiral

[62] Imperiali, *Diario*, pp. 380, 386.
[63] DDI, 5, VII, doc. 481, Imperiali to Sonnino, 15 March 1917.
[64] Imperiali, *Diario*, p. 372.   [65] Limpus MSS, Thursby to Limpus, 20 May 1916.
[66] Stevenson, *1917*, pp. 21–27.

Figure 10.2 British Field-Marshal Sir Douglas Haig, with Sir George Dixon Grahame and Admiral David Beatty

David Beatty, who replaced John Jellicoe as the Commander of the Grand Fleet when the latter became First Sea Lord at the end of 1916, recognised that the rules of the game at sea had changed. Whereas in 1915–1916 British priorities had been to support the Grand Fleet against the German High Seas Fleet and equip the BEF, now 'the real crux lies in whether we blockade the enemy to his knees, or whether he does the same to us'.[67] Thus, an Allied priority was to re-formulate their anti-submarine strategy and to strengthen as much as possible their own blockade on the Central Powers.

In the Mediterranean, this meant finding a comprehensive strategy that addressed both the deficiencies of the Otranto line and the defence of the Mediterranean trade routes.[68] As usual, France, Italy and Britain had different views on how to do this. The French proposed shifting the Otranto line northwards to reduce the space of manoeuvre for the U-boats

[67] J. H. Morrow, *The Great War: An Imperial History* (London: Routledge, 2005), p. 202.
[68] Halpern, *Royal Navy*, pp. 65 ff.

based at Cattaro, but the British and the Italians considered the proposal too risky.[69] Instead, the Italians proposed an extensive fixed barrage at Otranto.[70] The British were equally unhappy with this, as they had little faith in fixed obstacles and favoured a mobile barrage based on drifters. They were further preoccupied that the British mission in the Adriatic lacked a clear aim, and was left there, in the words of a ship's lieutenant, 'to buck-up the Anglo-Italian Alliance'. In the spring of 1916, Rear-Admiral Mark Kerr, who replaced Thursby as the Commander of the British Adriatic Squadron, was frustrated at having 'no executive work or command to do'.[71] The poor results of the barrage convinced him that the British battleships in Taranto could be better used elsewhere.[72]

At the January 1917 naval conference the French, happy to reduce the number of ships under Italian command, supported the British. Ferdinand De Bon (French Chief of Naval Staff) argued that 'the presence of the English battleships had an object which no longer exists, for the hypothesis of a big general engagement is now most improbable'. The Italian Navy Minister, Camillo Corsi, consented only as far as the British battleships were replaced by British anti-submarine light craft. Admiral John Kelly, the British delegate, asked: 'Do you not think that you have all the forces you need in the Mediterranean with two fleets?' Jellicoe, who presided over the conference, was more explicit: 'With the French fleet at Corfu is not the Adriatic perfectly secure?' Corsi replied that the Italians had lost five ships in the early phases of the campaign, and that their light craft were already stretched to the limit escorting troops to Salonika: the Adriatic was not as secure as his allies believed.[73]

Such differences emerged from the divergent strategic views of the scope of the Adriatic campaign. The Italian Naval Staff had become convinced that it would be a long war of attrition, which mirrored the land operations, and that the Allies needed to invest massive human, financial and material resources. The Italians saw the Adriatic as the main front in the Mediterranean, because it was the base of both Austro-Hungarian and German Mediterranean forces. The other allies now tended to see the rest of the Mediterranean as the real battlefield and believed that Adriatic distractions should not jeopardise their strategy elsewhere. In the end, it was agreed to pay off Thursby's battleships. In order to meet Italian objections, the French promised that a squadron of

---

[69] Jackson MSS, Kerr to Jackson, 4 November 1916.
[70] TNA, ADM137/1414, Kerr to Admiralty, 20 April 1917.
[71] Halpern, *Battle of the Otranto Straits*, p. 18.
[72] TNA, CAB24/10, Memorandum by Jellicoe to the War Cabinet, 17 April 1917.
[73] AUSM, b. 827, f. 6, Conferenza di Londra. Allied Naval Conference Report, 23–24 January 1917.

French battleships would be available at Corfu.[74] The combination of the British withdrawal and an increase of the French fleet in Corfu would result in the strengthening of French naval influence: an idea as unpopular with the British as with the Italians. To prevent such an outcome, the British and the Italians agreed to put another British officer, Commodore Algernon Heneage, in command of the Otranto barrage under the supervision of the Italian command, with the right to call on Allied support when necessary.[75] The Allies established ad hoc bilateral convergences – an Anglo-French collaboration to reduce British vessels under Italian command at Otranto and use them elsewhere, and an Anglo-Italian agreement to inhibit French control at the mouth of the Adriatic – which prevented each party from becoming preeminent in the Mediterranean. This of course impeded any coherent tripartite strategy, which had been one of the objectives of the London Conference. The re-formulation of Allied anti-submarine strategy was equally unsatisfactory.

The plan for the defence of the Mediterranean trade routes had been discussed at an early Allied conference in Paris in December 1915, when eighteen patrol zones were delineated, later reduced to eleven at the Malta Conference in March 1916.[76] The latter conference had also adopted the principle of fixed patrol routes for maritime traffic. The routes would be established by Allied Commander-in-Chief in the Mediterranean Dominique-Marie Gauchet, who had replaced Fournet in December 1916, with each nation responsible for patrolling its own zones.[77] Vice-Admiral Arthur Limpus, superintendent at Malta, considered the conference a success because it confirmed freedom of interference from Gauchet in each Allied zone. The British hoped this would make the French supreme command in the Mediterranean 'one in name only'.[78] But the crisis brought about by the resumption of unrestricted submarine warfare provoked major changes in the Entente strategy. The Admiralty decided upon a new formula to counter the menace. In January 1917 it ordered that the discredited system of fixed patrolled routes be abandoned for British ships. In the western basin British ships would keep as close to the shore as possible; west of Cape Bon they would 'spread as

---

[74] TNA, ADM137/1420, Report of Allied Naval Conference, London, 23–24 January 1917.

[75] Halpern, *Royal Navy*, pp. 209 ff.

[76] The Navy Records Society, *The Keyes Papers*, 3 vols. (London: Allen & Unwin, 1979), I, Halpern ed., doc. 135, Commodore Keyes to his wife, 30 December 1915, p. 299.

[77] De Robeck MSS, DRBK 4/36, Limpus to De Robeck, 26 January 1916; Jackson MSS, Limpus to Jackson, 2 February 1916; Limpus MSS, De Robeck to Limpus, 16 February 1916; De Robeck MSS, DRBK 4/36, Limpus to De Robeck, 23 February 1916.

[78] Halpern, *Royal Navy*, p. 210.

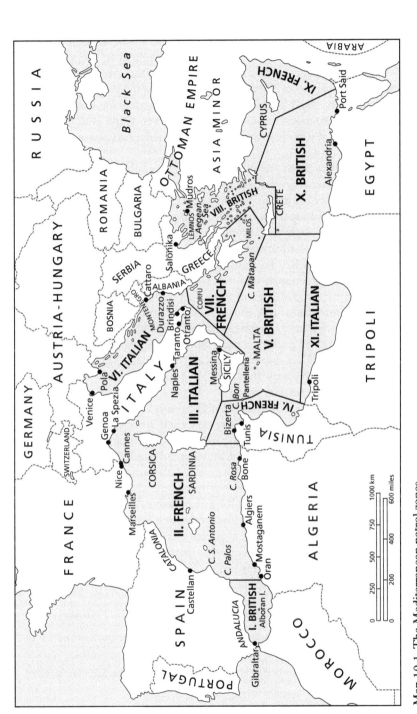

Map 10.1 The Mediterranean patrol zones

widely as possible', keeping well clear of Malta if not actually bound there.[79] At the London Naval Conference the British proposal was approved and extended to all Allied shipping in the western basin. In the eastern basin, however, there would be a trial of the two systems. The French scheme of fixed patrol routes would be used for traffic in the Aegean, while 'dispersion' would be used between Cape Bon and Port Said.[80] In March, it was clear that these experiments had not worked any better.[81]

Allied difficulties in overcoming Germany's counter-blockade were coupled with increasing British frustration over flaws in the Allied blockade. A memorandum in January 1917 expressed confidence that 'with some minor exceptions, practically no goods coming from overseas are getting through to Germany', but it also revealed that those exceptions were not at all insignificant and allowed the Central Powers to survive. The main British method to implement the blockade had been to establish agreements with the neutral countries limiting 'to any amount we think proper the imports [of] military value' into those countries. In some cases, like Sweden, it was only possible 'to secure agreements [on] cotton and lubricating oil'. This was considered 'satisfactory' in the case of goods coming from the British Empire but for goods coming from other overseas neutrals, principally North and South America, the difficulty was that British authorities had 'no right in international law to restrict trade ..., unless we can show that any particular consignment is destined for Germany'. To some extent, this problem was overcome through the so-called navicert system under which the British embassy in Washington received applications from intending shippers from the United States in advance; British-approved cargoes were given a 'letter of assurance' allowing passage through British patrols. When this system was not applicable, the British tried to detain the goods intercepted as long as possible,[82] but acknowledged that such policy could not 'be maintained much longer'.[83]

The biggest gap in the blockade concerned the import into Germany of the home products of the neighbouring neutrals, which the British had unsuccessfully tried 'to stop completely'.[84] And then there was Italy. For Rome, defending Allied shipping and ensuring imports of vital goods

---

[79] TNA, ADM137/1412, Minute by Admiralty War Staff (O.D.) 10 January 1917; Admiralty to Mediterranean Authorities, 11 January 1917.

[80] Ibid., 137/1420, Agenda and Conclusions, Allied Naval Conference, London, 23–24 January 1917.

[81] Halpern, *Naval History*, p. 390.

[82] TNA, CAB1/22, f1-2, Memorandum in regard to the present position of the blockade, by Carson, 1 January 1917.

[83] Ibid., 23/1 War Cabinet, 57, *cit.*   [84] Ibid., 1/22, f1-2, *cit.*

were only one aspect of submarine warfare. The other was the traumatic collapse of exports. In 1914 Italian exports covered 75.6 per cent of imports, but the figure fell to 53.9 per cent in 1915 and to 20 per cent in 1918. Italy was not selling anymore, as the nation's efforts were mainly put into the production of the wherewithal required by the civilians and the army. The consequent lack of income caused serious financial problems by 1917.[85] It was difficult to find markets that could ease this and the only option was to turn to the neutral countries.[86] Italy therefore maintained close trading relations with Switzerland, Holland, Denmark and Sweden – countries under strong German influence. Through these countries, Italian goods (sometimes presented as home products of Germany's neighbours) still reached the Central Powers.[87]

Italy was bound by the dictates of the Paris Economic Conference, signed by the Allies in June 1916. They provided regulations prohibiting trade with all persons and businesses in neutral countries 'subject to enemy influence', whose names were to be included in the so-called blacklist.[88] However, Italy sought various *escamotages* to maintain its commerce with neutral countries, in some cases openly violating the Paris agreements – not least by delaying the creation of its blacklist.[89] This caused increasing annoyance in Britain, which was in charge of the blockade. British recriminations were related to particular goods. Italy had agreed to limit cotton exports, but it did export silk to the countries of the Baltic Sea basin, which then exported it to Germany. Cecil explained to Rodd that this allowed the German textile industry to overcome the lack of cotton by replacing it with silk. The British were even more frustrated that Italian exports were sometimes sent to neutrals, regardless of the need for the same products in Entente countries – the case of sulphur sent to Sweden was symptomatic.[90] The same problem applied to Italian commodities sent to Holland and, in a recurring British motto, 'Holland means Germany'.[91] The discovery that Italian wines still reached Germany infuriated Cecil:

We have reasons to suppose that Germany is very short of alcohol. ... We have therefore after considerable trouble induced the French and the Spaniards to agree that the import of their wines into Denmark and Holland shall be subject to

---

[85] Einaudi, *Condotta economica*, p. 85.   [86] Crespi, *Alla difesa*, p. 127.

[87] For the development of British policy of blockade see: E. W. Osborne, *Britain's Economic Blockade of Germany 1914–1919* (London & New York: Cass, 2004).

[88] Brown Scott, 'Economic Conference', p. 847.

[89] For further details on Italy and the blockade see Caglioti, 'Dealing with enemy aliens in WWI: security versus civil liberties and property rights', *Italian Journal of Public Law*, II, 2, 2011, pp. 180–194.

[90] Rodd papers, Cecil to Rodd, 17 January 1917.

[91] TNA, CAB/23/1, War Cabinet 12, War Cabinet minutes, 20 December 1916.

rationing and other guarantees. The Italians have just concluded an agreement with the Danes by which their wines are to go into Denmark. . . . It is very difficult for us here to understand the working of a belligerent mind that does these things.[92]

Italy returned the accusation with intelligence obtained through the Greek embassy in Rome. The Italian Government protested that Holland had imported from Britain an amount of grain some twenty times higher than usual in 1915, exporting to Britain an amount of aniline twelve times as high as usual the same year. And since 'Holland means Germany', one might conclude that Britain, for its own stake, was trading with Germany indirectly.[93] Rodd desperately tried to mediate over this embarrassing question, re-stating in Rome, Britain's honest commitment to the blockade, and explaining to London that the Italian trade policy was motivated by serious economic needs, and that it was the trading restrictions imposed on Italy by Britain, that had pushed Rome to turn to those markets, which paid better prices.[94] This was, of course, an indication of how costly blockading an enemy could be for the blockader, especially when it did not command the vast resources of the British Empire; but Cecil replied that the Italians, 'however excusable they may be', were putting 'the blockade in great difficulties'.[95]

British complaints continued for the reminder of the war. The blockade by the Italians proved porous not only at sea but also on land. For example, a long-lasting controversy broke out over the dealings of the Italian representatives in Berne. According to British intelligence, they failed to guarantee with the Swiss Government that Italian imports were being used exclusively in Switzerland and not then exported to Germany. Sonnino replied succinctly to the criticism, stating that the accusation that Italy was not participating with the necessary determination was incorrect: the Italian chemical industry, which had just taken off thanks to wartime industrial mobilisation, desperately needed Swiss chemical components to keep going, as the British were not in a condition to provide them. Cecil noted to Rodd that Sonnino 'was missing the point':

We do not complain that the Italians refuse to be dragged by us into a 'forward' blockade policy as regards Switzerland, nor that, when we are sometimes in favour of drastic actions, they are sometimes in favour of compromise. . . . What we do complain is . . . that, as regards the carrying out of the details of an agreed policy, their representatives at Berne have consistently shown not merely slackness and incapacity, but willful obstructiveness.[96]

[92] Rodd papers, Cecil to Rodd, cit.   [93] Martini, Diario, p. 596.
[94] Rodd papers, Rodd to Balfour, 29 January 1917.
[95] Ibid., Cecil to Rodd, 12 February 1917.   [96] Ibid., Cecil to Rodd, 15 April 1918.

The British became convinced that the 'only chance of striking at the root of the system of frauds on the Italian-Swiss frontier' and to limit Italian indirect damage to the blockade, was to create a new ministry in Rome to deal specifically with the Allied coordination of this crucial aspect of the war. Such organisation 'should control the customs and licensing authorities and be more or less independent of the less reliable elements in the Italian administration'.[97] Despite the British pressure, no such ministry was created. Under Boselli a Ministry for Maritime and Rail Transport was set up to better supervise exports and imports, and the Italian blacklist was eventually drawn up[98] – but nothing more. All considered, the blockade worked well enough to suffocate the Entente's enemies progressively. The very decision to re-launch unrestricted submarine warfare is an indication of how desperate the situation was becoming in the Central Powers. Italy's trading policy did not prejudice the success of the blockade, but it did slow down its effectiveness.

The fiascos of the Rome, Petrograd and London Conferences, as well as the limited results in naval and economic warfare, delivered a serious blow to the British Cabinet's self-confidence. A Government which had come to power pledging to reconcile and coordinate Allied strategies to speed up victory had so far badly failed its call of duty.

---

[97] Ibid., Heverton Hamis [unclear] to Rodd, 7 May 1918.
[98] ASMAE, Archivio ordinario e politico di gabinetto, Ambasciata Londra, 1917, b. 422, Lista delle persone, ditte e società commerciali con le quali è vietato il commercio (Cabinet decree n. 960, 8 August 1916, and n. 1406, 23 August 1917, published in the *Gazzetta Ufficiale* on 17 September 1917).

11 Italy's Empire Project Accepted

11.1 St Jean de Maurienne: Out of the Colonial Tunnel

The unprecedented degree of mutual hostility caused by the recent colonial and maritime polemics provoked both Lloyd George and Boselli to intervene personally in Allied relations. The former quite possibly began to wonder how effective Balfour and Hardinge's policy really was towards Italy. In any case, he was not ready to embark on a permanent diplomatic battle against Rome, not least, because he feared that Italy might even leave the Alliance, if it were further humiliated.[1] Lloyd George wished to exert greater influence on Italian public opinion so as to reawaken in the Italian people a trust in their allies and in the idea of a coalition war. He instructed Rodd to strengthen British propaganda in Italy with the following objectives: to reinforce Italian confidence in Britain as the main Entente partner by stimulating greater appreciation of London's indefatigable mediation between Italy, France and Russia; to challenge the increasing Italian disapproval of British pro-Yugoslav sympathy; to reassert Britain's reputation by instilling, in those Italians who still thought of Germany as a strong and generous ex-ally, the idea that London was an even stronger, more reliable and generous ally. This was to be done without making any specific reference to colonial promises to Italy – rather, by emphasising British commitment for a 'just' peace as the natural product of Anglo-Italian shared liberal values. Lloyd George hoped that this propaganda would diminish Italian appetites and somehow modify Italy's war aims.[2]

Rodd reluctantly accepted this new task. He repeated that British propaganda in Italy had, up to then, been very successful, especially in countering pro-German sentiments, and no further effort was needed. He held that 'all decent people in this country are of one mind. ... The majority of these need no convincing, and they are all on our side

---

[1] Riccardi, *Alleati*, p. 465. [2] Rodd, *Memories*, III, pp. 289–291, 307–311, 315.

enthusiastically'.[3] Lloyd George however insisted in his plan, which could influence the broader Italian political sphere, including Boselli, his ministers and Italian MPs, thus bypassing Sonnino. Rodd was given these new guidelines in late February, after the creation of a new British Department for Propaganda under John Buchan within the Foreign Office, which expanded the office previously at Wellington House[4] and changed the very nature of British propaganda. Where Wellington House had largely aimed at intellectual elites and the business sectors, Buchan sought a mass response, combining the distribution of printed material, such as pamphlets, books, government papers, ministerial speeches and all the old tools adopted by Wellington House from the beginning of its activity, with new and more effective forms of publicity such as films, meetings organised by local British committees and the local press.[5]

Rodd began his campaign in March. He was anxious that the Italians would not feel they were being cheated, however. So he insisted that the larger part of the work be done by Italians, 'who are believed to be doing what they do for their own reasons. No one suspects them of being agents of the Embassy'. In particular, he enjoyed the collaboration of his friend, Pietro Santamaria, who translated and printed suitable material and distributed it through public libraries. A propaganda bureau was set up in Florence, with the aim of organising lectures and social activities and promoting frequent visits of British sympathisers all around the country, exercising 'a quiet, unobtrusive influence on Italian opinion'. The British staff sent to handle propaganda in Italy increased steadily to include experts in every field. Within three months, a director of propaganda in Italy had been appointed in the person of Algar Thorold, to supervise the work of Rodd, and to extend greatly the scale of operations throughout the peninsula.[6] The British considered propaganda almost a scientific-fighting tool, but however scientific and well-organised, it could not 'work miracles' overnight, wrote Buchan to Carson.[7] So, Lloyd George's ambitious Italian programme did not have an immediate impact on Anglo-Italian relations.

Boselli, for his part, realised that Italy seemed to have lost its preferential relations with Britain. Italian needs in supplies and the prospect of fatal isolation at the end of hostilities spurred Boselli to offer to contribute a force to the Anglo-French mission to the Hejaz in the Arabian Peninsula,[8] and

[3] C. Seton-Watson, 'British Propaganda in Italy 1914–1918', in *Inghilterra e Italia nel '900. Atti del Convegno di Bagni di Lucca (Ottobre 1972)* (Florence: La Nuova Italia, 1973), p. 120.

[4] TNA, INF4/1b, Memorandum to the Cabinet, 3 February 1917.

[5] Sanders, 'Wellington House', pp. 123 ff.

[6] C. Seton-Watson, 'British Propaganda', pp. 121–123; Rodd, *Memories*, III, pp. 307–311, 315.

[7] TNA, CAB23/WC75, War Cabinet minute, 20 February 1917.

[8] Ibid., FO371/3050/46706, note by the Italian ambassador, 28 February 1917.

another to Palestine. This initiative met Lloyd George's expectations of greater Allied military cooperation, and of shifting focus to the peripheral fronts. Of course, it also aimed to dispel the objection frequently made by the other Allies that Italy was not justified in asking for a significant share of Ottoman territory if it did not take a greater part in bringing about the Ottoman defeat. Moreover, news that a French contingent was about to embark for the Holy Land served as further stimulus to Boselli: if the French took part in the campaign, Italy must also join in.[9] Cadorna was unhappy about this new endeavour, but Sonnino pressed him on the grounds that the Italian participation in the Palestinian campaign would greatly support Italy's diplomatic efforts in the colonial question:[10] war aims drove strategy. On 14 March Imperiali presented Balfour with Sonnino's offer for an Italian contingent to be put under British command.[11] To the surprise of Imperiali and Sonnino, the British reacted rather coldly. The political purpose of the offer was all too obvious and few in the British Cabinet were happy to improve the Italian diplomatic standing on the colonial issue. On the contrary, Italian offers in Arabian matters were invariably seen with suspicion and 'unanimous opposition'.[12] No reply was given to Italy until June, when the Foreign Office found a formula that could reject the proposal without being disrespectful: Rodd informed Sonnino that operations by Arab rebels should be carried out by their leaders without foreign assistance and, confidentially, that Britain was trying to secure the withdrawal of the small French contingent in Hejaz.[13] As far as Palestine was concerned, Lloyd George himself was little interested in Italian support. The war in the Middle East was now more encouraging than in the past. In Mesopotamia, the British had counter-attacked the Turks throughout January and February, taking Baghdad on 12 March. In the same month the British invaded Palestine and Lloyd George expected a triumphal march into Jerusalem. In this case, it was war developments that set the context for war aims and peace planning. Lloyd George was less disposed to share oriental laurels with others, and became also more assertive about the faith of the Holy Land: 'We shall be there by right of conquest, and shall remain', he held.[14] British consent to Italian participation came only on 9 April, but with usual anti-Italian acrimony, Hardinge commented:

---

[9] DDI, 5, VII, Salvago Raggi to Sonnino, 12 March 1917.
[10] A. Battaglia, *Da Suez ad Aleppo. La campagna Alleata e il Distaccamento italiano in Siria e Palestina (1917–1921)* (Rome: Nuova Cultura, 2015), pp. 115–120.
[11] DDI, 5, VII, doc. 473, Imperiali to Sonnino, 14 March 1917.
[12] Fisher, *Curzon*, p. 76.
[13] TNA, FO371/3050 *cit.*, n. 1209, FO to Rodd, 23 June 1917; n. 125480, note by Hardinge, n.d.
[14] C. Andrew, S. Kanya-Forstner, *France Overseas: The Great War and the Climax of French Imperial Expansion* (London: Thames & Hudson, 1981), p. 124.

The Italians seem to be unduly fussy. . . . We are quite ready to agree to the presence of a small Italian contingent in the international zone. We want neither them nor the French, but since one has been admitted we cannot shut the door upon the other, and all we ask is that the Italian contingent should be merely for the purpose of showing their flag and should be reduced to the smallest possible number.[15]

Boselli was rather disappointed by the limited success of his Palestinian policy. Lloyd George too grew dissatisfied with the Middle East developments, as by late March the British advance towards Gaza bogged down to yet another stalemate. Lloyd George's real problem here was less his allies than his own generals. Robertson, in particular, did all he could to prevent a shift of British – and Allied – priorities from the western front. To boycott Lloyd George's plan, he had General Archibald Murray, the British commander in the Middle East, make the impossible demand that thirteen extra divisions be sent to him in order to capture Jerusalem – thus driving Lloyd George to give up his dreams of a rapid success in Palestine.[16]

Unexpectedly, the Austro-Hungarians provided the British premier with another card to play. Emperor Franz Joseph died on 21 November 1916 and his successor Karl on 24 March 1917 sent the new French Prime Minister, Alexandre Ribot, a secret offer of a separate peace. Ribot consulted with Lloyd George. The Austro-Hungarian proposal found eager ears in both of them.[17] Vienna's terms looked reasonable: a secret armistice with Russia in which the question of Constantinople would not be made an issue; Alsace-Lorraine and Belgium to be restored; and the formation of a Southern Slav monarchy, embracing Bosnia-Herzegovina, Serbia, Albania and Montenegro. Italy's claims, however, were altogether ignored.[18] In a meeting at Folkestone on 11 April, Lloyd George and Ribot agreed to organise a new Allied meeting with the aim of pushing Rome to accept a compromise. They would put Smyrna on the table in exchange for the withdrawal of Italian designs on Trieste. Subsequently, they were confident of bringing home Vienna's separate peace on the basis of Austria-Hungary surrendering Trentino alone.[19] When they invited Boselli and Sonnino to join them, Lloyd George and Ribot made no mention of their objective, using the pending question of Asia Minor as the ostensible *façade* of the new meeting.[20]

The summit took place in a railway carriage beside the station of St Jean de Maurienne (Savoie), on 19 April 1917. For the first time, it brought

[15] Rodd papers, Hardinge to Rodd, 15 April 1917.
[16] Woodward, *Sir William Robertson*, pp. 155–159.   [17] Riccardi, *Alleati*, p. 460.
[18] Lloyd George, *Memoirs*, II, pp. 1179–1182.
[19] See: A. Ribot jr., *Journal de Alexandre Ribot et Correspondances inédites* (Paris: Plon, 1936).
[20] Lloyd George, *Memoirs*, II, pp. 1175–1204; Ribot, *Lettres à un ami* (Paris: Bosard, 1924), pp. 67–73.

together the heads of government of Britain, France and Italy – Russia was excluded due to its convulsed domestic situation.[21] This is indicative of the growing mistrust that the promoters, Lloyd George in particular, had of the regular diplomatic channels. The British premier had consulted neither the Foreign Office nor his War Cabinet – only Hankey had been informed of the recent developments.[22] The exclusion of both Balfour and Hardinge from the meeting, as well as Lloyd George's decision to give up Smyrna was a veiled criticism of the poor results obtained by the Foreign Office on the colonial question. When he knew of the forthcoming meeting, Hardinge lamented the protagonism of Lloyd George who 'knows nothing about Oriental politics or even geography'.[23] Rodd and Imperiali were also disappointed at being excluded from the summit.[24]

The meeting proved unexpectedly fruitful. In the first round of talks, Sonnino accepted the Anglo-French plans for Greece, demanding Smyrna in exchange. He believed it was a fair *do ut des*: Smyrna to Italy, power in Greece to Venizelos, to the inevitable abdication of King Constantine.[25] The Italian move – which opened the path to the Greek intervention alongside the Allies on 28 June – was enthusiastically greeted by a jubilant Lloyd George who was happy then to introduce his new plan for the partitioning of Asia Minor: half the Aidin Vilayet and Smyrna passed to Italy, together with French-allotted coastal territory west of Mersin – which remained French together with Adana; Konya was to be ceded to the new Turkish state.[26] Sonnino observed that this proposal contradicted Balfour's project, which, though excluding Smyrna, had included Konya and its territory in the Italian area. Lloyd George justified this change on ethnic grounds, but eventually he and Ribot agreed that everything that had been offered to Italy under the Balfour proposal would be honoured, with the addition of Smyrna.[27] Sonnino seemed to have won right across the board, but the accommodating behaviour of the British and French leaders was preparatory to introducing the other issue, which was dearer to them: separate peace with Austria-Hungary, which Lloyd George presented as the potential turning point in the war – no doubt worth, in his opinion, Italy's surrender of Trieste. But Sonnino held that a peace without

---

[21] The participants were the three Prime Ministers, plus Sonnino, and their respective aides.
[22] R. Warman, 'The Erosion of Foreign Office Influence in the Making of Foreign Policy, 1916–1918', *The Historical Journal*, XV, 1, 1972, p. 142.
[23] Rodd papers, Hardinge to Rodd, 17 April 1917.
[24] Rodd, *Memories*, III, p. 311; Imperiali, *Diario*, pp. 390–392, 426.
[25] DDI, 5, VII, doc. 778, Note by Sonnino, 19 April 1917.
[26] Toscano, *Gli Accordi*, pp. 272–274.
[27] ADMAEF, Guerre 1914–1918, Dossier Général, vol. 884/28–30.

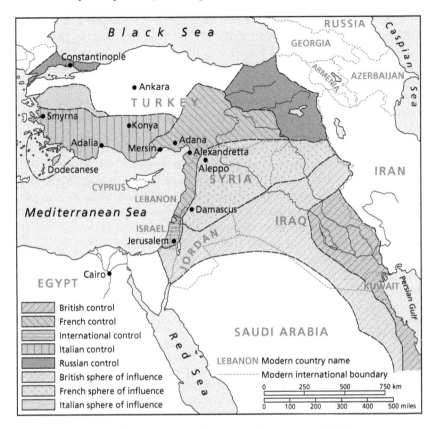

Map 11.1 The St Jean de Maurienne Agreement of 1917

Trento, Trieste, Dalmatia and the Adriatic islands would result in a revolution in Italy; he also reminded his colleagues that enemy proposals of a separate peace only had the purpose of dividing the Allies and that there could be no alternative to total victory; and finally, because an Anglo-French peace with Austria-Hungary violated the Entente agreement of 5 September 1914, which had later been signed by Italy and which bound the Allies not to conclude a separate peace, Sonnino threatened to make peace with Germany 'tomorrow' had Britain and France given further consideration to the Austro-Hungarian offer. A disheartened Lloyd George later commented: 'Where you are working with allies, it is just as difficult to negotiate an honourable peace as to wage successful war'.[28] At this point, Lloyd George and Ribot tried to link the agreement

---

[28] Lloyd George, *Memoirs*, II, pp. 1175–1188; Sonnino, *Diario*, III p. 395.

on Asia Minor to a more active role for Italy in the Balkans and against Turkey. Sonnino was adamant that Italy could not 'absolutely give anything more'. The discussion ended with the British and French delegates entering their appeal for greater Italian military effort into the records.[29]

Notwithstanding Anglo-French recrimination at the end, a solution to the Greek question and an agreement on Asia Minor were a remarkable result. Sonnino was enthusiastic.[30] Yet two issues remained on the table: the absence of Russia and the Allied request for greater support from Italy. These were confirmed at the British War Cabinet discussion on 23–24 April, when the new agreement was analysed for approval. Its content was received coldly. The general impression was that the Italian contribution to the war against Turkey hardly justified 'such large territories of the Ottoman Empire', and that Britain needed to avoid antagonising the new Russian regime by making a pact behind its back.[31] Such complaints were echoed in the Imperial War Cabinet, which included representatives of the British dominions. Lloyd George had convened it for the first time on 20 March to 'exercise control and supervision over the direction of the war and to formulate the terms of peace which the Empire as a whole would regard as a reasonable and equitable settlement to be aimed at'.[32]

The Imperial Cabinet had three sessions, the first of which in March–May 1917 discussed the Tyrrell-Paget memorandum and decided to establish a committee on Terms of Peace comprising two sub-committees assigned – quite tellingly – to the two prominent imperialists in the War Cabinet, Curzon and Milner. Curzon's committee dealt with British territorial desiderata, whilst Milner's analysed economic and non-territorial desiderata.[33] The Imperial War Cabinet discussed their reports on 1 and 2 May. Whereas Milner focussed on terms to be imposed on Germany,[34] Curzon re-stated earlier petitions in favour of the principle of nationality as a condition for a lasting peace. He also recommended reducing the growing influence of Britain's allies and stressed that the dominions claimed a share in the captured German colonies.[35] In the Arabian Peninsula, he insisted that 'no restoration of Turkish sovereignty or suzerainty should be permitted. ... The ultimate connection by

[29] DDI, 5, VII, doc. 784, Sonnino to Imperiali, Salvago Raggi and Carlotti, 20 April 1917.

[30] Ibid., doc. 851, Sonnino to Imperiali, Salvago Raggi and Carlotti, 29 April 1917.

[31] TNA, CAB23/2, War Cabinet 126, 25 April 1917; FO371/3043/1142, n. 748(D), Balfour to Rodd, 25 April 1917.

[32] Lloyd George, The Truth, I, p. 52.   [33] Goldstein, Winning the Peace, p. 15.

[34] TNA, CAB29/1/P-15, Imperial War Cabinet, Report of the Committee on Terms of Peace (Economic and Non-Territorial Desiderata).

[35] Ibid., 29/1/P-16, Report of the Committee on Terms of Peace (Territorial Desiderata), 28 April 1917.

railroad of Egypt, Palestine, Mesopotamia, and the Persian Gulf is an object to be kept steadily in view'.[36] Finally, he considered it 'of primary importance to the safety of the Empire to retain control of Palestine'.[37] General Jan C. Smuts agreed that Britain should keep the whole of Palestine – the Sykes–Picot Treaty notwithstanding – in order to prevent 'a very serious menace to our communications'.[38] During the discussion, the Imperial Cabinet protested the 'rather wild project' of France in the colonies,[39] and expressed 'disbelief' at Lloyd George's concessions to Italy.[40] Four additional reports submitted by Mallet even suggested expanding the British Empire at the expense of its allies by acquiring 'French Somaliland, French India, and St-Pierre and Miquelon', plus 'Portuguese Timor'.[41] Needless to say, the general sentiment was that Britain should 'milk the contingent clauses' of the St Jean de Maurienne arrangement 'to prevent the conferring on Italy of a position of equality in those areas covered by Sykes–Picot'.[42]

This shows not only that Britain's primary interests continued to be extra-European, despite the continental focus of the war, but also that the binding nature of all treaties so far signed was relative for most of the British and Imperial Cabinet members, their main preoccupation being to find formulas that could bypass London's commitments where necessary. Inevitably, this put Lloyd George in a crossfire for what he had acknowledged to his allies at St Jean de Maurienne. According to many British officials, Sonnino had exposed Lloyd George as a diplomatic amateur. Hardinge wrote to Bertie: 'We at the Foreign Office are very disgusted with the results of Lloyd George's recent visit to St. Jean. … The only comforting point about it is that the Italian programme is not likely to be realised now or even in the distant future'.[43] Such criticism of the premier was unfair. No doubt, Lloyd George had given up extensive territories, but his decision can only be appreciated if put in the context of the war. When the St Jean de Maurienne Treaty was signed in April, the Allies were going through a dreadful period in the conflict. The sinkings of Allied cargos even exceeded German monthly predictions – 874,140 tons.[44] The U-boats would never repeat that success, but, of course, Lloyd George could not know it. Coupled with the Russian Revolution and the slow US mobilisation, this made the Allied cause waver as never before. Lloyd George better than many others appreciated the importance of detaching Austria-Hungary from

---

[36] Ibid., 21/77/P-16.   [37] Ibid., 21/77, Curzon Committee report, 24 April 1917.
[38] Stevenson, *1917*, p. 338.
[39] TNA, FO371/2937/11293, n. 483, Balfour to Bertie, 2 July 1917.
[40] Fisher, *Curzon*, p. 78.   [41] Goldstein, *Winning the Peace*, p. 14.
[42] Fisher, *Curzon*, p. 78.   [43] Hardinge MSS, 3, Hardinge to Bertie, 27 April 1917.
[44] J. M. Waters, *Bloody Winter* (Princeton: Nostrand, 1967), pp. 6–8.

Germany or, at the very least, to reconcile the Allies[45] – which were his goals at St Jean de Maurienne. To calm his advisers and ministers, Lloyd George made a statement to the House of Commons on 10 May, in which for the first time – in contrast to earlier declarations in the Cabinet – he made it plain that under no circumstances would Britain return Mesopotamia, Palestine or the German colonies to their former rulers.[46] In a symbiotic circle, now war aims influenced British strategy. Lloyd George decided to appoint a new commander in Palestine, Edmund Allenby. Reinforcements were sent to the Gaza front – Allenby estimated that he could take Jerusalem with seven infantry and three cavalry divisions. By the end of the summer, Allenby commanded 120,000 men from the British Empire and Egypt and was ready to resume British advance on the Holy City.[47]

In addition to strengthening British claims in the Middle East and re-launching the Palestinian campaign, Lloyd George partly accepted his Cabinet's objections to the St Jean de Maurienne Agreement. Its ratifi-cation was made subject to three conditions: the consent of Russia; the establishment of Smyrna as a free port; and greater Italian participation in the Middle East campaign. On 10 May, Barrère declared that the French Cabinet aligned itself with the British adding one more French condition for the treaty approval – namely a 'satisfactory delineation' of Franco-Italian zones in the area west of Adana and Mersin.[48] The latter seemed a minor affair, but the British reservations regarding Russian consent and Italian commitment in the Middle East caused great irrita-tion in Rome.[49] Sonnino believed that Britain was playing a dirty game. Italy had offered its collaboration in Palestine in March, but it had been rejected apart from a 500-men contingent.[50] The British U-turn, after little more than a month, appeared an *escamotage* to make conditional an agreement that Lloyd George had already accepted. Sonnino would rather be considered stubborn – even grasping – but honest in his demands, than accommodating but hypocritical. Furthermore, he pro-tested to Rodd that the Sykes–Picot Agreement was not subject to any military clauses, and he would not accept differential conditions for the

---

[45] TNA, CAB21/78/IWC13, 1 May 1917; DDI, 5, VII, doc. 990, Imperiali to Sonnino, 15 May 1917.

[46] French, *Strategy of Lloyd George*, p. 91.

[47] J. Gooch, B. H. Reid eds., *Ottoman Army Effectiveness in World War I: A Comparative Study* (Abingdon: Routledge, 2007), p. 128.

[48] P. C. Helmreich, 'Italy and the Anglo-French Repudiation of the 1917 St. Jean de Maurienne Agreement', *The Journal of Modern History*, XLVIII, 2, June 1976, pp. 99–139.

[49] Imperiali, *Diario*, p. 396.

[50] F. E. Manuel, 'The Palestine Question in Italian Diplomacy, 1917–1920', *The Journal of Modern History*, XXVII, 3, 1955, pp. 263–80.

St Jean de Maurienne Pact.[51] Finally, given that Italy had offered its services in the Hejaz – the offer had not yet been answered – Sonnino sent Imperiali a memorandum claiming for Rome a position of equality with London and Paris in the Arab Peninsula.[52]

Italian complaints met with little sympathy in the British Cabinet – even less so did Sonnino's Arab memorandum. The Cabinet reiterated the traditional criticism that Italy was engaged only where its direct interests were at stake. Sonnino responded with British irony: 'The practical consequence of the British War Cabinet statement ... would be that Italy should at the earliest withdraw from Salonika its current contingent of 40,000 men, as she is not aspiring to any part of Bulgaria or Macedonia, and transport it to Asia Minor'.[53] Unable to move Sonnino, Lloyd George passed responsibility for the negotiation on the St Jean de Maurienne ratification onto Cecil. The colonial agreement was Lloyd George's first significant achievement in Allied matters, but the Prime Minister now sensed the slippery ground beneath his feet. It may be assumed that he wished to avoid any responsibility for another possible stalemate. Lloyd George may also have hoped that Cecil would establish better relations with the Italians than the Balfour–Hardinge duo. He was misled, for Imperiali had a negative impression of Cecil from their first chat on the colonial question. On 14 May, the latter asked Imperiali: 'What if, for argument's sake, you should have to choose between Dalmatia and Asia Minor?' The ambassador, incredulous, noted in his diary: 'If they start talking about revision ..., I shan't be accountable for what happens. Let's be careful we don't smash the whole Alliance'. He concluded: 'I do not trust Cecil. He's a Utopian!'[54] On 19 May Cecil tested Imperiali again. The accounts of that meeting by the two protagonists are slightly different and stimulate some thoughts. Cecil proposed to find a formula stating that the Allies were agreed 'in principle' on the Asia Minor question, but for the moment 'it was not possible to conclude a definite agreement'. He justified that with the need to appease the Russian Provisional Government, committed to a non-annexationist policy; from the debates in the British and Imperial cabinets, we can safely assume that he was talking in the interest of Britain more than Russia. Cecil continued:

I then hinted to the Ambassador that I thought it quite possible that all the international agreements would have to be revised. This was a great shock to the Ambassador. He jumped to the conclusion that I meant that none of the

---

[51] BOD, Sonnino papers, reel 41, doc. 635, Sonnino to Imperiali, Salvago Raggi and Carlotti, 29 April 1917.
[52] TNA, FO371/3044/95567, Memorandum by Imperiali, 11 May 1917.
[53] DDI, 5, VII, doc. 851, Sonnino to Imperiali, Salvago Raggi and Carlotti, *cit.*
[54] Imperiali, *Diario*, p. 405; DDI, 5, VIII, doc. 60, Imperiali to Sonnino, 23 May 1917.

advantages secured to Italy would be insisted on. I told him that was not what I had intended, but that I thought it quite possible that we should have to reconsider all the questions involved, or at any rate express our readiness to reconsider them. He seemed very much disturbed at this intimation, but promised to convey it to Baron Sonnino.[55]

Imperiali reported:

Cecil added that his impression ... was that all the various agreements already stipulated on Asia Minor will indistinctively end up being subject to revision, and that perhaps it will also be necessary to manoeuvre skilfully to reply to the potential Russian demands to revise the agreements, in a way that can placate the impatient exigencies of those [Russian] statesmen, and can buy time.[56]

The Italian ambassador did not mention his astonishment and his suspicion – noted by Cecil – that Italian promises, albeit recognised in Allied treaties, might be dropped. There is of course a possibility that Cecil invented that part of his report, but one sees no reason why he should have. It seems more likely that Imperiali did in fact react in dismay but preferred not to tell Sonnino; nor did he mention his personal mistrust of Cecil – which he put down in his diary. Instead, he emphasised the responsibility of Russia. Imperiali was a scrupulous diplomat. On this occasion, however, he seems to have delivered a tame version of the facts to Sonnino. Why so, can only be speculated. It is possible that Imperiali tried to prevent being blamed for the inadequate British collaboration in the ratification of the colonial agreement; he might have tried to avoid another Anglo-Italian polemic; or he might have simply been misled by his own biases. As an aristocrat, Imperiali was decidedly anti-socialist;[57] on the other hand, he was a determined supporter of an Anglo-Italian special partnership. He might have harboured some doubts, but in the end concluded that it was not the British, but the Russian socialists who were opposing Italy. Cecil of course encouraged that conclusion, which Imperiali re-stated to Sonnino on 23 May.[58] In any case, Sonnino, who was equally prejudiced towards the Russian revolutionaries,[59] received from London reports that did not question his assumption that securing agreements was a sufficient method to safeguard Italian interests.

Rodd, in the meantime, was desperate for clearer explanations from London about the nature of 'increased Italian support' in the Middle East. He realised that both the British military authorities and the War

---

[55] TNA, FO371/3044/102248, n. 112, FO to Rodd, 19 May 1917.
[56] DDI, 5, VIII, doc. 26, Imperiali to Sonnino, 19 May 1917.
[57] Imperiali, *Diario*, p. 490.   [58] DDI, 5, VIII, doc. 60, Imperiali to Sonnino, *cit.*
[59] Sonnino, *Diario*, III, pp. 357–363.

Cabinet were hostile to greater Italian involvement in the region. Rodd had to assume a sibylline and rather embarrassing position when he communicated to Sonnino that London did not imply any specific military involvement of Italy in the Middle East; rather, the War Cabinet only meant 'to point out in general the comparative efforts of Britain, France and Italy in that area'. This feeble argument was no more acceptable to Sonnino than the earlier one, and he rejected it point-blank.[60] On 14 June, London reluctantly agreed to eliminate any military clauses from the St Jean de Maurienne Agreement.[61] The question of Russian consent, though, remained a serious issue. On 15 June, Cecil suggested that Sonnino re-draft the text of the colonial agreement 'excluding any use of the words "occupation", "annexation" etc.',[62] to make it acceptable to the Russians. However, the disastrous result of the Russian offensive of 1 July – the so-called Kerensky offensive – together with the subsequent collapse of the eastern front and the steady growth of the Bolsheviks, made the prospect of Russian defection ever more real. Thus, Sonnino urgently needed to ensure that 'the agreements concluded among the three Allies will be in full force' regardless of Russian consent.[63] To this end, Sonnino accepted a new Allied conference on 25 July 1917 aimed at formalising the St Jean de Maurienne Treaty.[64]

In preparation for the conference, Sonnino corresponded extensively with Cecil so as to gain British support. In personal letters between 2 and 4 July Cecil proposed two slightly different notes to be attached to the official text of the colonial agreement, each containing further assurances about the maintenance of the principle of equilibrium and the 'equitable proportionality of territorial acquisitions', regardless of Russian consent to the treaty. Sonnino accepted both versions.[65] We will never know whether Cecil had abruptly changed his mind and was now willing to support Sonnino, or whether he was playing dilatory tactics. According to historian John Fisher, Cecil 'was on firm ground and had only to allow events to take their natural course to derail Italian ambitions'.[66] This seems confirmed by subsequent events; the memorandum approved by the British Cabinet on 23 July and presented to Britain's allies in the opening stage of the 25 July conference differed

---

[60] Helmreich, 'Italy and the Anglo-French', p. 112.
[61] Sonnino papers, reel 50, Cecil to Imperiali, 14 June 1917.
[62] TNA, FO371/3044/110579/1142, Nobokoff to Cecil, 8 June 1917; and Cecil to Imperiali, 15 June 1917.
[63] Helmreich, 'Italy and the Anglo-French', p. 122.   [64] Sonnino, *Diario*, III, p. 128.
[65] Sonnino papers, reel 47, First proposal of Lord Cecil; Translation of Lord Cecil's proposal n. 2; Cecil to Sonnino, 7 July 1917, and Sonnino to Cecil 4 July 1917.
[66] Fisher, *Curzon*, p. 80.

from Cecil's promises to Sonnino. The text had the Russian consent clause discarded, but included the equilibrium clause:

> It is understood that if at the time when peace is declared the total or partial possession of the territories contemplated in the agreements come to between France, Great Britain, Italy and Russia ... cannot be fully accorded to any one or more of those Powers, then in any alterations or adjustments of the provinces of the Turkish Empire consequential on the war, equitable consideration shall be given to the preservation of the equilibrium of the Mediterranean in accordance with article 9 of the London Agreement of May 1915.[67]

The British Government approved Cecil's equilibrium clause, because it referred only to the Mediterranean; territorial arrangements in Mesopotamia and Arabia, which were integrated in the Sykes–Picot Agreement, now fell outside the new pact. Thus, the new clause effectively freed Britain's hands in terms of its actions in the Middle East, potentially allowing London to expand its influence beyond the limits of the Sykes–Picot Agreement without having to compensate either France or Italy. Moreover, it also served to keep additional French territorial ambitions in Cilicia and Palestine in check, since such claims would necessitate further compensations to Italy.[68]

The final Allied colonial conference fell into two stages. The first took place in Paris at which Sonnino and Ribot reached agreement on the Italo-French frontier in Anatolia.[69] The second took place in London from 28 July to 8 August. Here Sonnino defended most of the St Jean de Maurienne Agreement, consenting to Smyrna being administered by the Italians as a free port. In turn, Cecil submitted through the Foreign Office a third proposal to remove Russian consent from the treaty. It read: 'If the Russian Government do not signify' their objections to the treaty, this 'shall be binding upon the parties thereto as though the Russian Government had consented to it'; if, however, Russian objections be made, all colonial agreements 'shall be deemed to have lapsed'.[70] This opened the question of validity of the Sykes–Picot Agreement too, which was now favoured in London where Balfour, Hardinge and Cecil dreamed of expanding British influence further but was obviously opposed in Paris. Thus, the French objected to Cecil's proposal. The final document approved by the Allies on 8 August contained the equilibrium clause, but it made no reference to the validity of the treaty removed

[67] TNA, CAB23/3, WC.193, Appendix g.t. 1474, Memorandum by Lord Cecil, 21 July 1917.
[68] Helmreich, 'Italy and the Anglo-French', p. 122.
[69] DDI, 5, VIII, doc. 737, Salvago Raggi to Sonnino, 27 July 1917.
[70] TNA, FO371/3044/153868/1142, Cecil to Sonnino, 3 August 1917.

from Russian consent.[71] Imperiali begged Sonnino not to give in to the French, but 'despite the force of my plea, Sonnino got irritated with me and did not insist'. Cecil's reiterated assertions and the equilibrium clause had convinced the Italian Foreign Minister that the question of Russian approval was just a technicality and that his allies, Britain above all, were truly committed to the colonial treaty they had signed. Imperiali's conclusion was in stark contrast to Sonnino's satisfaction: 'He'll regret it!'[72] Despite the ambassador's scepticism, the results of August 1917 apparently marked a triumph of Italian foreign policy.

11.2   Strategic Implications

Even before it was ratified the colonial agreement began to have important strategic consequences. First, Lloyd George hoped that renewed Allied synergy could lead to better cooperation against U-boats – a greater Italian commitment was especially needed, and now that Rome had been satisfied in the colonies, Britain expected it. Lloyd George had good reasons to insist on that. In March a full 25 per cent of all Britain-bound shipping was sunk. After the U-boat feat in April, sinkings in May amounted to 596,629 tons, in line with German predictions[73] – and Germany lost only nine submarines in the first trimester of the unrestricted campaign.[74] Allied imports collapsed. In Britain, this added to a growing economic suffering from labour shortages, a worsening balance of payments and inflation. Food and coal shortages; the consequent high price of goods compared to earnings; the terrific losses in human lives; and the War Cabinet's decision to abolish the trade card scheme and to extend dilution to private work caused protests culminating in strikes in the engineering industry in May. Lloyd George was obsessed that quasi-revolutionary sentiments inspired by the Russian Revolution were permeating civil society.[75] Increasingly harsh German air raids on British cities had also created a collective paranoia that the Germans 'may begin now at any moment' to 'employ poison germs in the bombs or vessels they drop over here from their Halberstadt aeroplanes by day or from their Zeppelins by night'.[76] And the British public was ever more convinced that shipping and trading companies where guilty

---

[71] BD, I, 4, pp. 639–642, Text of final version of St Jean de Maurienne Agreement as modified in subsequent discussions, plus letters of ratification, 18–22 August 1917.

[72] Imperiali, *Diario*, p. 433.

[73] M. Clodfelter, *Warfare and Armed Conflicts: A Statistical Encyclopedia of Casualty and Other Figures, 1492–2015* (Jefferson: McFarland, 2017), p. 428.

[74] Morrow, *The Great* War, p. 202.

[75] French, *Strategy of Lloyd George*, pp. 67, 85–86.

[76] TNA, CAB23/1, War Cabinet 59, War Cabinet minutes, 9 February 1917, Appendix II, 'Use of Bombs containing Poisonous Germs by Enemy and proposed Forms of

of profiteering – the Government being unwilling to stop this. Lloyd George tried to prevent an open revolt by implementing a food policy designed to conciliate the consumer. He conceded a subsidy and decided to requisite basic foodstuffs and to issue a list of fixed wholesale and retail prices for them.[77] But in June U-boat sinkings grew to 687,507 tons, again exceeding German predictions.[78] Had the trend continued, the prospect of starvation was real.

In May the Admiralty approved convoying all shipments coming through the North and South Atlantic. A convoy was a group of merchant-men or troopships travelling together with a naval escort. Allied naval authorities were slow to endorse this system: some of them miscalculated the number of escorts required, assuming that a 1:1 ratio between escorts and merchant vessels was needed – whereas a single escort ship could defend multiple merchant vessels; others believed that convoys presented larger and easier targets to U-boats. In fact, they reduced the number of available targets for U-boats, compared to a swarm of individual vessels, and forced the submarines to attack well-defended formations. After some successful experiments, the Allies approved the system at a naval conference in Paris on 24 July 1917, but the convoys' real impact only became evident in the second half of the year.[79] As for the Mediterranean, an Allied conference in Corfu, established a central authority for anti-submarine activities to arrange transport routes and escorts. Based in Malta under British command and made up of representatives of Allied navies, it opened the way for British direction of the anti-submarine war.[80] It was the first Allied step towards unification of command; results were slow however, for the Malta central authority did not have a magic wand to produce effective counter-measures to the submarine threat. The expedi-ents they tried included rather unsuccessful 'hunts' for U-boats and escort of individual merchant vessels.[81] In the Mediterranean, convoys were not introduced until the autumn, and the situation was exacerbated by the flaws in the Otranto barrage, through which U-boats continued to pass. On top of that, on 15 May 1917, the Austro-Hungarians launched a major raid against the Otranto line with their three fastest cruisers, *Novara*, *Helgoland* and *Saida*. The attack came by night and resulted in the sinking of fourteen

Retaliation' (Copy of Letter from Colonel Sir Arthur Davidson to Lord Hardinge of Penshurst, 18 January 1917).

[77] French, *Strategy of Lloyd George*, pp. 88–90.   [78] Clodfelter, *Warfare*, p. 428.

[79] French, *Strategy of Lloyd George*, pp. 74–77. After July the monthly losses never exceeded 500,000 tons, although they remained above 300,000 tons for the remainder of 1917: Morrow, *The Great War*, p. 202.

[80] TNA, ADM137/1421, Minutes of the Corfu Conference, 28 April-1 May 1917.

[81] A. Marder, *From the Dreadnought to Scapa Flow: The Royal Navy in the Fisher Era, 1904–1919*, 5 vols. (Oxford: Oxford University Press, 1961–1978), IV, p. 177.

Figure 11.1 The Austro-Hungarian U24 (former German UC12) submarine, captured by the Italians and renamed X1, returning to sea after repairs

of the forty-seven drifters in the line – and damage to another four. The Allied reaction was slow and confused, and the Austro-Hungarians escaped. The British realised that, until they could provide destroyers to protect the drifters, the line was likely to be raided again. As the destroyers were not available, the Admiralty ordered the drifters to be withdrawn, thereby making the barrage even less effective.[82]

With the Central Mediterranean now more open than ever to U-boats Allied naval losses increased dramatically. The inefficient Allied anti-submarine strategy affected Italy particularly since it was the most exposed Entente power in the Mediterranean. Proportionally, Italy lost the highest number of merchant vessels among the belligerents: 57.52 per cent as opposed to Britain's 42.63 per cent and France's 39.44 per cent.[83] These were superimposed on a merchant fleet, which was already chronically weaker than those of Britain and France: 617 ships in total (2,500,000 tons). Such a fleet, stated the Italian delegates at the Allied Shipping Commission, was 'absolutely insufficient for our needs in the matter of essential supplies, notwithstanding the restrictions in the consumption of bread, meat, sugar, coal etc. already imposed on our population, and the fact that importation of luxuries in Italy is stopped'.[84] Incidentally, Italy was also the Allied country more depend-ent on importation by sea of vital goods. The closing of the Dardanelles prevented Italy from obtaining grain from Russia and Romania, and the diversion of British traffic from the Mediterranean to the route around the Cape of Good Hope led to a drop of 33.9 per cent in Italian imports of fossil fuels.[85] Coal imports fell from 11 million tons in 1915 (90 per cent of which came from Britain) to 6 million tons in 1916 and by 1918 the figure was down to 5 million tons.[86] At the onset of the unrestricted submarine campaign a report of the Shipping Commission stressed that Italy must import monthly 'an absolute minimum' of 800,000 tons of coal. The shipping currently employed was sufficient for the importation of 465,000 tons monthly, so Italy had found it necessary 'to consume about 600,000 tons of different stocks, including navy stocks'.[87] These material difficulties were one reason why Italian naval authorities were reluctant to pool their forces in a systematic patrolling of Italian high seas, which the Entente allies tended to attribute to Italian cowardice.[88] Another was the limited capability of Italian dockyards to provide quick repairs, due largely to a lack of raw materials.[89] Of course, patrolling

---

[82] TNA, ADM137/782, Kerr to Admiralty, 21 May 1917.
[83] AUSM, b. 498, f. 3, La guerra degli Alleati, doc. 2107, 'Elenchi Navi italiane perdute durante la guerra. Tonnellaggio mercantile affondato durante la Guerra'.
[84] They would increase to 771 by the end of the war: USM, *Marina italiana*, VI, p. 564.
[85] Einaudi, *Condotta economica*, p. 59.   [86] USM, *Marina italiana*, VI, p. 563.
[87] Total stocks were 1,500,000; naval stocks were 800,000: AUSM, b. 827, f. 3, Allied Naval Conference Report, 23–24 January 1917.
[88] Morabito, *Marina italiana*, p. 150.
[89] AUSM, b. 827, f. 6, *cit.*, Revel a Rey di Villarey, Addetto navale all'ambasciata italiana in Londra, Memorandum per Lloyd George, 31 September 1917.

sporadically only favoured U-boat activity, in a deadly vicious circle. In May 1917, the Italian mission to Washington concluded that, without increases in coal deliveries, 'Italy would soon be out of the war'.[90] And Italy was undergoing a social crisis of its own. It sailed in more troubled waters than Britain; the latter was the world's largest capital exporter at the war's outbreak, whereas Italy was a net capital importer before a single shot was fired, so the supply crisis had greater impact on its people.[91] Strikes and anti-war protests multiplied throughout the spring.[92]

Rome therefore needed immediate support in both supplies and merchant vessels. Similar requests by France transformed the British supply crisis into an interconnected emergency in shipping, food, morale and provisions to Britain's allies.[93] Italian difficulties were discussed at an Allied conference in Paris (24 July). Revel, who was reinstated as the Chief of Naval Staff in February 1917, protested that the Malta commission had overlooked the Adriatic; he still considered it the key front in the Mediterranean – and he believed Austro-Hungarian raids proved him right.[94] Subsequently, Revel repeated his request for British cruisers arguing that the arrival of American and Japanese destroyers should have allowed the Royal Navy to provide more assistance.[95] The British were amused at the ineffability of the Italians – in their eyes 'children at the game of the sea'[96] who wanted an empire and were not even capable of defending their own waters. The Admiralty pointed out that the American destroyers had not reinforced the British fleet in the North Sea, but were engaged in defending Allied trade in the Atlantic, while the Japanese were fully occupied escorting troopships in the Mediterranean. The Royal Navy could not, therefore, spare anything more for the Adriatic.[97] On the contrary, it was the British who approached the Italians for reinforcements. Sir Eric Geddes, Admiralty First Lord, while dismissing Revel's Adriatic preoccupations, asked him for at least eleven destroyers to be used to escort Allied supplies to Italy. If provided with Italian escort, the British promised to send 700,000 tons of

---

[90] A. Caracciolo, 'La crescita e la trasformazione della grande industria durante la prima guerra mondiale', in G. Fuà ed., *Lo sviluppo economico in Italia* (Milan: Angeli, 1969), p. 203.

[91] D. J. Forsyth, *The Crisis of Liberal Italy* (Cambridge: Cambridge University Press, 1993), p. 321; Galassi and Harrison, 'Italy at War', pp. 4, 18.

[92] TNA, FO170/1005, n. 889, Rodd to Balfour, 1 November 1917; V. Zamagni, *The Economic History of Italy, 1860–1990* (Oxford: Clarendon, 1993), pp. 227–229.

[93] Stevenson, *1917*, p. 80.

[94] AUSM, b. 498, f. 18, Definition and Allocation of the Japanese and United States Reserves and their maximum contribution in the Mediterranean.

[95] TNA, FO371/2946, Memorandum from Imperiali, 26 June 1917.

[96] Halpern, *Naval War*, p. 236.   [97] Halpern, *Royal Navy*, pp. 213 ff.

coal a month to Italy. Revel politely opposed providing the eleven destroyers, as he explained to Sonnino:

We have only 40 destroyers, 21 of them antiquated and worn-out by long use, to fulfil the multiple obligations from the Tyrrhenian to the Adriatic, or the protection of communications to Libya and Albania. The 11 destroyers requested by the British represent more than a quarter of their already insufficient strength, and the request comes from the most powerful maritime nation in the world that has more than 375 destroyers, reinforced by American and Japanese craft.[98]

These statistics encouraged Revel's prejudice that the British wanted to exploit Italian resources to their own benefit.[99] In reality, the Royal Navy was already overstretched. In January 1917, a total of 70 British vessels where used for military transportation; 335 for provisioning overseas forces; 350 supplied the munitions and army clothing industries; 30 fuelled and provisioned the Royal Navy; 500 supplied Britain's allies and 750 supplied the British isles.[100] As noted by Stevenson, Britain struggled to satisfy its supply requirements even before the unrestricted submarine campaign, and its hindrance was aggravated when U-boat attacks intensified.[101] Revel did not appreciate this, whereas his British counterpart failed to appreciate that Italy's problem of defending trade did not end when large ships reached the major Italian ports; it was even more difficult to defend traffic between the large and small Italian ports. Consequently, Revel found it impossible to diminish the means he had to defend this traffic.[102] Once again, Italian reluctance to meet Allied requests was not caused by egoism or lack of collaborative spirit, but by serious material difficulties. Revel's refusal to comply with British naval schemes infuriated Geddes, who began to say openly to his subordinates that he saw the Italians as villains, and he threatened to interrupt supplies to Italy if the latter did not start to collaborate. Revel, in turn, reminded him that if shipments of coal ceased, he would be forced to suspend naval operations.[103] In Rodd's opinion, the fundamental problem was that 'Italy thinks she is a Great Power, but she is nothing of the sort'. Yet he begged the British naval authorities to appreciate Italy's efforts in really doing 'the little that she can'.[104] Rodd's tireless mediation, together with Revel's concession of twenty-eight Italian merchant vessels to be included in British convoys,

---

[98] AUSM, b. 740, f. 1, Revel to Sonnino, 24 September 1917.

[99] Marcuzzi, 'From the Adriatic', p. 479.

[100] NMM, DFF/6, Duff MSS, Duff memorandum, 1931.   [101] Stevenson, *1917*, p. 68.

[102] AUSM, b. 740, f. 1, Revel to Sonnino, *cit.*

[103] TNA, ADM137/1412, Ballard to Admiralty, 21 August 1917.

[104] Ibid., 137/499, Notes by Vice-Admiral Limpus, 15 March 1916.

allowed Rome to obtain an immediate despatch of 50,000 badly needed – though insufficient – tons of coal.[105]

The net situation was, quite simply, that Allied resources were strained, but all parties seemed unprepared to recognise that and tended to shoulder responsibility for the frustrating developments in the naval war onto their partners. The British assumed that the Italians kept asking for aid because they were either incapable or unwilling to commit themselves fully to the Allied cause (or both), which was not true; the Italians assumed that the British were disinclined to go beyond a limited assistance to Italy because they wanted to exploit the recourses of their allies without compromising their own, which was also not true. So, we see a recurrent discrepancy between Allied diplomatic negotiations – even when successful – and their strategic effect. Italy's commitment to the Entente's war formally increased between 1916 and 1917, but practically the impact was weaker than expected. It continued to be contested by reality: after Rome fully embraced the world war in 1916, Allied solidarity was hampered by colonial disharmony; when the latter was apparently resolved in the spring–summer of 1917, Allied collaboration was hindered by persisting material difficulties no less than diverging strategic views.

This is confirmed in land warfare. Another consequence of the St Jean de Maurienne Agreement was that it implied the rejection of Austria-Hungary's peace offer. Despite the fact that negotiations between Britain, France and Austria-Hungary were kept alive behind the scenes, the opportunity had for now passed.[106] Yet Lloyd George believed that the Austro-Hungarian card could still be played in a different way: since Austria-Hungary could not be extracted from its alliance with Germany diplomatically, it must be broken. He continued to sponsor greater efforts on peripheral fronts, and resumed his plan for a joint operation in Italy.[107] The Italians provided him with fresh arguments. Since the Seventh, Eighth and Ninth Isonzo battles (between September and November 1916) had failed to capitalise on the Gorizia victory, Rome welcomed a joint tenth offensive in May, in compliance with the Chantilly scheme.[108] This was Lloyd George's chance to offer the British public outstanding results at lesser cost in British lives.[109] He was further encouraged by the disastrous offensive of the new French Chief of Staff, Robert Nivelle, which, between 16 April and 9 May, led to 187,000 casualties with minimal gains in Northern France. The British had also

---

[105] USM, *Marina italiana*, VI, p. 18.   [106] Stevenson, *1917*, pp. 243–244.
[107] G. Sheffield, J. Bourne eds., *Douglas Haig: War Diaries and Letters, 1914–1918* (London: Weidenfeld & Nicolson, 2005), pp. 259–260.
[108] DDI, 5, VIII, doc. 44, Sonnino to Imperiali and Salvago Raggi, 21 May 1917.
[109] French, *Strategy of Lloyd George*, p. 53.

been involved in the attack under Anglo-French arrangements established at two conferences in Calais and Compiègne,[110] and had taken their own toll of losses – some 160,000. Lloyd George was determined that no such mistake should be made again.

Lloyd George's main problem was, once again, his generals. Both Robertson and Haig kept opposing any diversion of British forces from the western front. They pointed at the Gallipoli fiasco as a case that suggested against overseas solutions. The French also reiterated Napoleon's principle that only by defeating the enemy's 'principal mass' could the war be decided. And that could be done only on the western front. Taking Trieste, Pola or even Vienna 'would have no influence on the outcome of the war'.[111] Lloyd George would not fold. The high number of French casualties led to widespread *mutineries* that handicapped the French army for months. This was aggravated by the collapse of the Briand Government in March, which inaugurated a period of instability in French domestic politics until November 1917. Lloyd George needed a victory that prevented a Russia-style collapse in France.[112] But he could manage to extract from his generals only ten batteries of British six-inch howitzers for the Italian operation, much to Cadorna's dissatisfaction – 'We have to count ... on our own forces and means alone', he commented.[113] The British batteries served under the 3rd Italian Army commanded by the Duke of Aosta.[114] Once in Italy, the British confirmed at large Trevelyan's comments on that front: the terrain was impossible, the Italian soldiers were brave, but their commanders usually poor. British gunners noted the inadequate cooperation between Italian artillery and infantry; the former neglected counter-battery work and was brought forward too slowly when the infantry broke through.[115]

In the Tenth battle (12 May–8 June), the Italians attacked after Nivelle's offensive had ended, and before the Kerensky offensive had started. Lloyd George's hopes for better Allied coordination had once again fallen short of expectations, but Cadorna was optimistic. He told Delmé-Radcliffe that he would unleash 'a great offensive from Tolmino to the sea, since it was only by an offensive on this scale that he could be sure of obtaining a decisive success'.[116] The main attack focussed on the

---

[110] TNA, CAB23/1, War Cabinet 82, War Cabinet minutes, 28 February 1917, Appendix III, Agreement signed at Anglo-French Conference held at Calais, 26 and 27 February 1917.

[111] Stevenson, *1917*, pp. 123–129.   [112] French, *Strategy of Lloyd George*, p. 122.

[113] Quoted in C. Seton-Watson, *Storia d'Italia*, p. 534.   [114] Trevelyan, *Scenes*, p. 124.

[115] TNA, WO106/761 and 762, Delmé-Radcliffe reports, 31 May 1917; H. Dalton, *With British Guns in Italy: A Tribute to Italian Achievement* (London: Methuen & Co., 1919), pp. 22–49, 72–87.

[116] TNA, CAB24/18/95, Delmé-Radcliffe report, 4 July 1917.

lower Carso aiming to reach Trieste. By 22 May, Mount Kuk, Mount Vodice and Mount Santo had been conquered. But on 3 June an Austro-Hungarian counter-attack re-captured Mount Santo and part of Mount Vodice. The battle was a tactical Italian victory – which cost 160,000 Italian and 125,000 Austro-Hungarian losses – but Trieste remained a mirage.[117] The Carso offered little possibility for decisive pushes. The plateau, which 'yields as little shade or water as the Sahara', was cut through by cup-shaped hollows, or *doline*, 'each 20, 50, or more yards across', worn 'by the action of water collected for ages in the flat limestone surface'. Trevelyan observed that the Italians were trying hard to overcome the traditional problem of slow artillery re-positioning to prevent the attack abating: 'A few days after its capture I saw on top of Mount Kuk some Italian "seventy-fives" that had been dragged up, Heaven knows how, by sheer strength of arms and will during the *mêlée* itself'. But when approaching the Hermada, the mountain stronghold blocking the road to Trieste, the Italians found themselves stuck in 'a reedy marshland … passable only by narrow causeways and long wooden footbridges over the sullen water'. Trevelyan concluded: 'Anyone viewing the region wonders not why the Italians failed to establish themselves on Hermada, but how they at any time succeeded in crossing the marsh'.[118]

The Italian infantryman, the worst-paid soldier in Western Europe,[119] usually coming from the lower classes, had for two years faced this apocalyptic scenario with a tenacity that was matched only by the resilience by which he had always endured his poor social condition as a civilian. But now, morale began to falter. Minor mutinies – possibly encouraged by Pope Benedict XV's note on 1 August calling for an immediate cessation of hostilities – revealed that discontent was worming its way in the army.[120] An anonymous song became popular with the soldiers:

Il General Cadorna / ha scritto alla Regina / [General Cadorna / wrote to the Queen] se vuol veder Trieste / la guardi in cartolina / [if you want to see Trieste / get a postcard].[121]

Cadorna's frenetic purging which prevented the Italian officers from identifying with their unit, and vice versa and his exceptionally harsh discipline did not help.[122] During the Tenth battle, Italian officers

---

[117] Isenghi, Rochat, *Grande Guerra*, p. 211.   [118] Trevelyan, *Scenes*, pp. 123–124, 133.
[119] Thompson, *White War*, p. 5.   [120] Mondini, *Il Capo*, p. 300.
[121] A. V. Savona, M. L. Straniero eds., *Canti della Grande Guerra*, 2 vols. (Milan: Garzanti, 1981), I, pp. 169–180.
[122] The Italian army saw the highest number of death sentences among the belligerents: Mondini, *Il Capo*, p. 232.

Figure 11.2 General Cadorna visiting the British batteries in 1917

noted that the *élan* of their troops was less pronounced, and for the first time more attackers surrendered than did defenders – 27,000 Italians as opposed to 23,000 Austro-Hungarians – which was alarming. Aosta judged that at this rate, it would take ten years to get to Vienna, and the Italian people would say '*basta* – enough'.[123] But Cadorna, 'disgusted and nauseated' by the success of the Austro-Hungarian counter-attack – 'the most shameful fact of the war'[124] – was not dissuaded from launching an additional offensive on Mount Ortigara in Trentino, on 10–25 June. It was a complete failure that only added some 25,000 Italians and 9,000 Austro-Hungarians to the casualty bill.[125]

From the British perspective, the shipping crisis, French mutinies, Italian failures, and in July, Kerensky's disaster only increased the urgency of a victory. But Lloyd George was running out of options as to where it could be achieved. As Cadorna's thrusts wore down, discouraging additional British investment in Lloyd George's favourite Austro-Hungarian option, British advance in Palestine also marked time – Allenby's offensive was postponed to October, and Jerusalem would not fall before

[123] Stevenson, *1917*, pp. 210–216.   [124] Cadorna, *Lettere famigliari*, pp. 202–203.
[125] G. Pieropan, *Storia della grande guerra sul fronte italiano* (Milan: Mursia, 2009), p. 315.

December.[126] Ultimately this led the British army straight into the German jaws on the western front – yet again.

Like Cadorna, Haig still believed in a decisive battle. He shared Lloyd George's apprehension about the social crisis in Britain and agreed that 'success ... will do more than anything else to cure the doubts and the restlessness' of war. Only, he wanted to achieve it on his front. Robertson was less confident in a decisive battle with France unable to participate. Nonetheless, he recognised that inactivity was just not an option: pressure from Germany could not be relieved until the next season. Every time the Entente had allowed the Germans to seize the initiative – in May 1915 at Gorlice, in September 1915 in Serbia and in February 1916 at Verdun – they had inflicted grievous losses on the Allies. Now they might crush Russia or Italy. Robertson simply suggested pursuing limited objectives to minimise losses – the British had an encouraging precedent in minor, well-prepared offensives at the Vimy ridge battle in April.[127] Haig, however, had a formidable card to play – the Royal Navy. The Admiralty had begun to doubt that it could protect the British coastline from direct German attacks or amphibious operations undertaken with U-boat support. The General Staff agreed that it could not guarantee 'that invasion is impossible' and consequently '500,000 men ... [are] still locked up at home'.[128] Belgian ports were also known to be excellent bases for U-boats. Haig therefore promised to clear the Belgian coast. For some time, Lloyd George remained more favourable to a limited offensive on the premise that, if it met with insurmountable resistance, more British artillery could be transferred to Italy in time to participate in another Italian offensive in August. Haig dismissed it as 'the act of a lunatic'.[129] In the end, the Flanders offensive provided a rare case in which the exigencies of the military and those of the navy converged. Against such a unanimous chorus, Lloyd George could not stand. On 21 June, he approved Haig's plan which, if successful, would cure Allied morale and deliver a blow to enemy submarines.[130]

The Third battle of Ypres (or Passchendaele) resulted in a confused series of attacks and counter-attacks that went on, with some pauses, until 10 November 1917. The main British effort began on 31 July, followed by two great pushes on 10 and 16 August on the Gheluvelt plateau and at Langemark. None of them succeeded in driving the Germans off their positions. Heavy rain reduced the battlefield to a quagmire, but Haig insisted on continuing even when he had realised that no decisive

[126] Woodward, *Sir William Robertson*, p. 167.
[127] French, *Strategy of Lloyd George*, pp. 93–97.
[128] TNA, CAB23/1, War Cabinet 40, War Cabinet minutes, 22 January 1917.
[129] French, *Strategy of Lloyd George*, pp. 110, 122–121.
[130] TNA, CAB27/6, War Policy Committee, 21 June 1917.

breakthrough would be achieved. When the offensive was called off, the British had advanced some 9 kilometres; they had not seen a single Belgian port, and had in fact not even captured all of the objectives set for them on the first day.[131] Losses for the battle are disputed, but some 260,000 casualties on each side seems a reasonable figure.[132] Unsuccessful operationally, Third Ypres was also strategically fruitless. True, it gave the French some badly needed respite, but it did not prevent the Germans from operating offensively elsewhere: the latter managed to pursue the Russians almost as far as threatening Petrograd and had still some reserves available if Austria-Hungary needed them. This was soon to be a key element on the Italian front.[133]

11.3   Apparent Rapprochement

The Allied strategic procurement in the summer of 1917 seemed to call into question Lloyd George's achievement at St Jean de Maurienne. Revived Allied solidarity had not led to better military integration, and Austria-Hungary was still unbeaten. Nonetheless, the colonial treaty impacted Anglo-Italian relations in ways that were less obvious.

In the first place, it re-launched the Anglo-Italian entente, especially in Italian eyes. Sonnino and Boselli thought the arrangement had cleared away previous conflicts. Moreover, the ratification of the treaty coincided with the peak of Rodd's propaganda campaign which, after three months, began, in Rodd's words, to produce 'its effect'.[134] The extent of this effect is difficult to quantify. It can be revealed by the excellent and widespread collaboration that Rodd and Thorold established with Italian agents. The British embassy employed first-class Italian intellectuals such as Mario Borsa, Guido Calza and Salvemini, who published articles and pamphlets emphasising British strength and achievements, as well as Anglo-Italian friendship.[135] The British also enjoyed the 'splendid work done at Milan by Donna Bettina di Casanova' who founded the Milan British Institute. This proved 'invaluable for maintaining contact between the subjects of the two countries by supplying information, correcting misapprehensions and organising lectures'.[136] On Thorold's initiative, it was later copied at Florence, Genoa and Rome. Each institute, Thorold told Buchan,

[131] French, *Strategy of Lloyd George*, pp. 125–126.
[132] Sheffield, *Forgotten Victory. The First World War: Myths and Realities* (London: Headline, 2002 [2001]), p. 216.
[133] Stevenson, *1917*, p. 204.   [134] Rodd, *Memories*, p. 311.
[135] The most 'effective' of these were *Che cosa fanno gli inglesi, L'esercito inglese, L'Italia e l'Inghilterra, La guerra illustrata*, and *La vita Britannica*: C. Seton-Watson, 'British Propaganda', p. 127.
[136] Rodd, *Memories*, pp. 311–315.

constituted 'an organised form of providing accurate information which, besides being itself propaganda, would create a propitious atmosphere for any special propaganda work'.[137] British propaganda pieces were regularly distributed in Italian circles, public libraries and frequently published in Italian newspapers such as *Il Corriere*. English books were also distributed throughout the country, progressively breaking Germany's monopoly in the foreign book trade. Rodd was surprised by the degree of 'demand for English books' both 'from the professorial world and a limited reading public'. To reach illiterate Italians, Rodd worked with his Italian agents and acquaintances, who travelled around Italy holding conferences, seminars and speeches in the public squares, promoting the ideals of the Entente and Britain's role in close partnership with Italy.[138] This intense pro-Britain mobilisation of the Italian public made the idea of a special Anglo-Italian partnership, which in 1915 was stronger at the elites level, widespread. The propaganda that emphasised British generosity seemed to be validated by Sonnino's speech in parliament on 16 June, when he stressed British support of the principle of 'equilibrium and equality among the Allied powers' in the colonial question.[139] This was much publicised by the Italian media; Trevelyan too noted that, in light of American indifference to Italy – Washington had not even declared war on Vienna – it was 'mainly to England that the Italian war party still looked'.[140]

The renewed emphasis on common Anglo-Italian liberal values also encouraged an ideological shift in some Italian elites – as Lloyd George had hoped. Intellectuals like Luigi Albertini and Salvemini began to suggest a partial revision of Italy's claims in Dalmatia, embracing the policy of nationalities sponsored by American President Woodrow Wilson and welcomed by Lloyd George. More importantly, the opening of the summer session of the Chamber revealed a growing rift between the two prominent Cabinet members, Sonnino and Bissolati, over foreign policy.[141] Bissolati had replaced Martini as the soul of Italian democratic interventionism, breathing the Risorgimento-like message into the policy of nationalities.[142] Sonnino was the representative of Italian imperialism. In the middle were a few young MPs such as Francesco Saverio Nitti, who understood the need to integrate the two centrifugal forces within the Government and in Italian diplomacy.[143] They tended to support

[137] C. Seton-Watson, 'British Propaganda', p. 128.   [138] Rodd, *Memories*, p. 315.
[139] Sonnino papers, reel 51, Text of Sonnino's Speech to Chamber, 16 June 1917.
[140] Trevelyan, *Scenes*, p. 139.
[141] Sonnino, *Discorsi Parlamentari*, 3 vols. (Rome: Tipografia della Camera dei Deputati, 1925), III, pp. 564–568.
[142] Martini, *Diario*, pp. 931–933.   [143] Riccardi, *Alleati*, pp. 516 ff.

Bissolati, even though for the moment this axis was not being rallied against the Boselli Government. Such politicians had realised that Russia's revolution, American 'new diplomacy' – which talked directly to the peoples – and the strengthening of national sentiment among the Slavs, were changing world diplomacy; Italy needed to adapt.[144]

To reconcile the two factions, Boselli relied on men like Romeo Gallenga Stuart, a fervent interventionist, but more dynamic and less grouchy than Sonnino, and closer to the liberals. Together with Salvemini and Bissolati, he supported a moderate policy towards the Slavs, but was nonetheless committed to the dream of 'the greater Italy'. Upon the suggestion of Orlando, the Interior Minister, Boselli entrusted Gallenga Stuart with a special mission to Britain, aimed at further strengthening the Anglo-Italian entente against potential American intrusiveness in Allied war aims. Boselli wanted to test the degree of Britain's renewed benevolence towards Italy. The warm reception London had given to the American nationality principle, and the ever-growing British sympathy for the Yugoslavs, contrasted with British promises to Italy, and caused him some concern. Gallenga Stuart's mission was the ultimate and most important of a series of propaganda missions that Boselli organised throughout the spring of 1917 to improve relations with his allies.[145]

Gallenga Stuart's mission, which began shortly after the signing of the colonial agreement in August, evolved into a broader attempt to encourage more sympathy in the British public for Italy and its war aims. Modelled on British propaganda in Italy, Gallenga Stuart sought to involve British intellectual and political elites as well as the wider public. He worked on three levels. First, he exploited his personal relations with influential journalists and intellectuals such as Steed and Seton-Watson to explain the Italian war more effectively than hitherto; second, he set out to persuade British entrepreneurs to invest in Italy; finally, he encouraged mediation on the Adriatic question with leading exiled Yugoslavs, such as Frano Supilo and Nikola Pašić.[146] In his report to Orlando who forwarded it to Boselli, Gallenga Stuart wrote: 'The entire British Yugoslav movement, with *The Times* at the forefront, can be an effective ally against the tendency, which still exists in certain political spheres in this country, to oppose the dismemberment of the Austro-Hungarian Empire'.[147] The latter was not part of Italy's original war aims but

---

[144] DDI, 5, VIII, doc. 718, Nitti to Sonnino, 23 July 1917; C. Seton-Watson, *Storia d'Italia*, p. 539.
[145] Tosi, *Propaganda*, pp. 130 ff.
[146] D. Šepic, *Supilo diplomat* (Zagabria: Naprijed, 1961), pp. 242–249.
[147] Albertini, *Venti anni*, II, pp. 534–538, 546–552.

Gallenga Stuart and Orlando now tended to see it as a precondition for the fulfilment of Italian irredentist and Adriatic aspirations. To overcome British resistance to the break-up of the Empire, Italy should first avoid hysterical reactions to anti-Italian provocations by the Yugoslavs, then pursue its goals with a friendly attitude, limiting imperialist slogans as much as possible: 'I believe that, with tactful insistence, the Yugoslav movement will end up resigning itself to Italian claims on Dalmatia'.[148]

Gallenga Stuart's evaluation of the state of Anglo-Italian relations was even more optimistic. It was significantly influenced by military developments on the Italian front, where Cadorna launched his Eleventh Isonzo offensive on 18 August. It was the largest of Cadorna's battles, involving three quarters of the Italian army supported by 3,750 guns and 1,900 *bombarde*. Cadorna aimed at seizing the Bainsizza plateau between Gorizia and Tolmino to cut in half the enemy front and turn Mount Hermada from north. The preparatory bombardment was tremendous, supplemented by what John Peaty called 'the first strategic bombing campaign in history'.[149] Contrary to claims that 'the Italians lacked the western allies' customary air superiority'[150] in the summer of 1917 they had gained command of the skies,[151] and made good use of it bombing the Austro-Hungarian rear, disabling command centres and wrecking communication lines. Then the Austro-Hungarian trenches on the plateau were 'stormed in the grand style'. Trevelyan, who witnessed the attack, wrote that Capello's 2nd Army pursued it 'with the dash characteristic of the Italians whenever they are well led'.[152] By early September, the Bainsizza was in Italian hands, though at a terrible cost: the attackers' losses totalled 166,000, and 400 of the 600 battalions involved lost half or more of their strength.[153] Although shorter a battle than Third Ypres, Eleventh Isonzo saw a higher daily casualty rate, and the forces committed where similar – fifty-two Italian divisions as compared to fifty British divisions. The Italian front, in the words of Stevenson, 'had become extraordinarily destructive'.[154] General Paul von Hindenburg later called it 'a front as harsh as the Western Front, indeed, in many respects worse'. Waging a war of attrition in the mountains was a nightmare for the

---

[148] ACS, Carte Orlando, b. 5, f. 236, Gallenga Stuart to Orlando, 13 August 1917.

[149] J. Peaty, 'The Place of Douhet: A Reassessment', in G. Montinaro ed., 'Airpower in 20th Century. Doctrines and Employment – National Experiences', *Rivista Internazionale di Storia Militare*, 89 (The Hague: International Commission of Military History, 2011), p. 107.

[150] Stevenson, *1917*, p. 219.

[151] R. Gentili, P. Varriale, *Reparti dell'aviazione italiana nella Grande Guerra* (Rome: Ufficio Storico dell'Aeronautica Militare [USAM], 1999), p. 21.

[152] Trevelyan, *Scenes*, p. 143.   [153] Thompson, *White War*, p. 282.

[154] Stevenson, *1917*, p. 213.

defenders no less than for the attackers. An Austro-Hungarian veteran, Colonel Georg Veith, recorded: 'For anyone who had fought once on the Isonzo, any other theatre of war was deprived of its horror'.[155] In the Eleventh battle, the Austro-Hungarians suffered again proportionally heavier casualties than the Italians – 140,000 – and were on the brink of collapse.[156] The Italians lacked the energy for a final assault that might have been the decisive one. Nonetheless, Lloyd George was elated by the news of 'Cadorna's victory on the Carso'.[157] The British press tended to see the Tenth and Eleventh battles as two stages of a single, great offensive and cheered at 'General Cadorna's triumph';[158] the *West Sussex Gazette* called it 'an Italian masterpiece ... , one of the greatest feats of the war so far, on any front'.[159] When the Italians finally took Mount Santo on 24 August, *The Times* hyped the enterprise:

The main attack was brilliantly successful. ... They [Italians] broke down all resistance. They stormed the machine-gun positions, careless of loss ... and reached the caverns. In less than an hour the Italians were in possession of the main peak.[160]

Imperiali was amused. Throughout the summer, he saw British praises as confirmation that the Anglo-Italian special partnership was alive. He wrote to Sonnino:

The cordial and ever more intimate friendship of Britain can be of great value to contain and counter-balance the pernicious intrusiveness of France. That this country [Britain] is widely [*in massa*] friendly to us seems to me demonstrated by the abundant and unanimous expressions of enthusiastic gratification for the recent glorious successes of our troops.[161]

In such context Gallenga Stuart was easily convinced that, despite past misunderstandings, London trusted Italy, and that British 'generous friendship' was real. The British, he claimed, had lost all hope in Russia; they had a barely disguised hostility towards France; as regards the United States, London hoped it would not have a major role in resolving the conflict. Therefore, all that was left for Britain was to embrace Anglo-Italian collaboration. For Italy too, cultivating British support was crucial because 'it is certain that our friendship with England will place us at the lead of the Europe of tomorrow'. Gallenga Stuart argued that Italian claims under the London and St. Jean de Maurienne pacts should not be Italy's priority: it was more important to

---

[155] Quoted in Pieri *L'Italia*, p. 88.   [156] Barbero, *Caporetto*, p. 6.
[157] French, *Strategy of Lloyd George*, p. 137.   [158] *The Morning Post*, 27 May 1917.
[159] *The West Sussex Gazette War Special*, 3rd year, n. 47, 1917.
[160] *The Times*, 3 September 1917.
[161] DDI, 5, VIII, doc. 181, Imperiali to Sonnino, 1 June 1917.

establish through the war, those ties that would make Italy Britain's partner of choice in the post-war leadership of Europe. Gallenga Stuart linked the positions of Bissolati and the wider liberal-oriented Italian political and intellectual circles, to those of Sonnino and the imperialists. The bond did not, however, rest on the democratic ideals, which would later take hold. Rather it was a liberal-nationalist project. Thus, Lloyd George's efforts, sustained by an unprecedented British propaganda campaign with the ultimate purpose of encouraging a shift in Italian foreign policy, led to a major misunderstanding. True, Gallenga Stuart encouraged Italy's policymakers to go beyond the technical content of Allied pacts, but nothing suggests that he ever envisaged a reduction of the Italian expansionist thrust. If anything, Gallenga Stuart spoke of an Italian hegemony on more ambitious lines, going beyond Adriatic supremacy to European.[162] Gallenga Stuart's report was much appreciated by Orlando, who found it 'of great accuracy and fairness'.[163] The most important point that Orlando gleaned was that Britain was really committed to a special partnership with Italy, and that it was enough to soften Italy's rigid attitude to gain everything that had been promised, and maybe more.

Now, this idea of an Anglo-Italian leadership of Europe shows a rather naïve enthusiasm on Gallenga Stuart's part. It did not consider the anti-Italian currents that existed in both the Cabinet and the Foreign Office, and it underestimated how important – albeit problematic and at times irritating – the London-Paris tie really was. But Gallenga Stuart's ideas reflected the confidence which, in the summer of 1917, was growing among Italian elites and public opinion, that Britain really was Italy's preferred partner, happy to support Italy's empire project. This misunderstanding, aggravated by Lloyd George's expectations that he could alter the fundamental lines of Italian foreign policy, had a traumatic impact on Anglo-Italian relations in the final act of the war.

---

[162] Tosi, *Propaganda*, p. 136.
[163] ACS, Carte Orlando, b. 5, f. 236, Orlando to Gallenga, 23 August 1917.

Part III

The Forked Road to Victory and Peace (Autumn 1917–Summer 1919)

12   Context

The Twelfth battle of the Isonzo, between 24 October and 12 November 1917, was a traumatic moment in Italian history and threatened the very unity of the country. It originated with the results of the earlier battle. Although they had failed to achieve a decisive break-through, the Italians had advanced some 10 kilometres, which by Isonzo standards was a remarkable result. The Austro-Hungarians communicated to their German allies that they could not withstand another Italian attack and Hindenburg, despite the opposition of his subordinates, including Erich Ludendorff, reluctantly decided to mount a German and Austro-Hungarian counter-offensive into Italy.[1]

The attack broke the Italian lines between Tolmino and Plezzo, above a village called Caporetto.[2] The outcome was a massive Italian retreat to the Piave River, some 150 kilometres deep into Italian territory. For the Central Powers, it was one of the greatest advances of the war. For Italy, it provoked a dramatic shift in Rome's position within the Entente, and made an impact particularly on the goals of the Anglo-Italian alliance. On the one hand, Caporetto ended Italy's strategic autonomy, turning Italy's war from offensive to defensive both militarily and diplomatically. Militarily, Italy was now an invaded country fighting for its own survival; diplomatically, the defeat weakened Italy's position in the Entente and forced Rome to defend its empire project from any potential revision of the London and St Jean de Maurienne pacts following the new diplomacy of the Americans. On the other hand, Britain's objectives for the alliance changed significantly: previously London's aim was to involve Italy in a wider war, now Britain had to concentrate on keeping Italy in the war.

The Italian crisis is an example of how a military *débâcle* can test the very nature of an alliance. After the Russian collapse and in the midst of Allied financial, naval and social watersheds, Caporetto seemed to be the

[1] Barbero, *Caporetto*, pp. 22–23.
[2] C. Falls, *Caporetto 1917* (London: Weidenfeld & Nicholson, 1996), p. 25.

final blow to the Entente. The Allies clashed over responsibility for such a disaster and about how to react to it. In the end, the Entente's response is worth considering as a most effective reaction to a military emergency in coalition warfare. The medium-term consequences in Allied grand strategy were also important. The crisis stimulated greater Allied integration, leading to military cooperation in Italy, improving naval coordination and bringing about the unification of command on land. The Allies managed to prevent another 'Russian collapse' in Italy also by adopting a new propaganda strategy to counter defeatism and undermine the unity of the Austro-Hungarian Empire. These Allied successes proved decisive when the Germans and the Austro-Hungarians launched their 1918 offensives, aimed at finishing the war before the United States could come in full force. It was not all plain sailing for the Allies, though. Solutions to some crucial issues, such as the creation of an Allied reserve and unification of naval command, remained chimerical. Mutual competition within the Alliance did not dissolve and impacted negatively on its capacity to challenge the rising American hegemony.

The American case reveals the difficulty of integrating a stronger power into the political blueprint of a coalition on its knees. The emergence of an external power – the United States did not join the Allies as a new Entente member, but as an 'associate power' – as the de facto leader of the Alliance produced a shift in the political hierarchies of the Entente, which altered the original goals of the Entente's war. The approaches of Britain and Italy to this situation were antithetical; equally antithetical were the preparations for the Peace Conference in the two countries. This cast a shadow over their relations during the conference, and beyond.

13   Clash of Responsibilities
The Caporetto Crisis

13.1   Why Caporetto?

In the first half of September 1917, as the Italians were still winning their way 'yard by yard'[1] on the Bainsizza, and Haig's Flanders offensive had clearly failed its main objective, Lloyd George resurrected his Austro-Hungarian plan. Contrary (again) to his generals, he believed that prompt support to Cadorna might reinvigorate his Eleventh offensive and – as Lloyd George told Ribot – '*porter l'Austriche à traiter*'.[2] On 4 September Ribot agreed to transfer hundred heavy guns attached to the French armies in Flanders to Italy.[3] The decision had come too late to reinforce Cadorna's Eleventh battle, yet Lloyd George was confident that Allied reinforcements could join the decisive attack in mid-October. Cadorna initially agreed, but by late September, he changed his mind. The Russian crisis favoured the transfer of enemy forces to the Italian front, and a counter-attack seemed likely.[4]

Cadorna's decision to postpone any offensive to the following spring spurred Balfour's protest that, 'it was solely to assist an early Italian offensive that the French and British Governments consented to send a hundred heavy guns from the Western front where they are sorely needed'.[5] Cadorna replied harshly on 23 September: 'I cannot have my general decisions conditioned by the presence of this artillery on our front'. Cadorna held that Allied artillery was needed to defend the advances made in his earlier offensive.[6] On 25 September, Lloyd George and the new head of the French Government, Paul Painlevé,

---

[1] Trevelyan, *Scenes*, p. 123.   [2] Sonnino, *Diario*, III, p. 174.
[3] French, *Strategy of Lloyd George*, pp. 137–139.
[4] Sonnino, *Carteggio*, Cadorna to Giardino, 18 September 1917.
[5] TNA, FO371/2947/184450, Balfour to Erskine, 21 September 1917; ADMAEF, Guerre 1914–1918, Italie, vol. 578/109–110, Notes on an Anglo-French Conference, 4 September 1917.
[6] DDI, 5, IX, doc. 121, Sonnino to Borghese, 26 September 1917.

met at Boulogne to consider the Italian position.[7] They agreed that the guns had been granted to Italy for offensive purposes and any other use would entail their withdrawal.[8] The following day Robertson, in a terse message to Cadorna, demanded the immediate return of the guns. Cadorna's complaints were ignored.[9] The military dispute turned political. On 28 September the Italian *chargé d'affaires* in London, Livio Borghese, begged the British Government to leave the guns in Italy, as their withdrawal on the eve of a likely counter-offensive would have a dangerous effect, 'both on the safety of our front', and 'on overall morale'.[10] Lloyd George politely reminded him that the British commander was Robertson; and Robertson could not be moved.[11] The new Italian ambassador in Paris, Giuseppe Salvago Raggi, had much the same response from the French.[12] It was not until the week before the Austro-German attack at Caporetto that some concern regarding the Italian front emerged in London. Still, it appears to have been little more than a vague apprehension of the growing Italian anti-war sentiment. On 19 October, Rodd wrote to Balfour that 'the position of the Government is critical owing to a general dissatisfaction with war'.[13] Delmé-Radcliffe reported that the Italian Government 'fears the growing discontent in the country', fuelled by German-financed propaganda.[14] British diplomats felt that, as long as Sonnino remained Foreign Minister, 'there is no danger of *combinazioni* designed to leave us in the lurch'. However, 'if Sonnino were to fall, one does not feel any security in this direction'.[15] The only mention of an imminent enemy offensive was news, which reached the Foreign Office on 17 October: 100,000 German troops had been spotted in Tyrol on their way to Italy.[16] But once again, the risk was underestimated, and British preoccupations remained in the Middle East and Russia.[17] The decision to keep a symbolic number of British guns in Italy, withdrawing the rest, was a sadly unsatisfactory compromise.[18] Prior to Caporetto,

---

[7] Riccardi, *Alleati*, p. 540.

[8] ADMAEF, Guerre 1914–1918, Italie, Dossier Général, vol. 997/5–6, Conclusions of an Anglo-French Conference held in the train at Boulogne, 25 September 1917.

[9] Riccardi, *Alleati*, pp. 538–540.

[10] TNA, FO371/2947/188288, Secret Memorandum from the Italian Embassy, 27 September 1917.

[11] DDI, 5, IX, doc. 132, Borghese to Sonnino, 29 September 1917.

[12] Poincaré, *Au Service*, IX, p. 307; DDI, 5, IX, doc. 139, Salvago Raggi to Sonnino, 1 October 1917. Tittoni was replaced by Salvago Raggi on 9 November 1916; Salvago Raggi was replaced by Lelio Bonin Longare on 24 October 1917.

[13] TNA, FO170/1005, n. 849: Rodd to Balfour, 19 October 1917.

[14] Ibid., CAB24/27/GT2182: Delmé-Radcliffe to Robertson, 21 September 1917.

[15] Ibid., FO800/173/It/17/1: Grahame to Bertie, 6 January 1917.

[16] Ibid., 170/1014, Foreign Office note, n. 1830.

[17] Ibid., FO170/1809, n. 804, Dallolio to Delmé-Radcliffe, 22 October 1917.

[18] Martini, *Diario*, p. 996.

then, Italy's allies failed to analyse the situation accurately, notwithstanding the recurring Italian alarms.

Cadorna's contradictions made things worst. He was not as solicitous in ensuring that his orders to Italian commanders had been properly executed as he was in asking for Allied assistance. Capello, the aggressive commander of the 2nd Army, developed an offensive plan that contrasted with Cadorna's defensive instructions: the Italians should respond to a possible Austro-German offensive with 'a mighty counter-offensive', so Capello deployed most of his forces well forward.[19] His subordinate, Alberto Cavaciocchi, commander of the 4th corps in the Caporetto sector, made very poor defensive preparations, but Cadorna realised it only two days before the battle because he had not visited the frontline in sometime.[20] Cadorna himself oscillated from apprehension to scepticism about an enemy offensive with winter approaching. And the Italian commanders displayed an unprecedented – and, in retrospect, bizarre – optimism; Cavaciocchi and Badoglio, who led the 17th corps adjacent to the 4th, believed they could easily repulse the offensive, whereas Capello, as days passed, grew doubtful that it would come at all.[21] Rodd recorded: 'A greater feeling of confidence as regards the military situation on the Austrian front exists today than probably at any time since the beginning of the war'.[22] In the opposite camp, the Germans and Austro-Hungarians were working on a battle plan of unprecedented ambition on the Italian front. In September, two experts from the German General Staff went to the Isonzo to find a site suitable for a gas attack. They proposed the quiet Caporetto sector – farther from the lower Isonzo where the main body of the Italian army was deployed – where a good road ran west through a mountain valley to the Venetian plain. Boroëvić's *Isonzo-Armee* would be supported by the newly formed 14th Army, made of nine Austro-Hungarian and six German divisions, commanded by Otto von Below. The plan included a major attack in the upper Isonzo, north of the Tolmino bridgehead, and a secondary attack from the Plezzo basin. Unfortunately for the Italians, the Germans used new infiltration tactics, which they would successfully replicate in the west in 1918 .[23]

At 2 a.m. on 24 October infiltration attacks began with a brief and violent bombardment made of explosive, gas and smoke projectiles on the

[19] L. Capello, *Per la verità* (Milan: Treves, 1920), pp. 238–241.

[20] Gatti, *Diario*, p. 197.

[21] Stevenson, *1917*, p. 221; A. Cavaciocchi, *Un anno al comando del IV corpo d'armata. Il memoriale dell'unico generale che pagò per Caporetto* (Udine: Gaspari, 2006), p. 72; Trevelyan, *Scenes*, p. 162.

[22] TNA, FO371/2947, Rodd to Balfour, 9 September 1917.

[23] Labanca, *Caporetto. Storia e memoria di una disfatta* (Bologna: Il Mulino, 2017), pp. 113–115.

Italian front and communication lines, aimed at disrupting roads, artillery and command posts, so as to isolate the frontline and reduce the defenders' capability to launch effective counter-attacks. The objective was fully achieved. Then the new elite Stormtroopers provided with anti-gas masks and the shocking flamethrower weapon, penetrated the Italians' weak points, bypassing their strongholds. The weather, characterised by a heavy mist that made visibility difficult for the defenders, facilitated the assault. The Italians put up a hopeless resistance: they were outgunned 2:1 and outnumbered 3:1 in the sector where the German *Durchbruch* fell – at the conjunction between the Italian 4th and 17th corps.[24] Furthermore, having sustained essentially offensive operations hitherto, the Italians were little accustomed to some fundamental elements of defence, such as elastic tactics – and the terrain inhibited them anyway.[25] So when the front was breached, the Italians could hardly avoid the catastrophe. Whilst German and Austro-Hungarian reserves followed up to deal with the isolated Italian strongholds, the Stormtroopers pushed forward to keep momentum, catching by surprise Italian reserves limping towards the frontline. These found the enemy around them and usually behind them when they thought to be in safe territory and were in marching formation. Cries of 'treason' mixed up with those of '*viva la Germania*' and 'the war is over', and many surrendered with little or no fight.[26] Von Below's secondary attacks on either side of the main offensive were staved off by the Italians. Similarly, Boroëvić made little progress in the south. Nevertheless, von Below's sweeping success in the centre put the bulk of the Italian forces in the lower Isonzo, in danger of complete encirclement. In the night between 26 and 27 October, Cadorna ordered the retreat of the 2nd and 3rd Armies to the Tagliamento River. This was soon accompanied by a spontaneous and chaotic migration of civilians – between 230,000 and 500,000 – from the Carnia and Cadore areas westwards, which incidentally contributed to hindering the movement of Italian reserves.[27]

These developments were not initially appreciated in London. The first reports from Delmé-Radcliffe were rather optimistic. He stated that Cadorna was facing the situation 'with resolution', and did not intend 'to be overcome by it'.[28] Rodd sent several telegrams to persuade the Foreign Office that the situation was difficult but was not irremediable. He stressed

---

[24] Barbero, *Caporetto*, pp. 200–244.   [25] Stevenson, *1917*, p. 219.
[26] Barbero, *Caporetto*, pp. 341 ff.
[27] R. Seth, *Caporetto: The Scapegoat Battle* (London: Macdonald, 1965), p. 147; Mondini, *Il Capo*, p. 284.
[28] TNA, CAB24/30/21, Operations. Telegrams to and from the French and Italian Fronts, Delmé-Radcliffe to Robertson, 26 October 1917.

that 'so far the [Italian] national spirit seems calm. No signs of panic'. He concluded: 'The first impression is ... that the unfortunate experiences of the last few days have fortified public determination and drawn the nation together'.[29] The day after the attack Lloyd George met Imperiali. The British premier was confident that the Italian army could hold and mentioned once again his plan for a joint Allied offensive on the Italian front the following spring: 'We must defeat Austria but afterwards you must help us against Germany'.[30] Given the British optimism, inevitably there was some panic in London when the real scope of the defeat became known. In three weeks, the Italian casualties were more than 300,000 men, including dead, wounded and prisoners, as well as 3,100 guns and a further 300,000 men deserted – as opposed to 50,000 losses of the Central Powers.[31] Cadorna, who was pleased to repeat that he was in command of the largest Italian army since the time of the Caesars, had suffered 'the worst defeat on Italian soil since the battle of Cannae', over two millennia before.[32]

Such disaster quickly led to a venomous inter-Allied debate over responsibility, which had a crucial impact on the Allies' subsequent approach to crisis-solving. Cadorna accused his counterparts in the Entente of having taken from him 'with such sudden decision, the greater part of their guns ... even though I, being fully aware of how the situation was developing, had begged them to leave [the guns] on this Front'.[33] In contrast, the British held Cadorna responsible for not having used the Allied artillery. Even Rodd, who held Cadorna in high regard,[34] complained that 'the disaster is in great measure due to the most unfortunate abandonment by General Cadorna of his intended further offensive in the middle of October'.[35] Cadorna's more recent conduct also came under fire. Robertson sent Delmé-Radcliffe a telegram around noon on the 27th, exhorting him to do all he could to steady the *Comando Supremo*: 'Cadorna should have no difficulty in stopping the hostile advance ... The Roumanians [sic] did so a few months ago and surely the Italians could do the same if the troops but fought moderately well. Apparently, a panic prevails regarding which you should take a firm and stout line'.[36] After

---

[29] Ibid., FO170/1005: ns. 879, 883, 884 and 897, Rodd to Balfour, 29 and 31 October, and 4 November 1917; Rodd papers, Rodd to Balfour, 1 and 2 November 1917; Rodd to Hardinge, 7 November 1917.

[30] Imperiali, *Diario*, p. 433.

[31] M. Silvestri, *Caporetto, una battaglia e un enigma* (Bergamo: Bur, 2006), pp. 229–232.

[32] Thompson, *White War*, p. 325.

[33] Quoted in: P. Pieri, *La prima guerra mondiale 1914–1918. Studi di storia militare*, G. Rochat ed. (Rome: USSME, 1986), pp. 147–149.

[34] Rodd, *Memories*, III, p. 256.

[35] TNA, FO371/2948/213890, Rodd to Balfour, 3 November 1917.

[36] Rodd papers, Robertson to Delmé-Radcliffe, 27 October 1917.

reprimanding his allies, Cadorna blamed his soldiers. His bulletin of 28 October attributed defeat to the 'cowardice' of some units belonging to the 2nd Army.[37] In reality, the troops in the frontline had fought as hard as they could. The chaos and panic, which led to the number of prisoners and stragglers, was a consequence of the breakthrough and ruthless enemy pursuit, not the cause of the rout. Works by Roberto Bencivenga, Nicola Labanca, Paolo Gaspari and Vanda Wilcox have also revealed that in the first 48 hours of the battle, panic was more common in the Italian commands than in the Italian ranks, as generals like Giovanni Arrighi, commanding the 50th division in the 4th corps, and Capello's deputy, Luca Montuori, ordered hasty withdrawals from key points that should have been defended energetically; Cavaciocchi and Badoglio, for their part, suffered what Bencivenga termed a 'paralysis of will ... passively submitting to the will of the enemy'.[38] After the general retreat had been ordered, war tiredness resurfaced and Italian ranks were gradually infected by the cry of '*andiamo a casa* – let's go home'. Still, it was not a universal sentiment; whereas the 2nd Army collapsed, the others retreated in relatively good order, and some units fought a draining series of rear-guard actions to buy time for their comrades to escape.[39]

Cadorna's unfair bulletin was a low blow from a commander desperate to save himself at the expense of his men. In so doing, he discredited both the Italian army and the whole country, and he managed to further infuriate Italian politicians – Sonnino remonstrated: 'We run the risk of being treated like Russia'.[40] Imperiali fumed with rage when he read the bulletin, which he considered a lie and a major diplomatic mistake.[41] With a few lines, Cadorna had nullified all efforts by both Imperiali and Rodd to avert panic in the Foreign and War Offices. Late on 28 October Imperiali received a second version of the bulletin which, following Sonnino's instructions, emphasised the enemy's irresistible strength as the cause of the defeat. Imperiali managed to prevent the first version from being published in the British press, but Cadorna's bulletin had circulated in the War Office. It had a devastating impact. It revived historic anti-Italian prejudices and encouraged an interpretation of events, which blamed the Italian people for the *débâcle*. Haig commented:

[37] Isnenghi, Rochat, *Grande Guerra*, p. 391.

[38] Bencivenga, *La sorpresa strategica*, p. 85; Labanca, *Caporetto*, pp. 97–98; V. Wilcox, 'Generalship and Mass Surrender during the Italian Defeat at Caporetto', in I. F. W. Beckett ed., *1917: Beyond the Western Front* (Leiden & Boston, 2009), p. 38; P. Gaspari, *Le bugie di Caporetto. La fine della memoria dannata* (Udine: Gaspari, 2011).

[39] Trevelyan, *Scenes*, p. 169; Labanca, *Caporetto*, pp. 118–125.

[40] DDI, 5, IX, doc. 320, Sonnino to Cadorna, 30 October 1917.

[41] Imperiali, *Diario*, p. 446.

'The Italians seem a wretched people, useless as fighting men but greedy for money. Moreover, I doubt whether they are really in earnest about this war. Many of them, too, are German spies'.[42] Some reports from Rome encouraged this interpretation. Rodd blamed the anarchists and socialists. In private letters to Hardinge, he pointed out that anti-war propaganda had spread disaffection in the Italian army well before the offensive.[43] Years later, when the British ambassador published his *Memories*, he was still convinced that Caporetto was a psychological, rather than military, defeat.[44] Delmé-Radcliffe, who 'had made a career out of scathing judgements on his hosts' military capabilities, and never missed an opportunity to put the boot in',[45] alleged that 'on the left flank of 2nd Army it was not a question of troops fighting moderately well, but of their fighting at all'.[46] Even Trevelyan saw Caporetto as the result of 'a previously formed intention' in 'a few regiments' to 'surrender on purpose'.[47] The legend of anti-war propaganda contaminating entire divisions became so widespread that even an obscure Canadian officer, Major M. S. Bohem, 'was quoted by some of the New York papers as stating . . . that half of the Italian army were pro-German, that it was little wonder that the Italians surrendered, and that their army was full of traitors'.[48]

The environment thus created doomed to failure Imperiali's task of preventing a temporary military emergency from producing lasting political weakness. He reassured the British that the Italian army and the whole country would do their duty, emphasising that 'it is likely that in the plains of Veneto the fate of the whole war will be decided'.[49] The British were rather cold. Italy's reputation lay in tatters. 'Here I hear every sort of rumour', Imperiali wrote. 'They say that the disbandment of the 4th corps came about through treason, involving the generals themselves. That is the result of Cadorna's bulletin!'[50] In a few days, rumours of an Italian official bulletin denouncing mass defeatism and mutiny as the main cause of the defeat were leaked from British military circles to the press. This produced a bitter debate in Britain, providing food for the never-ending Lloyd George-Robertson confrontation. Part of the press, supporting Lloyd George, attributed Caporetto to the overwhelming strength of the enemy, while the rest of it, closer to Robertson and led

[42] Cassar, *Forgotten Front*, p. 321.
[43] Rodd papers: Rodd to Hardinge, 15 and 26 November 1917; Rodd to Balfour, 16 December 1917; Hardinge to Rodd, 22 January 1918.
[44] Rodd, *Memories*, III, p. 278.   [45] Wilcox, 'Generalship', p. 31.
[46] TNA, CAB24/30, quoted in Ibid.   [47] Trevelyan, *Scenes*, pp. 163–166.
[48] TNA, FO170/1080, 29/18, Spring-Rice to Balfour, 21 December 1917.
[49] DDI, 5, IX, doc. 337, Imperiali to Sonnino, 31 October 1917.
[50] Imperiali, *Diario*, p. 450.

by the *Morning Post*, ascribed the defeat to the feeble resistance of the Italians – thereby hammering Lloyd George's fascination for peripheral fronts.[51] Any reply by the Italian media would heat the debate instead of melting it. Imperiali believed the only action to be taken was an official communiqué by the Italian Government clarifying the military circumstances behind the *débâcle*.[52] Unfortunately, the Boselli Government had collapsed on the first day of the enemy attack[53] and the new Government led by Orlando took some time to elaborate a line of action. This was limited to an appeal to the military convention of 1915 which made Italy's effort against Austria-Hungary complementary to the Russian, thus attributing to Russian defection the 'overwhelming local numerical superiority' the Central Powers were able to pit against Italy. Further details regarding such an overwhelming force were not issued. Imperiali found this line rather weak and complained that it did not stress British negligence in withdrawing their guns against Cadorna's request.[54]

The debate over responsibility for the Caporetto disaster had extensive consequences. The overall Allied failure to address the Austro-German threat to Italy, and the new German tactics were not appreciated by either the British or the French, who attributed the catastrophe to Italian spinelessness. Cadorna's criticism of his Anglo-French colleagues fuelled the enmity of the British and French headquarters towards the Italian commander, who was already regarded with some hostility by Lloyd George. Cadorna's accusations against his own soldiers strengthened the worst stereotypes, which depicted the Italians as weak, greedy and rather useless allies. Contradicting such ideas, restoring Italy's reputation and defending Italy's stance as an aspiring great power, would be the main goals of Italian diplomacy in the final year of the war.

13.2   Taking Control of Italy's War

In early November Lloyd George realised that his plan for an Allied offensive on the Italian front was no longer plausible. Rather, it would now be necessary to act quickly to prevent Italy abandoning the war. Imperiali and Eric Drummond, Balfour's private secretary, discussed the possibility of a British expeditionary force to Italy (IEF). Two British divisions were despatched immediately.[55] Lloyd George urged the French premier, Paul Painlevé, to contribute.[56] An Allied Supreme War Council (SWC) was

---

[51] DDI, 5, IX, doc. 425, Imperiali to Sonnino, 12 November 1917.
[52] Imperiali, *Diario*, pp. 450–455.   [53] Albertini, *Venti anni*, II, pp. 590–597.
[54] DDI, 5, IX, doc. 369, Imperiali to Sonnino, 4 November 1917.
[55] Imperiali, *Diario*, p. 446.
[56] TNA, FO371/2948, Balfour to Bertie, 28 and 29 October 1917.

Figure 13.1 Italian troops retreat along the Udine–Codroipo road in north-east Italy after the Caporetto breakthrough

formed to deal with the shortcomings in organisation and political-military coordination, which had dogged the Entente. Italy had always opposed such a solution, which limited its freedom of action. Now, however, Rome could no longer oppose it. Meetings were immediately scheduled, with an Allied command on the agenda. The first was held on 5 November in Rapallo, a symbolic gesture to reassure Italy of its place in the team.[57]

In his memoirs Orlando remembered the conference, which brought together the Italian, British and French prime ministers, as a difficult test for his new Government.[58] Younger and more energetic than his predecessor, Orlando had formed a patriotic national-front Government, confirming most of Boselli's ministers, including Sonnino, at their posts. Lloyd George described the new Prime Minister as 'a learned, cultured and eminent lawyer, possessing considerable oratorical gifts, ... an extremely pleasant man to do business with'.[59] The business they had in hand was the toughest possible. Orlando's goal was to rally the country

[57] Riccardi, *Alleati*, p. 551.   [58] Orlando, *Memorie*, p. 294.
[59] Lloyd George, *The Truth*, I, p. 253.

to 'resist, resist, resist' the invasion.[60] The preservation of Italy's war aims was equally important, so his line at Rapallo was to minimise the impact of the military crisis – 'Allied help is necessary only for the time required for us to reorganise'. His report at the opening of the meeting did not encourage Allied trust, for Orlando had to inform his colleagues of a new Italian retreat from the Tagliamento to the Piave.[61]

Lloyd George planned to take advantage of Caporetto to gain 'control of the war' – at least in Italy.[62] At Rapallo, he promised further Allied support to Italy, but on one condition. The Italian command, said the British premier, had shown it was not up to the task; he had no intention of entrusting British troops to the same poor command. Painlevé shared his view. Orlando was probably the last person in the world to want to protect Cadorna. He resented Cadorna's overbearing manner and his stubborn refusal to submit to political supervision. Moreover, while serving as Interior Minister, Orlando had been severely criticised by Cadorna for 'failing to deal with the defeatism of many clerics and socialists'.[63] In his memoirs, the Italian premier claimed that past conflicts made his coexistence with Cadorna impossible, thus the replacement of the Chief of Staff was inevitable even without Caporetto and Allied pressure.[64] But Orlando's memoirs were written during World War II, and the author had a long time to re-elaborate his thoughts on World War I events; his account of Cadorna's replacement must be taken cautiously. Other sources record Orlando's sense of humiliation at the Allied *diktat* to sack the Italian commander. Colonel Gatti, Cadorna's secretary, remembered Orlando's dismay on 8 November: 'You cannot imagine how I felt humiliated today', the Prime Minister told Gatti. 'I felt treated like a servant. They [British and French] kept me waiting outside the door and called me at their disposal. But what can we do? We may be starving in two months if we do not accept'. And the new Italian War Minister, Vittorio Alfieri, confirmed that Italy's allies had made the dismissal of Cadorna a precondition of any help. Gatti concluded that the Allies were 'already speaking as our masters'.[65] Their role in Cadorna's firing was key. By complying, Orlando snatched the promise that Allied reinforcements would be put under Italian command. The new commander would have to be more of a diplomat, able to maintain a rapport with Italian politicians and with Italy's allies. The choice fell on

---

[60] ASCD, Atti Parlamentari, Discussioni, sessioni 1913–1917, vol. XIV, p. 154.
[61] Aldrovandi Marescotti, *Guerra diplomatica*, p. 140.
[62] Woodward, *Sir William Robertson*, p. 191. Hankey echoed Lloyd George: Britain now could 'get control of our allies': quoted in Burgwyn, *The Legend*, p. 111.
[63] Cassar, *Forgotten Front*, p. 80.   [64] Orlando, *Memorie*, pp. 227–240.
[65] Gatti, *Caporetto*, p. 254.

Armando Diaz. Lloyd George now promised Diaz eight Anglo-French divisions and more, if necessary.[66]

Subsequently, an outline constitution of the new SWC was drawn up. It would be formed by the head of government and the foreign minister of each of the three powers, who would also nominate a permanent military representative. To temper somewhat the replacement of Cadorna, Hankey proposed that he should be the Italian representative, *promoveatur ut amoveatur*. At the end of the conference, the climate was still strained. Though a recent study suggested otherwise,[67] the British and French seemed not to have much faith in the possibility of Italy redeeming itself. From Lloyd George's point of view, however, the conference was a success: Cadorna had been replaced, Italian autonomy weakened with the creation of the SWC, and it was now possible to establish Allied cooperation in Italy.[68] For this to be effective, however, Diaz's freedom of decision needed to be more nominal than real.

Lloyd George aimed to achieve this goal at the following conference, held on 8 November at Peschiera[69] to put into effect the Allied cooperation agreed at Rapallo. Victor Emmanuel III was present, for the first time, bringing all his authority to prove to the British and French allies that Italy had the strength necessary to pull together. He defended the Italian decision to stand firm on the Piave to prevent the occupation of Venice – following a plan which dated back to 1880[70] – while the other allies believed that the Mincio would be a more defensible line.[71] Italian accounts of the meeting described the King's 'impressive, calm and resolute' intervention as the turning point, which re-established Allied trust in Italy.[72] Yet Victor Emmanuel could not oppose Lloyd George's interference in Diaz's strategy. The British premier claimed that, 'complete discretion should be given to Generals [Henry] Wilson and [Ferdinand] Foch [British and French military representatives at the SWC] to move the six Allied divisions now in Italy to sectors of the Italian front where they thought the best use could be made of them'.[73] Lloyd George raised the question of Anglo-French

---

[66] Aldrovandi Marescotti, *Guerra diplomatica*, p. 160.

[67] M. McCrae, *Coalition Strategy and the End of the First World War: The Supreme War Council and War Planning (1917–1918)* (Cambridge: Cambridge University Press, 2019), pp. 98–99.

[68] Lloyd George, *Memoirs*, II, p. 1400.

[69] Orlando, Sonnino, Bissolati, Lloyd George, Smuts, Painlevé and Franklin-Bouillon took part in the conference.

[70] F. Cappellano, *Piani di Guerra dello Stato Maggiore italiano contro l'Austria-Ungheria (1861–1915)* (Valdagno: Rossato, 2014), pp. 43–55.

[71] Orlando, *Memorie*, pp. 244–247.

[72] Aldrovandi Marescotti, *Guerra diplomatica*, p. 177; Riccardi, *Alleati*, p. 556.

[73] DDI, 5, IX, doc. 391, Processo Verbale della Conferenza tenuta al Quartier Generale italiano a Peschiera, 9 November 1917.

freedom of action so as to gain control of the Italian front indirectly. Anglo-French divisions numbered about 12 per cent of the Allied forces in Italy, but they were indispensable to Italian command strategy and by placing conditions on their use, Lloyd George would be able to control Diaz. Italy had no real say in the matter. The independence of Generals Herbert Plumer, commander of the British force, and Foch – who kept direct command of the French contingent until 27 November when he handed it over to Emile Fayolle – was confirmed by their behaviour after the Peschiera Conference. Doubtful that the Piave front would hold, Plumer and Foch decided not to commit their forces to the frontline to avoid being caught up in another Italian disaster.[74]

Victor Emmanuel protested vehemently: the enemy was approaching the Piave and a major effort was expected on the part of the German and Austro-Hungarian pursuers to breach the improvised Italian line along the river. On 11 November, the King rallied Orlando to 'undertake diplomatic measures to support military action so as to push Allied troops, the British in first place, into the front line'.[75] The same day, Diaz had a long meeting with Foch and Sir Wilson to drive home his case.[76] His arguments fell on deaf ears, and he realised that the British and the French were unwilling to take suggestions let alone orders, from an Italian. The Allies' low impression of Italians was reciprocated. Gatti described Robertson, who was also visiting, as an 'illiterate English buffalo', jealous of his whisky. Foch was 'brilliant', but very annoying; he kept giving suggestions – some of which Gatti found 'dull' – and monopolised every conversation by repeating '*Taisez-vous, laissez-moi parler*'.[77] Allied scorn for Italians was so solid that when Diaz's scattered divisions managed to halt the Austro-German offensive in the so-called *battaglia d'arresto* on the Piave (13–26 November), the other allies gave hardly any credit to the Italian performance.[78] From these events we can conclude, first, that Allied mistrust of Italy was stronger than ever; second, that Allied troops in Italy enjoyed unusual independence of Italian command, whilst being able to affect its decisions significantly.

As they were attempting to take indirect control of Italian land forces, the British were trying to do the same with the Italian fleet. At the peak of the Caporetto crisis, the Admiralty ordered Vice-Admiral Somerset Gough-Calthorpe, the new British commander in the Mediterranean,[79]

[74] Aldrovandi Marescotti, *Guerra diplomatica*, p. 80.
[75] Sonnino, *Diario*, III, p. 385, Victor Emmanuel III to Orlando, 11 November 1917.
[76] Ibid., Diaz to Orlando, 11 November 1917.   [77] Gatti, *Caporetto*, pp. 222, 286–289.
[78] Imperiali, *Diario*, pp. 460–462.
[79] NMM, Fremantle MSS, FRE/301, Memorandum of Conference at the Admiralty, 14 August 1917.

to prepare for the possible fall of Venice and even for a separate Italian peace. Calthorpe's contingency plans for the re-deployment of British forces in the Mediterranean and the protection of trade show that he hoped to acquire at least a portion of the Italian fleet, mainly destroyers. Calthorpe feared that, should Italy make a separate peace, the Allied base at Corfu would be untenable. The British priorities, he wrote on 13 November, should be to occupy Valona and prevent Albania from falling to the Central Powers, to make every effort to reinforce and hold the Otranto barrage and to acquire at least those Italian ships in the Adriatic, which were 'of the utmost importance', without giving 'the enemy the chance of laying his hands on what is left'. The British were to keep 'as many of these latter as we can hope to man, and all the rest should be sent to the west coast of Italy before Italian neutrality becomes an accomplished fact'. The method of acquisition would be 'purchase or agreement, backed perhaps by a show of *force majeure*'. Finally, the admiral proposed that British shipping en route to Italy should be withdrawn or diverted to pre-arranged ports – ships bound from Gibraltar to Genoa be diverted to Marseilles, and those bound from Port Said to Italy to Malta.[80] The Admiralty replied briefly on 4 December, approving the draft of the plan and promising Calthorpe that he would receive further comments.[81] Calthorpe then forwarded his plans to Howard Kelly stressing that it was 'of the utmost importance that the Italians shall be unaware that the question is under consideration by us, and every precaution is to be taken by you to avoid the fact coming to their knowledge'.[82] The student of World War II will see a similarity with the situation in 1940, when the British attempts to acquire or neutralise the French fleet led to the tragedy of Mers-el-Kébir.[83]

The Italians too were concerned about the naval situation. An emergency Allied conference was called in Rome on 21 November to consider an Italian request for twenty destroyers to counter a potential naval or amphibious offensive by the Austro-Hungarians directed at the rear and seaward flank of the Italian army on the Piave.[84] Fortunately, for the Allies the contingency never arose, and the Central Powers postponed the final offensive against Italy to the following spring. Rosslyn Wemyss – who became First Sea Lord in December – participated in the meeting and believed the Italians had recovered their confidence, as demonstrated by their acceptance of the British refusal to send any naval reinforcements.[85]

[80] TNA, ADM137/2180, Calthorpe to Admiralty, 13 November 1917.
[81] Ibid., Admiralty to Calthorpe, 4 December 1917.
[82] Ibid., Calthorpe to Kelly, 14 November 1917.   [83] Halpern, *Royal Navy*, p. 216.
[84] TNA, ADM137/1420, Minutes of Naval Conference at Rome, 21 November 1917.
[85] Ibid., Memorandum by Wemyss, 26 November 1917.

However, there is little evidence that anyone else expected the Italians to resist. Balfour wondered: 'Who knows, indeed, whether our difficulty may not be to induce her [Italy] to go on fighting *even* for "Italia irredenta"'.[86]

Throughout December, the British secretly brought arms and munitions to their only battleship left in Taranto, the *HMS Queen*, which was being used as a depot. Those weapons were to be used to arm the drifters' crews, who would sabotage the Italian ports of Taranto and Brindisi in the case of an Italian separate peace. The *Queen* would then be scuttled in the channel between the Mar Grande (big port) and the Mar Piccolo (small port) at Taranto, to trap the Italian dreadnoughts in the harbour. The plan did not escape Italian Navy intelligence. Revel reinforced Italian garrisons in Taranto and Brindisi by transferring marine units from La Spezia, Naples and Messina. The *Queen* was isolated and the fresh water supply was cut off – officially 'due to technical difficulties', in reality to force the British crew to give up the ship. The Italian marines took control of it and immobilised it. All British weapons on the ship, including the 305 mm guns, were transferred to Italian depots. The *Queen* was released a few months later, but its guns remained in Taranto 'for the protection of the port'. Revel insisted that these actions must not be made public so as to avoid serious diplomatic repercussions at a delicate moment, when Allied synergy seemed the only card left to the Entente to save Italy and win the war.[87] He repeatedly opposed, however, the persistent British suggestion that Italian dreadnoughts be 'temporarily' transferred to Corfu. His excuse was that 'the voyage between the two ports was too dangerous' – which encouraged the British conclusion that Revel was 'an altogether contemptible person' and that his crews were afraid to leave their ports for even the safest of journeys.[88] Revel undoubtedly used a specious justification, but his real preoccupation, as he revealed to Admiral Carlo Bergamini some twenty years later, was that at Corfu his battleships would be at the mercy of the French; and he was 'as determined to prevent the ships being taken by the Allies' as he was to 'avoid surrendering them to the Germans'.[89] Despite the failure of the Taranto coup and Revel's opposition to the transfer of Italian battleships, the Admiralty kept updating its secret plans to intercept and neutralise Italian vessels: their final version is dated 8 January 1918.[90]

Although none of this happened, the British were clearly sceptical about an Italian recovery – which suggests that the impact of Victor

---

[86] TNA, FO800/202 Balfour to Wilson, 31 January 1918.

[87] Cernuschi, *Battaglie sconosciute*, pp. 203 ff.

[88] Hankey's Diary, 2 June 1918, quoted in Halpern, *Naval War*, pp. 485–486.

[89] Cernuschi, *Battaglie sconosciute*, pp. 203–205.

[90] TNA, ADM137/2180, Admiralty to Calthorpe, 8 January 1918.

Emmanuel III at Peschiera should be reassessed. Notwithstanding the King's intervention, the British kept trying to gain some control, direct or indirect, of Italian land and sea forces, and in part they succeeded. For the rest, they gave up the attempt in view of a slow but gradual improvement in the general situation. But the Caporetto crisis had virtually marked the end of Italian strategic autonomy.

14   Response to Military Emergencies
Keeping Italy Alive

14.1   Reorganising the Italian Army

Keeping Italy in the war was a military and economic challenge for the Allies. Militarily, it was crucial to ensure that the Italian army would hold together, and then reorganise to full efficiency. Economically, a further effort was required to give Italy the material and financial support necessary for its recovery. The first of these challenges was met and won in the space of a few months, whereas the second remained pressing throughout the last year of the war and terminated what (little) economic and financial independence Italy still enjoyed.

The First Battle of the Piave showed that the cowardice-accusations onto the Italian soldiers were unfounded. Nonetheless, Allied support troops remained crucial and by the end of the year, they numbered 130,000 French and 110,000 British.[1] The contribution of Allied officers to the reorganisation of the Italian army was important: for the first time, there was close and regular discussion among Allied commanders, with a frank exchange of opinions and shared solutions to the various problems. Plumer, who had been one of Haig's most reliable army commanders, aimed at setting 'an example of organisation, training, etc., which we hope the Italians will imitate'. After his initial scepticism about Italian military virtues, he managed to establish good relations with his Italian colleagues. He understood that the Italians were proud people and that the recent defeat had shattered their pride. Consequently, he treated Diaz and his subordinates with the utmost courtesy. Diaz reciprocated Plumer's goodwill and did everything he could to accommodate the British. The pioneer of IEF studies has commented that two Allies have seldom worked so well together.[2] Diaz's relations with the French were

---

[1] To be reduced to 45,000 and 80,000 by April 1918: Isnenghi, Rochat, *Grande Guerra*, p. 446.
[2] Cassar, *Forgotten Front*, pp. 103, 113.

less collaborative. Some of Fayolle's subordinates did not bother to disguise their contempt for the Italians and acted as if only their intervention had saved Italy. This made Diaz more inclined to cooperate with the British – little did he know that Plumer's staff and senior officers had a similarly low regard for Italians, but the British masked their feelings better.[3]

At Diaz's invitation, Plumer often inspected Italian troops. He viewed the poor attention devoted to training as a major obstacle to reorganising the army. Boys as young as seventeen had been called up and sent to the front after barely a month of camp drill[4] and Plumer pointed out to the Italian authorities that serious training was crucial. He encouraged Italians to attend training camps established by the British behind the frontline where Italian recruits were trained with particular regard for the concept of deep defence and anti-gas defence.[5] The British also provided the Italians with three million new British gas masks.[6] Despite some persistent weaknesses – such as the deeply ingrained habit of Italian officers to neglect supervision of the orders' implementation[7] – the Italian army improved fairly quickly. Infantry regiments were reduced from 3,500 to 2,600 men and equipped with a flamethrower section and 36 machine guns instead of 30, thus improving manoeuvrability and firepower.[8] The artillery was reorganised and commanders were ordered to concentrate more carefully on the positioning of their guns and on coordinating their action with light artillery and infantry in the frontline.[9] Divisions would no longer be broken up – a process which had fragmented the army and weakened morale. Infantry tactics became more elaborate, amending Cadorna's obstinacy for frontal assaults, and the new elite corps of shock troops, the *Arditi*, created the previous summer, was expanded.[10] Both the flexibility and military doctrine of the *Regio Esercito* were improved significantly.

Mountain combat was not a part of British training, and in this they could learn from the Italians. Another challenge that the British had not anticipated was the hairpin bends on the Italian mountain roads that made their supply vehicles unsuitable. The Italians had to provide them

---

[3] CUL, Hardinge papers, vol. 38, Rodd to Hardinge, 2 July 1918.
[4] Cassar, *Forgotten Front*, p. 115.
[5] TNA, CAB24/39, Plumer to Robertson, 13 January 1918.
[6] Stevenson, *With our Backs to the Wall. Victory and Defeat in 1918* (Cambridge, MA: Harvard University Press, 2013), p. 104.
[7] TNA, CAB24/39, Plumer to Robertson, 20 January 1918.
[8] Gooch, *Italian Army*, p. 273.
[9] AUSSME, E2, b. 132, n. 8094, Schieramento d'artiglieria per la difesa ad oltranza, 1 February 1918.
[10] Ibid., n. 6977, Deployment of forces in depth, 26 December 1917.

with hundreds of short-wheelbase Fiat trucks which the British found 'unequalled' as hill climbers.[11] Not many Tommies were much impressed by the Italian efforts, however. For most of them, the Italian campaign was a relief from the western front, and some openly referred to it as a picnic. This is understandable since the British had not experienced the cauldron of the Carso or the harshness of winter warfare on the Trentino peaks. From their letters and reports, the widespread idea emerges that victory in Italy would have been easily achieved, had the Italians been better fighters.[12] Plumer, for his part, formed a more balanced opinion of his allies. Many Italian officers were brave and maintained their calm under fire, but their knowledge of staff work was 'too theoretical', and few showed compassion for their men. The troopers, Plumer felt, lacked confidence in their officers. Still they were excellent material, capable of 'making a brilliant attack or a stubborn defence', and their morale was good notwithstanding the ordeal they had gone through.[13] Many, however, still lacked the training necessary to sustain 'prolonged efforts', so Plumer opposed London's plan to withdraw some British divisions from Italy after the situation had stabilised. Hardinge and Robertson suspected that Plumer would want to maintain his position to win laurels in Italy, and complained that, by following Plumer's suggestions, Britain 'shall never be able to withdraw our troops which are so badly needed in France'.[14] London decided to transfer Plumer to the dismay of Diaz who, given the 'excellent understanding' he had with his British colleague, urged Rodd intercede with Robertson to change his mind.[15] The latter replied that, in view of the German spring offensive expected on the western front, he could not refuse Haig's request for the general's return. On 10 March, Plumer handed over command of the British troops in Italy to Frederick Cavan.[16]

Cavan confirmed that the military emergency in Italy had passed, but he remained worried that a new Austro-German attack could lead to another Caporetto. It was therefore imperative to establish an emergency plan to send reinforcements to Italy.[17] A solution was found through the Inter-Allied Transport Council (IATC). Set up to propose improvements to land and sea communications,[18] the IATC focussed particularly on transport

---

[11] Trevelyan, *Scenes*, p. 66; J. Dillon, *'Allies are a Tiresome Lot'. The British Army in Italy in the First World War* (Solihul: Helion & Co., 2015), p. 150.

[12] Dillon, *'Allies'*, pp. 55–56, 64, 105–112.

[13] TNA, CAB24/57, Plumer to Robertson, *cit.*

[14] Rodd papers, Hardinge to Rodd, 28 January 1918.

[15] TNA, FO800/202, Rodd to Balfour, 3 March 1918.

[16] Cassar, *Forgotten Front*, pp. 129–136.

[17] TNA, CAB23/5, War Cabinet minutes, 5 March 1918.

[18] AUSSME, E8, b. 10, f. 2, Nota collettiva n. 8, 8 January 1918.

between France and Italy.[19] During the Caporetto crisis, there were forty-two military trains a day entering Italy from France. In spring 1918, however, fewer than half that number could be used for military transportation, because they competed with trains of materials for Italian industry and for the Anglo-French divisions in Italy. The Italian delegation calculated that, in the case of another military emergency, Diaz needed at least eight additional Allied divisions, which made a daily rate of forty-two trains a bare minimum. The IATC's final report was issued on 10 April.[20] After considering three options for reinforcements from France to Italy – entirely by train; by train and road across the Alps; by train to Marseilles, then by sea to Italian ports in the Northern Tyrrhenian Sea – it recommended reinforcements be sent entirely by train along the Modane–Ventimiglia line at a rate of forty-five trains a day. This implied suspension of goods delivery for a few days, which in turn required adequate stock-piling.[21] Upon Italian consent,[22] the SWC approved the report on 18 April.[23]

Another crucial issue in the Italian recovery was the strengthening of morale. It concerned both the army and the Italian people. In the military sphere, it was largely addressed by Gallenga Stuart who was appointed by Orlando as the new Under-Secretary for Propaganda, replacing Scialoja. Gallenga Stuart aimed 'to make ourselves aware and convinced of our true value'.[24] He counted on experienced workers to improve the effectiveness of the Italian propaganda machine. Among these were his friend Borgese, several journalists, writers and officers with new ideas, as well as Lombardo Radice, an educationalist, and Salvemini – all Italian democrats. Italian nationalists were also involved. Among them, Gioacchino Volpe who expounded Italy's moral right to resist the invasion, but held that countries were fighting to guarantee a greater future for their peoples, so he would not ignore Italy's expansionist aims.[25] Together, these people boosted the *Servizio P*, an organisation in embryo since the summer of 1917 under the aegis of the armed forces, which became more important in early 1918. It promoted a new type of propaganda among Italian troops. Italian intellectuals and *Servizio P* officers would address the soldiers not in the abstract

[19] Ibid., E9, b. 18, f. 114, Relazione sulla situazione generale dei trasporti sul fronte occidentale del Generale Sir P. A. M. Nash, 15 March 1918.
[20] AUSSME, E2, b. 81, f. Consiglio interalleato supremo di guerra, Risposta del Consiglio interalleato dei trasporti, 10 April 1918.
[21] A. Gionfrida, *L'Italia e il coordinamento militare 'interalleato' nella Prima Guerra Mondiale* (Rome: USSME, 2008), pp. 144–145.
[22] Crespi, *Alla difesa*, pp. 28, 47–54.
[23] AUSSME, E2, b. 21, f. Consiglio interalleato supremo di guerra, Nota collettiva n. 22, 18 April 1918.
[24] ACS, Carte Gallenga Stuart, b. 1, f. 7, 'La propaganda all'estero. Novembre 1917–giugno 1918'. Relazione a S. E. il Presidente del Consiglio.
[25] G. Volpe, *Fra storia e politica* (Rome: De Alberti, 1924).

Figure 14.1 Protecting a monument against enemy bombardments in Veneto.

rhetoric of lectures delivered by rather unlikely 'professors', but in the language of everyday conversation in the routine of trench-life, discussing the Italian war and shared Allied values and sacrifices. Trench newspapers were published and many soldiers contributed by writing, drawing and creating cartoons.[26] The main message was 'we shall make it'.[27] The papers emphasised the need for a new 'National Risorgimento'.[28]

The British participated by countering anti-war feelings in the civilian population. The last thing Britain wanted was pro-peace strikes, which would bring the factories in Turin and Milan to a halt, or defeatist ideas

[26] G. Lombardo Radice, 'Dopo Caporetto', in Id., *Nuovi saggi di propaganda pedagogica* (Turin: Paravia, 1922), pp. 28–29.
[27] P. Jahier, 'Perché vinceremo', *L'Astico*, n. 13, 9 May 1918.
[28] *Volontà*, ns. 5–6, 2 November 1918.

that would infect the army. Samuel Hoare was entrusted with preventing this from happening.[29] An MP and MI5 man in Rome, Hoare headed a staff of a hundred British intelligence officers and financed an anti-pacifist campaign led by Mussolini's *Il Popolo d'Italia*. Mussolini was paid £100 a week – the equivalent of about £6,000 today – from autumn 1917 for at least a year. The British subsidised *Il Popolo* but also, unofficially, funnelled money directly to Mussolini for the purpose of organising militant opposition to anti-war groups. British money was used to pay thugs – as Mussolini himself explained to his British benefactors – to 'break the heads of any pacifists who try to hold anti-war meetings in the streets'.[30]

These measures successfully prevented the spread of defeatism. They might not have been enough to keep the Italian people united, however, had there not arisen a fairly spontaneous revival of Italian patriotism. The invasion and the prospect of total defeat cemented the home front.[31] Croce wrote that 'the war really becomes our war at last'. Even the Catholic paper *Osservatore Romano* incited Italian Catholics to resist.[32] Now the Italians understood much better than hitherto, what they were fighting for – their homes and their land. In their minds, World War I became a crusade for Italian survival. To win it, they desperately needed more supplies and money.

14.2   Escorting Allied Manna

The Italian supply crisis emerged vividly from a report by Silvio Crespi, Italian Provisioning Commissioner, who, on 11 November 1917 for the first time, drew up a complete estimate of Italian requirements. He stressed that wheat and coal provisions, in particular, were critical. Wheat supplies had fallen to 70,000 tons per month, less than 20 per cent of the country's needs, whilst coal imports, down to 250,000 tons per month were 33 per cent of its needs. Crespi's conclusion was blunt: 'Italy does not have enough to eat', and had very little to keep its war machine going, too.[33] Italian necessities were discussed at an Allied conference in Paris between 29 November and 3 December, when the Allies established five councils to deal with logistic issues: Armaments, Maritime Transport and Imports, Finances, Supplies and Blockade. At the conference, Orlando and Sonnino met the new French Prime Minister, Georges Clemenceau. He proved nothing like the meek and mild Painlevé. Called *le Tigre* by his supporters, Clemenceau was

---

[29] Rodd, *Memories*, III, p. 397.
[30] CUL, Templewood papers, Part III, Italy and the Vatican, 1917–1918, fs. 1–5; S. Hoare, *Complacent Dictator* (New York: Knopf, 1947).
[31] Isnenghi, Rochat, *Grande Guerra*, pp. 410–424.
[32] C. Seton-Watson, *Storia d'Italia*, p. 557.   [33] Crespi, *Alla difesa*, p. 16.

famous for his hatred of Germany and his dislike of Italy, and he insisted on keeping a significant part of the equipment and supplies destined for Italy, on the French front, deaf to the protests of the new Italian ambassador to France, Lelio Bonin Longare.[34] Orlando admitted in his memoirs that his relations with Clemenceau 'were not always easy, let alone peaceful'.[35] Orlando and Sonnino urged Lloyd George to put pressure on the French, but the Italian statesmen realised that Clemenceau was a tough nut for Lloyd George as well. The latter's difficulties in involving France in the Allied supply chain to Italy aggravated the Italian position. The result was that Italy leant even more on Britain.

The British approach to the Italian supply crisis was linked to the anti-submarine campaign. On 3 November 1917, the Allied Maritime Transport Council was established, bringing together delegates from Britain, the United States, France and Italy to provide 'an international administration' for more efficient management of both shipping and distribution of supplies.[36] In three meetings held in London in December, the Allies estimated Allied and neutral shipping losses to U-boats in the following four months at two million tons. The Allies expected to balance them by 1 March.[37] Crespi, representing Italy, stressed that without immediate support, Italy would not survive through March. Italian merchant fleet losses had risen from 36,405 tons in 1915 to 190,385 tons in 1916 and to 312,242 tons in 1917 – which meant the loss of 420,382 tons of cargo. Food shortages were causing riots and protests[38] and Crespi concluded that the Central Powers were concentrating their Mediterranean operations on Italy 'to reduce it to starvation and to provoke a revolution'.[39] To prevent it, the British aimed to improve the Mediterranean convoy system, launched a new anti-submarine campaign and opened up alternative routes via river shipping.

The Mediterranean proved a more difficult zone for convoying than the Atlantic, because its routes were more complex and easier to spot by U-boats. Calthorpe began introducing the convoy system for the route from Port Said to Britain in mid-October 1917, but he remained short of escorts and was unable to cover all Mediterranean trade. The Allied solution to their Mediterranean difficulties was to increase the tonnage

---

[34] Sonnino, *Carteggio*, Bonin Longare to Sonnino, 23 November 1917, pp. 340–343.
[35] Orlando *Memorie*, pp. 360, 362.
[36] See: A. J. Salter, *Allied Shipping Control: An Experiment in International Administration* (Oxford: Clarendon Press, 1921).
[37] Crespi, *Alla difesa*, pp. 16–21.
[38] Hardinge suspected that the Italians were exaggerating their difficulties and blamed Italian disorganisation for food shortages: Rodd papers, Hardinge to Rodd, 18 January 1918.
[39] Crespi, *Alla difesa*, p. 176.

per convoy. Where the first convoys comprised 12 ships, they numbered 36 by the end of the year. The Allies also established new routes and frequently changed them, in the way that had proved successful in the Atlantic. The most important route was Gibraltar–Genoa. In the spring of 1918, a total of 1,088 vessels in 69 convoys – about 70 per cent of the traffic to Italy – reached Genoa from Gibraltar, and 1,044 vessels left Genoa for the Atlantic.[40] With the gradual success of the Mediterranean convoys, the Central Powers began to concentrate on attacking shipping in Italian coastal waters, as convoyed vessels dispersed to their individual ports. The Allied response to this new submarine tactic was multifaceted. Calthorpe suggested a renewed anti-submarine offensive in the lower Adriatic, moving slowly towards Revel's position. The latter continued to preach focussing on the core of the problem, the U-boat bases in the Adriatic, and planned to hit them with air strikes. Calthorpe proposed to the Admiralty the deployment of a hydrophone-hunting flotilla, using decoy ships working in concert with Allied submarines, and stressing the need to join Revel's air campaign.[41] For Italian and British naval commanders, assuming that the solution to their problem could lie in exploiting a different weapon than their own – especially an experimental arm such as the air force – was a not insignificant shift in their mindset. British air forces based at Taranto increased steadily in the last year of the war, and they provided crucial support to the Italian air campaign. 'Continuous joint air strikes' launched 'with energy' over the Austro-Hungarian submarine bases, Cattaro in particular, brought the enemy to its knees.[42]

In addition to these Allied initiatives, the Italians established their own measures to defend traffic in Italian waters. They endorsed the *motobarca armata silurante* (MAS), a fast torpedo motorboat with a ten-man crew and armament composed of two torpedoes, machine guns and occasionally a light gun. Designed in 1916, in late 1917 it became the main Italian device for patrolling national waters and anti-submarine activities, compensating for the lack of Allied support in light craft, and freeing some Italian escort vessels for convoy duty.[43] The MAS also proved highly effective for daring attacks against major units of the *k.u.k. Kriegsmarine*. On 10 December 1917 a MAS managed to sink the

---

[40] AUSM, b. 827, f. 6, Establishment of convoy system in the Mediterranean. Necessity for this system in order to ensure adequate supply of coal to Italy and to economise tonnage.

[41] TNA, ADM137/1413, Calthorpe to Admiralty, 28 October 1917.

[42] AUSM, b. 479, f. 2, Opera della Rega Marina in Eritrea e Somalia. Cooperazione interalleata durante la guerra in Mediterraneo.

[43] See Italian complaints about limited Allied support in: Ibid., b. 497, f. 2, Cooperazione interalleata durante la guerra marittima mondiale in Mediterraneo, Memorandum di Revel, 8 August 1917.

battleship *Wien* in Trieste harbour, while another damaged *Wien*'s twin *Budapest*.[44] Such striking successes were massively publicised by the Italian media, strengthening Italian morale and self-confidence – D'Annunzio famously renamed the MAS by the Latin motto *Memento Audere Semper* (remember to dare always). The Italians also established a specialised anti-submarine organisation, the *Ispettorato per la Difesa del Traffico Nazionale* (IDTN), which became a crucial component in surviving the crisis in the winter of 1917–1918. IDTN commands were based at La Spezia, La Maddalena, Genoa, Livorno, Civitavecchia, Naples and Palermo to coordinate and defend convoys in Italian waters. Each IDTN command had its own naval forces and could use them independently, according to circumstances. By the end of the war, the Inspectorate had 392 ships of all types, including 26 cruisers, 101 minesweepers and 167 MAS.[45] Semaphore stations on shore, aircraft patrol and protection by heavy naval batteries and armed trains were provided. Despite the usual Allied scepticism about Italian initiatives, the Italian system of traffic defence eventually proved very effective – quite possibly the most effective among the Allies, since Allied losses in Italian waters were a mere 20 per cent of those in extra-Italian waters. Thanks to all these measures, Italian naval losses in 1918 dropped to 138,175 tons.[46]

Further Allied efforts were made to encourage combined rail and river transport. Navigation on the Sile River was improved and the Bacchiglione River was made navigable between Padua (the new headquarters of the *Comando Supremo*) and Vicenza. At Piacenza, Cremona, Mantua and Pontelagoscuro, railway stations were connected to river wharfs. Goods transported by river grew from 38,526 tons in 1915 to 483,226 tons in 1917 and to 784,339 tons after the retreat to the Piave.[47] As a result, monthly wheat deliveries to Italy increased from 88,000 tons in September 1917 to 140,000 tons in late December: 'A significant improvement' rejoiced Crespi, who informed parliament on 22 December: 'Now I can guarantee that the country will live for another thirty days'. At the same session, Orlando rebuffed the socialists' complaints declaring: 'Before Italy talks of peace, we shall withdraw all the way down to Sicily!' On 26 January, an Anglo-Italian agreement on supplies covered Italian needs for the whole of 1918. The British guaranteed thirty-four million hundredweight of wheat, four million of which were shipped in the spring; excluding losses to torpedoing, 3,770,000 were landed. Wheat shipments received are shown below:[48]

---

[44] Morabito, *Marina italiana*, pp. 262 ff.
[45] C. Manfroni, *Storia della marina militare italiana durante la Guerra Mondiale, 1914–1918* (Bologna: Zanichelli, 1925 [1923]), p. 284.
[46] USM, *Marina italiana*, V, p. 469; VI, p. 191.
[47] Einaudi, *Condotta economica*, pp. 95–98.   [48] Crespi, *Alla difesa*, pp. 27, 88.

December 1917	140,000 tons
January 1918	223,000
February	230,000
March	218,000
April	323,000
May	377,000

The food emergency might have been solved, but the coal shortage remained dire. Coal stocks, which had been around 780,000 tons at the beginning of 1917, amounted to 360,000 tons in the winter.[49] The navy alone used around 50,000 tons a month and considering the emergency needs of the army meant that the stock would be exhausted within six months. 'It would be catastrophic', said Crespi. In early January 1918, Milner – who would become Secretary of State for War in April – invited Crespi to London to negotiate an Allied coal agreement. Crespi's team arrived on the 17th, including Riccardo Bianchi, Italian Minister of Rail and Maritime Transport; Salvatore Orlando, Commissar-General of the Italian merchant fleet; and their aides. In addition to the 250,000 tons of Allied coal supplied to Italy by sea, Milner proposed an extra 450,000 tons monthly by rail via France, which would have freed some British naval cargoes to be used for shipping food to Italy. The French however, refused to deliver 'even a kilogram' of French coal to Italy unless they received an equal quantity of British coal.[50] The Italian delegates were further annoyed because 'in this way we burn the bad French coal and the French burn the good British coal'.[51] But they were unable to propose an alternative solution. Both Milner and Cecil were disappointed by the Italians' lack of initiative. Except for Bianchi and Crespi, who were 'not so bad', they found the other Italian delegates 'really pitiable'. Against these men, 'the French had sent three or four really competent people', who managed to bring the talks to a stalemate with the pretext of their own 'infinite needs'.[52] Imperiali intervened in Crespi's support, warning Milner: 'Be careful for you will lose Italy'.[53] Given the inadequate contribution of the Italian delegation, Imperiali's complaints were inappropriate and caused Cecil's grumbles that the Italians 'are rather a hopeless set of people', and that he could 'only hope that they are not so incompetent in other matters as they appear to be in these'.[54] French vetoes continued

[49] Einaudi, *Condotta economica*, p. 91.   [50] Crespi, *Alla difesa*, p. 47.
[51] French coal 'is apparently from 10 to 20 per cent lower in calorific value than English coal:' Rodd papers, Cecil to Rodd, 18 March 1918.
[52] Rodd papers, Cecil to Rodd, 18 March 1918.   [53] Imperiali, *Diario*, p. 484.
[54] Rodd papers, Cecil to Rodd, *cit*.

at a second meeting on 9 February, but Cecil, irritated, threatened to halt British coal supplies to France, if the French did not collaborate. Eventually, the French Commerce Minister Etienne Clémentel reluctantly gave the green-light to the coal agreement, which was signed on 18 February. Italian needs were set at the figure presented by Crespi and Bianchi: 690,000 tons – 240,000 of French coal by rail and 450,000 tons of British, delivered in part by rail across France and in part by ship.[55] The British, once again, had taken on the greater share of the burden in supporting Italy.

Such burden was aggravated in May when the Italians approached the British for additional coal deliveries destined to create an army stock to be used in the event that a military emergency forced the Allies to replace coal-carrying trains with military reinforcements.[56] On 13 June, an Anglo-Italian coal convention was signed: the British would despatch by sea '150,000 tons of good quality coal taken from the railway reserve stocks [in Britain] for a period of six weeks from the 20th of the current month'.[57] This convention proved that Allied logistic coordination was beginning to produce results.[58] Complaints from the Italians were still recurrent due to British difficulties in providing the full amount of coal promised – the same applied to foodstuff[59] – but Diaz managed to offset some of the problems by imposing a strict discipline on Italian civilian authorities: the Italian commander prevented his military stock from being used by Italian public transport, despite recurring appeals from the Minister of Transport, Giovanni Villa.[60] Crespi enthused: 'The Allied nations have become a giant common body which combines every resource, of blood, energy and raw material and distributes them according to need'.[61] No doubt, that giant body had a British mind, though the Italians were rarely ready to appreciate how much it was working to their benefit in 1918.

14.3   The Financial Challenge

Italy's final problem in the crisis was how to finance the wealth of goods necessary for its survival. This issue was addressed by Emilio Morandi

---

[55] Crespi, *Alla difesa*, pp. 48–54.

[56] AUSSME, E2, b. 81, f. Consiglio interalleato supremo di guerra, n. 1092, 16 May, 1918; n. 754, Orlando to Di Robilant, 22 May 1918; n. 1450, Di Robilant to Levi, 31 May 1918.

[57] Ibid., b. 81, f. Riserva strategica di carbone, n. 2039, 'Accordi per la provvista di una riserva strategica di 150,000 tonnellate di carbone in Italia', 17 June 1918.

[58] Ibid., Diaz to Levi, 26 June 1918.

[59] Rodd papers, Hardinge to Rodd, 18 January 1918.

[60] Gionfrida, *L'Italia e il coordinamento*, p. 150.   [61] Crespi, *Alla difesa*, p. 117.

and Vincenzo Giuffrida, Italian provisions supervisors, who drew up a financial plan for 1918 setting out a total turnover (adding income and outgoings together) of 15 billion lire.[62]

Ten days after Caporetto, the Bank of Italy issued *una tantum*, money equal to 11 per cent of existing circulation to forestall a run on the banking system. In the following months, though, the policy of relying on debt finance, rather than taxation or the printing press, was restored. The Fifth National Loan issued in January–February 1918 reached its target subscription, mainly thanks to Nitti's massive propaganda campaign, which emphasised the need to reassert the national will to fight to the end. National loans, however, were not enough. At the beginning of 1918, the Italian Government and the Bank of Italy became involved in difficult negotiations over inter-Allied war debts that were to cast such a long shadow over the following decade. The Bank's preoccupation now shifted from finding domestic finance for the war effort, to managing a weakening external position. Early debt issues had reassured Stringher of the domestic market's ability to absorb large loans without unsettling the financial system. As public consumption climbed from around 10 per cent of GDP in 1913 to more than 40 per cent in 1917, and as Italy's weak endowment of raw materials bit deeper into its balance of payments, the Bank focussed increasingly on the exchange rate problem.[63]

Already in spring 1916 Stringher was advised that future borrowing would inevitably have to be raised on the US market. But it was not until late summer 1917 that the Bank secured an agreement with the US Federal Reserve.[64] Among the currencies of the Allied powers, the lira was 'falling fastest and farthest'.[65] Foreign debt slightly exceeded 16 per cent of total indebtedness at the time, so there was not much concern for the real burden of the debt. Rather the problem with depreciation was its inflationary impact, which caused high price increases for producer goods: from 1914 to 1917, retail prices rose 89 per cent but wholesale prices went up by 186 per cent.[66] Stringher realised that this would cause problems in the future, as financial intermediaries would have trouble re-adjusting to normality at the end of the war. Thus, while inflation would eventually reduce the real value of domestically held public debt, in the short term it would render necessary further

---

[62] Domestically, Crespi's recipe for facing the increase in prices on the Italian market, approved by Orlando, was to 'stabilise and curtail imports to reduce consumption': Ibid., pp. 20, 79.

[63] Galassi, Harrison, 'Italy at War', pp. 17–18.

[64] G. Toniolo ed., *La Banca d'Italia e l'economia di guerra* (Bari: Laterza, 1989), p. 50.

[65] Galassi, Harrison, 'Italy at War', pp. 18–19.

[66] V. Zamagni, 'Italy: How to Lose the War and Win the Peace', in M. Harrison ed., *The Economics of World War II* (Cambridge: Cambridge University Press, 1998), p. 213.

borrowing.[67] Galassi and Harrison revealed how much Nitti's view of the exchange rate problem was shaped by his political prejudices. He saw a lack of confidence in Italy's final victory underlying the depreciation and blamed the defeatism of Italian bankers and financiers who were avoiding repatriation of foreign revenues. Therefore, he decided to set up a clearing office, the *Istituto Nazionale Cambio* (INC), with a monopoly on foreign currency trading – despite the opposition of the main bankers. The INC, however, lacked the resources to sway the markets because Italy's foreign reserves were limited. Nitti resorted to looking for further foreign loans and aimed straight at the American market.[68]

With some 35 per cent of Allied early-war purchases in America being financed on the New York exchanges – some $2.4 billion in total – by 1917 all Entente powers had mortgaged themselves heavily to the United States. Britain was no exception: after America entered the war, London's almost exhausted credit line was extended further, with about 69 per cent of Allied purchases being financed on credit thereafter.[69] Nitti's negotiation for a loan from the US Treasury in the spring of 1918 took place in London in the presence of Henry Crosby, the American delegate. A joint INC-Fed committee would examine Italian credit needs in the US market and provide support for the lira, while the US Treasury would finance dollar-denominated Italian import bills. In return, all Italian-owned dollar balances would be earmarked for settlement of Italy's debts with the US Treasury. Similar agreements with Britain and France followed. The announcement of this agreement on 22 July strengthened the dollar and weakened sterling. The former rose from 11.38 lire in April to 12.48, going up to 12.71 in August while the latter fell from 38.47 lire, the record reached in February, to 37.15 lire.[70] The new agreements would give Italy 6 billion lire, to be spent primarily on the South American markets where prices were more favourable.[71]

On the other hand, this brought all Italian purchases abroad under the control of Allied authorities and ended Italy's independence in the allocation of foreign balances. Since the dollar was becoming the main means of international settlement, the agreement with the US Treasury also terminated Italy's ability to run its own monetary policy. Besides, access to the American market did not end Italy's problems. The financing, so expensively acquired, proved inadequate. Britain insisted on being paid in dollars for purchases that involved American raw materials and components. In September 1918, Italian dollar-denominated purchases in third

[67] Toniolo, *La Banca d'Italia*, pp. 46–47.
[68] Galassi, Harrison, 'Italy at War', pp. 19–20.   [69] Philpott, *Attrition*, p. 77.
[70] Galassi, Harrison, 'Italy at War', pp. 19–20. A hundred lire were worth 67 francs.
[71] Crespi, *Alla difesa*, p. 127.

countries caused resistance in London once the original line of credit granted by the US Treasury came to an end. Cecil ordered British shipping firms to halt operations, pending renegotiation of the financial agreements with Italy. Douglas Forsyth described Italy's position at the time as that of 'a beggar', whose financial weakness gave British and American diplomats room to obtain important trade concessions.[72]

Italy managed to survive the crisis of 1917, reorganise its army, increase its industrial production and find the funds to keep up the enormous effort of the final act of the war. But this occurred at the price of its autonomy, which, in economic terms, was even greater and longer lasting than in military terms. As Galassi and Harrison put it, 'fighting a war with one hand while holding out a hat with the other is a difficult act to carry through'.[73] It was yet another blow to Italy's ambitions as an imperial power.

---

[72] Forsyth: *The Crisis*, pp. 149–192; Galassi, Harrison, 'Italy at War', p. 20.   [73] Ibid.

15 Re-shaping Allied Grand Strategy

15.1 Strategy, Peace Feelers and Peace Planning

The developments of 1917 imposed a significant revision of the Allied approach to grand strategy. Lloyd George's ambitious strategic design had met with disaster in Russia, paralysis in France, crisis in Italy and failure in Flanders. American entry into the war compensated for all this, but it would take time before the United States could bring their resources into the European theatre – in January 1918, fewer than 60,000 American soldiers were in France.[1] A small British victory at Cambrai on 20 November 1917 – which was greeted by the ringing of church bells in Britain, but which was nullified ten days later by a German counter-attack – could not change the arithmetic of attrition.[2] In early 1918 the Central Powers still had the upper hand, and clearly they would try to bring the war to an end before the Americans could turn the tables on them. The Allies expected an unprecedented enemy offensive in France and in Italy. This stimulated a largely defensive strategy for the Entente in 1918, to 'wait for the Americans and the tanks',[3] the new weapons that could unlock the tactical stalemate of trench warfare and unleash the power of mobile offence.

Peculiar political and diplomatic developments shaped and challenged this postulation, leading to some significant contradictions and to a partial revision of the overall plan. Politically, late 1917 saw a growing centralisation of power within Allied countries; the chronic military–civilian conflict over the direction of war was progressively solved with the unenthusiastic recognition by the military of political primacy in the making of strategy, within both individual states and the coalition. At the state level,

---

[1] French, *Strategy of Lloyd George*, p. 237.

[2] Miles, *Military Operations, France and Belgium 1917: The Battle of Cambrai*, in *History of the Great War*, III, p. 278.

[3] Poincaré, *Au Service*, IX, pp. 394–395.

Lloyd George had concentrated wartime power in his small War Cabinet, and in the winter 1917–1918 he secured military compliance, not least by dismissing both the service Chiefs, Jellicoe and Robertson in December 1917 and February 1918 respectively. In France, Clemenceau took firm direction of the war effort giving it a military, political, economic and social unity following the advice of his aide, Henri Mordaq: 'In order to win this war . . . there must be a close alliance between policy and strategy, the latter being the continuation and the result of the former'.[4] In Italy, Orlando enjoyed greater authority over Diaz than either Salandra or Boselli had had over Cadorna. At the coalition level, the same power shift emerged in the creation of the SWC. It proclaimed the united front from Belgian to the Adriatic coast, strengthening the political alliance and compensating for the previous lack of coordination.[5]

The development of such relatively mature systems for bringing strategy planning under overall political control by uniting military and political sources was not accomplished without friction. Quite the opposite; civil–military conflicts occasionally resurfaced at both strategic and lower – such as the operational – levels. The SWC defensive plan for 1918, for example, was opposed by Foch, who wished to retake the offensive earlier than 1919, at least in France. He managed to have Allied plans revised, combining a purely defensive stance in the early months of 1918 with a more offensive footing – 'the only one which could lead to victory' – in the second half of the year, deploying French, British and American forces in France.[6] Further civil–military conflicts followed on the question of an Allied reserve, as we shall see. The SWC failed to iron out the fundamental differences at the heart of the Entente. In particular, Italy had little faith in the SWC and sent delegates of secondary importance to the council. The first was Cadorna, who after Caporetto was deprived of any real authority; the second was General Gaetano Giardino, former War Minister under Boselli, whose reputation was flying low after Boselli's fall; the third was General Mario Nicolis Di Robilant, who was a capable man but little known abroad. This was a huge contrast to Wilson and Foch, the British and French representatives. It reveals the different importance that the Allied powers gave to the new coordinating body.[7] Italian dissatisfaction with the SWC was aggravated as strategic divergences between Rome and the other allies deepened.

[4] J. J. H. Mordacq, *Le ministère Clemenceau: journal du témoin*, 4 vols. (Paris: Plon, 1930–1931), I, p. 6.
[5] French, *Strategy of Lloyd George*, pp. 161–162.
[6] Ministère de la Guerre, Etat Majour de l'Armée, Service Historique (EMA), *Les Armées Françaises dans la grande guerre*, 10 tomes (Paris, 1936), VI, n. 1, pp. 50–51.
[7] Riccardi, *Alleati*, p. 578.

Such differences largely originated with specific diplomatic tensions, which, in early 1918, began to damage Anglo-Italian relations irreparably.

From the British perspective, the increased possibility for Germany to redeploy forces from the eastern front to the western was the key strategic problem for the 1918 campaigning season, but it was not the only consequence of Russia's collapse. The latter hampered the Allied blockade by opening Russian resources to German exploitation; it threatened to upset Allied naval predominance both in the North Sea and the Eastern Mediterranean; and it created 'a new strategic geography' that exposed Britain's Empire in the Far East.[8] On 17 December 1917 Sir J. E. Shuckburgh, Head of the Political and Secret Department of the India Office, warned the War Cabinet that the Germans had abandoned 'the Berlin–Baghdad line, as a means of striking at the British Empire in India, in favour of the pan-Turanian project ... of uniting all the Turkish-speaking peoples, of course under German guidance and control, in one continuous chain from Constantinople to Samarkand and beyond'.[9] Milner recognised that the Turks might establish communications with the Turkish population of Northern Persia and with the Russian Muslims, which 'would present a new and very real danger to our whole position in the East'. Thus, Milner planned a British military mission in the Caucasus to support pro-Allied authorities in Tiflits establish an autonomous security force. Equally, Curzon, without compromising the pre-eminence of the western front, urged Lloyd George to have greater consideration for the Middle East and Africa, re-stating the need to keep all German colonies under British rule.[10] Imperialist designs of this kind, however, were somehow more difficult to implement now, because the Bolsheviks, after overthrowing the Russian Provisional Government with the October Revolution, disclosed secret Allied treaties – and the imperialist thrust they embodied. Vladimir Lenin loudly condemned it, with the Decree on Peace of November 1917 calling for a just and democratic peace.[11] American President Wilson too had repeatedly and publicly denounced 'secret covenants' between belligerent powers, affirming that the United States was not bound by them.[12] Growing indignation in the international community for the betrayal of Allied-stated principles of democracy and international justice called for a 'moral redemption' in Allied war aims. Lloyd George however agreed with Curzon that, while

---

[8] French, *Strategy of Lloyd George*, p. 174.
[9] L. P. Morris, 'British Secret Missions in Turkestan, 1918–1919', *Journal of Contemporary History*, XII, 3, 1977, pp. 365–366.
[10] French, *Strategy of Lloyd George*, pp. 176–177.
[11] C. Seton-Watson, *Storia d'Italia*, p. 567.   [12] *The New York Times*, 2 April 1917.

maintaining a defensive footing in France, something had to be done to harass the Central Powers elsewhere.[13]

Perhaps unsurprisingly, he once again looked to Vienna. He remained convinced that 'the best chance for the Allies would appear to lie in a separate peace with Austria, in which case Italy might have to be compelled to acquiesce'.[14] The weakening of Rome's stance within the Entente suggested that a reduction in Italian claims in non-Italian territories could favour an Austro-Hungarian compromise peace; it could also remove some of the international blame on the Allies by eradicating an embarrassing commitment that violated the principle of nationality.[15] Cecil agreed that Britain could limit its support to the 'reasonable demands' of its allies, including Alsace-Lorraine and 'some rearrangement of Trentino'.[16] Trieste and Dalmatia were not mentioned. The War Cabinet on the whole shared this view, believing that, if the British public was to be asked to fight for one or two more years, it should be told exactly for what purpose; and the public would not be prepared 'to continue the war in order to win certain islands in the Adriatic for Italy'.[17] Despite Italian protests, in Geneva on 19 December 1917 Smuts and Count Albert Mensdorff, a former Austro-Hungarian ambassador to Britain, negotiated the withdrawal of Vienna from the war.[18] Smuts asked Vienna to slow down, if not openly boycott, the transfer of German forces from the eastern front to the west for the spring offensive. This military clause was difficult to implement, but even more difficult was the question of territorial settlement. Mensdorff consented that Bosnia-Herzegovina should be added to Serbia (though he did not openly commit himself), but he became 'somewhat excited' when Smuts mentioned Romania and Italy.[19] Mensdorff was not happy to bow to the former, which had just signed an armistice on 9 December; and 'after the treachery of Italy' Vienna did not wish to make any concession to Rome. Yet Smuts made an optimistic report to Lloyd George that 'the Austrian mind was in an accommodating mood'.[20] However, it was necessary to give Vienna greater guarantees.

Lloyd George began to consider a public statement that served the present British strategic and diplomatic issues. On 3 January, the War

---

[13] French, *Strategy of Lloyd George*, p. 180.
[14] TNA, FO371/3134/13977, Hankey memorandum quoted in Ibid., p. 109.
[15] Lloyd George, *The Truth*, p. 68.
[16] TNA, FO800/207, Cecil to Balfour, 28 December 1917.
[17] Ibid., CAB23/16, War Cabinet 239A, 27 September 1917.
[18] Valiani, *La dissoluzione*, pp. 378, 468–469.
[19] G. Egedy, 'Lloyd George and the Dual Monarchy, 1917–1918', *Central European Papers*, II, 2, 2014, pp. 36–50.
[20] Lloyd George, *Memoirs*, II, p. 1485.

Cabinet, discussing the possibility, concluded that such a statement should be unilateral, to avoid amendments from the other allies. It should emphasise British liberal war aims and support for the principle of nationality without totally alienating Britain's allies – especially France – and without committing Britain to reducing its own ambitions. For example, British doubts that France could realise 'the whole of her war aims' should not be mentioned, while support to the Italian claims should be limited to the reunification of Italian territories under Austro-Hungarian rule 'without a specific reference to the whole of the Italian war aims'. Regarding the German colonies, the Cabinet was eager to 'remove the impression' that Britain was 'airily trying to annex more territory to an over engorged empire'. The proper course of action 'would be to express our willingness to accept the application of the principle of self-determination to the captured German colonies'. Precisely how the principle was to be applied 'need not now be discussed'.[21] The British premier gave his speech before a group of trade union representatives at Caxton Hall, on 5 January 1918. Outlining British war aims, he claimed that 'a break-up of Austria-Hungary' was not part of them; instead, he emphasised the need for its reorganisation according to the principle of nationality. He also did not exclude the survival of the Ottoman Empire. These statements nullified both the London and the St Jean de Maurienne agreements. Moreover, while promising to 'support until death French democracy's claims for Alsace-Lorraine', Lloyd George made only a sybylline reference to 'Italy's legitimate claims' as an object of British support. Lloyd George's statement was received with much satisfaction in Austria-Hungary[22] – and with astonishment in Italy. Imperiali telegraphed Sonnino that Lloyd George was now speaking 'like President Wilson'.[23] This highlighted the antithetical approach that Britain and Italy had towards the recent developments in international relations.

Lloyd George's speech had the double purpose of responding to Bolshevik and American cries for a truly democratic peace and of favouring Austria-Hungary detachment from Germany. By reaffirming solemnly, the liberal values that officially motivated Britain's war, Lloyd George wished to present himself as the champion of liberalism and democracy. Italy, on the other hand, rejected both Lenin's ideologies and the American new diplomacy. Given the respective strengths of Russia and America in early 1918, the latter certainly was more threatening to Italian interests. Wilson, to be sure, had never concealed his ideas;

---

[21] TNA, CAB23/5, War Cabinet 312, 3 January 1918.

[22] Ibid., FO371/3133/2002, Draft by Balfour of telegram to President Wilson, 28 December 1917.

[23] DDI, 5, X, doc. 37, Imperiali to Sonnino, 6 January 1918.

but Rome reacted in dismay to the apparent dismissal of Allied agreements by Lloyd George. In Italian eyes, guarding against potential revision of Allied pacts was a key purpose of the Anglo-Italian 'special partnership'. Now, however, Imperiali sensed 'a treacherous wind' blowing in Britain. On 7 January, he spoke to Hardinge 'harshly and privately', criticising the 'inconsistent, sporadic and contradictory' British policy.[24] The British justified their superficial reference to Italian promises with the need to 'drive a wedge' between Austria-Hungary and Germany.[25] The ambassador protested that Britain was in fact undermining the Entente, 'significantly weakening the indispensable solidarity among the Allies'.[26] The next day, Sonnino protested to Rodd that Lloyd George had suddenly thrown 'all our war aims ... out of the window, with the sole exception of the purely Italian territories. ... On the defence of the Adriatic and guarantees for our security there was not one word'.[27]

The Anglo-Italian dispute preceded by a few days President Wilson's address to the US Congress on 8 January, with the formulation of the famous Fourteen Points.[28] They rejected any imperialist ambitions by the belligerent powers, endorsing the principle of self-determination – without saying the term – in the peace settlement, and called for the creation of a League of Nations to preserve it. Lloyd George was unhappy with some of the points, in particular point 2 on 'freedom of the seas', which denied the possibility of implementing naval blockades and which he saw as a threat to British command of the waves. Lloyd George was also suspicious of an international league limiting British foreign policy (point 14), and of an 'impartial adjustment of all colonial claims' (point 5). Yet he chose to please Wilson and supported his declaration.[29] The rest of Wilson's points, after all, were similar to Lloyd George's aspirations.[30] In retrospect, it is also possible that the British premier felt he could eventually fool the American statesman, who had no experience of European politics, by supporting the principle of self-determination in Europe, but removing it from colonial affairs. Sonnino, by contrast, would not accept Wilson's points. Following the principle of 'clearly recognisable lines of

[24] Ibid., doc. 42, Imperiali to Sonnino, 7 January 1918.

[25] Imperiali, *Diario*, pp. 479–486.

[26] ASSR, Fondo Imperiali, b. 1, f. 6, Corrispondenza, t.gab. 18, Imperiali to Sonnino, 11 January 1918.

[27] DDI, 5, X, doc. 61, Sonnino to Imperiali, 9 January 1918; TNA, FO371/3229/8430, Rodd to Balfour, 10 January 1918.

[28] L. Salvatorelli, *Un cinquantennio di rivolgimenti mondiali (1914–1976)* 2 vols. (Florence: Le Monner, 1976), I, pp. 238–246.

[29] Lloyd George, *The Truth*, I, pp. 78 ff.

[30] President Wilson had been encouraged to denounce Allied secret treaties when Balfour visited him in April 1917, informing Wilson of the content of the London Pact and remarking that Balfour disliked it: Burgwyn, *The Legend*, p. 136.

nationality' in the shaping of Italy's new borders (point 9), Rome would have little claim to Istria, less to Dalmatia, and none to South Tyrol or the Isonzo valley above Gorizia, let alone African territories and Asia Minor.[31] Wilson reassured the Italians that 'Italy was entitled to the irredenta and also entitled to establish proper strategic boundaries'.[32] Orlando believed that meant American support for the whole Italian war aims.[33] However, in an interview with the Italian ambassador to Washington, Vincenzo Macchi di Cellere, Wilson clarified that it was through the League of Nations, that the strategic security of each country was to be guaranteed.[34] Nothing was farther from Sonnino's position. He thought the League of Nations would be useful only when 'every country has found, in the geographical demarcation of its political borders, that minimum of defensive conditions sufficient to give it the time [in case of attack] to resort to the protection' of the League.[35] Relations between Italy and France were no better, as the French Minister of Armaments, Louis Loucheur, openly preached 'a conciliatory' agreement between Italians and the Slavs on the Adriatic question.[36]

In this context, a visit by Orlando to London was urgent to ascertain whether Britain would keep its word and support Italy's promises under the London and St Jean de Maurienne agreements. On 24 January the Italian Prime Minister met with Lloyd George. The latter admitted that the Caxton Hall speech had been made to 'encourage the pacifist tendencies in Austria'. Then he added '*scherzosamente* [as a *boutade*]', that the need to extract Turkey from its alliance with the Central Powers might require a reduction of Allied colonial claims. Clemenceau, Lloyd George stated, agreed, and seemed ready to give up Syria. Imperiali, who was present as interpreter, noted in his diary that Orlando spoke 'well', eliciting British confirmation of ratified Allied treaties. Lloyd George was deliberately ambiguous. He insinuated the possibility of revising the Allied pacts but, when pressed, he reaffirmed the agreements. In conclusion, Lloyd George declared 'with intense cordiality', that he was ready to consider alternative means – perhaps a joint Anglo-Italian declaration – to rectify the unfortunate impression his speech had had on the Italian public.[37] Quite tellingly, this was never done. On the same occasion, Balfour and Hardinge too gave clear assurances to Italy about the validity of Allied pacts, claiming that they could not understand the Italian alarm

[31] C. Seton-Watson, *Storia d'Italia*, p. 567.
[32] DDI, 5, X, doc. 87, Macchi di Cellere to Sonnino, 15 January 1918.
[33] Thompson, *White War*, p. 336.   [34] Riccardi, *Alleati*, p. 604.
[35] DDI, 5, X, doc. 129, Imperiali to Bonin Longare, 23 January 1918.
[36] Ibid., doc. 104, Imperiali to Sonnino, 18 January 1918.
[37] Ibid., doc. 141, Orlando to Sonnino, 25 January 1918; Imperiali, *Diario*, p. 488.

regarding Allied 'partial support' of Italy's war aims, since these were ratified in a treaty, the London Pact, 'with regard to which no one can even think the British Government might consider withdrawing'.[38] It is difficult to read the minds of Lloyd George, Balfour and Hardinge here – in particular, why they confirmed British promises to Italy if they harboured the idea of revising Allied pacts. But there is no doubt they did so, and quite emphatically, too. The likely explanation is that British policymakers wanted to keep Italy committed to the Entente in a moment when the fate of the war was hanging by a thread, at the same time riding the wave of America's new diplomacy to limit as much as possible Anglo-American diplomatic frictions.

The feeble nature of British promises is however revealed by the renewed debate on peace-making in Britain. This was stimulated by expectations of an imminent Russian armistice – which indeed materialised at Brest-Litovsk on 3 March 1918. The Foreign Office reasoned that Russia's defection changed the fate of Constantinople. It reshuffled the cards of Allied colonial agreements,[39] spurring Hardinge's idea that preparations for the peace 'must necessarily be made in advance'.[40] Hardinge, therefore, set to organise a single department – the Political Intelligence Department (PID) – staffed by experts within the Foreign Office to speed up, update and rationalise British options for peace-making, which had been discussed since the summer of 1916.[41] Hardinge filled the PID with the best personnel he managed to poach from the Naval Intelligence Historical Section – overcoming the opposition of Cecil – and from the new Ministry of Information that Lloyd George had entrusted to William Aitken, 1st Baron Beaverbrook who unsuccessfully opposed Hardinge's manoeuvres. Bureaucratic warfare slowed down the activity of British peace-planning machinery, which would produce its reports by January 1919 – just in time for the Peace Conference. The PID was not supposed to suggest policy, but to support policymakers by providing them with all necessary information and possible solutions to the various issues; but from the onset, the environment gradually generated in the Imperial and War Cabinets as well as in the Foreign Office channelled PID's activity into a distinctively revisionist track towards Allied treaties. Harold Nicolson, Second Secretary at the Foreign Office, addressed a memorandum to his superior urging him to 'consider the means by which some modifications of our existing treaties

---

[38] DDI, 5, X, docs. 96 and 100, Imperiali to Sonnino, 17 and 18 January 1918.
[39] Ibid., doc. 75, Imperiali to Sonnino, 11 January 1918.
[40] TCC, Prothero papers, 'Peace Negotiations', 31 October 1917.
[41] Goldstein, 'The Foreign Office and Political Intelligence 1918–1920', *Review of International Studies*, XIV, 4, October 1988, p. 281.

with Italy' could be re-examined. It analysed the possible 'mortality' of the treaties of London and of St Jean de Maurienne. The former, albeit anachronistic, still had elements of validity, which made an agreed modification desirable; the latter should be considered lapsed. Beside the sentences about the St Jean de Maurienne Agreement, Hardinge noted: 'It is dead as far as Italy is concerned'.[42]

None of this was known in Italy, of course. Orlando had been relieved by his London trip. But Imperiali remained suspicious, because the British press continued to query the discrepancy between the 'cynical London Treaty' and the increasingly anti-imperialistic flavour of Allied war aims. The London Pact jeopardised the emerging claim of autonomy for the nations of the Habsburg Empire, and some British MPs such as Philip Snowden and Charles Trevelyan publically condemned 'the secret Italian Treaty'. Forcing injustice onto non-Italians, they held, would have bad repercussions inside Italy: 'By the acquisition of German, Slovene, Serbo-Croat, Albanian, Greek, Turkish and possibly Abyssinian subjects, Italy would become an Empire doomed to racial unrest and firm government'.[43] Imperiali was increasingly concerned by such attacks, which he believed hid 'intrigues and plots against us'.[44]

The unexpected diplomatic confrontation on war aims seriously impacted on the Italian approach to the Entente's grand strategy. Where Italy – given its military procurement – was initially in favour of a purely defensive strategy for 1918, it was soon confronted with the need to defend its empire project in a dramatically altered strategic and geopolitical situation. Italian policymakers therefore set up three new priorities. The first was to reclaim Italian strategic autonomy and control of operations in Italy. The second was to regain the initiative, knock the enemy out of Italy and occupy as many non-Italian territories as possible before the war ended: given the ever-changing diplomatic scenario, this seemed the best guarantee to Italian territorial claims thereafter. It was also imperative that Italy gained credit for its participation elsewhere, especially on the western front. This reversed Italy's traditionally low enthusiasm for operations abroad. Orlando and Sonnino thought it would allow them to repay the debts they had run up with their allies after Caporetto, and to claim rewards for the Italian contribution to the final victory over Germany.[45] Each of these goals conflicted with the general strategy of the Entente. The first Italian priority undermined the

[42] TNA, CAB24/4, g.t. 182, Memorandum by Curzon, 5 December 1917; FO371/3250/42599, Possible Revision of Our Treaty with Italy, 2 March 1918.
[43] Thompson, *White War*, p. 337.   [44] Imperiali, *Diario*, p. 491.
[45] A. Caselli Lapeschi, G. Militello eds., *1918. Gli italiani sul Fronte Occidentale* (Udine: Gaspari, 2007), pp. 13–15.

process of integration of Allied military effort, the second contradicted the essentially defensive character that the Italian campaign had in the eyes of the other allies and the third jeopardised Anglo-Franco-American management of the western front.

Unfortunately, Italian military strength was insufficient to achieve these goals. Diaz welcomed the efforts of Orlando and Sonnino to strengthen the authority of the Italian command, but he disagreed with their expectations for an offensive unless the other allies contributed significantly. As a result, Italian aspirations for a counter-attack in Veneto increased Italian demands for Allied assistance. Orlando's determination to participate in the western campaign, which stretched Italian resources to the limit, also led to him opposing strenuously any plan to reduce Allied contingents in Italy.[46] In other words, Rome sought Allied support to achieve strategic results that could serve Italian war aims, and this is further proof of how military strategy and aspirations for the peace were tangled. In view of the imminent German offensive, however, the other allies preferred to leave Italian divisions in Italy and transfer some of theirs to France; they never understood Orlando's case for a key role for Italy in France when Austro-Hungarian forces were encamped 30 kilometres north of Venice. Though largely reactive to events, Orlando's decisions reinforced Allied impression that Rome 'cared nothing for the common cause, only for "Italy's war"'.[47] These contradictions and misunderstandings generated frequent inter-Allied clashes over the implementation of the Entente's grand strategy.

15.2   The Phantom Allied Reserve

Further inter-Allied, and more specifically Anglo-Italian conflicts arose over the creation of an Allied reserve, which was discussed at the first SWC meeting in Versailles between 30 January and 2 February 1918.[48] The reserve would have crucial operational relevance in military emergencies. At Versailles the Allies created an Executive War Board (EWB) under Foch, with the authority to determine the strength of the reserve, its location and the measures necessary for its transportation and concentration.[49] Sonnino and Orlando objected that the EWB would interfere with the SWC, but their real concern was Italy's secondary role. Italian resistance was overcome when the other Allies accepted an Italian participation in the western

---

[46] Riccardi, *Alleati*, pp. 583–599.   [47] Burgwyn, *The Legend*, pp. 171–174.

[48] DDI, 5, X, docs. 166, 168 and 170–173, Consiglio Supremo di Guerra, Prima seduta, 30 January–2 February 1918.

[49] AUSSME, E8, b. 9, f. 2, Resolutions Passed at the Third Session of the Supreme War Council, January to February 1918.

campaign.[50] The 2nd corps of General Alberico Albricci would be transferred to France together with 60,000 militarised workers.[51]

On 3 February the EWB set the number of Allied divisions in the reserve at 'at least 30' made up of 9–10 British (three from the Italian front), 13–14 French (four from the Italian front) and the rest Italian.[52] Most Allied troops in Italy, therefore, could be moved at very short notice, although reserve divisions would for now remain on their current front.[53] Foch was happy that this scheme allowed him to exert indirect control on both the French and the Italian fronts, thereby creating an embryo of unified command.[54] Both the British and French Chiefs of Staff, Robertson and Philippe Pétain, respectively, plus Haig, strongly disagreed.[55] They claimed that a general reserve consisting of their troops but under an authority different to their own would limit their command. Diaz, on the other hand, was willing to participate with six divisions; in return, he asked that Allied forces in Italy be assigned under his direct command.[56] Diaz's position isolated Haig and Robertson, to Foch's benefit. In retaliation, Robertson opposed Diaz's request for the reorganisation of Allied forces in Italy, and on 17 February he declared his intention to withdraw two British divisions from Veneto.[57] Rome protested that the Austro-Hungarians were preparing their own spring offensive in Italy, and that the weakening of the Italian front would impede the transfer of Albricci's corps to France.[58] Clemenceau used the Anglo-Italian friction to impose himself and jump at any opportunity to boycott Orlando's French plan. He ordered the withdrawal of three French divisions from Italy. Orlando wrote to Imperiali that the strategy agreed at Versailles was 'slowly losing any sense'.[59] Imperiali's plea to the British, predictably, were ignored; without London's support, the Italians were deprived of any room for diplomatic manoeuvre. Orlando suspected that

---

[50] DDI, 5, X, doc. 172, Consiglio Supremo di Guerra, Terza Sessione. Conclusions: 'The Supreme War Council remits to the Executive Committee for the General Reserve, the study of the question of the employing Italian troops on the Western front'.

[51] The Italian 2nd corps was transferred to France on 18 April 1918: Caselli Lapeschi, *Militello, 1918*, p. 43.

[52] AUSSME, E8, b. 9, f. 3, Verbale della prima seduta del Comitato esecutivo del Consiglio Supremo di Guerra, 3 February 1918.

[53] Ibid., Verbale della terza seduta del Comitato esecutivo del Consiglio Supremo di Guerra, 6 February 1918.

[54] Gionfrida, *L'Italia e il coordinamento*, p. 111.

[55] EMA, *Les Armées Françaises*, VI, n. 1, pp. 71–75.

[56] USSME, *L'Esercito italiano nella Grande Guerra (1915–1918)*, 7 vols. (Rome: USSME, 1980) VII, n. 2, pp. 4–5.

[57] TNA, FO371/3230/30509, Balfour to Rodd, 16 February 1918; DDI, 5, X, doc. 248, Sonnino to Orlando and Giardino, 17 February 1918.

[58] Ibid., doc. 275, Orlando to Imperiali, 22 February 1918.

[59] Ibid., doc. 315, Orlando to Imperiali, 28 February 1918.

'the creation of the reserve' was an excuse that the other Allies would exploit to move the bulk of their forces from Italy.[60]

Behind this fresh Anglo-Italian antagonism lay a fundamental difference: British military leaders opposed the reserve, whilst Lloyd George considered it to be indispensable. Privately, he hoped it helped rein in the power of his generals; publicly he said the reserve was essential to match Germany's superiority on the French front.[61] Confronted by Lloyd George, Robertson handed-in his resignation and was replaced by General Wilson, whose seat in the SWC was taken by Henry Rawlinson.[62] The Italian position was the reverse: the Government disapproved of the creation of the reserve, whereas the Chief of Staff was in favour of it, at least in principle. Diaz's problem was to avoid that reserve being used solely on the French front. On 4 March, however, Haig openly refused to provide any of his forces for the reserve. General Tasker Bliss, the US permanent military representative, suggested bypassing the problem by leaving the number of reserve divisions on the various fronts undefined. Such a decision would have hammered the very idea of an Allied reserve; Foch rejected it. But faced by Haig's opposition, the EWB recognised that it 'had been unable to form a general reserve'. It reported this state of affairs to the SWC and awaited instructions.[63] At the following meeting of the SWC on 14–16 March, the British and the French made a common declaration asking the EWB to give greater attention to the Italian front,[64] and reluctantly accepted that Albricci's corps be transferred to France provided, however, that two French and one British divisions also be withdrawn from Italy. The Italian divisions would leave first to acclimatise to the French theatre and French military doctrine. Orlando was happy to see his French campaign confirmed but commented that the removal of the Anglo-French divisions was 'a total contradiction' of Allied commitment to give greater consideration to the Italian front.[65]

The lack of a coherent plan for the formation and the movement of the reserve revealed its faults when the German spring offensive came in the west. Codenamed *Kaiserschlacht*, it unleashed a series of attacks lasting, with some interruptions, from 21 March to mid-July. They marked the deepest German advance since 1914.[66] The first offensive, *Michael*, was

---

[60] Ibid., doc. 264, Orlando to Imperiali, 20 February 1918.
[61] Gionfrida, *L'Italia e il coordinamento*, p. 114.
[62] P. E. Wright, *At the Supreme War Council* (London: Nash, 1928), pp. 38–43.
[63] AUSSME, E8, b. 9, f. 3, Verbale della sesta seduta del Comitato Esecutivo del Consiglio Supremo di Guerra, 8 March 1918.
[64] DDI, 5, X, doc. 411, Orlando to Sonnino, 16 March 1918.
[65] Riccardi, *Alleati*, p. 591.
[66] There were four German offensives, codenamed *Michael, Georgette, Gneisenau* and *Blücher-Yorck*.

intended to break through the Allied lines at the conjunction of the French and the British armies between Arras and St Quentin-La Fère, outflanking the latter forces and beating them in detail. Once this was achieved, Berlin hoped that Paris would seek an armistice. The other offensives were subsidiary to *Michael* and were designed to divert Allied forces from the main attack. In the opening phases of *Michael*, the Germans made spectacular progress. They exploited infiltration tactics, advancing some 65 kilometres deep into British lines, taking 65,000 prisoners and 975 Allied guns. In retrospect, it can be argued that the Allies had failed to learn the tactical lesson of Caporetto. So, when the British 5th Army was broken, Clemenceau was astonished: '*C'est pire qu'a Caporetto*', he stated.[67] Lloyd George wrote to Orlando that he could not wait 'even a day' to remove a large part of the British artillery from Italy.[68] Orlando agreed in the name of 'perfect Allied solidarity', stressing that Italy was putting its allies' needs before its own. He also pointed out, in a slightly argumentative tone, that Allied arrangements would have imposed a very different procedure; finally, in concert with Diaz, he insisted that the other seven British and French divisions left in Italy should be put under the complete control of the Italian command.[69] Such divisions had already been deployed either on the Altopiani west of the Piave, or in the Venetian plain as a reserve: any changes to this deployment would be deleterious.[70] Between 25 and 26 March twelve batteries of British artillery left Italy. Between 27 and 30 March the 21st French corps, and between 31 March and 3 April the 7th British division followed suit. On 15 April, after the withdrawal of the 46th and 47th French divisions, only three British and two French divisions remained in Italy. On 18 April Albricci's corps also left.[71] Orlando was upset: he complained that the transfer of the French troops was very one-sided and had violated Allied military agreements, which foresaw a gradual withdrawal of the Allied troops *after* the transfer of the Italian.[72] Giardino protested to Foch, who refused any responsibility saying that French instructions came directly from Clemenceau. Giardino resigned in protest, and was replaced at the SWC by Di Robilant.[73]

Two conclusions can be drawn from these developments. First, that it was easy to speak abstractly of a 'united front', but the political conflicts at

---

[67] F. Foch, *Memorie* (Mondadori: Verona, 1931), pp. 361–363.

[68] TNA, FO371/3230/30509, Lloyd George to Orlando, 23 March 1918.

[69] DDI, 5, X, doc. 483, Orlando to Imperiali, 30 March 1918.

[70] AUSSME, E8, b. 10, f. 9, n. 9360, Diaz to Giardino, 25 March 1918.

[71] USSME, *L'Esercito italiano*, VII, n. 2, p. 8.

[72] AUSSME, E8, b. 10, f. 9, n. 392, Orlando to Giardino, 1 April 1918.

[73] Gionfrida, *L'Italia e il coordinamento*, p. 131.

the heart of the Entente remained. Crossing vetoes and clashes between politicians and generals, and also between one politician and another or one general and another, caused the key project of the Allied reserve to crack. This led to a rather chaotic and improvised movement of Allied reinforcements to France when the emergency came. Second, Anglo-Italian frictions favoured the French – frequently allowing them to impose their own ideas – and crippled the new Allied coordinating bodies. The failure of the EWB to create a general reserve is symptomatic: at the end of March 1918, its functions were entirely overtaken by events – specifically the appointment of an Allied Generalissimo.[74]

15.3   The Unification of Command

The Allies compensated for their failure to create an emergency reserve by establishing a unified command. The decision was taken by the British and French to overcome the faulty coordination between Pétain and Haig, which had favoured the overwhelming initial success of *Michael*. On 26 March, Poincaré, Clemenceau, Loucheur, Foch, Pétain and Maxime Weygand had a feverish meeting with Milner, Haig and Wilson at Doullens. Most of them believed that Foch had shown the best leadership and perseverance, and therefore appointed him coordinator of all the Allied armies on the western front.[75] At Beauvais on 3 April, Foch was given the title of Allied Commander-in-Chief following American consent.[76]

Foch immediately formed a reserve with a dozen Allied divisions, using it to plug the fatal gap that was about to open between the French and British armies after the German breakthrough in the British sector. The Germans were unable to move supplies and reinforcements fast enough to maintain their advance. The Stormtroopers leading the attack could not carry enough food and ammunition to sustain themselves for long, and the German attack petered out, partly, thanks to Foch's mastery of the battle.[77] Rawlinson remarked: 'I am overjoyed at [Foch's] methods and far-sighted strategy'.[78] Clemenceau was jubilant. Rarely had an Allied command reacted so quickly and decisively. In the wake of such events, Clemenceau demanded that such command be extended to the Italian front. Further German thrusts were expected and Foch needed to

[74] Greenhalgh, *Victory through Coalition*, p. 182.
[75] Gionfrida, *L'Italia e il coordinamento*, pp. 165 ff.
[76] EMA, *Les Armées Françaises*, VI, 1, pp. 401–404.
[77] L. H. Addington, *The Patterns of War Since the Eighteenth Century* (Bloomington: Indiana University Press, 1994), pp. 167–168.
[78] D. Winter, *Haig's Command: A Reassessment* (New York: Viking, 1991), p. 275.

have the overall control of Allied operations.[79] The military situation led Orlando and Diaz to welcome Foch's appointment on the Belgian-French front; but they opposed it in Italy, pointing out that it would be inappropriate given the geographic features of the Italian front and the huge disproportion between Italian and Allied divisions in Italy. Orlando therefore demanded that the aforementioned peculiarities of the Italian front should convert the de facto tactical independence of Diaz into strategical independence de jure.[80] Imperiali presaged that Italy's position might be interpreted as an attempt by Orlando to boycott the unified command.[81] In reality, Orlando had two reasons to avoid a head-on confrontation on the matter. First, the military emergency really cried for unity; second, Rome could not stand up against a decision that London had already approved. Rather, the Italian Prime Minister aimed at a political compromise. Italy would accept the Beauvais Agreement and a coordinating role for Foch, provided that the distribution of Allied forces on the various fronts be re-examined – which implied further Allied support to Italy after the emergency had passed.[82] Since Lloyd George too was eager to restrain Foch, he supported Orlando's point that coordination over the Italian front was good enough.[83] Clemenceau accepted.[84] At another Allied conference in Abbeville on 12 May, Orlando recognised Foch's authority as Allied coordinator on all fronts, including the Italian, 'but nothing more' as Milner observed.[85] By conceding coordination, not command, Orlando managed to defend the relative independence of the Italian command without isolating Italy from the other allies.[86] Yet Foch was satisfied as he now was officially recognised as Allied Generalissimo, and exulted that the British and the Italians had not conspired to boycott his role entirely.[87]

[79] AUSSME, E8, b. 10, f. 9, n. 579, Giardino to Orlando and Diaz, 31 March 1918; n. 606, Giardino to Orlando, 4 April 1918; G. Giardino, *Rievocazioni e riflessioni di guerra*, 3 vols. (Milan: Mondadori, 1929–1930), II, *L'armata del Grappa. La battaglia difensiva del giugno 1918: studio sul diario personale del comandante*, pp. 422–424.

[80] DDI, 5, X, doc. 490, Orlando to Imperiali, 2 April 1918; doc. 512, Orlando to Sonnino, 6 April 1918.

[81] Ibid., doc. 518, Imperiali to Orlando, 6 April 1918.

[82] ADMAEF, Guerre 1914–18, Dossier Général, vol. 986/226, Clemenceau to Barrère, 18 April 1918.

[83] DDI 5, X, doc. 628, Consiglio Supremo di Guerra, 5th session, second seating, Abbeville, 2 May 1918; Sonnino, *Carteggio*, p. 275, Orlando to Sonnino, 2 and 3 May 1918.

[84] ADMAEF, Guerre 1914–18, vol. 986/241, Barrère to Pichon, 27 April 1918.

[85] DDI, 5, X, docs. 621, 628 and 629, Consiglio Supremo di Guerra, verbale.

[86] Italian troops in France, though, were under Foch's command: AUSSME, E8, b. 10, f. 9, Orlando to Bonin Longare, 6 April 1918.

[87] Foch, *Memorie*, p. 383.

Imperiali nonetheless noted that the British press 'had a bitter taste' at the extension of Foch's power, and that Lloyd George privately repeated: 'Clemenceau has won the point'.[88] In a telegram to Sonnino, the ambassador recorded: 'The medicine is hard to swallow for the British', but on the whole 'now in this tragedy ... the Government is willing to put in place any measure it sees necessary to achieve the final victory'.[89] Instead of openly opposing Foch, the British tried to counter-balance his authority by exploiting the SWC.[90] The British disapproved that Foch operated through his own staff rather than through the SWC representatives. The Generalissimo saw the latter as his subordinate. The British, however, considered Foch merely as 'the commander of the Allied front in France and the strategic coordinator' of Allied operations, but they did not accept his power in the Balkans, Africa and Asia. On 11 July Rawlinson prepared a resolution, supported by Di Robilant and approved on 18 July, re-stating the SWC's complete and free executive power: the permanent military representatives should be intended as a technical and consulting organ for coordination of all fronts, following the suggestions of the commanders at each front – Foch being one of them. It marked a minor British success over the growing French military influence.[91]

The British hoped to further counter-balance Foch's command by appointing Jellicoe as Allied Admiralissimo in the Mediterranean. Milner proposed this privately to Imperiali on 10 May, stating that the French were too grasping. It was the fault of the British, Imperiali replied, 'for you always gave in to them', while 'I would advise [you] to proceed in a more intimate agreement with us [Italians], more moderate and rational. It is the only way to hold off the Gallic intrusiveness'.[92] Three days later, Orlando supported the British proposal, which would deprive the French of naval command. Despite the apparent security of the Anglo-Italian arrangement, the Allied naval conference of 1–3 June at Versailles went against expectation.[93] The Italians inverted the positions they had adopted on the Allied reserve when the military had been in favour and the politicians against: Orlando was now in favour of a British Admiralissimo, Revel was firmly opposed.[94] The Italians therefore tried the same manoeuvre that had

[88] Imperiali, *Diario*, p. 514.
[89] DDI, 5, IX, doc. 485, Imperiali to Sonnino, 30 March 1918.
[90] Gionfrida, *L'Italia e il coordinamento*, pp. 175 ff.
[91] USSME, *L'Esercito italiano*, V, n. 2, doc. 10, Di Robilant to Diaz, 18 July 1918.
[92] Imperiali, *Diario*, p. 530.
[93] AUSSME, E8, b. 9, f. 10, Verbale della prima seduta della sesta sessione del Consiglio Supremo di Guerra, 1 June 1918.
[94] Halpern, *Royal Navy*, pp. 184–188, doc. 209, Heaton-Ellis to Admiralty, 22 May, 1918; doc. 211, Admiralty to Heaton-Ellis, 24 May 1918; doc. 213, Clemenceau to Lloyd George, Most secret, 23 May 1918; doc. 214, Geddes to Lloyd George, 24 May 1918.

worked at Abbeville: accepting in theory a single command – guaranteeing the British complete authority over the Italian naval force in the Central Mediterranean and control of the convoys to and from Libya – but keeping on a practical level 'the little naval war of the Adriatic' out of Jellicoe's hands.[95] Infuriated, Lloyd George abruptly interrupted the discussion.[96] In turn, this offended the Italians. Hankey recorded:

'The end of the *séance* was screaming farce. Orlando, Sonnino, and . . . Revel were all shouting at the top of their voices at once, and gesticulating like monkeys. Sonnino's brick-red face looked like apoplexy, his eyes were bulging out of his head and flashing fire-real sparks and his body was lolling about with his gesticulation. . . . The meeting broke up in some confusion'.[97]

Imperiali commented: 'As usual they ended up playing the game of the French. . . . Now it's down to me . . . to pick up the pieces'.[98] On 8 June, the Italian ambassador saw Balfour at the Foreign Office and pointed out that 'the impulsiveness and briskness of Lloyd George were unjustified and had more offended than distressed Orlando'. Rodd too tried to recommence the discussion, convinced that the root of the argument was an unpleasant misunderstanding.[99] Revel's veto, however, left the matter on ice through the summer. Geddes was furious and repeated: 'Admiral Di Revel and he alone is responsible for the present state of affairs'.[100] Apparently, Geddes did not appreciate that the French were equally averse to surrendering any naval authority to 'Perfidious Albion' and found Italian objections very useful.[101]

Unification of command on land remained the chief Allied achievement in terms of integration of their military efforts in 1918.[102] Once again, Italy was portrayed by historians as the main cause of Allied coordination flaws,[103] whereas the matter was more complex than that, and the real issue lay with inter-Allied mutual rivalries across the board. The week following the failed appointment of Jellicoe as Admirallissimo the Austro-Hungarians attacked on the Piave. That battle would mark the turning point of the war in Italy, influencing the development of Allied strategy in the final months of the conflict.

[95] DDI, 5, XI, doc. 12, Orlando to Imperiali, 14 May 1918.
[96] TNA, FO371/3231/85586, Rodd to Balfour, 14 May 1918; AUSSME, E8, b. 9, f. 2, Resolutions Passed at the Sixth Session of the Supreme War Council, June 1918.
[97] TNA, ADM116/1649, fs.72–78, Hankey to Geddes, 1 June 1918.
[98] Imperiali, *Diario*, pp. 539–41.
[99] Halpern, *Royal Navy*, p. 504, doc. 226, Rodd to Geddes, 27 June 1918.
[100] Halpern, *Naval War*, p. 252.
[101] SHM, Es-19, De Bon to Saint Pair, 15 June 1918; Halpern, *Naval War*, p. 525.
[102] H. Mordaq, *Le Comandement unique: comment il fut réalisé* (Paris: Tallandier, 1929), pp. 57–91.
[103] Burgwyn, *The Legend*, pp. 177–182.

16 Propaganda As a Strategy

16.1 The Debate on Italian Adriatic Imperialism and the Fate of the Habsburg Empire

In the weeks that preceded the second Austro-Hungarian offensive on the Piave, the Italians had to compensate for the weakening of their front to the benefit of the French front. Italy's allies, on the other hand, considered how to beat Austria-Hungary without sending further reinforcements to the Italians. The Allies chose to concentrate on a more sophisticated use of propaganda, aimed at undermining Austria-Hungary's multi-ethnic army. On 8 April, an unprecedented Allied anti-Austrian propaganda campaign was launched mainly by Italy and Britain. It was the culmination of a long process of partial re-orientation of the Italian approach to Adriatic imperialism.

This originated chiefly with Gallenga Stuart, Borgese and intellectuals such as Luigi Albertini and Salvemini. As new director of Italian propaganda, Gallenga Stuart intended to pursue the 'policy of nationalities' in moderation. Thus, Italy could present its war as inspired by the same ideals of liberty and democracy that Wilson and Lloyd George preached, which Gallenga Stuart considered the best way to improve Italy's reputation. Borgese, for his part, believed a revision of the London Pact was likely and Italy should not submit to it passively but rather take the initiative, call for a conference of nationalities ruled by the Habsburgs to reach an agreement and impose it on Britain and the United States: 'America shall not withstand the will of the peoples', he wrote.[1] In the *Corriere*, Albertini proposed concessions to the Slavs to prove Italy's liberal posture. At this stage, he claimed, not even the alliance with Britain would safeguard Italian interests: 'We must begin to convince

---

[1] G. A. Borgese, Memoriale, 10 January 1918, in Albertini, *Epistolario*, pp. 849–851.

the democratic masses, if we want to influence the governments'.[2] Salvemini held similar ideas.[3] After the Caxton Hall speech, even Imperiali opined that an Italian agreement with the Slavs on Dalmatia was 'in our interest ... since we are not going to take it this time, anyway'.[4] These ideas stimulated a split in the Italian irredentist movement. Irredentists closer to Wilson founded the *Democrazia Sociale Irredenta* (DSI), which was opposed by Sonnino and the nationalist irredentists. The latter, led by Giorgio Pitacco and Giovanni Lorenzoni, responded to the birth of the DSI by founding the *Associazione Politica degli Italiani Irredenti* (APII). With the *Trento e Trieste* and the *Dante Alighieri*, it offered its services to Sonnino to prepare the ground for the Peace Conference by promoting Italian claims.[5]

These developments are indicative of the huge difference in approaches in Britain and Italy on peace preparations. In Britain, committees had been working on the matter for a year and a half and now new bureaus were being created to ensure that British peace planning was as grounded, flexible and coordinated as possible, capable of securing British interests in a volatile geopolitical context. Similar initiatives, though on a 'far less elaborate scale',[6] were inaugurated in France and the United States. In Italy, none of this happened. Sonnino remained solely responsible for the shaping of foreign policy, and his plan for guaranteeing a successful peace was to gain formal recognition of Italian claims in Allied treaties; improving Italy's reputation through propaganda, greater information on Italy's war and greater military commitment had long sounded bizarre – and even annoying – to him. Now that the possibility dawned on some Italian officials and intellectuals that Allied treaties might not be enough to secure Italian interests, Sonnino set to defend the letter of those treaties. Even so, he entrusted the task to Italian nationalist associations, without providing his ministry with a department staffed by experts – which suggests that, at this stage, he quite possibly had not fully realised the danger. The problem with Italian associations was quite predictable, that they tended to promote their own aspirations, lacked coordination and engaged in battles with rival organisations. This was especially true for Italian associations abroad, with the nationalist committees undermining the newly created DSI.[7]

---

[2] Albertini, 'L'Italia e l'assetto orientale', *Il Corriere della Sera*, 29 January 1918; 'L'Italia e i popoli dell'Austria', *L'Unità*, n.d.

[3] 'Il Problema dell'Austria', *L'Unità*, 24 January 1918.

[4] Imperiali, *Diario*, pp. 474–479.

[5] G. Giurati, *L'opera della 'Trento e Trieste' nell'ultimo periodo della guerra*, Relazione al XII Congresso nazionale, Trieste, 1–3 June (Rome, 1919), pp. 10–11; G. Pitacco, *Passione adriatica*, p. 288.

[6] Goldstein, *Winning the Peace*, pp. 99–111; Smith, *Sovereignty*, pp. 110–113.

[7] Burgwyn, *The Legend*, pp. 152–164.

For some time Orlando wavered between the two groups. The Italian premier never considered going as far as Gallenga Stuart, but he did consider indulging somehow the policy of nationalities at a delicate moment in Italy's war. Orlando was obsessed with the possibility of a separate Austro-Hugarian peace when Austro-Hungarian forces occupied North-Eastern Italy. Comments in the British House of Commons, such as 'we never had any quarrel with Austria', were still recurrent; and America had waited until 7 December 1917 before declaring war on Vienna.[8] Italian promotion of the principle of self-determination of the so-called oppressed nationalities of Austria-Hungary might convince Italy's allies to accept the dissolution of the Habsburg Empire. Furthermore, it could be a decisive propaganda tool against the Austro-Hungarian army in Italy. Orlando's visit to London in January had encouraged such conclusions, because reiterated assurances by Lloyd George, Balfour and Hardinge about the validity of Allied pacts had convinced him that the British were coming round on the question of dismantling Austria-Hungary. A limited Italian propaganda in favour of self-determination might speed up such a process.[9] In subsequent instructions to the Italian ambassadors in London, Paris, Washington and Corfu – where the Serbian Government was based – Sonnino stressed that he welcomed an agreement with the Slavs on the Adriatic question to precipitate an Austro-Hungarian crisis. Such agreement, however, should not imply any reduction in Italian claims. It would be an informal consultation – especially as there was no official Yugoslav authority to sign a treaty. Sonnino's aim was to have the London Pact accepted by the Slav minorities, instead of it being imposed upon them.[10] Italo-Slav negotiations, in other words, could either be concluded – if the Yugoslavs were willing to accept Italian claims – or dropped, if they were not. In both cases, the scheme of territorial partitioning in the region remained that sanctioned in the London Pact – as confirmed by the British Government to Orlando on his London trip.

As mentioned, these ideas were divorced from the real expectations of British policymakers. Yet Lloyd George came to support Italy's anti-Austrian propaganda because he wished to encourage a further round of secret peace negotiations with Vienna. Talks about an Austro-Hungarian separate peace had been kept alive thanks to Lloyd George's Caxton Hall speech, but in early March 1918 Germany's imminent offensive in the west had raised hopes in Vienna for a large-scale German success, and

---

[8] Sonnino, *Diario*, III, pp. 217–218. [9] Tosi, *Propaganda*, pp. 153–170.
[10] DDI, 5, X, Sonnino to Imperiali, Bonin Longare, Macchi di Cellere and Sforza, 31 January 1918.

Lloyd George's private secretary Philip Kerr suspected that Austria-Hungary now preferred 'to do business via America because the USA was not tied to Italy by treaty'.[11] Lloyd George's last hope to force Emperor Karl to negotiate on British terms was to press Vienna further psychologically. A propaganda campaign in favour of the policy of nationalities in the Empire served this scope.[12]

Two parallel propaganda efforts by Italy and Britain were initiated to undermine Austria-Hungary. In February 1918 Orlando granted Gallenga Stuart 9 million lire for the year 1918 to launch a massive campaign in favour of dismantling the Danube Empire. It was a record Italian investment in propaganda in the war – though the British allocated that figure in a month.[13] Gallenga Stuart used it to open offices in Allied and neutral capitals to build up a press office, which delivered mass communication overseas, and to activate an efficient information service. Entrusted to Borgese, the latter monitored the international press and public opinion, so that Italian propaganda could target it more efficiently. In the last year of the war, millions of postcards and 700,000 booklets were produced illustrating events of the Italian war. These publications kept battle illustrations to the minimum, focussing instead on the Italian recovery, Italian liberal values and the Italian struggle against the invader.[14] Britain, where pro-Austrian sympathies were stronger, was a special focus of the campaign. Imperiali was instructed to remove from the London scene, the main advocates of nationalist propaganda, Lieutenant Vittorio Fresco and Luigi Caprara.[15] Lieutenant-Colonel Filippo De Filippi and journalists Emanuel and Francesco Prati from the *Corriere*, took over the propaganda duties. Compared to those elsewhere, the offices in Britain were the most active, and their initiatives, such as the publication of the *Anglo-Italian Review*, enjoyed significant success.[16] Lloyd George, for his part, appointed Alfred Harmsworth, 1st Viscount Northcliffe, to supervise an Enemy Propaganda Department within the Information Ministry presided over by Beaverbrook and based at Crew House, London. Its aim was to spread dissatisfaction among the subject nationalities of Austria-Hungary. There was to be no official call for an end of the Habsburg Empire, but denials that its break-up was not an Allied war aim ceased.[17] Thus, Lloyd George remained open to both options: that Austria-Hungary, undermined by Northcliffe's campaign,

---

[11] Lloyd George, *Memoirs*, II, pp. 1498–1502.
[12] A. Palmer, *Victory 1918* (New York: Grove, 1998), pp. 154–156.
[13] Tosi, *Propaganda*, p. 226.   [14] ASCD, Carte inchiesta sulle spese di guerra, b. 11.
[15] ACS, Carte Gallenga Stuart, b. 1, f. 18; ASMAE, Carte Italia, 1916–1918, b. 111, f. 1152.
[16] Tosi, *Propaganda*, pp. 159–164.   [17] Sanders, 'Wellington House', pp. 127–129.

would eventually re-open discussions for a separate peace on British terms; or that it would, indeed, collapse.

The Italian and British campaigns progressively overlapped, thanks to the unprecedented cooperation that began between British, Italian and Slav anti-Austrian activists in London. On the British side, the more resolute were the members of the Pro-Serbian Society, Steed and Seton-Watson. Steed sponsored the creation of an independent Czechoslovakia, an autonomous Poland, and a strong Southern Slav kingdom: 'Serbia reborn will no longer be Serbia, but a United States of Yugoslavia'.[18] The dissolution of Austria-Hungary was the prerequisite of this scheme.[19] Seton-Watson deemed the creation of a united Yugoslavia vital for the interests of the British Empire.[20] In autumn 1916, he founded a weekly periodical bearing the optimistic title *The New Europe*, to stimulate 'an alert, organised and eager' public understanding, which would influence the making of peace. The journal was read by many MPs and by journalists and intellectuals on both sides of the Atlantic – it was frequently quoted by the *New York Times*, *Spectator*, and *Punch*. Throughout 1917, Steed and Seton-Watson won to their cause an increasing number of British intellectuals, including Trevelyan, Robert Ensor, Herbert G. Wells and J. Ellis Barker.[21] Trevelyan was notoriously pro-Italian, but he disliked Italian claims that contradicted the Risorgimento tradition; the others had been fervent adversaries of Italian Adriatic ambitions since the signing of the London Treaty. Now, however, their campaign for an Austro-Hungarian dissolution coincided with that of De Filippi, Emanuel and Prati.[22] The latter, unaware of Sonnino's instructions to his ambassadors, thought that Italo-Slav talks should be promoted to find an agreement based on mutual concessions. Emanuel, together with Mola, wrote several articles in the British press to convince the British public of Italy's good faith.[23] Steed, impressed by Italy's apparent change in its approach to the Adriatic question, offered to collaborate. Emanuel, De Filippi, Steed and Yugoslav representatives in London made repeated joint declarations claiming that Italians and Slavs would both benefit from the dismembering of Austria-Hungary; that Italy should give up claims on

---

[18] *The London Times*, 31 March 1916.
[19] Steed, 'A programme for peace', *Edinburgh Review*, CCXXIII, 456, April 1916, pp. 373–392.
[20] R. W. Seton-Watson, 'The Pan-German Plan and its Antidote', *Contemporary Review*, CIX, 1916, pp. 422–428.
[21] A. J. May, 'R. W. Seton-Watson and British Anti-Hapsburg Sentiment', *The American Slavic and East European Review*, XX, 1, February 1961, pp. 40–54.
[22] Tosi, *Propaganda*, pp. 168–169.
[23] Albertini, *Epistolario*, pp. 852–853, Emanuel to Albertini, 10 January 1918.

the Dalmatian coast; Zara should be a free city; and the Yugoslavs should drop claims on Carso and Istria.[24]

Sonnino was furious. He repeatedly reprimanded Imperiali for not having successfully monitored and contained the activity of De Filippi, Mola and the *Corriere* correspondents in London. Reiterating his guidelines, Sonnino insisted that 'approaches to the Yugoslavs ... should not mean giving up the Adriatic claims on the basis of which Italy entered the war'.[25] Orlando gave assurances to the Italian nationalist committees, upset by the London developments: 'From no declaration or act of mine preceding or subsequent to the beginning of this "policy of the oppressed peoples of Austria" can it be claimed that I have shown a tendency to give up, even partially, what Italy was guaranteed under its treaty with the Allies'.[26] Nonetheless, the British-Italian-Slav London team was achieving significant successes. Joint events, conferences and public meetings were held encouraging British policymakers to commit themselves openly to the dismembering of Austria-Hungary, and to promote an official Italo-Slav agreement on post-war settlement. The Italian people were now described by Steed, Seton-Watson and their supporters as another oppressed people of Austria-Hungary, fighting for their own independence, in a revival of the most positive images of Italy made in Britain during the Risorgimento.[27] In *The Times*, Steed praised Italy's recovery and called for a more determined British support at the Italian front in view of Austria-Hungary's final thrust,[28] while Seton-Watson declared: 'Trieste and Pola must be Italian'. The Italians drew the conclusion that the leading Yugoslavs and their British supporters had implicitly recognised Italy's rights to have strategically sound frontiers.[29]

Encouraged by these developments, Gallenga Stuart imagined that greater coordination of Allied propaganda was possible. He welcomed an Allied propaganda conference in Paris on 6 March 1918 and headed the Italian delegation.[30] The Allies agreed that they needed to coordinate their information services in Switzerland and speed up the detachment of Turkey from the Central Powers by supporting Ahmed Djemal Pasha over Enver Pasha.[31] Next on the agenda was propaganda aimed at Austria-Hungary. French delegates declared that the Italian overtures

---

[24] Such ideas replicated the content of an early talk between Mola and Slav representative Ante Trumbić on 18 December 1917: Tosi, *Propaganda*, pp. 105–106.

[25] ACS, Carte Orlando, b. 46, Sonnino to Imperiali, 17 June 1918.

[26] Pitacco, *Passione adriatica*, pp. 128–137.

[27] ACS, Carte Gallenga Stuart, b. 1, f. 1, Mola all'Ufficio Staccato, Relazione, 15 Februrary 1918.

[28] Albertini, *Epistolario*, pp. 852–853, Emanuel to Albertini, 10 January 1918.

[29] Burgwyn, *The Legend*, pp. 131, 149.   [30] Tosi, *Propaganda*, p. 177.

[31] ACS, Carte Gallenga Stuart, b. 1, f. 6.

to the Yugoslavs had paved the way for a new propaganda strategy to which the British adhered and, at Beaverbrook's invitation, a new meeting in London was agreed upon to organise it.[32]

16.2 The Allied Propaganda Offensive against Austria-Hungary

At the London meeting (12–15 March), a sort of Chiefs of Staff of Allied propaganda was formed by Steed, Borgese and Henri Moysset – *Chef de Cabinet* for the French Navy Ministry and an expert in German propaganda techniques. Moysset emphasised that the enemy must be beaten ideologically, not only militarily. As far as the anti-Austrian propaganda was concerned, it was agreed to target primarily the Austro-Hungarian army in Italy. The campaign would combine dissemination of anti-war slogans with appeals for mass desertion amongst the non-Austrian troops, driven by the promise of independence to the ethnic minorities of the Empire.[33]

This Allied initiative coincided with the final crackdown of Lloyd George's negotiations with Austria-Hungary. Greater pressure on Vienna had indeed stimulated one last round of Anglo-Austrian talks in Geneva, starting on 9 March 1918. Austro-Hungarian Foreign Minister Ottokar Czernin met with Smuts and Kerr promising to conclude '*une paix immédiate, juste et durable*', but only if '*l'Italie et la France abandonnaient leurs buts de conquêtes*'.[34] His concessions were as follows: 'Herzegovina and part of the Dalmatian coast [be ceded] to Greater Serbia, and Trentino to Italy, plus other minor rectifications and [Austrian recognition of] Italian claims to Valona and a protectorate over Albania'.[35] However, Czernin made a huge political mistake (which led to his resignation) when on 2 April – as negotiations were still ongoing – he boasted in the Municipal Council of Vienna that the French had asked for peace-talks. A furious Clemenceau unilaterally disclosed the letter of Emperor Karl, dated 24 March 1917, proposing separate negotiations between Austria-Hungary and the Allies. It proved 'a political bomb' that discredited Austria-Hungary in the eyes of Germany and forced it to cut Anglo-Austrian talks. Balfour recognised that the French had hampered 'any chance of Allied negotiations with the Austrian Emperor'.[36] Wemyss commented: 'Our dear allies the French and the Italians are really almost more difficult to deal with than is the

---

[32] Ibid., Carte Presidenza, b. 19-11-11, Gallenga Stuart to Orlando, 8 March 1918.
[33] Steed, *Through Thirty Years*, II, pp. 191 ff.
[34] TNA, FO371/3133/2002, n. 429, Rumbold to Balfour, 26 March 1918.
[35] PA, Lloyd George papers, Memorandum by Smuts, 14 March 1918.
[36] Egedy, 'Lloyd George', p. 49.

enemy'.[37] Vienna's preparations for the Piave offensive were probably ultimate proof that a separate Austro-Hungarian peace was unrealistic. Thus, the case for breaking up the Monarchy of the Danube finally prevailed in the top echelons of the British Government.[38]

On 8 April, therefore, the Allied anti-Austria propaganda campaign was officially inaugurated with a congress of the nationalities subject to Vienna, held in Rome, which solemnly proclaimed the right to independence of the Empire's minorities.[39] An Allied commission for propaganda in enemy countries was created, based in Padua. It included a French officer, Commander Gruss; a British colonel, Granville Baker; an American, Lieutenant Wanger; and Ojetti as general supervisor, with Stevan Hristić and Ante Trumbić representing Austria-Hungary's 'oppressed nationalities'.[40] This commission was the real mover of propaganda in Italy, despite the subsequent legend, springing mainly from the memoirs of Sir Campbell Stuart – a Canadian newspaper magnate who ran propaganda operations for the British during both World Wars – and Steed, that: 'President Wilson and Northcliffe's team were the destroyers of the Danube Empire'.[41] Both Stuart and Steed made much of the role of Crewe House in the anti-Austrian campaign, but the real manager of the whole operation was Gallenga Stuart, who controlled the Padua commission through Ojetti.[42] Baker complained to London that Ojetti was insisting on a purely Italian organisation of anti-Austrian propaganda.[43] On 18 June he warned Crewe House that: 'Everything is being done to deprive this commission of its inter-Allied character'. Steed opposed the overabounding power of the Italians but failed to turn the commission into a British-led body.[44] He managed, however, to encourage Diaz to raise a Czechoslovakian division made of prisoners of war in Italian hands willing to fight alongside the Allies against their former Austrian masters. This, in turn, generated further complaints by the French and American representatives that they were merely 'witnesses' to Anglo-Italian initiatives.[45]

Despite such frictions, the propaganda offensive against the Austro-Hungarian army was one of the greatest Allied propaganda successes of

[37] CCC, Wemyss MSS, WMYS11, Wemyss to Beatty, 29 May 1918.
[38] May, 'Seton-Watson', pp. 52–54.
[39] Amendola, 'Il Patto di Roma e la polemica', *Quaderni della 'Voce'*, 38, 15 September 1919, pp. 20–21.
[40] Rodd, *Memories*, III, pp. 398–401.
[41] M. Cornwall, *The Undermining of Austria-Hungary: The Battle for Hearts and Minds* (Basingstoke: Macmillan, 2000), p. 174.
[42] Albertini, *Epistolario*, pp. 924–925, Ojetti to Albertini, 31 March 1918.
[43] BOD, Milner MSS, Box 108, Delmé-Radcliffe to DMI, n. 10474, 18 June 1918.
[44] Steed, *Through Thirty Years*, II, pp. 208 ff.
[45] R. Mock, C. Larson, *Words that won war. The Story of the Committee on Public Information 1917–1919* (Princeton: Princeton University Press, 1939), pp. 256–257.

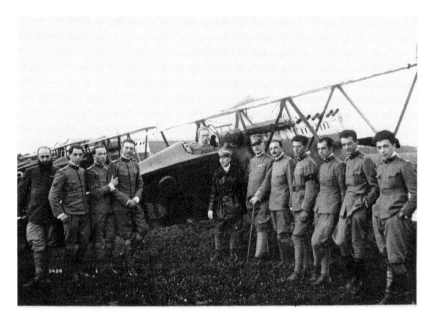

Figure 16.1 D'Annunzio and the pilots who flew over Vienna, August 1918

the war. From May to November, the printing works at Reggio Emilia produced some 60 million copies of 643 brightly coloured flyers, as well as 2 million copies of 80 news-sheets.[46] The material was dropped largely by aircraft on the enemy rear lines and cities – the Italian air force was re-gaining control of the skies after a brief period of Austro-Hungarian superiority following Caporetto.[47] These aerial missions, of which the most famous would be D'Annunzio's flight over Vienna, Graz, Ljubljana and Trieste on 9 August, also delivered the idea that the Danube Empire was completely exposed to enemy attacks: 'We are dropping leaflets, we might drop bombs instead', read Italian flyers.[48]

In addition to aerial missions, the Allies pioneered the so-called trench propaganda.[49] Mixed Czech-Italian patrols approached Austro-Hungarian positions and, making use of whatever cover they found, they launched

[46] Cornwall, *The Undermining*, p. 209.
[47] See: R. Gentili, A. Iozzi, P. Varriale, *Gli assi dell'aviazione italiana nella Grande Guerra* (Rome: USAM, 2002).
[48] V. Martinelli, *La Guerra di D'annunzio: da poeta a dandy, eroe di guerra e comandante* (Udine: Gaspari, 2001), p. 326.
[49] Cornwall, *The Undermining*, pp. 235 ff.

leaflets in Serbo-Croat, Czech, Polish and Romanian into enemy trenches – by hand or through slingshots. Such leaflets spread news of German defeats, of anti-German insurgency, and of famine, strikes and revolts within the Habsburg Empire. Alongside short, crude and colourful material, there were messages appealing more deeply to a national patriotism of the oppressed nationalities. Sometimes, the Czech would start conversations with their co-nationals encouraging them to desert. Thus, Allied propaganda not only exploited anti-war or social discontent but also, in the words of Major Aldo Finzi, 'spread dissension and mistrust among the various races', striking in this way at 'Austria's real weakness'. To circulate fast and accurate news, an Italian press agency was created in May in Berne answering to Gallenga Stuart and directed by Borgese. It soon became the main information centre of the Italian propaganda machine, and the intelligence gathered was shared with Italy's allies. This strategy soon proved worthwhile. In early May, Conrad, now Austro-Hungarian commander in Trentino, was alarmed. He warned that the enemy seemed to be pursuing 'an extremely dangerous form of propaganda which (if true) might have a demoralising effect on the men of Slav minority'.[50] Desertions from the Austro-Hungarian army before, during and after the battle of the Piave exceeded 22,000.[51] The growing domestic crisis in the Empire accelerated Austro-Hungarian preparations for a final offensive in Italy, but the widespread discontent in the army hampered it.

For Vienna, the Piave was the last card to play. Ambitions were high: medals had been coined to celebrate the conquest of Venice and Milan. With Russia out of the war, the Austro-Hungarians concentrated all of their reserves in Italy – 58 divisions supported by 5,000 guns, as opposed to 55 Allied divisions, including 5 Anglo-French divisions, supported by 4,500 guns. However, some Austro-Hungarian divisions were incomplete and suffering shortages of munitions and supplies. Conrad mounted a preliminary attack to conquer the contested Tonale pass at the western edge of the front on 13 June, but made little progress. The main offensive began two days later with a two-pronged attack by Conrad's Army Group Tyrol (10th and 11th Army) in the north, and Boroëvić's Army Group Piave (6th Army and 5th *Izonzo-armee*) across the river. The Italians had gathered precise intelligence on the enemy plan and opened up half an hour before the Austro-Hungarians, slaughtering their forces as they moved into position for the attack. Nonetheless, the northern thrust stormed the Asiago plateau, it broke into British and French lines and

[50] E. Egoli, *I legionari cecoslovacchi in Italia, 1915–1918* (Rome: Tipografia Segraf, 1968), pp. 44, 300, 443.

[51] ACS, Carte Presidenza, b. 19-4-6, f. 150, Servizio Informazioni to Orlando, 27 June and 25 July 1918.

overwhelmed the Italian 9th corps on Mount Grappa. When they sensed victory, the Austro-Hungarian veterans were ferociously counter-attacked by the 9th *Arditi* Assault Group under Major Giovanni Messe, and pushed back.[52] Boroëvić's southern attack too seemed full of prom-ise, as 100,000 Austro-Hungarians successfully crossed the Piave estab-lishing bridgeheads on the western bank in the early stages of the battle. However, the Italians adopted elastic defensive tactics and absorbed enemy assaults in a deep system of trenches. Having contained the northern threat, Diaz made good use of interior lines, deploying his reserves (nineteen divisions) southwards against enemy bridgeheads. The Italians attacked the Austro-Hungarian pontoons with aircraft and artillery fire. The Piave flood contributed to smashing the pontoons, becoming part of the Italian 'legend of the Piave'. After nine days of fighting, Boroëvić ordered the retreat across the river to avoid the com-plete annihilation of his bridgeheads.[53] Italy was saved.

The battle cost 85,000 Italian and 143,000 Austro-Hungarian losses, making the Piave as intense a battle as western front battles.[54] Although an essentially defensive victory, it was celebrated across Italy as a miracle by a jubilant population, which swore a collective oath 'to resist, bearing any sacrifice, until victory'.[55] The Italian triumph was greeted with relief by the Entente allies.[56] It dispelled their remaining fears of an Italian collapse and allowed the Allies to concentrate on the western front. Also, the Piave had proved the crucial impact of trench propaganda in under-mining the Austro-Hungarian army. Remarkably, most of the 25,547 Austro-Hungarian prisoners confirmed they had read or seen propaganda material disseminated by the Italians. Many indeed held propaganda leaflets, notwithstanding the severe measures by the Austro-Hungarian Command to prevent circulation of such material.[57] This was so encour-aging that many Allied representatives in Padua came to the over-optimistic conclusion that the Austro-Hungarian army would, in a little while, simply melt away, without any need to attack it. In consequence, they wished to push their campaign further, making greater promises to the ethnic minorities of Austria-Hungary. In particular, Steed and Baker insisted on an explicit Italian statement in favour of Slav claims. Vague

---

[52] Pieri, *L'Italia*, p. 189. Cadorna's purging, though it had undermined amalgamation between officers and soldiers, had nonetheless favoured the emergence of a younger generation of officers, some of whom, like Messe, proved their worth also in the next wars.

[53] Thompson, *White War*, p. 345.   [54] Stevenson, *Backs to the Wall*, p. 104.

[55] Gooch, *Italian Army*, p. 282.

[56] AUSSME, E8, b. 9, f. 2, Procés verbaux des trois séances de la septième session du Conseil supérieur de guerre, tenue à Versailles, les 2–4 julliet 1918.

[57] ACS, Carte Presidenza, b. 19-4-6, f. 150, Servizio Informazioni to Orlando, 27 June and 25 July 1918.

promises by Italian delegates, they held, were one thing; an official communiqué from Rome was something very different. But the Italian Government lingered.[58]

The anti-Austrian propaganda campaign, then, was spoilt by a major misunderstanding between Italy and its allies, as well as within the Italian political elite. Gallenga Stuart's men and the *Corriere* reporters had supported the principle of self-determination alongside Italy's allies in good faith while Orlando and Sonnino had indulged it at a propaganda level, without any intention to follow it up politically.[59] The British were further frustrated by what they held to be routine Italian inefficiency slowing down the work of the Padua commission.[60] In this case, at least, it was not poor organisation but deliberate inefficiency. The commission had enemies within the *Comando Supremo*: officers who shared Sonnino's ideas and who did not like the new strategy promoted by Gallenga Stuart and Steed with Diaz's approval.[61] Among these was Colonel Domenico Siciliani. Sonnino had managed to have him appointed president of the Padua commission – Ojetti having an executive but not an independent role. Siciliani hampered the commission's activity with delays and useless discussions.[62] Revel, for his part, advanced spurious technical excuses to deny navy seaplanes for the dropping of leaflets in Serbo-Croat on the Dalmatian coast to promote anti-Austrian insurgencies.[63]

Allied frustration with Italy erupted at the second Allied propaganda conference attended by some fifty delegates, including Northcliffe, Steed, Seton-Watson, Borgese, De Filippi and Emanuel.[64] In the opening session, on 14 August, Northcliffe and Steed demanded an explicit Italian declaration in favour of Yugoslav independence; this, they insisted, was indispensable to direct anti-Austrian propaganda 'into the best channels to attain the goals desired'.[65] It was 'an outright frontal attack on Italian foreign policy: and of a threatening and almost brutal nature'.[66] Borgese replied that the Italians were in favour of concessions to the Yugoslavs but not yet ready to abrogate the London Treaty unilaterally, 'for on the other side there is no authority competent to negotiate'. Moreover, Italy's unilateral surrender of its territorial claims would have been seen as an admission of weakness: it would have sparked nationalist recrimination in Italy and re-ignited hope in Austria-Hungary, which was not yet

---

[58] Burgwyn, *The Legend*, p. 152.   [59] Sonnino, *Diario*, III, pp. 265–266.
[60] Cornwall, *The Undermining*, p. 222.   [61] Tosi, *Propaganda*, pp. 187–189.
[62] ACS, Carte Orlando, b. 8, Ojetti to Albertini, 6 July and 18 September 1918.
[63] Ibid., Carte Presidenza, b. 19-11-10, Diaz to Orlando, 29 April 1918.
[64] Tosi, *Propaganda*, p. 203.   [65] Cornwall, *The Undermining*, p. 209.
[66] Albertini, *Epistolario*, pp. 960–970, Emanuel to Albertini, 17 August 1918.

defeated.[67] Borgese was convincing and managed to save his Government's ambiguous policy, though he did not share it; but on 16 August he received bad news from Orlando. The congress of Slav minorities held on the 15th in Ljubljana had shown marked hostility towards Italy: the 'moderate' current had claimed Dalmatia, Istria and Gorizia; the 'radical' had added Trieste to the list. Orlando telegraphed Borgese recommending that no further concessions be made to the Yugoslavs. Rather, 'it would be wise not to trust them'.[68] Conference resolutions had already been passed, however, which included a joint Allied appeal to the Rome Government 'to take the initiative to promote a common and public declaration' in favour 'of a free Yugoslav state including Serbs, Croats and Slovenes as one of the conditions for a fair and lasting peace . . . in Europe'.[69] Borgese warned Orlando that rejecting the Allied resolution would be unwise.[70]

These developments infuriated Sonnino. On 4 September he wrote to Orlando that the unilateral approval given by Gallenga Stuart's men to an Allied declaration sponsoring a reduction of 'vital Italian interests connected to our war aims', was unacceptable. Sonnino demanded that all propaganda offices be put 'under the direct and immediate responsibility of the Minister for Foreign Affairs'.[71] For the first time, after having long overlooked (and opposed) Italian propaganda, Sonnino determined to take control of it, revealing that only now, two months away from the end of the war on the Italian front, did he acknowledge the need for an institutional body supporting his diplomatic strategy in preparation for the Peace Conference. Of course, he intended such support as an abrupt reversal of any flexible and compromising attitude that had recently emerged in Italian foreign policy. Criticised by Sonnino, Gallenga Stuart advised Orlando that if propaganda were to be transferred to the Consulta, it would be a good idea to look for another Foreign Minister, incidentally proposing Bissolati as a candidate.[72] These tensions resurfaced at the council of ministers of the Italian Government on 7–8 September. Gallenga Stuart managed to keep his office autonomous, and the meeting closed with a favourable, albeit vague, declaration for a united Yugoslavia.[73] This appeared to be a victory for the Italian

---

[67] ACS, Carte Orlando, b. 49, Atti della Conferenza; Carte Gallenga Stuart, b. 1, f. 8, Erskine to Gallenga Stuart, 20 August 1918.
[68] Martini, *Diario*, p. 1279.
[69] ACS, Carte Gallenga Stuart, b. 1, f. 8, Relazione sommaria sulla conferenza interalleata di Londra 14–17 agosto 1918.
[70] Ibid., Borgese to Orlando, 17 August 1918.
[71] ASMAE, Carte Italia 1916–1918, b. 111, f. 1152; Sonnino, *Diario*, III, pp. 291–292.
[72] Tosi, *Propaganda*, p. 213.   [73] Sonnino, *Diario*, III, pp. 294–298.

democrats. In reality, the winner was Orlando, who had bought time to continue with his deliberately ambiguous policy.

The efforts of Gallenga Stuart, Steed and their men had contributed to convincing the British Government that the dissolution of Austria-Hungary was necessary. The Allies also realised that support should be given to the Empire's ethnic minorities to achieve that. Propaganda at the front was where these efforts merged. In mid-1918 trench propaganda secured itself a place in the overall strategy of the Italian army, becoming an important strategic tool. It was 'the most sophisticated example of front propaganda in the war',[74] sharpened by Allied advisers, but always with a solid Italian base and outlook. It certainly contributed to the failure of the Piave offensive, despite the meticulous Austro-Hungarian preparations for the attack. Victory in the field, though, was one thing. Political victory at international level was something different, and Italian ambiguities would eventually prove counter-productive. It was to Orlando's credit that he understood the need for a change in Italian propaganda; his limitation was that he considered the policy of nationality purely as a propaganda tool. Orlando lacked, as did Sonnino, a clear vision of the diplomatic and cultural changes that were taking shape. It is fair to say, however, that both Italian statesmen were encouraged in their assumptions by the no less ambiguous attitude of Lloyd George's Government. Hence, Allied relations looked set for greater collision after the war.

[74] Cornwall, *The Undermining*, p. 440.

17   Divided at the Finish Line

17.1   Race to the Armistices

Between 15–23 July Germany's last push in the west failed. In six months, the strength of the German army had fallen from 5.1 million fighting men to 4.2 million.[1] German manpower was exhausted, and an Allied counter-attack was approaching. The Italian contribution in the last Allied defensive battle of the war was important. Albricci's corps repulsed the Germans at Bligny, preventing the fall of Eparnay – and thence the encirclement of the Allies in Reims. In the effort, Albricci lost some 10,000 men – one third of his force.[2]

The Italians also scored a point in their favour in the endless inter-Allied confrontation over the question of naval command, preventing the establishment of a British Admirallissimo one last time.[3] The question resurfaced in July when the Americans proposed to adopt the Italian scheme for a fixed barrage at Otranto, in exchange for Italian acceptance of a British Admirallissimo. This seemed indispensable in light of the usually low evaluation that Italy's allies made of Italian naval activity. The Americans described the Adriatic as 'practically an Austrian lake', reinforcing Anglo-French deep-ingrained prejudice that the *Regia Marina* was basically inactive.[4] Statistics of Adriatic operations rebut such myth. The *Regia Marina* had maintained an offensive attitude, launching twenty sorties in 1918 largely unaided – the British and French contributing to just two of them – whereas Austro-Hungarian sorties had been decreasing throughout the war, dropping to just three in the whole of 1918. Moreover, supplies shipped by the Italians through the Adriatic increased from 61,900 tons in 1915 to 524,956 tons in 1916;

---

[1] Woodward, *Sir William Robertson*, pp. 187–189.
[2] Caselli Lapeschi, Militello, *1918*, p. 37.
[3] Halpern, *Royal Navy*, doc. 218, Geddes to Rodd, 13 June 1918.
[4] AUSM, b. 1191, Revel to Grassi, 30 April 1918; Halpern, *Naval War*, p. 439.

769,500 tons in 1917; and 1,381,900 tons in 1918, with a steady increase in war-related goods for both the Italian army on the Piave, and for Allied forces in the lower Adriatic. The idea of the Adriatic being an Austrian lake in 1918 is simply unrealistic, the reality being that the *Regia Marina* was in control of the greatest part of the sea and the *k.u.k. Kriegsmarine* tried to challenge its supremacy occasionally with raids and submarine attacks; but by mid-1918, it was practically immobilised in its ports. Even so, it was not immune. Contrary to the *k.u.k. Kriegsmarine*, which kept repeating the same type of bombardment raids, the *Regia Marina* diversified and updated its tactics and even developed a new doctrine. Called *battaglia in porto* or in-port battle, it responded to the Italian need to inflict decisive losses to an enemy that was less inclined to emerge. With ingenious devices such as the *Grillo*-class *barchini saltatori* (jumping boats) designed to overcome port defences and the MAS, the Italians managed to violate the ports of Trieste, Pola, Parenzo, Pirano, Fasana, Fiume and Buccari Bay to strike at anchored ships; additionally, the Italians pioneered manned-torpedo tactics that were likewise to score spectacular feats in World War II, allowing bold Italian *incursori* – towed by bigger boats in the vicinity of enemy bases – to swim deep into enemy waters to attack patrolling vessels. Such attacks proved increasingly successful and led Revel to rely more on such small devices than on larger ships. He was proven right when on 10 June 1918 a MAS sank the dreadnought *Szent István* off Premuda island in the upper Adriatic.[5] Land and naval successes made the Italians less disposed to accept unpleasant compromises. At an Allied naval meeting in Malta in August, the fixed Otranto boom was finally asserted. It comprised an uninterrupted 66 kilometres of nets between Otranto and Fano Island, plus an additional 14 kilometres between Fano, Somatraki and Corfu, and was made of 180 kilometres of steel nets, 429 buoys and 1,200 mines. Italy, France and Britain shared the astronomical cost of 3,238,345 lire. The barrage was completed in September 1918 and proved quite effective in blockading the remaining enemy submarines in the final months of the conflict, but it did not lead to the unification of naval command.[6] The question of a British Admirallissimo remained unsettled to the end of the war.

On land cooperation, the Italians appealed to the Beauvais Agreement, which provided for a re-distribution of forces on the land fronts in exchange for Italian consent to Foch's supreme command.

[5] Marcuzzi, 'From the Adriatic', p. 468

[6] Morabito, *La marina italiana*, pp. 319; Manfroni, *I nostri alleati navali: ricordi della guerra Adriatica, 1915–1918* (Milan: Mondadori, 1927), pp. 253–258.

Rome required immediate Allied support to exploit the Piave victory and launch a decisive counter-offensive. The only dissenter in the Cabinet was Nitti. The Treasury Minister was very influential in military circles. He knew Aosta and Diaz, and was anxious to avoid wearing down Italian manpower.[7] He wrote numerous letters to Diaz, insisting that the latter should plan the Italian army's stance – either offensive or defensive – exclusively according to his own military judgement. Italy 'was playing its last card and had to play it wisely'.[8] Diaz welcomed Nitti's pleas. In his eyes, the Piave had proven that the Austro-Hungarian war machine was still powerful and he was as well concerned that Italy was running out of men. The call-up of the 1900 contingent, he reasoned, would guarantee about 200,000 new recruits, to which 50,000 replacements already available could be added, while Austria-Hungary could count on 40,000 replacements immediately, plus 350,000 men between the 1900 contingent and prisoners returning from Russia. Therefore, he supported Orlando's request for Allied aid, but he reiterated that his outlook remained essentially defensive. Only when a decisive superiority in men and *matériel* was achieved, would he consider an offensive.[9] Paris and London drew different opinions. First, victory was to be won over the main enemy, Germany, on the main front, the French. Second, Austria-Hungary was disintegrating and would not be able to mount another offensive. Hence, no reinforcements would be sent to Italy – if anything, Allied forces should be withdrawn from Italy and Italy should counter-attack on its own.[10] Cavan alone objected to such plan, unhappy with the reduction in his contingent that it implied. He proposed to Lloyd George an Allied offensive in Italy supported by twenty-five British tanks and six extra Anglo-French divisions. Cavan's hope was that the Prime Minister would take the opportunity to realise his old project.[11] Clemenceau, however, was adamant in refusing any further aid to Italy. Germany was bleeding: any dispersion of Allied forces was counter-productive.[12] Diaz, for his part, insisted that reinforcements were a precondition for any offensive[13] because the Germans could transfer troops from France to Italy twice as fast as could the Allies, and he, unlike the French, had no American reserves as a fallback. Lloyd George commented bitterly

---

[7] Gooch, *Italian Army*, p. 271.
[8] Nitti to Diaz, 18 May 1918 and 2 June 1918, quoted in A. Monticone, *Nitti e la Grande Guerra* (Milan: Angeli, 1961), p. 280.
[9] Gooch, *Italian Army*, p. 284.
[10] TNA, CAB28/4, Notes of a Conference held at 10 Downing Street on Wednesday, 24 July 1918.
[11] Cassar, *Forgotten Front*, p. 171.   [12] Poincaré, *Au Service*, IX, p. 401.
[13] Rodd papers, Delmé-Radcliffe to Wilson, 10 August 1918.

that the Italians had 'lost their nerve so completely' because of Caporetto.[14]

If not manpower, Italy tried to get some support in *matériel* through the Allied Tank Committee.[15] Established on 8 January, it had to assess each country's need for tanks, the creation of an Allied reserve and its use.[16] Di Robilant requested fifty tanks for the Italian front. He got four, and they were used for training only.[17] Since French or British forces were not available, Rome maintained that American troops should be sent.[18] Macchi di Cellere gained overall approval from Wilson regarding American military collaboration.[19] General John Pershing, the US commander, differed.[20] On 28 July he wrote to Foch that his position was 'very firm' and identical to that of the French Generalissimo, who replied on the 30th confirming that 'it has not entered my mind to divert any American forces to another region'.[21] Some mere 1,500 American soldiers were sent to Italy,[22] whose marginal deeds were nonetheless celebrated by the most famous of them, Ernest Hemingway. The last Italian hopes to get Allied reinforcements vanished at the SWC meeting of 10 September where Allied military representatives presented their proposals for the 1918–1919 Allied strategy.[23] The proposal of Di Robilant included a major offensive in Italy by twenty-five Allied divisions.[24] The final note of the meeting, however, confirmed the priority of the French front.[25] The Italians were considered to have the upper hand on their front and should exploit it offensively as soon as they could. An Allied offensive in France was scheduled for the autumn, if the situation was favourable; otherwise, a general offensive was to be launched in France and Italy the following spring.[26] Despite recent

---

[14] Stevenson, *Backs to the Wall*, p. 156.

[15] USSME, *L'Esercito italiano*, VI, n. 2, pp. 419–127.

[16] Gionfrida, *L'Italia e il coordinamento*, pp. 151 ff.

[17] L. Ceva, A. Curami, *La meccanizzazione dell'Esercito italiano dalle origini al 1943*, 2 vols. (Rome: USSME, 1994), I, pp. 67–69.

[18] DDI, 5, XI, doc. 370, Attachment, Orlando to Macchi di Cellere, 8 August 1918.

[19] Ibid., doc. 409, Sonnino to Imperiali, Bonin Longare and Macchi di Cellere, 19 August 1918.

[20] J. J. Pershing, *My Experiences in the World War* (London: Hodder & Stoughton, 1931), p. 227.

[21] EMA, *Les Armées Françaises* VII, pp. 364, 380; Greenhalgh, *Foch in Command. The Forging of a First World War General* (Cambridge: Cambridge University Press, 2011), p. 417.

[22] F. Lazzarini, 'Col 332nd sul Piave', in Società Italiana di Storia Militare (SISM) ed., *Over There in Italy. L'Italia e l'intervento americano nella Grande Guerra* (Rome: Nadir Media, 2017), p. 269.

[23] AUSSME, E8, b. 10, f. 2, Nota collettiva n. 37 dei Rappresentanti militari permanenti al Consiglio supremo di guerra, 10 September, 1918.

[24] USSME, *L'Esercito italiano*, V, p. 2, n. 63, Di Robilant to Diaz, 3 September 1918.

[25] Ibid., n. 50, Nota collettiva n. 37, pp. 229–237.

[26] AUSSME, E2, b. 81, f. Consiglio interalleato di guerra di Versailles, n. 3788, Di Robilant to Diaz, 14 August 1918.

claims that British, French and American representatives 'did not dominate' allied conversations about strategy, allowing for significant Italian exploitation of inter-allied bodies,[27] the final plan approved was in Di Robilant's view, nothing else than the result of the western powers' political hegemony.[28] The immediate consequence was that the War Office ordered the British infantry battalions in Italy to be reduced from four to three in each brigade. Such a reduction of British brigades in the west had been approved in February, but Plumer and Cavan had successfully avoided it for their own troops in Italy, on the grounds that it would have had 'a bad morale effect on the Italians'.[29] The exceeding battalions would now be transferred to France.[30]

In Rome, irritation grew. Not only was Italy's request for reinforcements not met, but Italy was also expected to attack. On 15 September Nitti sent Rodd a blunt memorandum: 'On its front Italy really fights with its own forces only ... and Allied divisions (including soldiers and auxiliary workers) here are inferior in numbers to the units Italy has sent to France'. Nitti continued:

Austria-Hungary has the superiority over Italy in three respects: in the number of troops, in its artillery ... and in geographical position. ... The Italian front has an essential value which it is a grave error to disregard. If Italy were to lose the war ... probably the Entente will lose it too. ... On the other hand, victory on the Italian front could precipitate events.[31]

The overall situation, however, was taking a turn favourable to the Entente. On 14 September, the final Allied offensive in Macedonia began under the new Allied commander at Salonika, General Louis Frenchet D'Espèrey. Between 19–25 September, Allenby broke through Turkish defences in Palestine and opened the way to Damascus, which he captured on 1 October. In France, the Allies met with one success after another. On 26 September, Foch launched his grand offensive on the Hindenburg Line, pushing back the Germans on a 400-kilometre front, and capturing 4,000–4,500 guns in one month.[32] 'Things may come to a head, and we should not find ourselves to be idle, and with the enemy still in the house, while the other allies will have driven it out of their territories', commented Imperiali. But, 'Nitti is in no hurry'.[33] Orlando, alarmed, went to Paris to plead Italy's cause once more. He met with

[27] McCrae, *Coalition Strategy*, pp. 137–138.
[28] Gionfrida, *L'Italia e il coordinamento*, p. 188.
[29] TNA, CAB23/5, War Cabinet minutes 340, 7 February 1918.
[30] Dillon, *'Allies'*, p. 170.   [31] Rodd papers, Nitti to Rodd, 15 September 1918.
[32] DDI, 5, XI, doc. 791, Consiglio Supremo di Guerra 349, ottava sessione, prima seduta, verbale, 31 October 1918.
[33] Imperiali, *Diario*, p. 575.

complete indifference: 'All means inevitably flow to where there is a fight. We are in this vicious circle: we are not fighting because we do not have the means, and we are denied the means because we are not fighting'.[34] Sonnino concluded that inaction was more detrimental to Italy than the risk of a battle without Allied reinforcements:[35] 'Even if it fails, it will always be better for us, not to have remained idle in this moment when everybody is fighting'.[36]

The final push to Diaz came from the east. On 29 September, Bulgaria asked for an armistice. D'Espèrey signed it unilaterally the next day.[37] This was in line with Allied arrangements that armistices should be signed by the Allied Commander-in-Chief in a given theatre. D'Espèrey, how-ever, had – on Clemenceau's instructions – altogether excluded his allies from armistice negotiations, as if France was the only Entente power to manage Balkan affairs.[38] D'Espèrey's British subordinate, George Milne, reported that 'the French are playing their cards in this theatre solely for their own purposes', and that 'the British Army, like the Italian, Serbian, and Greek, is merely one of the cards'.[39] Such idea exacerbated British suspicion – which had been reinforced by Foch's management of the western front throughout the summer – that France was willing to exploit Allied resources to secure its national ends.[40] In response, Lloyd George removed Milne's contingent from D'Espèrey's command and placed it under Allenby. If the latter entered Anatolia, the two British forces could make a combined assault on Constantinople and secure British predom-inance in the crumbling Ottoman Empire. On 3 October, Lloyd George told the War Cabinet that 'Britain had won the war in the Middle East, and there was no reason why France should profit from it'.[41] The Cabinet agreed that 'there was now nothing in front of General Allenby to prevent him reaching Aleppo or Alexandretta',[42] which meant that 'we had con-quered the country, and the French wanted the spoils'.[43] The Admiralty too was anxious to keep the Mosul oil fields in British hands, in spite of Sykes–Picot assigning Syria to France.[44] Thus, the armistice must be imposed on Turkey by Britain 'alone & at once', in Milner's words. The

---

[34] DDI, 5, XI, doc. 539, Orlando to Sonnino, 18 September 1918.

[35] Ibid., doc. 519, Sonnino to Orlando, 16 September 1918.

[36] Imperiali, *Diario*, pp. 577–578.   [37] French, *Strategy of Lloyd George*, p. 262.

[38] C. Seton-Watson, *Storia d'Italia*, p. 576.

[39] French, *Strategy of Lloyd George*, p. 261.

[40] TNA, WO106/1456: Grant, notes made at General Foch's HQ, 7 August 1918; CAB23/44A/IWC29A: Committee of Prime Ministers, 8 August 1918.

[41] Ibid., CAB23/14/WC482A: War Cabinet minutes, 3 October 1918.

[42] Ibid., 23/8, War Cabinet 490, War Cabinet minutes, 24 October 1918, p. 3.

[43] Ibid., War Cabinet 492, War Cabinet minutes, 29 October 1918, p. 3.

[44] French, *Strategy of Lloyd George*, p. 266.

next day, the Germans appealed to President Wilson to mediate a peace on the basis of the Fourteen Points, to which the US Secretary of State Robert Lansing replied positively on the 9th – much to Entente irritation.[45] As for the Italians, Diaz was finally convinced that Italy also needed an armistice to flaunt, and began preparations for an offensive on the Piave.[46] An inter-Allied race had been ignited to exploit the war armistices as political tools in inter-Allied post-war competition.

On 7 October, at a SWC meeting, Lloyd George and Clemenceau 'spat at one another like angry cats';[47] the next day Cecil informed Stephen Pichon, the French Foreign Minister that the changed military situation in Palestine, Mesopotamia and Syria, Russia's collapse, and the entry of the United States into the war, meant that the Sykes–Picot Agreement 'does not appear suitable to present conditions'.[48] On 14 October, the Italians had a similarly bad surprise when Borghese met Balfour to discuss the settlement of Anatolia. The imminent Turkish armistice raised the question of how to manage the occupation zones to be assigned to the Entente. Greek ambitions on Smyrna threatened Italy's claim on the same province, so Borghese asked the British ally for guarantees. Balfour replied that the British Government, while willing to remain faithful to the Treaty of London, no longer saw the St Jean de Maurienne Agreement as valid because it lacked Russian consent.[49] This took Sonnino by surprise. Throughout the summer, he had prepared a new line of defence for Italy's war aims, but since repeated British assurances had made him confident of British support, he had focussed on Italian responses to American objections. He reasoned that Rome could exploit Wilson's hostility to imperialist endeavours. Unfair treatment of Italy by the British and the French in the Eastern Mediterranean would be a manifestation of the very imperialism that Wilson had resolved to fight. Equity of treatment – and therefore of expansion in the Eastern Mediterranean – between the three Entente powers, would, instead, guarantee a 'democratic peace'. As an *extrema ratio*, Italy might even give up its claims in Asia Minor – provided that the other allies did the same.[50] Now, however, Imperiali informed Sonnino that London seemed willing to make a *tabula rasa* of all past agreements.[51] Sonnino adopted an inflexible line regarding any revision of 'the compensations agreed upon

[45] Melchionni, *Vittoria mutilata*, p. 12.
[46] DDI, 5, XI, doc. 605, Orlando to Bonin Longare, 2 October 1918.
[47] TNA, FO800/201, Cecil to Balfour, 7 October 1918.
[48] Ibid., CAB27/24/EC-1915, Cecil to Pichon, 8 October 1918.
[49] Riccardi, *Alleati*, p. 613.
[50] DDI, 5, XI, doc. 134, Sonnino to Macchi di Cellere, 27 June 1918.
[51] Ibid., doc. 141, Imperiali to Sonnino, 27 June 1918.

with us'. He claimed that the clause regarding Russian consent on the St Jean de Maurienne Agreement was a technicality designed to bolster the morale of Russian Provisional Government and keep Petrograd as an active participant in the war. Russia's decision to leave the war obviously rendered this condition meaningless.[52] Imperiali presented Sonnino's objections to Hardinge, but found the latter 'in one of his *patronizing mood* days'. The Foreign Under-Secretary refused to discuss the subject. 'What a way to observe treaties', commented Imperiali.[53] The rejection of the colonial agreement signified that the entire political foundation for Italy's entry to the Entente was crumbling.

That Britain meant business became clear on 20 October when Constantinople requested an armistice with London. The tendency in Entente countries to go each its own way in pursuit of national interests was exacerbated and accelerated by the sudden collapse of the enemy. Two days later, the War Cabinet decided to inform the French and Italians 'of the Turkish approach and of the terms that the British would offer them, but to exclude [the French and Italians] from further consultations'.[54] British terms secured London's control over the Bosporus forts, the Straits and the Black Sea limiting Allied disembarkations into Anatolia to those cases where 'Allied security' was threatened – which left management of the territories promised to Italy and France largely to Turkish authorities.[55] At the following SWC meeting, Lloyd George and Clemenceau 'bandied words like fish-wives'.[56] The former insisted on entrusting the Turkish negotiation to Calthorpe with the argument that 'except for Great Britain no one had contributed anything more than a handful of black troops to the expedition in Palestine. . . . The British had now some 500,000 men on Turkish soil'.[57] As observed by Margaret MacMillan, it was an unfair argument because the British had sent correspondingly fewer troops to the western front.[58] Furthermore, the Allies had always agreed that 'fighting in one theatre of war, where there was little to gain, might be just as important a contribution . . . as much easier fighting in other theatres where great successes were achieved'; thus, 'any territories that the Allies might acquire should be pooled and should not be regarded as

---

[52] Ibid., doc. 694, Sonnino to Imperiali and Bonin Longare, 18 October 1918.
[53] Imperiali, *Diario*, p. 555. Official rejection was communicated on 30 October.
[54] French, *Strategy of Lloyd George*, p. 265.
[55] G. Caccamo, 'Esserci a qualsiasi costo: Albania, Mediterraneo Orientale e Spedizioni minori', in R. Pupo ed., *La vittoria senza pace. Le occupazioni militari italiane alla fine della Grande Guerra* (Bari: Laterza, 2014), p. 183.
[56] Quoted in MacMillan, *Peacemakers*, p. 385.
[57] DDI, 5, XI, doc. 784, Conferenza interalleata, verbale segreto, 'The Armistice with Turkey', 30 October 1918.
[58] MacMillan, *Peacemakers*, p. 386

the property of the nation which had won them'.[59] And finally, Clemenceau objected that Calthorpe was not the Allied commander in the Mediterranean theatre – he was subordinate to Gauchet. Balfour, however, argued that 'the Dardanelles, Bosporus and Sea of Marmara were not in the Mediterranean'; Lloyd George concluded bluntly that, should the other Allies object to the British decision to charge Calthorpe with armistice negotiations in Anatolia, Britain would insist on a British representative being present at any other case: 'For example, in the case of the western front the armistice terms would have to be signed not by Marshal Foch only, but by the generals of all the nations represented on that front. ... [An] Italian armistice ... would be signed, not by General Diaz alone, but by the Allied commanders of all the armies on the Italian front'.[60] The French and Italians reluctantly backed down on the Turkish issue.[61]

The matter increased Italian anxiety about their own victory. This was needed to counter-balance the successes of the French and British elsewhere, but also to secure Italian war aims vis à vis revisionist tendencies in allied countries. The only one opposing an offensive, until the very last, was Nitti, who reminded Diaz that defeat would mean ruin.[62] The numbers seemed to justify Nitti's pessimism. At the start of October, Diaz's army numbered about 2,160,000 men: for the final offensive, sixty divisions were available (including three British, two French and one Czechoslovakian), supported by 7,700 guns and 663 aeroplanes – as opposed to 6,145 Austro-Hungarian guns and 564 aircraft.[63] Far from enjoying the three-to-one superiority held to be necessary for a successful attack, Diaz was one division weaker than Boroëvić, although the latter's forces suffered severe shortages of supplies and munitions.[64] Colonel Tullio Marchetti, Chief of the *Ufficio Informazioni* in the Italian 1st Army and a pioneer of Italian intelligence, metaphorically described the Austro-Hungarian army in October 1918 as 'a pudding which has a crust of roasted almonds and is filled with cream'. If the Italians managed to pierce the crust, they would advance smoothly in the Austro-Hungarian rear, infected by anti-Habsburg agitation. The problem was to break the best Austro-Hungarian units in the frontline.[65] Diaz's plan included a northern attack on the Grappa to draw in the Austro-Hungarian reserves, followed by the main blow across the Piave. A particularly important task was given to Cavan's 10th Army, consisting of two

[59] TNA, CAB23/14, War Cabinet 482A, 3 October 1918.   [60] DDI, 5, XI, doc. 784, *cit.*
[61] MacMillan, *Peacemakers*, p. 386. The armistice came into operation on 31 October.
[62] Aldrovandi Marescotti, *Guerra diplomatica*, p. 188.
[63] Stevenson, *Backs to the Wall*, p. 157.   [64] Gooch, *Italian Army*, p. 293.
[65] T. Marchetti, *Ventotto anni nel servizio informazioni militari* (Trento: Museo del Risorgimento, 1960), p. 382.

British and two Italian divisions: breaking the Austro-Hungarian defences at Papadopoli Island, a crucial sector of the line.[66]

On 24 October, the anniversary of Caporetto, the action commenced. It developed differently from the usual World War I battle. This generally saw an initial success of the attacker that faded over time as the defender's resistance hardened and his reserves intervened. For three days, however, the Austro-Hungarians prevented any significant Allied progress and inflicted some 40,000 losses; Marchetti's almond crust was tough, indeed. Then the defenders ran out of reserves, some of whom were swallowed up in the cauldron and decimated, whilst others refused to move to the frontline, preventing the Austro-Hungarian command from launching effective counter-attacks. On 27 October, after successfully seizing Papadopoli Island, Cavan won a foothold on the eastern bank of the river. It was an important movement that breached the Austro-Hungarian front, but the subsequent British claim that Cavan had won the battle for the Allies was a gross exaggeration. The Austro-Hungarian collapse was determined by constant pressure, across the entire line, by the Italian divisions. Victory came on 29 October when the Italian 8th Army occupied the small town of Vittorio Veneto, which gave the name to the battle, separating the Austro-Hungarian army groups and causing a rout of the defenders.[67] Nonetheless, the British newspapers saluted it as an Allied victory, attributing the outcome of the battle to Cavan's action and to Yugoslav and Czechoslovakian agitation. Imperiali protested: the Allied contingent in Italy was too small 'to mark as an "Allied" success the efforts of three quarters of the Italian army'. He went on to list the numbers: '5,000 guns and 500,000 prisoners. No army can boast such a success'.[68] It was, by all means, Caporetto reversed. The debate on the battle did not fade away, and the respective historiographies later reflected this division. Italian scholars called Vittorio Veneto the decisive battle of the war, no less, because the surrender of Austria-Hungary accelerated that of Germany. They emphasised the light casualties suffered by Italy's allies (1,800 British and 500 French) and shouted about a 'conspiracy of silence' on Vittorio Veneto hatched by the western powers.[69] The British tended to describe the battle as an affair taken for granted because of the Austro-Hungarian

---

[66] Cassar, *Forgotten Front*, p. 188.

[67] S. Rovighi, 'Una "battaglia fortunata": Vittorio Veneto', in Labanca ed., *L'istituzione militare in Italia. Politica e società* (Milan: Unicopoli, 2002), pp. 101–106.

[68] Imperiali, *Diario*, pp. 591–592.

[69] Rovighi, 'Battaglia fortunata', *cit.*; P. P. Cervone, *Vittorio Veneto, l'ultima battaglia* (Milan: Mursia, 2007); E. Rosati, A. M. Carassiti, *Dizionario delle battaglie di terra, di mare e di cielo, assedi, rivoluzioni, colpi di stato, guerre civili. I conflitti che sconvolsero la storia dell'Umanità* (Genoa: Gulliver, 1996), p. 328; M. Caracciolo, *L'Italia e i suoi Alleati*, p. 310.

political and morale crisis.[70] Some British scholars openly supported the
'Cavan's victory' thesis[71] – failing to appreciate that Cavan's crossing of
the Piave was made on pontoons built by Italian engineers, who bravely
kept repairing them under enemy fire, and was made possible by the
covering fire of the Italian artillery. Only recently did Gooch concede
that Vittorio Veneto was not a *passeggiata* (promenade).[72]

This sort of historiographical derby has prevented a balanced and complete understanding of the battle. The largely Italian success of Vittorio
Veneto certainly deserves more attention on the part of non-Italian scholars,
particularly as no comparably clear victory was achieved in autumn 1918 by
the Allies against the German army, which the British War Cabinet by now
acknowledged to be 'the most fatigued of all the armies fighting on the
Western Front'.[73] Italian accounts need integrating with the crucial contribution of Italy's allies to the reconstruction and supply of the Italian army
that made the final battle possible in the first place. It was only through
increasing Allied collaboration during 1918 that victory was achieved. In
this regard, frontline cooperation no doubt worked better than political
cooperation. The Allies in Italy fought together, suffered together and won
together, each according to its potential.

The domestic collapse of Austria-Hungary was another factor in the
outcome of the campaign. On 28 October, Czechoslovakia declared
independence from Vienna, followed by the Slav minorities on the 29th,
and Hungary on the 31st. This had little influence on the fight, as news
was slow to come to the frontline; but it had a huge impact on the
disintegration of the Austro-Hungarian army during the rout that followed, thus contributing to Diaz's overwhelming success. On
29 October, Austria-Hungary was compelled to ask for an armistice.
Sonnino had required briefs from Diaz and Revel about military and
naval clauses for an armistice favourable to Italy since the early hours of
the Italian offensive, emphasising that such clauses should be justified on
'defensive and security' grounds. This reveals Sonnino's intention to
obtain through armistice negotiations peace terms that included Italian
claims under the London Treaty, but possibly also others that went
beyond it. This can be read as evidence of Sonnino's greediness or as
a response to the revisionist current in Allied countries, which encouraged
Italy to secure its interests by alternative means. Expectedly, the requests
of both Diaz and Revel, presented to Sonnino on 27 October, exceeded
the London Pact. Diaz asked permission to surpass the London Pact line

---

[70] Thompson, *White War*, p. 343.   [71] Cassar, *Forgotten Front*, p. 215.
[72] Gooch, *Italian Army*, p. 297.
[73] TNA, CAB23/8, War Cabinet 487, War Cabinet minutes, 16 October 1918, p. 2.

Figure 17.1 General Armando Diaz, Italian Chief of Staff after Caporetto

where 'necessary strategically', assigning occupied areas to Italian administrators. Revel demanded seizure of the whole of Istria, Dalmatia and their islands. Sonnino's armistice draft adopted many of these requests, though it did not mention the whole of Dalmatia nor an Italian administration of captured territories.[74]

Contrary to the Bulgarian and the Turkish armistices, the Austro-Hungarian was to be approved by all the Allied and associated powers. This originated in Lloyd George's desire, communicated to Sonnino at an Allied conference in Paris on 29 October, to 'consider the peace and armistice' of both Austria-Hungary and Germany together, 'and treat both on the same principles'.[75] This posed a problem because Germany had requested an armistice based on the Fourteen Points. So, the Allies

---

[74] Melchionni, *Vittoria mutilata*, pp. 27, 31–42.
[75] DDI, 5, XI, doc. 776, Conferenza interalleata, verbale segreto I.C.83, 29 October 1918.

needed to discuss how the Points related to armistice negotiations, and how the latter related to peace terms. Apparently detrimental to Italian interests, this actually provided Italy with the possibility to defuse the impact of Wilson's points on its war aims. If Italy could gain armistice conditions, approved by its partners that eluded Wilson's 9th point on the ethnical delineation of Italian borders, it could bring this juridical precedent to bear at the peace table. Lloyd George, for his part, wished to clarify early on that he would not 'under any conditions' accept the question of freedom of the seas as an armistice term – like the Italians, he wanted to establish a precedent for the Peace Conference; and Clemenceau yearned for military clauses that allowed him to extend French influence beyond Alsace-Lorraine – thus beyond Wilson's 8th point.[76]

On 30–31 October Lloyd George, Clemenceau, Sonnino and Colonel Edward House, Advisor of President Wilson, discussed the matter in Paris. Presenting his armistice draft, Sonnino proposed that the interpretation of the Fourteen Points for future armistices be extended to include not just the principle of ethnicity but also those of 'security', 'geography' and 'history'.[77] It was a distortion of Wilson's 9th point that the other partners would not accept. Instead, Lloyd George proposed an armistice text for Austria-Hungary that comprised – among obvious clauses such as the evacuation of enemy-occupied territory and the restitution of prisoners of war – an Italian occupation of the London Pact area and 'freedom of movement' for Allied forces, including to 'occupy strategic points in order to protect oppressed nationalities', provided that such occupation be made in the name of the Allies and not Italy alone.[78] It seemed a huge concession to Rome because it exceeded the London Treaty, and Sonnino happily accepted;[79] the proposal was equally important to the British and French, who wished to establish the principle that territorial terms for cease-fires should be determined by Allied military commanders according to the situation on the ground, which the United States disputed.[80] This allowed the French to claim the temporary holding of bridgeheads over the Rhine in the German text, 'with a radius of 30 miles on the east bank, and the Allied occupation of certain cities, such as Cologne',[81] to be restored after the peace treaty. In turn, the question

---

[76] Melchionni, *Vittoria mutilata*, p. 27.
[77] Aldrovandi Marescotti, *Guerra diplomatica*, pp. 191–192.
[78] Malagodi, *Conversazioni*, II, p. 427.
[79] DDI, 5, XI, doc. 791, *cit.*, Annex A: 'Conditions of Armistice with Austria-Hungary', Military conditions.
[80] Melchionni, *Vittoria mutilata*, p. 21.
[81] TNA, CAB23/8, War Cabinet 496, War Cabinet minutes, 4 November 1918, p. 4; DDI, 5, XI, doc. 797, Consiglio Supremo di Guerra, ottava sessione, seconda seduta, verbale 350: Annex B, 'Military conditions of an armistice with Germany', 1 November 1918.

of freedom of the seas was excluded from armistice terms to both Austria-Hungary and Germany.[82] House, for his part, accepted that Italy occupied the London Treaty territories to avoid a future Italian veto on the League of Nations, but barred 'the treaty itself' from being mentioned in the Allied text.[83] Finally, Clemenceau had his proposal accepted that 'terms of an armistice must not be confused with terms of peace'. The object of armistices, he held, was 'to place the victorious armies in such a position that their superiority was clearly established. . . . Our conditions of armistice did not prejudice our terms of peace'.[84] Overall, Sonnino had failed to have the Treaty of London accepted as a precondition for an armistice; he had gained temporary occupation of enemy territories under the London Pact and potentially beyond that, but possession of such territories would still have to be discussed at a general Peace Conference.[85] In the following days, Orlando tried to have Italian objections to the Fourteen Points attached to the armistice text, or at least jointly communicated to Wilson. Lloyd George, Clemenceau and House vetoed both proposals;[86] thus, Italian reservations to the Points as juridical basis for armistices were never presented to Wilson.[87]

Diplomatic setbacks notwithstanding, the Italian advance was in full swing. The crowning day of triumph was 3 November, when the Italians simultaneously took Trento with a rush and landed in Trieste. By midnight, the Austro-Hungarian armistice was signed, coming into effect on the 4th. Rome was 'wild with enthusiasm'. Finally, 'after a century of effort, of alternating progress and disillusion, the dream of Italian unity had been realised'. Rodd recorded:

No similar struggle accompanied our national evolution, and those who have not lived among . . . the Italian people can hardly conceive the exultation of that hour. Late in the evening there was a demonstration in front of the Embassy, and I had to improvise a speech. . . . It is good to feel the heart of a people at such moments. They knew I had done my best for them acting as an interpreter between the two

---

[82] Ibid., doc. 791, *cit.*, Annex B: 'Armistice with Austria-Hungary', Naval conditions; doc. 795, Conferenza interalleata, verbale segreto I.C.85, 'Naval conditions of an armistice', 1 November 1918.

[83] Orlando, *Memorie*, pp. 461–462.

[84] DDI, 5, XI, doc. 791, *cit.*, Verbale 349, 'Conditions of a military and naval armistice with Austria-Hungary', 31 October 1918.

[85] Malagodi, *Conversazioni*, II, p. 429.

[86] TNA, CAB28/5/5178, British note of a conversation at House's house, 3 November 1918.

[87] 'Colonel House thought it would be better to say nothing at all on this subject to President Wilson:' DDI, 5, XI, doc. 814, Conferenza interalleata, verbale segreto I. C.91, 3 November 1918. House, in fact informed Wilson that the Italians were solidly behind the President's principles: Burgwyn, *The Legend*, p. 188.

nations in the long and grim struggle, and in the hour of relief and triumph they did not forget it. Such experiences are worth living for.[88]

For the British ambassador, 24 May 1915, when Italy entered the war, and 4 November 1918, were 'the crowning days in a life'. Imperiali cried 'tears of joy' when he knew of the victory. He noted: 'It seems a dream, but it is reality. ... The unity of our country is fulfilled'. For Rodd and Imperiali their rejoicing was complete a few days later when they were informed of Germany's armistice.[89] On 11 November, the war was over.

17.2   The War Is Over?

In the night between 31 October and 1 November 1918, everything was quiet in Pola harbour. Earlier that evening, Admiral Miklós Horthy, the commander of the *k.u.k. Kriegsmarine* appointed in March, had solemnly turned over what remained of the Austro-Hungarian navy and its naval facilities to the National Committee of the newly self-proclaimed State of SCS (Slovenes, Croats and Serbs) – the apparent epilogue of the war and of repeated anti-Habsburg protests and mutinies that had shaken the *k.u. k. Kriegsmarine* in recent months. Around 05:00, as faint light started to appear on the horizon, two Italian *incursori* were spotted close to the dreadnought *Viribus Unitis*, which had been the flagship of the *k.u.k. Kriegsmarine* and was now considered by its crew the flagship of the SCS navy under a Croatian officer, Janko Vuković de Podkapelski. The Italian raiders, Raffaele Rossetti and Raffaele Paolucci, had accomplished one of the boldest military actions in modern times, swimming through the port naval defences and patrolling submarines riding a modified torpedo propelled by two compressed-air propellers and wearing self-made waterproof rubber suits; they had reached the flagship and had attached a 200-kilogramme mine to its hull. Captured, they told Vuković that the battleship would blow up at 06:30 and that he should save the crew but refused to locate the mine – even when they were informed that the *Viribus Unitis* had struck the Imperial flag. A delay in the explosion meant that part of the crew which had begun to abandon the ship, had returned on board when the mine set off at 06:44. The *Viribus Unitis* sank with 300 men, including Vuković, who had commanded the SCS fleet for only 12 hours.[90]

[88] Rodd, *Memories*, III, p. 370.
[89] Imperiali, *Diario*, pp. 448, 595; Rodd, *Memories*, p. 372.
[90] Halpern, *Naval War*, pp. 449, 567; see also F. Favre, *La Marina nella grande guerra* (Udine: Gaspari, 2008).

The sinking of the *Viribus Unitis* was the death blow to the Austro-Hungarian fleet-in-being, which by the end of the war had lost fourteen ships, including some of its strongest battleships, and had another forty-six damaged – even without a Nelsonian battle.[91] But it was also a sign that a smooth and peaceful post-war transition in Istria and Dalmatia was nearly impossible. Sonnino vetoed Allied recognition of Yugoslav committees as representatives of an allied people, declaring that he would never allow the Austro-Hungarian navy to escape capture with the 'expedient' of Vienna passing it over to the Yugoslavs.[92] On 5 November an Italian naval squadron under Admiral Umberto Cagni entered Pola harbour and proclaimed Italian seizure of its naval facilities and of all the ships that had belonged to Austria-Hungary. This was in line with the Austro-Hungarian armistice terms, but both Yugoslav committees and Italy's allies protested.[93] The Italians were particularly annoyed by British Yugoslav sympathies and asked the British naval representatives in Corfu – where negotiations over Yugoslav claims were being held – how they would feel if the German High Seas Fleet suddenly raised the Danish flag.[94] The fate of the Austro-Hungarian military and merchant fleets became a long-lasting question that was solved in Italy's favour only in 1920. Implementing the armistice terms proved equally difficult for Italy on land. The Italian advance into Istria stirred celebrations by Italian communities and demonstrations by the Slavs. Dalmatia posed greater problems as the Slav majority was utterly opposed to Italy. Diaz was convinced that Italian amphibious operations in Dalmatia to satisfy Revel would lead 'to another Gallipoli'.[95] The Italian advance then slowed to a crawl and the armistice line was reached only on 19 November after bitter skirmishes with Serb troops around Knin and tensions in the coastal cities. War, which had left Dalmatia and Istria largely untouched, in a sense came to the region after the end of hostilities in the shape of ethnic conflicts, incidents involving civilians from both sides and occasionally all-out fights between regulars.[96]

Matters were aggravated by Italian ambitions beyond the London Pact, especially in Montenegro and at Fiume. In the first case, Italian actions were largely reactive to those of the Serbs and the French. The former

[91] Italian total losses were: eight ships sunk and twenty-eight damaged. The British and French had four and two light ships damaged in the Adriatic, respectively: Cernuschi, *Battaglie sconosciute*, p. 242.

[92] DDI, 5, XI, doc. 795, *cit.*, 'The Handing Over to Yugo-Slavs of the Austrian Fleet'.

[93] Melchionni, *Vittoria mutilata*, pp. 65–67.   [94] Sondhaus, *Great War*, p. 349.

[95] C. Seton-Watson, *Storia d'Italia*, p. 660; Pupo, 'Attorno all'Adriatico: Venezia-Giulia, Fiume e Dalmazia', in Pupo ed., *Vittoria senza pace*, pp. 77–78, 81, 98.

[96] Melchionni, *Vittoria mutilata*, p. 80.

tried to occupy as many territories as possible to annex them to a united Yugoslavia; Paris was hostile to Italian Balkan appetites and openly favoured Slavs and Greeks to get better borders at Italy's expense. Rome, on the other hand, was determined to turn the Adriatic into an 'Italian lake' and needed to ensure that the advancing *Armée d'Orient* would not occupy Northern Albania and Montenegro, or it might cede them to Greece and Serbia later. Forerunning the French was difficult because Italian forces in Albania were shrinking as some units were being transferred to Dalmatia. Carrying out military occupations in a wide area from Istria to Albania and in a race against local competitors was proving a logistic nightmare. This forced Sonnino to revise his plans in the region. Though the Treaty of London provided for a partition of Albania amongst Italy, Serbia and Montenegro, he began to consider the possibility of an independent Albania under Italian protection. This mirrored an Italian promise made to Albanians with the Argirocastro proclamation of 3 June 1917, and Sonnino thought it would keep anyone else out. To 'protect' Albania, Italy nonetheless needed military bases, so Italian troops maintained control over key cities like Valona and occupied many others including Tirana and Durazzo, then moved into Antivari to prevent the whole of Montenegro being annexed to Yugoslavia.[97]

Italian actions at Fiume were motivated less by foreign competition and more by Italian appetites because the city itself was for the greatest part Italian and the municipal council had, since 28 October, appealed to Wilson's points to be united 'to its Italian motherland'; by contrast, the local Yugoslav committee required annexation to the SCS state on the grounds that the countryside was Slav.[98] On 31 October, Orlando declared to parliament that 'Fiume is more Italian than Rome', officially starting a dispute for possession of the city that was to last until 1924.[99] He authorised Revel to take Fiume, and an Italian naval squadron under Rear-Admiral Guglielmo Rainer entered the city port on 4 November.[100] Immediate complaints by the French and Slavs erupted to prevent an Italian disembarkation.[101] Imperiali asked Balfour to get Britain to show 'tangibly its friendship for Italy' by accepting the occupations of Durazzo,

---

[97] DDI, 5, XI, doc. 771, Diaz to Sonnino and Zupelli, 28 October 1918; G. Caccamo, 'Esserci a qualsiasi costo', pp. 161–171; C. Seton-Watson, *Storia d'Italia*, p. 582.

[98] Pupo, 'Attorno all'Adriatico', p. 84.

[99] Aldrovandi Marescotti, *Guerra diplomatica*, p. 199.

[100] Melchionni, *Vittoria mutilata*, p. 86.

[101] DDI, 6, I, doc. 101, Bonin Longare to Sonnino, 11 November 1918; F. Le Moal, *La France et l'Italie dans les Balkans 1914–1919, le contentieux adriatique* (Paris: L'Harmattan, 2006), p. 279.

Zara, Pola, Sebenico and Fiume for Italy.[102] But His Majesty's Government had received the same request from Yugoslav committees.[103]

Such Slav claims became the basis for Orlando's decision to reject any previous concessions made to the Slavs by Gallenga Stuart's team.[104] Most probably, he had always harboured this, but he waited for military victory to be achieved before dropping his ambiguous policy of nationalities and realigning himself with Sonnino. The Italian army had received orders to 'collect evidence of all excesses and abuses of which Yugoslav individuals are guilty against us'[105] since the eve of Vittorio Veneto. The propaganda Under-Secretary too was involved. In late October Northcliffe sent Gallenga Stuart, through De Filippi, a memorandum about the Allies' war aims, which echoed Wilson's 9th point on 'lines of nationality' as criteria for the future Italian borders.[106] The reply came on 7 November and it had an unexpected tone. Gallenga Stuart rejected the memorandum with arguments he had never used before. He claimed that Italy's strategic needs in the Adriatic were insufficiently protected.[107] The same day, Gallenga Stuart ordered Borgese to cease any reference to Italian 'territorial renunciations'. The task of Italian propaganda was 'in this hour to affirm the legitimacy of Italy's aspirations'.[108]

Borgese reacted in dismay. He proposed to Gallenga Stuart that promoting a nationality policy would enable Italy to claim Italian territories not covered by the London Treaty, such as Fiume, while international public opinion would respond badly to an annexationist programme in Dalmatia.[109] Borgese concluded that he was ready to resign, if Orlando's Government persevered in its old-fashioned policy. Gallenga Stuart's problem was that Orlando's radical shift towards Sonnino had left him isolated. He probably feared being dismissed (indeed, he was soon pushed to resign), had he not followed the premier's line; and he was also disheartened and irritated by the wild Yugoslav claims.[110] So he rejected Borgese's suggestions. The Anglo-Italian democratic alignment established around *The New Europe* group rapidly fell apart. The entire Italian propaganda apparatus (the offices of the navy, the *Comando Supremo* and Under-Secretary) was re-oriented as anti-Yugoslav.[111] In

---

[102] Imperiali, *Diario*, p. 582.   [103] Rodd papers, Rodd to Cecil, 3 November 1918.

[104] Tosi, *Propaganda*, p. 215.

[105] ACS, Carte Presidenza, b. 19-28-1, Orlando to Diaz, 18 November 1918.

[106] Ibid., Carte Orlando, b. 49, De Filippi to Gallenga Stuart, 29 October 1918.

[107] Ibid., Carte Gallenga Stuart, b. 1, f. 18; ASMAE, Carte Ambasciata d'Italia a Londra, 1918–1919, b. 463, f. 1, Gallenga Stuart to De Filippi, 9 November 1918.

[108] Albertini, *Epistolario*, Gallenga Stuart to Borgese, 9 November 1918, p. 1180.

[109] Ibid., Borgese to Gallenga Stuart, 15 November 1918, p. 1186.

[110] ACS, Carte Orlando, b. 102, Gallenga Stuart to Borgese, 9 November 1918.

[111] Ibid., Carte Presidenza, b. 19-28-1, Badoglio to Sonnino, 15 December 1918.

the propaganda missions abroad, where in previous months representatives of the irredentist associations had been replaced, members of the
DSI were now expelled and replaced with irredentists and nationalists.
Among these, Giorgio Pitacco, Felice Bennati, Roberto Ghiglianovich
and Riccardo Zanella were sent to London with the task of starting the
campaign for an Italian Fiume. They were inspired by D'Annunzio's
motto 'Victory, you shall not be mutilated!'[112]

To avoid the victory's mutilation, Italy needed British support.[113]
Thus, although the London team of British and Italian liberals was
disintegrating, the Italian Government tried hard to overcome past
conflicts with London and relaunch the Anglo-Italian 'special partnership'. To this end, Italy adopted a *laissez-faire* policy towards Britain in
Anatolia. Here an Italian naval squadron, made of the pre-dreadnoughts
Roma and *Vittorio Emanuele* and the cruisers *Piemonte* and *Libia*, had
reached Mytilene and was ready to disembark contingents heading
towards Smyrna, Adalia and Konya. The plan would almost certainly
have annoyed the British, so Sonnino exceptionally decided to postpone
any such operation and recommended the Italian command in Rhodes
to 'avoid actions that seem opposed to the terms recently signed
between England and Turkey'.[114] Additionally, Revel extended an invitation to Wemyss[115] to join Italian naval units in Istria and Dalmatia.
British ships were welcomed, but not so were American and, 'above all'
French vessels.[116] In Italian eyes, it was a huge concession to London
and a way to establish fruitful collaboration. Unfortunately for Italy,
Revel's telegram was leaked to Clemenceau, increasing Italo-French
polemic.[117]

Britain tried to stay *super partes*. Balfour did not condemn Italian
actions undertaken under the armistice terms, but suggested avoiding
harsh anti-Yugoslav propaganda. The same opinion was expressed by
Milner and Northcliffe.[118] The latter sent a long telegram to Eugenio
Chiesa, the commissioner of Aeronautics, suggesting 'strongly' that
'Italy's official policy' be 'without any delay' brought in line with the
principles of President Wilson and 'the great mass of the British public'.
If this was carried out '*immediately, publicly* and *spontaneously*', he

---

[112] D'Annunzio, 'Vittoria nostra, non sarai mutilata', *Il Corriere della Sera*, 24 October 1918.
[113] Imperiali, *Diario*, p. 598.
[114] DDI, 6, I, doc. 22, Sonnino to Imperiali, 6 November 1918.
[115] Ibid., doc. 88, Bonin Longare to Orlando, 10 November 1918; doc. 161, Imperiali to Orlando, 14 November 1918.
[116] Imperiali *Diario*, p. 597.
[117] DDI, 6, I, doc. 187, Imperiali to Orlando, 16 November 1918; doc. 202, Orlando to Imperiali, 18 November 1918.
[118] Tosi, *Propaganda*, pp. 217–219.

concluded, 'it may be of great advantage to Italy'.[119] Orlando asked Rodd to meet him, 'not officially but as a friend', to protest Northcliffe's words – which he in fact attributed to Steed 'since the letter was written in Italian'. Orlando complained that 'old friends and allies and their interests seemed to count for much less than the newly-discovered Yugo-Slavs'. Italy, he continued, had been fighting for almost a century to accomplish its destiny and obtain a 'liveable frontier', and had always had the sympathy of Britain in these efforts; and now suddenly 'a state which had hardly been heard of before the war, some of the components of which have been among the hardest fighters against the Allies, seemed to have a monopoly of sympathies and suffrages'.[120] Rodd tried to explain to London the reasons for Italian nervousness in the face of Slav claims: 'The traditions in which a young nation has grown to maturity are slow to die. It was perhaps not sufficiently appreciated at home how closely the Croat neighbour had been identified in Italy with the two-headed eagle'.[121]

On 13 November Imperiali had a long conversation with Balfour. He explained that Britain now had a 'unique chance to win over the deep and lasting sympathy of the Italian nation', and reminded him that 'Italy is a factor in European affairs; Yugoslavia is a hypothesis'. Balfour 'agreed', and Imperiali enthusiastically informed Sonnino that Britain had 'no intention' of embracing the Yugoslavian hypothesis to the detriment of Italy.[122] Spurred by the arrival in Fiume of two Serb battalions and quite possibly by Imperiali's assurances, the Italians landed in Fiume four days later to 'maintain public order'.[123] The volley of objections that followed from Italy's allies likely surpassed Italian expectations. Paris demanded that their flag be raised over the city together with the Italian, and insisted that a Serb mission be established in Fiume; Washington required that the Italians immediately accepted Allied contingents into the city; and London encouraged an Italian recognition of the SCS state. Of all these critiques, those coming from Britain were especially annoying to Italy. Imperiali looked for explanations but was unable to find any British diplomat available for a meeting until 22 November, when he finally met Balfour and remonstrated: 'Why do you want to ruin Italy's friendship? [You shifted] from positive assertions to the opposite'.[124] In the

---

[119] Rodd papers, Northcliffe to Chiesa, 3 November 1918.
[120] Ibid., Rodd to Balfour, 11 November 1918.   [121] Rodd, *Memories*, III, p. 289.
[122] DDI, 6, I, doc. 160, Imperiali to Sonnino, 14 November 1918; Imperiali, *Diario*, p. 956.
[123] Pupo, 'Attorno all'Adriatico', p. 85; Melchionni, *Vittoria mutilata*, p. 108.
[124] The British press demanded a recognition of Yugoslavia. See, for example, Evans' article on the *Manchester Guardian* on 18 November. Further anti-Italian comments appeared in the *Daily Telegraph*, *Morning Post* and *Globe*; Imperiali, *Diario*, pp. 598 ff.

end, Balfour approved Italy's occupations, provided that they be mixed and inclusive of the Serbs.[125]

The situation continued to degenerate. By December, in order to contrast what he termed 'a veritable persecution' of scattered Italian communities, attacks on Italian soldiers and on Italian women wearing Italian colours, Orlando approved a plan by Badoglio, which aimed at bringing about the disintegration of Yugoslavia before its unification became an accomplished fact. This would be done by steering up conflict among the Serbs, Croats and Slovenes, between peasants and their land-lords and between Muslims and Orthodox Christians.[126] In the mean-time, an Allied naval conference in Rome on 26–30 November established a partition of the Eastern Adriatic coast in four zones, each under the responsibility of one of the four Allied and associated powers until the signing of the peace treaty. Cattaro was assigned to France, Spalato to the United States, Sebenico to Italy and Fiume to Britain. Orlando tried to revise the scheme by proposing that Clemenceau keep Hungary under France's influence and leave Austria, including its former Adriatic possessions, under Italy's. But Clemenceau refused. Finally, the Allies established a commission of admirals tasked with investigating the current crisis in Croatia and put forward solutions to avoid an armed escalation. By late December it appeared clear that the commission would submit a report hostile to Italy, so the latter withdrew from the commission.[127]

On the eve of the Peace Conference, therefore, the Yugoslav question turned critical and quickly became a focal point in Italy's foreign policy, overshadowing other Italian claims elsewhere. The Italian Government, however, had to reckon with the situation where France and the United States were distinctively unsympathetic to it, and Britain was at best ambiguous. Hardinge informed Rodd on 6 December that if Italy did not 'at least show some moderation', it would be completely isolated at the peace table.[128] These proved prophetic words.

---

[125] ASMAE Carte Imperiali, b. 1, n. 407G, 25 October 1918.
[126] Quoted in MacMillan, *Peacemakers*, pp. 293–295.
[127] Melchionni, *Vittoria mutilata*, pp. 93, 105, 118–132, 135–136; DDI, 6, I, doc. 699, Thaon di Revel to Mola, 29 December 1918.
[128] Rodd papers, Hardinge to Rodd, 6 December 1918.

18 Versailles 1919
Italy's Empire Project Repudiated

18.1 Diplomatic Approaches

The peacemakers who met on 18 January 1919 in Versailles to arrange the post-war global order faced 'a Himalayan task'. They settled to do nothing less than fundamentally change the way the international system functioned, imposing lasting peace terms on the defeated powers while legalising new states and establishing new rules of the international concert aimed at preventing future conflicts.[1] As Churchill recalled, however, each statesman also sought 'to produce a triumph for himself and his party and give satisfaction to national fears and passions, well-founded or not'.[2] This book cannot study the Peace Conference. My aim is to analyse how Anglo-Italian relations played out during the conference, its preparatory phase and its immediate aftermath and vice versa – what impact the outcome of the conference had on those relations. As in pre-war and war events, the relevance of the bilateral relation during the peace negotiations was greater for the weakest party. As we shall see, Britain was key in Italy's peace-making strategy, whereas Italy was now little more than a pain in Britain's neck.

Rome's partners drew remarkably similar accounts of Italy's outlook at the conference. First, that Italy presented incredibly wild claims. President Wilson repeatedly inveighed about the 'greedy Italians',[3] assuming that they 'entered the war with a demand for loot' and were 'utterly incapable [of] taking any position of principle'.[4] Clemenceau agreed that the Italians in 1915 had made 'a *magnifique coup de chapeau* of the 17th century type', and Cecil echoed him lamenting 'the greediness of Italian foreign policy'. Second, the Italians proved 'absolutely inflexible' and refused a reasonable

---

[1] Mayer, *Politics and Diplomacy*, pp. 3–5.
[2] W. Churchill, *The World Crisis. The Aftermath* (London: Macmillan, 1941), pp. 120–121.
[3] Quoted in MacMillan, *Peacemakers*, p. 310.
[4] Quoted in R. S. Baker, *Woodrow Wilson and World Settlement. Written from His Unpublished and Personal Material*, 3 vols. (New York: Doubleday, Page & Co., 1923), III, pp. 278–280.

compromise, thus precipitating an inter-Allied crisis.[5] This was largely due to what Lloyd George called an 'unconcealed hostility of the Italian delegates towards the new Yugoslav Confederation'. Sonnino was especially troublesome. Lloyd George, who had been so positively impressed by him in 1917, now saw the Italian Foreign Minister in a completely different light: 'He was dour, rigid and intractable'.[6] Hardinge found him 'extremely tiresome',[7] and Clemenceau reproached Sonnino for 'remaining too faithful to the Italian method of which the Grand Master was Machiavelli'. Such stubborn voracity on the part of the Italians was added to what Lloyd George termed a 'huckstering spirit',[8] and irritating negotiating tactics that ultimately alienated anyone else and that made the 'settlement of the new frontiers of Italy' the most 'intractable' problem of the conference in British eyes.[9] During the negotiations in Paris, Cecil summarised the issue for Rodd: 'Sonnino's stubbornness and the extravagant nature of Italy's claims have had as a result that it is now literally true that Italy has not a friend in Europe except ourselves and she is doing her best to make her isolation complete'.[10]

Based on such unanimous narratives, historians have largely agreed that Italy marched into diplomatic defeat at Versailles because of its insatiable claims, its irritating attitude and its unreasonable inflexibility. MacMillan wrote that 'it was clear from the moment the Peace Conference opened that the Italians were in no mood to compromise with the Yugoslavs or anyone else'.[11] Mayer argued that Sonnino 'gradually isolated his delegation within the conference. ... He would settle for nothing short of his maximum aims'.[12] The Italian attitude, pointed out Christopher Seton-Watson, pushed Wilson to become 'the protector of Yugoslavia' – to Italy's doom.[13] Goldstein remarked that the Italians 'expected to receive anything they demanded', and seemed 'more interested in generating problems for the conference than in finding solutions'; this caused 'a pervasive anti-Italian attitude' among the great powers.[14] Italian sources reinforced the idea that Italy's failure occurred at the peace table. Sonnino admitted so in his diary[15], and Orlando, presenting the

---

[5] Quoted in MacMillan, *Peacemakers*, pp. 292, 295, 307.

[6] Lloyd George, *The Truth*, I, p. 253; II, p. 881.

[7] Rodd papers, Hardinge to Rodd, 17 June 1918.

[8] Quoted in MacMillan, *Peacemakers*, pp. 291–292.

[9] Headlam-Morley minute, 'Fiume and the Adriatic', 13 April 1923, quoted in Goldstein, *Winning the Peace*, p. 265.

[10] Quoted in MacMillan, *Peacemakers*, p. 295.   [11] Ibid., pp. 291, 301–302.

[12] Mayer, *Politics and Diplomacy*, p. 679.   [13] C. Seton-Watson, *Storia d'Italia*, p. 607.

[14] Goldstein, *Winning the Peace*, pp. 276, 269. Burgwyn made similar remarks: *The Legend*, pp. 273, 275.

[15] Sonnino, *Diario*, III, pp. 397–398.

problems he was facing at Versailles to the Italian parliament on 24 April 1919, claimed that trouble had started only very recently – namely, when a memorandum by President Wilson barred Italy from Dalmatia and Fiume.[16] Italian historians too, therefore, tended to see the peace settlement as a result of the mediocre negotiating skills of the Italian policymakers; Sonnino above all proved 'an obstacle to any reasonable compromise'.[17]

This book argues that such interpretation is partial and misleading. Italian mistakes during the conference were not at all irrelevant, but they were only the last – not the main – blow to Italy's empire project. By taking a broader and comparative analysis of the process of peace-making during and after World War I, two arguments can be made. First, Italy's allies did not resign themselves to reduce Italian claims because they had been expanded: that decision had essentially been taken when the conference started (equally, Italy's isolation had occurred before the conference began because of conflicts and misunderstandings developed during the war and because of inter-Allied competition). Second, the Italians were in fact ready to compromise as part of a diplomatic strategy in which London was a key factor, but this was not how the British saw it. An analysis of British and Italian approaches to the conference is necessary to appreciate these questions.

In Britain, revisionist tendencies towards Allied pacts had increased throughout the war, but after the armistices, they officially became part of London's diplomatic strategy for the conference. Such strategy was influenced by the general election that Lloyd George called on 14 December 1918. He wished the electoral campaign to focus primarily on domestic issues, and took advantage of the disarray in Asquith's Liberal Party to promote a liberal electoral reform that doubled the electorate. But Labour battled him on foreign policy, advocating 'a peace of reconciliation' and 'the extension of liberty and democracy in Europe'. On the other hand, Lloyd George was pressed by the newly founded National Party, which enjoyed the vocal support of Northcliffe's editorial group, and which articulated a programme 'of revengeful jingoism', in Mayer's words.[18] Lloyd George was obliged to discuss Britain's and the Empire's security publicly and asked the electorate 'for a vote of confidence to press England's national and imperial interests at the peace conference'.[19] He proved successful. His coalition won 382 seats (57.2 per cent) in

---

[16] Mayer, *Politics and Diplomacy*, p. 709.

[17] A. Di Michele: 'L'Italia in Austria: da Vienna a Trento', in Pupo ed., *Vittoria senza pace*, p. 22.

[18] Mayer, *Politics and Diplomacy*, pp. 133–134, 148, 150–153.

[19] *The Morning Post*, November through mid-December, quoted in Ibid., 151.

parliament, three times as many as Asquith's Liberal Coalition.[20] Lloyd George called it 'a sensational victory . . . much more complete than any of us had anticipated'.[21] Apprehension about the Empire's security, and especially revolutionary developments in Eastern and Central Europe had contributed 'by frightening otherwise moderate and sensible people into taking momentary refuge in super-patriotism'.[22] Now, however, Lloyd George, the re-appointed Prime Minister, was bound to his own triumph. As Keynes recalled, having consented to the British electorate being bamboozled, he found it difficult, if not impossible, to de-bamboozle it.[23] Lloyd George had to bring home a successful peace that served both British imperial security and domestic politics.[24]

British preparations for the Peace Conference were made through two main channels: the Foreign Office and the Imperial Cabinet. Some inter-departmental committees and the armed forces also played a role, especially in colonial questions. Amongst the departments of the Foreign Office involved, the most important were the PID and the Historical Section. The PID gathered 'a glittering cast' under Tyrrell – including Harold Temperley, an expert on Austro-German relations; Headlam-Morely, a German expert; Arnold Toynbee, a Middle Eastern expert; Louis Namier, a political historian; and Seton-Watson.[25] According to Imperiali, Tyrrell spoke as a friend of Italy;[26] yet the work of his team was not quite in line with Imperiali's assumption.

By early January 1919 the PID produced 175 peace memoranda, 12 of which concerned Italy.[27] As mentioned, they were supposed to outline viable solutions without suggesting policy. But, perhaps inevitably, the PID ended up suggesting policy in various cases. On 19 November 1918 Headlam-Morley submitted a memorandum on British desiderata in Europe. These encompassed the need to prevent a single power dominating the continent, according to the traditional British notion of balance of power; a new territorial redistribution very much in line with the expectations of the *New Europe* group; and the need to guarantee free trade and British maritime supremacy. As far as Britain's allies were concerned, Headlam-Morley mentioned only two territorial concessions, namely the return of Alsace-Lorraine to France and the cession of the Polish districts of Prussia to a new Poland. In all other territorial disputes, London should assume the role of 'honest

[20] E. David, 'The Liberal Party Divided 1916–1918', *Historical Journal*, XIII, 3, 1970, pp. 509–532.
[21] Lloyd George, *The Truth*, I, p. 179.   [22] Mayer, *Politics and Diplomacy*, p. 166.
[23] House to Scott, 10 March 1919, quoted in J. L. Hammond, *C. P. Scott of the Manchester Guardian* (London: Bell, 1934), p. 260.
[24] Mayer, *Politics and Diplomacy*, p. 152.   [25] Smith, *Sovereignty*, p. 105.
[26] Imperiali, *Diario*, p. 681.   [27] Goldstein, *Winning the Peace*, p. 63.

broker' in 'cordial cooperation' with the United States. Headlam-Morley emphasised that this provided Britain with the opportunity 'for the legitimate extension of British influence'.[28] The PID memoranda on South-Eastern Europe and the Balkans, prepared by Allen Leeper and Harold Nicolson, as well as those of Seton-Watson on Eastern Europe, endorsed the principle of self-determination as the one that 'offered the greatest possible opportunity for long-term peace'. Leeper and Nicolson analysed various options for Albania and expressed a preference for a partition of the country assigning its northern part to Greece and the rest to Italy as a mandate. In return, the Italians would neutralise the Albanian coast and the Corfu channel. This would benefit Britain by 'preventing the Italians from turning the Adriatic into an Italian Lake', while allowing them 'the dubious glory of ruling Albania'.[29] Greece was further to receive Smyrna and the Dodecanese islands, as well as Bulgaria's Aegean littoral, becoming Britain's main partner in the region.[30] These proposals violated both the London and the St Jean de Maurienne treaties, albeit inexplicitly. Together, Leeper, Nicolson and Seton-Watson advocated a united Yugoslavia,[31] whilst the memoranda on Italian claims, again written by Leeper and Nicolson, found an ambiguous formula, which, though recognising the Treaty of London, suggested informing the Italians that it would be advantageous not to adhere too rigidly to the treaty.[32] Unless, however, 'Italy herself . . . takes the initiative in proposing a revision, some means must be found of bringing her to reason'.[33] As far as Italy's northern frontiers were concerned, Headlam-Morley acknowledged that, in order to counter German influence, and especially in the event that Germany and Austria united, Italy needed a stronger frontier to the Brenner.[34]

Balfour found these proposals useful and grasped from them that the confrontation between Italians and Yugoslavs could become the lever to 'break the entire [London] Pact'.[35] He declared: 'The Italians must somehow be mollified',[36] and informed House that no matter how many times the British assured Italy that they would stand by the London Pact, they counted on President Wilson to dispute Italian claims;[37] but he also emphasised that

---

[28] TNA, FO371/4353/f23/PC55, quoted in Ibid., p. 130.

[29] R. W. Seton-Watson, *Making of a New Europe*, pp. 324–332.

[30] Goldstein, *Winning the Peace*, pp. 133–137.

[31] TNA, FO371/4355/f68/PC68, quoted in Ibid., p. 136.

[32] TNA, 4356/f131/PC131, Allen Leeper and Nicolson, 'The question of Italian claims', 18 December 1918.

[33] Ibid., CAB21(9)/8/139 PID Memorandum, P.C./016, 24 December 1918.

[34] Goldstein, *Winning the Peace*, p. 140.   [35] Melchionni, *Vittoria mutilata*, p. 102.

[36] Quoted in MacMillan, *Peacemakers*, p. 302.

[37] YU, House MSS, vol. 121, Cobb to House, 19 November 1918; TNA, FO371/3137/147786/195820, 23.

'the only people who can urge [a revision] with a good grace are the Americans; and it is for them, not for us, to explain to the Italians'.[38] Rodd desperately tried to change the Foreign Office attitude. His point was that 'the new Yugo-Slavia ... would be, and would remain, very remote from us' and 'no British interest could be served by the adoption of a partisan attitude on issues of relatively little concern to ourselves'. On the other hand, the Mediterranean was 'of the utmost importance', and it was imperative for Britain not to break its traditional friendship with Italy.[39] Rodd also repeatedly warned that Italy would be driven into the arms of Germany if not given what had been promised to it in the Adriatic. He was ignored. Hardinge noted: 'I think we ought not to listen to this from Sir R. Rodd'.[40]

Outside Europe, the PID focussed on the partition of the Ottoman Empire and the German colonies. From the Middle East memoranda entrusted to Toynbee emerges, once again, a clear eagerness to escape British promises made in wartime colonial agreements. Britain's goal was to 'persuade France and Italy to renounce their claims under the secret treaties, while retaining British control of the Middle East without any overt annexations'.[41] Toynbee proposed to do so through an application of Wilsonian principles and an artful interpretation of the agreements themselves. Middle Eastern peoples should be allowed 'to invite what power they like' as a mandatory nation.[42] Toynbee assumed that local communities in the Middle East would choose Britain, thanks to its imperial reputation or – in the worst case – the United States. Thus, the spirit of the secret agreements would be met by allowing all the Allies equal mandatory opportunities, while in fact Britain would emerge as the unchallenged colonial power. Nicolson's report on Turkey came to similar conclusions. Balfour and Hardinge approved the reports.[43] The former stated: 'We consider the advantage to the natives, the advantage to our prestige',[44] whilst the latter, who in 1915 had dismissed the very idea of self-government as 'ridiculous and absurd',[45] was happy to see it from a different angle.[46] These developments reveal how the work of regional experts could help policymakers in shaping, and, at times, re-shaping

---

[38] Ibid., Balfour MSS, Balfour to House, 26 February 1919.
[39] Rodd, *Memories*, pp. 373–374; DLG MSS, F/56/2/15, Rodd to Hardinge, 14 December 1918.
[40] TNA, FO698/39,12671, Crowe minute, quoted in Burgwyn, *The Legend*, p. 285.
[41] Goldstein, *Winning the Peace*, pp. 152–153.
[42] TNA, FO371/3385/f747, Toynbee, 'Peace Settlement for Turkey and Arabian Peninsula', 21 November 1918.
[43] Goldstein, *Winning the Peace*, pp. 155, 167.
[44] Quoted in MacMillan, *Peacemakers*, p. 409.
[45] J. Brown, *Gandhi's Rise to Power: Indian Politics, 1915–1922* (Cambridge: Cambridge University Press, 1974), p. 125.
[46] Goldstein, *Winning the Peace*, p. 68.

their plans. The PID proposals were reinforced by the 174 handbooks (called 'peace books') produced by the Foreign Office Historical Section, seven of which concerned Italy. They proposed a classic divide and rule policy for Britain, which implied a revision of Allied pacts.[47] Were it to be embraced by the British Government, Italian interests would be threatened especially, because the weakest of the Allied powers had no other guarantee to secure its claims.

Yet Lloyd George was unhappy to leave the Foreign Office to dictate the British line at the conference. He had been trying to strengthen his own role in foreign policy since 1917, and intended to keep his hands free now more than ever.[48] To the surprise of many, he entrusted the final peace brief for the British negotiators not to Balfour but to Smuts, who had the advantage, unique in the British Cabinet, of having participated in peace negotiations at the close of the Second Boer War.[49] Smuts, however, was exposed to Foreign Office proposals in Curzon's Eastern Committee, an inter-departmental group, where Foreign Office options on Middle Eastern and Asian affairs were 'more clearly defined'.[50] Furthermore, Smuts was astonished at having to prepare the brief rapidly from scratch, so he opted to pass Foreign Office proposals largely unchanged onto the Imperial War Cabinet with his imprimatur.[51]

The Cabinet met repeatedly between late November and early January 1919. On 20 December it endorsed many of Curzon and Foreign Office proposals based on the need to contain London's allies by retaining as many Ottoman and German colonial possessions as possible.[52] This idea was made possible by wartime events that had given Britain control of many of such territories – Lloyd George enthused that 'possession was nine-tenths of the law'.[53] It reveals once more the strict connection between war strategies and peace-making. Now those war conquests could be kept using self-determination as a tool. 'What we want', said a senior official at the India Office, 'is some administration with Arab institutions which we can safely leave while pulling the strings ourselves; something that won't cost very much, which Labour can swallow consistent with its principles, but under which our economic and political interests will be secure'.[54] Lloyd George recognised that this particular

---

[47] Ibid., pp. 42 ff.   [48] Warman, 'The Erosion of Foreign Office', pp. 133–159.
[49] Goldstein, 'The Foreign Office', p. 283.
[50] Goldstein, 'British Peace Aims and the Eastern Question: The Political Intelligence Department and the Eastern Committee, 1918', *Middle Eastern Studies*, XXIII, 4, 1987, pp. 419–436.
[51] Goldstein, 'The Foreign Office', p. 283.
[52] TNA, CAB23/42/IWC44, 20 December 1918.
[53] Steed, *Through Thirty Years*, II, p. 245.
[54] Quoted in MacMillan, *Peacemakers*, p. 409.

interpretation of self-determination might antagonise President Wilson, whose goodwill was 'essential'. But since it was assumed that the United States would decline any mandatory responsibility, Lloyd George decided to offer Washington such responsibility, which London could 'reluctantly assume' at Wilson's decline.[55] Not only was the St Jean de Maurienne Agreement considered lapsed, but also no one mentioned the need to give colonial compensations to Italy under the London Treaty. On the contrary, said Lloyd George, the Admiralty had submitted an 'egregious document' opposing 'giving up any of our African conquests'; the military conceded that Togoland – deemed insignificant – could be given to France in exchange for Djibouti, whilst the air staff demanded German East Africa 'to provide an "all red" air route from Cape to Cairo'. The only concession to Italy should be French Somaliland.[56] As far as Italy's Adriatic claims were concerned, the War Office had submitted in December, a detailed memorandum which recommended that the London Treaty be re-shaped so as to draw the Italo-Yugoslavian border perpendicularly from the Arsa channel to Pola, leaving Cherso, Lussino and Lissa islands to Italy, and the whole of Dalmatia to Yugoslavia.[57] Once again, these proposals were very much in line with the view of the Foreign Office that 'the whole situation had changed since 1915', and that there were 'irresistible reasons for modifying the arrangement then entered into between the Allies and Italy'. The Imperial Cabinet discussed the possibility of using America to 'get us out of our bargain with Italy'. According to Lloyd George, he opposed this,[58] but the option was undoubtedly there in reserve in the minds of many. Smuts himself admitted that he had grasped the chance to 'shoulder onto Wilson' the responsibility to unravel the knots of 'one of the most difficult territorial questions to have emerged from the war'.[59]

The conflict between the Foreign Office and the premier, therefore, was solved with the latter's acceptance of many ideas of the former. Lloyd George's priorities for the conference were in the end identical to Headlam-Morley's: protect the Empire, British trade, British naval dominance and preserve the balance of power in Europe.[60] Smuts' peace brief proved to be essentially a summary of PID proposals together with reports from the Board of Trade and

---

[55] MacMillan, *Peacemakers*, p. 50; Goldstein, *Winning the Peace*, p. 189.
[56] Lloyd George, *The Truth*, I, p. 121; TNA, CAB29/2/P-100 quoted in Goldstein, *Winning the Peace*, p. 187.
[57] Melchionni, *Vittoria mutilata*, p. 157.   [58] Lloyd George, *The Truth*, II, pp. 791–800.
[59] See: Memorandum by Smuts and War Cabinet of 3 December 1918 and n.d. in TNA, CAB29-2,5178, respectively; Melchionni, *Vittoria mutilata*, p. 53.
[60] MacMillan, *Peacemakers*, p. 50.

the Treasury.[61] And many of the British delegates to the conference, including Balfour, Hardinge, Tyrrell, Crowe, Nicolson, Leeper, Headlam-Morely, Toynbee and Mallet were from the Foreign Office or shared its views.[62] Quite tellingly, Rodd was not included, and remained overshadowed throughout the conference.[63] The line of the British delegation was incompatible with Italy's war aims.

Tendencies to reduce Italian claims had developed in France as well. The *Comité d'études* for the future peace, established by Briand in February 1917, produced policy suggestions aimed primarily at downsizing Germany; but it also encouraged an expansion of Greece into Smyrna, its hinterland, and the Dodecanese – to Italy's detriment.[64] Clemenceau, who preferred not to renew parliament before entering the Peace Conference,[65] was pressed by France's colonialist lobby to 'stand firm' about French imperialistic gains,[66] and was little inclined to give Italy any colonial compensations. Even less disposed was he to concede on Balkan affairs. In November 1918, Clemenceau promised Trumbić: 'The Adriatic cannot become an Italian lake. There will be no *Mare Nostrum*'.[67] And a French diplomat, Philippe Berthelot, told Trumbić explicitly that Paris counted on American objections to the London Pact to reduce Italian claims at the Peace Conference.[68] Italy's position was aggravated by the diminished role of some eminent Allied military leaders after the armistices, including Foch and General Wilson. Curiously enough, they were both quite sympathetic to Italy. Foch was anxious to see the security principle solemnly recognised from the Adriatic to the Rhine, while General Wilson remarked that the war was not over. Regional conflicts were continuing in Russia and in the former Ottoman Empire, and new conflicts were erupting in Finland and Poland, so he advised against opening a rift between the Allies. But Lloyd George and Clemenceau would have none of that.[69]

---

[61] Goldstein, 'Britain: the Home Front', in M. F. Boemeke, G. D. Feldman, E. Glaser, *The Treaty of Versailles: A Reassessment After 75 Years* (Washington & Cambridge: Cambridge University Press, 1998), p. 158.

[62] Goldstein, *Winning the Peace*, p. 112.   [63] Rodd, *Memories*, p. 374.

[64] Smith, *Sovereignty*, pp. 110–113.

[65] E. Bonnefous, *Histoire Politique de la Troisième République*, 8 vols. (Paris: Presses Universitaires de France, 1956–1987), III, *L'après guerre (1919–1924)*, p. 1.

[66] MacMillan, *Peacemakers*, pp. 395–403.

[67] See: Pupo, *Fiume città di passione* (Bari: Laterza, 2018).

[68] See: Memorandum by Berthelot of a conversation with Trumbić on 31 October 1918, in ADAR Série A Paix, vol. 200, p. 51 quoted in Melchionni, *Vittoria mutilata*, pp. 60–61.

[69] See: J. C. King, *Foch versus Clemenceau. France and German Dismemberment, 1918–1919* (Boston: Harvard University Press, 1960); C. E. Callwell, *Field-Marshall Sir Henry*

Thus, all the great powers arrived in Versailles with distinctly revisionist purposes towards Italian promises. Italy's partners had come to such a
conclusion independently of one another and each for its own reasons.
The Americans had tried to coordinate American, British and French
peace-planning since the visit of Major Douglas Johnson to London in
April 1918. If successful, Johnson's visit would have produced a more
coherent peace-making strategy amongst the Big Three, leaving Italy in
the lurch. No such coordination was established, since Johnson realised
how jealous Britain and France were of their peace preparations, and how
ignorant they were 'of each other's work'.[70] Though not embodied in a
coordinated anti-Italian plot, expectations for the peace settlement in
Britain, America and France were remarkably similar as far as Italian
claims were concerned; they ought to be reduced, and everyone knew that
American hostility towards Allied secret treaties could be the picklock to
do it. Italy was therefore virtually isolated before the conference started.

Italian policymakers were unaware of their partners' intentions; but they
expected trouble. The American position was well known and was re-
stated by House in a meeting with Sonnino on 15 November.[71] Wilson,
said House, would pursue self-determination in the shaping of the new
Italian borders, but exactly what self-determination meant was unclear.
Contrary to a widespread assumption, Sonnino was not altogether insensi-
tive to the idea of a new international order based on the principles of
nationality and even self-determination, but he recognised quite lucidly the
limits of those fancy words.[72] In a handwritten note, he observed:

The principle of nationality must undoubtedly underpin any order which deserves
to be made stable and lasting. But in extreme cases ... the security of an entire
nation can be threatened by the fact that some single positions, perhaps sparsely
inhabited but of great strategic and military importance, are occupied by a
powerful and threatening enemy and then how, with what guarantee of liberty
or equity, will the popular will be displaced? ... In other words, there are a
thousand distinctions to be made.[73]

In another handwritten note, Sonnino wondered:

Principle of self-determination – not contestable in theory, but all depends on the
forms and criteria of application. ... What's the smallest or largest territorial unit

Wilson, bart., G.C.B., D.S.O., His Life and Diaries (London: Cassel, 1927); Burgwyn, *The
Legend*, pp. 252–258; DDI, 6, II, doc. 934, Orlando to the King, 23 March 1919.
[70] Goldstein, *Winning the Peace*, pp. 102–103.
[71] Melchionni, *Vittoria mutilata*, pp. 143–146.
[72] See: M. Cattaruzza, *Il confine orientale italiano, 1866–2011* (Bologna: Il Mulino, 2007)
and *L'Italia e la questione adriatica. Dibattiti parlamentari e panorama internazionale (1918–
1926)* (Bologna: Il Mulino, 2014).
[73] Handwritten note by Sonnino found by F. Caccamo in ASMAE, Carte Sonnino, b. 3.

whose majority can determine the fate of an area? What's the electoral district for which this majority speaks? What guarantee is preventing violent or fraudulent manipulations of the electorates' liberty and will? Or the sincerity of their vote? The integrity of the count? The formulation of the question on which the vote is held? See Turks in Armenia – Serbs in Montenegro'.[74]

Orlando, for his part, saw a 'dialectical impossibility' in Wilson's programme for the Peace Conference aiming at re-affirming state sovereignty while at the same time re-straining state behaviour.[75] He also noted that Wilson had never explicitly called for the break-up of either the Habsburg or the Ottoman Empire, evoking nebulous concepts such as the 'freest opportunity of autonomous development' (point 12). How could this be implemented in practice? When Sonnino approached House for clarification, he realised that American diplomats were as unclear as the Italians regarding Wilson's ideas.[76] What, Wilson's subordinates wondered, made a nation? Political unity or ethnicity? And did self-determination really apply everywhere? How to reconcile the interests of colonisers and colonised, for example, if both had equal weight?[77] House had no answers to those issues. On the one hand, this made it difficult for Sonnino to challenge self-determination, but on the other, it provided a window for action. For example, House recognised that Britain had invoked the security principle to object to freedom of the seas[78] – so why not appeal to the same principle to defend Italy's Adriatic claims under the London Treaty? Sonnino was encouraged by Macchi di Cellere. After a meeting with Wilson on 24 November, the Italian ambassador assured Sonnino that the President was sympathetic to Italian security needs.[79] He omitted that Wilson had re-stated his intention to reject the London Treaty. In so doing, Macchi di Cellere stimulated Sonnino's deduction that the Treaty could be defended by playing around Wilson's contradictions.[80]

First, however, Sonnino needed to find out his allies' real intentions about the Treaty. Both France and Britain were ambiguous. On the one hand, Barrère had categorically denied that French sympathies for the Yugoslavs could invalidate the London Pact. Equally, Pichon had assured that Italian claims would be held in the same consideration as Alsace-Lorraine. Yet on 28 November, Barrère proposed to discuss post-war order from scratch, regardless of past treaties, which of course Sonnino

---

[74] Ibid., Carte Sonnino b. 3: F. Caccamo, 'Italy, the Adriatic', pp. 141–142.
[75] Smith, *Sovereignty*, p. 31.   [76] MacMillan, *Peacemakers*, p. 19.
[77] Smith, *Sovereignty*, p. 83.   [78] Sonnino, *Diario*, III, p. 314.
[79] DDI, 6, I, doc. 349, Macchi di Cellere to Sonnino, 26 November 1918.
[80] Macchi di Cellere to Sonnino, n. 2446/344G., 26 November 1918, quoted in Melchionni, *Vittoria mutilata*, pp. 143–151.

opposed.[81] Similarly, the British had repeatedly confirmed their loyalty to the London Pact, but Orlando lamented Lloyd George's limited support of Italy in Balkan affairs, and Colosimo blamed the 'dilatory responses' of both Allied Governments about 'the implementation of the London Treaty'.[82] This left Orlando unclear as to what diplomatic strategy Italy ought to follow at the Peace Conference. He confessed to Bissolati that Sonnino's policy during the armistice negotiations and since, had proved 'a total failure'; but he lacked an alternative, and preferred to play for time.[83] On 20 November, delivering his 'victory speech' to parliament, Orlando carefully avoided envisaging either an annexationist or a revisionist peace programme. On the same occasion, Sonnino sponsored a 'cordial and friendly collaboration and co-existence between our race and the Slav'.[84] Shortly after these vague speeches, the Chamber and the Senate suspended sitting until 1 March 1919. Like the war, also the peace would be planned in Italy by a handful of policymakers.[85] Free from parliamentary scrutiny, Sonnino and Orlando could explore their allies' intentions without pressure. They largely ignored France whose aloofness was marked and which they mistrusted,[86] and instead looked to London. Orlando, like many Italian statesmen, considered Anglo-Italian friendship one of the two pillars of Italy's foreign policy – the other being the containment of Austria – and had a special admiration for Lloyd George.[87] And Sonnino had held Britain its main diplomatic partner since 1915. Now that 'special partnership' ought to bear fruit. Sonnino instructed Imperiali to look for 'a preliminary confidential understanding between Italy and England'.[88]

Imperiali embarked on a series of feverish meetings, mainly with Balfour, Hardinge and Lloyd George. To the former, he stressed that the British attitude was at times 'surprising and painful', in 'strident contradiction' to the 'loyal and friendly purposes' repeated by Balfour. According to Imperiali, the British Foreign Minister replied that 'no attention should be given to the display of some irresponsible people who, in the present question, seem to have become advocates of the

---

[81] Ibid., pp. 36, 94, 151, 242.
[82] DDI, 6, I, doc. 187, Imperiali to Sonnino, 16 November 1918; doc. 161, *cit.*; doc. 202, *cit.*; doc. 475, Colosimo to Sonnino, 6 December 1918.
[83] L. Bissolati, *Diario di guerra* (Turin: Einaudi, 1935), pp. 137–138.
[84] Sonnino, *Discorsi parlamentari*, III, pp. 578–579.
[85] Melchionni, *Vittoria mutilata*, p. 176.
[86] Mayer, *Politics and Diplomacy*, p. 679. A final attempt to gain French support for Italy's Adriatic claims in exchange for Italian support for French designs along the Rhine failed: C. Seton-Watson, *Storia d'Italia*, p. 586.
[87] Orlando, *Memorie*, pp. 118, 358.
[88] DDI, 6, I, doc. 486, Sonnino to Imperiali, 7 December 1918.

German theory of the "scrap of paper"'. Something similar was expressed by Hardinge, who promised: 'In any event, of one thing [Imperiali] must be assured, that England will keep its undertakings scrupulously'.[89] Balfour's version of the conversation, however, includes a sibylline sentence: 'Clearly we could not modify the [London] pact without Italian consent'. Balfour also reminded Imperiali that there were powers, like the United States, that were not bound to the treaty. Imperiali omitted both sentences in his report, and he did not make any reference to Balfour's reluctance to promise a British declaration aimed at containing Yugoslav pretensions.[90] The discrepancy between the Italian and the English version might never be solved. Once again, we can only speculate whether Imperiali wittingly tamed Balfour's words, or whether the latter were intentionally equivocal. To Imperiali's credit, it must be said that he kept looking for confirmation of British good faith for weeks. On 11 December he discussed the colonial settlement with Balfour. The latter re-stated British objections to the St Jean de Maurienne Agreement, but he added: 'This exception must not in any way be interpreted as a mutilation of Italian rights under article 9 of the Alliance Treaty, which, in one way or another the British Government intends to execute meticulously'.[91] On 19 December Drummond blamed the recurrent pieces in the *Manchester Guardian* and *The Times*, which criticised the 'Metternichian' Italian policy and which held that the Rome Pact of April 1918 had replaced the London Pact of 1915.[92] And Lloyd George was more explicit than ever when he promised '*England will support Italy* [italics by Imperiali]'.[93]

Overall, it cannot be said that Imperiali took his task superficially. He repeatedly tested the main British policymakers and he was always reassured. True, he held some doubts. At times he called Lloyd George 'mellifluous', while at times suspected him of being a 'demagogic barker', that 'leans whichever way the wind is blowing', and was 'capable of anything'. There were also precedents – above all the British rejection of the colonial treaty – that suggested taking British promises with a pinch of salt. But in the end, Imperiali concluded that 'naturally I did not

[89] Ibid., doc. 294, Imperiali to Orlando, 23 November 1918. Balfour referred to the German dismissal of the 1839 treaty on Belgian neutrality as a 'scrap of paper' shortly before invading Belgium in 1914.

[90] TNA, FO371/3137, 5244, d. 195820, n. 488, Balfour to Rodd, 23 November 1918; Melchionni, *Vittoria mutilata*, p. 95.

[91] DDI, 6, I, doc. 521, Imperiali to Sonnino, 11 December 1918.

[92] Ibid., doc. 641, Imperiali to Sonnino, 24 December 1918; doc. 597, Imperiali to Sonnino, 19 December 1918.

[93] Imperiali, *Diario*, p. 615.

imagine that the good faith of the British Government in observing scrupulously their undertakings with us should be questioned'.[94] He found further confirmation of it in the British decision to support the Italian request that the Yugoslavs should be barred from the permanent meetings of the Peace Conference.[95] So, the ambassador revised his recent suggestion to surrender Dalmatia unilaterally and returned to his original diplomatic scheme of 1915 – based on the alleged special Anglo-Italian partnership. He told Sonnino that, despite predictable American opposition, British 'perfect loyalty' towards the 'execution of the [London] Treaty' was 'explicit',[96] and 'the British Government will use . . . all of its influence to ensure the [Treaty's] integral application'.[97] This conclusion was reinforced by Lloyd George's 'outstanding' electoral success, which made the British leader 'omnipotent, and . . . destined to have a position in the conference perhaps even more prominent than Wilson's, who cannot count on a [comparable] electoral support in America'. From such an 'exceptional position', Imperiali believed Italy 'could obtain positive advantages'. Hence, he recommended no immediate compromise on the London Pact, but 'speak loud . . . and stand firm on a strict execution of the treaty'. Then if circumstances required it, Italy could negotiate a compromise counting on British backing and safeguarding it further by supporting London desiderata where not incompatible with Rome's.[98]

In formulating Italy's line at the conference, Sonnino embraced Imperiali's suggestion at large. On 15–16 December he told his colleagues in the council of ministers how he would proceed methodically. He would first call on his allies to respect wartime agreements. Those pacts were less a manifestation of imperialism than a guarantee of Italian good faith, for under them Italy renounced spontaneously the city of Fiume 'whose Italianess cannot be contested by anyone'. He would raise the security principle to defend 'our military needs under the London Pact', including the Brenner Pass and 'some islands and channels in the Adriatic'. Once the London Pact was approved, Italy could bargain parts of the treaty with territories outside it.[99] Given what Sonnino knew from Macchi Di Cellere and Imperiali, his plan was rational – and not unreasonably obdurate as traditionally understood;

---

[94] Ibid., pp. 483, 494, 605, 652; DDI, 5, X, doc. 230, Imperiali to Sonnino, 14 February 1918.
[95] Melchionni, *Vittoria mutilata*, p.156.   [96] DDI, 6, I, doc. 521, *cit.*
[97] Ibid., doc. 531, Imperiali to Sonnino, 12 December 1918.
[98] DDI, 6, I, doc. 714, Imperiali to Sonnino, 31 December 1918; Imperiali, *Diario*, pp. 615, 652.
[99] Sonnino, *Diario*, III, pp. 397–398.

but it could work only if the treaty was accepted by the other Allies – which, unbeknownst to him, was not the case.

Sonnino gained the support of Zupelli – who had been re-appointed War Minister in March – and Colosimo, but was opposed by Bissolati and Nitti. Bissolati urged Sonnino to renounce the London Treaty, claiming that the more moderate, the more Italy would get. In Dalmatia, he claimed only Zara and was prepared to give up the Brenner and even the Dodecanese, which was largely Greek. But he demanded Fiume under the nationality principle.[100] Cooperation with Wilson was at the heart of Bissolati's policy. He realised that Italy not only needed American support for its desiderata, but it also depended on the US economically. Like many other countries after the war, Italy was undergoing a socio-economic crisis, which in Italy was arguably the most serious among victor nations. Italy had a public debt equal to 119 per cent of its GDP, which was five times the value of Italy's annual export trade;[101] 56 per cent of Italian external debt was owed to Britain, 40 per cent to the United States, and the rest to France.[102] Overall, it amounted to £700 million, aggravated by higher inflation than in any country except Russia.[103] These astronomical problems were superimposed on a fragile economy where the taxation required to balance the books fuelled long-standing grievances.[104] Furthermore, the end of the war had brought a dramatic drop of Allied supplies to Italy – from an annual 12 million tons of coal and grain to 6 million.[105] The cost of living in Italy was higher than in any of its partners; the wholesale price index was 25 per cent higher than in France, twice as high as in Britain, and 57 per cent higher than in the United States.[106] Unemployment was rampant, with inevitable strikes and an alarming growth in organised labour strength.[107] Bissolati held that Italy needed American supplies and credits, and it must also side with Washington against a concrete Bolshevist threat. Nitti made similar observations.[108] Sonnino rebutted them. By surrendering Italian rights under the London Treaty unilaterally, Italy would lose its sole legal anchor to its claims. Instead of withdrawing 'in advance', Italy should

---

[100] Melchionni, *Vittoria mutilata*, pp. 104–105, 174, 200–204.

[101] Toniolo, *La banca d'Italia*, p. 14. By comparison, Italy's debt was proportionally smaller than Britain's 140 per cent, but British foreign debt reduced the domestic pressures for inflation whilst the Italian increased the trade gap.

[102] Kindleberger, *A Financial History*, p. 307.   [103] MacMillan, *Peacemakers*, p. 289.

[104] Galassi, Harrison, 'Italy at War', p. 22.

[105] I. Montanelli, *L'Italia di Giolitti 1900–1920* (Milan: Bur, 2011), p. 327.

[106] E. Lémonon, *L'Italie d'après la guerre, 1914–1921* (Paris: Alcan, 1922), pp. 120–121; L. Hautecoeur, *L'Italie sous le ministère Orlando, 1917–1919* (Paris: Bossard, 1919), pp. 206 ff.

[107] Mayer, *Politics and Diplomacy*, p. 674.

[108] Melchionni, *Vittoria Mutilata*, pp. 196–204; Mayer, *Politics and Diplomacy*, p. 224.

'concede based on requests [and] in exchange for compensation'.[109] The final decision lay with Orlando. He called the hypothesis of entering the conference with an aprioristic renunciative programme 'a crime'. He would act empirically so as to preserve the 'spirit' of the London Pact and reconcile it with the broader 'needs of the country'. It was nebulous language that showed how unclear Orlando was about his goals, and only served to precipitate a cabinet crisis. Bissolati resigned on 28 December and Nitti followed on 2 January. This reduced conflict in government but aggravated a confrontation in the public between those who read the war in Risorgimento terms, and those yearning for imperialist expansion.[110]

The latter were a minority in the country but – as in 1915 – they were very noisy and enjoyed the support of the armed forces, which not only allowed anti-British and anti-French pamphlets to be distributed in the Italian army, but also favoured the creation of a voluntary Istrian para-military legion under a nationalist, Giovanni Host Venturi, which claimed Fiume for Italy. D'Annunzio urged the annexation of both Fiume and Dalmatia, and openly boasted about a new 'Radiant May' to lead the 'true Italy' into Rome and the institutions.[111] When Bissolati's ideas were exposed to the Italian public through an interview the former minister gave to *The Morning Post*, this magmatic scenario turned to fire. Italian conservatives and nationalists started a campaign against the *rinunciatari* (defeatists). *Il Resto del Carlino* called the Treaty of London 'the Great Charter of the Alliance', and misinformation was increased by claims in *Il Giornale d'Italia* that the treaty had been recognised by the Allies when they had decided to exclude Yugoslav representatives from the permanent meetings of the imminent conference.[112] The *Corriere*, *Secolo*, *Messaggero* and *Tribuna* stepped forward in defence of Bissolati. The latter had 'never denounced a single one of Italy's legitimate claims: he defends the Italianess of Trieste, of Fiume, of Zara'.[113] *Il Resto* and Mussolini's *Popolo* rebutted denouncing Bissolatians as Slavophiles. And since neither France nor Britain intended to give up their Mediterranean and colonial possessions or claims, Mussolini continued, why should 'only Italy and Italy alone' renounce its own? Imperialism need not be 'aristocratic and military: it can be democratic, pacific, economic and spiritual'. Under this

---

[109] Sonnino, *Diario*, III, pp. 318–319.

[110] Melchionni, *Vittoria mutilata*, pp. 180,209; Mayer, *Politics and Diplomacy*, p. 223.

[111] Caviglia, *Il conflitto di Fiume* (Milan: Garzanti, 1948), pp. 69–71; G. Rumi, *Alle origini della politica estera fascista, 1918–1923* (Bari: Laterza, 1968), p. 14.

[112] Melchionni, *Vittoria mutilata*, pp. 156, 213–214; Mayer, *Politics and Diplomacy*, pp. 198–199.

[113] *Il Secolo*, 28 and 30 December 1918; *Il Messaggero*, 30 December 1918; *La Tribuna*, 29 December 1918.

definition, Mussolini argued that President Wilson was 'the greatest and most prosperous of all imperialists'.[114]

Wilson's visit to Italy aggravated matters. The President had embarked on a tour of Allied countries preliminary to the conference, starting in Paris on 14 December, then moving to London on the 26th, and arriving in Rome on 1 January. His visit exacerbated nationalist protests, and it also proved misleading to Wilson in that he met mainly with Wilsonians, and grasped that they represented the broader Italian public.[115] The cheering of Italian democrats in the streets of Milan, which Orlando hoped would win the President's benevolence over to Italy, only reinforced Wilson's assumption.-[116] Wilson made a poor impression on both Orlando and Sonnino. The former described the President as a man affected by 'spontaneous hypocrisy' – meaning that 'hypocrisy was such a second nature in him that it was free from premeditation and consciousness'[117] – while Sonnino called Wilson 'a usurer' that wanted to dictate the peace.[118] Wilson, in return, was amazed by the 'limited political horizons' of Orlando and Sonnino.[119]

Unimpressed by Wilson, and very much impressed by nationalist agitation, Orlando decided to replace Bissolati with Zupelli – ad interim – and Nitti with Stringher. Together with Gallenga Stuart's departure, this left Sonnino unchallenged and his hegemony was confirmed by the eventual submission of Italy's propaganda apparatus to the Consulta at the end of December 1918[120] and throughout the peace negotiations.[121] This does not mean that Orlando had cleared his head about what line to follow at the conference. He acknowledged that the London Pact was 'a double-edged weapon which we cannot use without wounding ourselves', and was still suspicious of Sonnino, whom he considered 'mentally rigid' and 'irascible';[122] but he lacked – or so he thought – the political support to get rid of him. Sonnino was now very influential politically and very popular in the *piazza*, where, as in Britain, the war had accelerated the emasculation of the moderate centre; by contrast, Wilsonians were divided. Bissolati and Nitti might have shared a similar peace programme, but they were not at all sympathetic to one another; Giolitti was now badly isolated and saw

---

[114] *Il Resto del Carlino*, 31 December 1918; *Il Popolo d'Italia*, 1, 10 and 11 January 1919.
[115] Mayer, *Politics and Diplomacy*, p. 213.
[116] Melchionni, *Vittoria mutilata*, pp. 234–235.   [117] Orlando, *Memorie*, pp. 353–354.
[118] Quoted in MacMillan, *Peacemakers*, p. 287.
[119] Melchionni, *Vittoria mutilata*, p. 166.
[120] ACS, Carte Presidenza, b. 19-28-2, Orlando to Sonnino, 28 December 1918; Sonnino to Orlando, 31 December 1918.
[121] The arguments were now explicitly annexationist: 'I confini d'Italia', *Bollettino del soldato*, n. 1, 1919.
[122] Malagodi, *Conversazioni*, II, Conversation with Orlando, 7 February 1919; Orlando, *Memorie*, pp. 381 ff.

Nitti – rightly so – as a rival rather than an ally. Orlando did not dare to roll the moderates in the Cabinet against Sonnino; instead, in a supreme case of domestic policy influence over foreign policy, Orlando opted to stabilise his own position by supporting the Foreign Minister – as he had done in the past.[123]

Orlando's political preoccupations were reflected in the Italian conference delegation. It comprised Sonnino, Salvago Raggi, former ambassador to France and former Governor of Eritrea, Salandra, the advocate of *sacro egoismo*, Salvatore Barzilai, an irredentist from Trieste, and two conservatives, Giuseppe Giardini and Vincenzo Riccio, whom Orlando needed to win support from the Right in case a stalemate in negotiations forced him to call for national elections; a liberal, Giuseppe De Nava, and a Giolittian, Luigi Facta, were included for political compromise; General Caviglia, who replaced Zupelli as War Minister in January, and Stringher were included for their military and economic expertise. This heterogeneity produced a schizophrenic set of peace aims. Sonnino, as mentioned, was attached to the London Pact and would raise further claims such as Fiume, only at a second stage. Orlando was sensitive to nationalist agitations and was inclined to claim Fiume immediately to calm the nationalists, sacrificing most of Dalmatia.[124] The armed forces pushed him opposite ways: the navy was obsessed with keeping Dalmatia – in Revel's words, its possession was 'so vital' that he was ready to 'sacrifice Fiume' and even 'the Dodecanese and part of the colonial possessions';[125] the military deemed Dalmatia difficult to defend, and preferred to get Fiume, provided that the border be moved eastwards, between Mount Nevoso and the sea.[126] Salvago Raggi sponsored Colosimo's line, which echoed Sonnino's idea to use the London Treaty as a base for bargaining; but he did not quite consider Fiume, rather he wished to exchange London Pact territories for wider colonial compensations.[127] Colosimo realised that recent developments made the fulfilment of wartime colonial promises difficult, but he suspected that Britain and France still thought in strictly imperialistic terms in the colonial theatre, and might exploit the theory of self-government to build up 'formidable economic monopolies'. Italy needed to respond by expanding its own colonial influence.[128] None of the Italian policymakers

[123] Mayer, *Politics and Diplomacy*, pp. 208, 224.

[124] Melchionni, *Vittoria mutilata*, pp. 207, 243–249; Burgwyn, *The Legend*, p. 248.

[125] Quoted in Melchionni, *Vittoria mutilata*, p. 242; Sonnino, *Diario*, III, p. 317.

[126] Salandra, *I retroscena di Versailles*, Gifuni ed. (Milan: Pan, 1971), pp. 26–27, 29–30.

[127] Melchionni, *Vittoria mutilata*, pp. 198–199.

[128] DDI, 6, I, doc. 393, Badoglio to Orlando, Sonnino and Colosimo, 28 November 1918; doc. 475, *cit*.

was ready to drop his own claims. So Italy sued for all territories promised in the London and St Jean de Maurienne treaties, with the addition of Fiume. Colonial gains in Africa and the Gulf were added to the list as compensation for the Anglo-French partition of the German colonies, stretching from the Arabian Peninsula, to which Italy should have economic access, via Kassala in the Sudan to the Jaghbub oasis on the Egyptian-Libyan border. The possession of the British port of Kisimaio (based on a claim going back to 1888) and the French port of Djibouti was also indispensable to secure the 'organic unity' of Italian colonies in the Horn of Africa – which ought to be further strengthened by some sort of protectorate over Abyssinia.[129]

Although the Italians were convinced that 'compared to the great advantages that France and England intend to realise in Africa and Asia, what we ask is very little',[130] Italian claims had undoubtedly expanded. But, other countries too increased their demands on the eve of the conference. Britain, as mentioned, planned to expand its Empire significantly. France confirmed its colonial claims under the Sykes–Picot Agreement and its right to Alsace-Lorraine, but wanted it with the wider 1790 frontier instead of the 1815 frontier; Paris also demanded control of the Eastern Rhine bank and high war reparations for the damage suffered.[131] Greece claimed Southern Albania (Northern Epirus), Thrace, the Dodecanese islands and a huge portion of Asia Minor stretching from a point halfway along the southern shore of the Sea of Marmara almost 400 miles down the southern coast to Smyrna – an amazingly ambitious project for a new Greece of the 'two continents and the five seas' draped around the Aegean.[132] The Yugoslavian State of SCS, which from 1 December 1918 became the Kingdom of SCS and now included also Macedonia and much of Montenegro, wanted Dalmatia, Istria down to Trieste, the Hungarian provinces of the Backa and the Barayna north of the traditional boundaries of Croatia, the Romanian-speaking parts of the Banat or the German-speaking areas around Klagenfurt – such a wild programme that even Yugoslav sympathisers found it out of proportion 'and good sense'.[133] The logic behind this was pretty much the same for everyone: claim 100 to get 70 or 75. As Goldstein wrote, 'no negotiated settlement gives any of

---

[129] Ibid., doc. 853, Colosimo to Orlando and Sonnino, 12 January 1919; Gooch, *Italian Army*, p. 307.

[130] DDI, 6, I, doc. 475, *cit.*

[131] TNA, FO371/2937/11293, Balfour to Bertie, 2 July 1917; Goldstein, *Winning the Peace*, p. 108.

[132] MacMillan, *Peacemakers*, p. 362.

[133] Quoted in Ibid., p. 131; Imperiali, *Diario*, pp. 632–637.

its signatories its maximum desiderata', so the key is to gain one's 'essential core of goals'.[134]

The problem with the Italian claims, therefore, was not their expansion. Rather, it was that such analysis of the 'essential core of goals' was never done. Orlando continued to fluctuate between Sonnino's plan, Colosimo's plan – both dependent on Allied recognition of the London Pact – and the possibility of a compromise with the Allies and the Yugoslavs without his Foreign Minister. Since December, Imperiali suspected that Orlando and Sonnino did not 'see eye to eye'. He desperately advised Orlando: 'Be [our] policy whichever you like, rinunciatory or intransigent … but make it one, firm and united – the policy of the Government, not that of Dick or that of Harry'. He was disappointed. Receiving reports from Paris, Imperiali later lamented: 'If we at least knew what we want'.[135] The Italian delegation lacked a clear peace-making strategy.

A second issue lay with the principles upon which Italian claims rested. Italy appealed to three separate rights: those pre-dating the war, those arising during it and those that were a 'necessary consequence' of the post-war situation.[136] Depending on the claim, Italian delegates would invoke the principle of self-determination, strategic exigencies, economic necessities, wartime merits or needs for reparation of the damage suffered during the Austro-Hungarian occupation of Veneto.[137] It was an inconsistent policy. Once again, it was not peculiarly Italian; Greece too appealed to conflicting principles – history, language, religion and self-determination – to justify its claims, and the Yugoslavs invoked 'reward for virtue' thanks to Serbian war efforts, self-determination and security.[138] The difference in the Italian case was that Italy had treaties, which it wanted to be respected, so claiming territories based on a gamut of altogether different arguments risked automatically delegitimising those treaties.

A final and formidable flaw in Italy's peace preparations was the dearth of alternative options if matters developed unexpectedly. This was largely the result of the lack of a peace-planning machine established well in advance. Italian delegates were ill prepared for head-on confrontation with their Allied counterparts. No committees of experts were ready to brief Italian negotiators on what to expect and how to react. The

---

[134] Goldstein, *Winning the Peace*, pp. 3–4.
[135] Imperiali, *Diario*, pp. 604, 611.
[136] G. Buccianti, *L'egemonia sull'Etiopia (1918–1923): Lo scontro diplomatico tra Italia, Francia e Inghilterra* (Milan: Giuffrè, 1977), p. 26.
[137] A parliamentary commission calculated 159,882 billion lire of damage: C. Fumian ed., *Il secondo Risorgimento delle Venezie. La ricostruzione dopo la Grande Guerra* (Venezia: Marsilio, 2015), p. 34.
[138] MacMillan, *Peacemakers*, pp. 131, 362.

exclusion of Imperiali from the delegation – which Imperiali attributed to Sonnino's dislike of him and inability to work with anyone who could hold his own with the Foreign Minister[139] – was especially deleterious: a delegation that had primarily to defend the London Pact was condemned to do so without one of the Treaty's main architects. It was left to the delegates and their aids to foresee conference developments, and even that was not done systematically – mainly because it was too late. Sonnino, for example, continued to misjudge the Americans. What he knew about the United States was 'so little that it might almost be termed nothing',[140] and without experts to provide information, he could follow only his own biases and the cryptic counsel of Macchi Di Cellere. Later, Orlando admitted that Sonnino was poorly served by his collaborators, and called Macchi Di Cellere 'a good man, but absolutely inferior to the task, to whom must be ascribed [the fact that] we Italians went into the conference in complete ignorance of Wilson's real sentiments'.[141] Even Imperiali, who was far more expert and efficient than Macchi Di Cellere, nonetheless failed to read developments in Britain with the necessary detachment and allowed himself to be deceived by British assurances about the London Pact – partly, no doubt, because he could not accept the possibility that all his work over the years had been in vain. Thus, neither Sonnino nor Orlando was encouraged to look for original solutions that bypassed American objections to the secret treaties – for example, by establishing early bilateral agreements with the Yugoslavs or at least the Greeks, as offered by Venizelos during his visit to Rome in early January 1919.[142] But in the end, it was more than this or that ambassador that failed Sonnino: it was Italy's diplomatic and cabinet peace-planning that proved inadequate, and that was Orlando's responsibility no less than Sonnino's.

British and Italian final preparations for the conference, then, reveal a last – and crucial – rift in their relations. Alienated by differences in wartime strategy, and by increasingly incompatible war aims, the British and Italians diverged in peace-making. London entered the conference with a clear set of goals and veritable options to achieve them; Rome lacked both, and the secret treaties remained its main anchor. Encouraged by deliberately misleading assurances from the British, the Italian diplomatic approach was divorced from reality. Unless Italian

---

[139] Imperiali, *Diario*, pp. 604–605, 620–621.

[140] Quoted in MacMillan, *Peacemakers*, p. 296.

[141] Orlando, *Memorie*, pp. 384–388. Justus tried, rather un-convincingly to clear Macchi di Cellere's name of such accusations: Justus, *Macchi di Cellere*, pp. 102, 162–180, 187.

[142] DDI, 6, I, doc. 788, Bonin Longare to Sonnino, 6 January 1919; Sonnino, *Diario*, III, pp. 326–332.

delegates performed exceptionally well, Italy's empire project was doomed before the conference commenced.

18.2 Turning the Bucket

From the outset, the Peace Conference suffered from confusion, over its organisation, its agenda and its procedures. On 12–13 January, the prime ministers and foreign ministers of the main victor nations, the United States, Britain, France, Italy and Japan – soon to be called the Council of Ten – inaugurated a preliminary summit to agree on the terms to be offered to the defeated. In so doing, they would hear representatives of the smaller nations and then embark on a full-scale conference to negotiate with the enemy.[143] But the preliminary summit soon turned into the 'real' conference because agreeing on peace terms among the Allies implied re-shaping the world's map and addressing all the big questions of peace-making; so more than a negotiation between victors and defeated, the Paris Peace Conference was a negotiation among victors, the results of which would then be presented to – or rather imposed upon – the defeated.

The Council of Ten discussed the various issues haphazardly, jumping from topic to topic, 'one day Czechoslovakia, the next Fiume, the day after Greece, and then back again'.[144] The first topic to be addressed in full was the League of Nations, which was approved rather smoothly on 25 January.[145] Greater difficulty erupted over reparation and indemnity, with heated contrasts between the promoters of a Carthaginian peace with Germany, mainly the French, and those preoccupied with avoiding killing Germany, such as the Americans and part of the British delegation; the shaping of the new German borders, which was entangled with the creation of Czechoslovakia and Poland, also proved hard to unknot; the final arrangement was agreed only in May.[146] Britain was in the frontline in these negotiations, whereas Italy was largely passive. Despite Rome's desire to assert its identity 'as an empire',[147] the Italian delegation made a parochial showing, joining conversations only when Italian interests were involved. 'I always lurk in these discussions', admitted Orlando amiably, 'and I do not enter them unless it is to further my own case, and to detail those things that will turn to our favour when our matters are discussed'.[148]

---

[143] TNA, CAB28/5/5178/IC-98A, Conclusions of inter-Allied conference, 2 December 1918.

[144] Goldstein, *Winning the Peace*, pp. 115.   [145] MacMillan, *Peacemakers*, p. 92.

[146] Goldstein, *Winning the Peace*, pp. 193–197, 235–236; MacMillan, *Peacemakers*, p. 490.

[147] Smith, *Sovereignty*, p. 54.

[148] R. Vivarelli, *Storia delle origini del fascismo*, 2 vols. (Bologna: Il Mulino, 2012), I, p. 403.

Italian matters were first discussed privately between Wilson, Lloyd George and Clemenceau before the opening of the conference. All agreed that Italian claims had become 'extreme' and were 'in contravention of the principles upon which we entered the war'. Clemenceau asked whether the Italians still stood by the Treaty of London; Lloyd George replied: 'They still adhered to the Treaty where it suited them'. Clemenceau observed that under that pact the Italians could not get Fiume, but if they renounced the treaty, they would have no or minimal rights in other areas, like Turkey. He was 'by no means disposed to discuss favourably Italian claims anywhere'.[149] As for Wilson, he was prepared to give the Italians the Brenner frontier, but in the Adriatic, he would concede the Arsa as a border, barring Italy from the mountains dominating Fiume and Ljubljana and from Dalmatia (except for the islands of Lissa and Lussino); Zara, Sebenico and Fiume would be neutralised. This came to be known as the Wilson line and was proposed to Orlando privately on 9 January. It was as incoherent as the extended Italian claims; it left about 365,000 Istrian Slavs under Italy, and the largely Italian city of Fiume outside it; Wilson denied the security principle in the Adriatic whereas he recognised it in Tyrol – transferring 230,000 Austrians under Italy.[150] Orlando rejected the proposal point-blank, making it clear that 'before such an offer Italy would have no choice but to withdraw from the conference'.[151]

Italian claims were officially brought to the table on 7 February. They were immediately challenged by a combination of ideological and technical objections complemented by a *summa* of the classic anti-Italian stereotypes stretched to the limit – namely that the Italians were an untrustworthy and greedy people, whose contribution to the war had been pitiable. Wilson began by blaming Italy's motives for entering the war: Rome entered 'to conquer territories'; Washington to make 'justice'.[152] Then he re-stated his concessions to Italy, and to prove his determination, he recognised the SCS Kingdom.[153] France supported American objections to Italian Adriatic ambitions for other reasons. Clemenceau knew that Italian possession of Dalmatia would have allowed Rome to control commercial traffic on the Danube,[154] and he called the formula 'the London Pact plus Fiume' an 'absurdity'. Lloyd

---

[149] Lloyd George, *The Truth*, I, p. 290; II, p. 764.

[150] Malagodi, *Conversazioni*, II, p. 478; Orlando, *Memorie*, pp. 438–439; Lloyd George, *The Truth*, II, p. 814.

[151] Melchionni, *Vittoria mutilata*, pp. 244–245.   [152] Smith, *Sovereignty*, p. 37.

[153] C. Seton-Watson, *Storia d'Italia*, p. 607. Britain and France recognised Yugoslavia in June: MacMillan, *Peacemakers*, p. 120.

[154] M. Gilbert, *The First World War: A complete History* (New York: Holt & Co. 1994), pp. 589 ff.; MacMillan, *Peacemakers*, p. 125.

George agreed, but for the moment, he limited himself to confirm British rejection of the St Jean de Maurienne Agreement. Lloyd George raised two fundamental objections to the agreement. The first was Italy's insufficient contribution to the defeat of the Ottoman Empire. The second was the lack of Russian consent. The first point had no legitimate basis whatsoever, since military clauses had been removed from the colonial treaty in June 1917, but the second was technically correct. What most offended the Italians, however, was Allied slander of Italian sacrifices. Clemenceau held that Italy's rights were inferior to those of France and Britain because Italy 'was not capable of much' in the war and suggested that the figure of 500,000 Italian war dead should not be taken 'too literally'.[155] He was right. Italian war dead were 651,000. It was still a lower figure compared with the French and British – 1,350,000 and 750,000, respectively. But for a smaller and poorer country like Italy, it signified a bloodbath of no less appalling impact on its society – especially as it occurred in a shorter period of active combat. Italian war dead were 10.3 per cent of all mobilised men, and 7.5 per cent of the Italian male population aged between 15 and 49 – compared with France's 16.8 per cent and 13.3 per cent, and with Britain's 11.8 per cent and 6.3 per cent.[156] Yet, Lloyd George joined his French colleague, claiming that he saw a contrast 'between the Italian attitude towards the spoils of victory and the Italian contribution towards achieving it'. The Italian army, he believed, had never really recovered from Caporetto, and in the last year of the war, 'it took no further effective part … until the very end, when the Austrian Army was disintegrating'.[157] Given Italy's contribution on the Piave and to the final battles in France and Macedonia, this was at best unfair. The French and the British also charged Italian ships with having 'rarely ventured out of port, in spite of repeated promises to patrol the Mediterranean and the Adriatic' – this was utterly false. And again, Italy had squeezed resources out of its hard-pressed allies, which it had then 'refused to use in the war'[158] – this accusation was also questionable. So, overall, Lloyd George felt free to conclude that, when compared with the experiences of the British, the French and the Americans, 'the Italians have no idea what the fighting meant'.

Italian delegates reacted in dismay. They defended their country's performance during the war, and repeated the badly unfair Italian argument that Rome had defeated Vienna 'nearly alone', hastening the peace by threatening Germany from the south – so, the Italian people were now

---

[155] Quoted in Gooch, *Italian Army*, pp. 308, 310; Burgwyn, *The Legend*, p. 283.
[156] Isnenghi, Rochat, *Grande Guerra*, pp. 470–471.
[157] Lloyd George, *The Truth*, I, p. 68; II, pp. 775–776.
[158] Quoted in MacMillan, *Peacemakers*, p. 292.

pervaded by 'legitimate pride';[159] but Italian representatives struggled to find a single line of action. This was due in part to Orlando's irresolution, and in part to the inefficient work of the delegates and their staffs. Orlando lamented that his subordinates, especially Salandra, Barzilai and Sonnino, were reluctant to engage with the mammoth work of the conference's sub-commissions – where documents were elaborated, and policy options outlined for the negotiators. This left Orlando with scarce arguments for discussions.[160] Once again, the absence of an efficient machine for diplomatic planning proved a serious weakness.

Divided along political lines, the Italian delegation was also handicapped by the divergent temperaments of Orlando and Sonnino.[161] Lloyd George observed: '[They] were not a good team. When trouble came Orlando was too emotional and not hard enough, Sonnino was too sulky and too rigid'.[162] In his memoirs, Orlando argued that such difference was in fact an advantage, for it permitted them to better adapt 'to the variety of political situations that had to be addressed'.[163] His point is not very convincing. The Italians performed ineptly by all accounts, including Sonnino's, who later admitted that the Italian delegation had been 'vague and unsteady'.[164] Italian representatives seemed to be acting 'without a logic', according to the particular tactical needs of a given situation.[165] To be sure, they were fighting against all the odds. A British diplomat reported: 'They were held in supreme contempt ..., attacked and criticised on all sides; they were told what was good for them, but not taken into real discussions'.[166] Sonnino's tactics exacerbated this situation. Upon House's suggestion, he preferred to wait until the Big Three as well as some smaller states secured terms, which involved dispensation of Wilsonian principles, confident that these infractions would 'legitimise and fortify' Italian demands.[167] That meant, however, that little was done to assert Italy's influence at the conference in the month following the submission of Italian demands.

In the second half of February, the conference took a break as Wilson, Lloyd George and Orlando returned home to deal with domestic issues.[168] On 4 March Imperiali, informed of the Paris developments, met Lloyd George; he told the British premier energetically that respecting the London Treaty was simply a duty for Britain, and urged him to move 'all

---

[159] DDI, 6, I, doc. 50, Imperiali to Sonnino, 8 November 1918; Imperiali, *Diario*, p. 608.
[160] Orlando, *Memorie*, pp. 377 ff.   [161] Crespi, *Alla difesa*, p. 242.
[162] Lloyd George, *The Truth*, I, p. 256.   [163] Orlando, *Memorie*, p. 386.
[164] Sonnino, *Diario*, III, pp. 397–398.   [165] Imperiali, *Diario*, p. 604.
[166] Quoted in MacMillan, *Peacemakers*, pp. 292, 297.
[167] Mayer, *Politics and Diplomacy*, pp. 679–680.
[168] MacMillan, *Peacemakers*, pp. 159–160.

sails set' in support of Italy's 'just requests'. Lloyd George replied: 'I will bear well in mind'.[169] Another contact of Imperiali, 'very close to Lloyd George', swore that 'Anglo-Italian positions were mutually supportive'. Once again, the ambassador trusted the British. He telegraphed Sonnino that he had for nine years worked to strengthen Anglo-Italian partnership and now it was necessary to dispel doubts in the Italian public that 'England [could be] passive ... or more or less indifferent' towards a possible 'incomplete realisation' of the Italian peace programme.[170]

Imperiali's apprehension about Italian public opinion was justified. Reports and rumours from Paris had increased nationalist recriminations. The *Idea Nazionale*, and the *Resto del Carlino* accused Orlando of appeasement.[171] Martini observed that Fiume had acquired a symbolic significance; if Fiume was not annexed, 'the Italian people, emotional as they are, shall feel they have won a fruitless victory. They shall feel they have been fooled by God knows what plots'.[172] Mussolini's followers met with the *Arditi* of Milan on 21 March, and then again on the 23rd, calling for a coalition (*fascio*, bundle) of all interventionists and frontline veterans in a nationwide organisation aimed at 'turning victory to full account'. The Italian Fascist movement was born.[173] Old-style diplomatists like Imperiali disliked such a heating of public passions. 'Once popular passions rage, we can expect anything', he wrote.[174] Sonnino shared this view. But Orlando was far more sensitive to popular sentiments; he was possibly caught up in the widespread 'intoxication of victory' that he found across the country, but also feared he would fall, had he not brought home a successful peace.[175] The King himself warned Orlando that the country would take it very badly if its 'just aspirations' were not met.[176] Inaugurating the new session of parliament, the Italian premier declared that 'Italy could not ignore the appeal which came from that most Italian city, the jewel of Quarnaro'.[177] By the time he returned to Paris in late March, Orlando had made Fiume an irrevocable claim.

At this point the conference sped up. It was decided that the main matters should be dealt with by the heads of government of the main powers, Wilson, Lloyd George, Clemenceau and Orlando. This became the Council of Four, which generally met in Wilson's study. The setting of Italy's borders was high on its agenda. Orlando soon proved isolated both

---

[169] Imperiali, *Diario*, p. 642.
[170] DDI, 6, II, doc. 337, Imperiali to Sonnino, 14 February 1919.
[171] *L'Idea Nazionale*, 2 March 1919; *Il Resto del Carlino*, 2 March 1919.
[172] Martini, *Diario*, p. 1280.   [173] Mayer, *Politics and Diplomacy*, p. 677.
[174] Imperiali, *Diario*, p. 623.   [175] C. Seton-Watson, *Storia d'Italia*, p. 606.
[176] DDI, 6, II, docs. 66, 123, 191 and 223, Victor Emmanuel III to Orlando, 23 and 27 January; 1 and 4 February 1919.
[177] Mayer, *Politics and Diplomacy*, p. 679.

Figure 18.1 The four premiers of Italy, Britain, France and America (left to right): Vittorio Emanuele Orlando, David Lloyd George, Georges Clemenceau and Woodrow Wilson at Versailles

physically – he usually found himself sitting on one side of the fireplace facing the other colleagues – and linguistically – unlike Sonnino, he did not speak English well. The new council began to gather just as disturbing stories began to circulate about the situation in Dalmatia. The Italians were suspected of trying to suffocate Slav communities economically and politically; they supplied food, a British report read, 'only . . . to those who signed a declaration of loyalty to Italy'; they arrested Slav activists; and arbitrarily closed down Slav newspapers.[178] Sympathy towards Italy declined further, especially in British eyes. Balfour found Italy's policy towards its eastern neighbours 'perfectly insane'.[179] Leeper was adamant:

[178] MacMillan, *Peacemakers*, pp. 282, 290, 300; Burgwyn called it 'a policy of starvation': *The Legend*, p. 270. The Allied blockade was becoming tighter against Germany too. See: A. C. Bell, *A History of the Blockade of Germany and of the Countries Associated with Her in the Great War, Austria-Hungary, Bulgaria, and Turkey, 1914–1918* (London: H. M. Stationery, 1937); C. P. Vincent, *The Politics of Hunger: The Allied Blockade of Germany, 1915–1919* (Athens, OH: Ohio University Press, 1985).
[179] Balfour MSS, Balfour to Rodd, 14 March 1919.

'Fiume is vital to Yugoslavia', and Crowe agreed: 'The Italians have no case as regards Fiume'.[180] Once again, it was widely hoped that 'if America could carry its views on this point it would help to liberate Britain from a whole series of unfortunate promises made under the duress of war'.[181]

On 14 April, Wilson gave Orlando a memorandum claiming that Italy had made peace with Germany based on the 14 Points, and America could not accept a different treatment for Austria-Hungary. It smashed the bulk of Italian ambitions in the Adriatic. The debate intensified in the following days. Sonnino told Wilson: 'It is not conceivable that we should return to a worse situation than before the war; certain islands of the Dalmatian coast were conceded to us even by Austria-Hungary to secure our neutrality. You would not even grant us these'. He protested that Wilson had gone from concession to concession towards Britain, France, Czechoslovakia and Poland, often violating his own Points, and now he wished to restore their 'virginity at Italy's expense by invoking the purity of principles'. Both Sonnino and Orlando also warned of civil wars, Bolshevism or anarchy in Italy – to which Balfour replied: 'But suppose Italy falls out with the United States, I do not see how her economic life can continue, and, in that event, how would you avoid the social revolution?'[182] Before the next Council of Four meeting, Orlando consulted with Imperiali, who had finally been invited to join the conference. The ambassador still refused to imagine a British U-turn and maintained that 'political wisdom suggests we entrench behind the London Pact, and insist on its integral execution, renouncing Fiume, if needed. Thus, we'll be in an impregnable position'.[183]

When confronted again by Wilson in the Council of Four on 19 April, Orlando retreated to the London Agreement, confident that Britain and France would honour it. The three Entente partners met separately to discuss the matter. Clemenceau and Lloyd George jointly re-assured Orlando that, if no compromise could be worked out, they 'were bound to uphold the Treaty of London' – a pledge they repeated on the 21st. Orlando did not understand where the problem lay, then. Britain and France simply needed to press the United States to accept the London Pact as a legitimate basis for discussion, after which Italy would happily consider a Fiume-Dalmatia exchange. Lloyd George warned that the United States would not be easily moved; instead, he proposed an

---

[180] TNA, FO608/51/117/1/6/5307; FO608/35/89/1/2/4334, Minute by Crowe, 17 March 1919.
[181] Goldstein, *Winning the Peace*, pp. 255–256.
[182] Mayer, *Politics and Diplomacy*, pp. 681, 691–692; MacMillan, *Peacemakers*, p. 306.
[183] Imperiali, *Diario*, pp. 649–651.

Adriatic scheme, which granted Italy the offshore Dalmatian islands –
except Pago – for security, with the rest of Dalmatia to be demilitarised;
Fiume, Zara and Sebenico would be free cities.[184] In retrospect, it was a
good proposal that was a grave mistake to reject. But Orlando and Sonnino
would not drop two claims in the Adriatic – Fiume and Dalmatia; they
would renounce only one of the two. The traditional view that Italy insisted
on the 'London Pact plus Fiume' scheme is therefore incorrect. Not even
the most stubborn of Italian representatives really considered getting both.
He in fact opposed it. 'When the dispute embittered', Sonnino wrote, 'I
held that we should retreat, as an ultimate and supreme exigency, to what
the London Pact granted us – which our allies could not deny us; and then,
once [this] was granted, go back to negotiate Fiume in exchange for our
concessions'.[185] On one point, Italy would not withdraw: giving up
Dalmatia 'without compensation'. Similarly, the Italians refused Lloyd
George's second proposal, which gave Italy Anatolian compensations
against an Italian surrender of both Fiume and Dalmatia. Italy had been
promised Anatolian territories under the London Pact; if it traded Anatolia
for Fiume, it would then claim Dalmatia.[186] A 1:1 trade was fair; a 1:2 to
Italy's disadvantage, was not.[187]

The key to the whole question in the end rested with the fate of the
London Treaty; this was discussed privately between Wilson, Lloyd
George and Clemenceau on the morning of 23 April. On that occasion,
neither the French nor the British premier pressed Wilson to approve
the pact. They still did not reject it. But because it was assumed the
Italians would leave the conference had Wilson insisted on his terms,
Clemenceau and Lloyd George were confident that it was possible to
shoulder the responsibility for a break onto the Italians; if the latter
withdrew in protest, they would break the Pact of London of 1914,
which bound the Allies not to make peace separately, and this, in turn
would invalidate the Treaty of 1915. Lloyd George's attitude is particularly worth considering. The man from whom the Italians expected the
greatest support did little to promote the Italian case. He limited himself
to repeating that 'If we felt scruples about the Italian claims they should
have been expressed before Italy had lost half a million gallant lives' –
which was an indirect gibe to his predecessor in Downing Street who
had negotiated the Treaty – and confirmed that Britain stood by the
London Pact. This, in Lloyd George's memoirs, is presented as proof of

---

[184] Lloyd George, *The Truth*, II, pp. 813, 827–828.
[185] Sonnino, *Diario*, III, pp. 397–398.
[186] Mayer, *Politics and Diplomacy*, pp. 692–694.
[187] See also: P. Alatri, *Nitti, D'Annunzio e la questione adriatica* (Milan: Feltrinelli, 1959),
      p. 39.

Lloyd George's good faith.[188] But the British premier apparently never asked Wilson to revise his policy and consider the Italian Dalmatia–Fiume exchange proposal. On the contrary, together with Clemenceau, Lloyd George gave Wilson a memorandum, drafted by Balfour, which made it 'unmistakably clear' that Britain and France sided with Wilson on the Fiume question.[189] This was largely motivated by geopolitical reasons. Lloyd George did not want the Adriatic to become an Italian lake. Probably, he was getting tired of Italian doggedness, which was spawning a number of imitators in Versailles, especially the Romanians, the Chinese and the Japanese – the latter also threatened to leave if they were not granted former German possessions in China; moreover, the German delegation was expected in May to be presented with Allied peace terms, and the last thing the Big Three wanted was the Germans to find the Allies stuck.[190] The British army also pressed Lloyd George to accelerate an Adriatic solution, for the British battalion stationed in Fiume was now needed to calm the turmoil in Egypt – and the British were also facing trouble in Iraq and the Caucasus.[191] Lloyd George concluded that Britain needed to detach itself from European affairs to focus on its imperial problems, and in those days, he was pressing the French – with the famous Fontainebleau memorandum – to moderate their terms on Germany. Moderation and balance of power should prevail in the Adriatic too.[192] Finally, Lloyd George was not prepared to embark on a confrontation with Wilson to defend non-British interests. If there must be a break, he confessed in his memoirs, one with Italy 'would be bad enough, but not a disaster; a break with the United States would be a disaster'.[193]

The same afternoon, fortified by Anglo-French backing, Wilson delivered to the press a manifesto he had been preparing for some days, addressed to the Italian people. It told the Italians that the United States was not bound by the London Treaty, and encouraged them to think in new terms: 'Interest is not now in question, but the rights of peoples, of states new and old, [and] of liberated peoples. ... These, and these only, are the principles for which America has fought. These, and these only, are the principles upon which she can consent to make peace'. Orlando responded with a counter-manifesto, which in

---

[188] Lloyd George, *The Truth*, II, pp. 816–818, 865.
[189] Mayer, *Politics and Diplomacy*, p. 694.
[190] Goldstein, *Winning the Peace*, pp. 82, 255; MacMillan, *Peacemakers*, p. 307.
[191] TNA, FO608/8/39/1/1/7262, Minute by General Wilson, 7 April 1919.
[192] H. Elcock, *Portrait of a Decision: The Council of Four and the Treaty of Versailles* (London: Methuen, 1972), p. 165.
[193] Lloyd George, *The Truth*, II, p. 866.

Italian papers was published alongside Wilson's, rebutting the President's arguments and re-stating Italy's 'good national rights'.[194] Then Orlando informed his colleagues that by appealing directly to the Italian people, Wilson had delegitimised the Italian Prime Minister, so he needed to go home and ask for a vote of confidence to parliament. Though Orlando specified that he was not breaking negotiations, his departure was interpreted as a theatrical protest, no less than a political necessity. No one was much surprised. Leeper commented: 'Well, one always knew the break would come sometime'.[195] Lloyd George echoed him: 'Well, the fat is in the fire at last!' And he warned Orlando that, should the Italians be absent when the German delegation arrived, it would be the end of the London Treaty.[196]

Orlando left in the morning of 24 April. Sonnino followed a couple of days later. In Italy they were welcomed by the ringing of church bells and by crowds crying '*Viva Orlando! Viva Fiume! Viva l'Italia!*' Wilson's manifesto proved counter-productive. It stimulated a unanimous chorus of disapproval against the American President. Not even Bissolati and Salvemini stood behind him – why, the latter wondered, was Wilson not asking Britain to abandon Gibraltar, Malta and Suez? Democratic and moderate papers such as *Tribuna, Stampa, Secolo* and *Corriere* reprimanded Wilson for having violated his own Points to the benefit of all other nations, going as far as vetoing the principle of racial equality – and now those principles that had been compromised in Paris could not be cleansed in the Adriatic.[197] Nationalist organs launched a new motto, *l'Italia farà da sè* – Italy will do it alone. Nations, held Mussolini's newspaper, had rights, and Italy had its own, clear and legitimate;[198] those who denied them 'will be our enemies'.[199] Mussolini addressed critiques not just to Wilson, but increasingly to the other 'ungrateful' allies. But where France could still be reconciled with by offering Paris Italian support against a possible resurrection of German power in exchange for French support of Italian 'national claims',[200] Mussolini was more bitter towards Britain – the nation that more than any other had wanted Italy by its side, and was now repudiating it. Mussolini envisioned an Italian action against British lines of communication to India, an Italian support to Egyptian insurgents, and threatened to 'blow up the British African-Asiatic

[194] Ibid., pp. 840–842.   [195] Quoted in Goldstein, *Winning the Peace*, p. 267.
[196] Quoted in MacMillan, *Peacemakers*, p. 126; Lloyd George, *The Truth*, II, p. 818.
[197] Salvemini, 'Il messaggio di Wilson', *L'Unità*, 3 May 1919; Mayer, *Politics and Diplomacy*, pp. 702–703.
[198] B. Mussolini, 'Diamo il benvenuto al Profeta dei Popoli. L'impero di Wilson', *Il Popolo d'Italia*, 5 January 1919.
[199] N. Bonservizi, 'Il Mediterraneo "lago inglese"', *Il Popolo d'Italia*, 24 May 1919.
[200] Rumi, *Alle origini*, pp. 36–41.

empire'.[201] He also brushed up irredentist cries: 'Italy is not one yet –
there are places that everyone knows [are] due to Italy. And among these
... we should not forget the isle of Malta'.[202] In the meantime, Orlando
obtained a stunning 382 votes in parliament (against 40 socialist votes).
Fortified by popular and parliamentary endorsement, he waited for a
conciliatory sign from Paris.[203] As for Sonnino, he tried to turn the
motto 'Italy will do it alone' into practice ordering – without consulting
Orlando – Italian amphibious operations in Anatolia. The Italians had
first landed in Adalia on 28 March in response to French occupations of
Adana and Mersin,[204] but now Sonnino wanted to secure Konya and
Smyrna.[205]

Orlando's prolonged absence and Italian unilateral moves in
Turkey – which Lloyd George called 'madness'[206] – only served as
further excuse for the French and the British to exclude Italy from
the colonial partitioning. In Asia Minor, Italy was to be confined to
Adalia – the only province explicitly mentioned in the London
Pact – counter-balancing the French in Eastern Anatolia; Konya
was assigned to Turkey, Smyrna to Greece and Constantinople
made an international zone. Thus, no power could exert a dominating influence in Anatolia, to the overall benefit of Britain. Moreover,
under the new formula of mandates, Britain was allotted
Mesopotamia, Palestine and Transjordan; France obtained Syria
and Lebanon – though the colonial settlement was only finalised at
the San Remo Conference in April 1920.[207] London and Paris also
divided German Cameroons and Togoland. Britain gained by far the
greater land mass of German East Africa, making British rule continuous from Cape Town to the Suez Canal – and London promptly
relaunched Cecil Rhodes's 'Cape to Cairo railway' project to prove
it. Minor portions of the former German colonies were given to
some British dominions, Belgium and Japan. In terms of such territories' population of 12.5 million people in 1914, a total of 42 per
cent were transferred to mandates of Britain and its dominions, 33
per cent to France and 25 per cent to Belgium.[208] Imperiali solicited
Lloyd George on 3 May: 'Won't you make us some offer?' Lloyd

---

[201] Mussolini, 'Ideali e affari', *Il Popolo d'Italia*, 20 April 1919.

[202] *Il Popolo d'Italia* editorials: 'Malta', 29 January 1919 and 'Viva Malta italiana', 13 June
1919.

[203] Mayer, *Politics and Diplomacy*, p. 711.   [204] Imperiali, *Diario*, p. 612.

[205] C. Seton-Watson, *Storia d'Italia*, pp. 610–611.

[206] Quoted in MacMillan, *Peacemakers*, p. 440.

[207] TNA, CAB24/100/898, Memorandum by Balfour, 15 March 1920; MacMillan,
Peacemakers, pp. 115, 417, 435.

[208] J. A. R. Marriott, *Modern England: 1885–1945* (London: Methuen, 1948), p. 413.

George replied: 'To whom shall we make it? Can you receive an offer?' Imperiali said no.[209] It was indispensable that Orlando and Sonnino returned. They did so on 7 May – and had an 'icy reception'.[210] In the month that followed their humiliation became complete.

They were first informed that Venizelos had been authorised to seize Smyrna. The Greeks, said Lloyd George, deserved it for ethnic reasons and because their leader had always consulted the other allies before taking any initiative. Orlando asked when exactly the Italians had been informed about a Greek landing in Smyrna. They were now, replied Lloyd George with disarming candour.[211] Then the Allies formed a commission to discuss Italian colonial compensations – or rather, in Goldstein's words, 'to counter' the Italians' 'curious colonial appetite'.[212] Initially, Lloyd George was prepared to give Italy a mandate in Adalia plus British Somaliland and Jubaland, provided that the French 'redeemed their part in the London Agreement by similar concessions'; but he ran into 'insurmountable opposition' from some of his ministers.[213] Balfour sent him a strong memorandum emphasising how dangerous it would be to partition Turkey.[214] Greek–Turkish conflict erupted immediately after the Greek landing, risking a regional crisis – indeed, it would soon turn into all-out war – and reports from Constantinople suggested that the Italians had already begun to support an emerging Turkish leader, Muṣṭafà Kemal, to have the Greeks expelled.[215] The Turks, for their part, made it clear that they wanted a united state. On 19 May Lloyd George concluded that 'it is impossible to divide Turkey proper', and in any ways 'to put the Italians into Asia Minor would be to introduce a source of trouble there'.[216] Adalia was allotted to Italy only as a 'zone of influence' that was going to last until 1922.[217] In Africa, France rejected the Italian demand for Djibouti. This left the greatest burden of Italian colonial compensations on Britain, as in the 1916 colonial talks. In Rodd's words, 'it looked as if we alone were to make any substantial concessions to Italy'.[218] Milner opposed it with a letter to Lloyd George on 16 May, in which he stressed 'the seriousness of giving away all, or almost all, Italians ask of us in Africa'. Jubaland could

[209] Lloyd George, *The Truth*, II, pp. 868–869.
[210] Malagodi, *Conversazioni*, II, pp. 653–685.
[211] G. Caccamo, 'Esserci a qualsiasi costo', p. 187.
[212] Goldstein, *Winning the Peace*, p. 270; Crespi, *Alla difesa*, pp. 562–579, 615–626.
[213] Lloyd George, *The Truth*, p. 897.   [214] MacMillan, *Peacemakers*, p. 446.
[215] G. Caccamo, 'Esserci a qualsiasi costo', p. 185.
[216] Quoted in MacMillan, *Peacemakers*, p. 447.
[217] See: G. Cecini, *Il Corpo di Spedizione italiano in Anatolia (1919–1922)* (Rome: USSME, 2010).
[218] Rodd, *Memories*, p. 373.

reluctantly be ceded to Italy, but Lloyd George should oppose strenuously giving British Somaliland and any Abyssinian protectorate:

One has only got to look at the map to see how serious the setting up of an Italian Empire, half as big as British India, in the north-eastern corner of Africa, would be. It would cut right into the heart of that great sphere of British influence extending from the centre of East Africa through the Sudan, Egypt, Arabia and the Persian Gulf to India.[219]

All Italy received were small slices from French Algeria plus Jubaland – which nonetheless took up to 1924–1925 to be implemented.[220] As for the pending Adriatic question, a series of Allied meetings produced little but bad feelings.[221] Orlando curtailed his demands, allowing Fiume to be a free city under Italian administration, and promised to finance a second port and a railway for the Yugoslavs to connect the city with Dalmatia – which would largely be granted to the SCS Kingdom. Wilson vetoed his proposal, insisting on his Wilson line.[222] In turn, the Italians rejected repeated proposals by Leeper and André Tardieu, Clemenceau's lieutenant.[223] House was resigned: 'It is perfectly hopeless to get Sonnino into anything progressive or constructive'.[224] And Orlando, said Lloyd George, was 'gentler, but equally fanatical'.[225] Wilson threatened to send an American battleship to Fiume.[226] Orlando made a final and desperate move. He appealed to British friendship through two personal letters to Lloyd George dated 25 May and 3 June. In Italy, he wrote, the impression was rising 'that its position is that of a conquered rather than of a victorious nation'; he restated that he was 'desirous of finding a compromise'; and asked Lloyd George to intervene personally and with greater energy.[227] In Sonnino's view, it was a mistake, for it gave Lloyd George the chance 'to openly side with Wilson in condemning all our exigencies based on the London Treaty, which significantly worsened our situation'.[228] The British premier cordially but firmly rejected Orlando's appeal, claiming that 'frontiers should be drawn, to the utmost extent practicable, in accordance with ethnic majorities'.[229] Orlando went as far as begging Lloyd George in person: 'I must have a solution.

---

[219] Lloyd George, *The Truth*, II, pp. 898–900.

[220] Del Boca, *Italiani in Libia*, II, pp. 12–13; Imperiali, *Diario*, p. 693.

[221] MacMillan, *Peacemakers*, p. 305.   [222] Sonnino, *Diario*, III, pp. 333–334.

[223] See Hankey's report in J. V. Fuller ed., *Papers relating to the Foreign Relations of the United States. The Paris Peace Conference*, 12 vols. (Washington: US Government Printing Office, 1942–1947), VI, pp. 78–81, 89–92, pp. 78–81, 89–92; Goldstein, *Winning the Peace*, pp. 267–269.

[224] Thompson, *White War*, pp. 336–341.   [225] Lloyd George, *The Truth*, II, p. 785.

[226] MacMillan, *Peacemakers*, p. 440.

[227] Full text in Orlando, *Memorie*, pp. 534–540; Lloyd George, *The Truth*, II, pp. 882–888.

[228] Sonnino, *Diario*, III, p. 337.   [229] Lloyd George, *The Truth*, II, pp. 890–891.

Otherwise I will have a crisis in parliament or in the streets in Italy'. Lloyd George asked: 'And if not, who do you see taking your place?' Orlando replied: 'Perhaps D'Annunzio'.[230]

On 3 June the British premier thought he had found a solution for his Italian colleague. It would not come in the Adriatic but in the Black Sea. The British had fifteen battalions in the Caucasus since November 1918, but the local population was mounting a stiff opposition to foreign presence, and now those British forces were needed in Egypt. Initially, Smuts had considered trading the Caucasus with further Middle Eastern territories from the French, but Clemenceau had insisted on getting Syria, so Lloyd George now proposed the Caucasus to Italy as a compensation for Italian territorial sacrifices elsewhere. The British even promised to provide the ships necessary to transport an Italian expeditionary force.[231] Orlando and Sonnino seemed enthusiastic to gain a vast – albeit unknown to most Italians – territory rich in oil and mines, and ordered the 32,000-strong 12th Italian corps to get prepared to leave from Taranto at the end of the month.[232] A couple of weeks later, however, the British informed their younger ally that the Royal Navy no longer had vessels available for the transportation, and the final dream of the Orlando Government was aborted.[233]

Unsurprisingly, Orlando eventually fell on 23 June. It was down to the rest of the delegation to sign the Treaty of Versailles on Italy's behalf on 28 June, after which both Wilson and Lloyd George left, and Allied delegations kept gathering at the various *châteaux* around Paris – St Germain, Neuilly, Triannon and Sèvres – to formalise agreements with the other defeated states.[234] In the end, Britain stood up best among the victors, at least on paper. The United States emerged from the war as the world's new economic superpower, but the Senate declined to ratify the Versailles Treaty; the League of Nations was especially indigestible to the Republican majority in the Senate, and this introduced a new period of American isolationism.[235] France obtained its irredenta and extended its colonial possessions, though it did not accomplish Clemenceau's goal of totally crushing Germany – Paris received from Berlin financial reparations inferior to those it had paid Germany after the Franco-Prussian War of 1870–1871.[236] Britain was triumphant in its *divide et impera* strategy, re-establishing the European balance of power and safeguarding its maritime and Mediterranean interests. It had not only defended, but

---

[230] Quoted in MacMillan, *Peacemakers*, p. 311.
[231] C. Seton-Watson, *Storia d'Italia*, p. 612.   [232] Crespi, *Alla difesa*, pp. 627–632, 682.
[233] G. Caccamo, 'Esserci a qualsiasi costo', p. 214.
[234] Goldstein, *Winning the Peace*, p. 277; MacMillan, *Peacemakers*, p. 311.
[235] Smith, *Sovereignty*, p. 224.   [236] MacMillan, *Peacemakers*, p. 490.

significantly expanded its Empire – and was even ready to replace the United States as the arbitrator of the League of Nations.[237] British efforts overseas during the war and the accuracy of British peace preparations had proven decisive. The undercurrent of a desire for independence that was to bring the Empire to an end would emerge in a few years. For the moment, Britain appeared as the unchallenged European superpower once again.

By contrast, Italy's mirage of imperial apogee lay in tatters. Italy was granted Tyrol up to the Brenner, and the Austrian littoral (Gorizia, Gradisca and the March of Istria); it got a permanent seat on the League of Nations Council and a share in German reparations.[238] But it lost most of Anatolia and of its colonial demands, Fiume and the greatest part of Dalmatia:[239] 'In October 1918, D'Annunzio had told the public that Italy's victory must not be "mutilated", in December, Revel had warned of the possibility that it would be, and now Orlando and Sonnino told the Italians that it had been'.[240] Sonnino regretted having trusted the Allies in the first place. 'For my part, I see my death in all this – I mean my moral death. I have ruined my country whilst believing that I was doing my duty'.[241] Orlando held little doubt that Britain was gravely responsible. It was chiefly Wilson who crushed Italian Adriatic ambitions, but it was the British and the French that denied the bulk of Italian colonial aspirations. And, more importantly, the Entente Allies had dropped Italian promises despite repeated assurances. Orlando expected above all Britain to rein in the United States; instead, 'no one opposed [Wilson], not even Lloyd George!' The British premier gave Orlando personal, but not political support. At Versailles, the Italian Prime Minister blamed a joint 'Anglo-Saxon' (not just American) veto.[242] Though he never denied Orlando and Sonnino's clumsiness, Imperiali shared with Orlando one point: 'Lloyd George could have and should have done much more, taking before Wilson an attitude more distinctly favourable to us'.[243] Lloyd George himself admitted: 'Italy would know quite well that if we really pressed her claims they would be obtained'.[244] He at times acted as a mediator, but only where Italian interests did not collide with the British – given that the latter where global, this meant rarely. After all, Lloyd George never revised his conviction that Italy did

[237] Imperiali, *Diario*, p. 723.
[238] C. Sforza, *Contemporary Italy: Its Intellectual and Moral Origins* (New York: Dutton, 1944), p. 187.
[239] Sonnino, *Diario*, III, p. 337.   [240] Gooch, *Italian Army*, p. 310.
[241] Quoted in MacMillan, *Peacemakers*, p. 306.
[242] Orlando, *Memorie*, pp. 355–358, 399, 431.   [243] Imperiali, *Diario*, p. 706.
[244] Lloyd George, *The Truth*, II, p. 800.

not deserve more. He commented on 26 June: 'I went through the entire war, and, unfortunately, I always saw Italy trying to do as little as possible. France, England – and the United States, when she joined us later – threw themselves into the battle without reserve. . . . Italy always carefully measured what she gave'.[245] Of course, in Italian eyes both France and Britain had abandoned Italy; but where one need not have been 'surprised' by French opposition, British sell-out shocked Italian policymakers: 'What about the famous Anglo-Italian relations?' Imperiali wondered. 'I fear that all my work to strengthen them will go awry. Sad! But these English gentlemen will regret it, and I hope to see the day when we can pay them back in their own coin'.[246]

The same feeling was running through the Italian public. 'They are, I am sorry to say, very sore and depressed here', Rodd wrote to a friend,[247] and so was Rodd himself, convinced that London had made a mistake in alienating Italy's friendship. Even Tyrrell acknowledged that 'the word of England so far was considered sacred; I fear it will not be equally so in the future' – at least in Italy.[248] Lloyd George realised that 'Italian public opinion regarded Great Britain as more hostile than she really was'. British officers were 'insulted in the streets of Italian cities, and the feeling was running strong against us'.[249] Italian nationalists, of course, made much of Italy's diplomatic defeat, blaming both Italian weak and inept politicians and Italy's allies. They called the new international order – and its guardian, the League of Nations – 'an imposition by the United States, England and France onto *gentes minores*'.[250] Inflated by the slogan of the 'mutilated victory', the Italian public considered the treatment of Italy by its western allies, and more specifically Britain, the supposed guarantor of Italian promises, a betrayal that, someday, would need to be avenged.

---

[245] Quoted in Burgwyn, *The Legend*, p. 233.   [246] Imperiali, *Diario*, p. 609, 632.
[247] Quoted in MacMillan, *Peacemakers*, p. 311.   [248] Imperiali, *Diario*, pp. 681, 684.
[249] Lloyd George, *The Truth*, II, p. 860.
[250] Hautecoeur, *Le ministère Orlando*, pp. 194, 231–245.

Epilogue: Bloody Christmas in Fiume

After the signing of the German Treaty, interest in the Peace Conference in international public opinion began to wane, and many governments shifted focus to post-war economic and social needs and demobilisation problems.[1] But not in Italy. The newly appointed Prime Minister was Nitti, who chose Tittoni as Foreign Minister. They had to cope with an increasingly desperate domestic situation. The United States was holding up a badly needed credit of $25 million[2] and increasing discontent in the Italian peasantry – largely caused by unfulfilled promises of land re-distribution – threatened the very institutional structures of the nation.[3] Nitti also realised that the cost of Italy's imperialist footing was becoming unbearable. Italy still had 54,000 men in Albania, 24,000 in Dalmatia, 4,000 in the Dodecanese, 40,000 in Macedonia, 10,000 in Asia Minor, 500 in Palestine, 35,000 in Libya, 1,000 in Eritrea, 10,000 in the Rhineland and small contingents in Silesia, Bulgaria, Austria, on the Barents Sea, in Siberia and at Murmansk.[4] It was a financial black hole that Rome could not afford. Nitti first cancelled the Caucasus operation, which Italy had for some time tried to carry out independently, then withdrew the Italian contingent from Russia; then he moved to Paris to negotiate what revision he could of Adriatic terms before the signing of the Austrian Treaty at St Germain.[5]

He never stood a chance. In Paris, Nitti was given an Anglo-French memorandum prepared by Balfour – who now managed what remained of the British delegation – which finally and formally rejected the London Treaty. It was 'a brutal blow' that significantly worsened Italy's diplomatic

---

[1] Goldstein, *Winning the Peace*, p. 277.   [2] MacMillan, *Peacemakers*, p. 310.
[3] Rumi, *Alle origini*, p. 6.
[4] Gooch, *Italian Army*, p. 313; Pupo, 'Premessa', in Pupo ed., *Vittoria senza pace*, pp. VIII–IX. On Nitti's foreign policy see Micheletta, *Italia e Gran Bretagna*, I, pp. 15 ff. and L. Monzali, "La politica estera italiana nel primo dopoguerra 1918–1922. Sfide e problemi", *Italia Contemporanea*, 256–257, September-December 2009.
[5] G. Caccamo, 'Esserci a qualsiasi costo', pp. 214–222; Pupo, 'Considerazioni e confronti', in Pupo ed., *Vittoria senza pace*, pp. 224 ff.

stance.[6] Tittoni tried to look for bilateral arrangements that bypassed Allied refusals. In July he signed the Tittoni-Venizelos agreement for the partition of Albania and the settlement of the Dodecanese – to be returned to Greece except for Rhodes.[7] Then he tried to secure a better Adriatic settlement. He ran into a new Wilsonian veto, but he opened a bilateral channel with the Yugoslavs that was much appreciated by both the British and the French, anxious to formalise the Austrian Treaty. When the St Germain Treaty was signed on 10 September, it was agreed that the contested territories, including Fiume, Zara and many Adriatic islands were excluded from it and considered separately between Italy and Yugoslavia. Nitti hoped he had gained some respite to face Italy's huge socio-economic emergency,[8] but he was misled. When news came that the Austrian Treaty had not granted any of the contested territories, few in Italy cared about the clause on future bilateral talks and popular passions reached new heights. On 12 September D'Annunzio marched into Fiume with a legion of volunteers claiming the city for Italy. Men from the 1st *Arditi* division, ordered to stop D'Annunzio, joined forces with him instead, and so did Host Venturi's men and many demobilised soldiers and sailors over the following weeks.[9] 'It's an act of revolt against the Allies!' rejoiced Mussolini.[10]

This came as a shock both in London and in Rome. 'We are now really out of the London Treaty', regretted Imperiali, who called D'Annunzio 'flagellum of God'. *The Times*, *Daily Chronicle*, *Daily News*, and *Manchester Guardian* unanimously condemned D'Annunzio's actions and foresaw 'possible conflicts' between Italian volunteers and the Allied garrison in Fiume, which for now had prudently withdrawn.[11] Rodd was ordered to protest D'Annunzio's coup vehemently, yet he was surprised 'that my own countrymen, who have generally a weakness of a great adventure, were not more indulgent in appraising the bold defiance of authority which made the poet for a time the uncrowned king of Fiume'. Rodd acknowledged D'Annunzio had 'overstepped the limits of moderation in denouncing the Allies individually and collectively', but confessed that 'I could not help feeling a certain romantic sympathy [for him]'. It may not come as a surprise that Rodd was

---

[6] DBFP, 1st series, vol. IV, pp. 2–6; Crespi, *Alla difesa*, pp. 683–685.
[7] Burgwyn, *Italian Foreign Policy in the Interwar Period: 1918–1940* (Westport: Praeger, 1997), p. 15.
[8] Malagodi, *Conversazioni*, II, p. 715; G. Giurati, *Con D'Annunzio e Millo in difesa dell'Adriatico* (Florence: Sansoni, 1954), p. 131.
[9] D'Annunzio found himself in command of some 8,000 men and 4 ships: Gooch, *Italian Army*, p. 315.
[10] Mussolini, 'La stolta vociferazione', *Il Popolo d'Italia*, 29 September 1919; Rumi, *Alle origini*, p. 50.
[11] Imperiali, *Diario*, pp. 688, 728.

encouraged by Curzon to leave the embassy in October and was transferred to Egypt. A strongly pro-Italian diplomat was the last thing the Foreign Office wanted to deal with the crisis. Rodd left Rome after eleven years, saddened by his progressive eclipsing, further revealed by the minimal attention devoted to him in the British press: 'If I had ever been disposed to overestimate the result of my activities ... a corrective would have been supplied by the two or three bald lines in the English Press which were the only comment on our departure after an exceptionally long and strenuous term of office'.[12] Buchanan, former British ambassador to Russia, replaced him unhappily. For the new ambassador, Rome was a second-rate destination after his long diplomatic career.[13] It was indicative of Italy's standing amongst the great powers.

While the United States seemed ready to dislodge D'Annunzio by sheer force,[14] the British sent reinforcements to the Adriatic, but for now informed Rome that they would not intervene militarily; London nonetheless required Nitti to take a firm action.[15] In early October Hardinge blamed Italy for its dithering and intimated to 'end the anomalous situation created by D'annunzio's action, a situation that cannot be tolerated long. The calm so far kept by the British Government should in no way be interpreted as acquiescence'.[16] Imperiali, increasingly 'annoyed' by British critiques, replied that such 'threatening' language might be used with 'a Balkan representative', but was unacceptable if destined to 'the ambassador of the King of Italy'.[17] Rome and its allies were on the brink of a military confrontation. Yet Nitti hesitated. He told the Chamber: 'For the first time, albeit for idealistic aims, sedition has penetrated the army'.[18] Not only Italian soldiers, but – perhaps more significantly – Italian military authorities were largely sympathetic to D'Annunzio, including Aosta, Giardino and Badoglio, who was made extraordinary commissioner for Venezia-Giulia and given full authority in the region. The Italian regular forces limited themselves on establishing a rather relaxed blockade of Fiume.[19]

---

[12] Balfour signified Rodd his appreciation for the ambassadors' service privately: Rodd, *Memories*, pp. 385–388.

[13] See: H. Rappaport, *Petrograd 1917. Caught in the Revolution* (London: Windmill, 2017); G. Buchanan, *My mission to Russia and other diplomatic memories* (London & New York: Cassell, 1923).

[14] DDI, 6, IV, doc. 493, President Wilson to Nitti, 24 September 1919; doc. 526, De Martino to Tittoni, 1 October 1919.

[15] C. Seton-Watson, *Storia d'Italia*, p. 618.

[16] DDI, 6, IV, doc. 539, Imperiali to Tittoni, 4 October 1919; doc. 551, Tittoni to De Martino and Scialoja, 6 October 1919; doc. 553, Tittoni to Imperiali, 6 October 1919.

[17] Ibid., doc. 576, Imperiali to Tittoni, 8 October 1919; Imperiali, *Diario*, p. 692.

[18] Gooch, *Italian Army*, p. 317.

[19] DDI, 6, IV, doc. 517, Nitti to Badoglio, 30 September 1919.

Thus commenced D'Annunzio's occupation of the city – which the poet renamed the Italian Regency of Quarnaro – that was to last fifteen months. Non-Italian historians generally referred to it as a 'comic opera occupation'[20] and 'a mad carnival of ceremonies, spectacles, balls and parties'.[21] It was much more than that; D'Annunzio promoted a new socio-political order based on his Charter of the Quarnaro – entrusted to union official Alceste De Ambris and based on *sindacalismo rivoluzionario* (revolutionary unionism). It would influence fascist social policies for decades to come.[22] D'Annunzio's enterprise also exposed the growing weakness of Liberal Italy's institutions. Unrestrained, the poet kept delegitimising publicly the 'anti-Italian Government of Nitti', encouraging Italians to overthrow it, while he expanded his paramilitary organisations. Nitti tried to strengthen his own position through national elections, held on 16 November 1919. He was disappointed, as the result was a triumph for the Socialist and Popular parties and a retreat of the moderate reformists; the sole good news for Nitti was Mussolini's defeat: overshadowed by D'Annunzio, the fascist leader failed to win a single seat in parliament. All over Italy, the *biennio rosso* (red biennium) started, intensified by demands for social and economic reforms, land seizures by the peasantry and the war veterans and widespread turmoil: 'Revolutionary Italy is born!' proclaimed the *Avanti!* In Nitti's eyes, this confirmed that Italy's problems were primarily socio-economic, and reinforced his desire to appease the Allies over Fiume in exchange for economic benefits. Re-appointed Prime Minister, Nitti proposed to D'Annunzio a series of compromises that rectified the Italo-Yugoslav border in Italy's favour, but none of which included an annexation of Fiume to Italy – it was useless, Nitti thought, 'to fight for possession of a backyard when the house was burning'. All attempts failed, in part for D'Annunzio's lack of cooperation, in part for further Yugoslav and American refusals.[23]

D'Annunzio was living proof of the Government's inability to bring home any solution in foreign as much as in domestic policy. 'There you have a country', Clemenceau told Lloyd George, 'where the king counts for nothing, where the army does not obey orders, while you have 180 socialists on one side, and 120 men belonging to the Pope on the other!'[24] As months passed, the Fiume affair, far from re-establishing Italy's good

---

[20] Goldstein, *Winning the Peace*, p. 266.   [21] MacMillan, *Peacemakers*, p. 312.

[22] See: L. Castellani, 'L'impresa di Fiume', *Storia illustrata*, XXII, 142, 1969; G. B. Guerri, *D'Annunzio* (Milan: Mondadori, 2008).

[23] Raul 'Attorno all'Adriatico', p. 119; C. Seton-Watson, *Storia d'Italia*, pp. 616–619, 626–646; Rumi, *Alle origini*, p. 44.

[24] Quoted in MacMillan *Peacemakers*, p. 313.

relations with its allies, stimulated further conflict, with Britain once again urged by Italy to intercede for it – and being blamed for failing to do so. Imperiali noted that British irritation was producing delays in the implementation of the colonial agreements – in late November it was unilaterally postponed by the British '*sine die*'.[25] Nitti was concerned by 'the outlook of the Allies'.[26] He appealed to Lloyd George for a diplomatic intervention that smoothed American and Yugoslav resistance. But British public opinion was unanimously against Italy: *The Times*, the *Pall Mall* and even 'the papers closer to Italy' like *Daily Telegraph*, *Globe* and *Westminster Gazette* called for the despatch of British warships to crush D'Annunzio.[27] The Italian nationalist press responded bellicosely. The *Popolo* kept denouncing 'British greedy economic speculation', and threatening Allied colonial interests;[28] but it also blasted Italian institutions, evoking their subversion.[29] Nitti wrote to Imperiali: 'The domestic situation created ... by Allied attitude in the Fiume question is becoming more and more dangerous, and steals from the Government complete control of the army. ... The Italians feel deeply humiliated'.[30] Imperiali could not believe that Lloyd George could be 'blind to the point of alienating forever Italy's friendship with England. It would be an act of folly'.[31] He told Hardinge, 'We expected something very different from England'.[32] Foreign threats made Nitti's position precarious when he was facing mounting opposition in his Government by the Populars, over Nitti's agrarian reform. The Cabinet fell on 20 April 1920. In May Nitti formed another Government, but the magmatic political arena brought him down for the last time on 15 June 1920. Italian reformists were in disarray, and the leading Italian communist Antonio Gramsci prophesied that the Italian Kerensky had fallen, and now it was the time for an Italian Lenin.[33]

For a few months, Giolitti seemed capable of preventing an institutional collapse. He assembled a Government of a gamut of socialist democrats, radicals, liberals and populars, which refused to repress social turmoil and strikes, trying to contain them with the minimal violence

[25] G. Caccamo, 'Esserci a qualsiasi costo', p. 193; DDI, 6, IV, doc. 657, Tittoni to Imperiali, 25 October 1919; doc. 690, Imperiali to Tittoni, 29 October 1919.

[26] Ibid., doc. 668, Nitti to Tittoni, 26 October 1919.

[27] Imperiali, *Diario*, pp. 714–715.

[28] N. Bonservizi, 'Aspetti della questione turca', *Il Popolo d'Italia*, 14 February 1920; 'L'Italia e l'Egitto', *Il Popolo d'Italia*, 1 February 1920.

[29] Mussolini, 'Navigare necesse', *Il Popolo d'Italia*, 1 January 1920; 'L'Ora e gli orologi', 6 April 1920.

[30] DDI, 6, IV, doc. 681, Nitti to Imperiali, 27 October 1919.

[31] Imperiali, *Diario*, p. 728.

[32] DDI, 6, IV, doc. 631, Imperiali to Tittoni, 21 October 1919.

[33] Alatri, *Nitti*, pp. 472–473; Rumi, *Alle origini*, p. 43.

possible. Giolitti did not realise that Italian nationalists could take advantage of the light-footed Government in defence of the bourgeoisie. He fuelled fascist propaganda with further withdrawals in foreign policy. Facing an Albanian rebellion against the Italian occupation, Giolitti broke the Tittoni-Venizelos agreement and supported the country's independence, confident that a friendly Albania would serve Italian interests better than an occupied Albania in all-out revolt.[34] Giolitti then turned to Fiume. On 12 November, he signed a bilateral agreement with the Yugoslavs at Rapallo, which granted Italy the Mount Nevoso border, Zara and four Dalmatian islands – Cherso, Lussino, Cazza and Lagosta. Fiume was made a free city.[35]

Italian nationalists arose in revolt.[36] A first coup to overthrow Giolitti, involving Rocco and Corradini with the complicity of part of the Italian business sector, D'Annunzio and Mussolini, had been foiled in October.[37] Now D'Annunzio sent De Ambris to meet Mussolini in Trieste and discuss a joint march of Fiume legionaries and Mussolini's fascists to Rome. But Mussolini was little interested in further compromising himself with D'Annunzio[38] whose fate was now in Giolitti's hands. The Italian premier was under renewed pressure from the Allies to end what Washington termed 'the Fiume nightmare'[39] – and, Buchanan repeated, 'We all obey America, unfortunately'.[40] Progressively abandoned by his legionaries, D'Annunzio was dislodged from Fiume by Italian regular forces under Caviglia in the 'Bloody Christmas' actions from 24 to 30 December 1920, which led to fifty-three dead.[41] Abroad it seemed that Italy 'at last had a Government worth the name'.[42] In Italy many saw the outcome as merely additional confirmation of Italy's devaluation – a symbolic surrender of Italian aspirations. Shortly after D'Annunzio's defeat, Imperiali left the embassy in London on a mournful note. Looking back on his own work, he concluded that Italy had been reduced from a victor nation to a second-rate power.[43] In the margin of his *Ricordi e appunti* in 1937, Imperiali noted that he felt he should 'significantly amend', for the better, his opinion of Orlando and

---

[34] Giolitti, *Memorie*, II, pp. 569–571.   [35] Lloyd George, *The Truth*, II, pp. 896–897.

[36] Yugoslav nationalists protested just as much: C. Seton-Watson, *Storia d'Italia*, pp. 663–664.

[37] E. Fonzo, *Storia dell'Associazione nazionalista italiana (1910–1923)* (Naples: Ed. Scientifiche, 2017), pp. 228–253.

[38] See: U. Foscanelli, *Gabriele d'Annunzio e l'ora sociale* (Milan: Carnaro, 1952).

[39] DDI, 6, IV, doc. 604, Macchi di Cellere to Lansing, 15 October 1919.

[40] Ibid., doc. 666, Sforza to Tittoni, 26 October 1919.

[41] Pupo, 'Attorno all'Adriatico', p. 119; D. Massagrande, *Italia e Fiume 1921–1924: dal 'Natale di sangue' all'annessione* (Milan: Ed. Cisalpino-Goliardica, 1982).

[42] C. Seton-Watson, *Storia d'Italia*, p. 665.   [43] Imperiali, *Diario*, p. 654.

Sonnino and of their actions, performed 'in good faith' at Versailles.[44] It was likely a self-absolution too. Imperiali attempted to defend the wider political and diplomatic elite of Liberal Italy, which had been made the scapegoat of fascist blame for having lost at the peace table what had been won on the battlefield. Such legend nosed up during the Fiume affair and after the loss of the city.[45] Italian nationalists and fascists cried that Giolitti had sold out Italy's sovereignty to the capitalists, surrendering to a plot of 'the great international economic interests against the legitimate Italian aspirations', giving up 'national dignity' and turning Italy into 'a protectorate of transatlantic bankers'.[46] They denounced the encirclement of Italy by France and Yugoslavia, Italy's 'bondage' to Britain, and used the 'mutilated victory' as a political manifesto to refute the rule of law and attack the crumbling Italian liberal institutions.[47] Fascist sections, which totalled 30 with 870 subscriptions, on 31 December 1919, increased to 88 sections with 20,600 subscriptions one year later, and to 834 sections with 249,000 members by 31 December 1921.[48]

Giolitti resigned in March 1921, leaving the country in the throes of political instability. The Italian gates were wide open for the fascist flood. D'Annunzio's occupation of Fiume – the first major breach in legality in Italy's public life after the war – provided a model for Mussolini but also taught him a lesson. Next time, unlike D'Annunzio, he would go not for a peripheral city, but for the grand prize – Rome.

---

[44] Imperiali later served as Italy's representative at the League of Nations between 1921 and 1922. He resigned after Mussolini's seizure of power in October 1922: Imperiali, *Ricordi e appunti sulla mia partecipazione alla conferenza di Parigi, maggio-luglio 1919*, Appendix of *Diario*, pp. 565 ff.

[45] Mussolini would annex the city in January 1924: MacMillan, *Peacemakers*, p. 313.

[46] *Il popolo d'Italia*, quoted in Rumi, *Alle origini*, p. 49.

[47] C. Seton-Watson, *Storia d'Italia*, pp. 613, 687; G. Sabbatucci, 'La vittoria mutilata', in G. Belardelli, L. Cafagna, E. Galli della Loggia, G. Sabbatucci eds., *Miti e storia dell'Italia unita* (Bologna: Il Mulino, 1999), pp. 101–106.

[48] R. De Felice, *Mussolini il rivoluzionario, 1883–1920* (Turin: Einaudi, 1965), pp. 595–607.

Conclusions

Anglo-Italian relations played a major role in shaping how Britain and Italy participated in World War I. This book reconstructed how the idea of a 'special partnership' between the two countries came to fruition in Italian and, to a lesser degree, British elites. This was a largely artificial concept based on history and cultural heritage, and was not complemented by a deeper mutual understanding, as revealed by the persistent stereotypes that characterised the perception the two peoples had of each other and that marred their relations, especially in British eyes. Italy was the most solicitous in emphasising Anglo-Italian traditional friendship because it needed a stronger partner to deter its European competitors, whereas Britain was more interested in ensuring the European balance of power and safeguarding its imperial interests. In London, Italy was widely considered a greedy and Machiavellian partner and indulged only as long as it did not challenge those premises. Developments in the war and at the Peace Conference showed that Anglo-Italian friendship was in fact a weaker bond than Italy (and the few Italian sympathisers in Britain) had hoped.

Both countries had expectations of their partnership that were not fulfilled because Britain and Italy had incompatible approaches to war aims, war strategy and peace-making. Britain fought to defend its empire and world supremacy against both enemies and allies, and thought Italy could be a counter-weight to France and Russia; Italy fought to forge its own empire, in emulation of the glorious tradition of ancient Rome, and sought Britain as the guarantor of its empire project as provided for under the London and St Jean de Maurienne agreements. In a nutshell, for Britain it was a strategy of imperial defence through coalition, while for Italy it was a strategy of imperial expansion through diplomacy. Not only were Britain and Italy motivated by differing aspirations when they entered the conflict, but, as the war progressed, their war aims grew more antithetical. Italy's claims increased to the point of challenging

Britain's interests in key areas of its Empire, whereas Britain embraced a concept of strategic defence that encompassed territorial annexations – not initially envisaged – as guarantees of imperial security. A bitter confrontation at the peace table was therefore inevitable.

Such confrontation occurred after war developments had strained the bilateral relation. In terms of war strategies, Anglo-Italian collaboration was crippled by their divergent priorities: Britain saw Germany as its main enemy, whereas Italy had Austria-Hungary as its main opponent. This made a coherent Allied grand strategy very difficult. Britain's expectation of Italy was that it would deliver the decisive blow to the enemy coalition; Italy considered Britain its main naval, financial and commercial partner. So a 'special connection' between the two countries did exist, but more than a 'special partnership' in the diplomatic and political spheres (which implies mutual synergy) it seems to have been a 'special dependence' of Italy on Britain. London was frustrated at having to sustain massively Rome's war effort in addition to those of the other Allies, especially after Italy's intervention had failed to bring about the war's end. The problem, of course, was that Italy could never have matched such expectation. Knock-out blows simply did not happen in World War I – until Vittorio Veneto. They had not worked in the operational scenarios of 1914, neither west, nor east, nor south, and there was nothing to suggest they would work in the Alps in 1915. This does not mean that Italy could not have done better than it did. It certainly could have – as could have all other belligerents. The geographic features of Italy's war, both on land and at sea, however, made a decisive outcome even less realistic than elsewhere. In this sense, British frustration originated in British miscalculations as much as in Italian fiascos. As John Whittam pointed out: 'A strategy which stands or falls on the success of third parties without an intrinsic chance of success is a poor strategy'.[1] But from the British perspective, Italy's failures to declare war on Turkey and Germany, or at least to break Austria-Hungary indicated only one thing: Italy was neither a worthy ally nor a great power. This has stimulated a view that 'on military strategy', the Italians were 'responding to their own interests and worried only about the Habsburg Empire', which made Italy's alignment with the Entente 'a *mésalliance*'.[2]

Such a view needs to be qualified. In the first place, it ignores the huge efforts made by Britain when, resigned to the prospect of a longer war, it used its influence on Italy to better integrate Rome's war into the

---

[1] Whittam, 'War and Italian society, 1914–1916', in B. Bond, I. Roy eds., *War and Society* (London: Routledge, 1975), pp. 152–154.
[2] Burgwyn, *The Legend*, pp. 2, 90, 182; Riccardi, *Alleati*, pp. 599 ff.

Entente's war, taking it beyond the national dimension of Italy's 'fourth war of independence' against Vienna. Results were slow, yet in August 1916, Italy was eventually committed to the world war and involved in the Allied blockade of the Central Powers, and after St Jean de Maurienne, the Allies seemed to have cleared their pending colonial issues and to be more united. It proved insufficient to establish a consistent Allied grand strategy however, despite British persistence. Why?

In part, this was indeed the consequence of Italian refractoriness – as evidenced by Italy's persistently self-reliant trade policy handicapping the blockade. At the same time however, Italy's insistence that there was no substitute for complete victory provides a clear example of loyalty and steadfastness to the Alliance. There were other causes for Allied strategic failures that have been less explored. One pertained to the peculiar way in which strategy was managed in the Entente. Italy's failure to be accepted as Britain's main partner left Anglo-French intimate military collaboration on the western front, and later Anglo-American political alignment as key drivers of Allied strategy. But in many questions – such as Balkan, colonial and Mediterranean issues – the Allies did not form permanent blocs within the Entente. They talked more one on one, and often ganged up in twos against a third. This was a consequence of inter-Allied competition: bilateral arrangements were formed ad hoc to prevent each party from becoming predominant in a given theatre. So the idea of the three original members confronting Italy *en bloc* is incorrect. The Entente did not work that way. Instead, it grasped for a strategy whilst at the same time trying to keep a relative internal balance of power. This reveals the importance of bilateral collaborations, but also their volatility, for two partners could be mutually supporting on one issue and in opposition on another. In such circumstances, Britain acted as a leader-mediator in the Entente, trying to coordinate Allied war efforts while at the same time stirring competition amongst the other allies to prevent them from conspiring against London.[3] It was a contradictory policy that hampered Allied collaboration as much as Italy's narrow focus on its own front. Thus, coordination between the Allies was almost nil until 1918. The Allies managed to agree only on minor issues – for example, the synchronisation of land offensives.

Another reason for the persisting Allied strategic frustrations was the reality gap. Allied efforts were often nullified by insurmountable odds on the ground. This was especially true for Italy. In fact, the Italian army's efforts on the Isonzo might well have spurred greater respect, had its

---

[3] Goldstein, *Winning the Peace*, p. 164.

meagre resources been compared with those available on the western front.[4] The performance of the Italian navy too, despite inevitable mistakes and chronic shortages of raw materials, successfully matched the challenges of modern naval warfare. The long-lasting effectiveness of MAS and manned torpedo tactics demonstrated the excellence that the *Regia Marina* was capable of achieving. No doubt, it was up to the Italians to show their worth to their allies. It was an Italian responsibility to promote Italy's war, detail its peculiarities, emphasise its sacrifices and parade its achievements. That was never done in any coherent and systematic way until it was too late – as Macchi di Cellere confessed, 'Italy has no propaganda of her own; she is too old a country and too proud a race'.[5] Thus, although Rome's partial collaboration over strategy was often caused by material difficulties and domestic problems – as opposed to a perceived limited Italian commitment to the Entente or Italian cowardice – Italy failed to dispel the traditional, malign stereotypes it was saddled with, even when they were unfounded or badly exaggerated. On the other hand, the Italians too complained that Britain was not pulling its full weight in the war and was trying to exploit Italian resources to its own benefit. These accusations, which were shared by the French,[6] were equally unfair.

Allied coordination improved after Caporetto and throughout 1918. Initially this was made possible by the British ability to control Italian strategy indirectly – the inevitable result when an asymmetrical alliance is made even more asymmetrical by war events. Britain did so by subordinating British reinforcements and supplies, to the replacement of Cadorna with a more accommodating Commander-in-Chief of the Italian army, Diaz, and later influencing the latter's strategy by setting conditions for the use of British troops in the field. It was in this way, taking advantage of its minor ally's hindrance that Lloyd George managed to speed up Entente integration. Caporetto also changed Britain's objectives for its bilateral relations with Italy. Earlier on, London aimed to expand Italy's participation to the war, whereas now it needed to keep Italy in the war. For Italy, on the other hand, Caporetto signalled an abrupt shift from an offensive war to a war for survival and British financial, commercial and military support proved crucial in restoring Italian forces and morale. The Italian front became one of the decisive theatres of the conflict, but despite its unexpected resurrection, Italy never managed to recover from its breakdown in reputation and political weight. Furthermore, greater integration did not completely remove inter-Allied conflicts,

[4] Gooch, *Italian Army*, p. 4.   [5] Quoted in MacMillan, *Peacemakers*, p. 297.
[6] French, *Strategy of Lloyd George*, p. 291.

which became more acute as the end of the war approached.[7] Recurring differences on Italy's commitment to the Entente's war, diverging strategic priorities, lack of mutual understanding, and disappointing Italian military performance left the British and French 'with fewer scruples about breaking the territorial promises included in the Treaty of London'.[8] By contrast, Britain felt that it should indulge the bulk of French claims in Europe because France had made 'very great sacrifices'.[9]

Other official reasons for the rejection by the Peace Conference of many promises previously made to Italy, were the 'increased size' and the 'extravagant nature' of Italian claims, and unreasonable opposition to any compromise. This volume disclosed the limits of such vulgate, offering a different reading of Italy's diplomatic strategy and suggesting that geopolitical competition was at the root of Versailles' outcome – especially between Britain and Italy. The key to appreciating this is to look at the final problem that ruined Anglo-Italian relations – namely the two countries' divergent approaches to peace-making. In Britain, reflection on war aims and the policy needed to achieve them developed at the hand of imperialist currents that in time came to dominate the Foreign Office and the British and Imperial War Cabinets. It flowed from war events and more specifically from British strategy in the colonial theatre, which led the British to conquer large portions of German and Ottoman possessions that British policymakers subsequently found too attractive to restore. They progressively envisaged a different peace settlement from that provided for under Allied wartime agreements, including those securing Italy's claims; and eventually these proposals were largely turned into Britain's final peace-making strategy. This left the weakest party in the Alliance dangerously isolated, because France was equally disposed to be freed from the London Pact's 'embarrassing undertakings'.[10] Given the US neglect of Allied secret treaties, one is led to conclude that Italy entered the Peace Conference with an almost impossible task. It is important to stress, however, that there was no coordinated anti-Italian plot; the United States, France and Britain decided to reduce Italian claims independently of one another. Quite simply, Italy lacked bargaining leverage – yet another consequence of the Caporetto disaster.[11]

Awareness of its own weakness spurred Italy to rely on British friendship to counter the revisionist tendencies of the other Allies, especially the United States. This made the Peace Conference the climax of

---

[7] Similarity with inter-Allied relations in World War II is patent: Ibid., p. 289.
[8] Sondhaus, *Great War*, p. 133.   [9] TNA, CAB23/5, War Cabinet 312, 3 January 1918.
[10] C. Seton-Watson, *Storia d'Italia*, p. 607.   [11] Burgwyn, *The Legend*, p. 235.

Anglo-Italian relations. Rome expected London to act as a full supporter of Italian rights, not just as a mediator. British policymakers
ostensibly pledged to support their young ally; but in reality, London
saw Italy's empire project – rightly so – as a threat to British supremacy
in the Mediterranean and the Red Sea, and was not prepared to risk
a clash with Washington to defend it. Victor Rothwell in his book on
British diplomacy during the war concluded: 'Always one comes back to
the point that British foreign policy in the era of the World War I was
truly concerned with the interests of the British Empire'.[12] There is no
reason why it should have been otherwise, or why one should expect
British policymakers to have jeopardised British interests by serving
Italy's empire project. After a hundred years, however, it is time for
a deeper appreciation of the origin of the clash between Italy and its
allies, especially Britain, in 1919 – and, indeed, in the years that followed. That such a clash originated in Italy's 'intransigent' attitude is
misleading, because in fact it originated in the secret intention of Italy's
allies not to adhere to their promises.

This does not absolve the inherently flawed Italian diplomatic strategy,
which aggravated the Italian position; rather, it contextualises it. If one
wonders whether it was still possible for Italy to gain more than it did at
the Peace Conference, the answer must be yes. This would have required,
first, a systematic effort to build up greater empathy with Italy's new allies
during the war, including by increasing Italy's commitment overseas and
Italian propaganda in Allied countries; and second, a more flexible Italian
foreign policy that could better adapt to the traumatic changes in international relations that occurred during the war. Why Rome failed in all
these can be appreciated by comparing the ways foreign policy was
formulated in Britain and Italy.

British foreign policy was not a product of central decision-making; it
evolved organically 'from those with knowledge of their particular
spheres, which were synthesised at Paris ... and which in turn allowed
effective negotiations against the ambitions of the other participants'.[13]
This provided London's diplomacy with enough flexibility to adapt to
circumstances unpredictable when wartime agreements on the future
peace settlement were being signed. For Britain, those pacts were never
fixed and definite agreements, but rather a basis for subsequent discussion, where the strongest power would have the final word; it was the
geopolitical context that should direct their implementation, not vice

---

[12] V. H. Rothwell, *British War Aims and Peace Diplomacy, 1914–1918* (Oxford: Clarendon,
1971), p. 287.
[13] Goldstein, *Winning the Peace*, p. 286.

versa. In Italy, by contrast, foreign policy remained in the hands of Sonnino with limited external influence, even by Italian premiers – only in late 1918 did Orlando try to advance his own line, without, however, completely renouncing Sonnino's. Wartime peace-planning for Sonnino meant getting the Allies to sign detailed pacts that could be ratified straight away at the peace table. He overlooked that a parallel diplomatic effort – no less complex, long and stressful than wartime negotiations – was needed to keep those treaties alive in the changing geopolitical context. As in Britain, this was linked to, and influenced by, Italy's war strategy, which was primarily concerned with its own front, delegating to Allied pacts the defence of Italian imperial aspirations. Sonnino awoke to the risk that treaties were insufficient a means to defend Italian interests only in the final months of the conflict, when it was too late; his failure to improve Italy's reputation throughout the war then proved fatal.

Equally fatal was Italy's insufficient preparation for the Peace Conference. In Britain, committees of specialists with specific expertise were formed well in advance 'so that the vast and complicated secretarial work of the British delegation ... may proceed with the greatest possible measure of coordination and despatch', in Hardinge's words.[14] Thus the British delegation went to Paris with clearly identified goals and good policy suggestions as to how they could be achieved.[15] Italian negotiators were not nearly so well served. Committees of experts capable of offering detailed analysis and alternative solutions of the issues likely to be discussed, would have been of vital assistance to the Italian delegation in helping to establish clearer goals and to speak with one voice, but they were never created. The Italian delegation remained divided and proved unprepared when unexpected developments challenged the assumptions of Orlando and Sonnino, the most important of which was that London would actively support Italy in the realisation of its claims. That Italian policymakers repeatedly counted on it is striking. They had several signs of British ambiguity and still were blinded by their own expectations and by British duplicity. This is illustrative of the limits of the young and unexperienced Italian diplomatic school, ill prepared for the inevitable intrigues of imperial competition. The supposedly Machiavellian, 'astute'[16] and devious Italian policymakers were crushed when confronted by their British counterparts, some of whom were veterans of imperial management and mastered the *divide et impera* tactic. Mussolini's newspaper sarcastically commented after the Peace

[14] Prothero papers, 'Peace Negotiations', *cit.*   [15] Goldstein, *Winning the Peace*, p. 229.
[16] Lloyd George, *The Truth*, II, p. 771.

Conference: 'We cannot but conclude that the Italians are no longer the sons of Machiavelli, but rather [they are] bastards'.[17]

Unfortunately, Italy's humiliation at the Peace Conference contributed to making fascism, in the eyes of many Italians, the only way to restore shaken Italian pride. The failure of the negotiations for Italian colonial claims is another key aspect in understanding Rome's foreign policy in the following years: it played a major part in the colonial expansion pursued by Mussolini between 1922 and 1936. The fascist dictator relaunched the Italian empire project. London remained an inevitable interlocutor, and in the 1920s it still seemed that the response to fascist imperialist ambitions would be played out largely through Anglo-Italian relations.[18] In a series of conferences, from Lausanne in 1923 to Locarno in 1925, Britain attempted to address the problem of the post-war balance of power, in which the Mediterranean – and more specifically Italy – had an important part.[19] Tyrrell, assistant Under-Secretary at the Foreign Office between 1925 and 1928, saw the lack of a reliable post-war balance of power as an issue that had remained unresolved since 1919.[20] Headlam-Morley observed that the old British 'balance of power' doctrine was 'fundamental ... just as much after the establishment of a League of Nations as it has been before'.[21] He meant to address the unease with the Versailles outcome in both Germany and Italy. Austen Chamberlain, Secretary of State for Foreign Affairs from 1924 to 1929, was also much concerned with the issue of a Mediterranean balance of power. He warned the Committee of Imperial Defence (CID) in December 1924 that the dominant sentiment in Europe was that another war was inevitable unless Britain could give Europe a sense of security and stability.[22]

Britain's policy towards Italy was therefore guided by basic security precautions. If North Africa and the Middle East were properly in equilibrium, any threat to Britain would be much reduced.[23] The result was a series of long and difficult negotiations with Italy over the fate of the Dodecanese islands, the Horn of Africa and the Libyan-Egyptian border. Italy was granted possession of the islands in 1923 and was given Kisimaio

---

[17] G. P. (Gaetano Polverelli), 'Miserie parlamentari e diplomatiche', *Il Popolo d'Italia*, 5 February 1920.

[18] I. Kirkpatrick, *Mussolini. A study in Power* (New York: Hawthorn, 1964), pp. 17, 160.

[19] M. Dockrill, B. McKercher eds., *Diplomacy and World Power. Studies in British Foreign Policy, 1890–1950* (Cambridge: Cambridge University Press, 1996), p. 135.

[20] TNA, FO371/11066/W6497/9/98, Minute by Tyrrell, 18 March 1925.

[21] Ibid., 371/4353/f23/PC55, minute by Headlam-Morley, n.d., quoted in H. Nicolson, *Peacemaking* (London: Constable, 1933), p. 210.

[22] TNA, CAB2/4/CID192, meeting of 16 December 1924.

[23] Dockrill, McKercher, *Diplomacy*, p. 124.

and Jaghbub in 1925. But London was adamant in denying Rome Sollum and refused to make concessions over Abyssinia, the real objective of Italian colonialists. The paucity of Italian gains caused further resentment towards Britain[24] and Mussolini's unilateral invasion of Ethiopia in 1935 virtually marked the end of the traditional Anglo-Italian friendship:[25] the apparently unshakable pillar of Italian foreign policy – that of not going to war with Britain on any account – was close to collapse.

---

[24] A. Giannini, *L'ultima fase della questione orientale* (Rome: Istituto per l'Oriente, 1933), pp. 334–359; C. Rossetti, 'Come l'Inghilterra ci portò via Sollum', *Nuova Antologia*, October 1940, pp. 238–246.

[25] Quartararo, *Roma*, pp. 55 ff.

Bibliography and Sources

Primary Sources

Archives & Libraries

Archive Diplomatique du Ministère des Affaires Étrangères Françaises (ADMAEF), La Courneuve
Guerre 1914–1918, Dossier Général, vols. 858, 884, 986, 988, 991, 992, 997.
Guerre 1914–1918, Italie, vols. 563, 571, 574, 578.

Archivio Storico del Ministero degli Affari Esteri (ASMAE), Rome
Fondo Ambasciata Londra, 1914–1919.
1916, b. 122; 1917, b. 422; 1918, b. 463.
Cabinet Telegrams (t.gab.) 1396, 2188/519, 2359/547, 2808/500.
Cabinet Secret Telegrams (t.gab.segr.), 184/29.
Carte Imperiali, b. 1.
Carte Italia, 1916–1918, b. 111.
Carte Sonnino, Reels 1–15.

Archivio Centrale dello Stato (ACS), Rome
Carte Gallenga Stuart: b. 1.
Carte Orlando: bb. 5, 8, 46, 49, 102.
Carte Presidenza del Consiglio: bb. 19-4-6, 19–11-10, 19–11-11, 19–28-1, 19–28-2, 19–29-7.

Archivio Storico del Senato (ASSR), Rome
Archivi parlamentari (AP), Senato del Regno, Legislatura XXIV, Discussioni, Tornata del 4 luglio 1916, 2590–2591.
Fondo Guglielmo Imperiali, bb. 1, 2; 33 volumi di memorie.

Archivio Storico della Camera dei Deputati (ASCD), Rome
Archivi parlamentari (AP), Discussioni, Sessioni 1913–1917, vol. XIV.

Relazione della Commissione d'Inchiesta sulle spese di Guerra XXI, Camera dei
  Deputati, XXVI Legislatura, vol. I.
Carte inchiesta sulle spese di guerra, b. 11.

Archivio dell'Ufficio dello Storico della Marina (AUSM), Rome

Bb. 354, 497, 498, 740, 827, 1191.

Archivio dell'Ufficio Storico dello Stato Maggiore dell'Esercito (AUSSME), Rome

Fondi E2, G29, H5, E8, E9.

Bodleian Library (BOD), Oxford

Asquith papers, MS Asquith 25.
Milner MSS, Box 108.
Rodd private papers [uncatalogued].
Sonnino MSS, Microfilms 874–927.
Clarendon private papers, Box C.136.

British Library (BL), London

Jackson MSS, British Library Manuscript Collection, ADD MSS-
  49035–49714.
Bertie papers, ADD MSS-63043.

Cambridge University Library (CUL)

Hoare papers, Templewood Collection.
Hardinge private papers.
Italy and the Vatican, 1917–1918, ff. 1–5.

Churchill Archives Centre, University of Cambridge (CAC)

De Robeck MSS, DRBK4/31-36-39.

Churchill College, Cambridge (CCC)

Tomkinson MSS, 170/2.
Wemyss MSS, WMYS 11.

Marshall Library, Cambridge (MLC)

Keynes papers, JMK/T/

National Maritime Museum, Greenwich (NMM)

Fremantle MSS, FRE/301.
Duff MSS, DFF/6.

National Museum of the Royal Navy, Portsmouth (NMRN)
Limpus MSS, 101–14.

Parliamentary Archives, London (PA)
Lloyd George papers, LG, NRA15700.

Service Historique de la Marine (SHM), Vincennes
Es-19.

The National Archives, Kew Richmond (TNA)
ADM 1, 116, 137.
AIR I.
Balfour MSS, 800/202–203.
CAB 1, 2, 17, 21, 23, 24, 27, 28, 29, 37, 41, 42, 45.
FO 45, 170, 268, 368, 369, 371, 382, 395, 608,
  800, 971.
INF 4.
WO 106.

Trinity College, Cambridge (TCC)
Prothero papers, Crawley collection.

Yale University (YU), Boston
House MSS, vol. 121.

Published Documents

British Documents on the Origins of the War 1898–1914 (BD), vols. I-IX, G. P. Gooch and H. Temperley eds. (London: 1926–1935).

British Documents on Foreign Affairs. Reports and papers from the Foreign Office confidential print, Part II, *From the First to the Second World War, Series H, The First World War, 1914–1918*, D. Stevenson ed. (Frederick, MD: University Publications of America, 1989).

Corbett, J. S., *History of the Great War Naval Operations, Based on Official Documents*, 3 vols. (London: Longmans & Green, 1920–1923).

Fuller, J. V. ed., *Papers relating to the Foreign Relations of the United States. The Paris Peace Conference*, 12 vols. (Washington: US Government Printing Office, 1942–1947).

Hancock, N. J., *Handlist of Hardinge Papers at the University Library Cambridge* (Cambridge: Cambridge University Press, 1968).

Marder, A. J. ed., *Portrait of an Admiral: The Life and Papers of Sir Herbert Richmond* (London: Cape, 1952).

Michel, P. H. ed, *La question de l'Adriatique, 1914–1918: Recueil de documents* (Paris: Costes, 1938).

Ministero degli Affari Esteri (MAE), *I documenti diplomatici italiani* (DDI), Series 4th (1908–1914), 5th (1914–1918), and 6th (1918–1922), E. Anchieri, et al. eds. (Rome: 1954 – ongoing).

Payot, F. ed., *Documents diplomatiques sécrets russes* (Paris: Payot, 1928).

Sabini, C. Count of, *Le fond d'une querelle. Documents inédits sur les relations franco-italiennes (1914–1921)* 2 vols. (Paris: Grasset, 1921).

Salvemini, G., 'La diplomazia italiana nella grande guerra', in Salvemini, *Dal Patto di Londra alla Pace di Roma. Documenti della politica che non fu fatta* (Turin: Gobetti, 1925).

Official Histories

Committee of Imperial Defence, *History of the Great War Based on Official Documents by Direction of the Historical Section of the Committee of Imperial Defence*, 36 tomes (London: CID, Imperial War Museum & Battery, 1922–2010).

Ministère de la Guerre, Etat Major de l'Armée, Service Historique, *Les Armées Françaises dans la grande guerre*, 10 tomes (Paris: EMA ed., 1936).

Naval Staff, Training and Staff Duties Division, *Historical Monographs. Mediterranean Staff Papers Relating to Naval Operations from August 1917 to December 1918* (January 1920); *Naval Operations in Mesopotamia and the Persian Gulf* (July 1921); *The Eastern Squadrons, 1914* (April 1922); *The Mediterranean, 1914–1915* (March 1923).

Ufficio Storico dello Stato Maggiore dell'Esercito (USSME), *L'Esercito italiano nella Grande Guerra (1915–1918)* 7 vols. (Rome: USSME, 1980).

Ufficio Storico della Marina (USM), *La marina italiana nella Grande Guerra*, 8 vols. (Florence: Vallecchi, 1935–1942).

Woodward, E. L., Butler, R. et al. eds., *Documents on British Foreign Policy, 1919–1939* (DBFP), 3 series (London: HMSO, 1946–1947).

Memoires, Diaries & Correspondences

Albertini, L., *Epistolario: 1911–1926*, 4 vols., O. Barie ed. (Milan: Mondadori, 1968).

Id., *Le origini della guerra del 1914*, 3 vols. (Milan: Bocca, 1943).

Id., *Venti anni di vita politica*, part 2, *L'Italia nella Guerra Mondiale*, 2 vols. (Bologna: Zanichelli, 1951).

Aldrovandi Marescotti, L., *Guerra diplomatica: ricordi e frammenti di diario* (Milan: Mondadori, 1938).

Id., *Nuovi ricordi e frammenti di diario 1914–1919* (Milan: Mondadori, 1938).

Ambrosoli, L., *Né aderire né sabotare. 1915–1918* (Milan: Avanti! ed., 1961).

Amendola, G., *Carteggio*, 5 vols., E. D'Auria ed. (Rome & Bari then Manduria, 1986–2006).

Asquith, H. H., *Letters to Venetia Stanley*, E. & M. Brock eds. (Oxford: Oxford University Press, 2014).

Avarna di Gualtieri, C. ed., *Il carteggio Avarna Bollati, luglio 1914-maggio 1915* (Napoli: Ed. Scientifiche, 1953).

Avogadro degli Azzoni, F., *L'amico del Re. Il diario di guerra inedito dell'aiutante di campo di Vittorio Emanuele III* (Udine: Gaspari, 2009).

Bagot, R., *My Italian Year* (London, 1911).

Baker, R. S., *Woodrow Wilson and World Settlement. Written from His Unpublished and Personal Material*, 3 vols. (New York: Doubleday, Page & Co., 1923).

Begbie, H. (as A Gentleman with a Duster), *Mirrors of Downing Street: Some Political Reflections* (New York & London: Knicherboker, 1921).

Bencivenga, R., *Saggio critico sulla nostra guerra* (Rome: Tipografia agostiniana, 1930–1938).

Id., *La sorpresa strategica di Caporetto* (Udine: Gaspari, 1997).

Bissolati, L., *Diario di guerra* (Turin: Einaudi, 1935).

Blake, R. ed., *The Private Papers of Douglas Haig 1914–1919* (London: Eyre & Spottiswoode, 1952).

Blaserna, P., *Cinquanta anni di storia italiana*, 3 vols. (Milan: Hoepli, 1911).

Buchanan, G., *My mission to Russia and other diplomatic memories* (London & New York: Cassel, 1923).

Cadorna, L., *Altre pagine sulla Grande Guerra* (Milan: Mondadori, 1925).

Id., *La guerra alla fronte italiana. Fino all'arresto sulla linea del Piave e del Grappa (24 maggio 1915–9 novembre 1917)* (Milan: Treves, 1923).

Id., *Pagine polemiche* (Milan: Garzanti, 1951).

Id., *Lettere famigliari*, R. Cadorna ed. (Milan: Mondadori, 1967).

Callwell, C. E., *Field-Marshall Sir Henry Wilson, bart., G.C.B., D.S.O., his life and diaries* (London: Cassel, 1927).

Cambon, H. ed., *Paul Cambon: Correspondance 1843–1924*, 3 vols. (Paris: Grasset, 1940–1946).

Capello, L., *Per la verità* (Milan: Treves, 1920).

Id., *Caporetto perché? La II Armata e gli avvenimenti dell'ottobre 1917* (Turin: Einaudi, 1967).

Cavaciocchi, A., *Un anno al comando del IV corpo d'armata. Il memoriale dell'unico generale che pagò per Caporetto* (Udine: Gaspari, 2006).

Caviglia, E., *La dodicesima battaglia (Caporetto)* (Milan: Mondadori, 1933).

Id., *Le tre battaglie del Piave* (Milan: Mondadori, 1934).

Id., *Il conflitto di Fiume* (Milan: Garzanti, 1948).

Churchill, W., *The World Crisis. The Aftermath* (London: MacMillan, 1941).

Cork and Orrery, W. H. D. Boyle, *My Naval Life, 1886–1941* (London: Hutchinson, 1942).

Cross, C. ed., *Life with Lloyd George: The Diary of A. J. Sylvester, 1931–1945* (London: MacMillan, 1975).

D'Annunzio, G., *Per la più grande Italia. Orazioni e messaggi di Gabriele D'Annunzio* (Milan: Treves, 1920).

D'Azeglio, M., *I miei ricordi* (Florence: Barbera, 1867).

Dalton, H., *With British Guns in Italy: A Tribute to Italian Achievement* (London: Methuen & Co., 1919).

Dellmensingen, K. von, *1917. Lo sfondamento dell'Isonzo* (Milan: Arcana, 1981).

Foch, F., *Memorie* (Mondadori: Verona, 1931).

Gifuni, G. B. ed., *Il diario di Salandra* (Milan: Pan, 1969).

Giolitti, G., *Memorie della mia vita* (Milan: Garzanti, 1945).

Giurati, G., *Con D'Annunzio e Millo in difesa dell'Adriatico* (Florence: Sansoni, 1954).

Id., *L'opera della 'Trento e Trieste' nell'ultimo periodo della guerra*, Relazione al XII Congresso nazionale, Trieste, 1–3 June (Rome, 1919).

Godfrey, J. H., *The Naval Memories of Admiral J.H. Godfrey*, 7 vols. (Hailsham: Privately printed, 1964–1966).

Grey, E., *Twenty-Five Years, 1892–1916*, 2 vols. (London: Hodder & Stoughton, 1925).

Halpern, P. G. ed., *The Keyes Papers*, 3 vols., vol. I, *1914–1918*. Publications of the Navy Records Society, vol. 117 (London: Navy Records Society, 1972 [Allen & Unwin, 1979]).

Hammond, J. L., *C. P. Scott of the Manchester Guardian* (London: Bell, 1934).

Imperiali, Di Francavilla, G., *Diario 1915–1919* (Soveria Mannelli: Rubbettino, 2006).

Keyes, R., *The Naval Memories*, 2 vols. (London: Butterworth, 1934–1935).

Krauß, A., *Il miracolo di Caporetto. In particolare lo sfondamento di Plezzo*, E. Cernigoi, P. Pozzato eds. (Valdagno: Rossato, 2002).

Lenin, V. I., *L'opportunismo e il crac della II Internazionale* (1916), in *Opere scelte in due volumi* (Moscow: Ed. lingue estere, 1947).

Lloyd George, D., *The Truth about the Peace Treaties*, 2 vols. (London: Gollancz, 1938).

Id., *War Memoirs*, 2 vols. (London: Odhams, 1938).

Malagodi, O., *Conversazioni della guerra 1914–1919*, 2 vols., B. Bigezzi ed. (Milan & Naples: Ricciardi, 1960).

Manfroni, C., *I nostri alleati navali: ricordi della guerra Adriatica, 1915–1918* (Milan: Mondadori, 1927).

Marchetti, T., *Ventotto anni nel servizio informazioni militari* (Trento: Museo Trentino del Risorgimento, 1960).

Martini, F., *Diario 1914–1918*, G. De Rosa ed. (Verona: Mondadori, 1966); P. Pastorelli ed. (Rome-Bari: Laterza, 1974).

Minozzi, G., *Ricordi di guerra* (Amatrice: Tipografia Orfanotrofio maschile, 1956).

Mordaq, H., *Le Comandement unique: comment il fut réalisé* (Paris: Tallandier, 1929).

Mussolini, B., *Scritti e discorsi*, 12 vols., vol. I, *Dall'Intervento al Fascismo (15 novembre 1914–23 marzo 1919)* (Milan: Hoepli, 1934).

Nicolson, H., *Peacemaking* (London: Constable, 1933).

Ojetti, U., *Lettere alla moglie 1915–1919*, F. Ojetti ed. (Florence: Sansoni, 1964).

Orlando, V. E., *Discorsi per la Pace e per la Guerra* (Foligno: Campitelli, 1923).

Id., *Memorie*, R. Mosca ed. (Milan: Rizzoli, 1960).

Pershing, J. J., *My Experiences in the World War* (London: Hodder & Stoughton, 1931).

Poincaré, R., *Au Service de la France. Neuf années de souvenirs*, 10 vols. (Paris: Plon, 1926–1933).

Premuti, C., *Come Roma preparò la guerra* (Rome: Società Tipografica Italiana, 1923).

Prezzolini, G., *Vittorio Veneto* (Rome: La Voce, 1920).

Id., *Tutta la guerra: antologia del popolo italiano sul fronte e nel paese* (Florence: Bemporad, 1918).

Id., *Italia 1912. Dieci anni di vita intellettuale (1903–1912)*, G. M. Simonetti ed. (Florence: Vallecchi, 1984).

Ribot, A., *Lettres à un ami* (Paris: Bosard, 1924).

Ribot A., Junior, *Journal de Alexandre Ribot et Correspondances inédites* (Paris: Plon, 1936).

Rochat, G. ed., La storiografia militare italiana negli ultimi vent'anni. Atti del convegno, Lucca 1984, Centro interuniversitario di studi e ricerche storico-militari (Milan: Angeli, 1985).

Id., 'Il Comando supremo di Diaz', in G. Berti e and P. delNegro eds., Al di qua e al di là del Piave. L'ultimo anno della Grande Guerra. Atti del convegno internazionale, Bassano del Grappa, 25–28 maggio 2000 (Milan: Angeli, 2001).

Rodd, Sir Rennell J., Social and Diplomatic Memories 1902–1919, 3 vols. (London: Edward Arnold & Co., 1925).

Salandra, A., La neutralità italiana 1914–1915. Ricordi e pensieri (Milan: Mondadori, 1928).

Id., La nostra guerra è santa (Rome: Tipografia del Senato, 1915).

Id., L'intervento, 1915: ricordi e pensieri (Milan: Mondadori, 1930).

Id., Memorie politiche 1916–1925 (Milan: Garzanti, 1951).

Id., I retroscena di Versailles, G. B. Gifuni ed. (Milan: Pan, 1971).

Salvemini, G., Carteggio 1914–1920, E. Tagliacozzo ed. (Rome-Bari: Laterza, 1984).

Sheffield, G., and J. M. Bourne eds., Douglas Haig: War Diaries and Letters, 1914–1918 (London: Weidenfeld & Nicolson, 2005).

Sonnino, S., Diario (1916–1922), 3 vols. (Bari: Laterza, 1972).

Id., Carteggio 1914–1922, P. Pastorelli ed. (Bari: Laterza, 1974).

Id., Discorsi Parlamentari (Rome: Tipografia della Camera dei Deputati, 1925).

Id., Scritti e discorsi extra parlamentari, 1903–1920, F. Brown ed. (Bari: Laterza, 1972).

Steed, H. W., Through Thirty Years, 1892–1922: A Personal Narrative, 2 vols. (London: Heinemann, 1924).

Terrail, G. as Mermeix, Le Commandement unique, 2 vols. (Paris: Ollendorff, 1920–1923).

Turati, F., Kuliscioff, A., Carteggio, 9 vols., F. Pedone ed., vol. IV, 1915–1918. La grande guerra e la rivoluzione, t. I (Torino: Einaudi, 1977).

Weldon, L. B., 'Hard Lying:' Eastern Mediterranean, 1914–1919 (London: Jenkins, 1925).

Wemyss, W., The Navy in the Dardanelles Campaign (London: Hodder & Stoughton, 1924).

Selected Bibliography

Volumes

Addington, L. H., The Patterns of War Since the Eighteenth Century (Bloomington: Indiana University Press, 1994).

Audoin-Rouzeau, S., and Becker, A., La violenza, la crociata, il lutto: La Grande Guerra e la storia del Novecento (Turin: Einaudi, 2000).

Ids. eds., Les sociétés européennes et la guerre de 1914–1918 (Nanterre: Université Paris X, 1990).

Alatri, P., Nitti, D'Annunzio e la questione adriatica (Milan: Feltrinelli, 1959).

Alberti, A., L'importanza dell'azione militare italiana. Le cause militari di Caporetto (Rome: USSME, 2004).

Id., Testimonianze straniere sulla Guerra Italiana 1915–1918 (Rome: Ministero della Guerra, 1933).

Anghelone, F. and Ungari, A. eds., *Gli addetti militari italiani alla vigilia della Grande Guerra 1914–1915* (Rome: Rodorigo, 2015).

Andall, J., Dunkan, D., *National belongings: Hybridity in Italian Colonial and Postcolonial Cultures* (Bern: Land AG, 2010).

André, G., *L'Italia e il Mediterraneo* (Milan: Giuffré, 1967).

Andrew, C. and Kanya-Forstner, S., *France Overseas: The Great War and the Climax of French Imperial Expansion* (London: Thames & Hudson, 1981).

Antonioli, M., *Armando Borghi e l'Unione sindacale italiana* (Manduria: Lacaita, 1990).

Askew, W. C., *Europe and Italy's Acquisition of Libya* (Durham, NC., 1939).

Aspinall-Oglander, C. F., *History of the Great War: Gallipoli*, 2 vols. in 4 (London: Heinemann, 1929–1932).

Augias, C., *Giornali e spie. Faccendieri internazionali, giornalisti corrotti e società segrete nell'Italia della Grande Guerra* (Milan: Bur, 1994).

Baio, G. L., *Il milite noto. Il generale Luigi Zuccari 'primo morto' della Grande Guerra* (Bergamo: Papini, 2015).

Balbo, C., *Le speranze d'Italia* (Napoli: Gemelli, 1848).

Id., *Pensieri sulla storia d'Italia. Studi* (Florence: Le Monnier, 1858).

Barbero, A., *Caporetto* (Bari: Laterza, 2017).

Battaglia, A., *Da Suez ad Aleppo. La campagna Alleata e il Distaccamento italiano in Siria e Palestina (1917–1921)* (Rome: Nuova Cultura, 2015).

Barnett, C., *The Swordbearers: Studies in Supreme Command in the First World War* (Cholcester: The Book Service, 1963).

Beckett, I. F. W., *The Great War* (Harlow: Longmans, 2007).

Id. ed., *1917: Beyond the Western Front* (Leiden & Boston: Brill, 2009).

Beesly, P., *Room 40: British Naval Intelligence, 1914–1918* (London: Hamilton, 1982).

Bell, A. C., *A History of the Blockade of Germany and of the Countries Associated with Her in the Great War, Austria-Hungary, Bulgaria, and Turkey, 1914–1918* (London: Stationery, 1937).

Berriedale, K. A., *War Government of the British Dominions* (Oxford: Claredon, 1921).

Biagini, A., 'Addetti Militari', in *Storia Militare d'Italia. 1796–1975*, Società di Storia Militare ed. (Rome: Editalia, 1990).

Boemeke, M. F., Feldman, G. D. and Glaser, E., *The Treaty of Versailles: A Reassessment After 75 Years* (Washington & Cambridge: Cambridge University Press, 1998).

Bompiani G. and Prepositi C., *Le ali della guerra* (Milan: Mondadori, 1931).

Bond, B. and Roy, I. eds., *War and Society* (London: Routledge, 1975).

Bonnefous, G., *Histoire Politique de la Troisième République*, 8 vols. (Paris: Presses Universitaires de France, 1956–1987).

Bonomi, I., *La politica italiana da Porta Pia a Vittorio Veneto (1870–1918)* (Turin: Einaudi, 1944).

Borsa, M., *Italia e Inghilterra* (Milan: Società Editoriale Italiana, 1916).

Bosworth, R. J. B., *Italy, the Least of the Great Powers: Italian Foreign Policy before the First World War* (London & New York: Cambridge University Press, 2005).

Id., *Italy and the Approach of the First World War* (London & Basingstoke: MacMillan, 1983).

Bovio, O., *L'Ufficio storico dell'Esercito. Un secolo di storiografia militare* (Rome: USSME, 1987).

Brignoli, L., *Il generale Luigi Cadorna, Capo di Stato Maggiore dell'esercito (1914–1917)* (Udine: Gaspari, 2012).

Brodie, C. G., *Forlorn Hope 1915: The Submarines Passage of the Dardanelles* (London: Bryce, 1956).

Brown, J., *Gandhi's Rise to Power: Indian Politics, 1915–1922* (Cambridge: Cambridge University Press, 1974).

Bruce, A., *The Last Crusade: The Palestine Campaign in the First World War* (London: Murray, 2002).

Buccianti, G., *L'egemonia sull'Etiopia (1918–1923): Lo scontro diplomatico tra Italia, Francia e Inghilterra* (Milan: Giuffrè, 1977).

Burgwyn, H. J., *The Legend of the Mutilated Victory: Italy, the Great War and the Paris Peace Conference, 1915–1919* (Westport, CT & London: Greenwood, 1993).

Id., *Italian Foreign Policy in the Interwar Period, 1918–1940* (Westport: Praeger, 1997).

Burk, K. ed., *War and the State: The Transformation of British Government 1914–1919* (London: Allen & Unwin, 1971).

Id., *Britain, America and the Sinews of War, 1914–1918* (London: Routledge, 1985).

Caccamo, F., *Il Montenegro negli anni della Prima Guerra Mondiale* (Rome: Aracne, 2008).

Cammarano, F. ed., *Abbasso la guerra! Neutralisti in piazza alla vigilia della Grande Guerra* (Milan: Mondadori-Le Monnier, 2015).

Cappellano, F., Di Martino, B. and Gionfrida, A., *Un esercito forgiato nelle trincee. L'evoluzione tattica dell'esercito italiano nella Grande Guerra* (Udine: Gaspari, 2008).

Cappellano, F., *Piani di Guerra dello Stato Maggiore italiano contro l'Austria-Ungheria (1861–1915)* (Valdagno: Rossato, 2014).

Caracciolo, A. ed., *La formazione dell'Italia industriale* (Bari: Laterza, 1969).

Caracciolo, M., *L'Italia e i suoi Alleati nella Grande Guerra* (Milan: Mondadori, 1932; [1925]).

Carina, D., *Dell'ozio in Italia. Osservazioni* (Forlì: Gherardi, 1871).

Carucci, P., 'Funzioni e caratteri del ministero per le armi e munizioni', in G. Procacci ed., *Stato e classe operaia in Italia durante la prima guerra mondiale* (Milan: Angeli, 1983).

Caselli Lapeschi, A. and Militello, G., *1918. Gli italiani sul Fronte Occidentale* (Udine: Gaspari, 2007).

Cassar, G. H., *The Forgotten Front. The British Campaign in Italy 1917–1918* (London: Hambledon, 1998).

Cattaruzza, M., *Il confine orientale italiano, 1866–2011* (Bologna: Il Mulino, 2007).

Id., *L'Italia e la questione adriatica. Dibattiti parlamentari e panorama internazionale (1918–1926),* (Bologna: Il Mulino, 2014).

Cavallini, F., *Il processo Cavallini. Storia di un delitto giudiziario* (Milan: Modernissima CEI, 1921).

Cecchin, G., *Con Hemingway e Dos Passos sui campi di battaglia italiani della Grande Guerra. Cronache particolari* (Bassano: Collezione Princeton, 1998).

Cecini, G., *Il Corpo di Spedizione italiano in Anatolia (1919–1922)* (Rome: USSME, 2010).

Cernigoi, E., *La cavalleria italiana nella Prima Guerra Mondiale* (Rome: USSME, 2009).

Cernuschi, E., *Battaglie sconosciute. Storia riveduta e corretta della Regia Marina durante la Grande Guerra* (Vicenza: Edibus, 2014).

Cervone, P. P., *Vittorio Veneto, l'ultima battaglia* (Milan: Mursia, 2007).

Ceva, L. and Curami, A., *La meccanizzazione dell'Esercito italiano dalle origini al 1943*, 2 vols. (Rome: USSME, 1994).

Charmley, J., *Splendid Isolation? Britain, the Balance of Power, and the Origins of the First World War* (London: Hodder & Stoughton, 1999).

Chatterton, K. E., *The Big Blockade* (London: Hurst & Blackett, 1932).

Clark, C., *The Sleepwalkers. How Europe Went to War in 1914* (London: Allen Lane, 2012).

Clodfelter, M., *Warfare and Armed Conflicts: A Statistical Encyclopedia of Casualty and Other Figures, 1492–2015* (Jefferson: McFarland, 2017).

Colajanni, N., *Italiani del Nord e italiani del Sud (con 133 tavole numeriche e 31 tavole geografiche)* (Turin: Bocca, 1901).

Coletta, P. E., *Sea Power in the Adriatic and Mediterranean in World War I* (Lanham, MD: University Press of Amer, 1989).

Conwell-Evans, T. P., *Foreign Policy from a Back Bench 1904–1918: a Study Based on the Papers of Lord Noel-Buxton* (London: Oxford University Press, Milford, 1932).

Cornwall, M., *The Undermining of Austria-Hungary: The Battle of Hearts and Minds* (Basingstoke: MacMillan & New York: St Martin's Press, 2000).

Corradini, E., *La patria lontana* (Milan: Treves, 1910).

Id., *La guerra lontana* (Milan: Treves, 1911).

Cooper, R., 'The Image of Italy in English Writing, 1815–1915' (unpublished M. A. thesis, University of Sydney, 1967).

Crespi, S., *Alla difesa d'Italia in guerra e a Versailles* (Milan: Mondadori, 1937).

Croce, B., *L'Italia dal 1914 al 1918: pagine sulla guerra* (Bari: Laterza, 1965 [Naples: Ricciardi, 1919]).

Id., *Storia d'Italia dal 1871 al 1915* (Bari: Laterza, 1927).

Cruttwell, C. R. M. F., *The Role of British Strategy in the Great War* (Cambridge: Cambridge University Press, 1936).

Id., *A History of the Great War, 1914–1918* (Oxford: Clarendon, 1936).

Cuoco, V., *Platone in Italia*, F. Nicolini ed., (Laterza: Bari, 1928).

Curami, A., 'Un grande mistero: la produzione italiana di artiglierie', in C. Curami., A. Massignani, *L'artiglieria italiana nella grande guerra* (Valdagno: Rossato, 1998).

Darwin J., *The Empire Project. The Rise and Fall of the British World-System 1830–1970* (Cambridge: Cambridge University Press, 2009).

Decleva, E. *L'Italia e la politica internazionale dal 1870 al 1914. L'ultima fra le grandi potenze* (Milan: Mursia, 1974).

Id., *L'incerto alleato. Ricerche sugli orientamenti internazionali dell'Italia unita* (Milan: Angeli, 1987).

Del Boca, A., *Gli italiani in Libia*, 2 vols. (Milan: Mondadori, 1993).

De Felice, R., *Mussolini il rivoluzionario (1883–1920)* (Turin: Einaudi, 1965).

Del Negro, P. ed., *Guida alla storia militare italiana* (Naples: Ed. scientifiche, 1997).

Id., *Esercito, stato, società* (Bologna: Cappelli, 1979).

Id. ed., *Lo spirito militare degli italiani*, Atti del seminario, Padua, 16–18 November 2000 (Padua: Università degli Studi di Padova, 2002).

De Sanctis, F., *Saggi critici* (Naples: Morano, 1890).

Id., *Storia della letteratura italiana*, 2 vols. (Naples: Morano, 1870–1871).

Dillon, E. J., *From the Triple to the Quadruple Alliance: Why Italy Went to War* (London: Hodder & Stoughton, 1915).

Dillon, J., '*Allies Are a Tiresome Lot*'. *The British Army in Italy in the First World War* (Solihull: Helion & Co., 2015).

Di Martino, B. and Cappellano, F., *I reparti d'assalto italiani nella Grande Guerra (1915–1918)* (Rome: USSME, 2007).

Dockrill, M. and David, F. eds., *Strategy and Intelligence: British Policy during the First World War* (London & Rio Grande: Hambledon, 1994).

Dockrill, M. and McKercher, B. eds., *Diplomacy and World Power. Studies in British Foreign Policy, 1890–1950* (Cambridge: Cambridge University Press, 1996).

Doughty, R. A., *Pyrrhic Victory: French Strategy and Operations in the Great War* (Cambridge, MA: Belkna, 2005).

Douglas, N., *Old Calabria* (London: Secker & Warburg, 1915).

Dudan, A., *La monarchia degli Asburgo. Origini, grandezza e decadenza: con documenti inediti*, 2 vols. (Rome, 1915).

Edmonds, Sir James E. and Davies, H. R., *Military Operations in Italy 1915–1919* (London: HMSO, 1949).

Egoli, E., *I legionari cecoslovacchi in Italia, 1915–1918* (Rome: Tipografia Segraf, 1968).

Einaudi, L., *La condotta economica e gli effetti sociali della guerra italiana* (Bari: Laterza, 1933).

Id., *La guerra e il sistema tributario italiano* (Bari: G. Laterza; New Haven: Yale University Press, 1933).

Id., *Preparazione morale e preparazione finanziaria* (Milan: Ravà & Co., 1915).

Ellman, B. A. and Paine, S. C. M. eds., *Naval Coalition Warfare. From Napoleonic Wars to Operation Iraqi Freedom* (London & New York: Routledge, 2008).

Elcock, H., *Portrait of a Decision: The Council of Four and the Treaty of Versailles* (London: Methuen, 1972).

Falls, C., *Caporetto 1917* (London: Weidenfeld & Nicholson, 1996).

Id., *The Great War* (New York: Capricorn, 1959).

Fasanella, G. and Grippo, A., *1915. Il fronte segreto dell'intelligence. La storia della Grande guerra che non c'è sui libri di storia* (Milan: Sterling & Kupfer, 2014).

Fayle, C. E., *The War and the Shipping Industry* (London: Milford, 1927).

Favre, F., *La Marina nella grande guerra* (Udine: Gaspari, 2008).

Ferraioli, G., *Politica e diplomazia in Italia tra XIX e XX secolo. Vita di Antonino di San Giuliano (1852–1914)* (Soveria Mannelli: Rubbettino, 2007).

Ferrante, E., *Il pensiero strategico navale in Italia* (Rome: Rivista Marittima, 1988).

Id., *La grande guerra in Adriatico* (Rome: USM, 1978).

Id., *Il grande ammiraglio Paolo Thaon di Revel* (Rome: USM, 1989).

Ferrari, P., *La guerra aerea '15–'18* (Valdagno: Rossato, 1994).

Ferrero, G., *L'Europa giovane. Studi e viaggi nei paesi del nord* (Milan: Treves, 1897).

Ferretti, S., Guarini, P., Giovannelli, A., Grimaldi, A., Tamborrino, L. eds., *Operare i forti. Per un progetto di riconversione dei forti militari di Roma* (Rome: Gangemi, 2009).

Fisher, J., *Curzon and British Imperialism in the Middle East, 1916–1919* (London & Portland: Cass, 2005).

Foerster, R. E., *The Italian Emigration of our times* (New York: Russel & Russel, 1919).

Fonzo, E., *Storia dell'Associazione nazionalista italiana (1910–1923)* (Naples: Ed. scientifiche, 2017).

Forcella E. and Monticone, A., *Plotone d'esecuzione. I processi della prima guerra mondiale* (Bari: Laterza, 1968).

Forsyth, D. J., *The Crisis of Liberal Italy: Monetary and Financial Policy, 1914–1922* (Cambridge: Cambridge University Press, 1993).

Foscanelli, U., *Gabriele d'Annunzio e l'ora sociale* (Milan: Carnaro, 1952).

French, D., *British Economic and Strategic Planning, 1905–1915* (London & Boston: Allen & Unwin, 1982).

Id., *British Strategy and War Aims, 1914–1916* (London & Boston: Allen & Unwin, 1986).

Id., *The Strategy of the Lloyd George Coalition, 1916–1918* (Oxford: Clarendon, 1995).

Fry, M. G., *Lloyd George and Foreign Policy*, 2 vols. (Montreal & London: McGill-Queen's University Press, 1977).

Fuà, G. ed., *Lo sviluppo economico in Italia* (Milan: Angeli, 1969).

Fumian, C. ed., *Il secondo Risorgimento delle Venezie. La ricostruzione dopo la Grande Guerra* (Venezia: Marsilio, 2015).

Fussell, P., *The Great War and Modern Memory* (Oxford: Oxford University Press, 1975).

Gabriele, M. and Friz, G., *La politica navale italiana dal 1885 al 1915* (Rome: USM, 1982).

Gabriele, M., *Gli Alleati in Italia durante la Prima Guerra Mondiale (1917–1918)* (Rome: USSME, 2008).

Id., *Le Convenzioni navali della Triplice* (Rome: USM, 1969).

Galassi F. L. and Harrison, M., 'Italy at War, 1915–1918', in S. Broadberry and M. Harrison eds., *The Economics of World War I* (Cambridge: Cambridge University Press, 2005).

Galli, G., *Fanti d'Italia in Macedonia* (Milan: Marangoni, 1934).

Ganapini, L., *Il nazionalismo cattolico. I cattolici e la politica estera in Italia dal 1871 al 1914* (Bari: Laterza, 1971).

García Sanz, C., 'British Patriots and Spies in Italy (1914–1915): Fighting the Enemy of the Neutral Front Line', in A. Biagini and G. Motta eds., *The First World War: Analysis and Interpretation*, 2 vols. (Newcastle: Cambridge Scholars Publishing, 2015).

Id., 'The End of Neutrality? Italy and Spain in the Mediterranean Theatre on the Great War', in J-L. Ruiz Sánchez, I. Cordero Olivero and C. García Sanz eds., *Shaping Neutrality throughout the First World War* (Saville: Editorial Universidad de Sevilla, 2015).

Gaspari, P., *Le bugie di Caporetto. La fine della memoria dannata* (Udine: Gaspari, 2011).

Gatti, A., *Caporetto. Diario di guerra* (Bologna: Il Mulino, 1997).

Id., *La guerra d'Italia nel 1915–1918* (Milan: Treves, 1932).

Id., *Un Italiano a Versailles, dicembre 1917-febbraio 1918* (Milan: Ceschina, 1958).

Id., *Uomini e folle di guerra* (Milan: Mondadori, 1932).

Gatti, G. L., *Dopo Caporetto. Gli ufficiali P nella Grande Guerra: propaganda, assistenza, vigilanza* (Gorizia: Ed. Gorinziane, 2000).

Gayda, V., *La crisi di un impero. Pagine sull'Austria contemporanea* (Turin, 1913).

Gentili, R. and Varriale, P., *Reparti dell'aviazione italiana nella Grande Guerra,* (Rome: Ufficio Storico dell'Aeronautica Militare [USAM], 1999).

Gentili, R., Iozzi, A. and Varriale, P., *Gli assi dell'aviazione italiana nella Grande Guerra* (Rome: USAM, 2002).

Giardino, G., *Rievocazioni e riflessioni di guerra,* 3 vols. (Milan: Mondadori, 1929–1930).

Giannini, A., *L'ultima fase della questione orientale* (Rome: Istituto per l'Oriente, 1933).

Gilbert, B. B., *David Lloyd George: A Political Life. The Organiser of Victory, 1912–1916* (London: Batsford, 1992).

Gilbert, M., *The First World War: A Complete History* (New York: Holt & Co., 1994).

Gioberti, V., *Del primato morale e civile degli italiani,* G. Balsamo-Crivelli ed. (Turin: Unione Tipografico-Editrice, 1920).

Gionfrida, A., *L'Italia e il coordinamento militare 'interalleato' nella Prima Guerra Mondiale* (Rome: USSME, 2008).

Giordani, P., *Per l'esercito serbo. Una storia dimenticata* (Rome: Informazioni della Difesa, 2014).

Giordano, G., *Cilindri e feluche. La politica estera dell'Italia dopo l'Unità* (Rome: Aracne, 2008).

Glanville, J. L., *Italy's Relations with England 1896–1905* (Baltimore: Furst, 1934).

Goldstein, E., *Winning the Peace. British Diplomatic Strategy, Peace Planning, and the Paris Peace Conference 1916–1920* (Oxford: Clarendon, 1991).

Gooch, J., *The Italian army and the First World War* (Cambridge: Cambridge University Press, 2014).

Id. and *The Plans of War: The General Staff and British Military Strategy c. 1900–1916* (New York: Wiley & Sons, 1974).

Id., Reid, B. H. eds., *Ottoman Army Effectiveness in World War I: A Comparative Study* (Abingdon: Routledge, 2007).

Gottlieb, W. W., *Studies in Secret Diplomacy during the First World War* (London: Allen & Unwin, 1957).

Greenhalgh, E., *Foch in Command. The Forging of a First World War General* (Cambridge: Cambridge University Press, 2011).

Id., *Victory through Coalition. Britain and France during the First World War* (Cambridge: Cambridge University Press, 2005).

Gregory, A., *The Last Great War: British Society and the First World War* (Cambridge: Cambridge University Press, 2008).

Grenville, J. and Wasserstein, B. eds., *The Major International Treaties of the Twentieth Century. A History Guide with Texts* (London & New York: Routledge, 2013).

Grienti, V. and Merlini, L., *Navi al Fronte. La Marina italiana e la Grande Guerra* (Parma: Mattioli, 2015).

Guerri, G. B., *D'Annunzio* (Milan: Mondadori, 2008).

Guinn, P., *British Strategy and Politics, 1914–1918* (Oxford: Clarendon, 1965).

Hadaway, S., *Pyramids and Fleshpots. The Egyptian, Senussi and Eastern Mediterranean Campaigns, 1914–1916* (Straud: Spellmout, 2014).

Halpern, P. G., *The Mediterranean Naval Situation 1908–1914* (Cambridge, MA, & London: Harvard University Press, 1971).

Id., *The Naval War in the Mediterranean 1914–1918* (Annapolis: Naval Institute Press, 1987).

Id. ed., *The Royal Navy in the Mediterranean, 1915–1918*, Navy Records Society Publications, vol. 126 (Aldershot: Temple Smith for the NRS, 1987).

Id., *A Naval History of World War I* (London: University College London, 1994).

Id., *The Battle of the Otranto Straits. Controlling the Gateway to the Adriatic in WWI* (Bloomington: Indiana University Press, 2004).

Hamilton, R. R. and Holger, H. H., *War Planning* 1914 (Cambridge: Cambridge University Press, 2010).

Hankey, M., Lord, *The Supreme Command, 1914–1918*, 2 vols. (London: Allen & Unwin, 1961).

Id., *Government Control in War* (Cambridge: Cambridge University Press, 1945).

Hardach, G., *La Prima Guerra Mondiale 1914–1918. Storia dell'economia mondiale del XX secolo* (Sonzogno: Bompiani, 1982).

Harrison, M. ed., *The Economics of World War II* (Cambridge: Cambridge University Press, 1998).

Heller, H., *Anti-Italianism in Sixteenth-Century France* (Toronto-Buffalo-London: University of Toronto Press, 2003).

Hirst, F. W. and Allen, J. E., *British War Budgets* (Oxford: Oxford University Press, 1926).

Haste, C., *Keep the Home Fires Burning: Propaganda in the First World War* (London: Allen & Penguin, 1977).

Hattendorf, J. B. ed., *Seventeenth International Seapower Symposium: Report of the Proceedings, 19–23 September 2005* (Newport: Naval War College Press, 2006).

Hautecoeur, L., *L'Italie sous le ministère Orlando* (Paris: Bossard, 1919).

Herwig, H. H., *The First World War: Germany and Austria-Hungary 1914–1918* (London: Arnold, 1997).

Hinsley F. H. ed., *British Foreign Policy Under Sir Edward Grey* (Cambridge: Cambridge University Press, 1997).

Hoare, S., *Complacent Dictator* (New York: Knopf, 1947).

Hunt, B. D. and Preston, A. eds., *War Aims and Strategic Policy in the Great War* (London: Croom Helm 1977).

Ingram, E. ed., *National and International Politics in the Middle East: Essays in Honour of Elie Kedourie* (London: Cass, 1986).

Isenghi, M. and Rochat, G., *La Grande Guerra, 1914–1918* (Florence: La Nuova Italia, 2000).

Isenghi, M. ed., *I luoghi della memoria. Strutture ed eventi dell'Italia unita* (Rome-Bari: Laterza, 1997).

Jameson, F. and Said, E. W. eds., *Nationalism, Colonialism, and Literature* (Minneapolis & London: University of Minnesota Press, 1990).

Jannacone, P., *La bilancia del dare e dell'avere internazionale con particolare riguardo all'Italia. Prezzi e mercati* (Turin: Einaudi, 1951).

Jeffrey, K. ed., *The Military Correspondence of Field Marshal Sir Henry Wilson 1918–1922* (London: Bodley Heady, 1985).

Jeromela, V. P., *1918–1921. Fuoco sotto le elezioni. Gli incidenti di Spalato, Trieste e Maresego* (Trieste: Luglio ed., 2018).

Justus, V. (alias Giulio Casalini), *V. Macchi di Cellere all'Ambasciata di Washington. Memorie e testimonianze* (Florence: Bemporad, 1920).

Killinger, C. L., *The History of Italy* (Westport: Greenwood, 2002).

Kindleberger, C. P., *A Financial History of Western Europe* (London: Allen & Unwin, 1984).

King, J. C., *Generals and Politicians* (Berkeley & Los Angeles: University of California Press, 1951).

Id., *Foch versus Clemenceau. France and German Dismemberment, 1918–1919* (Boston: Harvard University Press, 1960).

Kirkpatrick, I., *Mussolini. A Study in Power* (New York: Hawthorn, 1964).

Labanca, N., *Oltremare. Storia dell'espansione coloniale italiana* (Bologna: Il Mulino, 2002).

Id., *La guerra italiana per la Libia, 1911–1931* (Bologna: Il Mulino, 2012).

Id., *Caporetto. Storia e memoria di una disfatta* (Bologna: Il Mulino, 2017).

Id. and Paret, P. eds., *Guerra e strategia nell'età contemporanea* (Genoa: Marietti, 1992).

Lasswell, H. D., *Propaganda Technique in the World War* (London: Paul, Trench, Trubner & Co., 1927).

Lawrence, J., *The Rise and Fall of the British Empire* (London: Abacus, 1995).

Le Moal, F., *La France et l'Italie dans les Balkans 1914–1919, le contentieux adriatique* (Paris: L'Harmattan, 2006).

Lederer, I. J., *Yugoslavia at the Paris Peace Conference: A Study in Frontiermaking* (New Haven & London: Yale University Press, 1963).

Lémonon, E., *L'Italie d'après la guerre, 1914–1921* (Paris: Alcan, 1922).

Lenci, G., *Le giornate di Villa Giusti. Storia di un armistizio* (Padua: Il Poligrafo, 1998).

Leon, G. B., *Greece and the Great Powers, 1914–1917* (Thessaloniki: Institute for Balkan Studies, 1974).

Leontaritis, G. B., *Greece and the First World War* (Boulder: East European Monographs, 1990).

Liddell Hart, B. H., *A History of the World War 1914–1918* (London: Faber, 1934).

Lombardo Radice, G., 'Dopo Caporetto', in Id., *Nuovi saggi di propaganda pedagogica* (Turin: Paravia, 1922).

Longo, G., *Le battaglie dimenticate. La fanteria italiana nell'inferno carsico del San Michele* (Bassano del Grappa: Itinera, 2002).

Louis, W. R., *Great Britain and Germany's Lost Colonies 1914–1919* (Oxford: Oxford University Press, 1969).

Lowe, C. J., *Salisbury in the Mediterranean* (London: Routledge & Keegan Paul, 1965).

Id., Marzari, F., *Italian Foreign Policy, 1870–1945* (London & Boston: Routledge & Keegan Paul, 1975).

Id., Dockrill, M. L., *The Mirage of Power*, 3 vols. (London & Boston: Routledge & Kegan Paul, 1972).

Lozzi, C., *Dell'ozio in Italia*, 2 vols. (Turin: Unione Tipografico-Editrice, 1870–71).

Luciani, L., *La riscossa dopo Caporetto. Le battaglie di arresto sul Piave, sul Monte Grappa e sull'Altopiano dei Sette Comuni* (Rome: Litos, 2013).

Lumby, E. W. R. ed., *Policy and Operations in the Mediterranean, 1912–1914*, Publications of the Navy Records Society, vol. 115 (London: Navy Record Society, 1970).

MacMillan, M., *Peacemakers. The Paris Peace Conference of 1919 and Its Attempt to End War* (London: Murray, 2001).

MacMunn, G. and Falls, C., *Military Operations: Egypt and Palestine, From the Outbreak of War with Germany to June 1917* (Nashville: Battery, 1996).

Mahan, A. T., *The Influence of Sea Power upon History 1660–1783* (Boston, 1890).

Id., *Sea Power in Its Relations to the War of 1812*, 2 vols. (New York, 1903).

Manfroni, C., *Storia della marina militare italiana durante la Guerra Mondiale, 1914–1918* (Bologna: Zanichelli, 1925 [1923].

Id. and Giglio, V., *Marina e aviazione italiana nella guerra mondiale* (Milan: Vallardi, 1937).

Mann, T., *Death in Venice* (London: Hamilton, 1932).

Marchetti, D., *Il servizio informazioni dell'esercito italiano nella grande guerra* (Rome: Tipografia Regionale, 1937).

Marder, A., *From the Dreadnought to Scapa Flow: The Royal Navy in the Fisher Era, 1904–1919*, 5 vols. (Oxford: Oxford University Press, 1961–1978).

Margiotta Broglio, F., *Italia e Santa Sede. Dalla Grande Guerra alla Conciliazione* (Bari: Laterza, 1966).

Marriott, J. A. R., *Modern England: 1885–1945* (London: Methuen, 1948).

Martinelli, V., *La Guerra di D'Annunzio: da poeta a dandy, eroe di guerra e comandante* (Udine: Gaspari, 2001).

Massagrande, D., *Italia e Fiume 1921–1924: dal 'Natale di sangue' all'annessione* (Milan: Ed. Cisalpino-Goliardica, 1982).

Maurin, J., *Armée, guerre, société. Soldats languedociens 1889–1918* (Paris: Publications de la Sorbonne, 1982).

Mayer, A., *Political Origins of the New Diplomacy, 1917–1918* (New Haven: Yale University Press, 1959).

Id., *Politics and Diplomacy of Peacemaking. Containment and Counterrevolution at Versailles, 1918–1919* (London: Weidenfeld & Nicolson, 1967).

McCrae, M., *Coalition Strategy and the End of the First World War: The Supreme War Council and War Planning (1917–1918)* (Cambridge: Cambridge University Press, 2019).

McGuirk, R., *The Sanusi's Little War. The Amazing Story of a Forgotten Conflict in the Western Desert, 1915–1917* (London: Arabian Publishing, 2007).

Meda, F., *I cattolici italiani durante la guerra* (Milan: Mondadori, 1928).

Melchionni, M. G., *La vittoria mutilata. Problemi ed incertezze della politica estera italiana sul finire della grande guerra (ottobre 1918-gennaio 1919)* (Rome: Ed. Storia e Letteratura, 1981).

Melograni, P., *Storia politica della Grande Guerra (1915–1918)* (Bari: Laterza, 1969).

Micheletta, L., *Italia e Gran Bretagna nel primo dopoguerra. Le relazioni diplomatiche tra Roma e Londra dal 1919 al 1922*, 2 vols. (Rome: Jouvence, 1999).

Migliazza, A. and Decleva, E. eds., *Diplomazia e Storia delle relazioni internazionali. Studi in onore di Enrico Serra* (Milan: Giuffré, 1991).

Miller, S. E., *Military Strategy and the Origins of the First World War* (Princeton: Princeton University Press, 1985).

Milza, P., *Garibaldi* (Milan: Longanesi, 2013).

Mitrasca, M., *Moldova: A Romanian Province under Russian Rule. Diplomatic History from the Archives of the Great Powers* (New York: Algora, 2002).

Mitrović, A., *Serbia's Great War: 1914–1918* (West Lafayette: PUP, 2007).

Mock, R. and Larson, C., *Words That Won War. The Story of the Committee on Public Information 1917–1919* (Princeton: Purdue University Press, 1939).

Mondini, M., *Il Capo. La Grande Guerra del generale Luigi Cadorna* (Bologna: Il Mulino, 2017).

Id., *Fiume 1919. Una guerra civile italiana* (Rome: Salerno, 2019).

Montalcini, C., *Sidney Sonnino* (Rome: Tipografia della Camera dei Deputati, 1926).

Montanari, M., *Politica e strategia in cento anni di guerre italiane*, 4 vols. (Rome: USSME, 2000).

Montanelli, I, *L'Italia di Giolitti 1900–1920* (Milan: Bur, 2011).

Monticone, A., *La Germania e la neutralità italiana (1914–1915)* (Bologna: Il Mulino, 1971).

Id., *Nitti e la Grande Guerra* (Milan: Angeli, 1961).

Id., *La battaglia di Caporetto* (Rome: Studium, 1955).

Monzali, L., "Sidney Sonnino e la politica estera italiana nell'età degli imperialismi europei", in Ballini, P.L. ed., La politica estera dei Toscani. Ministri degli Esteri nel Novecento (Florence: Polistampa, 2012).

Morabito, N., *La marina italiana in guerra, 1915–1918* (Milan: Maranzoni, 1934).

Id., *Le ministère Clemenceau: journal du témoin*, 4 vols. (Paris: Plon, 1930–31).

Morrow, J. H., *The Great War: An Imperial History* (London: Routledge, 2005).

Mulligan, W. M., *The Great War for Peace* (New Haven: Yale University Press, 2014).

Murray, W., Knox, M. and Bernstein, A. eds., *The Making of Strategy: Rulers, States, and War* (Cambridge: Cambridge University Press, 1997).

Murray, W., Sinnreich, R. H. and Lacey, J. eds., *The Shaping of Grand Strategy. Policy, Diplomacy, and War* (Cambridge: Cambridge University Press, 2011).

Neilson, K., 'Reinforcements and Supplies from Overseas: British Strategic Sealifts in the First World War', in G. Kennedy ed., *The Merchant Marine in International Affairs 1850–1950* (London & Portland: Routledge, 2000).

Neglie, P. and Ungari, A. eds., La Guerra di Cadorna, 1915-1917 (Rome: USSME, 2018).

Id. *Strategy and Supply: the Anglo-Russian Alliance 1914–17* (Boston: Allen & Unwin, 1984).

Nicolson, H., *Peacemaking 1919* (London: Methuen, 1964).

Northedge, F. S., *The Troubled Giant. Britain among the Great Powers, 1916–1939* (London: Political Science/G.Bell, 1966).

O'Brien, P., *Mussolini in the First World War: The Journalist, the Soldier, the Fascist* (Oxford: Berg, 2004).

O'Connor, M., *The Romance of Italy and the English Political Imagination* (New York: St Martin's Press, 1998).

Oriani, A., *Fino a Dogali* (Milan: Galli, 1889).

Id., *La lotta politica in Italia* (Turin: Roux & Frassati, 1892).

Id., *La disfatta* (Milan: Treves, 1896).

Id., *La rivolta ideale* (Naples: Ricciardi, 1908).

Osborne, E. W., *Britain's Economic Blockade of Germany 1914–1919* (London & New York: Cass, 2004).

Ottinger, D. ed., *Futurism* (Paris & Milan: Five Continents, 2009).

Page, T. N., *Italy and the World War* (New York: Scribners, 1920).

Palmer, A., *Victory 1918* (New York: Grove, 1998).

Parmalee, M., *Blockade and Sea Power: The Blockade, 1914–1919, and Its Significance for a World State* (New York: Crowell, 1924).

Pastorelli, P., 'Le relazioni fra l'Italia e la Serbia dal luglio 1914 all'ottobre 1915', in Pastorelli ed., *Dalla prima alla seconda Guerra mondiale. Momenti e problemi della politica estera italiana (1914-1943)* (Milan: LED, 1996).

Patriarca, S., *Italianità. La costruzione del carattere nazionale* (Bari: Laterza, 2010).

Petracchi, G., *Diplomazia di guerra e rivoluzione. Italia e Russia dall'ottobre 1916 al maggio 1917* (Bologna: Il Mulino, 1974).

Petrignani, R., *Neutralità e alleanza. Le scelte di politica estera dell'Italia dopo l'Unità* (Bologna: Il Mulino, 1987).

Philpott, W., *Attrition. Fighting the First World War* (London: Little Brown, 2014).

Id., *Bloody Victory: The Sacrifice on the Somme and the Making of the Twentieth Century* (London: Little Brown, 2009).

Pick, D., *La guerra nella cultura contemporanea* (Rome-Bari: Laterza, 1993).

Pickering, M., *Stereotyping. The Politics of Representation* (Basingstoke & New York: Pelgrave, 2001).

Pieri, P., *La prima guerra mondiale 1914–1918. Studi di storia militare*, G. Rochat ed. (Rome: USSME [1947]).

Id., *L'Italia nella Prima Guerra Mondiale (1915–1916)* (Turin: Einaudi, 1965).

Id. and Rochat, G., *Pietro Badoglio* (Turin: Utet, 1974).

Pieropan, G., *Storia della grande guerra sul fronte italiano* (Milan: Mursia, 2009).

Pitacco, G., *La passione adriatica* (Bologna: Cappelli, 1928).

Playne, C. E., *The Pre-War Mind in Britain* (London: Allen & Unwin, 1928).

Ponteil, F., *La Méditerranée et les Puissances* (Paris: Payot, 1964).

Porisini, G., *Il capitalismo italiano nella Prima Guerra Mondiale* (Florence: La Nuova Italia, 1975).

Prior, R. and Wilson, T., *The Somme* (Boston: Yale Universty Press, 2005).

Pupo, R. ed., *La vittoria senza pace. Le occupazioni militari italiane alla fine della Grande Guerra* (Bari: Laterza, 2014).

Id., *Fiume città di passione* (Bari: Laterza, 2018).

Quaroni, P., La politica estera italiana dal 1914 al 1945 (Rome: Società ed. Dante Alighieri, 2018).

Quartararo, S., *Roma fra Londra e Berlino* (Rome: Bonacci, 1980).

Rappaport, H., *Petrograd 1917. Caught in the Revolution* (London: Windmill, 2017).

Renzi, W. A., *In the Shadow of the Sword: Italy's Neutrality and Entrance into the Great War, 1914–1915* (New York: Lang, 1987).

Reynolds, P. A., *British Foreign Policy in the Inter-War Years* (London: Longmans & Green, 1974).

Riccardi, L., *Alleati non amici. Le relazioni politiche fra l'Italia e l'Intesa durante la prima guerra mondiale* (Brescia: Morcelliana, 1992).

Robbins, K., *Sir Edward Grey. A Biography of Lord Grey of Fallodoon* (London: Cassell, 1971).

Id., *The First World War* (Oxford: Oxford University Press, 1984).

Id., *Politicians, Diplomacy and War in Modern British History* (London & Rio Grande: Hambledon, 1994).

Rocca, G., *Cadorna* (Milan: Mondadori, 1985).

Rochat, G., *L'esercito italiano in pace e in guerra* (Milan: Rara, 1991).

Id., *Gli arditi della Grande Guerra. Origini, miti e battaglie* (Milan: Feltrinelli, 1981).

Id., *Il colonialismo italiano* (Turin: Loescher, 1973).

Id., *L'Italia nella prima guerra mondiale. Problemi di interpretazione e prospettive di ricerca* (Milan: Feltrinelli, 1976).

Rommel, E., *Fanterie all'attacco* (Milan: Longanesi, 1972).

Rosati, E. and Carassiti, A. M., *Dizionario delle battaglie di terra, di mare e di cielo, assedi, rivoluzioni, colpi di stato, guerre civili. I conflitti che sconvolsero la storia dell'Umanità* (Genoa: Gulliver, 1996).

Roskill, S., W., *The Strategy of Sea Power* (London: Collins, 1962).

Rossi, M., *Irredenti giuliani al fronte russo* (Udine: Del Bianco, 1998).

Rothwell, V. H., *British War Aims and Peace Diplomacy 1914–1918* (Oxford: Clarendon, 1971).

Rovighi, S., 'Una "battaglia fortunata': Vittorio Veneto', in N. Labanca ed., *L'istituzione militare in Italia. Politica e società, Questioni di Storia Contemporanea*, n. 11 (Milan: Unicopoli, 2002).

Rumi, G., *Alle origini della politica estera fascista, 1918–1923* (Bari: Laterza, 1968).

Sabbatucci, G., "La vittoria mutilata," in G. Belardelli, L. Cafagna, E. Galli della Loggia and G. Sabbatucci eds., *Miti e storia dell'Italia unita* (Bologna: Il Mulino, 1999).

Salter, A. J., *Allied Shipping Control: An Experiment in International Administration* (Oxford: Clarendon, 1921).

Salvatorelli, L., *La Triplice Alleanza. Storia diplomatica 1877–1912* (Milan: Istituto per gli Studi di Politica Internazionale, 1940).

Id., *Un cinquantennio di rivolgimenti mondiali (1914–1976)* 2 vols. (Florence: Le Monner, 1976).

Salvemini, G., *La politica estera italiana dal 1871 al 1915* (Milan: Barbera, 1944).

Sanders, M. L. and Taylor, P. M., *British Propaganda during the First World War, 1914–18* (London: MacMillan, 1982).

Savona, A. V. and Straniero, M. L. eds., *Canti della Grande Guerra*, 2 vols. (Milan: Garzanti, 1981).

Scaglione, E. ed., *Primavera italica. Antologia delle più belle pagine sulla guerra italo-turca* (Naples: Bideri, 1913).

Schindler, J. R., *Isonzo: The Forgotten Sacrifice of the Great War* (Westport: Praeger, 2001).

Semmel, B., *Liberalism and Naval Strategy: Ideology, Interest, and Sea Power during the Pax Britannica* (Boston: Mass, 1986).

Šepic, D., *Supilo diplomat* (Zagabria: Naprijed, 1961).

Serra, E., *L'intesa mediterranea del 1902* (Milan: Giuffré, 1957).

Seth, R., *Caporetto: The Scapegoat Battle* (London: Macdonald, 1965).

Seton-Watson, C., *Storia d'Italia dal 1870 al 1925* (Bari: Laterza 1967).

Id., 'British Propaganda in Italy 1914–1918', in *Inghilterra e Italia nel '900. Atti del Convegno di Bagni di Lucca (Ottobre 1972)* (Florence: La Nuova Italia, 1973).

Seton-Watson, R. W., *The Balkans, Italy, and the Adriatic* (London: Nisbet & Co., 1915).

Id., *R. W. Seton-Watson and the Yugoslavs. Correspondence 1906–1941*, British Academy & the University of Zagreb eds., 2 vols. (London & Zagreb: Institute of Croatian History, 1976).

Sforza, C., *Contemporary Italy: Its Intellectual and Moral Origins* (New York: Dutton, 1944).

Shanafelt, G. W., *The Secret Enemy: Austria-Hungary and the German Alliance 1914-1918* (New York: Columbia University Press, 1985).

Sheffield, G., *The Somme* (London: Cassell, 2003).

Id., *Forgotten Victory. The First World War: Myths and Realities* (London: Headline, 2001).

Id., *The Chief: Douglas Haig and the British Army* (London: Aurum, 2011).

Silvestri, M., *Caporetto, una battaglia e un enigma* (Bergamo: Bur, 2006).

Smiles, S., *Self-Help. With Illustrations of Character and Conduct* (London: Murray, 1859).

Smith, L., *Sovereignty at the Paris Peace Conference of 1919* (Oxford: Oxford University Press, 2018).

Società Italiana di Storia Militare (SISM) ed., *Over There in Italy. L'Italia e l'intervento americano nella Grande Guerra* (Rome: Nadir Media, 2017).

Sokol, A. E., *The Imperial and Royal Austro-Hungarian Navy* (Annapolis: Naval Institute Press, 1968).

Sondhaus, L., *The Great War at Sea. A Naval History of the First World War* (Cambridge: Cambridge University Press, 2014).

Id., *The Naval Policy of Austria-Hungary: Navalism, Industrial Development, and the Politics of Dualism, 1867–1918* (West Lafayette: Purdue University Press, 1993).

Soutou, G.-H., *L'or et le sang* (Paris: Fayard, 1989).

Stefani, F., *La storia della dottrina e degli ordinamenti dell'Esercito Italiano*, 5 vols. (Rome: USSME, 1983–1989).

Stevenson, D., *The First World War and International Politics* (Oxford: Oxford University Press, 1986).

Id., *With our Backs to the Wall. Victory and defeat in 1918* (Cambridge, MA: Harvard University Press, 2011).

Id., *1914–1918: The History of the First World War* (London: Penguin, 2012).

Id., *1917. War, Peace, and Revolution* (Oxford: Oxford University Press, 2017).

Stone, N., *Eastern Front, 1914–1917* (New York: Scribner, 1975).

Strachan, H., *The First World War: A New Illustrated History* (London: Simon & Schuster, 2003).

Id., *The First World War, Volume I: To Arms* (Oxford: Oxford University Press, 2001).

Id., *The First World War in Africa* (Oxford: Oxford University Press, 2004).

Id., 'The War Experienced: Command, Strategy, and Tactics, 1914–1918', in Horne, J. ed., *A Companion to World War One* (Chichester: Wiley-Blackwell, 2010).

Stringher, B., *Su le condizioni della circolazione e del mercato monetario durante e dopo la guerra* (Rome: Toniolo, 1920).

Sumida, J. T., *In Defense of Naval Supremacy: Finance, Technology and British Naval Policy, 1899–1914* (Boston: Unwin Hyman, 1989).

Suttie, A., *Rewriting the First World War: Lloyd George, Politics and Strategy 1914–1918* (Basingstoke: Palgrave MacMillan, 2005).

Talmon, J. L., *The Myth of the Nation and the Vision of Revolution: The Origins of Ideological Polarization* (Berkeley & Los Angeles: University of California Press, 1982).

Tamaro, A., *Il trattato di Londra e le rivendicazioni italiane* (Milan: Treves, 1918).

Thomazi, A., *Guerre navale dans l'Adriatique. La marine française dans la grande guerre 1914–1918* (Paris: Payot, 1925).

Thompson, M., *The White War. Life and Death on the Italian Front (1915–1919)* (London: Faber, 2008).

Tilley, J., *London to Tokyo* (London: Hutchinson, 1942).

Tommasini, F., *L'Italia alla vigilia della guerra: la politica estera di Tommaso Tittoni* (Bologna: Zanichelli, 1934).

Toniolo, G. ed., *La Banca d'Italia e l'economia di guerra* (Bari: Laterza, 1989).

Id., 'La Banca d'Italia e l'economia di guerra, 1914–1919', in F. Cotula, M. de Cecco, and G. Toniolo eds., *La Banca d'Italia: Sintesi della ricerca storica 1893–1960* (Rome-Bari: Laterza, 2003), pp. 171–207.

Id., *Storia economica dell'Italia liberale, 1850–1918* (Bologna: Il Mulino, 1988).

Toraldo-Serra, N. M., *Diplomazia dell'imperialismo e questione orientale: la spartizione dell'impero ottomano e la nascita del problema palestinese, 1914–1922* (Rome: Bulzoni, 1988).

Toscano, M., *Gli accordi di San Giovanni di Moriana* (Milan: Giuffré, 1936).

Id., *Il Patto di Londra* (Pavia: Pubblicazioni della Facoltà di Scienze Politiche, 1931).

Id., *La Serbia e l'intervento dell'Italia in guerra* (Milan: Mondadori, 1939).

Id., *Pagine di storia diplomatica contemporanea*, 2 vols. (Milan: Giuffrè, 1963).

Tosi, L., *La propaganda italiana all'estero nella Prima Guerra Mondiale: Rivendicazioni territoriali e politica delle nazionalità* (Udine: Del Bianco, 1977).

Trevelyan, G. M., *Garibaldi's Defence of the Roman Republic* (London: Longmans Green, 1907).

Id., *Garibaldi and the Thousand* (London: Longmans Green, 1909).

Id., *Garibaldi and the Making of Italy* (London: Longmans Green, 1911).

Id., *Scenes from Italy's War* (London: Jack Ltd, 1919).

Trumpener, U., *Germany and the Ottoman Empire 1914–1918* (Princeton: Princeton University Press, 1968).

Turiello, P., *Governo e governati in Italia. Saggio*, 2 vols. (Bologna: Zanichelli, 1882).

Ungari, A., 'La scelta di un Re', in G. Orsina and A. Ungari eds., *L'Italia neutrale 1914–1915* (Rome: Rodorigo ed., 2016), pp. 79–100.

Vv. Aa., *La battaglia di Vittorio Veneto. Gli aspetti militari*, L. Cadeddu and P. Pozzato eds. (Udine, Gaspari, 2005).

Valeri, N., *Dalla «Belle époque» al fascismo* (Rome-Bari: Laterza, 1975).

Valiani, L., *La dissoluzione dell'Austria-Ungheria* (Milan: Il Saggiatore, 1966).

Vandervort, B., *Verso la quarta sponda, la guerra italiana per la Libia (1911–1912)* (Rome: USSME, 2012).

Varsori, A., Radioso maggio. Come l'Italia entrò in guerra (Bologna: Il Mulino 2015).

Id. and Zaccaria, B., Italy in the New International Order, 1917–1922 (Cham: MacMillan, 2020).

Veneruso, D., *La grande guerra e l'unità nazionale. Il ministero Boselli, giugno 1916-ottobre 1917* (Turin: Società editrice internazionale, 1996).

Vigezzi, B., *Da Giolitti a Salandra* (Florence: Vallecchi, 1969).

Id., *L'Italia di fronte alla Prima guerra mondiale (1914–1915)* (Milan & Naples: Ricciardi, 1966).

Villari, L., *La Campagna di Macedonia* (Bologna: Zanichelli, 1922).

Vincent, C. P., *The Politics of Hunger: The Allied Blockade of Germany, 1915–1919* (Athens, OH: Ohio University Press, 1985).

Vivarelli, R., *Storia delle origini del fascismo*, 2 vols. (Bologna: Il Mulino, 2012).

Vollman, A. and Brazzale, F., *Grande Guerra. Britannici sull'Altopiano dei Sette Comuni* (Valdagno: Rossato ed., 2012).

Volpe, G., *Fra storia e politica* (Rome: De Alberti, 1924).

Id., *Il popolo italiano tra la pace e la guerra (1914–1915)* (Milan: Ipsi, 1940).

Id., *L'Italia in cammino* (Milan: Treves, 1927).

Id., *L'Italia nella Triplice Alleanza (1882–1915)* (Milan: Ipsi, 1939).

Yokell, M. A., *Sold to the Highest Bidder? An Investigation of the Diplomacy Regarding Bulgaria's Entry into World War I*, M.A. thesis (Richmond: UR Scholarship Repository, 2010).

Wallach, J. L., *Anatomie einer Militärhilfe: die preussisch-deutschen Militärmissionen in der Türkei 1835–1919* (Düsseldorf: Droste, 1976).

Waters, J. M., *Bloody Winter* (Princeton: Nostrand, 1967).

Watson, A., *Ring of Steel: Germany and Austria-Hungary at War, 1914–1918* (London & New York: Allen & Basic, 2014).

Whittam, J., *The Politics of the Italian Army, 1961–1918* (London: Croom Helm, 1977).

Wilcox, V., *Morale and the Italian Army during the First World War* (Cambridge: Cambridge University Press, 2016).

Id. ed., *Italy in the Era of the Great War* (Leiden & Boston: Brill, 2018).

Wilks, J., & E., *The British Army in Italy, 1917–1918* (Barnsley: Cooper, 1998).

Williamson, S. R., *The Politics of Grand Strategy: Britain and France Prepare for War, 1904–1914* (London: Ashfield, 1990 [1969]).

Wilson, K., *The Policy of the Entente: Essays on the Determinants of British Foreign Policy 1904–1914* (Cambridge & New York: Cambridge University Press, 1985).

Winter, D., *Haig's Command: A Reassessment* (New York: Viking, 1991).

Woodward, D. R., *Field-Marshal Sir William Robertson: Chief of the Imperial General Staff in the Great War* (Westport: Praeger, 1998).

Id., *Lloyd George and the Generals* (Newark: University of Delaware Press, 1983).

Wright, P. E., *At the Supreme War Council* (London: Nash, 1928).

Zamagni, V., *Dalla periferia al centro. La seconda rinascita economica dell'Italia, 1861–1981* (Bologna: Il Mulino, 2003).

Id., *The Economic History of Italy 1860–1990* (Oxford: Clarendon, 1993).

Zingales, F., *La conquista di Gorizia* (Rome: USSME, 1925).

Zugaro, F., *Il costo della guerra italiana* (Rome: Stabilimento poligrafico per l'amministrazione della guerra, 1921).

Reviews & Journals

Astuto, R., 'Ferdinando Martini e l'Inghilterra', *Rivista delle Colonie*, IV, 287, April 1943.

Amendola, G., 'Il Patto di Roma e la polemica', *Quaderni della 'Voce'*, 38, 15 September 1919.

Breganze, G., 'Preliminari della nostra Guerra (Diario aprile-maggio 1915)', M. Brignoli ed., *Il Risorgimento*, XIII, 1–2, 1982.

Brignoli, M., 'Edoardo Greppi. Londra 1914–1915', *Studi Storico-Militari*, 1999 (Rome: USSME, 2000).

Brown Scott, J., 'Economic conference of the allied powers', *The American Journal of International Law*, X, 4, October 1916.

Burgwyn, H. J., 'Italy's Balkan policy, 1915–1917. Albania, Greece and the Epirus Question', *Storia delle Relazioni Internazionali*, 1, 1986.

Caglioti, L. D., 'Why and how Italy invented an enemy aliens problem in the First World War', *War in History*, XXI, 2, 2014.

Id., 'Dealing with enemy aliens in WWI: Security versus civil liberties and property rights', *Italian Journal of Public Law*, II, 2, 2011.

Castellani, L., 'L'impresa di Fiume', *Storia illustrata*, XXII, 142, 1969.

Ceva, L., 'Parliamo ancora di Caporetto', *Nuova Antologia*, CXXXI, 2206, April-June 1998.

David, E., 'The liberal party divided 1916–1918', *Historical Journal*, XIII, 3, 1970.

Di Martino, B., Review to: Piero B., 'Bombardieri Caproni: le ali della Vittoria' (Rome: Settimo Sigillo, 2006), *I Quaderni della Rivista Aeronautica*, 3, 2008.

Di Nolfo, E. 'Il mancato matrimonio di Vittorio Emanuele II con la Principessa Mary di Cambridge', *Il Risorgimento*, XIX, 1967.

Dockrill, M. L. and Steiner, Z., 'The foreign office at the Paris peace conference in 1919', *The International History Review*, II, 1, January 1980.

Egdy, G., 'Lloyd George and the Dual Monarchy, 1917–1918', *Central European Papers*, II, 2, 2014.

Fatutta, F., 'Macedonia 1915–1919', *Rivista Italiana Difesa*, 9, September 1999.

French, D., 'The meaning of attrition, 1914–1916', *English Historical Review*, CIII, 407, 1988.

Gabriele, M., 'La Convenzione navale italo-franco-britannica del 10 maggio 1915', *Nuova Antologia, 1972–1973*, April-May 1965.

Id., 'Il contrasto fra Italia e Francia alleate (1915–1918)', *Storia Militare*, 167, August 2007.

Garzía Sanz, C., 'El poder de John Bull en la Gran Guerra. Visiones de la diplomacia italiana sobre la neutralidad', *Historia y Política*, 33, 2015.

Goldstein, E., 'The foreign office and political intelligence 1918–1920', *Review of International Studies*, XIV, 4, October 1988.

Goldstein, 'British peace aims and the Eastern question: The political intelligence department and the Eastern committee, 1918', *Middle Eastern Studies*, XXIII, 4, 1987.

Halpern, P. G., 'The Anglo-French-Italian Naval Convention of 1915', *Historical Journal*, XIII, 1, March 1970.

Helmreich, P. C., 'Italy and the Anglo-French repudiation of the 1917 St. Jean de Maurienne agreement', *The Journal of Modern History*, XLVIII, 2, June 1976.

Horne, J., 'La società britannica e la prima guerra mondiale', *Ricerche storiche*, 3, 1991.

Jedlicka, L., 'L'armistizio di Villa Giusti nella storiografia austriaca', Atti del primo convegno storico italo-austriaco, Innsbruck, 1–4 October 1971, *Storia e politica*, 3, July-September 1973.

Le Moal, F., 'La politique adriatique de l'Italie vue par les attachés navals Français à Rome, 1914–1919', *Bulletin d'études de la Marine*, July 2003.

Leproni, E., 'Aeroplani e cammelli in Tripolitania', Parte 1a, *Storia Militare*, 32, May 1996.

Id., Parte 2a, *Storia Militare*, 33, June 1996.

Lowe, C. W., 'Britain and Italian intervention, 1914–1915', *The Historical Journal*, XII, 3, 1969.

Manuel, F. E., 'The palestine question in Italian diplomacy, 1917–1920', *The Journal of Modern History*, XXVII, 3, 1955.

Marcuzzi, S., 'From the Adriatic to the Mediterranean. Italy in the Allied Naval Strategy (1915–1918)', *War in History*, XXVII, 3, 2018.

Id., 'The Battle of Gorizia (6–17 August 1916): A Turning Point in Italy's War', MWP Working Papers, 14, *Cadmus*, 2017.

Marks, S., 'Behind the scenes at the Paris peace conference of 1919', *Journal of British Studies*, IX, 2, May 1970.

May, A. J., 'Seton-Watson and the treaty of London', *The Journal of Modern History*, XXIX, 1, March 1957.

Id., 'R. W. Seton-Watson and British Anti-Hapsburg sentiment', *The American Slavic and East European Review*, XX, 1, February 1961.

Menoni, G., 'La Campagna di Macedonia 1916–1918', *Storia Militare*, 33, June 1996.

Montinaro, G. ed., 'Airpower in 20th Century. Doctrines and Employment – National Experiences', *Rivista Internazionale di Storia Militare*, 89 (The Hague: International Commission of Military Mission, 2011).

Monzali, L. "La politica estera italiana nel primo dopoguerra 1918–1922. Sfide e problemi", Italia Contemporanea, 256–257, 2009.

Id., "Il governo Orlando-Sonnino e le questioni coloniali africane alla Conferenza della Pace di Parigi del 1919", Nuova Rivista Storica, 1, 2013.

Morris, L. P., 'British secret missions in Turkestan, 1918–1919', *Journal of Contemporary History*, XII, 3, 1977.

Mosca, R., 'Autunno 1918: Sonnino, la Francia e la vittoria da spartire', *Storia e Politica*, XV, 1, 1976.

Pelagalli, S., 'Italiani in Palestina', *Storia Militare*, 31, April 1996.

Renzi, W. A., 'The Russian foreign office and Italy's entrance into the Great War, 1914–1915: A study in wartime diplomacy', *Historian*, XXVIII, 4, 1966.

Ricerche storiche, 'Studi Recenti sulla Prima Guerra Mondiale', ed. monografica, 3, 1991.

Ricerche storiche, 'Grande Guerra e Mutamento', ed. monografica, 3, 1997.

Rochat, G., 'La preparazione dell'esercito italiano nell'inverno 1914–1915 in relazione alle informazioni disponibili sulla guerra di posizione', *Il Risorgimento*, XIII, 1, 1961.

Id., 'L'efficienza dell'esercito italiano nella Grande Guerra', *Italia contemporanea*, 206, 1997.

Id., 'La convenzione militare di Parigi (2 maggio 1915)', *Il Risorgimento*, VIII, 3, 1961.

Id., ed., *La storiografia militare italiana negli ultimi vent'anni*. Atti del convegno, Lucca 1984, Centro interuniversitario di studi e ricerche storico-militari (Milan: Angeli, 1985).

Id., 'Il Comando supremo di Diaz', in G. Berti e and P. del Negro eds., *Al di qua e al di là del Piave. L'ultimo anno della Grande Guerra*. Atti del convegno internazionale, Bassano del Grappa, 25–28 maggio 2000 (Milan: Angeli, 2001).

Rossetti, C., 'Come l'Inghilterra ci portò via Sollum', *Nuova Antologia*, October 1940.

Sanders, M. L., 'Wellington house and British propaganda during the first world war," *The Historical Journal*, XVIII, 1, March 1975.

Seton-Watson, R. W., 'The failure of Sir Edward Grey', *English Review*, XXII, 1916.

Id., 'The pan-German plan and its antidote', *Contemporary Review*, CIX, 1916.

Silberstein, G. E., 'The Serbian campaign of 1915: its diplomatic background', *American Historical Review*, LXXIII, 1, 1967.

Steed, H. W., 'A programme for peace', *Edinburgh Review*, CCXXIII, 456, April 1916.

Strachan, H., 'The battle of the Somme and British strategy', *The Journal of Strategic Studies*, XXI, 1, 1998.

Id., 'The strategic consequences of the world war', *The American Interest*, IX, 6, June 2014.

Threlfall, T. R., 'Senussi and his threatened holy war', *Nineteenth Century*, XLVII, 227, March 1900.

Taylor, A. J. P., 'British policy in Morocco, 1886–1902', *The English Historical Review*, LXVI, 260, 1951.

Taylor, P. M., 'The foreign office and British propaganda during the first world war', *Historical Journal*, XXIII, 4, 1980.

Toscano, M., 'L'inizio della Rivoluzione sovietica visto dall'ambasciata d'Italia a Pietrogrado', *Nuova Antologia*, 2009–2010, May-June 1968.

Towle, P., 'The European balance of power in 1914', *Army Quarterly and the Defence Journal*, CIV, 3, 1974.

Ungari, A., 'The Italian air force from the eve of the libyan conflict to the first world war', *War in History*, XVII, 4, 2010.

Ventunesimo Secolo, 'Nuovi interrogativi e nuove risposte. La storiografia sulla Prima Guerra Mondiale', ed. monografica, XVI, 41, 2017.

Venturi, F., 'Il movimento riformatore degli illuministi meridionali', *Rivista Storica Italiana*, 74, 1962.

Villari, P., 'Di chi è la colpa? O sia la pace e la guerra', *Il Politecnico*, IV, 2, 1866.

Yang, H-Y., 'A study on role-based approach to bilateral alliances in Northeast Asia', *Journal of International and Area Studies*, XXIII, 1, June 2016.

Walters, W., 'Lord Salisbury's refusal to revise and renew the Mediterranean agreements', *The Slavonic Review*, 29, 1950.

Warman, R., 'The erosion of Foreign Office influence in the making of foreign policy, 1916–1918', *The Historical Journal*, XV, 1, 1972.

Woodward, D. R., 'Britain in a continental war: the civil-military debate over the strategic direction of the Great War of 1914–1918', *Albion*, XII, 1, 1980.

Newspapers

Avanti!
Il Corriere della Sera.
Il Corriere delle Puglie.
Il Giornale d'Italia.
Il Messaggero.
Il Popolo d'Italia.
Il Regno.
Il Resto del Carlino.
Il Secolo.
Italia Nostra.
L'Idea Nazionale.
L'Osservatore Romano.
La Stampa.
La Tribuna.
L'Unità.
The Daily News.
The London Gazette.
The Morning Post.
The Observer.
The Spectator.
The Times.
The Westminster Gazette.
The West Sussex Gazette.

Trench Newspapers

Il Bollettino del Soldato.
L'Astico.
Volontà.

Websites

Cellamare, D., "La preparazione e la mobilitazione generale dell'esercito italiano all'inizio della Prima Guerra Mondiale," Ministero della Difesa, Carabinieri Official Website: www.carabinieri.it/editoria/rassegna-dell-arma/la-rassegna/anno-2006/n-2–aprile-giugno/studi/la-preparazione-e-la-mobilitazione-generale-dell'esercito-italiano-all'inizio-della-prima-guerra-mondiale.

Index

www.ingramcontent.com/pod-product-compliance
Ingram Content Group UK Ltd.
Pitfield, Milton Keynes, MK11 3LW, UK
UKHW020453010325
455719UK00016B/559